HARRIET BEECHER STOWE

A Life

JOAN D. HEDRICK

New York   Oxford
Oxford University Press
1994

Oxford University Press

Oxford   New York   Toronto
Delhi   Bombay   Calcutta   Madras   Karachi
Kuala Lumpur   Singapore   Hong Kong   Tokyo
Nairobi   Dar es Salaam   Cape Town
Melbourne   Auckland   Madrid

and associated companies in
Berlin   Ibadan

Library of Congress Cataloging-in-Publication Data
Hedrick, Joan D., 1944–
Harriet Beecher Stowe : a life / Joan Hedrick.
p.   cm.   Includes bibliographical references and index.
ISBN 0-19-506639-1
1. Stowe, Harriet Beecher, 1811–1896—Biography.
2. Women and literature—United States—History—19th century.
3. Authors, American—19th century—Biography.
4. Abolitionists—United States—Biography.
I. Title.   PS2956.H43   1993   813'.3—dc20   [B]   93-16610

Permission to use Chapters 8, 14, and 22, which have been published in
slightly different form, is acknowledged on page xiv.

2 4 6 8 9 7 5 3 1

Printed in the United States of America
on acid-free paper

Harriet Beecher Stowe

Harriet Beecher Stowe, late 1870s. Photograph by Sarony. (*Stowe-Day Foundation, Hartford, Connecticut*)

For Travis

Preface

"Are there any lives of women?"
"No, my dear," said Mr. Sewell; "in the old times, women did not get their lives written, though I don't doubt many of them were much better worth writing than the men's."

Harriet Beecher Stowe,
The Pearl of Orr's Island

Few in the nineteenth century could have doubted that Harriet Beecher Stowe's life was worth writing. When she met Abraham Lincoln at the White House in 1862, the lanky, angular president is said to have greeted Stowe, who stood less than five feet high, with the words, "So you're the little woman who wrote the book that started this great war!" Catapulted to international fame with the publication of *Uncle Tom's Cabin* (1852), Harriet Beecher Stowe became one of America's best-paid and most-sought-after writers. At the World's Columbian Exposition in Chicago in 1893 Stowe's works were accorded a position of honor in the library of the Woman's Building. Displayed in an elliptical mahogany case with glass all around were first editions of *Uncle Tom's Cabin* and *The Key to Uncle Tom's Cabin*, a special edition of twenty volumes of her works bound in calf, translations of *Uncle Tom's Cabin* into forty-two languages, including Armenian, Illyrian, Servian, Russian, and Welsh, and a letter announcing two editions of *Uncle Tom's Cabin* in the Island of Java.[1]

Stowe's very success has made it difficult to evaluate her role in our cultural history. In a life that spanned all but fifteen years of the nineteenth century Stowe spoke to a nation deeply divided by race, sex, region, and class. Speaking to the masses meant negotiatiating diverse and even contradictory cultures. How successfully she accomplished this, and with what cost to various subcultures, continues to be a subject of fierce debate. In her time southern readers objected to her portrayal of slavery in *Uncle Tom's Cabin*. In our time African Americans have objected to Stowe's racial stereotypes. To engage her life is to engage the plurality and contradiction of American culture.

It is also to challenge twentieth-century notions of art and excellence. *Uncle Tom's Cabin* was not only translated into foreign tongues, it was transmuted into song, theater, statuary, toys, games, handkerchiefs, wallpapers, plates, spoons, candlesticks, and every form of kitsch that the commercial mind could imagine—a phenomenon that puts it on the level of the Davy Crockett fad of the 1950s or the Ninja Turtle craze of the 1980s. Can anything so popular be considered "art?" By the canons of academic scholarship, "popular" writers cannot pretend to the status of "artists." Yet Stowe's nineteenth-century popularity was not framed by such notions of cultural hierarchy.[2]

Stowe began her career in the parlor, writing stories for a Cincinnati literary club. Writing during the transition of literature from an amateur pastime to a business, Stowe's career marks both the flowering and the passing of what I call "parlor literature." Written for entertainment, instruction, and amusement, meant to be read aloud, these domestic literary productions were an integral part of polite society in antebellum America and were as accessible to women as to men. Before literature split into "high" and "low" forms in the 1850s and 60s, best-selling novels were extensions of parlor literature.

At a time when literature was not a particularly respected or lucrative occupation, Harriet Beecher was one of many women who began writing sketches and stories for magazines. Speaking in the conversational voice of a parlor letter writer, she addressed a nation in the throes of a vast transformation: the creation of a national culture. It is not incidental that her first book was a geography. Her 1830s sketches of regional types introduced the American West and the American East to one another, pioneering the use of dialect. Although she wrote a volume of religious poetry, Stowe's "hankering for slang" and delight in the rhythms of everyday speech made prose her natural element. "Did you ever think of the rythmical power of prose," she wrote to George Eliot, "how every writer when they get warm fall into a certain swing & rhythm peculiar to themselves the words all having their place and sentences their cadances."[3] In 1839 her stories began appearing in *Godey's Lady's Book*, the only periodical that, by soliciting and paying for original material, supported the development of American authors and American literature.

As the national culture and the publishing business reached the takeoff stage in the 1850s, women were strategically placed to profit from a sphere of activity that had been inadvertently left to their busy hands. Precisely because literature had not been professionalized, because it was only just beginning to be recognized as an occupation that might honorably support an independent life, women were allowed to practice what became for many a highly lucrative and influential career. "The ninth wave of the nineteenth century is the Destiny of Woman," concluded Sarah Josepha Hale, editor of *Godey's Lady's Book*, as she surveyed at midcentury the extraordinary burst of literary activity: "Within the last fifty years more books have been written by women and about women than all that had been issued during the preceding five thousand years."[4] Writing women were both a symptom of the social history of the nineteenth century and a powerful force in shaping it.

With the emergence of best-sellers like Susan Warner's *The Wide, Wide World* (1851) and Stowe's *Uncle Tom's Cabin*, women showed how much could be achieved. "It is women who read," wrote Nathaniel Willis in 1859. "It is women who give or withhold a literary reputation. It is the women who regulate the style of living. . . . It is the women who exercise the ultimate control over the Press."[5]

Just as Stowe's rise had to do with her apprenticeship in the parlor, so her decline resulted from the removal of literature from the parlor to institutions to which women had limited access: men's clubs, high-culture journals, and prestigious universities. As literature became professionalized, the voice of the novelist became depersonalized and the standards of art became matters for aesthetic consideration rather than political passion. Influencing public opinion became less important than creating a beautiful product. As the standards for judging literature changed and the voice of the novelist became more formal and distanced, Stowe's writing was judged to be amateur, unprofessional, and "bad art."

This did not happen, however, without a political struggle. It is revealing to read in the pages of the *Nation* reviews so hostile to women writers that one contemporary observer suggested the magazine should have been called the "Stag-Nation." In savage reviews of Rebecca Harding Davis and other literary realists, the young Henry James, cutting his literary teeth in the *Nation*, articulated the agenda of what became known in the twentieth century as the "new criticism," a formalistic approach to literature that focused on the internal, aesthetic properties of the work and eschewed biography, politics, and cultural analysis. Anyone who harbors the belief that this approach to literature has no political implications will be surprised to see the overtness of the struggle in the 1860s between the dominant women writers and the rising literary establishment of men who were determined to displace them.

This struggle was well underway when Florine Thayer McCray wrote the first full-length biography of Stowe in 1889. Raising the question of *Uncle Tom's Cabin*'s artistic merits, McCray contrasted a Jamesian notion of the "rules of art" to Stowe's shoot-from-the-hip attack on the reader's sensibilities. "It must be a technical mind which can learnedly discuss the work as tested by the criteria of modern art criticism," she wrote. Contrasting Stowe's strongly marked moral and social types with the "emasculated" characters of modern fiction whose virtues and faults were elaborated with "finical anxiety," McCray observed, "[s]he had no inclination to reduce her strong points to the polished level obtained by many writers. Their indecision (which they mistake for liberality) prevents them from making an enduring impress upon the age."[6] Making an "impress upon the age" was what all of the Beechers aimed to do.

When Stowe learned of McCray's intent to publish a biography of herself, she reacted with alarm. This had nothing to do with McCray's interpretation, which was not unbalanced, nor McCray's unreliability with dates, which

matched that of her subject. It had rather to do with the question of who
could claim her life as literary property. All of the Beechers had made a good
deal of literary capital out of their daily doings and sayings; from pulpit
pronouncements to travel letters to tips on gardening or memorials for the
dead, they regularly transformed the material of their everyday lives into
magazine copy, and they were as careful stewards of their lives as they were
of American culture. After the success of *Uncle Tom's Cabin*, Stowe's life
was much in demand. In 1868 a literary promoter had urged the Rev. E. P.
Parker of South Church in Hartford to write Stowe's biography. The promoter let it be known that if Stowe would not cooperate with Parker, there
was another party prepared to write her biography without her consent. Calvin Stowe, suspecting that this other party was Leonard Bacon, editor of the
Independent, advised Harriet to choose Parker as the lesser of two evils:
"Parker, with your consent & aid, would do it faithfully, delicately & well;
and if it must be done, would n't that be better than to be paved over with
Bacon fat?"[7] Stowe managed to limit Parker's incursions into her life to a
brief sketch compiled from published materials.[8]

Stowe had understood that Florine McCray, an occasional visitor in her
Hartford home, had intended to do a similar short sketch, and she sent her
a two-sentence letter acknowledging her project. When she learned that
McCray's intent was considerably more ambitious, she denounced this puta-
tive "authorized biography" by placing the following notice in the newspaper:
"Permit me to say, that all reports with regard to any authorised edition of
my life, are without foundation. I have placed all the letters & documents
for this purpose in the hands of my *son* & neither he nor I have authorised
any one to circulate such reports as have appeared of late in various papers."[9]
She sent out an alert to European friends to retrieve her letters so that she
could place them in her son's hands.[10] They complied, and in 1889 Houghton Mifflin published Charles Stowe's *Life of Harriet Beecher Stowe, Compiled from Her Letters and Journals*. A European visitor who called on her
during these final years described her as "a wonderfully agile old lady, as
fresh as a squirrel still, but with the face and air of a lion."[11]

After her death in 1896 friends and family closed ranks around her literary remains. Annie Fields, her close friend and wife of her publisher, issued
her *Life and Letters of Harriet Beecher Stowe* (Boston: Houghton Mifflin,
1897) the following year. "The moment has at last arrived when the story of
Mrs. Stowe's life can be given in full," she announced in her preface, yet her
portrait of "one who led the vanguard" in the "great sacrifice" of the Civil
War continued the hagiographical mode of Charles Stowe's account of his
mother's life. Nor was it interrupted when Charles Stowe coauthored, with
Stowe's grandson, Lyman Beecher Stowe, *The Life of Harriet Beecher Stowe*
(Boston: Houghton Mifflin, 1911). There has since been only one attempt
at a definitive biography, Forrest Wilson's *Crusader in Crinoline* (Philadelphia: J. B. Lippincott, 1941), now over fifty years old. Since then a wealth
of new material has come to light. These include many new letters from

Harriet Beecher Stowe, the letters of Calvin Stowe to Harriet, the "circular letters" the Beecher family wrote to one another in the 1830s and 40s, the diary Charles Beecher kept of Stowe's 1853 European tour, and many more items. In addition, the civil rights and women's movements have created new constituencies to contend Stowe's reputation and significance. It is time for a new biography of Stowe.

A deeply reserved woman, Harriet Beecher Stowe did not reveal herself easily. Her brother Charles remarked that her letters were not "the artless expression of spontaneous emotions. She is not in her letter pouring forth feeling merely because she feels it but planning by the combination of such and such feelings and thoughts to produce a given effect."[12] Like her father, Harriet was energetic, optimistic, an inveterate believer and a natural preacher. She believed not only in the Christianity of her heritage, but in almost every fad of the nineteenth century. She dabbled in mesmerism and spiritualism and became an avid devotee of the water cure, electricity treatments, and the movement cure. Her uncritical appetite for whatever was in the air led her to mix the profoundest currents of American democracy and religion—such as abolition and perfectionism—with the snake oil of popular culture. Her ready response to currents in her culture enabled her to intervene in that culture and shape it.

Thought of as a "genius" in a family of eccentrics, Stowe was an odd and whimsical woman. Daguerreotypes and photographs of her show a heavy-lidded woman with large cheekbones and full, sensuous lips; those who knew her said that she looked owlish or beautiful, depending on whether she was withdrawn or animated. An irrepressible sense of humor often compressed her lips into a wry expression. She was driven by the Beecher family sense of mission, but she pursued it with a more tolerant and open temperament than Lyman and Catharine, even though she often fell into family and class chauvinisms. She prized individuality and difference though she freely generalized about classes and races. Her approach is well summarized by her conclusion to her sermon on "Intolerance": "Every human being has some handle by which he may be lifted, some groove in which he was meant to run; and the great work of life, as far as our relations with each other are concerned, is to lift each one by his own proper handle, and run each one in his own proper groove."[13] By placing Stowe's life in the context of her times, I have tried to lift her by her own proper handle, and run her in her own proper groove. At the same time I have tried to place her in frameworks that illuminate the literary history of America during the century in which American literature came into being.

Middletown, Conn.   J. H.
April 1993

Acknowledgments

I am very grateful to the institutions that provided me the time to work on this book. A fellowship from the Rockefeller Foundation provided a crucial year in which I began inching my way through the mountain of archival material left behind by the Beechers, who knew they were famous and saved abundant documentation of their strenuous efforts to reform the world through Beecherism. A National Endowment for the Humanities Fellowship enabled me to write the first half of the book. For a sabbatical and research leave that enabled me to write the second half, I am grateful to the trustees of Trinity College.

The cooperation of many libraries has made this project possible. I wish to thank the staffs at the American Antiquarian Society, Worcester, Massachusetts; the Beinecke Rare Book and Manuscript Library, Yale University; the Boston Public Library, Department of Rare Books and Manuscripts; the Cincinnati Historical Society; the Clements Library, University of Michigan; the Connecticut Historical Society; Dr. Williams's Library, London; the Houghton Library, Harvard University; the Henry E. Huntington Library, San Marino, California; the Library of Congress; the Middlesex County Historical Society, Middletown, Connecticut; the New York Public Library; the Schlesinger Library, Radcliffe College; the Smith College Library; Sterling Memorial Library, Yale University; Trinity College Interlibrary Loan; the Clifton Waller Barrett Library, University of Virginia; and the Watkinson Library, Trinity College.

I am grateful to the Stowe-Day Foundation, Hartford, Connecticut, for permission to quote from the papers of Harriet Beecher Stowe and other Beecher family members. I thank James Parton for permission to quote from Ethel Parton, "Fanny Fern: An Informal Biography." For permission to quote from the Mark Twain Papers I thank the Mark Twain Memorial and the University of California, Berkeley. I am grateful to the Boston Public Library for permission to quote from letters in the Anti-Slavery Collection and to the Clements Library for permission to quote from the Weld-Grimké Papers.

Much of the research for this book was conducted at the Stowe-Day

Library, Hartford, Connecticut, and I wish to give special thanks to their staff, particularly to Roberta Bradford and Tom Harkins, who were there in 1983 when I began my research, to Joseph Van Why, the former director, to Earl French, and to Beverly Zell, Diana Royce and Suzanne Zack, who provided efficient, professional, and extremely knowledgeable support.

Several chapters have been published in slightly different form: chapter 8 in *Signs* (Winter 1992), chapter 14 in *Women's Studies* (1991), and chapter 22 in *American Quarterly* (September 1988). I am grateful to the editors of those journals for their assistance and for permission to use these materials.

I am fortunate to have a wonderful set of colleagues whose support has been consistent and sustaining. Barbara Sicherman's help and encouragement were key in the early stages of this biography and she has remained a steady advisor, counselor, and friend, ready to read a chapter at the drop of a hat. Joseph W. Reed's high standards of narrative biography shaped my initial view of the book. He also read the first half of the manuscript and made helpful suggestions, as did Robert L. Edwards, Paul Lauter, and Margaret Randall. I am grateful to the late Carol B. Ohmann for teaching me about the importance of voice to nineteenth-century women writers. The Feminist Writers Group—Ann duCille, Farah Griffin, Gertrude Hughes, Barbara Sicherman, Indira Karamcheti, and Laura Wexler—read several chapters and many drafts of the preface; their spirited responses were clarifying and encouraging. J. Ronald Spencer read the entire manuscript with a care and thoughtfulness for which I am extremely grateful. Maurine Greenwald and Gertrude Hughes provided suggestions that improved chapter 9. I am grateful to Mary De Jong for her helpful suggestions on chapter 14 and to Ann duCille for her perceptive comments on chapters 17 and 18. Many people have generously shared their knowledge: Lynette Carpenter, H. Bruce Franklin, Patricia Hill, Daniel Hurley, Carolyn Karcher, E. Bruce Kirkham, Peggy McIntosh, Marianne L. Novy, Cynthia Reik, Lyde Cullen Sizer, and William Stowe. John Gilchrist, a descendant of John Pierce Brace, generously made available a list of books from Brace's library.

Tammy Banks-Spooner and Ann Morrissey provided wonderful research assistance. In the final stages of this project, Ann tracked down undocumented quotations and bits of arcane information with unrelenting zeal. I am truly in her debt. At Oxford University Press, my editor, Liz Maguire, and her assistant, T. Susan Chang, gave me steady support, while Paul Schlotthauer and Phillip Holthaus read the manuscript with a care and engagement that inspired me to persevere through the minutiae involved in the final preparation of the book for press.

Friends and family have sustained me over the ten years of this project. Jane and David Ruhmkorff provided hospitality on a trip to the Cincinnati Historical Society. Neighbors Anna Salafia and Virginia Keene have been unflagging in their support and encouragement. Mary Simunich's eagerness to read this book was a spur to finish. My daughters, Jessica and Rachel, have buoyed me by their respect for and interest in my work, as have my brother, Michael Doran, and sister, Patricia Doran Wombacher. For twenty-five years of companionship and support I am grateful to Travis Hedrick, to whom this book is dedicated. More pages than I can count bear the imprint of his reference books, his fund of general information, and his sense of style.

Contents

Note on the Text

I have retained original spelling and punctuation in quoting from manuscript sources, making small changes (indicated by brackets) when the meaning might be unclear.

Following is a list of abbreviations used in the notes and parenthetically in the text.

BL	Beinecke Rare Book and Manuscript Library, Yale University
BPL	Boston Public Library
CES	Calvin Ellis Stowe
D	*Dred: A Tale of the Great Dismal Swamp*
HBS	Harriet Beecher Stowe
HL	Huntington Library, San Marino, California
HO	Houghton Library, Harvard University
HP	*Household Papers and Stories*
LF	*Little Foxes*
MW	*The Minister's Wooing*
NYPL	*The New York Public Library*
OF	*Oldtown Folks*
POI	*The Pearl of Orr's Island*
PP	*Poganuc People*
SchL	Schlesinger Library, Radcliffe College
SD	Stowe-Day Library, Hartford, Connecticut
SM	*Sunny Memories of Foreign Lands*
SML	Sterling Memorial Library, Yale University
UMi	Clements Library, University of Michigan
UTC	*Uncle Tom's Cabin*
UVa	Clifton Waller Barrett Library, University of Virginia

Harriet Beecher Stowe

CHAPTER ONE

New England Beginnings:
1811–1816

In the northwestern corner of Connecticut the roads rise gradually through heavily forested hills toward the town of Litchfield, Harriet Beecher Stowe's birthplace. Like much of her writing, Litchfield bears the strong stamp of geography and local culture. This is emphatically a New England town. The tall chimneys of the stately Georgian houses march in procession toward the green, which is laid out on the crest of a hill. On the green is the Congregational church, a two-story, white-clapboard building with shuttered windows, its simplicity set off by tall pillars and one of the most beautiful steeples in New England. This orderly, Federal-era town was built around shared values that included a godly hierarchy. Walking from the green down the left side of North Street one comes upon the Tallmadge house. A splendid building with a set of well-proportioned pillars recessed at either side, it bespeaks wealth and cultivation. Like many of the eighteenth-century houses in Litchfield, the Tallmadge house was built around the time of the American Revolution. Just a block down from Major Tallmadge's house is the site of the Litchfield Female Academy, the first women's school in the new nation.

A block beyond the academy, past a fine Georgian house built in 1771 by Lynde Lord, stood a much plainer edifice that was the parsonage for the Congregational minister. Here Lyman Beecher settled his family in 1810. In this two-story, L-shaped frame house, Harriet, the seventh child of Lyman and Roxana Beecher, was born on June 14, 1811. The parsonage has since been moved a few blocks away, where this large building now serves as a dormitory for the Forman School. During Harriet Beecher's childhood, it was likewise a boardinghouse. The front door opens on a steep stairway to the second floor, where a sloping hallway connects the original structure to the series of additions that Lyman Beecher made to accommodate his growing family and a large number of boarders.

In contrasting ways, Harriet Beecher's parents embodied important spirits of the age. Born in 1775, Lyman Beecher attempted to play a central role in defining the parameters of the emerging national culture. He combined enormous confidence, stamina, and intellect with religious convictions of prophetic intensity. The son and grandson of blacksmiths, he entered the ministry at the beginning of the religious revival called the Second Great Awakening, convinced that "the conversion of the world to Christ was near."[1] Against the secular, revolutionary forces of Tom Paine and the French deists, he arrayed himself in the shining armor of a soldier of Christ. In place of political revolution he enshrined the cataclysm of religious conversion. The first sermon to bring him into national prominence was an attack on the aristocratic institution of dueling, yet he would always be something of a Federalist and a theocrat at odds with the more pluralistic, democratic society that was spreading faster and farther than the fires of religious revival could burn. Describing himself as "harnessed to the chariot of Christ,"[2] he spent his life winning souls in what turned out to be a futile attempt to outflank the enemy. He died in 1863, just before the onslaught of material and secular excess called the Gilded Age.

Lyman's considerable skills as a military strategist in the crusade for Christ were combined with a remarkable lack of sensitivity to the personal feelings of others and an almost total lack of organization in his private life. As his religious zeal spread in ever-widening circles, from his parish to the nation and the world, it created at home a vortex of paper, books, and ink-blotted notes as well as a residue of moral earnestness and religious perplexity that would become for some of his children an almost intolerable burden. His high spirits, warm and impulsive nature, and extraordinary integrity of vision made him a father and husband to be reckoned with. He wore out two young wives and had been with his third twenty-seven years when he died at the age of eighty-eight. He was married a total of sixty-two years, letting only one year lapse between each wife.

He shrewdly chose women whose family connections and cultivation added polish to his rusticity—and who were highly socialized into women's proper role. He selected his first wife, Roxana, from the lively granddaughters of General Andrew Ward, of Guilford, Connecticut, who served under George Washington in the Revolution. General Ward, who took charge of his daughter's ten children when their father, Eli Foote, died of yellow fever, characterized the three eldest girls in this fashion. When Harriet came down in the morning, she would briskly call, "Here! take the broom; sweep up; make a fire; make haste!" Her sister Betsy would say, "I wonder what ribbon it's best to wear at that party?" But Roxana would say, "Which do you think was the greater general, Hannibal or Alexander?"[3] Fluent in French, Roxana's ready taste in literature made her the "queen" of a circle of home-educated girls who eagerly awaited the arrival of each new book from England. Novel reading was not frowned upon in this worldly circle. Samuel Richardson, Maria Edgeworth, even the bawdy adventures of Fanny Burney's *Evelina* were read and discussed by the girls as they spun flax together. Roxana Foote used to tie books by the best French authors to her distaff and study as she spun.

Judging that Roxana's was the best mind in the family, Lyman Beecher chose her over her sisters. He may have also judged that her gentle and compliant spirit would be more companionable than the satiric wit of her sister Harriet, whom Lyman described as "smart, witty; a little too keen."[4] Roxana's analytic mind was yoked to a spirit so timid that she could not speak in public without blushing, a reticence so great that even the public duties of a minister's wife were too much for her. But Lyman needed only a sounding board and a domestic regulator; in religious matters, he was general of his own campaign. He declared himself pleased with his choice: "she entered into my character entirely."[5]

Like the good and true heroine of Harriet Beecher Stowe's *The Pearl of Orr's Island*, Roxana Foote Beecher died young, of an excess of true womanhood. In 1799 she followed her husband to his first parish in East Hampton, Long Island, a raw settlement in which carpets were a rare luxury, many of his parishioners were Montauk Indians, and ministers were expected to live on $400 a year. There she bore six children in the space of ten years and ran a family school in the house, taking in student boarders from the community. As minister to a sprawling and undeveloped parish, Lyman was, as Roxana wrote to her sister Harriet, "every body's man." Everybody's, that is, but hers. "Last week, for example," she wrote in the winter of 1799, "he preached twice in town and two lectures, besides a funeral sermon on Gardiner's Island, and five sermons to the Indians and white people down at Montauk. He every week lectures at some one of the villages adjoining." He made the circuit of Wainscott, Amaghansett, Northwest, and the Springs, and when at home held meetings two and three times a day while Roxana prepared meals and set the house in order—no small task in the midst of Lyman's whirlwind of activity. "This uncommon attention to religion," she remarked, "has brought a good deal of company."[6] The constant visitors made it impossible for her to write, nor did she have time to spin, let alone to read the books she used to combine with that activity.

In 1808 she gave birth to her fifth child, Harriet. When the baby was a month old she caught whooping cough. Characterized by a spasmodic nightly cough that terminated in a convulsive gasping for breath, whooping cough was epidemic in particular localities every two to four years. It was especially hazardous to infants, who were more likely to wake up choking than coughing. After Roxana had been up night after night with the baby, Lyman told his exhausted wife to get some sleep; she obeyed, and while she slept the child died. For posterity, Lyman Beecher reported in his *Autobi-ography* her total absense of "agitation" upon finding her dead baby: "I never saw such resignation to God; it was her habitual and only frame of mind; and even when she suffered most deeply, she showed an entire absence of sinister motives, and an entire acquiescence in the Divine will."[7]

When his parishioners refused to increase his salary, Lyman Beecher left East Hampton in 1810 to answer a call to Litchfield, Connecticut. About a year after his family's arrival in Litchfield, Roxana gave birth to another daughter. Like the baby who had died, she was named Harriet—after Rox-ana's spirited sister, Harriet Foote. Two years later Henry Ward was born, followed by Charles in 1815. "The first child in a family," Harriet Beecher Stowe would later remark, "is its poem . . . the tenth . . . is *prose*."[8] Born seventh and eighth in a lineup of thirteen children, the two Beechers who were to become most famous, Harriet and Henry, had to make a loud clamor indeed in order to be recognized. Besides their elder siblings Catharine, William, Edward, Mary, and George, the Litchfield household included Betsy Burr, an orphan cousin who lived with the Beechers until she married; Rachel and Drusilla (Zillah) Crooke, bound servants; several students from Tapping Reeve's Litchfield Law School and as many as eleven boarders from the Litchfield Female Academy; Aunt Mary and Uncle Samuel from Guilford who visited regularly and for lengthy periods; and Grandma Beecher and her unmarried daughter, the legendary Aunt Esther, who came to live in a house close by. To all of these full-time and part-time residents must be added the constant flow of visitors making themselves at home in the minister's house, and the high level of social activity that obtained in this sophisticated town. Who can blame the five-year-old Harriet if she hardly understood after her mother's death that she was gone?

For Lyman Beecher, Litchfield, with its orderly tree-lined streets of white houses marching in straight lines from the centrally located white Congre-gational church, represented God's plan for the new world. With a law school, a female academy, and some of the most talented and entertaining society in America, Litchfield was a far cry from the sandy beaches of East Hampton, where the Beechers looked across the street to a scene of Indians selling baskets and brooms. Catharine Beecher remembered the first five years of Lyman Beecher's ministry there as a period of "unalloyed happi-ness" in which Roxana "enjoyed perfect health, and sympathized thoroughly with him in all his tastes and employments."[9]

The texture of Roxana Beecher's days, however, did not change signifi-cantly. In the telegraphic style of a busy mother, Roxana explained to her sister-in-law why she has not written:

> Would now write you a long letter, if it were not for several vexing circum-stances, such as the weather extremely cold, storm violent, and no wood cut; Mr. Beecher gone; and Sabbath day, with company—a clergyman, a stranger; Catharine sick; George almost so; Rachel's finger cut off, and she crying and

groaning with the pain. Mr. Beecher is gone to preach at New Hartford, and did not provide us wood enough to last, seeing the weather has grown so exceedingly cold. . . . As for reading, I average perhaps one page a week, besides what I do on Sundays. I expect to be obliged to be contented (if I can) with the stock of knowledge I already possess, except what I can glean from the conversation of others. . . . Mary has, I suppose, told you of the discovery that the fixed alkalies are metallic oxyds. I first saw the notice in the "Christian Observer." I have since seen it in an "Edinburgh Review." The former mentioned that the metals have been obtained by means of the galvanic battery; the latter mentions another, and, they say, better mode. I think this is all the knowledge I have obtained in the whole circle of arts and sciences of late; if you have been more fortunate, pray let me reap the benefit.[10]

What must it have been like to have been curious, intelligent, and a woman in 1815? (And Roxana Foote was among the privileged—what of Zillah and Rachel in the kitchen?) In the days before the common school the level of a woman's education depended on the level of her family culture, and among the Footes of Guilford this culture had been worldly and elevated. Roxana learned French from an émigré from the French West Indies, she learned of distant lands and strange customs from her world-traveling brother Samuel, she heard the novels of Scott read aloud and read extensively on her own. Then such a one "graduates"—marries and sets up housekeeping on her own. Vision turns inward. Nine babies. One of them always nursing, or on the way, or teething, or ill. Constant visitors. No time to read and reflect, except on the Sabbath, when work was forbidden and she *could* pick up the *Christian Observer*—that is, when she wasn't attending the morning and afternoon Sabbath meetings and listening to her husband preach. After seventeen years Roxana Beecher was worn out. In 1816 she grew pale and luminous and died of tuberculosis. She was forty-one years old.

At the time of her death Lyman Beecher was involved in some of the most strenuous activity of his career. On the one hand he was leading a highly successful revival in the Litchfield Female Academy, where he was assiduous in holding prayer meetings and counseling students.[11] On the other hand he was facing a political and religious crisis such as he had not experienced before: the fall of the Standing Order in Connecticut. The disestablishment in 1818 of the Congregational Church was to Lyman Beecher "the worst attack I ever met in my life"—excepting only, he said, the heresy trials he withstood in the 1830s, when, not coincidentally, his second wife was carried off.[12]

The Beechers accorded Roxana the sainthood her meek and resigned spirit had seemed to court. In the words of one biographer, she "became pure spirit with them all, an ideal, the family's Virgin Mary, the symbol of all that was most perfect in womanhood."[13] Roxana's beatification began on her deathbed. Although she had shown the signs of consumption for a year, no one noticed her condition until one day, on the way back from a visit to a parishioner, she announced to Lyman that she had had "a vision of heaven and its blessedness" and would not be much longer with him. Symptoms of rapid consumption soon appeared. She was taken by a chill, followed by fever and exhaustion. Her mind wandered. Acute spastic pains in the pit of her stomach marked her final day. She tried to speak to her children, but could not make her voice heard over their cries and sobs. Her deathbed, however, was not lacking in the Protestant rituals that allowed onlookers to say, after the fact, that her death had been happy. In spite of the fever and the effects of the laudanum she was taking, she had a lucid interval shortly before her death. Gathered around her bed were her good friend and neighbor, Elizabeth Reeve, her sister Harriet, her husband, and all of her children and servants. She told them of "her views and anticipations of heaven" and shared a personal religious triumph that was calculated to reassure them: she had not once, during her illness, prayed for her life. She then dedicated her sons to the ministry of God and prayed, with Lyman leading: "You are now come unto Mount Zion, unto the city of the living God, the heavenly Jerusalem, and to an innumerable company of angels; to the general assembly and Church of the first-born . . . and to the spirits of just men made perfect."[14]

Nineteenth-century readers of *Uncle Tom's Cabin* would have recognized in Stowe's depiction of the death of Eva this distinctively Protestant liturgy. They would have been able to supply, from their own experience, what the liturgy was meant to cover and evoke: the smell of the sickroom, the terror of departure, the awe of eternity. Having scrupulously pruned away the sacramental rituals with which the Roman Catholic Church eased the passage of human beings into and out of this life, evangelical Protestantism reinvented them after its own fashion. It is not surprising that, as they stood on the brink of eternity, with the awful knowledge that the state of one's heart determined for all time one's banishment from or reunion with the elect, these mere mortals embroidered some human assurances of divine favor— and invested the final words of the departed with prophetic power. In such intimate scenes too where death was a common visitor in the house, a close companion for days and nights and weeks, there was comfort in the orderliness of such rituals. In her experience and in her art, death was to be for Harriet Beecher Stowe a source of energy and vision, a transforming event that allowed her to fuse and transcend the gender-coded examples of Lyman and Roxana. One of her favorite hymns was "O mother dear, Jerusalem." Set to a plaintive, lullaby-like German melody in the hymnal of Henry Ward Beecher's Plymouth Church, its nine stanzas describe a vision of heaven embodied in reunion with a mother who ends all sorrows and comforts all griefs:

> O mother dear, Jerusalem
> When shall I come to thee?
> When shall my sorrows have an end?
> Thy joys when shall I see?[15]

In one respect, Roxana represented a wider circle than the son of the blacksmith. The Episcopal, novel-reading daughter of the well-traveled Foote family was quite a prize, in secular terms, for a humble evangelical minister—and one might well ask what Lyman Beecher thought he was doing in such worldly company. The pity is that this appealing cultural richness almost did not matter later on, so overshadowed was it by the demands of a large household and the rigors of childbearing. But Harriet Beecher Stowe, who went to Europe three times, learned French, and became an avid writer as well as reader of novels, showed herself to be her mother's daughter. She also succeeded, better than her father, in shaping the cultural agenda of the new nation, and a large part of her success was due to the inheritance from her mother. Lyman Beecher's dreams of a united Christian nation foundered on the reality of an emerging pluralistic culture in which his was only one voice among many. He remained to his death a provincial, whereas Harriet was better able to comprehend and translate the competing voices and cultural values of the geographically diverse nation. In part this was the heritage of the seafaring Foote family, in part it was the distinctive heritage of a nineteenth-century women's culture in which mothers were expected to translate the dialects of the spirit in order to smoothe the social interchange in the family.

In one of her novels, Harriet Beecher Stowe described the way this process worked:

> In the midst of our large family, of different ages, of vigorous growth, of great individuality and forcefulness of expression, my mother's was the administrative power. My father habitually referred everything to her, and leaned on her advice with a childlike dependence. She read the character of each, she mediated between opposing natures; she translated the dialect of different sorts of spirits, to each other.[16]

Here is a matter in which the training of the "angel in the house" has potential for application beyond the domestic sphere, for she who is "a common interpreter, who understands every dialect of the soul" and thus translates "differences of individuality into a common language of love" may also find a way to speak a common language to a mass readership. Combining the prophetic intensity of her father with the literary and cultural heritage of her mother, Harriet Beecher Stowe fused the best of her paternal and maternal heritage. She transformed the role of the angel in the house from a purely self-denying (and ultimately fatal) script into one in which she was a facilitator of and minister to the spirits of others.

CHAPTER TWO

Nutplains:
1811–1816

Women writers, *Virginia Woolf reminds us,* remember through their mothers.[1] This act of remembering represented a significant literary enterprise for Harriet Beecher, for she admitted that her recollections of her mother were "blurred and confused."[2] When the Beechers collected their family memories in the joint effort that would be called *The Autobiography of Lyman Beecher,* Harriet wrote to her brother, "I was between three and four years of age when our mother died, and my own personal recollections of her are therefore but few."[3] She did not even recall her age correctly, for Roxana died in September 1816 when Harriet was five. While this error is not surprising in one who rarely dated letters and often miscalculated her age by a year or two, it is significant. Lodged in the prehistorical recesses of childhood, Harriet's memories of her mother were susceptible to mythic reworkings.

Lyman Beecher took a strong hand in shaping the family memory of Roxana. "In every scene of family joy or sorrow, or when father wished to make an appeal to our hearts which he knew we could not resist," remembered Harriet, "he spoke of mother." These ritual invocations led Harriet to believe that Roxana's "memory and example had more influence in moulding her family, in deterring from evil and exciting to good, than the living presence of many mothers." Harriet directed the reader to "[t]he passage in 'Uncle Tom,' where Augustine St. Clare describes his mother's influence." It is, she said, "a simple reproduction of this mother's influence as it has always been in her family."[4]

Harriet had only a few fragmentary recollections of her mother. In one, Roxana says cheerfully, "Remember the Sabbath day to keep it holy." In another, Roxana gently reprimands the Beecher children for eating a bag of tulip bulbs under the mistaken impression that they were onions, allowing "not even a momentary expression of impatience" to cross her face.[5] These fragments confirm the image of Roxana as the Christian mother, quick with precept and example and, like Louisa May Alcott's "Marmee" in *Little Women*, a stranger to anger and self-assertion. Given the frequency with which this image of Roxana was held forth by Lyman as an example to the Beecher children, it is likely that these two memories were themselves structured through the family's oral tradition which cast Roxana in the role of the perfectly submissive, pious, and domestic wife. Lyman Beecher's Roxana could have stepped from the pages of a nineteenth-century advice book for young women in which wives were urged to "become as little children," to "avoid a controverial spirit," "to repress a harsh answer, to confess a fault, and to stop (right or wrong) in the midst of self-defense."[6]

The only other fragment Harriet could recall in later years—and this one is perhaps closer to direct experience—is literary: "I have a recollection of her reading to the children one evening aloud Miss Edgeworth's 'Frank,' which had just come out, I believe, and was exciting a good deal of attention among the educational circles of Litchfield."[7] Between 1801 and 1825 Maria Edgeworth published a series of children's stories designed for education and entertainment. Featuring a precocious child named Frank, mixing dialogue, information, and loosely plotted narrative, each of her *Early Lessons* was designed to take the child through a body of information while at the same time shaping character. Her *Frank*, published in 1801–1802, endeavored to teach six-year-old children some fundamentals of science—and may have been as close as Roxana Beecher was able to get during these years to scientific knowledge.[8]

Harriet's richest memories of Roxana were entangled with her visits to her mother's childhood home in Guilford, Connecticut, in an area called Nutplains. By contrast with the Roxana of Litchfield, who was Lyman Beecher's wife, the Roxana of Nutplains emerged from her own family culture and from a women's culture thick in associations. Here Roxana was daughter and sister and domestic artist. In Nutplains Harriet's memories of her mother were shaped by Grandmother Foote (also named Roxana) and her aunts, particularly her mother's favorite sister, Aunt Harriet.

Grandmother Foote had been beset with a terrible series of family tragedies. In the two-year period following the death of her husband from yellow fever she lost three of her oldest children: a daughter Martha, aged twelve, and two of her sons, Henry, aged sixteen, and Ward, aged seventeen.[9] In 1813 a fourth child, Mary Ward Hubbard, died of consumption at the age of twenty-eight. When the untimely death of her daughter Roxana was added to her sorrows, she felt a special bond toward this daughter's children. Edward Beecher reported to his sister Catharine after a visit to Nutplains,

[Grandmother] seems very glad to see me & wishes to hear every word I say & hardly lets me go where she cannot see me—I look she says like mother & to see me recalls to her mind the days when Uncles Samuel John & George with mother & the rest who are gone were young and around her—It always makes me feel melancholy to think of the time when all her children were blooming around her & the valley of Nutplains was cheerful with their sports.[10]

The valley of Nutplains did bloom again, in a small way, when in 1816 Grandmother Foote took into her home little Harriet, Roxana's daughter, who was draped in mourning for her mother. Harriet remembered that when she arrived, "Grandmama took me into her lap & cried & I wondered what made a great grown up woman cry to see me."[11] Whereas this first visit after her mother's death could have been associated in her later years with the painful memories of loss, for Harriet her visit to Nutplains only increased her sense of belonging and connectedness. Her loss quickly "faded from [her] childish mind."[12] In her account she is wondering at the grief of her grandmother—even as she herself is enfolded within that grandmother's care.

In temper, tone, and religious conviction Nutplains represented a colorful contrast to Litchfield. Nutplains was Episcopal and aristocratic, a place of refinement and culture where children were taught to sit straight in their chairs and say "Yes, Ma'am" and "No, Ma'am." Litchfield was Congregational and democratic, a place of "racket and tear" where rosy-cheeked, rough farm children vied with one another in blackberry picking and wood-chopping. Here things went along in "a free and easy way of living, more congenial to liberty and sociality than to conventional rules." At Nutplains Harriet's grandmother read from her English prayer book the prayers for the king and queen and the royal family; even more piquant, Aunt Harriet worried over the "uncovenanted" state of Lyman Beecher's soul—a lovely reversal for a father whose preoccupation with the "stupid" religious state of his children cast a dark shadow on their young lives. While Harriet's father preached sermons against the "unscriptural" practice of keeping Christmas, her mother's relatives festooned Nutplains with greens and sent the children Christmas presents. The contrasting cultures of Litchfield and Nutplains were dark and light threads woven into the texture of Harriet Beecher's young consciousness.[13]

It is not clear how long Harriet stayed with the Footes in Nutplains, but it was probably at least a year, until Lyman Beecher remarried. Long visits were the norm in those days, and children were frequently distributed at relatives' homes for a season or two. Even before Roxana's illness Harriet had made a long visit at Nutplains, as evidenced by this letter from Roxana to her sister, Harriet Foote:

April 17, 1814

I have not sent for little Harriet on account of the joiner's work we are going to have about soon; but if any circumstance unknown to me makes it expedient she should come home, you must send her with Mr. Beecher. I should have sent her a flannel slip if I could have found an opportunity, but it is now too late in the spring. You must get shoes for her, and Mr. Beecher must pay for them; and if he should forget it, I will remember. . . . Write me an account of all matters and things respecting both yourselves and little Harriet, whom you must tell to be a good girl, and not forget her mamma, and brothers, and sisters. I hope to come for her some time in the summer or autumn.[14]

Thus for the better part of 1814, when she was three years old, Harriet was under the care of Aunt Harriet at Nutplains; the following year Roxana was busy with her new baby, Charles, and Henry Ward, aged two; the year after that she died. Harriet Foote nursed Roxana for six weeks before her death and took little Harriet back to Nutplains with her afterward. It is not surprising that Harriet Beecher's memories of her busy and often physically distant mother paled before those of the aunt for whom she was named and with whom she maintained a relationship into adulthood.

Aunt Harriet never married. It is possible that other men formed the same estimate of her that Lyman Beecher had when he chose her more tractable sister. She was "an acute and skillful controversalist," and her practice of matching her knowledge of the Episcopal Church's history and doctrines against the theological talents of young Presbyterian ministers would have given pause to fainthearted suitors.[15] It is also possible that this strong-minded woman chose not to marry. She "took the lead in the family" and was much appreciated at Nutplains for her wit, her droll way of telling stories, and her "stock of family tradition and of neighborhood legendary lore." Harriet Beecher remembered visits during which the nieces and nephews were so convulsed over her stories "that they would call for a truce, and request Aunt Harriet to be silent at least long enough for them to drink their tea."[16] No one, including the aged Grandmother Foote, was safe from her crisp and pointed remarks; though couched in humor, they were Aunt Harriet's way of keeping folks in line and letting them know where she stood. She was decisive, principled, an efficient household manager and a strict disciplinarian.

Aunt Harriet instructed the young Harriet Beecher in the useful arts of knitting and sewing and regularly catechized her. "A more energetic human being," Stowe later remarked, "never undertook the education of a child."[17] In the matter of religious instruction, however, Harriet Foote's principles conflicted with her sense of delicacy and propriety. "A vigorous English-woman of the old school," she belonged to the Episcopal Church and accordingly instructed the young Harriet in the church catechism. Although the child showed herself a ready pupil and could soon intone the answers with "old-fashioned gravity and steadiness," Aunt Harriet was troubled by the picture of this daughter of a Congregational minister being led "out of the sphere of [her] birth." Her solution was a victory of energy and discipline: she decided that her charge should learn *two* catechisms, the Presbyterian (the same as the Congregational) *and* the Episcopal. This must have proven too much for both Harriets, for the younger was relieved to hear her aunt mention privately to Grandmother Foote that "it would be time enough for Harriet to learn the Presbyterian Catechism when she went home."[18]

Harriet and Roxana Foote were members of the last generation of New England women who did their own spinning and weaving. Describing a typical day, the nineteen-year-old Roxana wrote to her sister, "I generally rise with the sun" and "after breakfast I generally take my wheel which is my daily companion."[19] Harriet Foote took her spinning and weaving seriously. During a visit to her brother George in New York, she cited as a reason for her to return to Nutplains "that I may see to the weaving of the vast quantities of yarn that I have spun during the past winter."[20] These traditional domestic arts, though often tedious, were an important source of self-definition for Harriet and Roxana Foote. Even in in their youth, however, the transition to factory production was beginning. This may be seen in a small way in the "spinning-mill" built by their grandfather, Andrew Ward, at the back of his house in Nutplains. "Castle Ward" was situated on the East River, which was navigable by rowboat right up to the Ward property. Here on this brook Andrew Ward built a small spinning mill "furnished with machinery for turning three or four spinning-wheels by water power."[21] Roxana and her friends gathered in this "favorite spot" to spin, chat, and read. Neither house nor factory, this neighborhood spinning mill bespoke the transition that was in progress.

The War of 1812 gave a boost to American manufactures, and by 1815 the transition from home spinning and weaving to the factory production of cloth was so far advanced as to threaten to displace Harriet Foote's supremacy in this quarter. In the same letter in which she mentioned her desire to return to Nutplains in order to oversee the weaving of the prodigious quantities of yarn she had spun, she noted that her brother John—employed by a commercial house in New York—had insisted that "he shall be able to furnish us with more and better cloth than we can make." A linen company there had spun a large quantity of yarn, and when it was put into the loom the weaver declared it to be "the strongest yarn he ever saw either in Europe or America."[22] The sheer quantities that technology made it possible to produce brought the price of cotton yarn down from 92 cents per pound in 1805 to 19 cents in 1845.[23]

Harriet Beecher grew up with the new industrial age, reaching her majority during the 1830s, the golden age of the Lowell Mills. Nutplains, however, remained connected to the mercantile and preindustrial past. Except for those employed in a handful of shoemaking shops, the people of Guilford made their livelihoods through agriculture or fishing and seafaring. Sea captains who built their vessels in Guilford often engaged in the lucrative and dangerous West Indies trade.[24] It was through this sea commerce that Mary Foote Hubbard came to marry a Jamaican planter and that Roxana Foote learned French from a West Indian émigré. Samuel Foote was directly engaged in this trade, along with travel to more far-flung ports.

In her capacity as family historian and collector of legendary lore, Aunt

Harriet made Nutplains come alive with memories: "There was Aunt Catharine's embroidery; there Aunt Mary's paintings and letters; there the things which Uncle Samuel had brought from foreign shores: frankincense from Spain, mats and baskets from Mogadore, and various other trophies locked in drawers, which Aunt Harriet displayed to us on every visit."[25] At Nutplains Roxana Foote was restored to life through the stories that were told about her, the love that was bestowed on her daughter, and the carefully worked objects she had left behind: "We saw her paintings, her needle-work, and heard a thousand little sayings and doings of her daily life."[26] If the children were good, some of the family portraits that Roxana had drawn on ivory would be taken out of places of safekeeping.[27]

Harriet Beecher Stowe remembered her visits to Nutplains as the "golden hours" of her childhood, and certainly there was rich material there for one of an imaginative temperament. The curtains around her bed were of an Indian linen and printed with "strange mammoth plants," in the convolutions of which were perched Chinese summer houses and giant birds—a scene brought from foreign shores by Uncle Samuel.[28] More than Litchfield, Nutplains was the mythic landscape of childhood where ordinary objects took on magical properties. The countryside surrounding the Foote farmhouse was alive with memory and feeling: "Every juniperbush, every wild sweetbrier, every barren sandy hillside, every stony pasture, spoke of bright hours of love, when we were welcomed back to Nutplains as to our mother's heart."[29] Some seventy years later Stowe's memories of Nutplains, aroused by her sister Isabella's visit there, were still sharp and warm:

> I *do wish* I could have been with you in your pleasant visit at Nutplains, where some of the most joyous days of my childhood were spent All the things that you mentioned I *have done* over & over again when I was a wild free young girl & *never got tired* of doing them. The room I slept in for the most part, was the *first right hand room* as you get to the top of the front stairs. . . .
>
> The room directly facing the head of the stairs was aunt Harriet's & Grandma's it had two large comfortable beds for them—I have slept with Aunt Harriet in her bed & *enjoyed* it as she always kept me so nice & warm
>
> Then there was the colored woman *Dine* was a great friend of mine & we had many frolics & capers together—she told me lots of stories & made herself very entertaining—Then there was the grave yard on Sandy Hill, the other side of the river where I often walked—I wonder if it is there now. It had a nice picket fence all round it then with a gate so I could easily get in & read the inscriptions on the grave-stones.[30]

Nutplains was the maternal home, and it exercised a powerful tug on Harriet Beecher Stowe's imagination. Presided over by Aunt Harriet, a woman of "faculty" who could spin and weave as well as challenge fledgling ministers to doctrinal debates, Nutplains was a woman's place in a preindustrial age in which women claimed a productive sphere. As the locus for memories of her departed mother, it was an evocative land where memory was embroidered by myth and imagination. In part, the legends passed on by her aunts and uncles confirmed the image of Roxana as the angel in the house: "Your mother never spoke an angry word in her life. Your mother never told a lie."[31] But physical objects Roxana had transformed into works of domestic art put Harriet in touch with a different reality: the smooth ivories on whose sensuous surfaces the faces of Aunt Harriet and Grandmother Foote miraculously looked out upon the world, the pieces of fine embroidery whose intricate, tiny stitches expressed a unique sense of design, fabric, texture, and color, as well as an art "which had almost passed out of memory"—these tangible remains made palpable the fingers of a woman artist.[32]

Out of this mixture of myth and sympathetic magic, Stowe on the one hand created a literary mother and on the other hand imagined a domestic landscape instinct with maternal love. Both appear in her novels, the former as a liability and the latter as a rich reservoir of vision and feeling. "Saint" Roxana was a secondhand creation that perhaps was as emotionally unconvincing to Harriet Beecher Stowe as St. Clare's dying exclamation, "Mother!," is to modern readers of *Uncle Tom's Cabin*. By contrast, Harriet Beecher Stowe's roomy New England kitchens, with their wide fireplaces, ample settles, faultless loaves of cake, and familiar conversation embody the ethos of a women's culture that was her mother's richest heritage to her. Located in a preindustrial world in which shadows fell picturesquely on the bare boards of a country kitchen, Stowe's love affair with the New England past was in some sense a literary transformation of her love affair with a distant mother. Just as significantly, Stowe created in her fiction a large panorama of mother surrogates who in their combination of realism and feeling are among her most interesting characters. Modeled on real-life women like Aunt Harriet and Grandma Foote, who warmed her with affectionate arms and taught her wayward and dreamy spirit to trace the neat cross-stitches of a New England daughter's education, these are the Aunt Ophelias and Miss Mehitabels and Widow Scudders of her fiction. Women without men—independent women—these mother surrogates provided an alternative model of womanhood more congenial to the needs of a woman artist than that of the saintly Roxana.

CHAPTER THREE

Litchfield:
1816–1824

*H*arriet described the parsonage in Litchfield as "a wide, roomy, windy edifice that seemed to have been built by a succession of after-thoughts."[1] This rambling affair in which kitchen gave rise to sink-room and sink-room to wood-house and wood-house to carriage house in "a gradually lessening succession of out-buildings" provided during the long Litchfield winters an interior landscape in which the large Beecher house-hold distributed itself. Harriet's favorite rooms were the kitchen and her father's study, both of which enfolded her in a welcome sociability. As she says of Dolly in *Poganuc People*, she had the misfortune "to enter the family at a period when babies were no longer a novelty, when the house was full of the wants and clamors of older children, and the mother at her very wits' end with a confusion of jackets and trowsers, soap, candles and groceries, and the endless harassments of making both ends meet which pertain to the lot of a poor country minister's wife" (PP, 8). Harriet was trained with a military precision to come when called, to do as she was told, to speak only when spoken to. As long as she was healthy, clothed, and fed, her caretakers assumed that all of her earthly wants were satisfied; listening to her ques-tions, musings, and small childhood tragedies was a luxury for which they had no time. For sociability Harriet turned either to the books in her father's study or to the society of the kitchen help.

In the kitchen she found black servants and white hired girls who, being "in the same situation of repressed communicativeness, encouraged her con-versational powers" (PP, 8). She may have remembered Zillah and Rachel

Crooke, who followed the Beechers from East Hampton to Litchfield to finish their indentures. Catharine Beecher described Zillah as "the smartest black woman I ever knew." Harriet recalled a black woman named Candace, hired to help out with the mountain of laundry generated by the Litchfield household. The terms in which she remembered Candace suggest that for Harriet the kitchen was a place of emotional expressiveness. Soon after the death of Roxana Beecher, while the family prayer service proceeded in the next room, Candace drew Harriet aside in the kitchen and, Harriet remembered, "held me quite still till the exercises were over, and then she kissed my hand, and I felt her tears drop upon it. There was something about her feeling that struck me with awe. She scarcely spoke a word, but gave me to understand that she was paying that homage to my mother's memory."[2] Candace joined in the eulogies to Roxana's "saintly virtues," but what struck the young child most forcibly was the direct physical expression of her feelings.

While her visits in the kitchen encouraged free expression, her ruminations in her father's study, located at the very top of the house in the third garret, gave flight to her imagination. Seated in a corner of this arched room, surrounded by the "friendly, quiet faces of books," she felt both sheltered and free. The presence of her father seated at his desk, mumbling over the preparation of a sermon she could not understand, represented the adult world that simultaneously protected her and excluded her from its mysteries. The questions that no one except the kitchen help had time for, only telling her that she would understand these things well enough when she was grown up, sent her to books for companionship and answers—but even here she was met with a bewildering array of adult titles: Bell's *Sermons,* Bogue's *Essays,* Bonnet's *Inquiries,* Horsley's *Tracts.* But when the bottom of a barrel of old sermons yielded up the hidden treasure of an intact copy of *Arabian Nights,* she discovered reading as a radical liberation:

> The "Arabian Nights" transported her to foreign lands, gave her a new life of her own; and when things went astray with her, when the boys went to play higher than she dared to climb in the barn, or started on fishing excursions, where they considered her an encumbrance, then she found a snug corner, where, curled up in a little, quiet lair, she could at once sail forth on her bit of enchanted carpet into fairy-land. (PP, 121)

Harriet's reminiscences of her youth are peppered with envy of her older brothers, from whose activities she was regularly excluded on the grounds of both age and sex. In Litchfield, her brother Charles remembered her "coming in with a six quart pail full of berries, and her dress wet up to her knees."[3] Harriet remembered how she, "sole little girls among so many boys," helped to chop wood.

> How the axes rung, and the chips flew, and the jokes and stories flew faster; and when all was cut and split, then came the great work of wheeling in and piling; and then I, sole little girl among so many boys, was sucked into the

vortex of enthusiasm by father's well-pointed declaration that he "wished Harriet was a boy, she would do more than any of them."

I remember putting on a little black coat which I thought looked more like the boys, casting needle and thread to the wind, and working almost like one possessed for a day and a half, till in the afternoon the wood was all in and piled, and the chips swept up.[4]

These outdoor exploits were clearly a way of gaining her father's coveted attention. Catharine, the eldest, enjoyed Lyman Beecher's companionship, but to Harriet her father was an idolized but distant figure.

While her brothers were treated to a fishing expedition at Pine Island with Lyman Beecher, she was likely to be assigned the task of sewing a long, straight seam on a sheet.[5] In *Poganuc People* Dolly's brothers go off to the Fourth of July celebration—a male affair in which mock battles generate great clouds of gunsmoke and noise—while Dolly sits at home manufacturing a great pool of tears, envying "the happy boys who might some day grow up and fight for their country, and do something glorious like General Washington" (PP, 134). Dolly's brothers were not above displaying their superiority; educated at the Academy, they came home spouting Latin phrases, sometimes deliberately displaying them to confound her. "There also were the boys' cabinets of mineralogical specimens; for the Academy teacher was strong on geology, and took his boys on long tramps with stone-hammers on their shoulders, and they used to discuss with great unction to Dolly of tourmaline and hornblende and mica and quartz and feldspar, delighted to exhibit before her their scientific superiority" (PP, 119). Surrounded by older people, Harriet grew up burning with ambition to enter the adult world with a flash of glory. She turned to books for solace and reward; in both a figurative and literal sense, they did finally enable her to climb higher than her brothers.

She was constantly on the prowl for reading matter which, though in plentiful supply in the Beecher household, was likely to be somewhat daunting: titles such as "Toplady on Predestination" stood out in the welter of sermons, essays, replies, and rejoinders that were the meat and drink of Lyman Beecher's combative ministry. He considered novels "trash" and did not allow them in the house. Harriet fed her taste for the imaginative by memorizing the Song of Solomon and reading lurid tales of the anticlericalism of the French Revolution. She recalled finding in a pile of religious pamphlets a dismembered section of *Don Quixote* "rising . . . [like] an enchanted island out of an ocean of mud." An even greater discovery was Mather's *Magnalia Christi Americana*. His tales of her native land inspired her just as they did her contemporary, Nathaniel Hawthorne. They were early examples of a Euro-American literature that drew on indigenous materials: here were Indians, witchcraft, the sayings and doings of everyday life—but mixed in with a high and holy purpose which made it permissible to be entertained by them.[6]

Novel reading was viewed in an entirely different light, however, by the

Foote family, and the Beecher household at Litchfield was not impervious to this influence. Catharine vividly recalled the visits of Uncle Samuel Foote, who was one of the most important intellectual influences on Harriet Beecher:[7] "After we moved to Litchfield, Uncle Samuel came among us, on his return from each voyage, as a sort of brilliant genius of another sphere, bringing gifts and wonders that seemed to wake new faculties in all." Captain of a his own vessel by age twenty, Samuel Foote had sailed all over the world. He brought to Litchfield not only Oriental caps and Moorish slippers, but appreciation of the diversity of cross-cultural customs and beliefs. He delighted in challenging Lyman Beecher's evangelical single-mindedness by exhibiting uncomfortably broad knowledge. "I remember long discussions," wrote Catharine, "in which he maintained that the Turks were more honest than Christians, bringing very startling facts in evidence." He defended the piety and learning of the Catholics in Spain and the heroic martyrdom of the Jews in Morocco. "The new fields of vision presented by my uncle, the skill and adroitness of his arguments, the array of his facts, combined to tax father's powers to their utmost."[8]

Samuel Foote also brought new voices to the literary circles of Litchfield, where he was viewed as "a sort of hero of romance" by the young women. He was fluent in French and he spoke Spanish with a flawless Castillian accent. It was through his agency, and that of Aunt Mary Hubbard, that novel reading was introduced into the evangelical household of Lyman Beecher. They always appeared with stacks of the latest romantic literature: the novels of Scott and the poetry of Byron and Moore were read and reread aloud to eager family gatherings. Faced with this domestic mutiny, Lyman Beecher made what at first may have been a tactical concession to an irresistible cultural force, but that later became an acquired taste of his own. Harriet remembered the day that Lyman Beecher spoke ex cathedra: "George," he declared, "you may read Scott's novels. I have always disapproved of novels as trash, but in these is real genius and real culture, and you may read them."[9] And read them they did, *Ivanhoe* seven times over, until much of it was committed to memory.

Sir Walter Scott became a Beecher family institution. Catharine wrote romantic ballads after his style, and with her friend Louisa Wait at the piano the parsonage "rang with Scottish ballads."[10] When the Beechers sat around the kitchen peeling apples for the cider apple sauce that would be frozen and cut in slices for use on the table in winter, they passed the time by seeing who could recall the most of incident and passage from Scott's novels.[11] As Harriet wrote in *Poganuc People*, "The young folks called the rocks and glens and rivers of their romantic region by names borrowed from Scott; they clambered among the crags of Benvenue and sailed on the bosom of Loch Katrine" (PP, 91). When Harriet had a household of her own it contained a "Walter Scott bookcase," and when she traveled to Scotland she made a point of visiting all the places whose names had invested the haunts of her childhood with a mysterious, romantic aura.[12]

Neither was Lyman Beecher immune to the appeal of romanticism. He followed with great interest the career of Lord Byron, though he covered his attraction by imagining himself Byron's evangelical savior. He did not attempt to hide his admiration for Napoleon. "Genius and heroism," Harriet remembered, "would move him even to tears." The courage and fortitude of Milton's Satan in *Paradise Lost* inspired him to read aloud the description of his marshalling his troops after his fall from heaven with such evident sympathy that Harriet was quite enlisted in Satan's favor. When he reached the passage, "Thrice he essay'd, and thrice, in spite of scorn, / Tears, such as angels weep, burst forth," he burst into tears himself.[13] Harriet loved these stories as much for their drama as for their religious sentiment, and not a small part of her hero worship was childhood's dream of ambition. Her first poetic attempt was an overwrought narrative called "Cleon," set in Rome during Nero's persecutions of the Christians. No doubt she was sure that *she* would have stood up to the emperor.

Lyman Beecher believed that there were two kinds of armor his children needed for the battle with the principalities and powers. The first was polemical skill. One of Harriet's most characteristic images of her father is a picture of him, apple peeler in hand, encouraging theological debate among the assembled apple peelers. He would deliberately take the wrong side of a question and spar with his sons. If they did not score a direct enough hit, he would stop and explain, "The argument lies so, my son; do that, and you'll trip me up."[14] Later victorious in two heresy trials, Lyman trained his sons for a litigious ministry that was sport, spice, and salvation all rolled in one. Speaking of his expertise in the ecclesiastical councils of Litchfield, he said, "I became quite a lawyer. Never succeeded better any where than in ecclesiastical courts."[15] In fact, he relished these battles. To Harriet, her father's heroism in battle was no less moving than Satan's: ["H]is name was 'Turn to the Right Thwack Away'— & thwack away he did lustily & with good courage."[16]

An even more essential armor than polemical skill was the experience of rebirth in Jesus Christ. A conversion experience was the capstone of a Beecher family education, an "anchor to the soul" without which it was foolish to "mingle with the world." A recently converted Edward Beecher chided Catharine for her neglect of this principle: "Do you think of going to Boston before you become a christian? It must not be—How can you think of it. The harvest may be passed for ever."[17] It was a source of considerable torment to Lyman Beecher that he could lead successful revivals in Litchfield, but he could not bring his own children to Christ. He continually told his children that his greatest anxiety was the state of their unconverted souls, and that the greatest happiness would be his when he heard the news that they had submitted to Jesus Christ. Under this weight of constant parental scrutiny many of the Beecher children experienced total paralysis of their spiritual faculties and delayed the crisis until well into adulthood. This only redoubled the watchings and warnings. Every Saturday Lyman Beecher held meetings with the students at the Litchfield Female Academy where student Caroline Boardman recorded his apocalyptic warnings: ["T]here were five who attended this school formerly that were now deprived of their reason, five who had become intemperate and two died every year."[18] While his graphic powers of description and his vivid portrayals of the tortures of hell spread his success as a revival preacher, at home his children remained "all stupid."[19]

After Roxana's death Esther Beecher, Lyman's half-sister, assumed the charge of the Beecher children out of sympathy with their motherless state, and in a spirit of duty and self-abnegation. Like Harriet Foote, Aunt Esther never married, but unlike Harriet Foote Esther had been an only child raised under the dark, critical eye of a mother whose neat and orderly house represented the horizon of her world. Yet Aunt Esther possessed formidable skills in the line of reading, writing, and the marshalling of ideas. Her inventiveness no less than her patience is suggested by the exclamation of a Beecher child who, during convalescence from an illness, was heard to say, "Only think! Aunt Esther has told me *nineteen rat stories* all in a string." (The old parsonage was so riddled with rats that even the cats ignored them.) Harriet believed Aunt Esther knew the sum of knowledge in the world, for never did she fail to answer a question put to her. "She had read on all subjects—chemistry, philosophy, physiology, but especially on natural history, where her anecdotes were inexhaustible."[20] A sermon that satisfied Aunt Esther represented to Lyman Beecher "the highest state of excellence in writing to which I ever aspire."[21] Her neat and shady parlor overhung by inviting bookshelves was one of Harriet's favorite retreats.[22]

The Beechers considered Aunt Esther "the peaceable fruits of righteousness"—the compensation and comfort that had grown out of their loss of Roxana.[23] She was loyal to the Beechers in all their vagaries and schemes. She worried over their debts and darned their socks. She followed the Beecher children to Hartford and then Cincinnati, and circulated among them after they were dispersed to points across the Western Reserve. When there was sickness or domestic need, Aunt Esther soon appeared. As adults, the Beecher children vied for her time, begging for a visit from Aunt Esther, that she might ease the domestic difficulties of their household with her calm and self-denying presence. In the epochs of the three successive Mrs. Beechers, Aunt Esther was a constant; the family memory and the chronicler, she was the one to whom the Beechers turned with questions about their childhood histories.[24] When she died, Harriet Beecher asked if she could have her work basket to remember her by.

Another of the "peaceable fruits" of Roxana's death was the spirit of independence and family competence that the children necessarily developed. As the oldest of the household of eight children, Catharine felt the mantle of responsibility descend on her shoulders. At sixteen, she became mother to her brothers and sisters. As she measured and cut the clothes for them—a task that perplexed Aunt Esther—she not only experienced the pride of accomplishment, she provided the cornerstone of a peer culture in which the Beecher children cared for one another. The extraordinary family loyalty of the Beechers was a deep reservoir of emotional and intellectual support upon which they all made large draughts during their ambitious and far-flung careers. "Remember that we shall never regret that we acted like brothers & sisters," Edward wrote to Catharine around this time.[25] When Harriet was eighteen she wrote, "I love to hear sisters speak of their brothers There is no pride I can so readily tolerate as pride of relationship."[26] The ability of the Beecher children to rally around one another was strengthened in the difficult year after Roxana's death. As one of the younger children raised by elder siblings, Harriet Beecher was particularly susceptible to this peer culture; when she was twelve, her father was nearing fifty and beginning, as he said, "to look back and lean on [my children] as once I looked up for support to those of the generation which is gone."[27]

In the fall of 1817 Lyman Beecher brought home his second wife. In terms of intellect and socialization, Harriet Porter was significantly like her predecessor. She was a woman of "vigorous and cultivated intellect" and her uncles were the governors, bishops, and congressmen of Maine. Moreover, she was well adapted to the job of domestic support for a ministerial husband. She wrote a few months after their marriage, "When I think what he is, and what he is doing in his study above, it helps in the discharge of duty below."[28] Catharine formally welcomed her stepmother into what had been her sphere of responsibility, but Harriet Porter remained an outsider to the Beecher children from Lyman's first marriage. Harriet remembered being in awe of this beautiful and delicate lady, who seemed a storybook princess: "I remember I used to feel breezy, and rough, and rude in her presence."[29]

Not intimately involved in the care of the Beecher children, Harriet Porter nevertheless appreciated their intellectual appetites. Soon after her arrival she described their prospects in a letter to her sister:

> It seems the highest happiness of the children (the larger ones especially) to have a reading circle. They have all, I think, fine capacities, and a good taste for learning. Edward, probably, will be a great scholar. . . . Catharine is a fine-looking girl, and in her mind I find all that I expected. She is not handsome, yet there is hardly any one who appears better. Mary will make a fine woman, I think; will be rather handsome than otherwise. She is twelve now, large of her age, and is almost the most useful member of the family. The four youngest are very pretty. George comes next to Mary. He is quite a large boy; takes care of the cow, etc.; goes to school, though his father expects to educate him. He learns well.
>
> Harriet and Henry come next, and they are always hand-in-hand. They are as lovely children as I ever saw, amiable, affectionate, and very bright. Charles, the youngest, we can hardly tell what he will be, but he promises well.[30]

The two oldest boys, Edward and William, soon left for college. The other children were completely under the care of Catharine and Mary morning and night and were away at school during the day. Harriet Porter's energies were soon taken up by children of her own; in 1818 she gave birth to the first of her four children, who would arrive in this order: Frederick, Isabella, Thomas, James.

Harriet Beecher had the good fortune to grow up in Litchfield at the height of its golden age. By becoming a supply depot during the Revolutionary War, Litchfield had developed commercial arteries to Boston and New York. In the decades following independence commercial development boomed. Litchfield was the county seat, and the regular court sessions held there added a population of lawyers to the merchants who had set up stores. A prosperous professional elite made Litchfield appealing to people of taste and intellect. The Rev. Dan Huntington, pastor of Litchfield from 1798 to 1809, described the town as he found it: "A delightful village, on a fruitful hill, richly endowed with schools both professional and scientific, with its venerable governors and judges, with its learned lawyers, and senators, and representatives both in the national and state departments, and with a population enlightened and respectable, Litchfield was now in its glory."[31]

Litchfield responded quickly to the changed manners that came with independence. In colonial times no theatricals were ever held in Litchfield, but after the war and the founding of the law school, "the infusion of a new spirit was so strong" that theatricals immediately sprung up.[32] Revolutionary thinking extended to women's rights and responsibilities in the new republic. Judge Tapping Reeve, a leading Litchfield citizen and intimate of Lyman Beecher, wrote a treatise on domestic relations that was thought to lean "too much to women's rights" to be considered law. He and other like-minded men of vision put up the subscription that enabled Sarah Pierce to build her female academy, for in republican America the intellects of its women were resources to be cultivated in the interests of rearing intelligent sons and daughters of liberty.[33]

In an address to Miss Pierce's class of 1816, teacher John Brace reminded the students of the privilege they enjoyed by living in an age distinguished by "the general diffusion of knowledge." He observed that education was "no longer restricted to our sex," but "shines equally upon both with the same rays and the same effects." Contrasting the present age with "the night of ignorance" that preceded it, he credited education with improving women's "rank in society, placing her as the rational companion of man, not the slave of his pleasures or the victim of tyranny."[34] Making allowances for his republican rhetoric, he was not exaggerating. Only about half of all New England women could sign their names in 1780, and probably many of these could not read. By 1840, however, literacy in New England was virtually universal.[35] Improvements in women's education, as one historian has observed, "form[ed] the basis of all the other major role changes experienced by women in the later nineteenth century."[36]

The story of Sarah Pierce's school, which the Beecher children attended gratis in exchange for their father's pastoral services, was itself a parable of the times. When their father died at the early age of fifty-three, Sarah

Pierce's brother, who had had a distinguished career in the Continental Army under George Washington, encouraged her to prepare herself to run a school. Although the talents he expected her to develop were more social than intellectual, the school she began in her Litchfield dining room in 1792 reflected the new cultivation of women's minds as well as the older, more aristocratic attention to women's accomplishments.[37] Her educational goal was to teach the art of thinking, her larger purpose, to "vindicate the equality of female intellect." While in step with the republican spirit of the times, this was, as Mary Beth Norton has observed, a radical philosophy.[38] In 1798 Miss Pierce moved her school into the building erected by the subscriptions of the town's prominent citizens, and this inaugurated the most successful period of the academy's history; during the next three decades the school enjoyed a national reputation and enrollments of as many as 140 students per session. One of the first female academies in the new nation, Miss Pierce's school attracted students from all over New England and from as far away as New York, Ohio, Canada, and the West Indies. The girls boarded with local families and abided by rules which remind us that while their minds were schooled in republican principles, their behavior was regulated by the canons of true womanhood: "You must suppress all emotions of anger, fretfulness and discontent," they were warned.[39]

Although not immune to evangelical earnestness, the school had a decidedly eigthteenth-century tone. In his address to the class of 1816, John Brace told the students that the school had endeavored "to teach you to feel but to feel in subordination to reason."[40] His personal library included works by Bunyan, Dryden, and Colley Cibber, as well as volumes of Addison and Steele's *The Spectator* and Fielding's *Tom Jones*.[41] The English classics were a favorite point of reference for both John Brace and Sarah Pierce, and the latter interspersed her daily counsels with quotations from them. Catharine Beecher recalled that "[e]ven the rules of the school, read aloud every Saturday, were rounded off in Johnsonian periods, which the roguish girls sometimes would most irreverently burlesque."[42]

John Brace, who had a significant influence both on the school and on the education of Harriet Beecher, was himself something of an eighteenth-century man. Possessed, as Harriet recalled, "of the most general information on *all subjects*,"[43] Brace had interests that ranged from heraldry to astrology; a poet and novelist, he became editor of the Hartford *Courant* after he retired from teaching. He was Sarah Pierce's nephew and was educated at Williams College for the express purpose of becoming her assistant. He became head teacher in 1814 and inaugurated important curricular expansions. An accomplished naturalist, he was in correspondence with learned men in England, Sweden, and Switzerland; Harriet remembered that his example inspired the boys (girls were apparently not included in rockhounding expeditions) to tramp over hill and dale in search of minerals to set up in their collections.[44]

Although Miss Pierce normally did not accept students until they were twelve years old, Harriet Beecher entered in 1819 at age eight.[45] Endowed with a "remarkably retentive memory," she had attended private primary schools since the age of six where she had learned to read fluently and had memorized twenty-seven hymns and two chapters of the Bible.[46] Miss Pierce's school, located one block from the Beecher family parsonage on North Street, was one large room, about seventy by thirty feet in size, containing an elevated teacher's chair, a piano, and small closets for cloaks and caps. Students sat on long, hard, pine benches without backs and wrote on plain pine desks.[47] The year Harriet entered, John Brace observed that the student body was "not as large as usual," about ninety-five scholars. Harriet had been preceded by her older siblings Catharine, Mary, and George (a few boys' names appear in the class lists of the Litchfield Female Academy); Henry and Charles were enrolled in 1823, the year before she left.[48]

Harriet's education was significantly different from that of Catharine, who attended the school when Miss Pierce was the sole teacher. "At that time," Catharine recalled, " 'the higher branches' had not entered the female schools. Map-drawing, painting, embroidery and the piano were the accomplishments sought, and history was the only study added to geography, grammar, and arithmetic."[49] With the arrival of John Brace, the curriculum at the Litchfield Female Academy resembled more nearly that of a boys' academy. He added higher mathematics, the sciences, moral philosophy, logic, and an occasional Latin tutorial.[50] The courses of study required for a degree in Harriet's time included "Morse's Geography, Webster's Elements of English Grammar, Miss Pierce's History, Arithmetic through Interest, Blair's Lectures, Modern Europe, Ramsey's American Revolution, Natural Philosphy, Chemistry, Paley's Moral Philosophy, Hedge's Logic and Addison [that is, Alison] on Taste."[51]

The inclusion of moral philosophy in the curriculum of the Litchfield Female Academy is evidence of the high intellectual aspirations of this pioneering school. It was not taught in the boys' academies because it was assumed that preparatory students would experience it in college, where, indeed, moral philosophy formed the capstone of their senior year. Paley's *The Principles of Moral and Political Philosophy* (1785), used at the Litchfield Female Academy, was the text most widely used in American colleges into the second quarter of the nineteenth century. In general the teaching of moral philosophy painted an eighteenth-century universe in which "[i]t was discovered that religious conviction and Christian ethics rested not only upon the word of God but upon the verification which man's reason found in nature."[52]

Harriet Beecher described John Brace as "one of the most stimulating and inspiring instructors I ever knew."[53] Although his work in the natural sciences was perhaps his most notable accomplishment, Harriet remembered his skill in moral philosophy and composition.[54] His approach to composition was at once progressive and rooted in eighteenth-century aesthetic principles. Believing that the first impulse to expression was the conviction that one had something of worth to say, he stimulated discussion on a wide variety of topics, and it was these debates that Harriet remembered most vividly in later years.[55] At the same time he encouraged the reading of the English classics to form his students' taste; Harriet Beecher followed his lead when she later prepared to teach composition at the Hartford Female Seminary.[56] A surprising amount of the organized reading at the Litchfield Female Academy was of novels, including Maria Edgeworth's *The Unknown Friend*, which Miss Pierce read aloud to the school in 1814.[57]

One of the youngest scholars, Harriet Beecher lost no time in proving her readiness to enter the grown-up world of the academy. Writing regular compositions was a staple of John Brace's educational regimen, and when she was only nine Harriet volunteered to write every week. The difference between Sarah Pierce and John Brace is illustrated in the topics they assigned for composition. Drawing almost exclusively from the British advice literature on the proper education of women, Sarah Pierce assigned essays on such topics as "Contentment," "Cheerfulness," "Charity," "Forgiveness," and other female virtues.[58] John Brace's first assignment to Harriet was an essay on "The Difference between the Natural and Moral Sublime"—a topic, Harriet noted, "not trashy or sentimental, such as are often supposed to be the style for female schools." The misspelled composition she handed in was a tribute to her ambition and to the excitement of John Brace's teaching. After two years of his tutelage in composition Harriet Beecher was selected to be one of the writers for the academy's annual exhibition. The topic, "Can the immortality of the soul be proved by the light of nature?," was calculated to call forth the best in the pupil of John Brace and the daughter of Lyman Beecher. She argued the negative. When at the exhibition the composition was read aloud "before all the literati of Litchfield," her father was sitting on high next to John Brace. She noticed that Lyman Beecher "brightened and looked interested" while her composition was being read, and at the conclusion she heard him ask Brace who wrote it. When the answer came, "*'Your daughter, sir!,'*" Harriet experienced "the proudest moment" of her life: "There was no mistaking father's face when he was pleased, and to have interested *him* was past all juvenile triumphs."[59]

In spite of this precocious essay, Harriet was not a consistent student. John Brace organized the school along military lines and encouraged a fierce competition among the different divisions, each headed by a "lieutenant."[60] In addition, Sarah Pierce "publicly rank[ed] students each week into a complex system of credit and debit marks and award[ed] coveted awards and prizes at the end of each school term."[61] It was Mary Beecher, the only child of Lyman Beecher to have no public career, who regularly won prizes and the privilege of being "head of papers."[62] Harriet excelled when her interests were engaged, but did not have the discipline and regularity of the prizewinning student. She had no mind for arithmetic and remarked in later years that "when I was a girl I thought I could not even make change in a store."[63] When she should have been applying herself to her lessons, she was listening to the recitations of the older children. "Much of the training and inspiration of my early days consisted, not in the things which I was supposed to be studying, but in hearing, while seated unnoticed at my desk, the conversation of Mr. Brace with the older classes." As she listened "from hour to hour" with "eager ears," she absorbed precocious intellectual frameworks, a love of ideas and expression, and a desire to excel in the handling of them.[64]

The influence John Brace exercised by virtue of his engaging and intelligent teaching was enhanced by the fact that in 1819 he married Lucy Porter, sister of Lyman Beecher's second wife, and lived for a time in the Beecher parsonage. As Catharine reported in a letter to her Uncle Samuel, "[Lucy] is a lovely girl about my age & has spent the winter here.—She will be married next fall to Mr. John Brace & will settle here which will be a great comfort to mama & all of us."[65] Two years later Brace and his wife were still boarding at the Beechers.[66] Thus Harriet had ample opportunity to observe her mentor in the parlor, where he cut quite a literary figure. "The poetical compositions of this gentleman," recalled Harriet, "were constantly circulating among the young ladies of his school and the literati of the place, and there was a peculiar freshness of enjoyment and excitement to us in this species of native unpublished literature." She remembered in particular the vogue for "ballads and poetical effusions" on the subject of the Bantam Indians who had lived in Litchfield.[67] In the summer of 1821 John Brace initiated a newspaper at the Litchfield Female Academy. It was called the "Holy-day Recorder" because it was read on Wednesdays, a holiday when students came to the school but no classes were held—the most interesting day of the week for many students. "Very many of the students wrote for it, as I did myself," Brace noted, "and it was very interesting." It is likely that Harriet Beecher, an eager writer in what Brace called this "literary loving school," participated in this venture, though no copies of the newspaper exist to confirm this supposition. Brace pointed out that this newspaper was the model for the one that Catharine later began at her Hartford Female Seminary, though she gave him no credit.[68]

Miss Pierce was a firm believer in the benefits of exercise and required her students to take morning and evening walks. Other forms of exercise included bowling on the green with young men from the law school, jumping rope, and swinging on swings.[69] Groups of young women strolling to such destinations as Chestnut Hill, Bantam Lake, and Prospect Hill would often be joined by young men from the law school. Many courtships were begun and pursued during evening strolls, and more than fifty marriages issued between women from the Litchfield Female Academy and men from the Litchfield Law School. Indeed, placing one's daughter in a position to marry well was one reason parents went to great trouble and expense to transport them to Litchfield. In the early republic, social life in Litchfield was relaxed and inclusive of all ages. Even children as young as eleven went to the balls. By the time Harriet entered school, however, Miss Pierce's rules stipulated that only girls sixteen and older might attend the balls.[70]

Although Harriet Beecher lived at home while she attended the Litchfield Female Academy, the Beecher parsonage was if anything more like a school boardinghouse than even Miss Pierce's home. In addition to the head teacher, John Brace, boarders included Louisa Wait, the music instructor, who lived with the Beechers for many years and became a close friend of Catharine, plus many student boarders attending the Litchfield Female Academy or Tapping Reeve's Litchfield Law School. During the winters a Russian stove heated three rooms down and three rooms up, drawing all inhabitants to the comparative warmth of these quarters. A large parlor had been added to the front of the house, but company always sat in "the little front room," which was warm.[71] The rich social life of the Beecher parsonage cramped their quarters but broadened their horizons. As Lynne Brickley has written, "The boarders served an important educational function in Litchfield's families, mingling the thoughts, habits and customs of places as different and distant as New York City, Savannah, Georgia, Middlebury, Vermont, Ohio and Canada. In a time of limited travel and communication, the boarding system broadened the townsfolks' exposure to national rather than to local customs, tastes and ideas."[72]

Harriet Beecher was born in an enlightened republican age and received the best education available to women at that time. Her first education was informal, and took place in the kitchen and common room and library of the Beecher household. Her second was formal, and proceeded most notably under the auspices of Sarah Pierce's nationally reknowned school. In both, it is striking that Harriet's most important lessons were not taught but overheard: Lyman Beecher's instructions to his sons on the art of debate, John Brace's conversations with the older children.

As a young girl, however, this heightened attentiveness often made her appear "odd." Imbued with a strong desire to please, she did not readily fall into ways of winning approval. It was easier to gain attention by making "wry faces" and exciting laughter than by adhering to the forms of proper girlhood.[73] In the winter of 1822 when the Beechers were struggling under the combined difficulties of Lyman's breakdown from overwork and Harriet Porter's approaching confinement with her second child, Harriet was sent to Nutplains. When Catharine wrote to her to announce the birth of Isabella, she told her, "We all want you home very much, but hope you are now where you will learn to stand and sit straight, and hear what people say to you, and sit still in your chair, and learn to sew and knit well, and be a good girl in every particular; and if you don't learn while you are with Aunt Harriet, I am afraid you never will."[74]

Lyman Beecher recognized the oddity of his daughter as the mark of "genius" in conflict with gender. His observations about Harriet in a letter to his brother-in-law stand out by contrast with the more ordinary remarks he offers about his other children:

> William is doing well in his clerkship at New Milford & now supports himself. Catherine is learning to play on the Piano with the intention of teaching Miss Pierces School & helping herself—Mary [hole in page] to be the best scholar in Miss Pierces school & at home does all the *chores*. Harriet is a great genius—

I would give a hundred dollars if she was a boy & Henry a girl—She is as odd—
as she is intelligent & studious—Henry is Henry—grown older & learning some
bad things from bad boys—but on the whole a lovely child—Charles is as
intellegent as ever & falls down 20 times a day—he will doubtless be a great
man.[75]

For all of the limitations of this response, Lyman Beecher's appreciation of
Harriet and his accessibility as a role model positioned her to overhear what
she needed to learn in order to find a channel of expression for both her
genius and her gender. In addition, she was exposed through the Litchfield
Female Academy and the contrasting cultures of Nutplains and Litchfield
to the pluralism of the new republic. Even before she left Connecticut, she
had had a more national experience than most of her contemporaries.

The completion of Harriet's Litchfield education came in the summer of
1825, when she reported to her father that Christ had taken her for his own.
Her imaginative temperament spared her the paralyzing doubts that posed
an obstacle to more strict and legalistic minds. Her conversion came gently,
naturally, in the afterglow of an inspiring sermon by her father. She was
thirteen years old.[76]

CHAPTER FOUR

The Hartford Female Seminary: 1824–1827

*O*n September 3, 1824, the city of Hartford turned out to welcome General Lafayette, who two weeks earlier had begun his triumphal tour of America. Revered for his heroism at Yorktown and his willingness to share the deprivations of the common soldier at Valley Forge, Lafayette turned Americans inside out in a frenzy of republican pride. Babies were named for him and held up at the processions that greeted him from New York to Washington, D.C. His visit was "an entrepreneur's delight."[1] In Hartford "triumphal arches were erected at the foot of Morgan Street and on the west side of the State House." The normally somber banks and commercial buildings were festooned with flowers and evergreens. Throughout the city citizens illuminated their houses in tribute to the Revolutionary War hero. In this city of seven thousand, eight hundred young schoolchildren marched in procession, the girls in white dresses pinned with ribbons that read "Nous vous aimons, La Fayette" ("We love you, La Fayette").[2] At the State House the governor's address welcomed Lafayette to Connecticut, "where a virtuous and enlightened people have, during nearly two centuries, enjoyed Republican Institutions."[3]

Some time during this week thirteen-year-old Harriet Beecher made her unobtrusive entry into the same city with her carpetbag stuffed with all her worldly goods. It is fitting that she made her entrance into Hartford at the same time as Lafayette, for she was embarking on a republican experiment in women's education. Catharine Beecher's Hartford Female Seminary, bravely begun in the spring of 1823 with seven students in a single room above the White Horse harness shop, was destined to take a significant place in the history of the education of women. Moreover, it sprang from Catharine's awareness of the contradiction between republican principles and the still-backward state of female education. In its prime the seminary boasted more than 160 students, eight teachers, two principals, and a governess—all of whom were female. Run by and for women, the Hartford Female Seminary provided a separate institution in which young women aged twelve and up could explore for themselves the meaning of republican sisterhood. From dawn until dusk they studied together, prayed, incited and quelled food rebellions, talked, sewed, and exchanged a welter of notes—notes of friendship, of personal distress, of religious concern. The seminary provided an all-female institution within the larger culture, a space within which young women could, for perhaps the first time in their lives, articulate a culture that spoke directly to and from their experience. Under Catharine's leadership, it became a testing ground for women's "moral influence." It provided Harriet Beecher's first lectern and pulpit, an opportunity to test her power to influence others. Here, in the winter of 1829, the students and the teachers engaged in a radical experiment in republican government. In this women's culture Harriet Beecher tentatively tried out her vocations of teacher, preacher, and writer. Harriet's eight years in the Hartford Female Seminary took her through the formative period of adolescence: when she emerged she was twenty-one. Although her career took a different path from Catharine's, it was profoundly shaped by her elder sister, who adroitly turned her own experience into practical experiments for the benefit of others.

When, in 1822, the expected course of her life was dramatically altered by the death of her fiancé, Alexander Fisher, Catharine Beecher experienced a rude awakening. She had had no preparation for the independent life she now found thrust upon her. She had attended Miss Pierce's Female Academy when the emphasis was on social rather than intellectual attainments. In addition, Catharine had beguiled her mentors with her charm and high spirits, thus avoiding confrontation with strenuous thought. She admitted in a letter to her father in 1822 that whatever knowledge she possessed had "walked into her head."[4] In the year following Fisher's death she set about remedying the deficiencies of what she termed a "domestic education"; she learned the rudiments of geometry, chemistry, geography, and moral philosophy with a view to defining an independent life for herself and teaching an improved curriculum. As she later wrote, "The most remarkable case of the culture of undeveloped or deficient intellectual faculties, in the Hartford Seminary, was my own."[5]

Catharine's educational mission began within the Beecher family. Bemoaning the indolence of her youth and casting about for a means of support, Catharine wrote her father, "I feel anxious that Harriets mind should not be left to run to waste as mine has & should feel a pleasure in taking care of her education."[6] This sentiment modulated naturally enough into thoughts of founding a female school in Hartford with her sister Mary.

Edward Beecher was already in Hartford; as principal of a primary school he could funnel likely students to Catharine and Mary when they reached the appropriate age. Lyman Beecher, who believed scholarship to be "the best use the Beechers can be put to," and a course of action likely to open the "greatest usefulness for you & perhaps for Harriet also,"[7] encouraged his daughter's plans and urged that she apprentice herself to the Rev. Joseph Emerson, known for his progressive views of female education. Catharine, however, declined to enlist a male mentor and set out alone, "equipped only with her own ideas."[8] Her ideas bore the strong imprint of her experiences at the Litchfield Female Academy, a point confirmed by the complaint of John Brace that Catharine had "all her life . . . taken my best ideas, and by her imitations run away with the credit."[9]

Catharine Beecher's first attempt at creating an American institution bears some characteristic features of her work: emphases on efficiency and professionalism, both of which were meant to promote greater freedom, dignity, and independence for women. Her first stroke was to accept no girls under the age of twelve—"all young ladies and no children"—thus relieving herself of many tasks which, while not unrewarding, required great stores of time and patience. Just a year after the school's inception her scholars numbered upwards of thirty and she and Mary "established a system of classification & mutual instruction so that we are confined only half the day."[10] As soon as increased staffing allowed, Catharine instituted a division of labor that enabled teachers to concentrate on one or two subjects in the curriculum, a system, she remarked, "of essential advantage both to pupils and to teachers."[11]

The most remarkable feature of Catharine's school, however, was its form of government—suggested by her phrase "a system . . . of mutual instruction." From its origins as a kind of Beecher family project to its self-conscious articulation under Catharine's visionary leadership, the Hartford Female Seminary exemplified a collegial, egalitarian polity.[12] The self-conscious valuation and articulation of a school of equals was the result partly of principle, partly of necessity. In the beginning necessity was uppermost. Catharine created from nothing a school that in a few years had a specialized curriculum, an imposing neoclassical building, and a national reputation. Because neither she nor any other woman had been educated for the work, she not only had to do it all herself, she had to learn how to do it as she went along. Thus she was principal, teacher, student, business manager, housekeeper, moral guide, and fundraiser all in one. These duties, she pointed out, in a well-endowed male institution would be divided among many qualified people. She had two choices: to continue to run the school on her own energies until she gave out in exhaustion, or to use her energy to train others in the tasks that she alone could not hope to sustain. She quickly turned first to her sisters and then to the likeliest pupils, making them "teachers" and "assistant pupils." This was all the more necessary because, owing to the deficiencies in her students' preparation, they came to her with no certain skills and she had to divide them into many different recitation classes, each of which required someone to hear and correct their work. With the aid of assistant pupils, an efficient and decentralized system of remedial education was put in place.[13]

Harriet Beecher was quickly drafted into this cadre of assistant pupils. As the beneficiary of John Brace's improved curriculum, Harriet's formal training surpassed Catharine's. When Catharine found her with time on her hands to write poetry, she set Harriet the task of teaching Joseph Butler's *Analogy of Religion, Natural and Revealed, to the Constitution and Course of Nature* , "a task for which she had been fitted by listening to Mr. Brace's lectures at the Litchfield school."[14] At the same time Catharine took seriously her intention to supervise Harriet's education. Her first assignment to her charge was anything but frivolous: Harriet Beecher would learn Latin. On September 10, 1824, soon after she had settled into her lodgings at Mrs. Bull's, Harriet wrote to her Nutplains relatives: "I do not study any thing but Latin for the present am almost through the grammar I study mornings and afternoons and *read* in the time between five oclock and dark and *work* the *evening*."[15] Catharine's decision to teach Harriet Latin was a bold declaration of her belief in the capacity of women's minds to cope with the most difficult of the traditional subjects in the male curriculum. Having herself learned Latin from her brother Edward, Catharine read with Harriet "most of Virgil's Aeneid and Bucolics, a few of Cicero's Orations, and some of the finest parts of Ovid."[16] Harriet's letters during the next few years are sprinkled with Latin flourishes.

Catharine probably felt more freedom to experiment with her sister's education than she did at first in her school at large. She was still feeling her way in an educational system that, even at the college level, relied mainly on rote recitation. She later recalled the task of checking how much students had memorized as "a painful and distracting dream." Her "only pleasant recollection" of her early experiments, she wrote, was "my own careful and exact training under my most accurate and faithful brother Edward, and my reproduction of it to my sister Harriet and two others of my brightest pupils."[17]

Catharine used her own family experience to gain leverage against the educational machinery of the larger culture. The Beecher family provided a mixed-sex culture in which, at the sibling level, a rough equality prevailed. Although gender distinctions were made within the family, daughters were often exposed to the same influences as sons. In addition, the fact that Catharine was the firstborn tended to equalize gender distinctions: she enjoyed the confidence and support of her father to an extent that probably would not have been the case had her birthorder been different.[18] It is undeniable that the sons enjoyed educational privileges in the outside world—Isabella remarked bitterly that, while all her brothers had college educations, "cost what it might," no daughter of Lyman Beecher "cost him more than $100 a year, after she was sixteen"[19]—but the Beecher children treated one another as equals and viewed greater age or experience not as prerogatives to be asserted but as privileges to be shared. The transmission of Latin is an example: Edward taught Catharine, Catharine taught Harriet, and Harriet taught Henry. Acting partly out of necessity, Catharine extended this model of brothers and sisters educating one another to a self-conscious program of peer education. She also had the benefit of Sarah Pierce's example, for Catharine had been one of her assistant pupils at the Litchfield Female Academy.

Catharine's school was one of a handful of female institutions where young women could get an education equivalent to a young man's. The curriculum she offered was essentially the same as that at the Young Ladies Academy in Philadelphia, the Litchfield Female Academy, and Emma Willard's Troy Female Seminary. The eighteenth-century model on which they all depended was Benjamin Franklin's proposal for an "English" school (as opposed to a "Latin" school). Designed to outfit young men for a practical vocation in the business world, his curriculum stessed the basics of grammar and spelling, reading for oral effect and comprehension, and rhetoric and oratory; next pursued were history, the natural and mechanical sciences, composition, ethics, and logic, capped by wide reading in the best English authors.[20] In addition to these subjects in the "English branches," the Hartford Female Seminary offered Latin, French, Italian, drawing, and music. Many academies for boys offered two courses of instruction, the "academical" and the "useful," the former comprising Latin, Greek, logic, rhetoric, and mathematics, the latter such subjects as bookkeeping, surveying, navigation, and shorthand.[21] The curriculum of the Hartford Female Seminary combined in one course the "academical," college-preparatory subjects, with subjects that could be classified as either ornamental or "useful," depending on their application. Painting could be an aristocratic accomplishment or it could be a practical way of earning one's living; parents were eager to have their daughters trained by teachers skilled in the decorative arts, and Catharine Beecher had to prepare herself in this area before she embarked on her teaching career.[22] In a period in which women's colleges had not yet emerged, this hybrid curriculum appropriately enough prepared young women for everything and nothing.

Tuition was dependent on how many subjects a student pursued.[23] In the beginning Catharine consulted parents as to the most desirable course of study, but by 1831 she had worked out a three-year sequence of courses for the "Primary Class," "Junior Class," and "Senior Class," though parents were still free to enroll their daughters without having them adhere to this "regular course." Those so enrolled, upon satisfactory examination, received certificates of membership in their class; upon the close of their studies they were given a "testimonial" indicating that they had completed the regular course.[24] Catharine considered geography, grammar, and arithmetic "essential" and insisted that students take them if they were not already well prepared in these subjects; these constituted the studies of the "Primary Class."

The natural sciences Catharine thought an important and often neglected area of study for women. She secured some laboratory apparatus and made the study of chemistry one of her particular preparations for beginning the school; she required Comstock's *Elements of Chemistry* and his *Natural Philosophy* for the Junior Class, along with astronomy and Euclidian geometry.[25] She did not, however, have the advantage of a well-trained naturalist such as John Brace, nor access to Amos Eaton, whose willingness to educate Emma Willard's students in his classes at the Rensselaer Polytechnic Institute greatly enriched the science curriculum of the Troy Female Seminary.[26] Having a strong natural science curriculum was dependent on the presence of male teachers, and the Hartford Female Seminary remained, until Catharine left, solely under the supervision of women. The capstone of the senior year was Paley's *Moral Philosophy*, taught in many female academies as it was in men's colleges by the president of the school.[27]

The subject to which female educators brought special attention was geography. One of Emma Willard's alumnae ranked her "spreading the idea of intelligent study of geography" as one of her greatest achievements.[28] In the eighteenth century geography, like history, was considered an ornamental subject. After the American Revolution, however, it became practical and patriotic to understand the vast geographic sweep of the new nation. Entrepreneurs and traders needed to know the routes on which products traveled to markets. Precisely because of their position on the margin, female academies were in a good position to transform the ornamental subject of geography into republican practice.[29] Besides considering it an "essential" subject, Catharine Beecher experimented with some new pedagogical strategies. Before students engaged in detailed investigations of land areas, they were required to draw maps from memory on the board and explain what they were drawing. Catharine complained of "the want of suitable schoolbooks," the difficulties of adapting those that were not congenial, and the sometimes easier course of writing one's own.[30] Sarah Pierce had done this at her school; when she discovered that the history texts were dry and unappealing to her students, she "set out and wrote her own," mixing moral with historical instruction.[31] Catharine Beecher's innovations in the teaching of geography led to the publication, in 1833, of her new geography text—which had been written by her sister Harriet.[32] Catharine Beecher's pioneering educational philosophy thus resulted in one of Harriet Beecher's first publications to the world.

Just as Benjamin Franklin's English school aimed to produce not classically trained gentlemen, but practical men of the world, so Catharine approached the study of Latin in a more practical spirit than was usual. Discarding the notion that knowledge of Latin grammar was a first step toward learning the English language, she believed that familiarity with the idioms, most common vocabulary, philosophy, and classification of the language was all that was necessary—and could be taught in six weeks.[33] It is striking that with the study of Latin Catharine simultaneously introduced an "exotic" topic into female education and swept away some of the cobwebs that made the study of Latin a torture to nineteenth-century youths such as Henry Ward Beecher. Harriet, who had charge of teaching her brother Latin, later condemned the pedantic mode of teaching it "which makes one ragged, prickly bundle of all the dry facts of the language, and insists upon it that the boy shall not see one glimpse of its beauty, glory or interest, till he has swallowed and digested the whole mass."[34] The pedagogical principle that Catharine applied throughout her curriculum was first to engage her students' attention and desire to learn by presenting an overview of the whole subject to be mastered.

As was increasingly the custom at men's colleges during the nineteenth century, the Hartford Female Seminary students boarded with local families rather than residing in dormitories. The "commons" system that prevailed in men's colleges in the eighteenth century was breaking down as older and often poorer students entered college; their demands for simple, affordable food led to conflicts, or "food riots," among the students; their need to work outside of school did not accord well with the inflexible schedules that students were once expected to march through. Pressures for change mounted during the three decades after 1830, when about one-fourth of the New England college graduates were older than twenty-five.[35] A boarding-out system allowed such students more freedom and independence. Catharine's students were younger and probably more economically homogeneous, and would have been likely candidates for a commons system. In 1829 she did attempt, unsuccessfully, to raise a subscription for a dormitory, perhaps with the thought of making her seminary more like a traditional men's college.[36]

The boarding-out system had the advantage of placing young men and women in a "family discipline."[37] Typically, two or three of Catharine's teachers boarded in the same house with half a dozen to a dozen scholars. The proprietors of these boardinghouses were eminently respectably women whom Catharine described as "nearly as valuable as teachers in many particulars." The ones Catharine saw fit to mention by name were of high social position:

> Of these, Mrs. Henry L. Ellsworth, daughter-in-law of our Chief-Justice and sister of Professor Goodrich of Yale College, took charge of ten of my scholars. Mrs. Dr. Cogswell, widow of the leading physician of the city and State, received another portion. Mrs. Major Caldwell, wife of a gentleman of reduced fortune, once one of the wealthiest shipping merchants of New England, gave me and several pupils a home for some years, and her daughters were among my most reliable teachers. Mrs. William Watson was a lady of equal position and character, and two of her daughters were my teachers, while several pupils boarded with them.[38]

That several of these formidable women were also the *mothers* of teachers in the seminary added to their likely influence, which, combined with that of the teachers, would surely have been the dominant force within the small groups of students housed on their premises.

Catharine's students were required to rise with the sun, to attend family worship, to be present for the grace said both before and after meals, and to attend the church of their parents' choice twice on the Sabbath. At sundown they were to be in their chambers. A bell was rung to signify a quiet time when no visiting or talking was to take place, and students were expected at this time to study for at least two (but not more than four) hours. All of their clothing was to be marked with their full name, no borrowing or lending was allowed, and they were required "[t]o spend the time immediately after dinner on Saturday in mending all articles of dress which are brought from the washerwoman, as needing it."[39] They were expressly forbidden to enter the kitchen without permission. On Friday evenings and Saturday afternoons they were permitted to "see company." They were not "[t]o walk or ride with gentlemen without permission from the principal teacher," nor "[t]o receive visits from gentlemen except in the presence of some lady of the family."[40] Weekly "levees" to which local grammar school teachers and other eligible young men were invited provided a carefully supervised introduction of the young ladies to society.[41]

The routine of the school day began at 9:00 A.M., when students were expected to be in their seats in study hall, equipped with books, paper, quills, penknife, pencil, india rubber, portfolio, and a small box for refuse and torn paper. Ink was provided by the school, and students were expressly forbidden from cleaning their quills by "throwing" the ink from the pen.[42] Catharine began the day by holding a forty-five-minute class in moral instruction, concluded by a prayer. When the bell rang, students assembled two by two in rows and walked to their recitation classes, past monitors who were stationed at the top and bottom of stairs to ensure order. Students who had no class at that hour remained in study hall where a teacher, later a specially designated governess, presided. She kept order, answered questions, mended pens, and sent the various classes to their respective recitation classes on the hour. The girls were forbidden to bring sewing to school, a departure from Sarah Pierce's practice at the Litchfield Female Academy, where her students were required to engage in needlework as a means of ensuring order while the class, under the care of one teacher, recited their lessons one at a time.[43] Another of Catharine's rules suggests that women's education was viewed, at least by the students' families, as subject to interruption for domestic cause: "If they are sent on errands at hours that interfere with these rules, they are expected to bring a *written* statement of the fact, signed by the person who sent them." The first period was followed by required calisthenics, after which there was a ten-minute break for talking and relaxation. Afternoon classes resumed at two o'clock, when girls were again expected to be in their seats in study hall. Another period of calisthenics followed the first recitation period of the afternoon.[44]

Strong bonds of friendship developed among schoolmates engaged in this common routine. As Ann Gordon has written, "[t]he girls became, in their own word, 'sisters.' They were on their own to work and learn."[45] The students at the Hartford Female Seminary left a richly textured record of their relationships. Some hastily scribbled notes passed during school hours merely registered momentary feelings: Harriet Beecher wrote in a young hand, "Oh Mary I am unhappy & I cannot find comfort in any earthly friend" and left this note upon her friend's seat in study hall where she had hoped to find her.[46] Another student in a letter "written . . . whenever [she] could get a moment's time in school" worried that her studies were interfering with her religious life; this note appropriately enough broke off with the declaration that it was time for her to study her lesson on Butler's *Analogy*.[47] Study hall and the evening study hours offered more extended opportunities for correspondence, and letters flew back and forth like shuttles, weaving a web of relationships that the young women treasured for the rest of their lives. After graduation they took it upon themselves to nurture and sustain these bonds, often transmitting messages for third parties, and sometimes acting as intermediary between two school friends who were in danger of misunderstanding or detachment.[48]

Religion played an important role in the strengthening of these schoolgirl friendships. In addition to the promotion of self-esteem and psychological autonomy, the experience of religious conversion, as Kathryn Sklar has observed, "promoted solidarity among young women by encouraging them to express their 'affection & tender solicitude' for one another."[49] The development of these bonds was made the more likely by Catharine's method of "mutual instruction," which she also employed to spread the fires of religious enthusiasm. Having led a successful revival in the school in 1826, she utilized a peer network to extend the work, as she explains in her *Educational Reminiscences*: "Each teacher and assistant pupil, and all the scholars who had commenced a religious life, were requested to select at least one member of the school who was not thus committed, and suggestions were made as to the best way to exert an influence either by conversation or notes. . . . Many were, thus, not only led to commence a religious life, but were taught the duty and best methods of influencing others."[50] If this peer outreach system had the virtue of impressing the evangelical character of religion upon neophytes, it also had obvious implications for *women* as ministers of the word. In the Hartford Female Seminary every woman was a potential Christian and lay minister. The most radical aspect of this system—which in effect takes Protestantism to its logical completion—was that it undermined male, clerical authority.

Harriet Beecher, who had experienced conversion in 1825, was by 1826 deeply engaged in this task of converting her peers. She wrote long and earnest letters to her fellow students, urging upon them the performance of their daily duties for the sake of Jesus Christ. Lyman Beecher remarked in a letter to his wife, "Harriet has written home a wonderful letter—for a child of her age is full of elevated & ardent christian experience & practical zeal." This is not surprising, for she was getting regular practice in such productions.[51]

Even in letters it was sometimes difficult for students to broach the highly charged subject of human salvation; when they succeeded, the result was a deepening of intimacy. Their hesitancy before this subject is evident in the cautious way in which they approached it. "I am about to write to you dear Sarah," began a school friend to Sarah Terry, "because we have never yet conversed on that subject which I believe lies nearest our hearts & engrosses our attention. . . . My heart is full, but untill you tell me how you feel, I cannot speak or write to you with freedom." The writer urged Sarah to sit down that very evening and write her a long letter. "I do not think I expect too much if I ask you to write to me, unreservedly, & with that perfect freedom you would use towards a sister—a sister that loved you tenderly."[52] Mary Talcott wrote to Harriet Grew, "You asked me in your note . . . if I am willing that you should write to me on the subject of religion—Yes my dear H. you know that I will not be offended, but will be grateful to you for any thing you will say or write to me." Mary also promised to write something of her own thoughts on the subject, as Harriet had requested.[53] In her next letter Mary was true to her promise, all the more difficult for her to keep in that she had to confess that she was neither converted nor pious. Surely the revivalistic heat in female seminaries made the unconverted uncomfortable—it was designed to—and one can legitimately ask whether the community forged by these methods was not to some degree coercive.[54] It is likely that some young women felt excluded—Catharine held evening meetings that were designed only for the "pious"—but even for those who felt only indifference and hardness of heart, the act of entrusting this confidence to the care of another deepened the intimacy between the correspondents. "I trust you will not show this to *any* one," wrote Mary Talcott at the end of her letter.[55]

Between 1826 and 1832 the young Harriet Beecher produced a small sheaf of letters on religion that were her first opportunity to try out a pastoral ministry.[56] In them we can see the emergence of an egalitarian value system that is implicitly at odds with the authoritarian methods of her father. This value system grew out of the women's culture of the Hartford Female Seminary in which young women were constantly engaged in sisterly counsel and mutual instruction.

The pastoral model she inherited from her father is vividly depicted in the letters Lyman Beecher wrote to Catharine after the death of Alexander Fisher. Approaching the mourning process as an exercise in right thinking, Lyman Beecher inadvertently did incalculable violence to Catharine's feelings.[57] In long, closely written letters that were unrelieved sermons on the necessity of submitting to God's will, he repeatedly counseled that she set aside her "wrong feelings" and murmurings.[58] While Catharine endeavored to explore the particularity of her loss by examining the personal artifacts of her dead lover, Lyman glossed over the edges of her pain by reminding her of her remaining blessings (himself included) and submerging her loss in the generality of the human condition. He charged that Catharine's tumultuous response to Fisher's death was causing her to remodel God's character, when in fact she should change herself, not God. He began with a theory about God and then derived from it a prescription for how human beings should feel and act (or, more likely, he inferred from *his own* intellectual approach to religion that God was a pedant—and then urged women to be apt scholars of God's unbending doctrines).[59]

Although she inherited the forms of evangelical Protestantism from her father, Harriet Beecher tried them out in a women's culture imbued with a less judgmental spirit. Just as Lyman Beecher did, and Catharine after him, she presided over souls awakened in revivals: "I feel a deep & peculiar interest in the character & welfare of those in this school who during the last interesting season began as I trust their christian course."[60] But she did not scrutinize the religious experience of these neophytes to make sure that it was of the right genus and species, as the Rev. Joel Hawes, a clerical friend of her father's, had done upon her conversion, and as she complained her brother Edward did when she wrote to him of her spiritual melancholy: "Your speaking so much philosophically has a tendency to repress confidence. We never wish to have our feelings analyzed down, and every little nothing that we say brought to the test of mathematical demonstration."[61] Instead of analysis, she provided her young spiritual charges with general exhortations to be "earnest" and specific admonitions from her own experience so as to "guard them," she said, "against temptations before which I have fallen."[62]

In her relationship to her flock she was not a shepherd but rather a wiser, more experienced sheep. The effectiveness of her counsel—and that of the other peer counselors—arose from her ability to identify with the spiritually troubled; having been there before them, she could guide them safely home. She encouraged one correspondent to think of Christ not as a "master" to "servants" but rather as a "near & confidential friend."[63] In another letter she attempted to cut through the "very puzzling" topic of free will by suggesting that there was no use in trying to reason it through: "If we *know* that we have power to do all that God requires—if we *feel* that we have—nay more, if we are so made that we never can *help* feeling it—what matter is it if we cannot see *how* it is."[64]

It is striking that so much of this religious concern was expressed on paper. Harriet, who was first an assistant pupil and later a teacher, provided one explanation for this literary mode. She wrote to student Sarah Terry, "By my duties as a teacher I am cut off from almost all modes of intercourse with the young ladies except by writing—but I think that by corresponding on this subject as much & perhaps more good might be effected than by personal intercourse."[65] Other evidence suggests that it was as much temperament as expediency that led Harriet to adopt the written word as her vehicle of religious persuasion. She admitted to her brother Edward, "It costs me an effort to express feeling of any kind, but more particularly to speak of my private religious feelings."[66] Writing to her brother George in a moment when the full burden of evangelical, millennial piety weighed on her young spirit, she burst out, "Oh that I could feel it enough to do away this timidity which I feel in addressing others—It seems to me as if the etiquette of society imposed unnatural barriers on this subject and as if *I* and all christians neglected duty upon it with wonderful indifference."[67] Like Nathaniel Hawthorne, who spent twelve years in his "solitary chamber" before opening what he called "an indirect intercourse with the world" through the publication of *Twice-Told Tales*, Harriet Beecher preferred a literary mode of communicating that preserved a measure of privacy and reserve.

Letter writing was not the only opportunity for extracurricular literary productions. Like the Yankee girls at the Lowell Mills who during the 1820s and 30s improved their spare time by writing *The Lowell Offering*, the students at the Hartford Female Seminary used their study halls for a literary endeavor, the *School Gazette*. The paper was begun in 1824, the first year Harriet was there. This was an election year, and the "prospectus" with which the *School Gazette* opened its first issue took ironic note of this fact in a disclaimer:

> In commencing a publication of this kind, it is customary to make something of a statement of the object of the paper, its politicks sentiments, & all the different bearings which it is intended to effect on the morals, literature, religion, & politicks of the country. In accordance with general practice therefore, the conductors of this paper wish to have it understood, that they are neither Moralists, nor Philosophers, nor Theologians, nor Politicians; but only a few harmless maidens, in a little retired nook which they call "Study Hall," where they meddle not with things too high, nor seek to step out of the little pleasant sphere in which they move, to busy themselves with the cares of the great world abroad. The object of this paper is merely to furnish a pleasant & profitable relaxation from the duties of the school; to give an opportunity for the indulgence of humour and the imagination; & to promote a readiness in easy & sprightly composition. . . . and it is hoped that neither Crawford, Adams, or Jackson or any of the other of the candidates for the Presidency or their partisans will be needlessly alarmed on the present occasion.[68]

The stance taken by the writers of this prospectus at once denies national ambitions and yet coyly invokes them; takes refuge in the "retired nook" of a study hall in a female academy, yet mockingly imitates the forms of publications to the world. The editors of the Hartford Female Seminary *School Gazette* perhaps needed to convince themselves that they were not overstepping the bounds of women's sphere, even as they tried out semipublic voices.[69]

The editor pro tem of the September 9, 1825 issue was H. E. Beecher. Of the fourteen issues of the *School Gazette*, Harriet edited two numbers and her close friends Georgiana May and Catherine Cogswell edited another three. As an exercise, this foray into journalism was significant, for periodicals were at the time the most important means of influencing public opinion. Harriet Beecher had witnessed the labors of her father for the *Christian Spectator*, a journal he had hoped would put to rout the forces of Episcopalianism and Unitarianism in Connecticut. No matter that the issues discussed in the *School Gazette* were mundane: Harriet was the editor of a newspaper—an opportunity she could have only in an all-female world.

In her maiden editorial Harriet continued the mock-heroic tone of the "Prospectus," complaining that the *School Gazette* had been so successful that it had "stimulated the ambition and cupidity of many to attempts of the same kind," in which she grandly included the recently announced *Connecticut Observer.* "The managers of this paper have with unblushing effrontery intimated to the public that there are some moral wants in the community which our paper has not supplied, that there are some departments of moral influence which we have not occupied,"[70] wrote the fourteen-year-old editor. The articles, notices, and reviews in the issue Harriet edited are typical *School Gazette* productions: a "Medical Report" on a study hall bench taken with "trembles;" a "Critical Review" of "The Death and Burial of Cock Robin," this last being a poem published in a previous issue of the *School Gazette.* These study hall journalists played with the literary forms of the public world, pretending to be doctors, editors, and critics. In the process they sharpened their wits and reinvented an ancient political weapon: satire. All that was needed to turn their mock-heroic gambits into a genuinely satirical mode was the conviction that the public world they invoked was less worthy than the semiprivate world they inhabited.

CHAPTER FIVE

Year of Decision:
1827–1828

The typical pattern of attendance at female seminaries and academies was for girls to enter at around age fifteen and to stay for one to three years.[1] Harriet Beecher, having entered the Hartford Female Seminary in 1824 at age thirteen, was ready in 1827 to move on—but to what? Enlightened republican minds agreed about the importance of educating young women, but there was less clarity about the future course such educated young women were expected to pursue. The emotional turmoil Harriet Beecher experienced in 1827 was felt by many young women of her time when they embarked upon the world freighted with a well-stocked mind, a sense of social duty, and no clear way in which to put their talents to use. Ann Gordon has remarked in her study of the Young Ladies Academy in Philadelphia that the contradiction between the education the girls had received and their future prospects was evident in their commencement addresses, which "offered no vision of life beyond school."[2] Having received an education equivalent to that given a young man, they faced a world that had conventional expectations for women.

This dilemma was heightened for graduates of the Hartford Female Seminary. The ideology of republican motherhood to some extent contained—though it did not resolve—this contradiction between education and "after-life." But Catharine Beecher had begun her school out of her personal awareness that not every woman would marry and have children. Unlike Sarah Porter, who would train her young ladies to be "useful wives," Catharine brought her students up in the belief that it was their duty to be "useful";

she left off the marital prescription and in its place encouraged preparation for an independent life.[3] Exactly what course this indicated for graduates of her school, however, was not clear.

Catharine herself provided a model, of course. As founder and head of a school, Catharine Beecher's example was so persuasive that she had trouble keeping her teachers; no sooner had they mastered her curriculum and established their reputations than they "left for more eligible situations." Teacher Julia Hawkes took two of Catharine's scholars with her and founded a female seminary in Springfield, Massachusetts. Mary Dutton left after a year and took a position in New Haven at Miss Peters's School.[4] After repeated years of training new teachers only to see them leave once their proficiencies were developed, Catharine characteristically formulated the contradictions of her experience into a plan affording her a wider sphere of influence. She would train teachers and send them forth into the West to train other teachers, and their refinement and culture would save the nation from the excesses and impieties of the foreign cultures that threatened the evangelical Protestant vision—a plan complementary to those Lyman Beecher was formulating at the same time.[5] This crystallization of her experience did not occur, however, until 1830. In the meantime the fifteen-year-old Harriet Beecher struggled to see what shape her life would have.

In 1826 Lyman Beecher had moved to Boston to rout the Unitarians on their own turf, and it was to Boston that Harriet went after completing her studies at the Hartford Female Seminary. All the older Beecher children were established in their niches in the world: Edward was installed as pastor of the Park Street Church in Boston, William was studying, George was a minister at Groton, Catharine and Mary were at the seminary. Harriet's move home to a place that had never been her home, to a stepmother who had had little to do with her raising, to a much-diminished group of her siblings, now increased by the addition of her half-sister Isabella and her half-brother Thomas, could not have been very satisfactory. She had no defined role in the family, no friends in Boston, and no career direction. In February of that year she wrote to Catharine, "I don't know as I am fit for anything, and I have thought that I could wish to die young, and let the remembrance of me and my faults perish in the grave, rather than live, as I fear I do, a trouble to everyone." She complained of feeling "wretched," of dragging out her days "so useless, so weak, so destitute of all energy," and then of being unable to sleep, of groaning and crying till midnight. She was tossed by waves of feeling, excruciatingly self-conscious, and uncertain of her purpose and direction. Her efforts to appear cheerful succeeded so well that her father reproved her for laughing too much. "Mamma often tells me that I am a strange, inconsistent being," she wrote Catharine. "I was so absent sometimes that I made strange mistakes, and then all laughed at me, and I laughed, too, though I felt as though I should go distracted." Like the young Benjamin Franklin, she attempted to put her life on paper and regulate its course. "I wrote rules; made out a regular system for dividing my time; but

my feelings vary so much that it is almost impossible for me to be regular."
Her letters bore no dates, being, as she later remarked, "only histories of the
internal."[6]

What options were open to her for service in the world? While Mary Beth
Norton is right to point out that the first generation of educated female
Americans included "teachers, missionaries, authors, and the early leaders
of such nineteenth century reform movements as abolitionism and women's
rights,"[7] such careers were not obvious choices in 1827; some of them were
recently invented or imagined, and none of them, with the exception of
authorship, were widely practiced or approved. The postseminary experiences of Mary Talcott, a student at Catharine's school from 1831 to 1833,
were perhaps more typical for educated women of the time than those of
more public figures such as Elizabeth Cady Stanton. A look at her brief
career will provide a context for Harriet Beecher's difficulties.

Mary Kingsbury Talcott was born in 1816 to Russell Talcott, a dry goods
merchant in Hartford, and Harriet Kingsbury Talcott. Her father died two
years after her birth, and her mother died three years later. Raised apparently
by her mother's family, the Kingsburys, Mary Talcott was well educated. As
an eight-year-old primary school child she was on hand to welcome Lafayette
to Hartford, and she preserved the ribbon that she wore on that day in 1824.
She attended Miss Rockwell's School and received a certificate on May 7,
1830, on which Miss Rockwell's signature testified that she had attained her
"entire approbation as a scholar and young lady." She entered the Hartford
Female Seminary the next year, at age fifteen, and attended until probably
1833, when she turned eighteen. Her best friend was Harriet Grew, who
was enrolled at the seminary the year before Mary's arrival. The letters Mary
Talcott wrote to her school friend between 1834 and 1837 testify to the
success of Catharine's curriculum in broadening the horizons of her female
students, and provide poignant witness to the smallness of the social world
that opened to receive them.[8]

After leaving the Hartford Female Seminary, Mary's friend Harriet Grew
moved to Philadelphia where she was swept up in abolitionist activity which
the presence of large numbers of Quakers helped to foment. On the eve of
her departure Mary Talcott wrote to her, "I shall often think of you. May I
ask in return dear Harriet that you will remember me when you think of
your *school friends* for those whom we have known at school seem *most dear*
to the heart." Perhaps quoting one of Catharine Beecher's adages, Mary's
parting wish for her school friend was "May you 'be useful, be good, and be
happy.' "[9] Mary Talcott stayed in Hartford and pursued a round of philanthropic activities typical for middle-class women of the time: Bible classes,
Education Society collection tours, temperance lectures, classes in which
free blacks were taught to read, Dorcas Society meetings where the busy
fingers of women made garments for the poor—these activities feature prominently in her letters. The proliferation of voluntary societies in antebellum
America ensured that the loose energies of educated young women would
readily be tapped.[10]

Mary Talcott's subscription to the conventional view that true woman-hood demanded reticence and decorum prevented her from considering two activities that provided the most public and wide-ranging lives for women of her time: promoting abolition and teaching. "You speak of abolition," she wrote to Harriet Grew. "I have never thought much on the subject—nor do I like to attend to a controverted subject . . . for I see so many who do becoming excited—& led to the indulgence of bitterness & warmth which seem to me quite wrong." She assured her school friend, "I do not mean to insinuate that your interest in this subject affects your temper—for I know you too well to *suspect that* of you." She continued, "I do not know but I ought to form some opinion of my own upon this point. And I *have half* an opinion—or more properly some prejudices—and to tell the truth they are contrary to *immediate abolition* but I am not sufficiently enlightened to know what is right."[11] Harriet Grew's interest in abolition challenged Mary Talcott to confront her prejudices, her lack of knowledge, and, most significantly, the shackles that the cult of true womanhood placed on free thought.

Mary Talcott observed the tendency of graduates of the Hartford Female Seminary to follow a teaching career—"S & A Tilley have left for Cincin-nati—expecting to be teachers in Miss Beecher's seminary there," she remarked to Harriet Grew[12]—but the same hesitancies that prevented her from considering action to promote abolition put teaching beyond her reach. Because teaching was clearly a more socially acceptable occupation than abolition work, however, the challenge it posed to Mary's conventional views provoked a harder contest. The contradiction between her republican edu-cation and the domestic ideology in which she sought to contain it is evident in the question she posed to Harriet Grew: "Do you think that mental acquirements and a high state of cultivation *need* interfere with the domestic usefulness of a woman?" She admitted that "there are many who uphold a contrary opinion," but offered her own, that "no woman who has a proper regard for her sex—for their true advancement & dignity—*can* oppose any thing which tend to promote it." She followed this brave statement by words in a different key. "Still I would not have any one ostentatiously display their learning—I do not approve of that Female college in Kentucky [perhaps the Lafayette Seminary in Lexington] for this very reason—I think however great the acquirements which a woman has made, they should never be blazoned to the world—should be kept in the shade and never exhibited or dis-played."[13] Such equivocation, while not unusual, effectively removed Mary Talcott from the ranks of those educated young women who were in the process of turning teaching into a female profession.

This is especially unfortunate because her letters reveal a curious intel-lect and a passion for reading, both of which were cultivated at Catharine's school. "Do you remember the pleasant hours spent in our class in Paley's Theology and Evidences," she asked Harriet Grew; "I love to recall them—to live my school days 'over again'—but that is vain pleasure I sometimes think 'to live in the past.'"[14] Her experiences in an all-female school stim-ulated her mind and enhanced her appreciation of women's mental capacities—and this subtly subverted her loyalty to the conventional view of women's diminished portion. She took pride in the accomplishments of literary women and sent eager reports of her latest reading pleasures to Harriet Grew. "Have you seen the 'Poetry of Life'—a very interesting and pretty work by Miss Stickney—The more pleasing, of course, as it comes from a female pen." She asked her schoolmate, "Do you not feel almost proud of the talents and acquirements of the distinguished ones in our own sex—I do—so much is the female mind decried and underrated—so often its inferiority asserted that I am delighted with any striking instances to prove the contrary."[15]

Unable to resolve the contradiction between her curious mind and her decorous self-image, Mary Talcott indulged in frequent daydreams of that time in her life when she did not feel her sex and her intellect at war: her school days at the Hartford Female Seminary. Responding to similar sentiments in a letter from Harriet Grew, Mary wrote back:

> I too, dear Harriet, love to retrace the scenes of my school days, *dearly* as I love to think of those who have been associated with me in treading the path of science, and I am sure that time & absence instead of diminishing my affection for them, serves to strengthen the ties by which my heart is bound to theirs—I often find the wish arising in my heart that I were again a school girl, but this is discontent or something like it.

Writing the year after she left school, Mary wondered whether "childhood is the happiest portion of our existence."[16]

Nostalgia for the happy scenes of her school days may have led her to organize the reading group that she mentioned in one of her last letters to Harriet Grew: "I have been very pleasantly occupied for some time past in the study of Paley's Moral Philosophy. A class of young ladies, numbering from fifteen to twenty have met weekly at the house of our dear pastor to recite and discuss the various topics comprised in this system of ethics." This class was the perfect vehicle for Mary Talcott's "proper" intellect.[17] On the one hand it allowed her the mental stimulation and female camaraderie she enjoyed at the seminary—and provided an opportunity to return to an author who evoked warm classroom memories. On the other hand it did not overstep the bounds; presided over by "our dear pastor," whom the ladies sometimes had "taken the liberty of dissenting from," but from whom Mary "profited by [his] many interesting and valuable remarks," this reading group posed no danger to the stability of the republic or to the fragile truce existing between Mary Talcott's restless mind and her notions of decorum. Unable to find work in the world that served both sides of her consciousness, Mary found a setting that duplicated and re-created the pleasures of her school days.

Her pastor's class on Paley's *Moral Philosophy* was as close as Mary Talcott ever got to finding where she belonged in the world. That same year Harriet Grew died of tuberculosis. Her sister Julia wrote to tell the news to Mary Talcott, assuring her of the "delightful state of feeling" that characterized Harriet Grew's spiritual state, but skipping over an account of her last week, which her "poor shattered nerves" prevented her from putting on paper. She told Mary she planned to send her "a memoir of Mrs. Judson, which was our dear Harriet's, and which she requested us to send to you, as her parting bequest." This memoir of a woman missionary was a fitting remembrance of Harriet Grew's enlarged vision of women's possibilities in the world (her sister Eliza had gone to Bangkok as a missionary), and an equally fitting memorial of the intimate intellectual companionship, so often intertwined with books, that Harriet and Mary had enjoyed. For Mary Talcott, orphaned at an early age, this loss of her childhood friend and schoolmate was a severe blow. Mary Kingsbury Talcott died the following year, perhaps of the same disease.[18] She was twenty-two.

Mary Talcott's life traced the arc of fifteen-year-old Harriet Beecher's desperate wish: to die young, to be no trouble to anyone, to be so good and useful that one was used up and out of the way. That this was the pattern of Roxana Beecher's life made this a particularly dangerous fantasy for her. Harriet lived a life that in many ways showed her loyalty to the memory of her mother's proper womanhood, and as she stood on the brink of her own maturity she consciously tried to model herself on her mother's ladylike example. Harriet Beecher lived to be eighty-five, but until she was past the age at which her mother died she lived with the conviction that her life would end soon. When her sister-in-law urged her to write a book depicting the horrors of slavery, Harriet responded, "I will if I live."[19] Declarations to this effect have puzzled biographers, but they may simply have been Harriet's way of expressing loyalty to her mother's memory—and perhaps they unconsciously acknowledged the danger posed by the model of the Victorian "Angel in the House." If women artists of Virginia Woolf's generation had to kill the angel in the house in order to claim the freedom and self-authorization to write, their nineteenth-century counterparts had to figure out how to avoid being killed by her.

Catharine Beecher recognized the dangers of Harriet's melancholy and was instrumental in extricating her from it. She wrote to Lyman Beecher, "I have received some letters from Harriet to-day which make me feel uneasy."[20] She quickly took matters in hand and suggested a cure for her sister's depressed spirits. To Edward she wrote:

> If she should come here (Hartford) it might be the best thing for her, for she can talk freely to me. I can get her books, and Catherine Cogswell, Georgiana May, and her friends here could do more for her than any one in Boston, for they love her and she loves them very much. Georgiana's difficulties are different from Harriet's: she is speculating about doctrines, etc. Harriet will have young society here all the time, which she cannot have at home, and I think cheerful and amusing friends will do much for her. I can do better in preparing her to teach drawing than any one else, for I best know what is needed.[21]

A confidante, books, friends, and a career—as an antidote for the melancholia of an educated young women, Catharine's recipe had a stunning

precision. Not incidentally, her prescription entailed Harriet's return to the
female institution from which she had recently separated herself. It would
not be necessary for her to daydream about her school days or to attempt to
find pale substitutes—or even to die young. Before she had a chance to
plumb the depths, she was on her way back to the Hartford Female Seminary.

During its first four years the Hartford Female Seminary twice outgrew
its lodgings. When the third-floor room on the corner of Main and Kinsley
Streets became overcrowded, Catharine moved her school to the basement
of the North Church. By 1827 her school was sufficiently successful that
she raised an endowment to erect a building. Situated nearly in the center
of the city at 100 Pratt Street, its tall pillars crowned by a neoclassical ped-
iment, the new Hartford Female Seminary building was a monument to
Catharine's vision of women's intellectual aspirations. Beyond the white
fence that enclosed the grassy yard at the front of the building, the front
steps led up to a door above which was a large window. The students entered
not by this front door, but by the east door which opened into a cloakroom
where the girls hung their garments on pegs labeled with their names. The
cloakroom gave way to a long hall that ran the length of the building, on
either side of which were three classrooms. At the far end of the building
was a large study hall capable of seating 150 students.[22]

Catharine's school had two terms of thirteen weeks each, a summer term
and a winter term. The winter term ran from the middle of November to the
middle of April. After a four-week vacation the summer term began in the
middle of May. Harriet spent the spring vacation of 1827 in Nutplains with
Grandmother Foote and her other relatives, accompanied by her best friend,
Georgiana May. When the winter term began in the middle of November
she returned to Hartford to continue her studies and to begin her career as
"Miss Harriet," a teacher.

Harriet's return to the Hartford Female Seminary was not without advantages to Catharine. The size of the school and the weight of her responsibilities had led her to consider taking a partner—a scheme her father had
advised her against. "Why should you divide & lessen the momentum of your
own energies?," he wrote her in February 1827. "Be the head," he urged. "*I
would not divide with any one but one of our own family.*" He was less clear
on how this might be arranged, for none of the other Beechers was in a
position to become a full-time coprincipal. He thought that perhaps "Mary
and William together one half day would be better than any possible help
you can get . . . & if Marys health should allow you may progress in this
manner untill Harriets age shall enable her to take his place Indeed she may
soon take as you say to her particular part."[23] Harriet's return was an important calculation in preserving the character of the Hartford Female Seminary
as a Beecher family institution.

Mary Beecher's health remained problematic; she had had consumptive
symptoms in the early 1820s and had recently taken a leave from the school

to rest. Nineteenth-century health fads tended to extremes, and Mary chose an approach diametrically opposed to Lyman Beecher's. When his health had broken from overwork in 1822, he took a year off from studying and preaching and became a full-time farmer—and this cured him after a trip to Niagara Falls had not. He remained to the end of his days a devotee of regular exercise as a balance to the intellectual pursuits that, he said, tended to give the Beechers dyspepsia. Mary chose a method more akin to the "rest cure," which led Lyman Beecher to inquire of Catharine, "How is Mary does her anti exercise scheme succeed any better than the agitation System unless it does she had better stick to the latter." He could not resist adding, "I would not live a week without the exercise of two or three hours a day in my wood-house & my jimnastics beside all my walking & riding which has been not less than 1200 miles since I came to Boston."[24] Catharine followed his example and in the height of her enthusiasm required calisthenics three times a day at her school.[25] Mary found something that worked better than either antiexercise or agitation. She decided to retire from schoolteaching and become a full-time housekeeper for Catharine. In 1826 Catharine had made the decision to rent a house independently instead of boarding, and this meant that the housekeeping duties were hers to attend.[26] This was not a problem during the first year, for Aunt Esther had come to preside over this "Hartford annex," composed of Catharine, Harriet, and Henry; but when Aunt Esther joined Lyman Beecher's ménage in Boston the following year, Catharine found herself in need of domestic help and took up Mary's offer. Catharine believed that five or six weeks of housekeeping might propel Mary back to the classroom and she prudently sought another housekeeper to guard against that eventuality.[27] Events confirmed Catharine's foresight, but not her understanding of Mary's motives. Having chosen a domestic role, Mary Beecher soon chose a husband to go with it. In the fall of 1827 she married Thomas C. Perkins, a Hartford lawyer; this marked the end of Mary's public career and of her health problems.

Mary's physical breakdown may have been in part a response to the burdens that Catharine too blithely passed on to her shoulders; Lyman knew his eldest when at the outset of her school project he warned her "to apply herself and not let the work fall on Mary."[28] As Kathryn Sklar has observed, Catharine Beecher was better on the windup than on the follow-through,[29] and her penchant for discovering ways to save her own energies sometimes encroached on the prerogatives of others. The strains on all the teachers must have been excessive in the early years of the seminary. Harriet wrote to her brother George, "[D]id you realize as I do how many other things 'we *female teachers*' have to do besides to exchange thought and feeling with our brethren, you would not wonder that you hear from me so seldom."[30] Catharine pointedly observed in her *Educational Reminiscences* the number of heads of female educational institutions whose health was broken by the incessant demands of their work.[31]

The long hours and hard work, however, were a balm to Harriet Beecher's

troubled spirit. A few months after the commencement of the winter term
she wrote to Grandmother Foote:

> I have been constantly employed, from nine in the morning till after dark at
> night, in taking lessons of a painting and drawing master, with only an inter-
> mission long enough to swallow a little dinner which was sent to me in the
> school-room.
>   You may easily believe that after spending the day in this manner, I did not
> feel in a very epistolary humor in the evening, and if I had been, I could not
> have written, for when I did not go immediately to bed I was obliged to get a
> long French lesson.

She was also "carrying two young ladies through Virgil" and planned if she
had time to begin studying Italian. One side effect of her return to the Hartford Female Seminary as a teacher was that she had an opportunity to extend
her studies beyond the normal three-year period for a girl's education. "I am
very comfortable and happy," she told her grandmother.[32]

Having given up their separate establishment after Mary Beecher's
departure, in 1828 Catharine and Harriet were boarding at Mrs. Strong's
with three other teachers and a number of scholars from the seminary. This
arrangement made school coextensive with home and friends and ensured
that few spare moments would remain for solitary reflection. Harriet's roommate was in fact her French teacher, Miss Degan, who made long lessons a
part of her evening routine. The other boarding teachers were Clarissa
Brown and Julia Hawkes, the latter of whom roomed with Catharine. Harriet
wrote to Grandmother Foote that Julia Hawkes "in some respects . . .
reminds me very much of my mother. She is gentle, affectionate, modest,
and retiring, and very much beloved by all the scholars."[33] The atmosphere
in Mary and Thomas Perkins's household, where Catharine and Harriet
boarded in 1831, was likewise quiet and refined. Angelina Grimké, who
stayed with the Perkins when she visited Catharine and her school that year,
left a description in her diary:

> The tea was handed round [at four o'clock] & immediately after, the door was
> closed and T[homas] P[erkins] read a chapter in the Bible & offered up a
> prayer. . . . 12 scholars board here, they are very genteel in their manners &
> appear to be under excellent management, the house is as quiet as tho' there
> were neither young children nor boarders in it. T[homas] P[erkins] and his
> wife are quite the gentleman & lady in their deportment.[34]

Running a well-regulated and genteel home was perhaps Mary Beecher's
way of honoring the memory of Roxana Beecher. Harriet absorbed this influence but asserted her continuity with her mother in another fashion. Roxana
Beecher had studied painting with a good New York artist secured by her
brother John. At Nutplains Harriet delighted in the "little works of ingenuity,
and taste, and skill, which had been wrought by her hand—furniture adorned

with painting; pictures of birds and flowers, done with minutest skill."[35] Now Harriet studied painting with the thought that she herself would become a teacher of painting. She wrote to Grandmother Foote:

> I propose, my dear grandmamma, to send you by the first opportunity a dish of fruit of my own painting. Pray do not now devour it in anticipation, for I cannot promise that you will not find it sadly tasteless in reality. If so, please excuse it, for the sake of the poor young artist. I admire to cultivate a taste for painting, and I wish to improve it; it was what my dear mother admired and loved, and I cherish it for her sake. I have thought more of this dearest of all earthly friends these late years, since I have been old enough to know her character and appreciate her worth. I sometimes think that, had she lived, I might have been both better and happier than I now am, but God is good and wise in all his ways.[36]

Harriet's drawing lessons afforded her many hours of pleasure and provided the foundation for a hobby she enjoyed to the end of her life. Some of her letters are charmingly illustrated with sprigs of flowers. In later life she sometimes gave a hand-painted fan as a wedding gift, and a number of her oil paintings—mainly of birds and flowers—survive. It was common for her to suggest illustrations to accompany her fiction, especially for her children's stories. Undertaken out of loyalty to the memory of her mother, drawing and painting remained for her "accomplishments," not a serious career. That they could be undertaken in a different spirit is illustrated by the rigorous standards that (somewhat ironically, given the domestic cast to her educational philosophy) Sarah Porter later brought to the study of the arts at her school; she recruited European-trained musicians and an art teacher trained at the Ecole des Beaux Arts, thus providing "depth and a certain rigor to the study of . . . subjects that educators such as Catharine Beecher despised as mere genteel accomplishments."[37] Catharine, however, was reacting to her own "domestic education." Her younger sister, having enjoyed a much more rigorous mental training from her early years, viewed drawing and painting as additions to her education, not substitutes for it. More importantly, this activity was part of Harriet's self-definition at age sixteen: she was her mother's daughter.

Another important element in her self-definition was her role as teacher. In 1828 she wrote to her school friend, Mary Swift, "As for me, I tell all my friends the same story, that I am a *real school ma'am*." With a characteristic mixture of lightness and seriousness she continued, "I do not mean by that that I am very grave, very precise, very learned, *or* very conceited—but simply that my school duties take up all my time—so that I cannot visit much nor read for amusement or write half what I wish to—I am obliged to sacrifice my own private feelings in many things." By comparison with the depression she had experienced in Boston, however, she was thriving on her busy days. She allowed that "in many things the performance of duty exactly accords with [my feelings] How many there are to whom the performance of duty involves constant self denial!—to me it comes in the form of *pleasure*—

certainly this is more than I deserve."[38] In the fall of that year she spent her vacation visiting in Boston and Franklin, Massachusetts, where her brother George was attending Groton. In Boston she found her father's household "all well" and recently increased by the addition of the last of Lyman Beecher's children, James, about whom she remarked, "he has nothing to distinguish him from forty other babies, except a very large pair of blue eyes and an uncommonly fair complexion, a thing which is of no sort of use or advantage to a man or boy." She was kept too busy in Boston to remember her earlier bad times there: "In the first place," she wrote to Georgiana May, "I was obliged to spend two days in talking and telling news. Then after that came calling, visiting, etc., and then I came off to Groton to see my poor brother George, who was quite out of spirits and in very trying circumstances." Then it was back to Boston for four or five days, and then back to Groton, where she spent the rest of her vacation. So concerned was she about her brother George's depression that she considered taking charge of a female school in Franklin so she could be of some "assistance and company" to him.[39] Harriet Beecher was still thinking seriously about her direction and life choices, but at this point her career identity was solidly established. She was a schoolteacher.

She ended up staying at the Hartford Female Seminary, but she did not become a teacher of drawing and painting. In 1828 or 1829 Harriet found her true subject: rhetoric and composition. This subject drew together the experiences that had had the most profound effect on her own education at the Litchfield Female Academy: her attraction to ideas and intellectual frameworks and her pride in expression. By February 1829 she was dividing her evening between preparing exercises for her composition class and studying French and Italian.[40] In her *Educational Reminiscences* Catharine Beecher gave her sister full credit for the systematic approach to the teaching of composition pursued at the Hartford Female Seminary.[41] Reduced to its essence, Harriet's method was to make sure students had something to say and the wherewithal to say it. She began by having them read and imitate passages from writers such as Samuel Johnson amd Washington Irving; this improved their stock of words and trained their ears in the rhythms of the language. The next step was to generate a stock of ideas. "A pupil is never required to write on any subject till she has first *obtained some ideas* on that subject."[42] To this end, Harriet led lively discussions on the topics proposed for compositions before her students took up their pens to write. In short, Harriet duplicated the method she had found so stimulating in John Brace's teaching at the Litchfield Female Academy. The "Exhibitions" held at the end of the school terms emphasized composition—to the unfortunate exclusion of other branches of study, in the opinion of one student.[43] This emphasis may have owed something to Harriet's memory of her triumph at the exhibition at the Litchfield Female Academy when her essay won the admiration of Lyman Beecher; it may also suggest the importance of the subject to the curriculum of the Hartford Female Seminary under Catharine and Harriet's leadership.

In the winter of 1829 Harriet roomed with teachers Ann Fisher, Susan Brigham, and Mary Dutton, the latter of whom was to become an important friend. So that he would know something of those "who must exert an influence over my character," Harriet described her roommates for her brother Edward:

> Miss Dutton is about twenty, has a fine mathematical mind, and has gone as far into that science perhaps as most students at college. She is also, as I am told, quite learned in the languages. . . . Miss Brigham is somewhat older: is possessed of a fine mind and most unconquerable energy and perseverance of character. From early childhood she has been determined to obtain an education, and to attain to a certain standard. Where persons are determined to be anything, they will be. I think, for this reason, she will make a first-rate character.[44]

Besides these strong-minded teachers, Harriet was influenced by her schoolmates. Her cousin, Elizabeth C. Lyman, boarded in the same family with her and became a close associate. Assuming fictive familial roles was a common practice among nineteenth-century schoolgirls, and Harriet followed suit by addressing Elizabeth as "wife" and "grandmama," and Mary Dutton as "mother."[45] Her other close friends were Catherine Cogswell, daughter of a prominent Hartford physician and quite popular at the seminary, and Georgiana May. Georgiana was one of the most intimate friends Harriet made, and one would like to know more about her. Harriet described her as "older and graver [than Catherine Cogswell], and less fascinating to the other girls."[46] Catharine Beecher rated her at the top of her student body and hoped to win her to the ranks of female teachers. According to Catharine, Georgiana May combined "genius" with "the discretion, piety, energy & steadiness that are seldom combined with genius."[47] Harriet named her fifth child Georgiana May Stowe.

Another student to whom Harriet was attracted was Sara Willis. If Mary Dutton and Georgiana May appealed to her serious side, Sara Willis tapped another sensibility. Born just a month after "Miss Harriet," pupil Sara Willis had much in common with her sixteen-year-old teacher. Under the pseudonym Fanny Fern she was to make quite a literary name for herself in later life.[48] Sara Willis and Harriet Beecher also shared an active sense of humor, which sometimes expressed itself in verbal wit, sometimes in practical jokes. On one occasion Harriet was aided in this department by a visit from her brother Henry, "recently of the Sheafe Street gang in Boston," and at the time enrolled in a school nearby in Hartford. While Catharine was occupied with other things Harriet and Henry slipped away and exchanged clothes. When they reappeared, "Henry had become Harriet and Harriet had become Henry." In Henry's coat and trousers Harriet "made a more than passable

Beecher youth," while Henry in hoopskirt, mantilla, bonnet, and veil "was the very 'spit and image' of Harriet."[49]

This was a mild escapade compared to the antics of Sara Willis. Sara came to the Hartford Female Seminary in 1827. She first appears in Catharine Beecher's correspondence in a letter to her parents, who receive the news that they are to pay for a desktop on which Sara has carved her initials.[50] Her most conspicuous exploits, however, centered on a subject of general fascination to adolescents: food. Sara lived at Mrs. Strong's, along with Catharine, Harriet, and a number of other teachers and students. All of the members of the boardinghouse "family" took their meals together at a long table. As an economy measure, the housekeeper had developed the practice of serving better quality food at Miss Beecher's end of the table and reserving a lower quality for those who sat "below the salt." One day Sara Willis interchanged the butter dishes so that Catharine Beecher tasted some rancid butter that was meant for the other end of the table. When Catharine commented that the butter was "not the same as usual," Sara Willis jumped up and revealed the switch, declaring, "[I]t's just as usual, only we have your dish, and you have ours." Besides demonstrating Sara's spirit, this story underscores Catharine's instinctive egalitarianism. According to Sara Willis's story, "There was no further discrimination. Miss Beecher had not been aware of the little meanness, and at once put a stop to it."[51]

Sara Willis was also a leader of the "pie rebellion" in Mrs. Strong's boardinghouse. The context for this food riot is to be found in Catharine's strict notions of diet. In periods of social reform and regeneration, new dietary laws seem to provide immediate access to self-transformation and moral purity. Isaac Hecker, resident of Brook Farm, was a transcendental baker whose "unbleached flour" survives on the market today; Sylvester Graham invented a yeastless wholewheat cracker that was part of an ascetic and wholesome diet. An advocate of "graham things," Catharine Beecher believed that rich foods led to "bodily grossness" and "the obscuring of the mental faculties." She discouraged second helpings and for a while insisted that the girls' rations be carefully weighed. Sara Willis's appetite and spirit rebelled against this regimen and she led a nighttime raid on Mrs. Strong's pantry, which yielded a sweet booty of several pies.[52]

As a teacher, Harriet Beecher could not condone such activities, but it was apparent to Sara Willis that she often "openly sympathized" with such high jinks—just as Miss Pierce had indulged Catharine's pranks at her academy in Litchfield. In later life, when Harriet Beecher Stowe and Fanny Fern were household names, these two literary women renewed their acquaintance; fondly and ironically reasserting their respective roles as "Miss Harriet" and "Sara Willis," they reminisced about their adventures in the seminary. In Stowe's account of Sara's transgressions there emerges a portrait of the willful Sara and the indulgent Miss Harriet. In a letter to Fanny Fern's husband, Harriet recalled Sara Willis, who, I grieve to say one night stole a pie at Mrs Dr Strongs and did feloniously excite unto sedition & rebellion some five or six other girls,—eating said pye between eleven & twelve o clock in defiance of the laws of the school & in breach of the peace—ask if it isnt so—& if she remembers curling her hair with leaves from her geometry?—Perhaps she has long been penitent—perhaps—but ah me when I read Fanny Ferns articles I detect sparks of the old witchcraft—& say, as poor Mrs Strong used to when any odd mischief turned up—Thats Sarah Willis I know[53]

Sara's granddaughter, who loved to hear her grandmother's stories about her escapades at the Hartford Female Seminary, summarized Miss Harriet's relationship with her students: "For any who really wished to learn, she was an excellent teacher, but less successful with those who did not. Compulsion came hard to her, and it was fortunate that she was so generally liked it was rarely necessary."[54] In matters of discipline, Harriet was her mother's daughter, not her father's. Her reluctance to discipline was temperamental, but added to this was the difficulty of asserting authority over one's peers. Catharine's system of "mutual instruction" had implications for the authority patterns of the school, ones that she codified in her theory of "moral influence."

CHAPTER SIX

A Republic of Women:
1829–1832

The educational priorities of Catharine's seminary were the building of character, the cultivation of the intellect, and the proper preparation of young ladies to enter society. The most important of these was character.[1] By 1828 Catharine was beginning to formulate her educational philosophy and to think of it as a "system." Early in 1829 she published her *Suggestions Respecting Improvements in Education*, which underscored her empasis on moral character.[2] Some events that began rather fortuitously in the winter of 1829 matured her philosophy and provided the most dramatic chapter in Catharine's experiment in republican education. In their aftermath, Catharine fully institutionalized her optimistic and romantic educational philosophy of women's "moral influence," and Harriet experienced a quantum growth in confidence and power. The events of December 1829 underscore the radical potential of Catharine's school.

In spite of the disclaimer made by the initiators of the school newspaper, the students at Hartford Female Seminary did concern themselves with national events. Under Catharine's leadership they organized on behalf of the Cherokee Indians, who in 1827 were ordered to vacate their lands in the state of Georgia. Throughout 1829 Catharine and her students were deeply involved in circulating petitions and circulars protesting this federal action. Harriet describes the mounting ferment:

> Last night we teachers all sat up till eleven o-clock finishing our Cherokee letters. We sent some to the principal ladies of New Haven by Martha Sherman, to put in the Post-office there. Margaret Brown says the circular is mak-

ing a great excitement in New York. The Hartford ladies have received theirs from several cities, we among the rest. There is great wonderment as to who composed the circular ["To the Benevolent Women of the United States," by Catharine Beecher]. The girls come and tell us such marvelous stories about a circular for the Cherokees around in Hartford. They say public meetings and petitions are getting up in New York and other places, and here they are moving for the same. The excitement, I hope, is but just begun. So "great effects come from little causes."[3]

On top of the day-to-day responsibilities of running the school, this heady foray into national politics pushed Catharine into a nervous breakdown that to her "seemed like approaching insanity." Her fellow teachers urged her immediately to cease her duties and get some rest. Totally incapacitated, she acceded to their wishes. Before her departure, however, she put in place a bold experiment: "I arranged with my teachers that during my absence the school should be resolved into a sort of republic, and attempt self-government at least for a short experiment."[4]

Catharine broke her authority into pieces and scattered it like grain. As she explained, "I divided the scholars into *circles*, with a teacher at the head of each, and to each circle was committed one department of my responsibilites." After she left, Harriet in daily letters kept her sister informed of the state of affairs in her "forsaken dominion." The report from the circle over which Harriet presided was positive: the students had proposed several plans to aid the school's government and "seemed to feel as if the weight of the nation were on them." As for the other circles, all but one, into which some of the most troublesome girls had been placed, were eager for the scheme to succeed. Harriet was optimistic: "On the whole, dear sister, I think this plan will be productive of great good. If nothing else, it will form a habit in the school of acting *with* the teachers and sharing some of their trials."[5]

Just as Catharine had enjoyed the responsibility that came to her at the age of sixteen when the death of her mother left her in charge of her younger siblings, so now Harriet felt her powers expanding. In Catharine's absence, she emerged as the leading voice of the school. She convened a faculty meeting at which the teachers agreed that Harriet should explain the plan in more detail to the whole school. Accordingly, Harriet addressed the assembled student body the following morning in study hall. "I found my confidence growing so fast that I actually stood and looked in the eyes of all and 'speechified' nearly half an hour," she wrote Catharine. Harriet urged her sister to stay away longer, for her absence enabled the teachers "to go forward with a confidence they would not feel in your presence." Having articulated the psychology of this new republic, she went on to express its philosophy and political theory: "The union of feeling and action among teachers and scholars in this emergency will produce great good. We are fast becoming acquainted with all, and I think we shall do wonders."[6]

Activities moved forward on many fronts: the teachers continued their letters on behalf of the Cherokees, social gatherings increased, and under the rising "affection and good feeling" Harriet took steps to produce a revival of religion. She extended the decentralized plan of the "circles" to her boardinghouse "family," where she interested three of the students in leading prayer meetings with the other students in their "entry." She expected that "[t]his influence will be felt in the family and extend to the school"and she increased the likelihood of an all-school revival by reconstituting the prayer meeting of the members of Mr. Hawes's church, which had not been held since the previous term.

Harriet's powers of speech continued to astound her, and her confidence grew apace. On December 12 she wrote Catharine, "I shall speak in the Hall again Monday. I now feel as if I could do anything." A few days later she wrote, "I shall become quite an orator if you do not come home too soon." Catharine had recently tried unsuccessfully to raise an endowment for the twin purposes of building a dormitory and hiring Zilpah Grant, associate principal of the Ipswich Academy, to oversee the department of moral instruction. Harriet assured Catharine that even without the services of Zilpah Grant, "means elsewhere" could be procured to forward Catharine's ambitions for women's influence. She was perhaps thinking of herself for the role Catharine had cut out for Zilpah Grant, for Harriet's next words were "I feel willing to devote my whole life to this institution, as I never did before."[7]

Harriet was a zealous convert to Catharine's scheme of moral influence. On December 16 she wrote, "This morning I delivered a long speech on 'modes of exerting moral influence'; showing the ways an evil influence is unknowingly exerted and the ways in which each and all can exert a good one." This gentle means of exerting power was suited to her temperament, and her training in moral philosophy equipped her with ready answers to the students' quibbles. As she explained to Catharine, "When the girls wish what is against my opinion they say, 'Do, Miss Beecher, allow just this.' '*Allow* you?' I say. 'I have not the power; you can do so if you think best.' Now, they cannot ask me to give up my opinion and belief of right and wrong, and they are unwilling to act against it." The principle that Harriet drew from this became the guiding star of her prophetic career: "Ere long they will find that under the dominion of conscience and a correct public sentiment they have rulers they cannot sway like teachers of flesh and blood." [8]

Other teachers sent Catharine notes testifying to "the prosperity of our Republic"—notes clearly meant to reassure her that she could safely remove the cares of the seminary from her weary brain. That this crisis unleashed a genuine outpouring of energy, competence, and cooperation seems certain. When she returned Catharine found that the "republican organization" of the school greatly reduced her work. The system of "mutual instruction" that she had adopted out of expediency when she created her school, had, in December 1829, flowered into a self-conscious Republic of Women.

Soon after the events of the December Republic, Catharine institutionalized these developments by announcing a new, antiemulationist policy.

The spirit of republican sisterhood called forth by that crisis was antithetical to the individualism implicit in competition. Concluding that competition and emulation were more productive of evil than good, Catharine "determined to banish every thing of the kind." The *Catalogue* of 1831 announced that "for some time past, this Institution has been conducted *entirely* without appealing to any such dangerous principles. No prizes are given; no reward is offered for any degree of *comparative* merit; no emulation has existed in any department of the school."[9]

Competition and prizes were an established fact in boys' education, and most female academies followed this practice until more romantic educational principles began to prevail in both boys' and girls' academies.[10] The Litchfield Female Academy had an elaborate scheme of awards. At the Hartford Female Seminary the best scholars had been awarded the "First Honour," the most improved were awarded the "Second Honour," and "other prizes [were] given according to the discretion of the teachers."[11] At the Young Ladies Academy of Philadelphia the best student in each subject won a prize paid for by her parents; the girls competed in Christian knowledge by vying for denominational prizes: the "Presbyterian Prize," the "Protestant Episcopal Prize," and so forth. Ann Gordon views this competition as a healthy preparation for the world the girls were about to enter and a useful counter to "the ideal of female delicacy."[12] Sarah Porter's opposition to competition both on the tennis court and in the classroom, on the grounds that women "were to be known for their simplicity and humility, not for their accomplishments,"[13] tends to bear out Gordon's interpretation. On the other hand, it is not clear that young women were being trained, in the 1820s and 30s, to enter the competitive marketplace. Certainly, Catharine Beecher's assumption was somewhat different. Training women for useful lives, in an experimental educational setting, she prepared them neither for entrance into a male sphere nor for confinement to a traditional women's sphere. She prepared them for a *new* sphere of usefulness that their educations and ambitions were calling into being.

In the place of emulation Catharine substituted "the personal influence of the teachers." Their example and their noncoercive expressions of duty and principle would, like an unobtrusive yeast, leaven the student body. This process was not left to chance in the afterschool hours. In order to secure their influence, teachers were expected to "mingle with the scholars as companions and friends." By "constant and unrestrained intercourse" teachers could discover "peculiarities of character" and diffuse "a constant, though unseen and unnoticed *moral influence*."[14] Catharine testified, "[I]t is much easier to govern a school of one hundred and fifty without emulation and competition, than it ever was, by their aid, to control one of twenty or thirty."[15]

Another significant change in the seminary's procedures may be attributable to the impact of the December Republic. As late as 1828 Catharine was still following the widespread practice of publicly admonishing students for their deficiencies.[16] Charlotte Brontë has left a memorable picture of this practice in Chapter 7 of *Jane Eyre*, in which her heroine is held up before the entire student body at Lowood School and castigated as a liar. At boys' boarding schools in America, even "family" institutions like St. James's School—a "Christian Household" where boys were "as much as possible under the personal influence of the instructors"—students were disciplined through public admonition.[17] By 1831 Catharine Beecher had discarded this humiliating practice and in its place instituted an alternative system. The teachers were required to keep a daily journal on each student, noting infractions of rules and lapses in scholarship. Twice a week the teachers met in the library to compare notes; as each student's name was called the teachers read aloud their comments. Students whose behavior warranted it were called privately before the teachers and asked to give an account of themselves. Catharine included her assistant pupils in these supervisory exercises; her system of mutual instruction was perhaps nowhere more effective than in this work of character formation. As Catharine shrewdly observed, the "sympathy and cooperation" of the assistant pupils sometimes exceeded that of the teachers, "owing to their more intimate access to their companions."[18] The gains thus made were consolidated by an honor code that sought to enlist the moral sympathies of the entire student body.

Did Catharine's system of "moral influence" employ what one critic has termed "psychological weapons with new orders of coercive power?"[19] Certainly, there were elements of peer pressure and surveillance in Catharine's honor code, but it appears that Catharine's republican experiment in education went beyond the limits of her toleration, and therein lies the proof of its success in creating self-governing citizens. Catharine's response to the December Republic was terse and cryptic: "But my strength continued to fail, and I foresaw that my career there was coming to a close, and that this method could not be made permanent, being only fitted to that special emergency."[20] Perhaps she saw that her career as *leader* of the school was at an end; structurally, after all, she was playing the role of King George III to this republican upstart. Indeed, evidence suggests that the December Republic led to more assertiveness and unruliness among the students. Subsequent school regulations make concessions to student desires and also attempt to contain what appears to be a growing insistence on student free speech.[21] It was doubtless easier to grant responsibility to the students than it was to take it back again upon the return of the principal. The fact that Catharine for the first time hired a governess whose responsibility was solely to keep order—while it is in keeping with her practice of efficiently dividing tasks—may also have been a response to the growing assertiveness of her charges.[22] While Catharine Beecher may have wanted her system of moral influence to subtly manipulate her students to her point of view, their experience of mutual instruction in a female institution untrammeled by hierarchical gender assumptions had a radical effect. As her study hall journalists, orators, and lay ministers found that they *could* govern themselves, they determined that they *would*. It was only by resorting to more traditional forms of discipline that Catharine contained the republican experiment she had set in motion.

Even as the events of the December Republic signaled the close of Catharine's Hartford career, they brought to fruition an important stage in the unfolding of Harriet's. Harriet's leadership during the crisis enabled her to consolidate her experience as teacher and pastoral guide, to try on the mantle of moral leadership, and to gain confidence in her eighteen-year-old self. Catharine's preparation of her younger sister for an independent life had had the desired result. A letter written five months after the events of the December Republic displays Harriet's easy confidence. "I am quite buisy preparing for my Composition class," she wrote her fellow teacher, Mary Dutton. "Have been reading Rasselas—& writing a little in imitation of Dr Johnson's style—Think it is improving me by giving a command of language." Although Harriet's habitual carelessness in matters of spelling and punctuation may not reflect the lessons she gleaned from her eighteenth-century prose model, there is no mistaking the energy and playfulness of her response: "I have been spouting at Catherine respecting '*general and transcendental truths*' and '*errors of exaggeration & declamation*' ever since For half an afternoon I was quite '*ora rotundo*' & could not even shut a closet door except in a double antithesis." Her delight in the exercise of rhetorical flourishes was doubtless intensified by the memory of her oratorical flights in study hall the previous winter. She concluded with an impressive assertion of professional intent: "My plan this summer is to have the Young ladies imitate the style of various authors & read the English Classics—Respecting composition I think that never yet have time & attention enough been given to it to have it well taught—I mean it shall be this summer."[23] This is the resolution of one who takes the art of writing seriously. Harriet was building on the skills she practiced under John Brace's tutelage. More importantly, she was pursuing self-culture and self-definition in tandem with her teaching duties, improving her own style and command of language, exercising her delight in language's possibilities. Such duties were indeed pleasure.

Harriet's playful assertion of the educational principles of the Hartford Female Seminary occurs elsewhere in this letter to Mary Dutton, when she introduces an allusion to the educational debate over "emulation." Harriet and Catharine were in the habit of riding on horseback every morning before breakfast, Harriet astride "a beautiful young white horse" and Catharine astride a similar black one. With obvious pleasure, Harriet related how her horse, imbued with "the evil spirit of emulation," broke into a canter and then a gallop when Catharine's horse attempted to draw near.[24] The image of the eighteen-year-old Harriet, bonnet flying behind, racing on her white horse ahead of the twenty-nine-year-old Catharine, is a striking emblem of their emerging relationship.

The role of pastoral guide was as complementary to Harriet's temperament as it was to the tone of the Hartford Female Seminary, and her powers in this department were significantly enhanced by the December Republic. When the mantle of moral leadership passed to Harriet in Catharine's absence, her earnestness was enshrined by moral authority, and with this came an expanded sense of her identity and vocation. A few months after the events of December 1829 Harriet wrote to her brother:

> You see my dear George that I was made for a preacher—indeed I can scarcely keep my letters from turning into sermons. . . . Indeed in a certain sense it is as much my vocation to preach on paper as it is that of my brothers to preach viva voce—I write note after note every day full of good advice & am used to saying "but you must consider" & "I wish you to remember"—& "think my dear" &c &c that you need not wonder to find me exhorting you.[25]

Her practice in pastoral counseling prepared her for a prophetic career in which she would "preach on paper" to the nation. What allowed her to affirm this as a conscious vocation and to encapsulate all of her pastoral and didactic experience into this prescient declaration of her vocation, however, may well have been the surge of confidence and exhilaration that the December Republic had unleashed.

When Catharine returned to the helm of the seminary, it was Harriet's turn to claim that ill health necessitated a break from her teaching duties. In July 1830 she wrote cheerfully to her brother George that she was staying at her sister Mary's "very domestic home-like" place, and was occupied in being "*nihil laboriose agendo.*"[26] The two terms of 1831–1832 were to be Harriet's last teaching stint in the Hartford Female Seminary, and they were busy ones. In April 1831 Catharine appointed Lucy Ann Reed as assistant principal and in September of that year Catharine resigned her post.[27] She claimed ill health, but she also made new plans to continue her educational scheme on a wider scale. "In *three years*," she wrote Mary Dutton, whom she asked to join her, "we could train both *principals* & teachers to go forth and establish similar institutions all over our country." She continued, "I see no other way in which our country can so surely be saved from the inroads of vice, infidelity and error. Let the leading females of this country become refined, well educated, pious and active, and the salt is scattered through the land to purify and save."[28] Perhaps no other statement so succinctly displays what Kathryn Sklar has called Catharine's "lifelong skill in altering the forms of her own culture even while she insisted that she was preserving them."[29] Of the four cardinal virtues in the cult of True Womanhood, Catharine retained only piety; for purity she substituted refinement; for submission, education; and for domesticity, activity in the world.[30] The landscape on which this program was to be enacted was the West.

In July 1831 Angelina Grimké spent a week in Hartford visiting Catharine and Harriet. She had written ahead to Mary Beecher Perkins, her hostess, to let her know of her arrival, but it seems that the writer arrived just after her letter, throwing the Perkins household into confusion. The first sight of the Quaker woman, with her strange cap and clothes, excited comment wherever she went; when she and her traveling companion, Sarah Whitall, appeared at the Perkins's door Mary was quite taken aback by their "plain" appearance. The Quaker women were "quite amused to find how our letter was received here & what surprise our unique appearance occasioned." The Beechers soon found that unconventional behavior went with the unconventional clothing. Angelina refused to participate in the family prayers led by Thomas Perkins; and at the seminary she remained seated during the opening exercise of Scripture reading and prayer as "a testimony against forms of worship."[31]

The purpose of her visit was to determine whether she should embark upon a career as a schoolteacher, and she spent the weekdays at the seminary participating and observing.[32] Harriet was apparently away during the early part of that week. By the time Angelina returned from the school in the late afternoon of July 15, Harriet had returned to her lodgings at the Perkins's house. Angelina found her "very sociable" and regretted that she had not had the opportunity to see her in school. The two of them did have an opportunity the following day to spend considerable time together during a seminary outing to Daniel Wadsworth's estate. July 16th dawned "uncommonly cool," providing perfect weather for the expedition. Catharine set out on her horse, while Harriet and Angelina went ahead in a hack in order to avoid the dust. Daniel Wadsworth's estate on Talcott Mountain offered a splendid view: forty miles away stood Mount Holyoke, "in bold relief on the northern sky"; in the other direction, thirty miles to the south, stood West Rock. Hartford, Farmington, Avon, Newington, and Litchfield could all be seen. Harriet was all the more delighted when, upon entrance into the country house, she saw on the wall of the dining room a painting that perfectly captured the view she had just been beholding without. After picnicking on the grounds, the other students and teachers wandered off to explore the sights while Angelina and Harriet ensconced themselves in an "embowered retreat." Here Harriet made several sketches of the scene and she and Angelina took advantage of their time alone together to have "a long talk about the [Society of] Friends." This was Harriet's first acquaintance with Quakerism, which was a significant nineteenth-century breeding ground for radical ideas. Unlike the mainstream Protestant churches, the Society of Friends had no strictures against women speaking in meeting, nor did they see any reason that women should not be educated to the same degree as men. Their commitment to a radical egalitarianism led them to eschew hierarchies and all forms of worship that embodied them. It has often been observed that many of the pioneers in the antislavery and woman's rights movements had a Quaker background. For example, Lucretia Mott, coinitiator of the Seneca Falls Convention of 1848, was a Quaker. The self-confidence and independence fostered by female seminaries paired well with Quaker notions of womanhood; not surprisingly, Lucretia Mott's coinitiator at Seneca Falls was Elizabeth Cady Stanton, educated at Emma Willard's. But, as Ann Firor Scott has argued, in the training and example women received at female academies, feminist principles were often inchoate and bound together with contradictory impulses.[33] While the conventionality of feminist educators like Emma Willard and Catharine Beecher did increase their influence, it also confused the consciousness of students like Mary Talcott. By making clear and conscious commitments to egalitarian principles, the Society of Friends made it more likely that their adherents could act on those principles. Angelina and Sarah Grimké were soon to issue radical challenges both to the institution of slavery and to the strictures against women speaking in public.

This expedition to Talcott Mountain with Angelina Grimké was one of the last memorable experiences Harriet was to have at the Hartford Female Seminary. Lyman Beecher had received an inquiry from Lane Seminary in Cincinnati. Catharine acompanied her father to Ohio in March 1832 to explore the prospects of moving there, leaving Harriet in charge of the seminary for several months during her absence. Before she left Catharine had held meetings every night for students interested in religion—and twenty to thirty came each night. According to Mary Talcott, Miss Harriet was so exhausted from having "the whole superintendence of the school" on her shoulders that she was "not well enough to attend them" and they ceased for the time being.[34] The reports Catharine and Lyman Beecher brought back from Cincinatti were glowing, and the Beechers prepared to emigrate.

Looking ahead to her departure, Catharine took special pains in the *Catalogue* of 1831 to elaborate her plan of instruction and educational philosophy so that her republican experiment could be continued. Nevertheless, the departure of the Beechers for Cincinnati marked the end of an epoch in the Hartford Female Seminary. When Catharine secured the services of Thomas Gallaudet and later, John P.Brace, the women's culture she had fostered and presided over was put under the leadership of men. Brace was a splendid teacher and well liked by pupils, but he had a difficult time making the seminary prosper. Because he required a salary sufficient to support a family, the funds that had procured the services of many single women were required for his keep alone. He reduced the teachers from eight to two or three, making the work more onerous for them and less satisfying educationally.[35] With a man at the helm, the benefits of Catharine's specialized curriculum were no longer economically viable. Catharine Beecher rightly predicted that the future of secondary education in America lay in the hands of single women. The heyday of the Hartford Female Seminary was over. As Harriet later remarked to Catharine, "There never was such a school as that!"[36]

CHAPTER SEVEN

The West:
1832–1833

W*hen the Beechers emigrated* to Cincinnati in 1832 Lyman Beecher was just past the prime of life and Cincinnati was poised for the enormous expansion that would make it by 1850 the sixth-largest city in America. In 1820 Cincinnati's population was 10,000—just a bit larger than Hartford's. By 1830 Cincinnati had leaped to 25,000 and it was entering a twenty-year boom during which it was the fastest-growing city in the nation. By the following decade, swelled by large numbers of German immigrants, the population was 46,000.[1] The growth continued during the 1840s as the Irish, who numbered only 1000 in 1842, fled the series of potato famines between 1846 and 1849; by 1850 the Irish alone in Cincinnati numbered 14,000.[2] The city's situation on the Ohio River, near the rich farm lands of Ohio and Indiana, was propitious to trade and to the development of the world's largest pork packing industry; in 1845 Cincinnati slaughtered and processed a quarter-million hogs, exceeding even Ireland.[3] By the time the Beechers began to move back East, in 1851, Cincinnati's population was 114,000, of whom 46 percent were immigrants. This was the city to which Lyman Beecher took his evangelical Christian crusade. But the provincial New England preacher was no match for this boomtown. "Like a mighty locomotive engine he had leaped his track in coming to the West," wrote one of his older students.[4]

The West had a different meaning for those young enough to grow up with it. Henry Ward Beecher was a student at Amherst College when he received the news from Harriet that Catharine and their father had gone out

to Cincinnati to assess the prospects for removing the Beecher tribe to western soil. "I fairly *danced* the first half hour after I read your letter," he wrote
back to Harriet. "I sang, whistled, flew round like a mad man Father's
removal to the West is my 'hearts desire' "—and he wrote "the West" in large,
flourishing letters as if it were the eighth wonder of the world. Certainly it
represented to him a wider arena of experience, which he trusted would be
enough to convince his father. "I do rejoice in his determination to *go on &*
see at any rate—Edward went on to *see* & was caught [Edward Beecher's
western career had already begun]—Eve went to *see* & eat some apples—
father I trust will go to *see* & come back & let we go & see—It will make the
people of the west think that Jacob & his family are again going down to
Egypt."[5] This is the patriarchal plot: men go west to discover a virgin land,
to "eat some apples," and like Jacob, whose sons became the progenitors of
the Twelve Tribes of Israel, to scatter their seed. The West of the male
imagination was a garden of possibility, an extension of the mission that had
drawn the Puritans to the rocky coast of New England.

Lyman Beecher was not under the illusion, however, that the West was
a vacant land. He understood that the great westward movement of the nineteenth century was dramatically altering the character of the republic, and
he planned to be a major actor in the battle for America's soul, a "competition
. . . in which Catholics and infidels have got the start of us." In July 1830
he expressed to Catharine his concern for "the character of the West": "I
have thought seriously of going over to Cincinnati, the London of the West,
to spend the remnant of my days in that great conflict, and in consecrating
all my children to God in that region who are willing to go. If we gain the
West, all is safe; if we lose it, all is lost." Drawn to the West as to Armageddon, he had "a feeling as if the great battle is to be fought in the Valley of
the Mississippi, and as if it may be the will of God that I shall be employed
to arouse and help to marshal the host for the conflict."[6] During the next
eighteen months he and Catharine conspired and planned their campaigns:
he agreed to become president of Lane Seminary, in response to the plea
that "one of their best generals should occupy the very seat of Western warfare while the enemy is coming in like a flood"; she planned to follow him
West and institute a female college.[7] Just as Lyman Beecher had viewed
Catharine's Hartford Female Seminary as a fortress against Episcopalianism
in Connecticut, so her female college and his male seminary would be bas-
tions against infidelism and Roman Catholicism in Ohio. Edward Beecher
had begun this western campaign by going to Jacksonville, Illinois, to assume
the presidency of Illinois College.

In October 1832 Lyman Beecher marshalled his troops. The Beechers
had not lived together since the Litchfield years. Now the Boston and Hartford contingents were reunited in New York, preparatory to their westward
march. They were a large group: Lyman Beecher and his wife, Aunt Esther,
Harriet, George, Catharine, Henry, Isabella, and James. Once in New York,
Lyman Beecher took advantage of the opportunity to raise funds for Lane

Seminary. So taken was he with the pyrotechnics of his performances, which included a night at the Chatham Street Theatre, that some in his party despaired of ever getting to Cincinnati. "Father says we are in the hands of Providence," wrote Harriet, "but mother and Aunt Esther seem to demur, and think they should rather trust Providence by the way."[8] The journey, once underway, was slowed by further fund-raising in Philadelphia, the loss of baggage that had been taken to the wrong wharf in New York, and poor horses crossing the Appalachian Mountains. A journey that normally took the mail-stage forty-eight hours took the Beecher family eight days. They passed the time by singing hymns, which recalled to Harriet the land they had left, the hills and the skies that she would see no more, the friends whom she had left behind. When they struck up "Jubilee" she remembered the times she had sung it with Georgiana May as they bumped over the rough Guilford roads. Her cousin from Nutplains who had emigrated to Cincinnati a few years earlier expressed feelings that Harriet may have shared: "[W]hen I saw those large covered waggons toiling along through Guilford, filled with women and ragged children with their heads out at every corner who I was told were emigrants to Ohio—that wilderness of savages and wild beasts—I little thought it would be my fate so soon to follow them."[9] Harriet resolutely turned her homesickness into a means of spiritual improvement: "Well, my dear," she wrote Georgiana, "there is a land where we shall not *love* and *leave*. Those skies shall never cease to shine, the waters of life we shall *never* be called upon *to leave*. We have no continuing city, but we seek one to come."[10]

Harriet Beecher does not seem to have shared her father's high sense of purpose in going west. While crossing Pennsylvania she observed to Georgiana that the *Philadelphian* had taken note of their patriarchal pilgrimage, "setting forth how 'this distinguished brother, with his large family, having torn themselves from the endearing scenes of their home,' etc., etc., 'were going, like Jacob' etc.—a very scriptural and appropriate flourish." She added, "I do hate this way of speaking of *Christian* people. It is too much after the manner of men, or, as Paul says, speaking 'as a fool.' "[11] The following day she continued, "Here we all are—Noah, and his wife, and his sons, and his daughters, with the cattle and creeping things, all dropped down in the front parlor of this tavern, about thirty miles from Philadelphia." Her impulse to deflate Noah by dropping him down in a tavern was continuous with the mock-heroic tone of her editorials in the Hartford Female Seminary *School Gazette*, with one significant change: her point was directed not at the insignificance of the female world, but at the patriarchal pretensions of the male world. Unencumbered by the weight of a divine mission, Harriet remarked on the food, the state of the roads, the scenery. The journey from Wheeling, then part of Virginia, to Cincinnati was her introduction to the western institution of the "corduroy road." Formed by laying rough logs over a path that would otherwise engulf the wagon wheels in deep mud, it was designed for practicality rather than comfort. As she jolted over the logs and saw around them the smooth, black mud, so different from the rocky soil of Connecticut,the acculturation of a New Englander had begun. Behind her lay picturesque New England villages, scattered like sheep on the hills. Before her the land gently undulated toward a distant horizon.

The eighteen years Harriet Beecher spent in Cincinnati encompassed her literary apprenticeship, her marriage, and the birth of all but one of her seven children. The West was the cradle of her career. Unlike her father, who campaigned to wipe out the cultural diversity of the Mississippi Valley, she studied ways to comprehend it and translate the accents each to each. Within a year her tolerant views of Catholics won her the praise of John Baptist Purcell, bishop of Cincinnati. She was a New Englander when she came; by the time she left she was an American.[12] Although she distanced herself from the social theories of her father and the sister who raised her, she remained bound by deep feelings of family loyalty and pride that would continue to be a source of strength. Moreover, her psychic energy to effect this intellectual break with her family was itself a product of Catharine's careful tutelage of her in an all-female environment, which gave her an identity and a culture separate from the patriarchal "reality."

By 1832 she was ready to leave the sheltered world of a female seminary and try a wider world. Using as her excuse the "wear & tear of feeling & nerves" she had undergone at the Hartford Female Seminary, she asked for "at least a year to recruit" before she joined Catharine's new educational venture.The more important reason was that she had found a new occupation. "[Harriet] has employed herself this winter in writing some books for children," Catharine explained to Mary Dutton, "& as she finds this will be a means of *usefulness* & of *money*, she has concluded to defer taking any responsible part in a school for the coming year & to continue her present employment."[13] Benjamin Franklin's English school curriculum had fitted Harriet for practical enterprise. In the summer of 1832 she began writing the geography book that would be her first, and quite successful, publication.

Harriet's *Primary Geography for Children* was published in Cincinnati in March 1833. It went through four editions in three months, and a fifth a few months later. The *Western Monthly Magazine* called it "a capital little book," observing that "[w]riting books for children is one of the most difficult, and surely one of the most useful branches of authorship."[14] Writing a textbook was a good way to effect a transition from schoolteacher to author. British novelist Maria Edgeworth had begun her career by writing a highly influential series of educational tracts for children, and Harriet remembered her mother reading aloud from her "Frank" stories. The literary strengths of Edgeworth's educational books, as summarized by her biographer, are strikingly similar to the techniques Harriet began experimenting with in her *Geography*: "[G]eneralization is supported with concrete illustrations; ideas are developed in the movement of the narrative; anecdotes, proverbs, snatches of dialogue, citations of authority, homely understatement, and an overall appeal to common sense enliven the work and protect it from the appearance of personal prejudice."[15]

Harriet's *Geography* also suggests the way in which her western experience expanded her horizons. Writing in the intimate narrative voice characteristic of her best work, Harriet invited her young readers to imagine the commercial riverfront in New Orleans: "Now just suppose you could go to that city, and stand on the banks of the Mississippi, and see all that goes on. There is a broad sort of wharf, built all along by the river, called the levee. This is the place where all the boats land, and a great part of the business is done." She described the flat-bottomed boats that came from all over the Mississippi Valley, laden with flour, with corn and meat, with cattle and horses. She had been in the West only a matter of months, but she understood the economic power of the fertile lands and the network of rivers and canals that flowed through the Mississippi Valley. "You can see on the shore, the merchants full of business, taking out of the steamboats, or putting on board ships, their sugar, or molasses, or tobacco, or other goods. You may hear the sound of all sorts of languages, French, Spanish, English, and German, spoken by negroes, mulattoes, or white people,—for here are people from almost every country."[16]

Harriet's description of the wharf in New Orleans, which she had not seen, owed much to the Cincinnati landing, where commerce was almost as brisk. Frances Trollope, who missed the ruined castles of Europe and thought Cincinnati lacked "domes, towers, and steeples," nevertheless recognized the nobility of the Cincinnati landing, the center of commerce in the Ohio Valley. "[E]xtending for more than a quarter mile," she observed, "it is well paved, and surrounded by neat, though not handsome buildings. I have seen fifteen steam-boats there at once, and still half the wharf was unoccupied."[17] From the landing one looked across the Ohio River to the wooded hills of Kentucky, which rose abruptly from the riverbed. From these hills came the Kentucky flatboat men. Riding the current to New Orleans, they deposited their cargo and then crowded the decks of the steamboats to return to the Cincinnati landing, "gambling and wrangling, very seldom sober," and periodically leaping ashore to carry wood to the engine to pay for their portage.[18] In 1831 a youth from Kentucky who had moved to Illinois with his family built a flatboat and navigated it to New Orleans and back: his name was Abraham Lincoln.

The "Queen City" during the heydey of the steamboat, Cincinnati was the commercial center of the West—attracting half of all the capital invested in manufacturing in Ohio.[19] The city's easy water routes to the rich farmlands of Ohio and Indiana gave the Queen City another title: "Porkopolis." The country lanes were thronged with herds of swine being driven in from the surrounding farms. One could hardly walk the streets of the city without encountering a hog or two, which, republican fashion, were allowed to roam freely, providing the city the service of eating the garbage that was heaped up in the middle of the street for their delectation. "Speaking of the temptations of cities," Harriet wrote to her sister Mary, "I have much solicitude on Jamie's account lest he should form improper intimacies, for yesterday or day before we saw him parading by the house with his arm over the neck of a great hog, apparently on the most amicable terms possible."[20]

In her *Geography* Harriet summarized the importance of the western states: "The land is much finer than in the eastern states. . . . Then the rivers make travelling easy, so that whatever is raised in one place can be taken to another, and sold; and thus you see it gives people an opportunity to grow rich."[21] A year later she projected her next book, to be called *New England*, "sketching the rise & progress of a good common sense New Englander from poverty & boyhood to universal respect & estimation & high office."[22] Harriet's attraction to this dream of ambition had had a long foreground in the Beecher family culture. In addition, she had a penchant for being in the right place at the right time. She had ridden the crest of Litchfield's post–Revolutionary War expansion and left for Hartford just as the tide was going out. By 1833 the Litchfield Law School was closed, the Litchfield Female Academy appeared old-fashioned by comparison with the new generation of schools founded by Emma Willard and Catharine Beecher, and improved roads to other places heralded the decline of this mountain town.[23] Similarly, Harriet came to Cincinnati when its development was taking off, and left in 1851 just as its rapid growth was coming to an end, when land travel via rail superseded the waterways and the steamboat. Cincinnati boosters who witnessed the takeoff of the city in the 1830s confidently predicted that "the London of the West" would, as Harriet wrote in her geography, "become one of the greatest [cities] in the world."[24] Success was in the air. Frances Trollope, who put her British nose up and sniffed the slaughterhouses, was less enthusiastic about the "rapid conversion of a bear-brake into a prosperous city." She observed that "every bee in the hive is actively employed in search of that honey of Hybla, vulgarly called money."[25] But in America, Harriet pointed out to her young readers, there were no noblemen: "And do you not think that it is a great deal better, for men to be honored for what they do themselves, than to be honored just because they had a title and estate left them by their parents?"[26] Harriet's *Geography* earned her $187, the equivalent of about 15 percent of her father's annual salary, and almost as much as Catharine Beecher earned in a year of tending school. The secularization of an evangelical Protestant was well under way.

This process had begun long before Harriet's emigration to the West, by virtue of her contact with her mother's relatives, the worldly Foote family. This influence came particularly from her Uncle Samuel, now retired from the sea, married, and established in a mansion in Cincinnati. Having married Elizabeth Elliott, a Guilford descendant of their common ancestor, Andrew Ward, Samuel Foote brought her to Cincinnati in 1828. His brother John had come some eight years earlier; a bookseller and typefounder, John Foote was active in a number of literary and educational organizations, including the Ohio Mechanics Institute, the Cincinnati Historical Society, and the Western Literary Institute. Pioneers in a boomtown, Samuel and John originated the Cincinnati Water Company. Samuel invested heavily in real estate and in 1829 built an elegant mansion on the corner of Vine and Third streets; his parlor became a center of cultural and social life until the Panic of 1837 wiped out his fortune even faster than he had made it. A shrewd businessman, he rebuilt his fortune and returned in the 1850s to Connecticut to retire in comfort.[27]

It was while visiting her Uncle Samuel in the summer before her removal to Cincinnati that Harriet came to a new resolve, to enter society rather than to sit in a corner scrutinizing it. A letter to Georgiana May provides a glimpse of the earnest, introverted schoolgirl she was about to leave behind:

> The amount of the matter has been, as this inner world of mine has become worn out and untenable, I have at last concluded to come out of it and live in the external one, and, as F[rances] S[trong] once advised me, to give up the pernicious habit of meditation to the first Methodist minister that would take it, and try to mix in society somewhat as another person would.
>
> "*Horas non numero nisis serenas.*" Uncle Samuel, who sits by me, has just been reading the above motto, the inscription on a sun-dial in Venice. It strikes me as having a distant relationship to what I was going to say. I have come to a firm resolution to count no hours but unclouded ones, and to let all others slip out of my memory and reckoning as quickly as possible. . . .
>
> I am trying to cultivate a general spirit of kindliness towards everybody. Instead of shrinking into a corner to notice how other people behave, I am holding out my hand to the right and to the left, and forming casual or incidental acquaintances with all who will be acquainted with me. . . . This kind of pleasure in acquaintanceship is new to me. I never tried it before. When I used to meet persons, the first inquiry was, "Have they such and such a character, or have they anything that might possibly be of use or harm to me."[28]

The joviality of Uncle Samuel's entertainments owed nothing to such Calvinistic calculations of self-improvement. Harriet's second Christmas in Cincinnati was celebrated at his fireside, where he wished everyone "good fires & plenty of apples & nuts—not to mention minced pyes & roasted Turkeys— long lives & Merry Evenings." The Christmas frolic he got up was a lively contribution toward the latter. Impressed by the Corpus Christi processions he had seen in Spain, Samuel Foote sponsored a secularized Protestant version in the Christmas procession that marched through his parlors: performing the function of standard bearer, Uncle Samuel led; after him followed Kate Foote with flageolet, John Foote with tin trumpet, Samuel Foote's three-year-old son with the bass drum, Catharine Beecher with poker and tongs, Henry Edward Foote with the artillery, Elizabeth Foote with the clarinet, Charly Richards with the rattle, Harriet Beecher with tin kettle, Katy Grum with whistle, "after which followed a long & gorgeous train of singers & shouters & talkers & laughers." A few bottles of champagne were soon expended and the party "hooted & halloed & laughed & talked & Danced," wrote Samuel, "till we were entirely fagged out." He summed up the frolic for the benefit of Grandma Foote and his Nutplains brother and sisters: "[I]t was like last Christmas only a great deal more so."[29]

This manner of celebrating Christmas appealed to Harriet, who recorded in *Poganuc People* the festivities from which she, as a daughter of a Congregational minister, was excluded. But just as Lyman Beecher had bowed to the power of an irresistible cultural force when he permitted novel reading, so he bent in Cincinnati to manners pagan and popish. A week after her romp at Uncle Samuel's, Harriet rode out to her father's parsonage in Walnut Hills, laden with "forty or fifty little bundles & notions" for the Beechers: "[T]wo humming tops—one for Thomas & one for James—and a most marvellous pussy cat with her neck made of wire so that it should be constantly in motion & a caro case for Bella & a present for Aunt Esther." She was met on the verandah by little James, who was as pleased as if she had "dropped from the skies." Harriet enjoyed playing Santa Claus to her younger siblings and providing them with some of the simple delights that she had longed for at their age. That this celebration took place on New Year's Day rather than Christmas was enough to preserve the Protestant forms.[30]

During the first two years in Cincinnati Harriet couldn't quite make up her mind who she was, a schoolteacher or a literary woman. She wrote stories and sketches but she also allowed herself to be impressed into the work of Catharine's school. The ill health and depressed spirits that plagued Harriet during this period probably owed much to her lack of enthusiasm for the duties of the schoolmarm. In May 1833 she wrote a letter to Georgiana May that revealed her mental depression and her boredom:

> Since writing the above my whole time has been taken up in the labor of our new school, or wasted in the fatigue and lassitude following such labor. To-day is Sunday, and I am staying at home because I think it is time to take some efficient means to dissipate the illness and bad feelings of divers kinds that have for some time been growing upon me. At present there is and can be very little system or regularity about me. About half of my time I am scarcely alive, and a great part of the rest the slave and sport of morbid feeling and unreasonable prejudice. I have everything but good health.[31]

When she was sixteen and in the depths of a depression, the many time-consuming tasks of a schoolteacher had pulled her into a busy routine and a ready-made society of half-a-dozen other teachers and many scholars of her same age. Catharine's new school, the Western Female Institute, was small and struggling and represented only the tedious side of teaching, unleavened by the energy and sociability that she had enjoyed in the heyday of the Hartford Female Seminary. "Now, Georgiana," she continued, "let me copy for your delectation a list of matters that I have jotted down for consideration at a teachers' meeting to be held to-morrow night. It runneth as follows. Just hear!," she mocked. " 'About quills and papers on the floor; forming classes; drinking in the entry (cold water, mind you); giving leave to speak; recess-bell, etc., etc.' 'You are tired, I see,' says Gilpin, 'so am I,' and

I spare you." Even the company of Mary Dutton and Elizabeth Lyman, who had come at Catharine's request, was not sufficiently diverting. In her dissatisfaction with the external world in which she had vowed to live, she again retreated to the inner world. She read Madame de Stael's *Corinne*, and the heroic feelings that de Stael's heroine kindled in her were a kind of torture, given the blandness of her days. She told Georgiana, "I have felt an intense sympathy with many parts of that book, with many parts of her character. But in America feelings vehement and absorbing like hers become still more deep, morbid, and impassioned by the constant habits of self-government which the rigid forms of our society demand. They are repressed, and they burn inward till they burn the very soul, leaving only dust and ashes." In contrast to Corinne, Harriet was "exhausted," "listless," and "sinking into deadness."[32]

Her sister Catharine had extricated Harriet from a similar depression—also caused by a removal from her former associates—by bringing her back into the society of young women of her age. Now Harriet effected her own cure, perhaps aided by the example of Georgiana, who had become quite a "woman of the world." Harriet envied her this busy social intercourse. "How good it would be for me to be put into a place which so breaks up and precludes thought."[33] Her determination to enter society brought her out of the female world of schoolteaching into the parlor, where men and women mixed, discussed the topics of the day, and entertained themselves by writing poems, stories, and sketches. Harriet's entrance into society was also her entrance into the world of parlor literature.

CHAPTER EIGHT

Parlor Literature:
1833—1834

P*arlor literature,* like parlor music, was a centuries-old institution. When books were still expensive and amusements were simple, people provided their own entertainments in their homes.[1] Typical activities included singing, playing the piano, and readings of specially produced essays and poems. These domestic literary productions often contained humorous references to people and events known to the participants. The literature produced at home had a strong affinity with what is called "occasional verse," lines written to commemorate an anniversary, an election, a memorable local event. Catharine Beecher was fond of such impromptu productions and contributed much to the hilarity of the Beecher household in Litchfield by such poems as her epitaph to a dead cat. Written at the request of Harriet, who was the "chief mourner" at funerals for animals, Catharine undertook her charge in her characteristic high spirits:

> Here died our kit,
> Who had a fit,
>   And acted queer.
> Shot with a gun,
> Her race is run,
>   And she lies here.[2]

"Scarcely any thing happened in the family without giving rise to some humorous bit of composition from her pen," remembered Harriet. These prose and verse productions were "read at the table, and passed round among the social visiting circles which were frequently at our house."[3]

Literary clubs—a feature of the Litchfield society of Harriet Beecher's youth—provided a bit more formal audience for domestic literature. Men and women gathered in the parlor and read aloud their essays and poems. The dramatic verse, ballads, and sketches produced in the parlors and salons of early nineteenth-century American homes display much in common with eighteenth-century taste: when satire was not the mode, interest in "antiquities"—which in America meant the Indians—was likely to take its place. Among the domestic compositions that were "much in vogue in the literary coteries of Litchfield," Harriet recalled that several recounted "[t]he history and antiquities of the Bantam Indians . . . one of which, by sister Catharine, and two by the head teacher of the Female Academy, Mr. John P. Brace, were in the mouths and memories of us all."[4] Sometimes the encouragement that an author received upon reading his or her work led to subsequent publication. Brace went on to publish two novels, *Tales of the Devils* (Hartford, Conn., 1847) and *The Fawn of the Pale Faces or, Two Centuries Ago* (New York, 1853). These literary gatherings provided entertainment, sociability, and a stimulus to amateur authors.

The production of literature was thus an integral part of polite society and domestic culture. "Becoming an author" was not a distant and mysterious process, but an everyday event continuous with polite forms of society such as writing letters. Letter writing, in fact, was a more public act than might be supposed, for letters were often read aloud, in the parlor, to an audience that might consist of family, friends, boarders, and servants. Correspondents took pains to make their letters entertaining, literary, amusing, and fit for such semipublic occasions. "This is not fit to show or read to any body," runs a typical disclaimer;[5] the number of times correspondents criticize their "stupid" letters suggests that epistolary productions were a much more self-conscious literary form than was later to be the case when published literature became more accessible and its home production declined. Indeed, "epistolary correspondence" was an item in the curriculum in a number of schools; recommended by Benjamin Franklin as a way of improving composition skills at the Philadelphia Academy, letter writing was encouraged at the Litchfield Female Academy: the 1832 *Catalogue* characterized it as as an activity "where, alone with few exceptions, women can manifest the extent of their information."[6]

In the 1830s the function of letter writing, domestic literature, and literary clubs began to expand. As Americans became more mobile, the domestic production of literature began to serve some of the same functions as the voluntary societies that proliferated at the same time. Just as temperance societies and fraternal orders provided a ready-made social group through which to effect one's assimilation into a new location,[7] so the literary clubs began to play this same role of integrating newcomers into the growing cities of America. While the activities of the literary clubs eased the adjustment of a move, letter writing became a signally important link with family and friends left behind. As Americans became more national in their geographic allegiances, the domestic literature they produced subtly reflected this shift. Writing increasingly in western parlors, Americans on the move recorded their growing awareness of a national culture, which at first they experienced as a loss of the regional culture they had recently left behind. Paradoxically, this loss was also a discovery, for only upon leaving their homes did they discover what was unique to their native region.

The heightened significance with which such domestic literature was viewed in a mobile society is illustrated by the highly ritualized reception the Beecher household in Cincinnati accorded the first letter from "the East"— now endowed with a power undreamed of by those who earlier envisioned "the majestic West." The originator of the letter was Mary Beecher Perkins. The most geographically rooted of all the Beecher children, she lived to the end of her life in Hartford. Her letter included notes and messages from many Hartford friends, including Mrs. Parsons, who "stopped in the very midst of her pumpkin pies" to think of the distant Beechers on Thanksgiving. All of the Beechers in Cincinnati had been waiting anxiously for the first news from the East, but it was Harriet who had made sure that someone inquired daily at the post office, and into her hands fell Mary's letter before the other family members were aware of its arrival. She immediately ran upstairs and began a reply. "The fact of our having received said letter is as yet a state secret, not to be made known till all our family circle 'in full assembly meet' at the tea-table," she wrote Mary. "Then what an illumination!" She thought it "too bad to keep it from mother and Aunt Esther a whole afternoon," but Harriet's subsequent production of the letter to the assembled family had the desired effect: as she read it aloud, the delight and warmth of each listener increased the pleasure of the group, and the Beechers had a kind of reunion with the family and friends left behind. This family ritual, around the ceremony of tea, strengthened the bonds of community in the "saving remnant" who had gone forth into the wilderness.

It also provided an opportunity for Harriet to engage in an epistolary response that captured this moment of family unity. Her letter to Mary, begun while she was in the midst of darning her brother George's socks, continued in stolen moments throughout the day.

> Evening. Having finished the last hole on George's black vest, I stick in my needle and sit down to be sociable. You don't know how coming away from New England has sentimentalized us all! Never was there such an abundance of meditation on our native land, on the joys of friendship, the pains of separation. Catharine had an alarming paroxysm in Philadelphia which expended itself in "The Emigrant's Farewell." After this was sent off she felt considerably relieved. My symptoms have been of a less acute kind, but, I fear, more enduring. There! the tea-bell rings. Too bad! I was just going to say something bright. Now to take your letter and run! How they will stare when I produce it!
>
> After tea. Well, we have had a fine time. When supper was about half over, Catharine began: "We have a dessert that we have been saving all the afternoon," and then I held up my letter. "See here, this is from Hartford!" I wish you could have seen Aunt Esther's eyes brighten, and mother's pale face all in a smile, and father, as I unfolded the letter and began.[8]

Besides capturing a wonderful moment of community feeling across a continent, Harriet's letter itself crossed the border between letter and epistolary novel, between the private and the public realms of discourse. "There! the tea-bell rings"—by such novelistic devices, she invited Mary into the parlor, to see the faces of the Beecher family, to lean over their shoulders as they listened to the reading of the letter from the East. Of course, Harriet knew that her letter would be read aloud in similar gatherings in Hartford: to the teachers and scholars boarding at the Perkins's house, to groups of friends and neighbors, like Mrs. Parsons, who had sent messages. As letter writing increasingly bore the burden of painting pictures of those who were absent, it became more novelistic and more firmly established within the domain of parlor literature.

Women's letters in particular, filled with details of everyday life and a concern with particular friends and family, took on a novelistic quality. The Beecher women often began their letters by invoking a scene: "So here you see me, after a world of trouble seated comfortably at our great red table with paper of all sizes and dimensions before me," Harriet wrote to former schoolmate Mary Swift. The parlor or common room was usually the setting for epistolary productions, and women often peopled their first paragraph with those among whom they sat: "I am seated upon one side of the table in our parlour Ann upon the other Mary between us darning a pair of stockings with her little basket before her, Mother is the other side of Ann making piping for her frock," begins an especially full catalogue; "Sarah is sitting on one side of the fire place knitting Uncle is in the rocking chair the other side Sarah has gone to bed Paddy & Frederick are in bed little George is asleep in the cradle in one corner of the room. We have just been laughing at an anecdote which Susy Adams told the other day to our girls."[9] By inviting the reader to "behold"—a verb with which Harriet often introduces such an epistolary scene—a picture is created that joins the reader to the situation of the writer. Such a "graphic sketch," as Harriet said in requesting one from her brother, gave the reader a specific setting within which "to locate [her] recollections."[10]

Such engaging epistolary openers were followed by detailed descriptions of people, rooms, and "trifles." "Pray be particular in your communications," runs a typical encouragement, "and, if they seem trifling, recollect the importance which affections gives to trifles, & that nothing which concerns you can be uninteresting to me."[11] Catharine Beecher urged a correspondent, "Do be particular for I think it is *trifles* that constitute the interest of a letter."[12] "I want to know if the kitchen is built & how the church progresses and about how the grapes succeeded and various other matters too numerous to mention," wrote Harriet to her cousin, Hannah Foote. "Now Hannah the beauty of your epistolary style consists in its minuteness of detail & telling just the things we women like to hear." Men were less satisfactory correspondents in this regard. "Charley's letters are generally what he is thinking of—subjects—impulses moods of mind," wrote Harriet to her daughter-in-law; "I want to here about details."[13] Harriet urged her son's wife, "Do dear

Susie write me a womans letter—tell me all about Mr & Mrs Hobson & Mrs Caliper. . . . Are you to have a piano—Please tell me about every body & every thing."[14] As Harriet wrote to Susie, it took "the graphic touch of a female pen to bring to sight those many little matters in which I am interested."[15] Women criticized men for neglecting the most important—which is to say the most particular and trifling—news. Catharine Beecher wrote to Louisa Wait that she had received "a long letter from John," who had gone to Portland to get married, and then complained, "His letter was a long one but it was all a description of his journey there he said nothing about Lucy or Portland or the family or any thing he ought to."[16]

Besides proffering a wealth of graphic detail, women's letters invited a familiar visit. "Now if you should ask why I take such a *big* sheet," Aunt Esther wrote to Harriet, "my answer is that I do not intend to have this a regular built letter but a real *talk* such as I would have if I were sitting by you in your nursery."[17] Catharine Beecher wrote to two school friends, "I want to know all about yourselves & the children & Katy & Elisabeth & Mason—so please to answer all the questions you think I should ask if I were sitting in your little breakfast room as in bye gone days."[18] The nursery, the breakfast room, and the parlor beckoned the letter reader to come and sit a spell: "I . . . am rejoicing in the light of my own fire & wishing you could look in upon me to share it."[19]

The continuity between the writer and the reader was ritually established through the exchanges of small items that often accompanied the letters: recipes, pieces of carpet, items of food, clippings of plants. Harriet Porter Beecher sent one of her letters tucked inside the mouth of a bag of apples.[20] "I am very busy just at present in transplanting flowers," Catharine wrote from Cincinnati to friends in Connecticut. "I have a noble variety & Mary if you wish to increase your stock & will just reach me a tin pan out of your pantry I will give you an abundance."[21] Catharine's whimsical request, "reach me a tin pan out of your pantry," recalled the familiar exchanges they had enjoyed as neighbors, even as it acknowledged the thousand miles that now stretched between them. As families became more mobile, these exchanges took on a heightened significance, just as the first letter from the East was no ordinary letter. In addition to elaborating the bonds between family, friends, and neighbors— attenuated and intensified through distance—these exchanges of flowers, fruits, and food transmitted local culture from one region to another and were a part of the process through which a national culture was elaborated.[22]

While the emigrants brought family recipes with them, they also adapted to new culinary customs. "Yesterday I made calves head soup and calves feet jelly," wrote Elizabeth Foote to her sister-in-law. "Don't tell Abigail—she would faint at the thought of such vulgar things as *calves feet*."[23] Edward Beecher's wife, Isabella, writing from their outpost at Illinois College, explained why she hadn't written: "[W]e have had to salt down pork, try out lard, cure bacon, make sausages & various other *literary* pursuits connected with *hog killing,* which some of my readers will no doubt think quite vulgar occupations, which nevertheless come within the line of a housekeeper's duties a housekeeper in *Illinois.*"[24]

In the absence of national holidays and national rituals, domestic rituals rooted emigrants to a material culture. With the exception of the Fourth of July, holidays were largely regional affairs. Thanksgiving was celebrated on a variety of days determined by the governor of each state, and had particular customs in particular locales.[25] Thus when the Beechers left New England in October 1832, they left behind a holiday that they could not re-create in Ohio. They talked about keeping the holiday New England style, but in the end let it pass as an ordinary day. "Perhaps," Harriet commented, "we should all have felt something of the text, 'How shall we sing the Lord's song in a strange land?' "[26]

In the pre-railroad times between 1830 and 1850, before a mass culture was articulated, women's culture was at the height of its influence. As the cooks and keepers of the hearth and heart, women had an important role to play in the elaboration of links between the regional culture that had been left behind and the new land to which families had removed. Weaving the material reality of everyday life into their letters, they created the ground from which emerged American realism, with its attention to particular accents, local peculiarities, and regional types. The trifles that were the delight of their letters were also the stuff of realistic fiction. A more abstract and allegorical tradition developed, naturally enough, from men's interests. "As to domesticals," wrote Charles Beecher to the Beecher family, "I'm going to insist on Sarah's inditing all that part—And it remains only for me to speak of philosophicals." While he explained his studies in "the philosophy of mind," his wife Sarah responded, "I wrote to you a short time since by way of Collinsville all about domesticals, as Charles is pleased to name common indoor arrangements."[27] Ralph Waldo Emerson, who wrote abstractly and philosophically about nature, called in 1841 for an American poet who would sing of the common and the everyday. He perhaps did not observe that women were seated in their parlors writing and reading aloud just such examples of native American literature.

Such literary realism served several purposes. As Annette Kolodny has argued, the novel of western relocation, in the hands of women, provided westering women with practical advice about what equipment and clothing to bring with them; it also prepared them psychologically for the rigors of western life. Their concerns almost totally ignored in the promotional literature for the West, women found an "emigrant's guide" in novels such as Caroline Kirkland's *A New Home—Who'll Follow?* This novel, which Kolodny describes as "the first realistic depiction of frontier life in American letters," originated in "Kirkland's attempt to share her new experience [in Michigan] in letters to friends and family in the east."[28]

A second function was to explain regional customs to readers who were vicariously, through fiction, entering another part of the country. In *Uncle*

Tom's Cabin Stowe pauses to explain to a reader whom she calls her "inno-cent Eastern friend" the intricacies of travel over "an Ohio road," made from logs precariously positioned over mud of "unfathomable and sublime depth." By such direct address Stowe acknowledged the heterogeneity of her audi-ence while at the same time creating a sense of intimacy. "Such direct remarks to the reader," as Robyn Warhol points out, "make novel-writing resemble a personal correspondence."[29] The great nineteenth-century novels were in fact letters to the nation, and the populace read them to see reflected back just who they were, in all their regional variety.

This points to the most important effect of women's epistolary realism: the creation of a national literature. The shift from local to a national liter-ature required a new content, and fiction, as Ronald Zboray has pointed out, "helped to unite the still heterogeneous national reading public."[30] Instead of reading about the particular doings of relatives who had moved away, readers were now treated to fictive aunts and uncles who bore some rela-tionship to all of them. Between 1830 and 1850 domestic culture and national culture were held in a dynamic suspension: the movement to new homes created an expanded sense of nation and culture and the search for a national identity was in some sense a search for a new home.

But how did letters produced for domestic consumption make their way from the parlor to the press? An important institution mediating between oral tradition and print culture was the literary club. The step from writing letters for domestic consumption to writing for a literary club was small but significant. The clubs met in the parlor, but when company came for a polite entertainment the parlor was transformed into a Parlor. Now one read not just for family and friends and boarders, but for distinguished guests whose critical tastes were not alloyed with the warmth of family feeling. Harriet Beecher's literary career formally commenced in the Semi-Colon Club, a Cincinnati literary society begun in the early 1830s. After the publication of the *Geography*, with which both Catharine and Harriet were credited, the Semi-Colon Club invited the Beecher sisters to join.[31]

The Semi-Colons met most frequently in Samuel Foote's mansion, sit-uated high on a bluff overlooking the city. Harriet and Catharine had lived with their father in Walnut Hills when they first arrived in Cincinnati, but soon they were living in town and spending much of their time at Uncle Samuel's house. His sponsorship of the Semi-Colons in his well-known par-lor helped to offset the somewhat intimidating assortment of intellects that assembled on Monday evenings. All of the professions were represented— and by people who were destined to make a significant mark. One of these was Salmon P.Chase, later to become Lincoln's secretary of the treasury and then chief justice of the Supreme Court. He was at this time recently estab-lished in law practice in Cincinnati and increasingly involved in antislavery activity; his insistence on defending the rights of escaped slaves earned for him the title of "attorney-general for runaway negroes." Another professional man of distinction was Dr. Daniel Drake; a well-known medical educator, he was also the family physician for the Beechers. "He is tall, rectangular, perpendicular sort of body," observed Harriet, "as stiff as a poker, and enunciates his prescriptions very much as though he were delivering a discourse on the doctrine of election."[32] Professor Calvin Stowe, the most learned biblical scholar in America and recently appointed as professor of biblical literature at Lane Seminary, came to the Semi-Colon with his twenty-five-year old wife, Eliza Tyler; she was one of the most popular members and Harriet soon fell in love with her. Education was also represented by Mrs. Peters, afterwards founder of the Philadelphia School of Design, and of course by the founders of the Western Female Institute, Catharine and Harriet Beecher. Caroline Lee Hentz had just made the transition from schoolteacher to author by publishing her first novel, *Lovell's Folly,* and Judge James Hall was the editor of the *Western Monthly Magazine.*

Many of the Semi-Colons were transplanted New Englanders. The core of the club consisted of Samuel and Elizabeth Foote and their neighbors, William and Abby Lyman Greene. William Greene had been a student at the Litchfield Law School while he courted Abby Lyman, a student at the Litchfield Female Academy. Another member, Edward D. Mansfield, had likewise been a student at the Litchfield Law School. Edward King, now established among the intelligentsia of Cincinnati, was a former beau of Catharine's from Litchfield and related to the Beechers by Lyman's marriage to Harriet Porter. In addition to these members of the Semi-Colon, there were in Cincinnati various friends from Litchfield and Guilford and even two former housemates from Hartford: Mr. and Mrs. Brigham, who had boarded at Mrs. Strong's with Catharine and Harriet. Surrounded by these old friends, Catharine concluded that Cincinnati was full of "intelligent, New England sort of folks." "Indeed," she continued, "this is a New England city in all its habits, and its inhabitants are more than half from New England."[33]

Whatever regional prejudices the New Englanders brought with them to the Semi-Colon met a strong challenge in the persons of Daniel Drake and James Hall. Although he had been born in New Jersey, Drake was well established in Cincinnati and was a vocal Ohio booster. He is credited with naming it the Buckeye State, after a speech he gave in April 1833 extolling the horse chestnut tree and its role in settling the Ohio Valley; at his house a leaf from this tree remained on display.[34] James Hall used his *Western Monthly Magazine* to puff the West. When Lyman Beecher preached of the need to save the West through eastern influence, James Hall took umbrage at his chauvinistic remarks and published a response in the *Western Monthly Magazine.* After the publication of Beecher's *A Plea for the West,* Catharine attempted to defend the family honor by dividing Cincinnati society along an East/West axis and expelling Drake and Hall. She failed miserably.[35] Cincinnati society, and the Semi-Colon Club in particular, was an engine of assimilation that swallowed up newcomers and turned them into Buckeyes. By 1839 even Samuel Foote was referring to his family as "us Buckeyes."[36]

The Semi-Colon was a decidedly mixed sex and heterosexual gathering. Men and women came as couples, either as husbands and wives or as a courting pair, and for the unattached there were opportunities for flirtation and more serious explorations of common interests; jokes about matrimonial prospects were so regularly bantered about that Harriet felt called upon to produce "a set of legislative enactments purporting to be from the ladies of the society, forbidding all such allusions in the future."[37] The Semi-Colons met every Monday evening at 7:30. A reader—apparently always male—was appointed for each meeting. Although some put their name to their productions, many wrote anonymously or under pseudonyms. After the readings there was discussion, followed by dancing, sandwiches and coffee, and, at Samuel Foote's, a fine brand of madeira. The evening finished off with "a gay Virginia reel led by the reader of the evening and a merry-hearted girl."[38] With little regard for formal unity, the Semi-Colon parties liberally mixed "the *conversazione*, the reading club, the musical recital, and the dance." Observed one, "Only in the youth of a city, before society began to crystallize into set forms, could these informal, unique assemblies exist."[39]

What did the Semi-Colons write about? "Anything," said John Foote, "that gave opportunities for the display of the tastes and opinions of the members."[40] Charles Beecher wrote an "Incantation," an anonymous member produced an essay on "Female Influence," and for the meeting of March 11, 1831, "Samuel Essence" speculated about music, in reply to "Hortensia." Occasional verse such as "Lines Written by a Father on the Occasion of His Daughter's Marriage" alternated with personal reminiscences.[41] The tone of the Semi-Colon papers was satiric and exaggerated; there is an element of self-conscious cultivation about them, very much like the mock-heroic gambits of the Hartford Female Seminary *School Gazette*. For example, a satiric poem, billed as "The Humble Petition of the Editors of the Cincinnati Chronicle and the Illinois Monthly Magazine to the Semi-Colons" begins:

> Fair and gentle Semi-Colons
> Bright as Hebe, wise as Solons,
> Famed for beauty, wit and learning,
> *Jeux d'esprit*, and deep discerning,
> Secret, social coalition—
> Listen to our poor petition
> . . . .
> Each whose footstep hither tends,
> Philosophic forty friends,
> "Favored and enlightened few,"
> Champions of the stocking blue,
> For your own, your country's sake
> List, oh, list to Hall and Drake![42]

Holding up the Semi-Colons as beacons of Greek culture in the American West (where towns with classical names like Athens and Gallipolis and

Cincinnati rubbed shoulders with towns with Native American names like Wapakoneta and Chillicothe), this "petition" simultaneously mocked the pretensions to culture it invoked, displaying a double consciousness very like that of the student editors at the Hartford Female Seminary. This doubleness arose from the ambiguous position of these semipublic voices; speaking both from the domestic center and the political periphery, parlor literature naturally broke into satire and parody—of itself and the public world to which it pointed.[43] All that was necessary for this parodic voice to slip into political satire (as *Uncle Tom's Cabin* demonstrates) was the conviction that parlor commonplaces were superior to the prevailing public morality.

Harriet Beecher's first Semi-Colon papers were in this satiric mode. She drew up a mock advertisement of the "wares" available at the Beecher family domicile. In its self-conscious mingling of literary and domestic productions, this ad suggests the multiple activities of the parlor:

Sign of Beecher Deveaux Petit & Co—At the Presbyterian Nunnery.
    Frocks aprons & Geographies got up in first rate style & at shortest
    notice—also
    Shoes mended cheap!—also
    Varses written & hairdressing executed gratis—also
    Bonnets made & trimmed &
      the English languages instructed in—also
    All sorts of sociable doings invented in a style never before seen—
    Those disposed to patronise are requested to call at the store of the firm
    & examine for themselves[44]

The humor of this arises from the unexpected conjunctions—"Frocks aprons & Geographies" are "got up" indiscriminately; verse writing and bonnet trimming are interchangeable activities. As we have seen, Harriet herself pursued letter writing and mending in alternate moments, and she had just published a *Primary Geography* for children. The needle and the pen were not that far apart. Indeed, as one observer remarked of the Semi-Colon, the "unceremonious nature of these parties was shown by the busy fingers of the ladies employed in pretty fancy or knitting work."[45] The self-consciousness of Harriet's advertisement, however, suggests that historical processes were already underway that would bring about the separation of writing from the parlor.

In a similar satiric mode, Harriet outlined for Georgiana May what she called "a history of my campaign in this circle":

My first piece was a letter from Bishop Butler, written in his outrageous style of parenthesis and foggification. My second a satirical essay on the modern uses of languages. This I shall send to you as some of the gentlemen, it seems, took a fancy to it and requested leave to put it in the "Western Magazine" and so it is in print. It is ascribed to *Catherine*, or I don't know that I should let it go. I have no notion of appearing in *propria persona*.
    The next piece was a satire on certain members who were getting very much

into the way of joking on the worn-out subjects of matrimony and old maid and old bachelorism.[46]

Harriet's reluctance to appear "in *propria persona*" was shared by many of her literary sisters (though not by Catharine Beecher, who was happy to put her name on Harriet's *Geography*). As Mary Kelley has demonstrated, literary women of the pre–Civil War period were often "secret writers" who were reluctant to betray their domestic socialization; even as their popular novels increasingly defined the emerging national culture, they adopted elaborate stratagems and pseudonyms to avoid stepping onto the public stage.[47]

Virginia Woolf observed that nineteenth-century women writers inherited a "male sentence" that was ill-suited to their voices.[48] If such a sentence did indeed exist, Harriet worked her way through it by deliberately and repeatedly imitating it until imitation tipped into parody and catharsis. Her next production was "a letter purporting to be from Dr. Johnson. I have been stilting about in his style so long that it is a relief to me to come down to the jog of common English." She soon had had enough of satire and began to shape a genre that allowed for more "serious and rational" productions. In the process, she began to reinvent both the epistolary novel of Richardson and the serial novel of Dickens.[49]

She "conceived the design of writing a *set of letters*." The first letter described "a house in the country, a gentleman and lady, Mr and Mrs Howard, as being pious, literary, and agreeable. I threw into the letter a number of little particulars and incidental allusions to give it the air of having been really a letter." Her purpose was to provide herself "an opportunity for the introduction of different subjects and the discussion of different characters in future letters." She not only wrote in a familiar epistolary genre, but even more significantly, in a colloquial style. She threw away the stilts of eighteenth-century male essayists and wrote in the ordinary voice of a domestic letter writer. This departure from the sprightly and humorous tone of the Semi-Colon was sufficiently risky that Harriet adopted an elaborate ruse, as she explained to Georgiana:

> Yesterday morning I finished my letter, smoked it to make it look yellow, tore it to make it look old, directed it and scratched out the direction, postmarked it with red ink, sealed it and broke the seal, all this to give credibility to the fact of its being a real letter. Then I inclosed it in an envelope, stating that it was a part of a *set* which had incidentally fallen into my hands. This envelope was written in a scrawny, scrawly, gentleman's hand.

She sent the letter to Samuel Foote's wife, Elizabeth, who was the only one Harriet let in on the deception. Elizabeth showed it to Samuel, who pronounced it a "real letter," and it was passed on to Mr. Greene, the reader, who developed a theory of authorship by reconstructing the names and dates Harriet had erased. Harriet's letter had passed the test of authenticity, yet still as she awaited the Monday gathering at which it would be read, she confessed to Georgiana that she was uneasy about its reception: "Elizabeth, after reading it, did not seem to be exactly satisfied. She thought it had too much sentiment, too much particularity of incident,—she did not exactly know what. She was afraid that it would be criticised unmercifully."[50] The "particularity of incident" that women demanded in their letters might be heard in a different key in the more formal setting of a literary club.

The reception of this letter and the fate of Harriet's projected series was not recorded by the Semi-Colons, but soon after this experiment stories and sketches flowed from her pen in creative profusion. Moreover, they soon made their way into print, through the agency of James Hall's *Western Literary Magazine.* "I wrote a piece," she explained to her brother George in January 1834, "a little bit of a love sketch & sent it in—thinking it was rather a contemptible little affair—& indeed much hesitating whether I would have it read at all—But somehow or other every body was mightily taken with it— & I have heard more about it since than any thing I ever did—Judge Hall wants to put it in his magazine & so I have promised it to him & so you will see it."[51] Her most memorable character sketch, "Uncle Lot," was written for the Semi-Colon Club in November 1833. James Hall was so taken with it that he suggested she submit it to the prize competition sponsored by his *Western Monthly Magazine.* Harriet won the substantial $50 prize and the story was published in the April 1834 number under the title "A New England Sketch." Based on the crusty New England farmer who had raised Lyman Beecher, "Uncle Lot" seems familiar only because, as Forrest Wilson has written,

> "[W]e have met him and his kind in dozens of stories, plays, and novels dating from Sarah Orne Jewett to the present. It was not commonplace on a Monday evening in November, 1833. Harriet was then introducing her New England to the American audience for the first time—the shrewd, pious, capable, humorous New England that has gone into our tradition rather than the tragic New England portrayed by her contemporary, Nathaniel Hawthorne."[52]

Harriet's ability to describe Uncle Lot's peculiarities and transcribe his manner of speech owed much to the oral tradition within the Beecher household; she had heard stories of Uncle Lot told over and over again, in dialect. Her ability to see him as a regional type, however, arose from the intersection of her eastern and her western experiences. In New England he was only Uncle Lot, a peculiar individual. In the West he became a social type, the New England farmer. But what enabled all of this to find expression in a fresh, colloquial voice was Harriet's bold adaptation of the rhythms of everyday speech to parlor literature of a more formal type.

Ten years later Harriet collected a number of her Semi-Colon papers and published them in a collection of stories and sketches entitled *The Mayflower.* When they were reprinted in 1855 Harriet noted in the introduction that there were some "scattered through the world" who would remember "the social literary parties of Cincinnati, for whose genial meetings many of these articles were prepared." With "affectionate remembrances," she dedicated the book "to the yet surviving members of The Semicolon." These sketches bear the marks of the gatherings for which they were created. They often begin with a local reference: "Since sketching character is the mode, I too take up my pencil, not to make you laugh, though peradventure it may be—to get you to sleep." Refracted by the dialects and customs of both the East and the West, they addressed an audience of western pioneers. "Were any of you born in New England, in the good old catechizing, church-going, school-going, orderly times?," begins one sketch. Another described the Sabbath as it used to be kept in New England—a custom that now appeared quaint from a western perspective. In "Uncle Lot" she deliberately worked a strain of New England nostalgia, aided by her graphic imagination: "Do you see yonder brown house? . . . You must often have noticed it . . . you recollect its gate, that swung with a chain and a great stone; its pantry window, latticed with little brown slabs, and looking out upon a forest of bean poles."[53] Harriet's narrative is punctuated by "You remember," and as she watched the faces of the Semi-Colons as they listened to the reading, she could see that many of them did indeed recall such domestic scenes from their New England past.[54]

Parlor literature afforded Harriet Beecher an advantage she never lost: an intimate relationship to her audience. Her stories were always read aloud—in later years to her husband and children and servants—and as she gauged their effect she developed a powerful capacity to move her audience. Although they were an unusually distinguished group, in some ways her initial audience, the Semi-Colons, were typical of the mass market her fictions would later address. They were intelligent men and women, gathered in the parlor; they were experiencing a rapidly transforming national culture; they looked to literature, and to domestic rituals in general, to root them momentarily in the flux. When *Uncle Tom's Cabin* burst on the national scene in 1851, the intimate narrative voice of that book, its appeal to domestic institutions and reader emotions, had had a long foreground in Harriet Beecher's apprenticeship in parlor literature.

CHAPTER NINE

Courtship and Marriage:
1834–1836

I *n December 1833 Charles Beecher* remarked to his father, "Seems to me its most time for a wedding somewhere or other—Isn't George most ready? *I* never would be so slow & awkward about it—He says Harriet is going to be an old maid—If she is I hope she'll be as good an one as Aunt Esther, & Sister Catharine."[1] Harriet was at this time twenty-two years old—the same age as Catharine when she had been betrothed to Alexander Fisher—and she had had no romantic interests. She had recently helped George navigate the storms of an abortive courtship with Cordelia Baldwin, assuring him that as she had no interests of her own, she was wholly free to devote herself to his troubles.[2] The unusual length and thoroughness of her education made her something of a "bluestocking." It was perhaps her book-ish predisposition that had led her father to hazard the opinion, when she was but a young girl, that teaching "opened the greatest sphere of usefulness" to her. In the forefront of women's education, Harriet was in a position that anticipated that of a later generation of college-educated young women who chose to follow a career rather than marry.

Harriet's eight years in a female seminary shaped by Catharine's philos-ophy of independence and usefulness had not particularly fitted her for the marriage market, nor was the arrangement of nineteenth-century men's and women's lives conducive to spontaneous relationships. The parlor was one of the few places where men's and women's spheres overlapped. In her *Geog-raphy* Harriet contrasted the veiling of Muslim women to the more favorable situation of women in republican America, yet it is significant that the only instances she cited of male and female interaction in this country were the "parties where men and women all meet together, and talk."[3] Frances Trollope commented on the absence of public places in which American women could be seen. Men did the marketing—even men in silk hats could be seen carrying a haunch of pork in one hand and a basket of turnips and cabbage in the other—while women, in the meantime, were "actively employed in the interior of their houses." There were "no public gardens or lounging shops of fashionable resort," and were it not for Sunday worship and the ritual of tea, Trollope concluded, "all the ladies in Cincinnati would be in danger of becoming perfect recluses."[4]

Given the separation of their spheres, it is not surprising that men and women were a bit awkward when they were thrown together. Trollope was appalled by her "evenings in company" in Cincinnati, where the women herded at one end of the room and the men at the other. "Sometimes a small attempt at music produces a partial reunion; a few of the most daring youths, animated by the consciousness of curled hair and smart waistcoats, approach the piano-forte, and begin to mutter a little to the half-grown pretty things, who are comparing with one another 'how many quarters' music they have had.'" The fate of the older crowd was even more dismal:

> The gentlemen spit, talk of elections and the price of produce, and spit again. The ladies look at each other's dresses till they know every pin by heart; talk of Parson Somebody's last sermon on the day of judgment, on Dr. T'otherbody's new pills for dyspepsia, till the "tea" is announced, when they all console themselves together for whatever they may have suffered in keeping awake, by taking more tea, coffee, hot cake and custard, hoe cake, johny cake, waffle cake, and dodger cake, pickled peaches, and preserved cucumbers, ham, turkey, hung beef, apple sauce, and pickled oysters than were prepared in any other country of the known world.[5]

It is possible that Trollope put such a damper on American parties that she was not in a position to judge their hilarity. Certainly a "romp" described by Harriet Beecher at her Uncle John's was of a different character. Present were Mary Dutton, Cordelia Baldwin, Janette Cooley, and Elizabeth Foote "of the feminine gender" and James Perkins, "Howe," and Benjamin Drake "of the masculine." Harriet wrote to her brother George, "as to what we did—dont ask me. . . . There was pulling of hair & cuffing of ears—& scampering, & screaming, —& pouring water on each other & dancing & hopping & every kind of ing." She slyly added, "of course—you may know that I took no part in such indecorums—not I to be sure—ask the girls if I did."[6]

Literary parties moderated between these two extremes. One of Daniel Drake's strongest motives for forming the Semi-Colon Club was to provide for the proper socialization of his two daughters, then entering womanhood.[7] The literary gatherings brought young men and women into regular, informally structured social intercourse that faciliated intelligent interaction between the sexes. The ringing of a bell was the signal for the Semi-Colons to convene around the announced agenda. Although the literary aspect of the club has been emphasized, the reading of poetry and stories was described by one member as "interludes" in the general plan of the group, "whose main object was the discussion of interesting questions belonging to society, literature, education, and religion."[8] Virginia Woolf was right to observe that "all those good novels" of the nineteenth century were written by "women without more experience of life than could enter the house of a respectable clergyman,"[9] yet the common room when occupied by the Semi-Colons was alive with the pressing topics of the day. "The subjects," recalled Edward Mansfield, "were always of the suggestive or problematical kind, so that the ideas were fresh, the debate animated, and the utterance of opinions frank and spontaneous."[10]

Harriet's *Geography* had broached a number of social issues, including the status of women, education, and religion. She was well primed for the wide-ranging discussions of the Semi-Colon, which, on a more sophisticated level, stimulated her much as had the discussions John Brace had led at the Litchfield Female Academy. She listened closely, content to let Catharine, "a far more easy and fluent conversationalist," have the floor in these debates. But when she did speak, observed Edward Mansfield, she "showed both the strength and humor of her mind."[11] Abby Lyman Greene, who was a frequent hostess for the Semi-Colons, wrote of her: "I do like Harriet Beecher very much. She has a truly liberal mind besides a real genius, and is the most perfectly unpretending person I ever met with." She compared her to Harriet Martineau, who was currently touring the country and gathering material for *Society in America*.[12]

Like many writers, Harriet was often more disposed to sit in a corner watching the behavior of others than to participate actively herself. The social and religious topics thrown open for discussion at the Semi-Colon, however, drew her in. At this time Cincinnati was just beginning to experience the effect of Irish and German immigration. By 1851, 46 percent of the populace would be foreign born. In 1835 there were fewer than a thousand Irish in the city, but their presence was viewed as a threat to the somewhat precarious claims of this pioneer town to culture.[13] The Irish were looked on askance for their peasant origins, their propensity for strong drink, and their spiritual loyalty to Rome. As a group, the Semi-Colons held more liberal views on this subject than did Harriet's father. Salmon P. Chase, described by his biographer as not a snob but "almost a snob," attended Lyman Beecher's church even though he did not socialize with him. In his journal entry of February 8, 1834, he summarized Beecher's dire predictions of America's ruin: "He adverted to the various devices of corrupting influence—the influence of infidel publications and organized infidel exertion; the struggles of papacy to establish an influence in the West; the tide of European emigration, augmented by existing agitations, and the theatre and other amusements of the same class."[14] In her *Geography* Harriet clearly stated her Protestant evangelical bias, but when she surveyed world religions, she treated Catholicism in the same objective way that she did paganism and Islam, as a system of belief subscribed to by one portion of the world's population.[15] Her strongly held republican principles moderated her evangelicalism. In a climate of opinion shaped by Lyman Beecher's rhetoric about the "Scarlet Woman of Rome," this was cause for comment. When Bishop Purcell visited the Western Female Institute in 1833, he praised not only the school but Harriet's textbook. "He spoke of my poor little geography, and thanked me for the unprejudiced manner in which I had handled the Catholic question in it."[16]

Harriet's views on Catholics drew her into dialogue with James H. Perkins, to whom she had apparently been attracted before his marriage in 1834 to Sarah Elliot of Guilford. She began thinking of him again at a literary party at Mrs. King's at which two of the men announced their engagements; this set her wondering "whether *I* had anything to think of." She confided to her brother Henry,

> I had a long talk with Perkins about the Catholics—He wrote a very pretty sketch of which my favorite M. Luther was the hero, & I went afterwards & shook hands with him on the subject,—& there ensued this Catholic discussion—He had a very pretty piece of poetry too some line of which touched my *heroic* feelings, so that I felt quite as I used to do last winter—I do love him— he is so sincere & so capable of understanding sincerity in others—& withal he understands some of my heroism better than almost any body—that is he loves what is high & strong—& noble as I do—I feel confidance in him more than I commonly do in men[17]

Harriet was searching for a soul mate, and James Handasyd Perkins bore a strong resemblance to the man she eventually married. Like most of the Semi-Colons, he was liberal in his views, literary, and benevolently inclined. He came to Cincinnati as a lawyer and for several years edited the Cincinnati *Chronicle*. He was most remembered, however, for his career as a Unitarian minister in which he acted as "minister at large" to the Cincinnati poor during the decade before his premature death in 1849. While his literary flights appealed to Harriet's heroic impulses, Perkins was personally unassuming, given to plain living and studious habits. An admirer wrote of him, "Mr Perkins was not an idler, but was not very energetic in his labors; so that, except for the 'Annals of the West,' he left nothing which might be called a monument to his literary labors."[18] Harriet was attracted to men who supported the strongest impulses of her nature, yet who themselves were somewhat lacking in worldly ambition.

In the summer of 1834 Harriet returned to the East to attend Henry Ward Beecher's graduation from Amherst. Railroad tracks were etched across the land in fitful strokes, but travel at this time usually involved successive couplings of stages and canal boats and steamboats, none of whose schedules were carefully coordinated. The journey from Ohio to Massachusetts took about nine days. It was considered improper for women to travel unaccompanied, though an exception was made in the case of travel by canal boats, perhaps because the more public nature of the accommodations was sufficient protection of a woman's reputation and safety. Harriet was accompanied by Mary Dutton. They traveled by stage to Toledo, and Harriet sent Elizabeth Lyman an entertaining description of her fellow passengers, among whom was an accommodating Irishman who was continually jumping up to give his seat to ladies. When he "fell into a little talk about abolition and slavery" with a fellow passenger, Harriet was delighted with the ensuing display. His antagonist was

> a man whose mode of reasoning consists in repeating the same sentence at regular intervals as long as you choose to answer it. This man, who was finally convinced that negroes were black, used it as an irrefragible argument to all that could be said, and at last began to deduce from it that they might just as well be slaves as anything else, and so he proceeded till all the philanthropy of our friend was roused, and he sprung up all lively and oratorical and gesticulatory and indignant to my heart's content. I like to see a quiet man that can be roused.[19]

Harriet, who loved the drama of conflicting temperaments and points of view, had the luck to be born into a large family of highly individualistic, assertive siblings in an age when sectional and ideological conflicts were mounting. She sometimes stirred the pot just to see the steam rise. Catharine wrote of her during the turbulent period of abolitionist activity in the 1830s, "Harriet sometimes talks quite *Abolitiony* at me & I suppose quite Anti to the other side."[20]

Harriet took advantage of her time in the East to return to Nutplains, the maternal homestead. Her Grandmother Foote was eighty-four years old and increasingly feeble. When Harriet took leave of her, she knew that it might be for the last time. The rhythms of her grandmother's life were closely linked to those of Harriet's mother. In a poem she transcribed for her grandmother during her visit, Harriet reflected on the meaning of these women's lives:

> The most loved are they,
> Of whom Fame speaks not with her clarion voice,
> The vale with its deep fountains is their choice.
> And gentle hearts rejoice
> Around their steps—till silently they die,
> As a stream shrinks from Summer's burning eye!

At the bottom of the paper Harriet wrote, "Signed by my aged grandmother in her 84th year" and after the shaky signature of Roxana Foote she recorded "Nutplains, August 1, 1834."[21]

While Harriet was in the East the Semi-Colon Club suffered the unexpected death of one of its most beloved members, Eliza Tyler Stowe. She and her husband were both New Englanders. They had met at Dartmouth College where Calvin Ellis Stowe had been a professor of Greek and she was the daughter of the president, Bennett Tyler. Calvin Stowe, whose father died when he was six years old, had obtained an education against the odds.

The deaths in childhood of seven brothers and sisters left only Calvin, his mother, and one brother. With the financial support of local ministers in Natick, Massachusetts, he graduated from Bowdoin College in 1824, valedictorian of his class. During the next few years he studied at Andover Theological Seminary and acquired French, Spanish, Hebrew, Greek, German, and Arabic, determined to be "a literary man." In 1829 he was twenty-seven-years old, had two scholarly books to his credit, and had been editor of the *Boston Recorder*.[22]

He courted Eliza Tyler with great insistence and candor. When she responded to his proposal by allowing that she *"could"* love him, he immediately wrote to her, "Now, if you *can*, it seems to me you *should*; for *I cannot help loving you*, & if you do not make me happy, I shall be wretched. It would make a new man of me to have your affection, & I should not only be happier, but better & more religious."[23] He wrote frankly of his slim prospects for worldly success and appealed to her to take care of him:

> I have always been entirely without property, & have no prospect of ever possessing any. . . . I am, from choice, very industrious, & simple in all my wishes as to living—but I have no *faculty* for saving things—I lose nearly as many clothes in a year as I wear out, and every body that deals with me, cheats me, (unless he is very particularly honest, wh[ich] is very rarely the case.) I have nothing to depend upon bu[t] my salary & my pen, which latter will probably amount [to] but very little in the course of a year.—You may now know what you have to calculate upon—& feeling my own incapacity to manage money, I shall put all my temporal concerns under your direction. I hope you will not decline the trust, for from my earliest youth my mind has been so entirely occupied with books that I have never learned the art of *getting a living*, & I fear it is too late to begin now. I have always needed a guardian angel to watch over me.[24]

Won by this or some other appeal, Eliza Tyler became his wife in June 1832.

Reading German scholarship did nothing to lighten the pessimism that, whether temperamental or the product of his unlucky youth, was a deeply engrained trait of character in Calvin Stowe. He predicted doom and death so regularly that it is perhaps not surprising that occasionally he was right. In April 1833, as they made their preparations to depart for the West, he warned Eliza to guard her health carefully: "In more senses than one we may *take our lives in our hand* when we go to Cincinnati."[25] The city was indeed not a very healthful place. Fevers and dysentery were chronic, outbreaks of typhoid not uncommon. The Beechers had been obliged to delay their arrival in the fall of 1832 because of the first epidemic of Asiatic cholera. Cincinnati was built without drains, and as the rainwater ran off the hills it settled in one of the main thoroughfares; whatever garbage had been scorned by the pigs was washed, in various stages of decomposition, into this stagnant water; the droppings of horses and pigs did the rest. Most of the large warehouses in town were located on this street, so it was heavily traveled. When the hot and humid days of July heated this fetid mixture, cholera bacteria multiplied and rapidly spread throughout the city. At the time, however, it was not understood that cholera was contagious, nor that contaminated water was the chief means of spreading it. Harriet Foote wrote from Cincinnati soon after her arrival, "I believe this is a very healthy place notwithstanding being obliged to drink dirty water—I had a slight attack of dysentary . . . which confined me to my room two weeks."[26]

In the summer of 1834 cholera again swept the city and reached Walnut Hills. The first student who was stricken at Lane Seminary survived, but three days after the onset of his symptoms thirty students were ill, of whom six or eight exhibited the severe convulsions that characterized the most malignant form of the disease. The professors lived in houses adjacent to the campus and were likewise at risk. Lyman Beecher's wife, writing to Harriet, Catharine, and Lyman in the East, created a memorable narrative of the events of August 1834:

[N]othing special occured the ten days preceeding your departure among our-selves, but the sickness in the city was dreadful one hundred & more deaths in one week & Edwards affecting letter came with the intelligence of the death of his second little boy, which letter I forwarded to Boston—next came the illness of our dear Mrs. Stowe. . . . She was taken ill of the dysentery the very day you left—The disease yielded to medicine well & on the following sabbath she was apparently entirely relieved & the Dr said she would be well in a day or two. On Monday morn⁸ she had a severe relapse & as it respected her own opinion, I believe all hope of recovery ceased—we had one of those great changes in the weather that night from heat to cold which occasioned hundreds to wake up, almost in ague fits—Everything within reach of medicine was applied, also of nursing & kind attention but without the least mitigating effect—Dr Drake was anxious for her case from the beginning on account of the chronic disease of her bowels from which she has suffered so much and which alone accounts for the entire inefficasy of medicine—She set all her affairs in order, gave messages to Mr Stowe for her friends & than said she wished to talk no more about these things, she wished the 23d Psalm to be read & to be quiet—Her heart seemed fixed & her face set—This Psalm com-forted her all the way down even through the dark vally When I left her at 4 o'clock monday afternoon she had revived some & hope revived some with us. Esther was with her that day constantly—The next morning we found no hope of recovery left—she was strugling with death when I entered, her brows were knit & a deadly paleness was gathering fast with distressing movements of convulsive throes I thought O Lord God can we go through this! Mr. Stowe said O my love, remember, remember The Lord is my shepherd I shall not want, he leads me in green pastures, beside the still waters, these comforts have delighted your soul they will do so still—She broke out O, how delightful! Her whole countenance brightened & glowed She waved her hands with joy, saying (I cannot tell how many times) O, how delightful, did you ever see anything like it—Mr Stowe said is it not joy unspeakable & full of glory! She repeated with a very strong voice "joy unspeakable & full of glory"! "There is not room enough to receive it" ["]there is not room enough to receive it"! She continued in this frame till she was entirely exhausted & than sank into a lethargic sleeplike state from which time I suppose she had no more consciousness—we sat by her in silence—it was the still chamber of death & nothing could be done—we had prayer & various redings of portions of scripture & repeating of Hymns I read the hymn

"Happy Soul thy days are ended.
"All thy mourning days below
"Go by angel guards attended
"To the sight of Jesus go.

The group gathered around Eliza Tyler Stowe continued in this manner "near two hours, when the only apparent change was she ceased to breathe."[27]

The obituary that appeared in the Cincinnati paper repeated many of the details of Eliza's last hours.[28] After the funeral Lyman Beecher's wife persuaded the grieving husband to come to their house where "we have all administered to his comfort as we could."[29] When Harriet returned she was in a natural position to support these efforts. She was a close friend of Eliza and appreciated what Calvin Stowe had lost. Moreover, she had considerable skill in pastoral counseling. The many letters of consolation that she wrote, particularly to grieving women, suggest that she pursued a self-conscious lay ministry to the bereaved and troubled.[30] Building on the peer counseling system Catharine had instituted at the Hartford Female Seminary, Harriet developed informal methods that were particularly effective in disarming the Calvinist scruples that often added an intolerable burden to those who suffered feelings of loss. Instead of scrutinizing the spiritual state of the sufferer to see if he or she fully submitted to God's will, Harriet simply accepted the pain, the anger, the confusion. As she wrote to a mother who had lost her daughter, "[w]hen the heartstrings are all suddenly cut, it is, I believe, a physical impossibility to feel faith or resignation; there is a revolt of the instinctive and animal system, and though we may submit to God it is rather by a constant painful effort than by a sweet attraction."[31]

Calvin Stowe appreciated Harriet's sympathetic and generous ways. "I thank God that he has given me a female friend to whom I can open my heart," he wrote her. "There are some feelings which a man cannot exercise, and my heart cannot rest in masculine friendship alone. I must be within reach of woman's love, or my own feelings will suffocate me."[32] When he missed Eliza he needed to be with Harriet, and she readily complied. They also saw one another at the Semi-Colon meetings, which they began attending together. In addition, that winter Calvin Stowe gave a series of sermons on the Bible that Harriet reported in detail in the pages of the Cincinnati *Journal*, a newspaper that was for all intents and purposes a Beecher family organ. These sermons displayed not only his vast scholarship but, concerning the New Testament, his remarkably simple focus on the historical Jesus. Thus Harriet saw Calvin Stowe not only as the grieving widower, but also as the learned professor, a role in which he showed to advantage. Elizabeth

Lyman, who observed that Calvin Stowe was "much admired by the literary circle here," attended all of his lectures and left this description:

> Professor Stow of Lane Seminary .. is now delivering a course of most interesting discouses on the Bible—various proofs of its authenticity—propper mode of its intrepetation—authors of its several books—& a great many other subjects connected with the scriptures, which cannot be gathered from books—or at least from books in the *English* language—such as could be read by ignorant people, like ourself. I suppose Prof. Stow is the *greatest scholar* of this side of the mountains. He's a delightful lecturer—not at all eloquent—but jsut what you *can't help liking*.[33]

Eight months after Eliza's death Calvin Stowe declared his love for Harriet Beecher: "My affection for you is no sudden caprice, and no sudden caprice will change it. It is of slow and natural growth, & true to its object as the needle to the polar star."[34] He freely expressed his emotional dependency: "I have a sort of feeling of *inseparableness*, as though my blood somehow circulated through your veins, and if you were to be torn from me I should *bleed to death*."[35]

In the fall of 1833, when Harriet was actively pursuing her "campaign" in the Semi-Colon Club, she had instigated a domestic literary effort of another sort. Charles Beecher reported receiving at Bowdoin College a "great letter" that had traveled from Hartford, Middletown, and Amherst, collecting news as it went. "Harriet was the writer, & if I understood her prospectus rightly, that was nothing but the first of a series of family sheets."[36] This was indeed the first of the round-robin letters that the Beecher family circulated from East to West and West to East. Instituted by Harriet just after the diaspora of the Beecher family, these circular letters kept the Beechers in touch with one another not only as individuals, but as a family. A typical letter began with news from Edward and Isabella Beecher at Illinois College; continued with notes from Harriet, Catharine, and sometimes Aunt Esther in Cincinnati; touched down in Putnam, Ohio, where William Beecher and his wife Katherine struggled against constant illness; continued to Batavia, New York, to glean the latest on George Beecher, who had taken to wife Sarah Buckingham; and finally settled in Hartford, where Mary Beecher Perkins devoured the long and closely written pages, took a fresh sheet, and started it on a return westward course. Looking at the successive scrawls of his brothers and sisters, Charles Beecher remarked, "This is the first time I ever heard of a folio sheet being in the family way."[37] By means of these circular letters, as one of the Beechers (probably Harriet) commented, "many families, wide asunder in locality, of independent and often antagonistic views, were bound together, year after year, in a more than patriarchal unity."[38]

Having initiated this serial epistolary form, Harriet did her best to keep it going. She rescued one fat folio from Lyman Beecher's study, where it "was in danger of sinking to oblivion in the vortex of Father's sermons."[39] These circular letters reveal the warm, witty family culture of this very articulate group of siblings. They also provided a ready vehicle for Harriet to share the news of her engagement and marriage, yet she was strangely quiet on this topic. In late December 1835 Mary Dutton attached a note, addressed to Catharine Beecher, sending a distress signal about the Western Female Institute, which was in a "state of emergency" for lack of teachers: "It is out of the question for Harriet to stay in school any longer—she is so bent on matrimony."[40] For her part, Harriet sent news of the violence that erupted between two competing schools of thought when Dr. Shotwell and some of his medical students attempted to remove cadavers from the Potter's field for medical research: "They were attacked & fired upon by five men— Dr S was wounded in the eye." She said almost nothing of Mr. Stowe, remarking only that "The semicolons are to be revived alternately between Mrs. Green's & Mrs. Stetson's Mr S & self are going to the first one at Mrs Green's next Wednesday even—I am writing a piece for it."[41] Two weeks later, on January 6, 1836, she was quietly married at home. Not even all her brothers knew of the marriage, and there was some confusion in the newspapers as to which sister Calvin Stowe had married, Catharine or Harriet. Harriet wrote to her family, "I suppose you have all heard that Kate & I have been *pitted* against each other in the newspapers as to who should have Mr Stowe to husband." She quipped, "he married *me*, & whether he married her too or not is no concern of mine—he does n't seem to remember whether he did or not."[42] Catharine rejoined, "I am flourishing in more respects than one—for besides flourishing with a new book & flourishing with Harriets husband, I am flourishing in health & spirits."[43]

It was easy enough to joke after the fact, but the weeks preceding her marriage had been emotionally stormy. She wrote on December 9, 1835, to Elizabeth Lyman that she had cried herself to sleep the night before and expected to do the same that night: "I feel as sad and as resigned as if I was going into a convent—I wish it *was over*—I can't bear this sort of uncertainty." Her feelings showed her to be a woman of her time. "From the 1780s to the 1830s," writes an historian of American courtship rituals, "diaries and correspondence are full of women who 'trembled' at the approach of their wedding day; who were 'anxious,' 'mortified,' 'fretful'; whose minds were 'loaded with doubts and fears'; or whose 'spirits were much depressed' as the day drew near."[44] Marriage often meant the separation of a woman from the family of her birth and her removal to a new home or even a new land. In addition, the hazards of childbirth made women acutely conscious of their mortality.

The uncertainty into which Harriet was thrown by her approaching change of state was heightened by the fact that she did not know exactly when she was to be married. Calvin Stowe, whose only personal property was a library of thousands of scholarly volumes, had been delegated the task of acquiring a library for Lane Seminary. He had also been appointed by the

Ohio legislature to study the Prussian public school system. For these dual purposes he planned a trip to Europe. "There has been some talk of my going also," wrote Harriet to Elizabeth Lyman; "if so I shall not be married till spring—If not, I shall be married in a month or so."[45] The tears and sleeplessness did not abate until the day of her marriage, when a profound calm that masked the depth of her feeling descended on her. As she sat awaiting the arrival of her bridegroom, she took a sheet of paper and began a letter to Georgiana May:

> Well, my dear G., about half an hour more and your old friend, companion, schoolmate, sister, etc., will cease to be Hatty Beecher and change to nobody knows who. My dear, you are engaged, and pledged in a year or two to encounter a similar fate, and do you wish to know how you shall feel? Well, my dear, I have been dreading and dreading the time, lying awake all last week wondering how I should live through this overwhelming crisis, and lo! it has come and I feel *nothing at all*.
>
> The wedding is to be altogether domestic; nobody present but my own brothers and sisters, and my old colleague, Mary Dutton; and as there is a sufficiency of the ministry in our family we have not even to call in the foreign aid of a minister. Sister Katy is not here, so she will not witness my departure from her care and guidance to that of another. None of my numerous friends and acquaintances who have taken such a deep interest in making the connection for me even know the day, and it will be all done and over before they know anything about it.
>
> Well, it is really a mercy to have this entire stupidity come over one at such a time. I should be crazy to feel as I did yesterday, or indeed to feel anything at all. But I inwardly vowed that my last feelings and reflections on this subject should be yours, and as I have not got any, it is just as well to tell you *that*. Well, here comes Mr. S., so farewell, and for the last time I subscribe
>
> > Your own
> >
> > H.E.B.

Whether or not she was given away by her father, it was the sisterly world of her school companions and a sister's guardianship to which she bade adieu.[46]

Calvin and Harriet began their married life with a separation, thus establishing what became the pattern in their relationship. On June 8, 1836, he sailed from New York to London, not to return until the following February. Harriet closed the house in which they had lived together for five months and went to live with her father's family in the president's house, which had been built for him after he came to Lane Seminary. Her expectant condition dictated against travel and the uncertainties of ocean liners' schedules. Calvin was enormously disappointed that she could not make the trip with him. Their separation reminded him all too poignantly of his permanent separation from Eliza, for the two women were still closely intertwined in his emotional life. He instructed Harriet to visit Eliza's grave at precise hours, synchronized with his London and German watches. Harriet's parting gesture was the presentation of a series of notes she had written for him to open

each Sabbath he was on board the ship. He was touched by this thoughtfulness and wished that he had done the same for her. Harriet knew that his
spirits would need lifting. He had written before the voyage of his misery in
sleeping alone, his nervous headaches, and his melancholy. "I have more
than half a mind to relinquish my aquatic journey and return with you to
Cincinnati, and enjoy myself, and let Vail go to Euope and get the books. I
think all the time of you and Eliza, and hardly know which I want to see the
most." In a note he opened during the voyage Harriet reminded him of the
pleasures that lay ahead of him: the German scholar, Tholuck, with whom
he planned to confer, "the great libraries and beautiful paintings," the "fine
churches": "My dear, I wish I were a man in your place; if I would n't have
a grand time!"[47]

For all his apprehensions, Calvin Stowe's European trip represented a
height of happiness and professional worth he would not reach again until
his serene old age. On board ship he had no sea sickness, though eating
breakfast in rough seas was a challenge, as he described for Harriet's amusement:

> Fixing myself at table and holding on with both hands I now watch the move-
> ment of things; and the passengers each make their entry in the manner fol-
> lowing: to wit, first: you lean against the inside of the door of each sleeping
> cabin a heavy body come up *aulong*—secondly the door flys open *crash*, thirdly,
> out pops a man's head, fourthly, whisk comes his body up to the breakfast
> table, which together with the chairs is made fast to the floor. And now the
> jingling of crockery, the dinning of knives & forks, the spilling of coffee to
> warm us & the pouring of sea water through the sky lights to cool us, the
> staggering of waiters and the scolding of passengers is utterly indescribable.
> "Waiter, ugh! ught! What did you turn that coffee down my back for?"—"Now
> waiter a'nt you ashamed you dumped that plate of butter right into my neck"
> "Why here comes the broiled chicken jumping into my lap."

In England he saw the sights, displayed a confident American perspective
on British institutions, and had his revenge on Frances Trollope. He had no
awe for the House of Lords, filled with what looked to him like "a parcel of
old *gracious grannies*." "I wish you could have seen some of those old with-
ered up, spindle-shanked, baboon-faced specimens of humanity, with their
big white perukes and long black robes *noble lording* one another." He preferred Shrewsbury on market day, where he entertained himself by observing
the *"whims and oddities"* of the common people. Wherever he went, he
recorded for Harriet's enjoyment the accents that he heard about him.[48]

While in London he frequented the cathedral services and hobnobbed
with the British antislavery people. "Many who come here return Episcopalians and Abolitionists, but I must say that I am farther from both than
ever before." Discussions with moderate antislavery people such as the Rev.
Dr. Philips of South Africa confirmed Calvin Stowe in his own views. "Ultra
Abolitionism here has the same *nasty Radicalism*, the same dogmatic nar-
rowness, that it has in America." He was pleased to find that no "rational

respectable" person in England approved of George Thompson, the radical British abolitionist who was then touring America.[49] Britain's abolition of the slave trade in 1833 had prodded the conscience of America, and there was some psychic relief in finding more moderate views on American slavery than were often attributed to the British abolitionists.

Calvin Stowe's views of the British antislavery movement passed through Harriet's mind and pen, for she was regularly working up portions of his letters for publication in the *Cincinnati Journal*. He had agreed to write, for "a consideration," a series of travel letters for that paper. "By the way," he told Harriet while enroute on the *Montreal*, "I do not believe I shall have time to write much to them; and now cannot you take my letters to you, and extract from them all that may [be] suitable and interesting, and fix them up & embellish them in your own way, and send them to the Journal under the head of 'Notes from a correspondent,' or some other appropriate title?" He provided the frameworks, she provided the "embellishments." He planned upon his return to write more of these himself, when questions from Harriet would push him "to make my recollections as minute as possible."[50] These two enjoyed an easy intellectual comradeship. As Calvin remarked to his mother, "Harriet is as well adapted to my present condition and character, as Eliza was to my former self. Her intellectual strength, her fruitful imagination and ready wit, the real kindness of her heart, the absorbing and self-devoting ardor of her affections, and her intelligent and deeply tried piety, are just what I need to sustain and encourage and hold me up."[51]

In Germany Calvin Stowe was in his element, buying books, talking with scholars, viewing the manuscripts of Goethe and Luther. In Halle he spent two days talking theology with Tholuck, coming away feeling "so full," he wrote Harriet, "that it is painful. . . . My feelings almost kill me because I have not you to feel with me." In Heidelberg he met with Professor Creutzer and Dr. Paulus and visited Heidelberg Castle. Calvin only regretted that Harriet was not there to enjoy it with him: "It seems to me that you would derive double the benefit from it that I do." Professor Creutzer had written a book on "The Mythology of the Ancients," in which he traced "the formation of the various mythological ideas of the ancients to the religious element essential to man every where." Calvin found this deeply interesting and assumed that Harriet would too: "When I get home we must read the whole work together." Does Calvin Stowe sound much like Dorothea's husband, Casaubon, who in George Eliot's *Middlemarch* spent his honeymoon in the dark and musty catacombs of Rome collecting material for his "Key to All Mythologies"? Upon reading *Middlemarch* Harriet assumed—much to Eliot's amusement—that she had modeled Casaubon on the man she lived with, George Henry Lewes.[52] Calvin Stowe *was* like Casaubon in his vast learning and the difficulty that he had, after marriage, in harvesting the fruits of his laborious scholarship. But his lusty enjoyment of physical pleasures set him apart from the bloodless Casaubon. He enjoyed the German beer and longed for his wife: "My arms & bosom are *hungry*."[53]

CHAPTER TEN

Free Men and Free Speech: 1834–1837

arriet Beecher Stowe embarked upon housekeeping during the turbulent decade of the 1830s when antislavery riots erupted in most of the major cities. As abolitionists were gagged, mobbed, and murdered, Harriet was drawn into abolitionist sympathies by her engagement in the free speech movement that sprung up in their defense. This tapped her republican principles and her heroic impulses.

In 1834 Harriet had witnessed a free speech battle at Lane Seminary that had long-range consequences for the future of that institution. The first class of seminarians comprised forty men who, like many college men of this period, were mainly older students. Lyman Beecher praised their piety and maturity, remarking that the "only inconvenience" of the latter was their "independence" and their lack of acquaintance with "the discipline and restraint of college life."[1] Among them was Theodore Weld, noted for his brilliance, eloquence, and leadership. In February 1834, while Lyman Beecher and Calvin Stowe were in the East, Weld organized an eighteen-day "protracted meeting" to debate the slavery issue. The first nine days were devoted to the antislavery position and the second nine to the colonizationist position. At the conclusion of these famous "Lane Debates," the students voted overwhelmingly against colonization and in favor of "immediate abolition."[2]

Lyman Beecher was caught in the middle between his radical students, his liberal benefactor, and his conservative trustees—a position that mirrored the murkiness of his own consciousness. Arthur Tappan, the wealthy

New York philanthropist who had urged the presidency of Lane on him and paid his salary, was under the assumption that Beecher was an abolitionist. In fact his position was considerably more conservative and ambiguous: he considered himself both an abolitionist and a colonizationist. In thus holding the views of both sides in the Lane Debates, Beecher did not perceive in himself "any inconsistency."[3] The sharp edges of difference between these camps were rapidly emerging in this period of polarization. William Lloyd Garrison, a member of Lyman Beecher's church in Boston, had declared himself a colonizationist in an address at Edward Beecher's Park Street Church in 1829. But in the first issue of the *Liberator* (1831) he recanted, begging pardon of his God and country for the "timidity, injustice, and absurdity" of his defense of the "pernicious doctrine of *gradual* abolition."[4] The colonizationists took the cautious position that if the slaves could be shipped back to Africa, slavery could safely be abolished. The position of the abolitionists was that slavery was a sin and must be unequivocally and immediately halted, come what may.

Lyman Beecher was unprepared for the radicalism and assertiveness of his students. When they first mentioned the idea of the debates to him he cautioned delay, hoping "that at a later period discussion might be either needless or safe." The worst was not that they went ahead with them, but that they proceeded to act on their principles. After the debates they formed an antislavery society and a colonization society and threw themselves into a wide range of educational and benevolent activities, all of which brought them into regular social contact with Cincinnati's black population. Beecher was increasingly alarmed. "If you want to teach colored schools," he told them, "I can fill your pockets with money; but if you will visit in colored families, and walk with them in the streets, you will be overwhelmed." The students' insistence on relating to black people as social equals caused the town to look upon Lane Seminary as a nuisance "more to be dreaded than the cholera or the plague."[5]

While Beecher was in the East raising money, the trustees took matters into their own hands. They changed the school rules, prohibiting meetings and addresses and specifically outlawing the abolitionist and colonization societies. The antislavery newspapers denounced this attack on freedom of speech, asking "In what age do we live?," "and in what country?" When he returned from the East, Lyman Beecher tried belatedly to achieve a reconciliation, but there was too great a gulf. The trustees and the town saw in the students' wanton association with black people a "spirit of insubordination" that conjured up images of riot and revolution, of "scenes of France and Hayti."[6] The young men of Lane Seminary viewed the unilateral action of the trustees as a tyrannical breach of their constitutional rights. Under Theodore Weld's leadership, they staged the "Lane rebellion." Weld and most of the Lane Seminary students walked out of Lane and went to Oberlin, where Arthur Tappan installed in the theology department Beecher's rival, Charles Grandison Finney.

Lyman Beecher's lack of clarity and leadership spelled disaster for Lane Seminary. As a result of this widely publicized event, Lane was regarded as anti–free speech and antiabolition by the rapidly growing evangelical movement for immediate abolition; Garrison labeled it "a Bastille of oppression— a spiritual Inquisition."[7] On the other hand, the trustees and townsfolk of Cincinnati deemed it to be a hotbed of anarchy and race mixing. The institution never fully recovered. Between 1836 and 1840 the average class size dwindled to five students. There were no students at all in 1845.[8]

The year following the Lane Debates marked a turning point in the national awareness of the slavery issue. Between July 1835 and the following May the American Anti-Slavery Society deluged the mails with over a million pieces of antislavery literature, making slavery an issue no one could ignore. The backlash against the abolitionists served to publicize the issue even more dramatically. Race riots broke out in New York City in July 1834, culminating in the burning of Lewis Tappan's house, the mobbing of a July 4 service in the Chatham Street Chapel commemorating the state's Emancipation Day, and the gutting of a black school and church and a dozen black homes. The city authorities were not alarmed until the homes of wealthy whites were threatened, at which point the mayor called out the militia. Southern governors demanded that Arthur Tappan be extradited and tried in the South for fomenting rebellion; northern newspapers increasingly supported free speech.[9] As racial violence spread in 1835, the orthodox clergy rejected colonization and gradualism for more militant measures. "During that fall," Robert Merideth writes, "riots, mass meetings, and suppression of the discussion of slavery had irritated the open sores of the country. What Garrison described as 'The Reign of Terror'—the beginnings of the gag rule in Congress, the suppression of abolitionist documents in the mails, major riots in Washington, Philadelphia, Baltimore—had culminated in the famous mob of 'respectables' who on October 21 dragged Garrison through the streets of Boston. With good cause, many Americans were beginning to link the antislavery issue to the freedoms: the freedom of speech, assembly, the press."[10]

In 1835 the abolition and free speech issues engulfed the Beecher family one by one. Edward wrote in November that in St. Louis his abolitionist associate Elijah Lovejoy was threatened with "tar & feathers or some form of Lynch Law—& his office with demolition by a mob." Strongly defending Lovejoy's right to speak, Edward feared that "all those who oppose slavery as a *sinful system* will be obliged to leave the slave states, although they are not immediate abolitionists, for even church members & elders in St. Louis are taking the ground that the Bible sanctions slavery."[11] In Putnam, Ohio, where abolitionist sentiment was strong, William and Katherine Beecher were developing views sufficiently alarming to Catharine Beecher that she cautioned, "I hope William will not be in haste about any Abolition movements till he sees a thing or two which I shall have to show him when I come on."[12] George Beecher joined the Anti-Slavery Society in 1836.[13] Harriet and Henry were swept into the controversy that July, when James Birney's newspaper office was mobbed and his printing press thrown into the Ohio River.

James G. Birney was a southerner who in the early 1830s converted to abolition and freed his slaves. He was eagerly recruited for the Anti-Slavery Society by Arthur and Lewis Tappan, who, not wishing to make a martyr of him, kept their support secret until he left Kentucky. In the winter of 1836 he moved to New Richmond, Ohio, and began publishing his weekly anti-slavery journal, the *Philanthropist*. Twice run out of this Ohio river town, he brought his printing press to Cincinnati in April 1837 and continued publishing antislavery broadsides. Cincinnati was in many ways a southern town, and it was violently proslavery. The *Philanthropist* soon became an "object of popular hatred and complaint." In July, while Calvin Stowe was in Europe and Harriet was home expecting her first child, violence erupted. At midnight on July 12 a mob attacked the office of the *Philanthropist* and damaged the press, threatening further violence if Birney did not cease publication. Birney replaced the press the next day and refused to be intimidated. While the hot weather had spurred the crowd on, this attack on freedom of the press was coolly fanned by a committee of the most respectable citizens of Cincinnati.

Soon after the attack, on July 21, a citizens' meeting was called to consider whether they "would permit the publication or distribution of abolition papers in Cincinnati." The mayor presided, and all the respectable and influential men of the town were invited by name. Writing to Calvin, Harriet described the four camps into which the town divided: revolutionary supporters of mob violence; anti-Birney men who hoped to accomplish their purpose without a mob; a muddled group who were ashamed of the proceedings but did nothing to stop them; and finally, a small group of outspoken defenders of freedom of the press. The Semi-Colon Club members were divided. William Greene and John P. Foote fulminated against the mob, but ended up participating in the attempt to suppress Birney, in the hopes of preventing further violence. E. D. Mansfield and Salmon P. Chase unequivocally defended Birney's right to publish.[14]

The large group of citizens gathered on July 21 resolved to use "all lawful means" to suppress any newspaper advocating "the modern doctrine of abolition." They reasoned that unless such dangerous ideas were suppressed, violence was bound to ensue. The committee, Harriet wrote Calvin, "in so many words voted a mob." This endorsement of "mobocracy," echoed by most of the Cincinnati papers, was genteelly covered by the formation of a committee to call on Birney to request that he cease publication of the *Philanthropist*. To Harriet's disgust, her Uncle John agreed to participate in this charade. This committee of thirteen, composed of "gentlemen of large wealth and commanding social position," met on the evening of July 28 with members of the Ohio Anti-Slavery Society, the sponsors of the *Philanthropist*. The Anti-Slavery Society members proposed that the issue be thrown open to public discussion. The citizens' committee refused. If Birney did not immediately cease publication, they predicted "a mob unusual in numbers, determined in its purposes, and desolating in its ravages." Judge Barnett, head of the committee, estimated it would include five thousand persons, including two-thirds of the property owners of the city. The Anti-Slavery Society members then asked these eminent property owners whether they would allow the *Philanthropist* to continue if they could be assured that violence would be averted. Several members of the citizens' committee immediately answered in the negative; they gave the Anti-Slavery Society until noon the next day to decide whether to suspend publication.[15] The eight members of the Anti-Slavery Society executive board met the following day and refused to comply with the committee's demand.

Under cover of darkness, the predictions of the citizens' committee were realized. A mob converged on Birney's office, destroyed the press, scattered the type, and dragged the whole down to the river and threw it in. They then went in search of Birney himself, who had prudently absented himself. When they reached the Franklin Hotel, where Birney lived, they were met on the front porch by Salmon P. Chase, who refused to let them pass. When the ringleader told Chase he would "answer for this," Chase replied, "I can be found at any time." The mob contented itself with destroying the homes of a number of respectable black families. After several hours of this random violence the mayor decided that the mob should be called off. This proved to be more difficult than inciting it had been. In a letter written to the *Cincinnati Journal* just after the first attack on Birney's press, Harriet had warned the respectable citizens who were willing to wink at mob violence as long as it fell in with their prejudices, "Don't you know that the same train of powder runs under your house and mine and every house in the city?" She went on, "Every man is glad of a mob that happens to fall in with his views, without considering that if the mob system gets once thoroughly running, it may go *against* as well as *for* them."[16]

When the mob refused to disperse and another night of violence threatened, the mayor swore in a vigilante committee and authorized them to shoot to kill. Many of the respectable men who had incited the mob now enlisted against it. They patrolled the city for three nights, during which Harriet feared "war to the knife" and witnessed her brother Henry pouring bullets into molds and leaving the house with a brace of pistols. She reported, "We were all too full of patriotism not to have sent every brother we had rather than not have had the principles of freedom and order defended." Harriet was thoroughly caught up in the excitement. Just two months away from delivery of twins, she wished Birney "would man [his office] with armed men and see what can be done. If I were a man I would go, for one, and take good care of at least one window."

Throughout this disruption Harriet and Henry had been exerting their powers of persuasion in the *Cincinnati Journal*, which, in the absence of Thomas Brainerd, was under the temporary editorship of Henry Ward Beecher Harriet's contribution was a letter to the editor, which she signed

"Franklin." Just as she had launched her "campaign" in the Semi-Colon Club with an elaborately disguised letter sent to her cousin, so she embarked upon her antislavery career under cover of a pseudonymous letter to an "editor" who was her brother. The deliberate creation of personae for both author and audience—a device that could undermine the clarity of her conscious-ness and the effect of her message—in fact operated to liberate her voice. Addressing a hostile, proslavery town through the medium of her brother had the advantage of cutting through barriers of reserve on both sides. Har-riet further dissimulated by pretending to relate a conversation she had over-heard at a dinner.

The dialogue between "Franklin" and his dinner-table host, "Mr. L.," opens with a self-satisfied comment from the latter. ' "So,' said Mr. L., flour-ishing his carver, 'I hear Birney's press is broken open at last. I knew it must be so. . . . It will teach him better than to be setting these ultra measures on foot in our city.' " Franklin expresses surprise that Mr. L. so readily concurs with mob actions that overturn not only "the laws of the city," but also—Harriet knew her audience—"the rights of private property." He then pro-ceeds to expose the questionable constitutional foundations of his host's reasoning.

> "Now, my friend, do you think the liberty of the press is a good thing?"
> "Certainly—to be sure."
> "And you think it a good article in our Constitution that allows every man to speak, write, and publish his own opinions, without any other responsibility that that of the laws of his country?"
> "Certainly, I do."
> "Well, then, as Mr.Birney is a man, I suppose you think it's right to allow *him* to do it in particular?"

Here we can observe a practical side to Harriet's adoption of a male pseud-onym. By custom and state laws, only white, propertied males enjoyed full civil rights. Unpropertied white men, all black men, and all women were denied suffrage. Whether or not these disenfranchised enjoyed the right to free speech was a matter decided by both law and custom. Married women and slaves had no legal identity in the courts, where their only mouthpiece was their husband or master. Single women were by custom expected to exhibit their marriageability by their decorous, discreet, and undemonstra-tive mien. Women whose wit was judged "too keen," like Aunt Harriet Foote, were passed over for more retiring models of womanhood. By becoming "Franklin," Harriet sidestepped this subversive issue, enjoyed the voice she was technically denied, and kept her audience focused on Birney and abo-lition.

It being incontrovertible that James Birney was a *man*, Mr. L. protested, "But Mr. Birney's opinions are so dangerous!" Franklin then suggests that perhaps the Constitution should be rewritten to read, "Every man in the State may speak, write, print, and publish his own sentiments on any subject, provided that nobody in the nation thinks they are dangerous." Mr. L., made increasingly uncomfortable by the logic of Franklin, reverts to that confession of defeat, pejorative labeling. "'Why,' said my friend, after an uneasy silence of a few moments, 'really you are getting be be quite a warm Abolitionist.' "[17] In striking contrast to Harriet's bold journalistic experiment is the deferential letter she wrote to her husband describing it. She characterized it as a "conversational sketch" written in a "light, sketchy style, designed to draw attention to a long editorial of Henry's in which he considers the subject fully and seriously." After praising the power of Henry's "well studied, earnest, and dignified" editorials, she made an obeisance to her husband: "I thought, when I was writing last night, that I was, like a good wife, defending one of your principles in your absence, and wanted you to see how manfully I talked about it."[18]

In this same year, 1836, Angelina and Sarah Grimké embarked on their abolitionist careers with stunning analyses of the relationship between two patriarchal institutions, slavery and the subordination of women: "The investigation of the rights of the slave has led me to a better understanding of my own."[19] When Angelina Grimké extended the free speech she had enjoyed in Quaker meeting to address "promiscuous" public gatherings, the Protestant clergy rebuked her for departing from "woman's sphere." In a "Pastoral Letter" the male clergy assured her she would gain a "greater power" by remaining "unobtrusive and private."[20] From this point on, the issues of women's rights and abolition were closely intertwined. When women were excluded from the World Anti-Slavery Convention in London in 1840, Lucretia Mott and Elizabeth Cady Stanton began to understand that they had a battle of their own to fight. They organized the first women's rights convention at Seneca Falls in 1848, at which a "Declaration of Sentiments," modeled on the grievances presented by the American colonists to King George III, enumerated the denial of women's civil rights.

Harriet Beecher, modeling herself on her mother's ladylike example, made no such challenge to the cult of true womanhood. Enjoying privileged access to the organs of public opinion—she referred to the *Cincinnati Journal* as "our *family newspaper*,"[21]—she had no desire to speak in public. Even after her international reputation was established, Harriet used Henry Ward Beecher's *Christian Union* to publish editorials on subjects she did not want to own by name. Early on she learned ways to speak both from women's sphere and from men's.

During the anti-Birney agitation, Harriet wrote to Calvin, "For my part, I can easily see how such proceedings may make converts to abolitionism, for already my sympathies are strongly enlisted for Mr.Birney."[22] As mob violence created martyrs, public sentiment rose behind the abolitionists. On November 7, 1837, abolitionist editor Elijah Lovejoy was shot and killed in Alton, Illinois, while defending his newspaper. National reaction reached a peak of intensity that would not be surpassed until the hanging of John Brown. The murder of Lovejoy moved Edward Beecher into full-fledged abolitionism; in 1838 he was elected manager of the Illinois Anti-Slavery Society.[23] Lovejoy's martyrdom made Catharine Beecher's temperate and pacifying *Essay on Slavery and Abolitionism*, published the previous year, a document of the past. Edward's wife, Isabella P. Beecher, wrote to her, "Stir up your stumps, you are quite behind the spirit of the age; you must become an *Abolitionist*, or you will be left in the background. The Alton murder has brought us all over to the faith."[24]

In family letters the Beecher women—daughters and wives—were if anything more outspoken on abolition than the men. "Do not be alarmed," Isabella assured Catharine. "I am not coming out in print like Miss Grimké, nor *Miss Beecher*." But in the freedom of family letters, she was outspoken, as was William Beecher's wife, Katherine. Katherine and William Beecher lived in Putnam, Ohio, which was "about half Abolitionist" and had a strong circulation of abolitionist newspapers. Katherine Beecher excoriated the *Cincinnati Journal* for ignoring abolitionist activities: "Why, Caty, you may read it from month to month & not find the word slave, slavery or even freedom of speech, or of the press hinted at, and if you read nothing else you would think all these agitating topics were in profound peace." She believed it was too late to attempt "to hoodwink enquiry." "[D]epend upon it, the subject is fairly up before the American people, & never will be at rest, until right & not might prevails."[25] When Harriet visited Putnam that summer, she read the abolitionist papers and witnessed firsthand the local ferment. A woman active in the Female Anti-Slavery Society called on Catharine and brought her the proceedings of their convention. Harriet thought them as "ultra" as anything she had seen, though marked by "a better spirit" than was usual in such documents. She wished for an *"intermediate society"* that would allow conscientious expression of feeling on the subject: "Pray what is there in Cincinnati to satisfy one whose mind is awakened on this subject? No one can have the system of slavery brought before him without an irrepressible desire to *do* something, and what is there to be done?"[26]

CHAPTER ELEVEN

Domestic Labor:
1836–1839

*I*n contrast to the republican impulses stirred by the free speech battles, Harriet Beecher Stowe's most intimate contact with black people was mediated through the unrepublican institution of household servants. From Rachel and Zillah, the bound servants whom the Beechers brought with them from East Hampton to Litchfield, to Candace, the family servant in Litchfield whose tears for Roxana Beecher fell on the young Harriet's head, to Dine, the "colored woman" at Nutplains who told Harriet stories and with whom she "had many frolics & capers," to the "black girl" who ate dinner with Uncle Samuel's family, to the former Kentucky slave whom Harriet hired in Cincinnati, Harriet's contacts with blacks were primarily with women in a serving capacity.[1] As such, these relationships were on a continuum with those of the white "help"—carefully distinguished from the black "servants"—who were increasingly girls of an immigrant class. Harriet's consciousness of slavery and abolition, to become so historically connected with her writing, was itself intertwined with domestic institutions over which women had immediate supervision. The complexities of Stowe's response to slavery and "the negro problem"— embroiled with racial prejudice for even ardent abolitionists—may be laid in part to these entangled domestic relations. During the formative period of the 1830s her consciousness was divided between that of republican defender of free speech and middle-class, white, household mistress. That she was herself trying to escape being a "mere household drudge" and "domestic slave" intensified the contradictions; she turned to her writing to make money that would enable her to hire household help—and she was dependent on household help to relieve her of duties so that she was free to write. The political economy of the household was intimately connected with the political economy of slavery. Both were patriarchal institutions that subordinated the labor of one group of people to the leisure and well-being of another. As a woman, Stowe's own labor was a commodity in this exchange.

The evening of September 29, 1836, was doubtless one of some drama at Walnut Hills, for while Harriet lay in one room giving birth, Aunt Esther lay in another, severely ill with cholera. If it had not been for the coincidence that Dr. Drake was on hand to attend Harriet, Henry thought that Aunt Esther "would be laid here for a corpse." It is even more remarkable that Dr. Drake did not spread disease to the new mother, for no one at this time understood the importance of sterile hands. At ten o'clock, Harriet gave birth to a baby girl. Much to everyone's astonishment, she then proceeded to give birth to another. Henry reported that one baby "is just like Harriet," the other, "the perfect image of Mr. Stowe."[2] The "Stowe baby" was called Eliza; she was thin and sickly and Catharine worried that Harriet would not be able to raise them both.[3] The "Beecher baby" was fat and healthy and retained throughout her life something of an advantage; it was she that her mother took on trips, leaving Eliza at home. Aunt Esther, left quite feeble by the cholera, recovered the more slowly because she insisted on doing things around the house—"& she *does* something," remarked Henry, she "tires and worries herself."[4]

While her sister Mary had chosen a domestic role and then found a husband to go with it, Harriet Beecher, the family "genius" and "bluestocking," chose a husband and then adjusted to the domestic role that went with wifehood. The Beecher family sat back and waited to see how this highly educated, intellectual young woman would manage her domestic duties. If Calvin Stowe was like George Eliot's Casaubon, there was also more than a little Dorothea Brooke in Harriet. Her production of twins was taken as confirmation of her eccentricity and was the occasion of much family merriment. A few days after the event Henry wrote to William and Katherine: "Harriet has got along bravely—& is quite forward after such a singular exploit, or rather I should have called a plural one."[5] Katherine wrote back to Harriet that she had served them "such a trick," but that she would excuse her for "making us all jump & laugh & shout & cry & feel glad & sorry 'all under one'—because—only because, you are a genius, and therefore cannot be expected to walk in a beaten track."[6] The twins plunged Harriet precipitously into a demanding domesticity, further piquing the curiosity of those who had imagined a different life course for one who had lived in a rarified literary and intellectual realm.

Upon his return from Europe Calvin Stowe reported to the Ohio legislature on his investigation of the Prussian school system. His *Report on Elementary Instruction in Europe*, circulated in every school district of Ohio and widely reprinted by the legislatures of other states, had an important influence on the development of common school education. His trip was a resounding success. He had purchased for the Lane Seminary library eight crates of books, two from London, two from Germany, and four from Paris. For an impoverished scholar there could be few pleasures greater than selecting—on someone else's budget—a choice collection of scholarly volumes. These included the works of the Greek and Latin Church Fathers, "a large assortment of the best volumes of engravings illustrating ancient Oriental architecture, costumes, [and] manners," volumes of German theology, French and German poetry, the *Proceedings of the Royal Society*, and various encyclopedias and reference works. There were 5,000 volumes in all. Calvin Stowe had been the librarian at Bowdoin College the year after his graduation and he now served as the librarian at Lane Seminary. He gave explicit directions that none of the volumes "be allowed to go out of the library till they all are labelled and entered in the library record." Lane Seminary was a manual labor school that required students to work three hours a day "to promote health and vigor of both body and mind"; Stowe planned to buy bookbinding tools and have two students engage in this otherwise expensive task. He also outlined a way of cataloguing books by author and subject, to allow for easy access.[7]

Calvin had written to Harriet on his journey out: "Take good care of yourself, and of the *little one* whom (as the Germans say) you are carrying *under your heart*. Remember, if female, the name is *Eliza E. Tyler* without hesitation, curtailment or addition. This is indispensible."[8] Children were easy. It was just a matter of naming and cataloguing them. After a return voyage of two months, Calvin learned upon arrival in New York on January 20, 1837, that Harriet had given birth to twins. "Bravo! You noble creature," he wrote to her. She had named one Eliza Tyler, following his wishes, and the other Isabella. Calvin Stowe overrode her second choice. "Eliza and Harriet! *Eliza & Harriet*! ELIZA AND HARRIET!"[9] Having had twin wives, it was only right that he had twin daughters to bear both of their names. He hurried home to see about this two-volume affair.

The first reports on her children from Harriet are written in the terse and telegraphic style of a mother who has little time to spare for the luxury of writing letters. "My children—One is fat—the other poor one pretty well the other feeble & sickly & either one of them more care than babies of their age in general."[10] Physical recovery from the birth of twins was bound to take some time, and sleep was in short supply. When one baby woke up and cried, the other baby woke up and cried to keep her company. Yet by the time the twins were six months old the reports from Walnut Hills were uniformly encouraging. Harriet wrote to Elizabeth Lyman, "Dont be discouraged by my example for I tell you seriously that tho I scarcely slept a wink last night & tho I have had one of two babies in my arms all day—tho money is scarce & times hard yet I never was happier on the whole than I am now."[11] Catharine wrote to the Beecher family, "Harriet manages better than folk would expect who are wont to think a genius & a blue stocking cannot be good for anything else."[12] The cozy domesticity into which the newly married pair had settled after their marriage was reestablished when Calvin returned from Europe, and he provided an extra set of arms for the twins. Harriet reported that this "worthy man" lectured and attended faculty meetings during the day and rocked the crib and tended "one baby or another nights—in consequence of which he is often tired & sleepy at both periods."[13]

In the midst of this double complication of their lives, Harriet and Calvin continued to lay the planks of their marriage, only five months old if reckoned by the time they had lived together. Perfectly matched intellectually, they quickly discovered that they were total opposites in temperament. While she rarely gave spontaneous expression to her feelings, Calvin was, he admitted, "altogether the creature of impulse. Every feeling that I have, however transient or trivial, comes out all over me and explodes like gun powder. What other people only feel for a moment without showing it, I proclaim to all the world."[14] His lack of what Harriet called "self-government" was made worse by the fact that, as he explained to her, "my good feelings are quiet & silent and my ill ones urgent & obstrusive."[15] Full of "bitter recollections" of his treatment of Eliza, he promised his new wife that he would reform, adding, "I hope you will try to help me."[16]

Calvin Stowe attributed the beginning of their difficulties to their housing situation. The rapid growth of Cincinnati meant that housing was chronically in short supply, and they were living in a small brick cottage while the trustees of Lane Seminary delayed on making good the promise of a house to accompany Professor Stowe's salary. Comparing their cramped living quarters to the situation of professors at less endowed institutions, he fulminated against the Lane board of trustees for their cavalier treatment of him. He told Harriet in the summer of 1837 that he would "throw Lane Seminary to the dogs if they do not justice to me in this respect, and you may tell them so. Our miserable accomodation, the covenant-breaking conduct of the board, and the degrading contrast between me and the other professors has been the cause of three fourths of my unhappiness since I returned from Europe."[17] That the president of Lane Seminary was Harriet's father of course added piquancy to these remarks.

The failure of the Lane board of trustees to honor their promises was part of a much larger economic failure: the Panic of 1837. Following a period of wild land speculation over six hundred banks failed, food and rent prices rose, and unemployment spread in ripples from failed businesses. In a way, the Stowes were better off than established couples, for they had less to lose. By contrast, Harriet's sister Mary, married for nine years, had a well-established home in Hartford which the panic took away, piece by piece. Aunt Esther wrote Harriet of Thomas Perkins's failure, "more trying now than at his former failure" for "then he had but two children and a regular salary of a thousand dollars a year for their support and his office rent free—now he has four children no salary and hires an office at a hundred dollars a year." The Perkins were forced to turn over all of their assets to their creditors—

"not only the out of doors property but the furniture of the front parlor is given up," including "Marys beautiful piano."[18] In Cincinnati the depression caused similar retrenchment among the well-to-do Foote brothers. Samuel Foote made plans to close his parlors and move to a smaller house; the Semi-Colon Club met on March 6, "our *last* Semi-colon . . . and probably the last time that we shall open our Parlors for company," wrote Harriet Foote. This rugged New England woman was not altogether unhappy at the retrenchment; she felt they could live for half what they did in a mansion where "the ceiling in my bedroom is thirteen feet high" and she couldn't "stand in a chair and reach cobwebs with a broom."[19] Two years later Catharine Beecher reported that John Foote had "sold out" and was planning "to join two of his little houses in one & live back of where he used to do."[20]

When the bank failed to honor Arthur Tappan's draft for Lyman Beecher's salary, the panic struck closer to home. The trustees advanced him salary from other funds, and also paid Calvin Stowe a $250 supplement in lieu of the house he should have had. The Beechers held on tight and waited for the Tappans to weather the financial storm; Catharine was confident that in the meantime John Tappan "with some others of the family will see that our supplies do not fail," and she hoped that "Aunt E[sther] will not worry or lie awake another night." Expressing the Beecher family philosophy about money, Catharine continued, "[I]t saves a great deal of trouble always to hope for the best."[21] This optimistic approach to financial management worked well when others stood by to cover shortfalls, but was less successful when the outcome depended on those who were dipping into the till, as Catharine was soon to discover. Her Western Female Institute, on precarious ground after Catharine alienated the families most likely to send their daughters, was one of the casualties of the financial panic. When she attempted to settle the accounts, everyone came up short. Catharine determined that the shortfall "was owing to Harriet's *overdrawing*"; she calculated that Harriet had spent $114 more than the $500 she was entitled to.[22] Harriet acceded to this interpretation, giving up her claims to the school furniture. Mary Dutton thought she was due $500, but by Catharine's reckoning, it was she, Catharine, who was owed money, for she had drawn only $200 a year in salary. Catharine complained that the school had "been more plague to me than all I suffered in Hartford for ten years" and that she pursued it only for the good of others: "because father wished it—because Harriet needed some means of immediate support—because I was urged by various friends." She counted as part of her losses the money she could have been earning "by my pen."[23] In point of fact, it was Harriet's plan, not Catharine's, to live by her pen. She had been drawn into Catharine's school against her inclinations. Katherine Sklar concluded from an examination of the documents that Harriet Beecher Stowe and Mary Dutton both lost money on the Western Female Institute.[24] The Panic of 1837 was the death knell, but the school was doomed from the start by Catharine's New England chauvinism. Catharine followed her father's blueprint for saving the West from barbarism through the influence of "the social and religious principles of New England,"[25] and the Buckeyes were not impressed. Harriet's *Geography*, on the other hand, was a resounding success; it had already reached a sale of 100,000 copies and had been introduced widely throughout the schools in the West.[26]

If the Panic of 1837 devastated those who had the most to lose, it pinched hard on those who had little margin. Ministers excused themselves from attending ecclesiastical conventions so that they could perform marriages—for which they earned a small fee. "Oh we are quite poverty struck out in this big West," commented one observer of this practice.[27] The panic also had implications for women's work in the household. Thomas and Mary Perkins were obliged to cut back on household help: "[I]nstead of keeping two girls and a man we now have one girl and no man," reported Aunt Esther, who expected to take up some of the slack. She went on, "if it be true that it is *only* for *idle hands* that *satan* finds some mischief still I think there is little danger of his forcing much work into my hands . . . with my broom my flat irons my bread tray and my knitting needles I think I shall be able to *keep him at bay*." As banks failed and money became scarce, women's unpaid labor took the place of household help. "As for leisure, reading, and social enjoyment out of the famaly," wrote Aunt Esther, "they must wait for a more convenient season."[28]

At a time when others were cutting back, Harriet Beecher Stowe's reliance on expensive household help was essential to the good management her relatives observed. She was obliged to pay $3 per week for her wet nurse and $1.25 for her "help." This cash outlay—exclusive of the room and board that was added for the help—on a yearly basis totalled $220, or 20 percent of Calvin Stowe's annual salary. Harriet Foote, who observed that Harriet Stowe "gets along with her two babies much better that we expected she could," and was "quite a good housekeeper," worried about this expenditure, especially as fuel was expensive and the cost of living "enormous."[29] But Harriet Beecher had grown up with household servants and simply assumed that one could not get along without them. This was not an uncommon assumption in a period in which there was one servant for every eight families in America.[30]

In 1837 Calvin's mother came to live with them, changing the balance of power within the household. Hepzibah Stowe was a tough New England woman whose family culture was spare and lean. She eschewed servants and did her own work, taking care of her house for so many decades and with so little adverse affect on her health that, Calvin wrote, "She is almost afraid that she shall never die at all."[31] Her presence gave weight to Calvin's point of view and brought to a boil the temperamental differences that had been simmering between the newlyweds. "Since that time," Harriet later wrote him,

> you have been *predisposed* to view me in a wrong light—It was never till after this that I heard any thing from you as if you had been too complying or I too exacting. . . . Since that time of Mothers stay in the family I have plainly seen two currents in your mind—one of morbid brooding almost vindictive blame

looking with a brooding & jealous eye on my faults—exaggerating them & predisposing to impatience—There were certain ideas that mother dwelt very much on that you were often repeating in moments of hasty impatience—& they were these That I was extravagant in expenses—that I needed much waiting on—that I inclined to keep too much help"[32]

In July 1837 Hepzibah Stowe abruptly cut short her visit and journeyed back to Massachusetts. "I hardly know what to think about Mother's going home," Calvin wrote, as he prepared to send her by steamboat when the Ohio River was so low that only small boats could travel without "sticking in the sand all the way up like flies in a streak of molasses."[33] But the household politics were clearer to Harriet; several years later when Calvin proposed to bring his mother to Walnut Hills permanently, she told him she did not think it was a good idea.[34] In an essay on "Intolerance," Harriet later wrote that religious intolerance was "only a small branch" of this streak of human nature:

> Physicians are quite as intolerant as theologians. They never had the power of burning at the stake for medical opinions, but they certainly have shown the will. Politicians are intolerant. Philosophers are intolerant, especially those who pique themselves on liberal opinions. Painters and sculptors are intolerant. And housekeepers are intolerant, virulently denunciatory concerning any departures from their particular domestic creed. (LF, 176–77)

"How does Harriet do?" asked Catharine Beecher rhetorically in a letter to Connecticut friends:

> "I wish you could just step across our garden into her little box & go up stairs into a little upper verandah & there you will see a little swing cradle suspended and at one end sits little Harriet playing, who looks up with bright blue eyes & an ever ready smile—she is a fat, easy, plump, quiet, little puss. At the other end lies little Eliza—smaller, more delicate, & quietly sucking her thumb."

The sketch Catharine drew of Harriet, Calvin, and Anna Smith, their domestic help, suggests the fragile equilibrium that prevailed during the first year of their marriage:

> Harriet sits by darning stockings & looking rather thin & worn. Mr. Stowe is in his little study busy with his books Anne—the mainstay is in the kitchen alternate nurse, cook & chamber maid. They live very snugly & have but little work to do compared with most families, & have as great a share of domestic enjoyment as ordinarily falls to the lot of married people, who are entirely satisifed with each other.[35]

The Stowes' domestic tranquility depended on the continued good health and stamina of Harriet, on the reliability of the help, and on the good management of limited household funds. "[I]f Mr. Stowe was not the most frugal content man in the world and so in love with Germany & German customs," observed Harriet Foote, "they could not get along so comfortably."[36] When the Lane trustees that year increased Calvin Stowe's salary to $1,100, Catharine reported that the Stowes were "out of debt and free from worry at on that account."[37] In the beginning his austere habits set the tone in the household, but as he withdrew more and more to his study and Harriet and Anna took charge of the children and the house, a more Beecheresque economy prevailed.

A complication was underway even as Catharine penned her sketch of Harriet's happy home life. Harriet was already expecting another baby, conceived when the twins were not yet seven months old. By the next January she would have three babies under eighteen months old. "Poor thing she bears up wonderfully well," wrote Catharine, "& I hope will live thro' this first tug of matrimonial warfare & then she says she shall not have any more children *she knows certain* for *one while*—How she found this out I cannot say but she seems quite confident about it."[38] This child was conceived within two months of Calvin's return from Europe. These circumstances may have suggested a strategy. Of the first fifteen years of their marriage, Harriet and Calvin spent approximately half apart, for they found sexual abstinence more likely to succeed under these circumstances. It was the only method they used to limit their family.[39]

In order to escape both the sickly heat of Cincinnati and the domestic cares that weighed more heavily as her pregnancy advanced, Harriet made a visit that summer of 1837 to William and Katherine Beecher in Putnam. She left around June 10, traveling by riverboat through Wheeling and Marietta. Calvin wrote to her on June 18, "You must remember that your only object is to regain health & bend all your efforts to that. I want you at home, but I want you to be well." He kindly reassured her about the babies: "They have never been in so good health or grown so fast. . . . They have both of them almost entirely forgotten how to cry."[40] On July 3 he sent her money for the return trip, advising her, "If you come without a gentleman in company, I should think it would be well to come by Marietta [that is, by water], if with a gentleman, by stage."[41]

While Harriet's health was at continual risk from unplanned pregnancies, there was little certainty to be had in the matter of domestic help. The rule of thumb was that good girls were hard to get and impossible to keep. Elizabeth Foote wrote to Eliza Foote expressing surprise at hearing from her,

for I thought if you had to bake, brew, wash put up dinner for workman, and tend baby some, you would feel very little disposed to write to your friends— but we were really rejoiced to hear that you had at last procured a good girl— the next important circumstance will be to keep her—if you have any more of the said article—good girls—than to supply yourselves we should like a cargo sent to the West, for we find it as difficult to get them here as you do in Guilford.[42]

Frances Trollope put the "servant problem" in both a local and a national perspective: "The greatest difficulty in organising a family establishment in Ohio, is getting servants, or, as it is there called, 'getting help,' for it is more than petty treason to the Republic, to call a free citizen a *servant*."[43]

Native whites in serving capacities were the first to object to the term "servant"—"Servant, that means what slave used to."[44] The operative distinction between "help" and "servant" was race: help was white, servants were black. This careful distinction put a republican veneer on what nevertheless remained a somewhat feudal relationship. Just as the association between blacks and slavery mutually reinforced the prejudice attaching to both race and servitude, so the assumption that servants "were descended from the serfs" reinforced the negative connotations of service. As Daniel Sutherland has observed, "[E]ven though the conditions of American service were not comparable to slavery, and the degree of feudalism present in its system of free labor was not as extreme as that found in serfdom or indentured servitude, Americans continued to accept and defend a relationship that irredeemably stigmatized servants and service."[45] The "medievalism" of the mistress–servant relationship made Americans uncomfortable with it, but few stopped to consider the continuity between the hired white help and the owned black slave, both of whom labored in a domestic economy. In between these two extremes were the indentured servants of all races and the free black servants. Zillah Crooke was bound to the Beecher family for thirteen years. The only difference between her servitude and that of slaves is that the latter were bound for life. Servants and help often lived in the household of their mistresses. This increased the dependency and the paternalism of the relationship, opening up the private life of the servant to the interference and domination of the mistress. The domestic setting also obscured the nature of the relationship, at least in the minds of the masters. Lyman Beecher remarked of Zillah and Rachel, much as a slaveholder might, that they were "a part of the family."[46]

This is the context for the republican rebellions reported across the land by women who could not keep their help. Most help were single women who worked for awhile and then left to marry and keep house on their own. The temporary nature of their employment gave them an identity separate from their servitude and endowed them with dignity. They refused to wear uniforms, to provide references, or to contract for the year. Many left unannounced within weeks of their hiring. Such behavior exasperated employers, who usually ascribed it not to the republican institutions of America but to the peasant origins of the help. Caroline Barrett White of Brookline, Massachusetts, left in her diary a trail of disappointments with her help: "My cook left today and the one I had engaged to take her place has failed to keep her engagement. *Irish fidelity!*" Faye Dudden observed that Mrs. White

repeatedly summed up her servant problems by professing herself "heartily sick of the Irish," or "sick of all the race." Despite the fact that she experienced similar difficulties with non-Irish domestics ... Mrs. White persistently recurred to the idea that her problems would be solved if only she could find "some good Protestant girls." ... Her husband Frank once joked that the best excuse a suicide could leave behind was *"I kept Irish domestics."*[47]

The inexperience of many recent immigrants made them appear ignorant, when in fact they were only unsophisticated and unused to the appliances of modern housekeeping.[48] Although most learned quickly and saved
up enough money to set up house on their own, it was the wide-mouthed
ineptitude of the green hand that made its way into the literature, reinforcing
nativist assumptions that hardly needed reinforcing. In Cincinnati the largest
immigrant population was German, and "Dutch" girls were most commonly
employed as help. In 1838, when the twins were two years old and Henry
eleven months, Harriet Beecher Stowe employed a German girl to do her
housework, thus freeing Anna Smith to look after the children and Harriet
to devote three hours a day to writing. She explained to Mary Dutton these
"new arrangements:"

> I have realised enough by my writing one way & another to enable me to add
> to my establishment a stout German girl who does my housework leaving to
> Anna full time to attend to the children so that by method in disposing of time
> I have about three hours per day in writing & if you see my name coming out
> every where—you may be sure of one thing, that I *do* it for *the pay*—I have
> determined not to be a mere domestic slave—without even the liesure to *excel*
> in my duties—I mean to have money enough to have my house kept in the
> best manner & yet to have time for reflection & that preparation for the edu-
> cation of my children which every mother needs—I have every prospect of
> succeeding in this plan & I am certain as yet that I am not only more com-
> fortable but my house affairs & my children are in better keeping than when
> I was pressed & worried & teased in trying to do more than I could—I have
> now liesure to think—to plan—contrive—see my friends make visits &c besides
> superintending all that is done in my house even more minutely than when I
> was shut up in my nursery.[49]

Elizabeth Foote, writing to relatives back East, confirmed that "Harriet
Stowe is getting on in the world very nicely now," and was in "better health
than she has been since her marriage—she nurses her baby yet and I hope
will find it convenient to a long time—she has Anna for nurse and another
very good girl in the kitchen. she writes stories for the Ladies book and makes
a good deal of money."[50] This specialization of labor was like the schemes
Catharine had instituted at the Hartford Female Seminary. Unlike those
schemes, however, it depended on a hierarchy of jobs and a corresponding
hierarchy of laborers. At the top was the native-born New England bluestocking, engaged in literary work; then came the immigrants in rank order:
Anna Smith, who was English, acted as governess and nurse; below her was
the nameless "German girl," who did the heavy housework.[51] In 1839 a yet-
lower servant was added to the train. It was common in Cincinnati to hire
slaves from across the river; their masters contracted their labor out and
collected a portion of their wages.[52] According to her authorized biography,
Harriet "received into her family as a servant a colored girl from Kentucky."[53]
These servingwomen of various races and cultures were intimately con-

nected with Harriet's literary productivity. They not only freed her time so that she could write, but they provided her with some of her best material. Looked at in class terms, they were exploited both as labor power and as material for art. Their own voices remained silent. Harriet's German girl provided her with material for a sketch which she published under the title "Trials of a Housekeeper." Addressed to "the lords of creation" who cannot fathom the difficulties women have in getting help, this sketch is narrated by a newly married young woman who lives a mile and a half outside of town—which is to say, a woman in Harriet's situation in Walnut Hills in 1837. Her description of the German girl who comes to help her invokes all the stereotypes about immigrant help. Kotterin is "a great, staring Dutch girl, in a green bonnet with red ribbons, with mouth wide open, and hands and feet that would have made a Greek sculptor open *his* mouth too." When she attempts to make a bed—"it never having come into my head that there *could be* a wrong way of making a bed"—her mistress realizes that Kotterin is *"just caught."* The "look of stupid wonder" that overtakes her face when the doorbell rings without the aid of human hands completes the picture of the ignorant help, who causes the mistress "almost as much work, with twice as much anxiety, as when there was nobody there."[54] In what Forrest Wilson called this "humorous and elegant discussion,"[55] Harriet allied herself with the patriarchal consciousness of the "lords of creation" whom she addressed.

The "colored girl" whom she hired in 1839 may have been a light-skinned, high-class black woman such as William Beecher's wife described as being in her employ in Putnam: "I have got some help—if you can credit me!—a tolerably smart & very pleasant colored woman—a sort of 'white coon' in these parts."[56] At the top of the hierarchy of slaves, mulatto women were desirable house servants. In some instances, employment in white homes facilitated escape from slavery. In what became a celebrated case, James Birney in 1837 employed a black woman named Matilda who, it turned out, was a fugitive slave. Her master had transported her from Virginia enroute to Missouri, but when they stopped at the Cincinnati landing Matilda made her way into the city and found employment. When her master attempted to recover her under the provisions of the Ohio Fugitive Slave Act of 1793, Salmon P. Chase defended Matilda, arguing that she was legally free when she set foot on the northern side of the Ohio River. The judge of the Common Pleas Court decided against Matilda, remanded her into slavery, and proceeded to hear a related case brought against James Birney for harboring a fugitive slave. He found Birney guilty and fined him $50, being supported in this as in his other decision by "the prejudices and sympathies of nearly the entire community."[57] These widely publicized cases influenced community awareness of the problem of fugitive slaves and the liability of employers; Matilda's was only the best known of many similar difficulties that arose in this border town.

If Matilda's legal claim to freedom hinged on her having been brought to Cincinnati by her master, so too Harriet's servant, having been brought into Ohio by her mistress, was by the laws of Ohio a free woman. As Matilda's case demonstrated, however, having the law on one's side did not matter if the judge and popular opinion were indisposed. After Harriet's servant had been with her a few months, Professor Stowe "received word . . . that the girl's master was in the city looking for her, and that if she were not careful she would be seized and conveyed back into slavery."[58] According to the family story, Calvin Stowe and Henry Ward Beecher armed themselves and drove the woman twelve miles by back roads to John Van Zandt's cabin, a station on the Underground Railroad, whence she made her escape. This unnamed black woman, hired to lighten Harriet's domestic labor, provided her with rich material that she later transformed into the story of Eliza's heroic escape in *Uncle Tom's Cabin*. In the real-life drama, however, Stowe was cast in the role of Mrs. Shelby, the white mistress who looks on help-lessly as white men decide the fate of her household help.

That this black woman was both a labor-saving device and a source of literary inspiration points to the complicated relationship in which Harriet Beecher Stowe stood to her help. But if her servant was doubly used, so too was Stowe called upon to march double-time in order to employ her pen. In a very real sense she too was a domestic slave. Her letters reveal that she gave considerable thought to employing her time as efficiently and econom-ically as possible,[59] yet in her best-laid plans she resembled a tiger chasing her own tail. Harriet escaped the nursery but she never escaped the circular treadmill: she wrote to get money to hire help to enable her to write (to get money to hire help, and so on). If she eventually escaped being "a domestic slave," she never escaped being a slave to her pen.

In "The Trials of a Housekeeper" a ray of sunshine appears in the form of "a tidy, efficiently-trained English girl; pretty, and genteel, and neat, and knowing how to do every thing, and with the sweetest temper in the world." The mistress rests from her labors as this English help keeps the house "as clean and genteel" as her pretty self.[60] In Harriet's sketch, this reprieve is short-lived, for the pretty English girl soon leaves to get married. Although this ending was highly realistic, in fact Harriet's English help, Anna Smith, came to her as a young woman and remained in her employ, unmarried, for more than eighteen years. Described by Catharine Beecher as the "mainstay" of the family, Anna Smith was as important to Harriet's career as Amelia Willard, Elizabeth Cady Stanton's devoted housekeeper for thirty years, was to hers. Both functioned as second mothers to the children and, despite the complexities of cross-class relationships, developed strong ties of affection with their mistresses.

CHAPTER TWELVE

The Nursery and the Parlor:
1838–1841

C<i>alvin Stowe was in many respects</i> an ideal husband for Harriet, and
the companionship they enjoyed tempered the difficulties of her
busy days. Their idea of a good time was to read together around
the stove and to have long talks, enabled by their agreement on fundamental
values. "On matters of religion and taste," Calvin told her, "our opinions and
feelings, though quite independent and different from the rest of the world,
are very much alike; and I believe there are very few husbands and wives in
the world, who have so many real good talks together on such matters as we
have."[1] They quietly separated themselves from the theological bickering that
absorbed so much of Lyman Beecher's time and talent. An ordained minister,
Calvin likened such battles to children's quarrels: "It is all—'I say you did'
& 'I say you didn't' 'Joe begun at me *first*.'"[2] Their love of books was a
continually renewed source of mutual pleasure. When she was in her seventies and Calvin in his eighties, Harriet sent thanks to Sarah Orne Jewett
for sending her latest novel, which she had just read, having been delayed
by "Mr Stowe's eagerness to read it."[3]

Unlike the male-dominated marriages of the eighteenth century, Calvin
and Harriet's union was a "companionate marriage"—increasingly the middle-class norm. As Lynn Brickley has observed, one of the effects of academy
attendance "was to increase the chances that a young woman would seek a
husband who would be her intellectual companion and tutor. . . . This marital concept of intellectual companionship, prevalent in the advice literature
of the period, was strongly enforced by the teaching of Sarah Pierce at the

122

Litchfield school."[4] Marriage to a highly educated man was a means through which intelligent young women extended their education. Sarah Josepha Hale described her hours with her husband, surrounded by chintz-covered furniture, a writing desk topped with bookshelves, in a parlor illuminated by a bright fire:

> We commenced, soon after our marriage, a system of study and reading. . . . The hours allotted were from eight o'clock until ten—two hours in twenty-four. How I enjoyed those hours! In this manner we studied French, Botany— then almost a new science in this country but for which my husband had an uncommon taste; and obtained some knowledge of Mineralogy, Geology, etc., besides pursuing a long and instructive course of reading. In all our mental pursuits, it seemed the aim of my husband to enlighten my reason, strengthen my judgment, and give me confidence in my own powers of mind, which he estimated more highly than I did.[5]

Sarah Josepha Hale was born a generation too soon to avail herself of a female seminary. Harriet's education in the parlor with the valedictorian of Bowdoin College, class of 1825, built on thirteen years of education: at the Litchfield Female Academy, at the Hartford Female Seminary, at the Western Female Institute, and at the Semi-Colon Club. Her definition of herself as a woman of intellect was strong when she married Calvin Stowe, and his assumption of her intellectual worth supported both their relationship and her continuing development.

"Here we are—me & my Professor, in the same old house," Harriet wrote to Mary Dutton in December 1838; "after all the vision of a house this fall proved a mirage of the desert to us—so after fussing & fuming awhile we have concluded to quirl up a while in our old lair." She described for Mary a parlor scene very like that between Sarah and David Hale:

> We have our Olmsted stove moved into the parlour & use only one part of it & it keeps the room delightfully warm here we eat our meals, near enough to the fire to toast our bread as we go along which I think is the ne plus ultra of a sociable cozy breakfast or tea—Mr Stowe reads german books & translates sometimes as he goes along—I'l tell you for your edification that he has read to me the story of "Blue Beard" "Puss in boot" & various others of the kind out of the old mother German to say nothing of Faust, of which by way of routing a fit of the blues the good man undertook a translation.[6]

Underlying the companionate marriage was a commitment to the autonomy and personhood of woman that would have been unheard of in the eighteenth century. Calvin Stowe assumed that women were individuals with their own unique destinies to discover. He had urged Catharine Hills, the first woman he was romantically interested in, to find out what she was meant to do in this life and to do it. In his twenties he declared his own design, "to live and die *a literary* man."[7] He courted Harriet Beecher in a literary club where the writings and opinions of women enjoyed equal consideration with those of men; he married her with the expectation that they would be partners in intellectual pursuits.

The gains for women in the new, companionate ideal were clear, but there were costs as well. Companionate marriages gave rise to more conflict, for the expectations and roles were less defined. With two literary careers in the family, the potential for conflicting priorities—and outright rivalry—was kept in check as long as the normal course of events transpired, which is to say, the husband's career took precedence. The democratic, companionate ideal grew up in the soil of a marital system based for centuries on male privilege—what Elizabeth Cady Stanton called "the aristocracy of sex." How far could it develop before it came into conflict with the old order? Then too, as Susanne Lebsock has pointed out, people who married for love "opened themselves up to new risks."

> Once husbands and wives thought they had a right to be loved, the potential for feelings of rejection and betrayal grew. Once the wife was allowed to voice opinions, the opportunities for overt conflict multiplied. The companionate ideal, in short, raised the emotional stakes in marriage. The rewards could be great, but the potential for disappointment had never been greater.[8]

This is the context for what Calvin Stowe called "the semitones of domestic life" that he and Harriet experienced during the first decade of their marriage.

Because he was a professor, Calvin worked in the house a good bit of the time, increasing not only the amount of companionship the Stowes enjoyed but also the daily jostling of unlike temperaments. Describing the incompatibility of two of her characters in *Oldtown Folks*, Stowe wrote, "A satin vest and a nutmeg-grater are both perfectly harmless, and even worthy existences, but their close proximity on a jolting journey is not to be recommended."[9] "There are certain points in which we are so exactly unlike," Calvin told her, "that our peculiarities impinge against each other and sometimes produce painful collisions when neither party is conscious of any intention to disoblige the other." And he methodically enumerated them:

> 1) I am naturally anxious, to the extent of needlessly taking much thought beforehand. You are hopeful, to the extent of being heedless of the future, thinking only of the present. . . .
> 2) I am naturally very methodical as to time and place for everything, and anything out of time or out of place is excessively annoying to me. This is a feeling to which you are a stranger. You have no idea of either time or place. I want prayers and meals at the particular time, and every piece of furniture in its own place. You can have morning prayer anytime between sunrise and noon without the least inconvenience to yourself; and as to place, it seems to be your special delight to keep everything in the house on the move, and your special torment to allow anything to retain the same position a week together. Permanency is my delight,—yours, everlasting change.
> 3) I am naturally particular, you are naturally slack—and you often give me inexpressible torment without knowing it. You and Anne have vexed me beyond all endurance often by taking up my newspapers, and then instead of folding them properly and putting them in their place, either dropping them all sprawling on the floor, or wabbleing them all up into one wabble, and

squulching them on the table like an old hen with her guts and gizzard squeezed out.[10]

Harriet admitted "the importance of system and order in a family," but urged on her husband the fact that both she and Anna "labor under serious natural disadvantages on the subject." She observed, "It is not all that is necessary to feel the importance of order and system, but it requires a particular kind of talent to carry it through a family. Very much the same kind of talent, as Uncle Samuel said, which is necessary to make a good prime minister."[11]

Harriet was right that her talents did not lie in domestic management. The good home manager must keep her eyes and ears alert to the motions and doings of a dozen people and contrivances; she must know that that thumping noise means that the dog has gotten into the garbage pail; she must keep the calendars of husband, children, servants, and shopkeepers in her head. The coordination of such detail requires attention to many things at once. Harriet's nature was different. Calvin created a memorable portrait of her in one of his letters of domestic complaint:

> When your mind is on any particular point, it is your nature to feel and act as if that were the only thing in the world; and you drive at it and make every thing bend to it, to the manifest injury of other interests. For instance, when you are intent on raising flowers, you are sure to visit them and inspect them very carefully every morning; but your kitchen could go for two or three days without any inspection at all, you would be quite ignorant of what there was in the house to be cooked, or the way in which the work was done. Your oversight of the flowers would be systematic and regular; of the kitchen, at hap-hazard, and now and then. You should be as regular in the kitchen as in the garden.[12]

Calvin urged her "to do things a little at a time and often, and not absorb and exhaust your whole strength on one thing at one time, as if your life were the life of a silk worm, just to spin one cocoon and then die."[13] Yet her capacity for total absorption was essential to her creativity. This single-minded focus— so hard for women to achieve—allowed her to see characters and scenes with an intensity that made them real. The photographs of Harriet Beecher Stowe all show a woman with an elusive, faraway look in her eyes. It is as if she is lying fallow, waiting for a stimulus that will totally absorb her sympathies.

Born a woman, Harriet Beecher Stowe was impelled by a restlessness and expansiveness more conventionally associated with men. The manic fury with which Harriet gardened both confirms Calvin's portrait of her and says much about the pent-up energies that she experienced within the confinement of the home. This passion broke loose soon after they moved into their new house in the fall of 1839. The house was nearing completion in July, when Calvin went East to deliver the Phi Beta Kappa address at Dartmouth College. Harriet accompanied him as far as Hartford, while Calvin went on to Natick, Massachusetts, to visit his mother. From there he wrote to her of a letter he had received from Samuel Fowler Dickinson, the treasurer of

Lane Seminary, assuring him that his house was to be finished "all to my liking in a few weeks" and that he was to have a salary of $1200. "[I]f so, I'll try it for a while longer," he told Harriet, who had continually urged him to stay at Lane despite the institutional setbacks the seminary had experienced, "though I must confess I have no very sanguine hopes of great success while Bigg's tallowy guts and muddy brains are to be saddled on the institution. This is a world of fools and madmen, and I suppose they will have their way in it." Harriet was supposed to come on to Natick to join him, but became ill; Calvin, having had one young wife snatched from him, tried to keep morbid thoughts at bay but could not help wondering whether, "just as I begin to know your feelings & susceptibilities, our union is to cease?"[14]

When they returned to Walnut Hills and moved into their new house, located on the other side of the seminary from the president's house in which her father lived, Harriet made creative plans to disburse a good portion of Calvin's $1,200 salary. Not for her were simple plots of a few local plants. Vying with the neighbors, she planned and executed grand gardens involving tons of manure and eight kinds of geraniums. She was constantly digging up and moving rose bushes, hedges, and bulbs. "Gardening is to be all the fashion among the ladies on Walnut Hills," she wrote her brothers and sisters. "We shall make it blossom as the rose." She asked George, her gardening brother, questions about the culture of bulbs: "What sort of soil do they favour—What is the speediest way of increasing them, when should they be taken up & when put out"—and in the easy way the Beechers had of turning their private writing into public instruction, she continued, "Suppose you write an article on the subject for the 'farmer'—a horticultural & agricultural paper we have here & for which I am writing."[15] Calvin took a dim view of the time and expense this hobby involved, and ventured that they "could wear themselves out on something more profitable to our fellow creatures than having home, pasture & garden like Uncle Sam and our neighbors."[16]

Faced with a rapidly expanding family and an even more rapidly shrinking income, Calvin Stowe reacted with an obsessive watchfulness over financial matters. Keeping strict accounts became for him an article of faith. Harriet complied in her own way with his wishes, writing down on scraps of paper approximate amounts, rounding off, estimating, and generally pursuing an optimistic plan that allowed her to buy whatever she wanted at the moment. She was endowed with a full measure of the Beecher family attitude toward money, which was summed up in a motto her father often quoted: "Trust in the Lord and Do Good."[17] God, or his earthly representatives, often bailed Lyman Beecher out of financial difficulties—which was only right since he had stumbled into them by keeping his eyes fixed on the millennium. Harriet scolded Calvin for his excessive material care: "My love you do wrong to worry so much about temporal matters—you really *do wrong*: you treat your Savior *ungenerously* & you ought not to do it."[18] Hard to answer, that, especially when Harriet combined it with astute observation of his slackness in matters of religion: when he was pressed with care, he made room in his day by eliminating family prayers.[19]

But mixed with her evangelical heritage were personal traits Harriet was less ready to acknowledge: sensuousness, a love of beauty, and a Victorian capacity for the accumulation of things. Harriet brought into Calvin's book-lined existence a welter of plants, servants, crockery, Russian stoves, doodads and gimcracks. Calvin found her bookkeeping methods "exceedingly vague and unsatisfactory." He pleaded with her, "Don't say . . . 'for Aunt Esther's bonnet and something else we borrowed of Mr Perkins 14.50' " or " 'there is a milliners bill of some 2 or 3 dollars'—that sort of loose, slip-shod statement is not at all sufficient for so small an income with so many and such big loop holes as mine."[20] In vain he urged her to write all her expenditures in one book kept for the purpose. When it came to expenses, he told her, "I can hear none of your words, but I can read your writing."[21] Her refusal to keep an account book was a continual point of contention in their marriage.

Harriet was better at earning money than keeping it, and while Calvin was criticizing her inexact accounting methods she was earning a steady stream of income from her writing. One of her stories, "Mark Meriden," published by *Godey's Lady's Book* in 1841, is an instructive counterpoint to her daily life. This is a Horatio Alger parable cast in Victorian terms: Mark Meriden, happily married, is continually invited by his friend Ben Sanford to evening frolics— those "clubs, oyster suppers, and now and then a wine party, and various other social privileges for elevating one's spirits and depressing one's cash, that abound among enlightened communities." The virtuous Mark Meriden—who has recently reformed his ways—resists these temptations and returns home every night to his bright-eyed wife, who keeps "the clean glowing hearth, the easy chair drawn up in front, and a pair of embroidered slippers waiting for him." But this is not enough. Stowe provides her hero with "a small account book" in which he faithfully records not what he *spent*, but what he *saved* by declining those wine parties and oyster suppers: at the end of the year he totals his account and shows it to Ben Sanford, who has complained that he lacks the money to get married. Stowe concludes her domestic morality tale with an admonition for wives: "If Mrs. Meriden had been a woman who understood what is called 'catching a beau,' better than securing a husband—if she had never curled her hair except *for company*, and thought it a degradation to know how to keep a house comfortable, would all these things have happened?"[22] The moral of this story is that Harriet could write about domestic tranquility more easily and profitably than she could bring it about. She would become one of the chief propagandists for the Victorian ideology of the home, prescribing for other women a role in which she herself had failed over and over again.

A greater stress on their marriage than their contrasting temperaments was the strain of closely spaced childbearing—a reality that compromised the ideal of the companionate marriage. In January 1838 Harriet had given birth to her third child, Henry Ellis. The management of three small children filled Harriet's days with a multitude of trifles, each of which had to be attended to or large consequences might ensue. These are fully depicted in a letter she wrote to Georgiana May:

My Dear, Dear Georgiana,

   Only think how long it is since I have written to you, and how changed I am since then—the mother of three children! Well, if I have not kept the reckoning of old times, let this last circumstance prove my apology, for I have been hand, heart, and head full since I saw you.

   Now, to-day, for example, I'll tell you what I had on my mind from dawn to dewy eve. In the first place I waked about half after four and thought, "Bless me, how light it is! I must get out of bed and rap to wake up Mina, for breakfast must be had at six o'clock this morning." So out of bed I jump and seize the tongs and pound, pound, pound over poor Mina's sleepy head, charitably allowing her about half an hour to get waked up in,—that being the quantum of time that it takes me,—or used to. Well, then baby wakes—quâ, quâ, quâ, so I give him his breakfast, dozing meanwhile and soliloquizing as follows: "Now I must not forget to tell Mr. Stowe about the starch and dried apples"—doze— "ah, um, dear me! why doesn't Mina get up? I don't hear her,"—doze—"a, um,—I wonder if Mina has soap enough! I think there were two bars left on Saturday"—doze again—I wake again. "Dear me, broad daylight! I must get up and go down and see if Mina is getting breakfast." Up I jump and up wakes baby. "Now, little boy, be good and let mother dress, because she is in a hurry." I get my frock half on and baby by that time has kicked himself down off his pillow, and is crying and fisting the bed-clothes in great order. I stop with one sleeve off and one on to settle matters with him. Having planted him bolt upright and gone all up and down the chamber barefoot to get pillows and blankets to prop him up, I finish putting my frock on and hurry down to satisfy myself by actual observation that the breakfast is in progress. Then back I come into the nursery, where, remembering that it is washing day and that there is a great deal of work to be done, I apply myself vigorously to sweeping, dusting, and the setting to rights so necessary where there are three little mischiefs always pulling down as fast as one can put up.

   Then there are Miss H____and Miss E____, concerning whom Mary will furnish you with all suitable particulars, who are chattering, hallooing, or singing at the tops of their voices, as may suit their various states of mind, while the nurse is getting their breakfast ready. This meal being cleared away, Mr. Stowe dispatched to market with various memoranda of provisions, etc., and the baby being washed and dressed, I begin to think what next must be done. I start to cut out some little dresses, have just calculated the length and got one breadth torn off when Master Henry makes a doleful lip and falls to crying with might and main. I catch him up and turning round see one of his sisters flourishing the things out of my workbox in fine style. Moving it away and looking the other side I see the second little mischief seated by the hearth chewing coals and scraping up ashes with great apparent relish. Grandmother lays hold upon her and charitably offers to endeavor to quiet baby while I go on with my work. I set at it again, pick up a dozen pieces, measure them once more to see which is the right one, and proceed to cut out some others, when I see the twins on the point of quarreling with each other. Number one pushes number two over. Number two screams: that frightens the baby and he joins in. I call number one a naughty girl, take the persecuted one in my arms, and endeavor to comfort her by trotting to the old lyric:—

"So ride the gentlefolk,
And so do we, so do we."

Meanwhile number one makes her way to the slop jar and forthwith proceeds to wash her apron in it. Grandmother catches her up by one shoulder, drags her away, and sets the jar up out of her reach. By and by the nurse comes up from her sweeping. I commit the children to her, and finish cutting out the frocks.

But let this suffice, for of such details as these are all my days made up. Indeed, my dear, I am but a mere drudge with few ideas beyond babies and housekeeping. As for thoughts, reflections, and sentiments, good lack! good lack!

I suppose I am a dolefully uninteresting person at present, but I hope I shall grow young again one of these days, for it seems to me that matters cannot always stand exactly as they do now.

Well, Georgy, this marriage is—yes, I will speak well of it, after all; for when I can stop and think long enough to discriminate my head from my heels, I must say that I think myself a fortunate woman both in husband and children.[23]

In March 1839 Catharine Beecher wrote to Mary Dutton, "Harriet is not well as to *nerves*, but no discouraging prospects yet in the maternal line. I hope she is to have an interval of rest from further services at present in that line."[24] Yet by September she was pregnant again, her fourth baby in three years. The winter was "very wet . . . and very cold-catching."[25] Harriet suffered from "periodic attacks of neuralgia." The pain in her head and eye was so severe, she wrote to Eunice and Henry Beecher, that she was "scarcely . . . able to get from my bed to the chair and back again" and was "deprived . . . of sight and almost of sense for the time of their continuance." When her neuralgia passed, Harriet bounced back to what she described as "excellent health."[26] With spring came the birth of Frederick William on May 6, 1840. The repeated childbearing, however, was beginning to take its toll: she "never had a good getting up," and this time she was confined to her bed for two months. Between that and the neuralgia, Harriet's literary activity was sharply curtailed. "For a year I have held the pen only to write an occasional business letter such as could not be neglected," she told Georgiana May.[27] "[M]y thoughts & longings & wishes evaporate and leave no trace on paper."[28]

In both the difficulties and joys of young motherhood Harriet was supported by her help, Anna Smith, a recently arrived English immigrant whom Harriet treated more as a sister than a domestic servant. Anna responded with a passionate loyalty. Anna joined the Stowe household in 1836, the year Stowe married and gave birth to twins. Anna was nineteen, Harriet twenty-five. The complex and interchangeable roles they assumed vis-à-vis one another are described in a letter Anna wrote her three years later:

My Dear Mama

You are only about 7 years older than me but I have as much right to call you Mother as you have to call me your oldest daughter it is very convenient to have 2 Mothers I think little Hatty and I are very well off in that respect I wish I could see you for just half an hour I would get you to sit down in the rocking chair and then I would fix your curls and brush your hair and make you feel very sleepy and comfortable and when your eyes were about half shut I would steal such a good kiss.[29]

Anna claimed Harriet as her mother, while at the same time acting as mother to Harriet's child Hatty—a vicarious doubling and identification across class lines. And most striking, while Anna dubbed herself Harriet's "oldest daughter," she as servant ministered to her mistress's personal needs, thus turning the "mother" into her child–lover. The intensity of Anna's bond with Harriet appears to have arisen in part out of their closeness in age and temperament. Like her mistress, Anna was confident, energetic, and spunky, more interested in the quality of human interactions than in the maintenance of a strict household regimen. By far their strongest bond, however, developed from their common mothering of Stowe's children. In Harriet's place Anna acted and responded much as Harriet herself would have done, in regard to both her children and the mothers' network of which Stowe was a part. When Harriet was in Chillicothe visiting her brother George, Anna reported that Mrs. Allen, Harriet's neighbor and the wife of a professor at Lane Seminary, had been to town and had taken the time to stop in and see Harriet's baby Frederick, who had been placed with a wet nurse in the city. "[F]or my part I like her a whole degreee more than I did before," Anna told Harriet.[30] A good vicarious mother, Anna liked Mrs. Allen for the care she exhibited toward Harriet's baby, much as the bonds between the two professors' wives were strengthened by their mutual solicitude for one another's children. On another occasion Anna recorded in loving detail and with a mother's ear all the new words of baby Henry—and told them to the absent mother, who thereby knew that in her absence her baby had been mothered (so well that one wonders who, indeed, was the vicarious mother, servant Anna or mother Harriet?).[31]

If Anna took on her mistress's roles, she also assumed some familiar prerogatives of her master. Much as Calvin Stowe did, Anna both supported Harriet's literary chareer and chided her for neglecting her health. "I hope you won't try to write more than one piece in a month for Mr Godey," Anna advised in 1839. "[I]f you do you will make yourself sick and you know you traveled for your health and not to get money. I wish the Lady's Book would come I want to see your story very much."[32] Her passionate attachment to her mistress drew the banter of the other servants, as Anna recounted:

I hope you will write again very soon I shall want another letter in a week Anne says I shall read this that came yesterday all up Jane says I shall look a hole through it. Mary Anna says Oh that precious letter they laught at me but I don't care when I get another they may laught more Mary Anna thinks that nobody can love each other much but husbands & wives but I know better than that.[33]

While Harriet remained in touch with Anna Smith long after she had left her employ, nowhere does she express a passion comparable to these expressions of love. But, then, rarely did she express her passionate feelings to anyone, even to Calvin.

In the fall of 1841 came the news of the death of Harriet's maternal grandmother, Roxana Foote. The passing of this link to her mother stimulated Harriet's mind and pen to a rich remembrance. "It is now about twenty-four years or so since I first came a little bit thing to Nut Plains—draped in mourning for my dear mother," she told Harriet Foote, "& I remember the first evening after I got there that Grandmama took me into her lap & cried & I wondered what made a great grown up woman cry to see me." As she remembered her own childhood and surveyed the children she now had, she linked her past and her present through the parlor culture in which both participated:

I remember as plain as if it was yesterday the great parlour where we used to sit & where you taught me to sew & to knit, where I executed a most miraculous garter & a stocking that you said grew wider & wider till it was almost big enough for Mammy Ward—My little Hatty is now exactly the same age that I then was & as she trots about hither & thither I think "was I ever such a little silly concern myself?"—Upon reflection I am convinced that I must have been a more tractable subject than she is, for I should as soon think of teaching a grasshopper to knit as she & as to sewing though she is very much in earnest to sew yet her utmost skill consists in puckering a piece of cloth into some most unheard of shape & then fussing & crying because her needle wont go through—Eliza & she & Henry keep up a Castle Misrule in the nursery where they read sing, have prayers, preach, say their letters keep school wash Carlo's face & comb his hair & pull his tail, & do everything that ever a patient dog allowed—They are rosy & healthy & tho backward in the useful arts of reading knitting & sewing I do not much grieve because I think life is long enough for them to learn all that there is any need of knowing and I am desirous that they should have a good growth of body first of all—Next year, if they live, will be time enough for commencing their education—As to my baby little Frederick William 1st he is in the city with a very good woman who can give him that which his mother cannot—& altho he was very puny he is growing into a fine little baby. He will be one year old on the sixth of May next & looks as much like the other children as one pea does to another.[34]

That winter Harriet described as "the very pleasantest" of her marriage thus far; a good portion of the pleasure came from the continuation of her parlor education. In January 1841 Harriet described for the Beecher family a familiar scene: "We have generally sewed in day time & read & studied in evening We have been reading Combe's physiological works & looking at some elegant anatomical plates out of the library & we are now commencing Robertson's Chart[s of the China Navigation]."[35] Calvin Stowe's vast scholarship and Harriet Beecher's seminary education made such evenings highly instructive. She turned to him for information, relying on his scholarly command to direct her to sources she used in her writing. He relied on her narrative skill and attention to detail to enliven his journalistic pieces and biblical lectures. Harriet once likened her scholar-husband to a cormorant, putting more and more learning into his bottomless bill; but while he was content to store knowledge, Harriet fashioned information into useful articles, editorials, stories that would touch a nerve in the reading public.[36] Calvin's marriage to Lyman Beecher's daughter was in part inspired by his admiration for the practical energy and confidence he himself lacked. When strangers admired his flock of children, he was known to remark proudly, "Yes, Beechers, every one of them." With his support and encouragement, Harriet became "a literary woman."

CHAPTER THIRTEEN

A Literary Woman: 1839–1843

*H*arriet Beecher Stowe's initial publications had been in the *Western Monthly Magazine*, which specialized in stories of self-made men who built the West while they built their fortunes. Between 1833 and 1834 she published five stories and sketches in James Hall's magazine. While becoming a westerner was an important step on her way to reaching a national audience, Stowe's literary power intensified when she began writing for Sarah Hale's *Godey's Lady's Book*, self-described as "a proud monument reared by the Ladies of America as a testimony of their own worth."[1] Beginning in 1839 with "Trials of a Housekeeper," Stowe published at least eight stories in *Godey's Lady's Book* during the three following years.

During the same period she began publishing in the *New-York Evangelist*, a weekly devoted to news about revivals, Sunday schools, and temperance societies. Her contributions alternated between morally instructive stories, such as the temperance tale "The Drunkard Reclaimed," to what are billed as "Parables," short homilies on Christian themes. All the elements she would later meld into a powerful mixture in *Uncle Tom's Cabin* are present in her periodical publications of the 1830s and 40s: the impulse to instruct, to use fiction as a vehicle for moral and cultural reformation, to write of domestic doings and sayings. But her audience was split: in one voice she addressed an audience of western pioneers, presumably men; in another she wrote domestic stories for the *Lady's Book*; in yet a third she addressed a Christian public in the *New-York Evangelist*. Not until she intertwined domesticity, religion, and reform in a national canvas would she have the range demonstrated in *Uncle Tom's Cabin*.

Even so, there are early indications of her impulse to merge her several audiences. "Uncle Enoch," one of her temperance tales for the *New-York Evangelist*, paid particular attention to women at a time when drunkenness was assumed to be a male problem. Uncle Enoch remarks, "A she drunkard is about the worst two-legged thing I know of, and there is a good many more of them in every place, than most persons think for."[2] At the same time, this tale appeals to the spirit of American inventiveness and go-ahead, compatible with the spirit of the *Western Monthly*. Uncle Enoch makes a speech lauding the temperance society as a "new plan":

> "We live in a country where they are continually finding out new things, and when a man has invented a new machine, if it's useful, we praise him and pay him too. Now if they have found out a way that will stop the increase of drunkards, if it appears to be a good invention, let us try it, especially as it don't cost any thing. I'm for trying it, as [it] was the patent rake that saved me the work of ten men. I want to see if it won't save money, and characters, and lives."[3]

Uncle Enoch's colloquial speech lends authority to his remarks, and couching temperance in terms of pragmatism and American ingenuity tagged the reform onto well-established cultural values. Stowe was "working" her audience like a revival preacher.

Indeed, her temperance tales may be seen as her homage to her father. Lyman Beecher had made a national splash by publishing *Six Sermons on Intemperance* in 1826. While scattered attempts at temperance reform had been made in the previous decade, the publication of Beecher's *Six Sermons* was the bugle blast of the national campaign against the staggering quantities of alcohol consumed in the early republic. In 1830 the consumption of absolute alchohol was 3.9 gallons per capita of total population—almost twice the level consumed in 1975.[4] Denouncing drunkenness as "a national sin," Beecher had sketched the consequences in terms of lost labor, broken homes, and wasted lives. Harriet Beecher Stowe fleshed out the details, created characters and situations, and, in "Uncle Enoch," a believable voice. Her training as a schoolteacher attuned her to the importance of catching her audience, and she knew many ways to engage the reader's ear. Using the *New-York Evangelist* as her pulpit, she mixed cultural reformation with individual salvation, linking both with an American ideology of self-help that, strictly speaking, a good Calvinist had no business embracing. In this she was in the vanguard of the temperance movement, which would take off in Cincinnati five years later, propelled by the self-help societies of artisans and shopkeepers who called themselves the Washingtonians. While her father had popularized an issue that would dominate nineteenth-century reform, he nevertheless cast temperance in aristocratic terms that neutralized its potential. Fearing the mob, hostile to the Catholic immigrants with their love of beer, Lyman Beecher preached temperance for *others*.[5] Using the colloquial voice of Uncle Enoch, Harriet deftly democratized and American-ized the issue.

In his newspaper days Walt Whitman likewise wrote a temperance tale— *Franklin Evans*—an unmemorable piece of boilerplate with stock situations and undeveloped characters. That Stowe had more novelistic talent—as well as more investment in reform—is clear in both "The Drunkard Reclaimed" and "Uncle Enoch." The former was republished in Stowe's *The Mayflower* under the title "Let Every Man Mind His Own Business," but "Uncle Enoch" is more original, carried along by the distinctive voice of Uncle Enoch. Both Whitman and Stowe came into their own during what critic F. O. Matthies-sen has called "The American Renaissance," that flowering of a national literature in the 1850s. Likewise, both experienced a personal rebirth between the earlier, relatively uninspired writing they did for periodicals and the visionary work for which they are remembered. But just as surely, their apprenticeship in the periodical literature of the 1840s was critical to their success in finding a national voice in which to speak.[6]

The *Lady's Book* introduced Stowe to an audience she would have par-ticular sympathies with: the women of America. Under the editorship of Sarah Josepha Hale, the *Lady's Book* became "the arbiter of the parlor, the textbook of the kitchen," reaching a circulation of 150,000 by midcentury.[7] It had its beginnings as the *Ladies' Magazine*, published in Boston between 1828 and 1836. After the great success of her first novel, *Northwood* (1827), Sarah Josepha Hale received a proposal to become the editor of a new mag-azine that would address exclusively the ladies of America. She accepted, having learned after the death of her husband nine years into their marriage some harsh realities of being a woman. Under her leadership the *Ladies' Magazine* championed such causes as improved working conditions for women, women's education, and married women's property rights. "The wish to promote the reputation of my own sex," she wrote, "was among the earliest mental emotions I can recollect."[8] In 1836 she merged her *Magazine* with a new venture of Louis Godey, who had the entrepreneurial talents and style of P. T. Barnum. This merger resulted in a phenomenally successful national magazine—the first of its kind.

At this time most American journals simply pirated material from English books and periodicals. The stories that began appearing in the 1830s in the *Token*, the *Pioneer*, and *Graham's Magazine* under the names of Nathaniel Hawthorne and Edgar Allan Poe were the exceptions. International copy-right laws would not be established until 1891, and filling up entire American journals with borrowed English fare was simpler and cheaper than support-ing American writers. This was the policy of Louis Godey until Sarah Hale took over the editorship with the January 1836 issue of *Godey's Magazine and Ladies' Book*. From this time forward, the promotion of American writers and American materials became the special distinction of the *Lady's Book*, proclaimed boldly on the back covers:

THE BOOK OF THE NATION
THE OLDEST MAGAZINE IN AMERICA
DEVOTED TO
AMERICAN ENTERPRISE, AMERICAN WRITERS, AND AMERICAN ARTISTS

The phrase appearing after a title, "Written expressly for the *Lady's Book*," called attention to the original material appearing in Mr. Godey's pages. The stimulus that the *Lady's Book* provided to indigenous American literature has not been fully appreciated; given the nature of the magazine and its audience, this stimulus was applied particularly to *women* writers. Moreover, Godey was the first publisher to *pay* authors for their work.[9] This was an important consideration for Harriet Beecher Stowe.

Harriet tasted the fruits of her literary labors in 1838 when Carey and Hart, Philadelphia publishers, notified her that they intended to send her $40 for a story she had written the previous year. "[T]his money Mr Stowe says he shall leave me to use for my personal gratification," Harriet told her sister-in-law, "as if a wife & mother had any gratification apart from her family interests."[10] The uncertain prospects of Lane Seminary, hard hit by the negative publicity surrounding the Lane Debates, were on Harriet's mind as 1838 drew to a close. "We are rather better in that we now know *exactly* the state of our accts—We are in debt—& embarrassed but have good hope by management to pay off—But few students—traveling expences great—cant afford to come from the east & not many to be found in this ungodly west—Must retrench."[11] As the fortunes of Lane Seminary tottered, Calvin Stowe's promised salary of $1,200 shrank to $1,100. This was the first of several retrenchment bites that would reduce his salary by about half the amount the board had originally agreed to pay him. To make up the shortfall, Calvin and Harriet counted increasingly on the extra $200–300 she could bring in through her writing. Harriet had written to Mary Dutton, "if you see my name coming out every where, you may be sure of one thing, that I *do* it for *the pay*." *Godey's Lady's Book* paid her $15 a page, which was "making money fast," as Calvin observed.[12]

To a greater extent than the *Western Monthly Magazine* or the *New-York Evangelist*, *Godey's Lady's Book* provided a forum from which Stowe could speak broadly, in spite of the presumed audience of "ladies." Men as well as women wrote for the *Lady's Book*: the 1840 volume sported stories by Harriet's brother Charles as well as by T. S. Arthur and James T. Fields, and Harriet interrupted one of her stories to address a comment to "our gentlemen readers."[13] Other evidence that Stowe's audience included men is suggested by her "Sketches from the Note Book of an Old Gentleman." Not only in her adoption of a male persona but also in her subject matter—recollections of growing up in Puritan New England—these sketches bear the imprint of the Semi-Colon Club; their origin in the parlor is the key not only to their ready acceptance at the *Lady's Book*, but also to their appeal to a diverse audience of both men and women. Indeed, Stowe drew on one of these sketches, "The Old Meeting-House," for Chapter 5 of *Oldtown Folks*, published in 1869 when Stowe was at the peak of her national reputation.[14]

Sarah Hale ascended to the *Lady's Book* one year before Queen Victoria ascended the throne, and both reigns were part of the dominance of institutions over which women presided: the home, motherhood, and the parlor. Through the periodical press, these institutions were exerting increasing influence over the tenor of public debate. In "The Canal Boat," an amusing sketch published in the *Lady's Book* in 1841, Stowe mischievously observed that the sex-segregated sleeping quarters aboard the canal boat were invaded by shoes of the opposite sex: "Let us not intimate how ladies' shoes have, in a night, clandestinely slid into the gentlemen's cabin, and gentlemen's boots elbowed, or, rather, *toed* their way among the ladies' gear."[15] The parlor and the magazines that issued from the parlor were like the ladies' shoes: they slid into a public space that was just opening up, through the new institution of the periodical press.

Consistent with Sarah Hale's policy of promoting the interests of her sex, Stowe used the *Lady's Book* to address women on temperance. In "The Coral Ring,"[16] she addressed women not as victims of drunken husbands, but rather as potential wielders of *female influence*. Florence Elmore is a wealthy, pampered, twenty-year-old who has no thought but for her own amusement. One day, however, her bachelor cousin has a serious talk with her about her self-absorbed existence. Bridling under his words that she is "only a parlor ornament," she resolves to make a difference in the world. Using her female influence, she prevails upon a man of her circle to sign the temperance pledge.

Besides helping her to focus her attention on women's issues, *Godey's Lady's Book* brought Stowe onto the ground floor of a publication that was determined to have a national voice in the shaping of American literature. Was she ambivalent about stepping out of the private sphere into the public eye? She had been content to let Catharine put her name to a number of her earlier writings, but at this stage in her career she was more assertive. While many of the writers for the *New-York Evangelist* signed only their initials to their work, Harriet's commonly appeared under her full name, Mrs. H. E. Beecher Stowe. She was enough of a propagandist to know what each of those names, "Beecher" and "Stowe," conjured in the way of authority and expectations, and she meant to use their influence.

In 1842 she was approached by Harper Brothers of Boston about the possibility of bringing out a collection of her short stories. For an American author to have a *book* published under her name was extraordinary recognition. In April Harriet gathered up her clothes, her manuscripts, and her daughter Hatty, and departed for Boston, full of the importance of this event. Her growing sense of professional identity is evident in the letters she wrote home to Calvin. Determined to collect all the money that was due her for her work, she consulted her brother-in-law, Thomas Perkins, an attorney, about ways to bring pressue to bear on recalcitrant publishers: "[H]e says if

Williams offered to pay me an equal compensation to the writers in the North
American, that the amount of that can easily be estimated & he is legally
bound for the sum," she wrote Calvin, requesting that "[i]f Williams letter
is not among your papers you must get Anna to look over all mine in the
sideboard drawer & in my bureau & see if it is there."[17] Not all publishers
were so difficult:

> I have seen Johnson of the "Evangelist." He is very liberally disposed, and I
> may safely reckon on being paid for all I do there. Who is that Hale, Jr., that
> sent me the "Boston Miscellany," and will he keep his word with me? His offers
> are very liberal—twenty dollars for three pages, not very close print. Is he to
> be depended on? If so, it is the best offer I have received yet. I shall get some-
> thing from the Harpers some time this winter or spring. Robertson, the pub-
> lisher here, says the book will sell, and, though the terms they offer me are
> very low, that I shall make something on it. For a second volume I shall be
> able to make better terms. On the whole, my dear, if I choose to be a literary
> lady, I have, I think, as good a chance of making profit by it as any one I
> know of.[18]

Calvin's response to this letter rode over the small questions of information
she had referred to him, and underlined her destiny. He told her:

> You must be a *literary woman*. It is so written in the book of fate. Make all
> your calculations accordingly, get a good stock of health, brush up your mind,
> drop the E out of your name, which only encumbers it and stops the flow and
> euphony, and write yourself only and always, *Harriet Beecher Stowe*, which is
> a name euphonous, flowing, and full of meaning; and my word for it, your
> husband will lift up his head in the gate, and your children will rise up and
> call you blessed.[19]

His spontaneous liturgy points not only to Harriet's prophetic career, but
also to the transformation that the companionate marriage was effecting
within households. "Your children will rise up and call you blessed" was a
biblical phrase commonly invoked to undergird the traditional expectations
of nineteenth-century motherhood; that Calvin Stowe used it to bless not
Harriet's domestic activities but her literary life suggests that women's place
and mission were wider than the cult of domesticity supposed. Without comment, he changed her "literary lady" into "literary woman" and proceeded to
baptize the former Mrs. H. E. Beecher Stowe into her literary identity, Harriet Beecher Stowe.

For Calvin, there were some immediate benefits to Harriet's being in
demand. He wrote her of the peace that had descended on the household
upon her departure. "[H]ow like clock work we get along in the family," he
crowed, "Aunt Esther sweeps and dusts my study every morning, and makes
it look so neat and nice, and keeps the front entry so clean and in such good
order, that I have no temptation to be cross. You have no idea how many of
my temptations to ill-humor arise from seeing my room unswept and things
about house out of place." But in the same letter he told her he missed the
good talks they had together in their chamber, she with her arms around his

neck, he with his arms around her waist: "I begin to find out, (what I knew very well before), that you are the most intelligent and agreeable woman in the whole circle of my acquaintance."[20] As April stretched into May and May into June, his admiration for his wife's talents shone more brightly than the discomforts of daily life with her:

> Who else has so much talent with so little self-conceit, so much reputation with so little affectation, so much literature with so little nonsense, so much enterprise with so little extravagance, so much to give with so little scold, so much sweetness with so little soft tommy, so much of so many some things with so little of many other things? Come, come, my sister, my spouse, my undefiled, and let us again read Solomon's Song together as in the days of our first espousals.

He urged her to come home "just as soon as you can," and, he promised in the words of their four-year-old, Henry, "I w-i-i-i-i-i-ll be g-o-o-o-o-o-d."[21] But Harriet did not come home until September.

Now that there was a distinct possibility that she might become a literary woman, Harriet expressed some ambivalence. "Our children are just coming to the age when everything depends on my efforts," she wrote Calvin. "They are delicate in health, and nervous and excitable, and need a mother's whole attention. Can I lawfully divide my attention by literary efforts?" But having raised this imponderable question, she tacitly set it aside: "There is one thing I must suggest. If I am to write, I must have a room to myself, which shall be *my* room." Anticipating by almost a century Virginia Woolf's observation that "a room of one's own" is essential for the woman writer, Harriet plunged ahead with the practical arrangements: "I have in my own mind pitched on Mrs. Whipple's room. I can put a stove in it. I have bought a cheap carpet for it, and I have furniture enough at home to furnish it comfortably, and I only beg in addition that you will let me change the glass door from the nursery into that room and keep my plants there, and then I shall be quite happy."[22] It surely did not escape Calvin's notice that even this seeming focusing of his wife's energies resulted in characteristic expenditure, accumulation of goods, and transformations of domestic space. Yet her destiny as a Beecher dazzled him, drew him in, just as Lyman Beecher had drawn him into his ill-fated plans for Lane Seminary. He replied to her letter by counting up her prospects: "You have written for the Evangelist, as near as I can make it out, between four and five columns, enough to make between 20 & 25 dollars. Why don't you write some more? We look in every paper for a piece from you."[23] A column of print in the *New-York Evangelist* was two feet long and contained a thousand words; that put her pay at a penny a word. Compared to the many hundreds of stitches in a pair of trousers, for which product women got between six and ten cents, this was good pay indeed.[24] But Calvin Stowe's main concern was not with money but with the influence she could wield over the culture; it was the same Beecheresque plan that had drawn him in Lyman Beecher's wake to the West: Beecher's vehicle was the pulpit and the schools; hers would be the periodical press: "You have it in your power, by means of that little magazine [the Souvenir] to form the mind of the West for the coming generation. It is just as I told you in my first letter, God has written it in his book, that you must be a literary woman, and who are we that we should contend against God? You must make all your calculations to spend the rest of your days with your pen."[25]

Harriet's calculations were much more shrouded in modesty and indirection in her letters to the Beecher family. In a circular letter written while she was in the East, Harriet struck a very different tone from the businesslike tattoo of her letters to her husband: "There is also a work to be expected from the press of Harper & Brothers from the pen of Professor Stowe's wife sometime this fall," she wrote; "so Mrs. Stowe told me sometime since—but I dont trouble my head much with any of these matters having taken this summer for a play day."[26] She pulled around her the cloak of Victorian femininity. How convenient to have a husband to hide behind when it suited her. Professor Stowe's wife, indeed.

While she was in the East Harriet stayed in Hartford at her sister Mary's house, from which she sent a glowing report of Mary's success in childrearing, owing, Harriet thought, to Mary's system of paying her children for their labor in the house and garden.

> The children have all become uncommonly amiable & obliging—& I think it is in a great measure the result of education—for they were naturally just like other children—So understand all of you that while the rest of us are producing our works big & little, bound in calf morocco muslin & so on, Mary like Mrs Cornelia Graccus must bring forward *her children* as her works on education—
>
> Now as to this matter of writing on education I dont mean to do it till my children are *grown up* then if they turn out well I'l write my system for the benefit of posterity—so those of you who are waiting for my views on this subject will go on I hope as well as they can without me—I shant expect as much of you as if you had all the light I could give if I should speak out now.[27]

Harriet never did write her views of childrearing, for by the most basic yardstick her brood did not "turn out well." Of her seven children, only three survived her. Samuel Charles died in infancy, Henry drowned at nineteen, Frederick was an alcoholic from the age of sixteen, and Georgiana was addicted to morphine and died in her forties. Would they have turned out better if she had not "divid[ed her] attention by literary efforts"? Probably not, except perhaps for poor Fred, upon whom his mother's fame sat heavily. The best adjusted of the lot was her last child, Charles, who was under the care of others (Calvin, part of the time) in the 1850s while Harriet made three tours of Europe. The domestic record suggests that Harriet's literary activity was her most effective means of channeling energies that otherwise she would have jittered off into ruffling dresses and gardening and voluntary societies and travel. She could not change her temperament and her education, both of which predisposed her toward activity in the world. Neither could she control her reproductive life. It was the stuff of tragedy. Between her absentminded tending to her flock, alternating between passionate involvement with her babies and total forgetfulness of their welfare, and Calvin's frequent but unpredictable explosions of temper, the Stowe household knew none of the follow-through and security that builds strong children. Capable of throwing herself into their amusements, Harriet lacked the generalship to curb their increasingly far-reaching campaigns. The Stowes' constantly transforming household produced highly individualistic children appreciated for their high spirits and vocal abilities, but not disciplined, secure, or relaxed ones. Harriet and Calvin Stowe were early converts to the theories of George M. Beard, a popular doctor who wrote a book called *American Nervousness*—an analysis of the national predisposition to neurasthenia. They knew firsthand the entire career of American nervousness, from "Nervous dyspepsia" and "Sick-Headache" to "Hypochondria" and "Hysteria." Beard attributed American nervousness to "modern civilization," by which he meant five things: "steam- power, the periodical press, the telegraph, the sciences," and, lastly, "the mental activity of women."[28] Progress had a cost. Isabella Beecher Hooker observed of Harriet's style of household management, "the imperfections . . . are so clearly traceable to the very qualities which render her so superior to most." Isabella continued, "I never saw so many strong points in any one family—father, mother & every child have as marked & unique a character as if there were no other human being created."[29] Harriet's tolerance and encouragement of individual temperaments and peculiarities was part of her expansive and emphathetic charm, but raising a garden of eccentricities was not compatible with the smooth ticking of the domestic clock. The unsettledness of modern life and of the Stowe household in particular would have been facts whether or not Harriet Beecher Stowe became a literary woman, but her becoming so allowed the tragedies of her private life to sink deep into her being and to emerge transformed in fictions of tremendous power.

In 1843 Harper Brothers brought out Harriet's collection of stories. It was entitled *The Mayflower; or, Sketches of Scenes and Characters among the Descendants of the Pilgrims* and it gathered in one place and marketed under her name fifteen stories and sketches that had appeared variously in the *Western Monthly*, the *Lady's Book*, and the *New-York Evangelist*. They are an uneven lot, ranging from her prizewinning tale and literary landmark, here called "Uncle Tim" rather than "Uncle Lot," to treacle like "The Tea Rose." Many of them begin tentatively; as the author searched for the right note, her voice cracked, revealing her uncertain but definitive movement from the eighteenth-century male prose models of her training to the American voice she would come to own. For example, "Frankness," first published in the *Western Monthly Magazine* as "By a Lady," begins with a stilted paragraph in which two definitions of frankness are set forth in a didactic, reasonable tone like that of Addison in *The Spectator*. Stowe then undercuts this voice with a frank address to her audience: "Now, if you suppose that this is the beginning of a sermon or of a fourth of July oration, you are very much mistaken, though, I must confess, it hath rather an uncertain sound."[30] She was trying out the voices that she had heard used in public. Among her most successful pieces is "The Canal Boat," based on her firsthand observations of a means of transportation that was linking East and West in a network that would, with the rise of the railroad, become transcontinental. With a well-trained ear, she caught the rhythms of the men, women, children, babies, and nurses who were crammed in the dark quarters "under hatches": " 'We shall be smothered! we shall be crowded to death! we *can't stay* here!' are heard faintly from one and another; and yet, though the boat grows no wider, the walls no higher, they do live, and do stay there, in spite of repeated protestations to the contrary. Truly, as Sam Slick says, 'there's a *sight of wear* in human natur'.' "[31] Her western voice clearly emerges here, just as surely as Sam Clemens's would a generation later. Her ability to hear and translate local accents to a national audience was the first step toward creating a national literature. In this sense *The Mayflower* was both a tribute to her New England roots and an acknowledgment that she had pushed off from another shore.

CHAPTER FOURTEEN

Signs of the Times:
1843

O n her way to becoming one of the most popular and well-paid authors of the nineteenth century, Harriet dipped her pen in the main currents of antebellum social and religious thought. Her ability to write what her audience wanted to read—a skill honed through her magazine writing—arose from her thorough immersion in the culture of which she was a part. Her life during the 1840s, on the surface a dreary record of illness, death, and small domestic defeats, was in fact a crucial time of spiritual transformation. Her passage through a religious experience fraught with millennial expectation placed her at the center of the cultural ferment of the 1840s, a decade filled with schemes secular and religious for the Total Improvement of Humanity. These ranged from the dietary fads of Sylvester Graham—adopted by Catharine Beecher at the Hartford Female Seminary—to temperance, revivalism, and the utopian communities of visionaries such as John Humphrey Noyes, who propounded at his Oneida Community a system of "complex marriage" in which every woman was the wife of every man in the community and vice versa. Such bold sexual schemes were outside the venue of the children of Lyman and Roxana Beecher, yet many of them experimented with new ideas. Edward Beecher became convinced of the pre-existence of souls—an idea dear to Mormon thought—and all of the Beecher children distanced themselves from the gloomy Calvinism of Lyman Beecher's sledgehammer sermons. Charles found it necessary to separate himself geographically from the family and took a job in a countinghouse in New Orleans, whence he sent reports of commercial slave trading that would later make their way into Harriet's fiction. Harriet and Calvin's adoption of sexual abstinence—to spare her from what still turned out to be closely spaced pregnancies—may be connected to the self-improvement schemes of utopian reformers, many of whom had ideas for new sexual arrangements; at Fruitlands, the short-lived experiment of Bronson Alcott, the community members eschewed all sexual contact, even between married couples. Such new ideas were motivated, as was temperance reform, the water cure, and dietary reform, by the belief that through self-regulation a more-perfect social order could be brought into being on earth. Stimulated not by Lyman Beecher's sermons but by the perfectionist striving of the age, Harriet Beecher Stowe somewhat paradoxically experienced what her father had always wanted for her and his other children: a real conversion experience.

The family story of Harriet Beecher's conversion at the age of thirteen portrays a rather mild affair in which the schoolgirl announced to Lyman Beecher after hearing one of his sermons that "I have given myself to Jesus, and he has taken me." It is likely that Harriet, eager to please and quite aware of the pressure and torment Catharine had suffered at her father's hands when she refused to submit to religious expectation, took her conversion much as one takes an innoculation: to save the trouble of the real thing. The pro forma nature of Harriet's early religious experience is, in the family biographies, somewhat obscured by the criticism of Calvinism in which it is encased. The interest of the story quickly shifts to the aftermath, when a clerical friend of her father questioned her minutely to determine whether the character of her experience qualified it as a bona fide conversion. This interrogation by the Rev. Joel Hawes reportedly took the religious pleasure out of the experience and "fixed the child's attention on the morbid and oversensitive workings of her own heart."[1] This aftermath may rightly be taken as a formative experience in Stowe's critique of Calvinism. As the evangelical emphasis on "experiential" religion and the necessity for a "second birth" became matters of dogma rather than experience, the conversion process was codified into a set formula and then held up as a yardstick against which to measure individual religious experiences. "Even her sister Catharine," the family story goes, "was afraid that there might be something wrong in the case of a lamb that had come into the fold without being first chased all over the lot by the shepherd; great stress being laid, in those days, on what was called 'being under conviction.' "[2] This version of Harriet's experience was recorded in 1889 in her authorized biography written by her son Charles. Calvinism had been long in decline by this time; the more developmental approach to Christianity that superseded it— explicated in Horace Bushnell's *Christian Nurture* (1861)—is reflected in Charles Stowe's sympathetic commentary on the young Harriet's religious experience. "If she could have been let alone," he wrote, "and taught 'to look up and not down, forward and not back, out and not in,' this religious experience might have gone on as sweetly and naturally as the opening of a flower in the gentle rays of the sun."[3]

This post-Calvinistic rendering of Harriet Beecher's religious experience obscures the extent to which Stowe herself was caught up in the Calvinist expectations of her age. Her story was not that of a smooth development from the converted schoolgirl into the mature woman who wrote *Uncle Tom's Cabin*, but rather a rough and stormy passage in which Harriet Beecher Stowe sought her religious identity in a society that had strong prescriptions both for Christians and for women. In some of her most powerful writing, Harriet Beecher Stowe would draw on the politics and experience of women's culture to challenge Calvinism's institutionalization of spiritual life and to recall evangelicals to the experiential religion they had once championed. Nevertheless, Joel Hawes was right—for reasons he could not fathom: Harriet Beecher's conversion at age thirteen was *not* sufficient to her adult spirituality, not because it fell short of the formula but because it left her heart wanting. Eighteen years later she found herself yearning for something deeper and richer, "a baptism of the spirit." The rebirth that she experienced in her thirties resolved the contradictions between expectation and reality in her image of herself as a woman and as a Christian. It replaced an unrealistic doctrine of perfection with a gospel of suffering that united her experience as a woman with that of an oppressed slave and a suffering Messiah.[4]

This religious experience took place at a time of cultural transformation when orthodox Calvinism was under attack from all sides, but most insidiously from the doctrine called "perfection." Popularized by Charles Grandison Finney and sometimes called "Oberlinism" after the college where he was president, this doctrine turned on its head the Calvinist notion of original sin and held that mortals could become perfect in this life. Whereas Calvinism held that one's "election" was predestined, emphasizing human depravity and the necessity of God's freely given grace, perfectionism put much of the burden of salvation on human effort. Lyman Beecher preached against this doctrine, but his brand of Calvinism, by opening the door for the exercise of free will, let perfectionism sweep in behind. In a period of evangelical energy during which reformers planted colleges, schools, temperance societies, and Sunday schools throughout the nation, perfectionism had a strong appeal; harnessed to reform energies at Oberlin, it brought moral pressure to bear against human outrages like the institution of slavery. It also encouraged individuals to bring an intensity to bear on their mortal lives that was, in some cases, intolerable. In this last respect it was continuous with Calvinism's intense introspection, criticized by Charles Stowe for turning his mother's childhood conversion into a scrutiny of "the morbid and over-sensitive workings of her own heart."[5] Turned outward on the world, perfectionism supported utopian communities and radical reforms like the abolition of slavery; turned inward on the self, perfectionism had enormous potential for self-destruction.

The self-destructive potential of perfectionism was magnified in the case of women by the ideology that restricted them to the private sphere; energies that might have been directed outward on the world were turned inward, just as in the 1980s, Joan Jacobs Brumberg has argued, eating disorders among young women may be understood as a secular form of perfectionism directed at the self.[6] For nineteenth-century middle-class women, perfectionism was both a social and a religious prescription in which women's domestic roles were closely linked with expectations of their piety.[7] Harriet Beecher Stowe was at particular risk from the self-destructive potential of perfectionism because of the saintly example of her mother. The Roxana Beecher whom Harriet knew through family tradition met the standards for womanly perfection—as a real mother could not.

While her childhood was shaped by the invocation of this perfect, self-denying mother, Harriet entered upon wifehood and motherhood just as the angel in the house was being institutionalized as the model of domesticity. The Victorian home was the storm center of a changing culture, and the Victorian mother was expected to harmonize both the conflicting temperaments of family members and the accumulated stresses of the emerging industrial order. "[It] drinks up all my strength to care for & provide for all this family," Harriet complained to Calvin, "to try to cure the faults of all—harmonise all—alas it is too much for me & an aching head & heart often show it."[8] This was perhaps the most stressful of all of her assignments, for as her consciousness was tattered by a thousand daily cares, she was to be the knitter-up of other peoples' days and ways. She complained to her daughters, "a word spoken harshly by any one to any other grates on me—I bear the blame of all—I feel for each & this tires me & wears me out more than writing or housekeeping."[9] In contrast to the eulogies of Roxana to which Harriet was treated by her father, her marriage to Calvin Stowe was punctuated by a continuous struggle, particularly marked in the decade of the 1840s, over housekeeping, bookkeeping, expenses, and domestic management, exacerbated by their attempts to limit their family through sexual abstinence.[10] "Harriet is not very well as to *nerves*," Catharine Beecher observed in 1839.[11]

Standards for housekeepers—like those for religious seekers—were being codified at this time; in 1841 Catharine Beecher published her widely read *Treatise on Domestic Economy*, in which she devoted an entire chapter to "The Preservation of a Good Temper in a Housekeeper." There she observed,

> It is probable that there is no class of persons, in the world, who have such incessant trials of temper, and such temptation to be fretful, as American housekeepers. For a housekeeper's business is not like that of the other sex, limited to a particular department, for which previous preparation is made. It consists of ten thousand little disconnected items, which can never be so systematically arranged, that there is no daily jostling, somewhere.[12]

Catharine was quick with suggestions for the harried housekeeper: "In the first place, a woman, who has charge of a large household, should regard her duties as dignified, important, and difficult." In the second place, she counseled the housekeeper "deliberately to calculate on having her best-arranged plans interfered with, very often."[13] Thus in addition to bearing the responsibility for making things right, the housekeeper was to expect to fail and to exercise the strictest control over her own feelings of disappointment and anger when this occurred. Under this conflicting set of demands, it is hard to imagine what perfection might look like.

While such tensions simmered in the home, they were intensified by developments in the public sphere. The heightening of religious expectations was evident in the revivals that swept over the towns of the West like prairie fires. In Cincinnati in January 1840 the Methodist preacher James C. Moffat drew large crowds; Isabella Beecher observed, he "is stirring the whole city with his *eloquence* as some say, but more with his oddity & excitement, I think."[14] Lyman Beecher and his sons did not stand idle on the harvest plain. From Batavia, New York, in the heart of what was called the "burned over" district because so many revivals had swept through, William Beecher's wife wrote "We are greatly in hopes that this place is about to witness another revival. . . . do pray for us, that the showers of divine grace, which are falling all around us in this region may not be withheld from this still very wicked place."[15] Henry Ward Beecher reported to his father on the revival in Lafayette, Indiana: "[T]ruly a wonderful work . . . between 60 & 70 conversions in three weeks I was there," signing his letter, "From the battlefield."[16] Harriet saw signs in Cincinnati that a revival would follow on the heels of temperance activity. "I have felt a presentiment of all this for a long time in deep & earnest desires for it which have sometimes been unutterable & other christians have felt the same."[17]

The hopeful watching and waiting intensified during the winter of 1842–1843, and the strain of this contributed to overwork on the part of the Beechers and illness among overwrought congregations. "We have had so much sickness in the family the past winter—and so much sewing & visiting & preaching & going to meetings of different sorts that I do not think I was ever more occupied," wrote William's wife.[18] George Beecher wrote from Chillicothe in January 1843 that his wife Sarah had been sick for four weeks; she was unable to eat and had severe diarrhea; at one point George "feared she would not recover." When the hired girl, "worn down by overwork anxiety & watching," came down with a "bilious fever," George had to take care of the baby, just weaned, and "to make fires cook & attend to everything besides having three or four meetings a week besides the Sabbath."[19] The winter of 1843 was by all the Beecher family accounts one of repeated, prolonged, and severe illness. The rash of revivals that accompanied it was both cause and effect, as the body and the soul burned in feverish anticipation of a better world.

For the less religiously inclined, energies spilled over in drunken and disorderly conduct. In September 1841 a race riot erupted in Cincinnati in which "a number of persons both black and white have been killed," Aunt Esther reported to the Beecher family.[20] Tensions had been high since the murder, in August, of a German farmer and the rape of a white woman—

crimes attributed to black men. Aunt Esther's account, written while the riot was still in progress and during a period in which she had not slept for three days, told of "skirmishing between the black and whites" on a Thursday, followed by a "real battle" on Friday which the civil authorities did nothing to prevent. On Saturday many blacks fled to surrounding areas for safety and those who remained were put in prison to protect them. When a mob gathered and threatened to storm the jail, "a strong guard of citizens and military" intervened. The mob then attacked the "property of abolitionists and negroes demolishing windows doors and furniture" and "then broke into the office of the Philanthropist and destroyed all they could lay hands on." It was a reprise of the 1835 mob action; like that mob, it was "composed of the most degraded portion of the community," led on, it was rumored, by Kentuckians avenging the support given to runaway slaves by "persons in the city." This time, however, the mob threatened to come out to Walnut Hills. After the raid on the office of the Philanthropist "the cry was raised Now for Lane Seminary." The Beechers braced for the assault, and defensive measures were taken: while large companies of armed citizens patrolled the streets of the city, the passes by which the mob could approach Lane were guarded by horsemen; a company of fifty armed and mounted citizens came out to guard the seminary. But the mob was too tired to attack this point on the outskirts of the city, and Lane was spared.

As people searched for explanations for financial crises, drunkenness, disease, and death, they sometimes found it quite comforting to look toward the Second Coming of Christ, an event that would both explain the rash of disasters and herald their end. The widely publicized predictions of William Miller, a revivalist convinced that the end of the world was at hand, increased the millennial expectation. "Soon, very soon God will arise in his anger and the vine of the earth will be reaped," he preached in his calm voice. Epidemics of disease were evidence that God's wrath was rising: "See! See!—the angel with his sharp sickle is about to take the field! See yonder trembling victims fall before his pestilential breath! High and low, rich and poor, trembling and falling before the appalling grave, the dreadful cholera."[21] Unknown in the Western hemisphere until the nineteenth century, cholera invaded suddenly, like the wrath of God, and moral explanations were more readily available than medical ones.[22] It was, to take the title of a millennialist newspaper, one of the Signs of the Times. Miller's preaching fell on fertile soil and released energies that mushroomed out of control. As 1843 drew to an end—the last "year of time" in Miller's calculations—the tension for some became insupportable. As Alice Felt Tyler has written,

> Suicides were attributed to despair over the necessity of facing the day of judgment. The state insane asylums reported the admission of several who had been crazed by fear of the end of the world. In Portsmouth, New Hampshire, a Millerite in voluminous white robes climbed a tree, tried to fly when he thought the fatal hour was near, fell, and broke his neck. A Massachusetts farmer cut his wife's throat because she refused to be converted to Millerism, and a despairing mother poisoned herself and all her children.[23]

Millennial expectations fell heaviest on those who demanded the most of themselves, and subscribers to the doctrine of perfection had a front seat. Nathaniel Hawthorne wrote a story about the search for perfection called "The Man of Adamant." Hawthorne's self-deluded protagonist won the spiritual battle but turned to stone. Those not so hardened either learned to bend, or broke. For George Beecher, who veered between strenuous attempts at spiritual perfection and plunges into fits of depression, it was to prove too much to bear. The difficult path he trod was both example and warning to his sister Harriet, who was drawn into the vortex of perfectionist striving.

William Miller's predictions were publicized widely in the Boston area while Harriet Beecher Stowe was in the East during the summer of 1842 arranging for the publication of *The Mayflower*. As she turned her face toward home and contemplated her re-entry into her turbulent family, millennial intensity mingled with her hopes for the future. She wrote to Calvin:

> Now by the grace of God I am resolved to come home & live for God— It is time to prepare to die—the lamp has not long to burn—the hour is flying—all things are sliding away & eternity is coming— Will you dear husband join with me in simplicity & earnestness to lead a new life—& to live no more as we have—allowing ourselves in sin here & there,—sorrowing with a feeble sorrow, half resolving, & again beguiled—Why look at it—Life is half gone!— What have we done?—We are both of us no longer young—We both of us have already the sentence of death in our members—The grey hair will never become black again but the black hair *will* become grey—Nay I feel in myself changes that I know will not *change back*—I see steps that I have taken downward that I shall never retrace—& are we ready to take the exceeding and eternal weight of glory— what have we done & suffered for Christ?[24]

Harriet had written letters of religious import before, but never one of such personal intensity. She was thirty-one years old—time was slipping away— perhaps only a few years remained before she followed Roxana Beecher to her reward—and what would that be? Surely she was not as good as her mother had been. Caught up in the widespread fever of religious expectation, Harriet was discontented with her former level of piety. Longing for a fiery renewal of faith, she carefully distanced herself from the heretical doctrine of perfection while eagerly embracing its emotional counterpart: "I do not believe in *perfection* in this life—but I do believe, & my thoughts have turned much to it this week, in a baptism of the spirit,—a second conversion that is to the Christian as real an advance, as his first regeneration."[25] She wrote of "the deep immortal longing" that pursues sensitive spirits—a longing that could, if no outlet were found for it, give way to "mania or moroseness."[26]

The pieces Harriet wrote for the *New-York Evangelist* during this period reveal her preoccupation with perfection and final judgment. In "The Dancing School" a mother gives in to the pleadings of her daughter for dancing lessons, against the better advice of her sister, who asks, "Could you preserve that watchfulness, self-recollection, that habit of constant readiness of death which the Savior enjoins, through such excitements?" Emerging from an overheated room after an evening of dancing, the daughter is stricken with a deadly fever. A presentiment of her daughter's imminent death is immediately superseded in the mother's mind by the more horrible thought that she will die "unprepared." The hapless mother had thought in the course of things "an acceptable time and day of salvation would come. She had not thought of this unexpected call—this coming of the Son of Man while she was not aware."[27] On the same page with this story appeared an article on William Miller's millennial predictions. In another sketch dramatizing "Old Testament Pictures," Stowe describes the appearance of the Lord to Abraham, who is greeted with the words, "I am the Almighty God! walk before me, and be thou perfect."[28]

While perfectionism drove the scrupulous to ever-more-demanding heights of self-sacrifice and self-repression, it also built up a reservoir of contrary feelings. The strain of watchfulness and self-recollection gave rise to intense longings for release. "Through the whole mass of struggling Christian mind," Harriet wrote in another piece, runs "a longing for some definite point of rest."[29] Perfectionism fed off millennial expectations in a constantly intensifying circle, winding sensitive spirits to intolerable levels of self-scrutiny and morbid watching that finally expended themselves in illness or catharsis. For some, weary of the constant struggle, despairing of victory over themselves, death appeared as a blessed deliverer.

George Beecher's interest in the doctrine of perfection had given only mild alarm to his brothers and sisters. Charles Beecher, warning him against the dangers of self-delusion and deceit, wrote to him, "That a Christian can be perfect is evident, else God commands impossibilities. Whether they ever are or not, who can decide?" Henry Ward Beecher joked, "As to perfectionism, I am not greatly troubled with the fact of it in myself, or the doctrine of it in you." He congratulated George on his prudent decision to resist publishing his views: "[A]fter we have *published*, if we do not hit exactly right, there is a vehement temptation *not* to advance, but rather to nurse and defend our published views." It was sage advice, couched in homely metaphors. "Apples that ripen early are apt to be worm-eaten, and decay early, at any rate; late fruit always keeps best. . . . I have seen men by an injudicious effort run so high up aground that there never was a tide high enough to float them again." His benediction for his brother was soon to be fulfilled in a way he could not foresee: "May God never let you run ashore until it is upon the shores of that land of peace where perplexities shall cease their tormenting flight, and all be joy!"[30]

Calvin Stowe traveled east early in September 1842 to bring Harriet home, leaving her in Buffalo with her sister Catharine. The women planned "to return more at leisure according to their strength."[31] Having been away from home since April, Harriet spiraled slowly back into her domestic orbit, staying a few days with friends, stopping in Cleveland, and then wending her way to Chillicothe to spend some time with George Beecher and his family. Formulating impromptu plans, she signaled her intent to George in a letter that specified her arrival only in terms of "Monday" or "Wednesday." George commented, "This letter has come dateless & placeless as vague & indefinite as a summer night's dream. I presume Harriet will be here to morrow within one day of the letter."[32]

When she finally returned to Walnut Hills she found her flock diminished in spirits by a series of illnesses that had fallen on Aunt Esther to nurse. The whooping cough had laid Henry and little Freddy quite low, and they were still recovering. Harriet's first act upon arriving home was to get sick herself: a mysterious nervous malady caused her to lose the use of her arms, the same malady, apparently, that had struck her sister Catharine a few months earlier. Catharine reported in early November that she had recovered the use of her hands and could sew, knit, and write as well as ever, but that Harriet had gotten worse again, "her arms . . . affected just as mine were so that she cannot do any thing with her hands."[33]

Harriet had no sooner recovered the use of her hands when the next crisis hit. In December an epidemic of typhoid turned Lane Seminary into a hospital and the houses of the professors into auxiliary nursing facilities. As of the end of the month, sixteen students had come down with the fever, one had died, and another "who for more than a month has been sick at Harriets is now near his end," Catharine reported.

> Some of Harriets & all of Prof. Allens children have had the fever too—not severely however For a fortnight all seminary exercises stopped as all the students were either nurses or patients. They appointed committees of five for each sick one who nursed & watched successively—All are now convalescent except the one who is at Harriets. The one who died was at Mr Moones.[34]

As the winter passed slowly into spring, one of the few letters Harriet wrote reflected tersely on the past events. "We, like you have had a winter of sickness & trial," she wrote to Sarah and George Beecher. "We have witnessed sickness & suffering more dreadful forms than you probably have ever seen— & death did not come among us with so gentle an aspect as with you."[35]

Then on July 1, 1843, the stunning blow fell. Catharine Beecher had arrived the night before in Chillicothe in time to join George and Sarah Beecher in family prayers, and "found all in unusual health & prosperity."[36] They had recently moved into a new house and their prospects appeared brighter than ever. George had just written exuberantly in a circular letter of his completed house and his wish that they would all come and see him that summer, concluding with an enumeration of the flowers and fruits that he was cultivating.[37] But early on Saturday morning he went out into his garden, put his double-barreled shotgun to the side of his cheek, and blew the top of his head off.

In a little volume of his writings compiled after his death by his brothers and sisters, George Beecher's "Views on Christian Perfection" appeared.[38] A tortured refutation of the doctrine of perfection, his essay includes long lists of what the Christian would have to do in order to be perfect. These perfectionist schemes, with their minute watching and examining and controlling of every stray thought and impulse, are elaborated in a detail that suggests a painful intimacy with the process; they speak eloquently of the pressures that drove George to pull the trigger.

George's death threw Harriet into a final struggle with perfectionism. "The sudden death of George shook my whole soul like an earthquake," she wrote her brother Thomas, "and as in an earthquake we know not where the ground may open next so I felt an indistinct terror as if Father brothers husband, might any or all sink next—These deep stunning agonies show us heart secrets before undreamed."[39] She wrote to her brothers and sisters,

> Is there any of us, that lives with our friends prepared for such a parting— without a moment of warning—a word of communion—a sign—a look—a farewell—I woke up last night from a troubled dream about funeral processions & accidents & alarms—& it came slowly over me, that it was so indeed, that on earth I had no more that brother—that I never should see his face, or hear his voice or exchange a word with him again & tho I have, or had, seven brothers it seemed as if it was more than I could bear. . . . Our circle has begun to break up—who shall say when it shall stop?[40]

Death and loss created special problems for nineteenth-century evangelicals. If they grieved too hard or too long, would not God think that they loved a mere mortal more than God himself? Sally Squire recorded in her diary just such an emotional dilemma after the death of her two-year-old son. Going through her "gloomy and silent" rooms and remembering the chirruping of the child that used to brighten them, she feared, "God is now saying . . . if I love God why do I mourn that his will is done? because of my wicked heart."[41] Failure to submit could lead to further chastisement. Another nineteenth-century diarist, Mary White, wrote this entry on July 2, 1842:

> My heavenly Father has been in different ways teaching me that this is not my house. . . . I have not heeded his warnings as I ought to have done. First he took my dear little Norman and laid me upon a bed of suffering for many months. He then sent whooping cough into my family and while some of the children had it lightly others were so severely ill as to cause us much solicitude. But my heart was not filled with gratitude as it should have been that they were all spared and now he has come and smitten down our healthiest and one of our loveliest ones. Oh that he would teach me the meaning of all this and help me so to profit by it that he will not need to send upon me a heavier chastisement.[42]

Coming just at that season when Harriet was filled with dissatisfaction over her Christian life, George's death fell on a soul troubled, doubting, and self-critical. Determined to profit by this warning, Harriet wrote to George's wife, Sarah,

> How different from all human wisdom is this which commands us to rejoice in suffering, as the seal of our adoption,—as a door of sympathy & communion

opened between us & a suffering saviour,—an evidence of the favour of Him who "chasteneth whom he loveth"—We will not then shrink from this, which we are warned, cannot for the present seem joyous but grievous, in hopes that afterward it shall yeild us the peaceable fruits of righteousness.

Even the fact that George gave in to depression at the moment of his seeming greatest happiness was an indication of "a special influence from the unseen world drawing & preparing him to go thither." The violent and bloody means by which he ended his life was likewise a calculation of a Calvinist God. "*Why* has God spoken to us in so decided a tone—& wrung our hearts as much by the *manner* of this event as by the death itself—Is it not his desire to produce on all of us an ineffaceable impression—to make us forever after different."[43] George's death was a very personal sign of the times, and Harriet endowed it with millennial significance: "Dear brothers, sisters, who is to be called next?—Are we ready—Have we put on the Lord Jesus?—are we all waiting with our lamp burning."[44]

Harriet's propensity to turn her letters into sermons led her brother Charles to remark that her epistles were not "the artless expression of spontaneous emotions. She is not in her letter pouring forth feeling merely because she feels it but planning by the combination of such and such feelings . . . to produce a given effect."[45] She used them as her pulpit and honed her skills in religious persuasion. As such, they afforded rich opportunities for the improvement of her readers, but only temporary relief from her loss.

This intensified her dissatisfaction with her Christian piety and put her on the same perfectionist road that proved too hard for George. "I wrote and spoke of Christ, the immovable and ever present portion, and while I wrote my heart *exulted*, yet when I had done writing all went down, as a fire burns itself out and I returned to grief and tears—Ah said I to myself, is my soul *fully* on God, to be so shaken?—I saw that my trust was *partial*,—and superficial—and that was one more element of self-discontent." While the waves of feeling washed over her, she berated herself for her inability to make "an entire IDENTITY of my will with God's." She asked herself, "Am I then a Christian?," and urged herself to submit—to give up her "seperate will" and unite her soul to Christ's; when time and again she proved incapable of such submission, she lashed herself to greater and greater efforts: "Why not?— ah why not? Words of deep meaning to any one who tries that vain experiment—Every effort breaks like a wave upon a rock—we reason reflect resolve pray weep strive love—love to despair, & all in vain—In vain I adjured my soul—Do you not *love Christ* why not then cut wholly loose from all other loves, and take his will alone."[46]

As Harriet tried to come to terms with this "bolt from heaven," she typically turned her private grief into a publication. A few months after George's death Harriet wrote to Sarah, "I was thinking of undertaking to compile a sort of memoir of George, with selections from his sermons & papers—He has been widely known & I think such a publication might be made interesting to many hearts—If you come do bring his papers with you & let us look them over & make such selections as may be suitable for this purpose."[47] *The Biographical Remains of Rev. George Beecher* was a response, as the introduction tells us, to "calls of the heart." "He is gone!—the affectionate son—the warm-hearted brother—the earnest Christian—the faithful minister; and with yearning hearts, they look around for memorials of the departed, that his spirit may yet seem to dwell among them."[48] This creation of *memorials* of the departed was one of the distinctive cultural elaborations of the nineteenth century, and women appear to have been dominant in the production of such funerary art: from braided wreaths of hair worked into intricate designs to daguerreotypes of babies in their caskets to such literary remains as Harriet compiled for her brother, the impulse to make a physical object that embodied the spirit of the departed was a spur to art. While the Calvinist theology under which they labored urged them to submit to the will of God, to accept the loss, to bring their wills into identity with that of a capricious Ruler whose sickle and sword brought a heavenly discipline, women busied themselves with *substitutes* for the departed, with consolations that were insistently material, not spiritual. For Protestants who knew nothing of Roman Catholic rites for the departed, these memorials provided opportunities for daily rituals in the home. Remembering her Litchfield childhood with the brother who was her next-oldest sibling, Harriet wrote to Sarah, "George & I were flower gatherers & garden makers together at that time—I cannot say how precious to me would be some of the plants he tended I wish also that you would give something of his to [brother] Henry for he has a longing desire to have some plant which he might nurse & cultivate for his sake."[49] As hands moved mechanically, then more purposefully and tenderly, watering plants, weaving strands of hair into braids and fashioning the braids into intricate knots and the knots into wreaths, a healing took place that was outside the discipline prescribed by Calvinism, perfectionism, or any other male theological scheme. It was a therapy, and one often closely linked with artistic creation.

Another memorial of George Beecher was the nomenclature of Harriet's fifth child. Born a few weeks after George's death, Harriet's daughter was named Georgiana May. "I did hope before her birth that I should have a little boy that I might call *George*—it seemed as if it would have been a comfort to do so—I made the nearest approach to it that I could bestowing on her the name of one of my dearest early friends." However comforting this living memorial was, the baby demanded much in the way of physical strength, and childbirth left her so feeble that she felt the weight of "every grain of dust."[50] For the next several years Harriet's health was seriously compromised by a series of miscarriages and the demands of her five small children. Striving to be a perfect wife and mother and Christian, Harriet found her efforts daily undermined by lack of sleep, physical exhaustion, sickness, and the mental distress of never being able to complete a task. "My recovery from my confinement was slow & interrupted," she continued to Sarah, my babe was eight weeks old this Tuesday & yet I am far from being fully restored. She is a dear little thing,—& I seem to love her more than any child I ever had—. . . . I am now making arrangements to fit up a room for a wet nurse for my baby—for alas after all my efforts & sufferings I am deprived of the ability to nourish her myself & she is so very dear to me that I cannot think of putting her out to nurse.[51]

The baby was colicky and Mrs. Richardson, the wet nurse, proved to "have a faculty for almost every thing else than nursing."[52] She made first-rate cornbread but she would neither care for Georgiana nor step aside so that her mother could assume control. While the nurse jealously guarded her position, Harriet feared to provoke a confrontation, torn between worry over the baby's welfare and the knowledge that she herself could not nurse it. In the winter after George's death Harriet was pushed to the limit of her physical and spiritual resources. "I often day & night was haunted & pursued by care that seemed to drink my life blood," she wrote:

[A] feeble sickly child a passionate unstable nurse, with whom I feared to leave it from whom I feared to withdraw it—slowly withering in my arms & yet I exerting my utmost care for it in vain—harrassed, anxious, I often wondered why God would press my soul longing for reunion with a weight of cares that seemed to hold it prostrate on the earth—I felt alone unsupported—& whom in former times I had found *very* present seemed to leave me entirely.[53]

Soon after this experience of total helplessness—within the sphere over which women were supposed to rule—Stowe ceased her perfectionist striving; at that moment she was washed, exhausted in body and spirit, onto the shores of Beulah. "When self-despair was final . . . then *came* the long-expected and wished help," she wrote of this experience:

My *all* changed—Whereas once my heart ran with a strong current to the world, it now runs with a current the other way. What once it cost an effort to remember, it now costs an effort to forget—The will of Christ seems to me the steady pulse of my being & I go because I can not help it. Skeptical doubt can not exist—I seem to see the full blaze of the Shekinah every where. I am calm, but full.[54]

Having attempted to be perfect according to the canons of both true womanhood and Christian perfection, Harriet Beecher Stowe was brought to the humbling realization that she was indeed helpless; at this very Calvinistic moment of human inability, the grace of God rushed in. This was her "Victory."

Harriet Beecher Stowe's rebirth in the 1840s convinced her that God uses lowly tools for his purposes. Not through human striving or vain schemes of perfection, but through the suffering of the lowliest and most oppressed did the kingdom of God arrive. As she sat in the pew of the First Parish Church in Brunswick, Maine, on a winter day in 1851, the eucharistic celebration of the body and blood of the suffering Christ brought a picture before her of a bleeding slave being whipped. That vision, which she put down on paper when she returned home, pictured the death of the hero in *Uncle Tom's Cabin*. "Have not many of us, in the weary way of life, felt in some hours, how far easier it were to die than to live?" Stowe rhetorically asks in the opening of Chapter 38, "The Victory." Much harder to bear than a martyr's death, Stowe suggests, is the daily struggle to live: "[T]o wear on day after day of mean, bitter, low, harassing servitude, every nerve dampened and depressed, every power of feeling gradually smothered,—this long and wasting heart-martyrdom, this slow, daily bleeding away of the inward life, drop by drop, hour after hour,—this is the true searching test of what there may be in man or woman." (UTC, 2:173) She came to this realization by having striven as a woman and a Christian to perform her duty, defined by impossible perfectionist standards. Out of the contradiction between expectation and human reality grew up a radical brand of Christianity that had transformative implications for American culture. Stowe replaced perfectionist strivings with the imitation of Christ. Her understanding of the life of Christ validated the common and the everyday, both in her personal life and in her literary realism. Out of the trials of this period she wrote "Earthly Care a Heavenly Discipline," a pamphlet that enjoyed a wide circulation in the 1850s.[55]

Her consolidation of realism and evangelicalism into a unified literary creed is evident in the essay she published at this time on Charles Dickens. Calling her critique "Literary Epidemics—No. 2," Stowe continued the evaluation of popular writers she had begun with an earlier essay on Scott, Byron, Bulwer, and Marryat. She compared Dickens's influence to that of Byron, whose romantic postures had led young girls to believe that "terribly black whiskers, and a lofty, morose contempt of God and man" were requisites for domestic happiness. Her sympathies are readily apparent: Byron was a sneering, atheistic aristocrat of the sort that she would portray in her characterization of Aaron Burr in *The Minister's Wooing*; Dickens's more democratic spirit validated the concerns of nineteenth-century women's culture and of the literary realism that Stowe and other women writers would develop from it. Unlike Byron and Bulwar, who scorned "the common sympathies, wants, and sufferings of every day human nature," Dickens "shows us that our coarse, common world, can be made a very agreeable and interesting place." Stowe's own struggles with "earthly cares" disposed her to value such activities in literature. She praised Dickens in particular for extending his vision of the common and the everyday to "the whole class of the oppressed, the neglected, and forgotten, the sinning and suffering" whom he drew "within the pale of sympathy and interest."[56]

Dickens, however, was a decidedly secular writer who rode roughshod over the concerns of the readers of the *New-York Evangelist*. Labeling his stories "anti-temperance tracts," Stowe took aim at the constant tippling and red-nosed exploits in which Dickens plunged his characters, objecting in *The Pickwick Papers* to "the burlesqued account of the temperance meetings in which the Rev. Mr Stiggins, the leader, is introduced on the stage, so drunk as to be unable to finish his speech." She reserved her most serious warning for the manner in which Dickens made light of religion. Sam Weller's father endeared himself to readers by his outrageous plays on the expression being "born again." In the millennial climate of the 1840s, Stowe was not amused: "The day of judgment—the retributions of eternity, or anything else most fearful or sublime in themselves, might all be treated in the same way, and with the same success—it only requires a sufficient amount of moral hardihood to do it."[57]

Stowe's originality and power arose from her skillful synthesis of literary realism—the "coarse, common world" validated in Dickens's novels—with an evangelical intensity. Under the pressure of poverty, pregnancy, and sickness in the 1840s, both her immersion in the everyday and her identification with the suffering Messiah deepened and intensified. When she was incapacitated by neuralgia, she took comfort in knowing "that the Saviour voluntarily suffered . . . that he might appreciate every trial of our suffering condition." She reflected that had Jesus been raised in wealth and ease and "ignorant from experience of the keenness of suffering and want how different a Saviour he would have been—How impossible would it have been for the neglected the forsaken the poor to have turned to him as they do now."[58]

The litigious ministry of Lyman Beecher did not appeal to her as powerfully as did the example of Martin Luther, who wrote "Jesus" at the top of all of his letters. Stowe observed that "the great body of Luther's preaching was not controversial, but consisted of such plain, practical efforts to lead the weak and ignorant to a Saviour, as would befit a city missionary of our own times." " 'When I preach,' " she quoted Luther, " 'I preach not for learned men and magistrates, of whom there are but few; but for the poor, the women, and children, and servants, of whom there are some thousands.' " Stowe pointedly asked the readers of the *New-York Evangelist*, "might not some modern ministers derive a useful hint from this?"[59]

Stowe urged the readers of the *New-York Evangelist*, "read the life of Jesus with attention—study it—inquire earnestly with yourself, 'What sort of a person, in thought, in feeling, in action, was my Saviour?'—live in constant sympathy and communion with him—and there will be within a kind of instinctive rule by which to try all things."[60] Speaking like an Old Testament prophet, Stowe repeatedly tried to awaken her readers by comparing the formal lip service paid to the Bible to the reality of primitive Christianity. Such "apostolic experience" must "become the common experience of all Christians, before Christ can subdue the world."[61] By identifying herself with the Man of Sorrows, "a captain whom suffering made perfect,"[62] Stowe turned her human weakness into a source of divine strength and fixed on a historical and religious reality that linked her experience as a woman with that of a slave. Simultaneously, all of her perfectionist striving was turned outward on the world rather than inward on the self. What humans could not accomplish, God could.

CHAPTER FIFTEEN

In the Tide-Mud of the Real:
1844–1845

It was not the exhaltation of religious experience nor the thrill of literary success that characterized Harriet's daily round. "[T]he *real* remained," Harriet would write, "the *real,* like the flat, bare, oozy tide-mud, when the blue, sparkling wave, with all its company of gliding boats and white-winged ships, its music of oars and chiming waters has gone down, and there it lies, flat, slimy, bare,—exceedingly real." (UTC, 1:202). In the fall of 1843 Harriet commented to Calvin, "Our straits for money this year are unparalleled even in our annals." Professor Diarca Howe Allen, who with his wife Sarah and family lived next door to the Stowes, estimated that the "very most" the Lane professors could expect to collect of their salary was $600.[1] In order to help bridge the growing gap between their expenses and their income, Calvin determined that Harriet should take in boarders for the summer. Thus began her brief career as boardinghouse mistress.

Taking in boarders was of course a traditional way for women to supplement the domestic income, always too meager in Lyman Beecher's household. Roxana Beecher had taken in boarders when Harriet was a young child; his second wife did the same. When Lyman calculated in 1823 that the five boarders for whom Harriet Porter Beecher was responsible were "clear gain," he did not calculate the costs to his wife, nor did he recall that Roxana's days were shortened by the burden under which she labored.[2] By 1835 Harriet Porter Beecher was laid in a grave next to Calvin's young wife, Eliza, but the symbolism of this was lost on Calvin, in spite of his morbid worry over

Harriet's health. Only visible when it was not done, housework was not, in a husband's calculations, exactly like *work.*

But, of course, the Beecher women did not do their own manual work; Harriet Porter Beecher had two "girls" in the kitchen while she kept boarders, and it was only up to her to manage them. Even this executive work was, under Calvin's scheme, to be removed from his wife's shoulders. He arranged for a husband-and-wife team, the Boardmans, to live in their house and direct the operation. Calvin then left for a fundraising tour of the East; with their domestic establishment on an income-earning basis and the coffers of Lane Seminary renewed by eastern philanthropy, the Stowes could reasonably hope for better times.

By early May 1844 Calvin was in New York; surveying his wife's prospects from this distance, he hoped that the "cheerful company" of the Boardmans, the family reunion planned with her brothers and sisters, "and other pleasant things this summer" would restore her health.[3] Harriet, who had been left to see the new arrangements through, found that taking in boarders required a total revolution of the domestic arrangements: "Since you have been gone," she wrote back, "I have had a great pressure of care upon me—The arranging of the whole house with reference to the new system—the cleaning &c— the children's clothes, & the baby often have seemed to press on my mind all at once. Sometimes it seems as if anxious thought had become a disease with me from which I could not be free."[4] All the rooms were shifted, the dining room floor was given a fresh coat of paint, and they ate in the parlor to save the new floor. Harriet arose early to oversee the setting of the breakfast table. At 6:00 A.M. they all sat down to eat: Harriet, Anna, their five children, the Boardmans, the "girl" they brought with them ("amiable" observed Harriet, "but not . . . very smart"), and the boarders—a Mr. and Mrs. McGuffie (he was "as accommodating & unselfish as she was the reverse") and their nurse and child.[5] Afterward came morning prayers for all who desired to attend.

Mrs. Boardman, the woman placed in charge of this domestic establishment, Harriet described as "ardent & executive, but not consecutive & systematic." When she had had a few days to see Mrs. Boardman in action, Harriet expressed some doubt as to whether she "realised what she undertook in taking this house, my family, & other boarders." Mrs. Boardman's lack of system did not keep the new boardinghouse from attracting guests; on May 23 Harriet noted that they had gained two more for a total of six. "How strange this mode of life seems to me!" she told Calvin, as she surveyed the new faces around her. "I scarce know myself & in the bewilderment scarce miss you since I feel as if I was somebody else—Whether *after all* we shall make any thing with all our trouble may be doubted." Remembering a more certain source of income, she told Calvin that the *New-York Evangelist* owed her money for "The Dancing School" and a couple of other pieces; could he collect it for her?[6]

Calvin wrote back that he was on his way to New York City to collect her money from the editors and raise "a little money for your father's salary." He found fundraising "onerous and trying" and not likely to lead to "pecuniary *affluence*." "At most it will just enable us to struggle through another year, and give us hope that we shall not be obliged through excessive poverty to quit our post."[7] He was now convinced of the necessity of hanging on at Lane Seminary to the "last gasp," admitting to her that her views on this subject "now appear to me more correct than my own have been heretofore."[8] Besides feeling the weight of her father's educational and evangelical mission, Harriet believed the West to be "the only fit place for living."[9]

By June 14 another boarder—a doctor friend of theirs—had agreed to join the burgeoning Stowe household; his presence would increase the weekly income of Mr. Boardman to $10. Harriet was unclear as to where they stood financially because, as she reminded Calvin, he had left without bothering to agree with Mr. Boardman on terms. But Mr. B. "keeps exact accounts" and Mrs. B. "is economical in her arrangements," she told Calvin, "& I think on the whole that we shall get on."[10] Calvin was encouraged that Harriet had Mr. Boardman's businesslike methods as a model; he urged her to follow suit and keep track of expenses "in a *book devoted solely to that purpose*, and not on loose bits of paper, or the fly leaves of other volumes."[11]

In the middle of the summer Harriet's energies were taxed by a week-long celebration of Lane Seminary's tenth anniversary. The *New-York Evangelist* marked the occasion with a laudatory notice, observing that the seminary had educated 256 young men, but for Harriet it meant more visitors, more places at the table, and more confusion. The Beecher clan descended on Walnut Hills for the occasion, and Lyman Beecher remarked happily, "We have had so much to do & think & say that we feel as if we had said nothing at all almost tho' we have talked one or two or all together every waking hour—We are all in good health & spirit & are quite garrulous & filled with laughter."[12] Harriet added to her table Henry and Eunice Beecher and their children, Hatty and Henry, plus Sarah Beecher, her little George, and his nurse—making in all ten children. She complained to Calvin, who complained to Lyman Beecher that Harriet should not have had almost the whole family at her house when there were other houses (his) that could have provided hospitality.[13] He also complained to Harriet for taking on much more than she could manage: "Will no experience and no suffering teach you, that there are certain boundaries which you have no right to pass over?"[14]

In this department Harriet was aided by the ardent and expansive Mrs. Boardman, whose chief talent lay in acquiring more boarders and whose domestic style remained "unsystematic to a degree that astonishes even your wife," Harriet told Calvin. Her "jumping into the quicksand & jumping out 'first rate' are perfectly characteristic of her." Harriet, who had understood that they were to take in just a few friends to help with expenses, found her home metamorphosing into an international hotel. Mrs. Boardman next accepted a certain Mr. and Mrs. Chase and their child and nurse, apparently promising Harriet, who had returned with Henry and Eunice to Indianapolis, that they were Mr. and Mrs. Salmon P. Chase. Then the McGuffies left and Harriet learned that in their place Mrs. Boardman had installed a Mr. and Mrs. Canoop—"Spanish people & nobody knows what." It also transpired that the Mrs. Chase was "no Salmon P's wife but some foreign body born in England & educated in Italy & speaking only broken English." Harriet threw up her hands. "[M]ercy on us,—what a home to return to."[15]

Her month-long visit with Henry and Eunice in July provided a much-needed respite. Here she had no responsibilities except to get herself to the table for meals; as she told Calvin, "the cottage is still & quiet & I hear the clock tick with quiet satisfaction."[16] It made her weary just to think of the full house she would return to—"is it necessary!" she exclaimed to Calvin. "I don't know what to say—I wish the summer were through & this boarding business closed, I am heartily sick of it—It is too noisy & disquieting & harassing." Anna was planning a trip to Charleston with Hatty and Eliza after her return, and Harriet thought wishfully of going off herself with the remaining children "& so be out of the scrape." But if, she told Calvin "you think it *necessary*, why I must try to bear with it till you return & then I should be glad to go back to our own family circle."[17]

Yet she could not keep her mind from embracing more attractive schemes for employing her time than being a boardinghouse mistress. Away from her family, situated in Indianapolis where the culture was newer and less developed than in Cincinnati, susceptible to Henry Ward Beecher's ambitions, Harriet dreamed of setting up a school. Adopting an arch and executive tone very like that of her sister Catharine, Harriet joked with Calvin that she was "seriously thinking of breaking up our *connection* & coming here to I[ndianapolis]—to take a class of young ladies & so influence the state— such pretty girls as they have here & *so* uncultivated." Her plan was "not merely of *teaching a school* but of forming the *centre* of female influence in the state—Henry says he wants only the woman & he can move the whole state for her."[18] She had long and absorbing talks with her brother, full of schemes and new ideas. They talked about education, revivalism, and the latest fad: mesmerism. Henry, whose charismatic preaching would eventually hold thousands spellbound, demonstrated his powers of magnetism by putting Harriet into an hypnotic trance on three different occasions. Harriet became a believer, urging Calvin to "[s]how this account to Edward & see if he does not think there is an animal magnetic fluid."[19] She urged the skeptical Eunice, her body broken by disease and childbearing, to see if she could be relieved by a few of Henry's mesmeric passes. ("But you wont will you Eunice—no you wont—all witchcraft.") She herself professed to have treated a nervous woman with a breast abcess by twice putting her into an hypnotic sleep.[20] In her state of "vegetation" in Indianapolis, Harriet reveled in the freedom from care and in the easy warmth of family feeling. "I have forgotten almost the faces of my children—all the perplexing details of home, and almost that I am a married woman."[21]

When Harriet returned in August she found her domestic establishment increasing by multiplication as well as addition. Mrs. Canoop, the Spanish boarder, gave birth to another Canoop, who was delivered in the absence of a physician by Harriet as "head nurse" and her neighbor, Mrs. Allen, as "surgeon 'accoucheur.'"[22] As the dog days of August set in and the thermometer stood at 90 degrees in the evening, Cincinnatians renounced all political excitement, religious enthusiasm, and intellectual exertion in favor of cold baths. For her part, Harriet felt "strange and homeless." "[T]his house full of strangers does not seem like my house—these Spanish French German folks tho quiet enough are not *my folks.*"[23]

It is hard to imagine such a response to keeping a boardinghouse among an earlier generation of women, and it points to the rapid changes underway in American society and in the Victorian family. The homogeneous population that settled in New England was, in the West, replaced by a heterogeneous mixture of Yankees and Europeans of various extractions and religions. Opening one's house to them meant inviting inside the very cultural forces defined by Lyman Beecher as the enemy. There were other significant factors, chief among them the changing status and economic roles of women, but surely the increasing isolation of the Victorian home was in part a response to this foreign threat. The more diverse and threatening the culture at large became, the more securely the doors were locked against the tide and the closer the chairs were drawn up to the Victorian hearth that increasingly was inhabited only by the immediate family members.[24] "I long for the time when we shall once more be a quiet united family with none but our own selves," Harriet told Calvin.[25]

Through one of her boarders, Harriet became acquainted with a Mrs. Bonneville, who with her husband created a sensation in Cincinnati the following summer with lectures and experiments on mesmerism. He was regarded as a humbug by people whom Harriet respected, like J. H. Perkins, but Harriet, struck by the force of Mrs. Bonneville's personality ("a singularly interesting woman," like "a Joan of Arc, or other enthusiast"), invited her to pass a few days with her and found herself "every day increasingly attached to her." Harriet allowed herself to be a subject for Mrs. Bonneville's experiments and reported that she "produced effects on me very marked & singular." Harriet began experimenting on herself and on others and became convinced "that neuralgic pains may be assuaged entirely by mesmeric passes."[26] In contrast to Harriet's enthusiasm, Catharine Beecher took a more scientific approach to the fads of the forties; upon hearing of the work of two clairvoyants in Boston, Catharine planned to visit the women and test their powers, instructing the Beecher clan to keep track of their sayings and doings during the period of her visit. Mary Beecher remarked, "I think animal magnetism will find its match in sister Kate."[27]

The island of serenity Harriet experienced at Henry and Eunice's cottage in Indianapolis she attempted to re-create at Walnut Hills by moving her writing desk and books and papers into a room that was located in a wing of the house. Here she attempted to separate the rhythms of her life from the daily convolutions of Mrs. Boardman and her tribe. "The whole boarding establishment I have left to take care of itself," she wrote Eunice from her enclave, "casting it off in a lump & just disconnecting my little wing suppose myself to be keeping house alone."[28] For the second time in two years she had set up a room of her own.

Calvin's five-month trip "on agency" for Lane was a total failure, as anyone who knew the temperament of the cautious scholar would have predicted. The more he worried about their financial straits, the less prepared he was to persuade easterners that they should invest their money in western education. Moody and self-critical, he was not the man to work up an audience into a pitch of enthusiasm, optimism, and philanthropy. At the beginning of July Calvin lost his voice and retreated into illness. "I can do nothing now but loll on the bed, straggle over the fields, read newspaper, and nibble a letter now and then," he wrote Lyman Beecher. "I am very nervous, my throat is sore, my lungs are weak, my stomach is exceedingly sensitive and rebellious; and though I am obviously mending, it is at a slow rate."[29] The doctor predicted he would be laid up for two or three weeks. He urged Harriet to arrange affairs within the family as she saw fit, and to act as if he were dead. "Indeed, as to all practical purposes I am dead for the present, and know not when I shall live again."[30]

He recuperated with Mary and Thomas Perkins in Hartford, where Mary reported he was "very comfortably sick"[31] and undergoing homeopathic treatment. Calvin's bodily ailments were soon compounded by spiritual ones. The professor of biblical literature and lecturer on church history was afflicted by doubts "as to the reality of experimental religion, and whether the whole Bible is not after all humbug."[32] He complained to Harriet that her recent letters had none of the "thrilling paragraphs" on religion that so inspired him but rather were such that "I or any professor of religion might write." He requested that she write him of her "own experience of the love of God."[33] She responded with a long sermon, almost novelistic in its rendering of a vision of God, and tried to reassure him about his spiritual crisis. "It is so much the fashion now a days for christians in good standing especially ministers to feel that they have paid their passage, got their ticket, & are of course on the rail road track to heaven [perhaps a reference to Hawthorne's "The Celestial Railroad"], that any man who groans & labours & doubts his salvation & is pressed with inward conflict is set down as nervous visionary & not quite sound in mind."[34] Harriet's talents as a preacher and spiritual guide were encouraged within her marriage as well as exercised within the Beecher family culture in which the views of family "divines and divin*esses*" were sought on topics moral, political, and social.[35] But as Calvin leaned heavily on his wife to support his soul as well as her own, she was drawn into her mother's role, that of the angel in the house. Harriet's role as spiritual and financial supporter of the family, while it widened her sphere, also intensified her domestic responsibilities and made increasing demands on her time and emotional resources.

The volatile mixture of religious intensity, human longing, and perfectionist schemes that characterized the 1840s made ministers susceptible not only to religious doubts but also to sexual indiscretions. More than professional feelings were sometimes evoked by the spiritual struggles of parishioners, and during this decade of experimentation such feelings were more likely than in other periods to find expression. Then too, as John Humphrey Noyes shrewdly observed, "Religious love is very near neighbor to sexual love, and they always get mixed in the intimacies and social excitements of Revivals."[36] Although Nathaniel Hawthorne set his 1850 tale of adultery in seventeenth-century New England, models for ministerial impiety were close at hand in the 1840s. Henry Ward Beecher, who several decades later would be involved in the most famous adultery trials of the century, took note of the many cases troubling the ministerial ranks in Indiana. In the East, similar stories were scorching ears and setting tongues to wag. Calvin wrote to Harriet in vivid detail of the fall from grace of five prominent ministers, concluding, "Is there any body we can trust? Are all ministers brutes?"[37] Whatever his motives in writing this to Harriet while they were separated and practicing a most severe sexual discipline within their marriage, these revelations had a startling effect on her.

A "horrible presentiment crept over me," she told Calvin:

> I thought of all my brothers & of you—& could it be that the Great Enemy had prevailed against any of you, & as I am gifted with a most horribly vivid imagination in a moment I imagined—nay saw as in a vision all the distress & despair that would follow a fall on your part till I felt weak & sick—I took a book & lay down on the bed, but it pursued me like a nightmare—& something seemed to ask Is your husband any better *seeming* than so & so—I looked in the glass & my face which since spring has been something of the palest was so haggard that it frightened me.

She warned him against sexual passion and denied that she had any—responses perfectly in keeping with what Nancy Cott has dubbed "passionlessness," a strategy through which Victorian women garnered some physical autonomy and moral capital.[38]

> What terrible temptations lie in the way of your sex—till now I never realised it—for tho I did love you with an almost *insane* love before I married you I never knew yet or felt the pulsation which showed me that I could be tempted in that way—there never was a moment when I felt any thing by which you could have drawn me astray—for I loved you as I now love God—& I can conceive of no higher love—and as I have no passion—I have no jealousy,— the most beautiful woman in the world could not make me jealous so long as she only *dazzled the senses*—but still my dear, you must not wonder if I want to warn you not to look or *think* too freely on womankind—If your sex would guard the outworks of *thought*, you would never fall.

Having set Calvin straight and denied her own passion, Harriet continued the conjugal sparring by telling her husband that she was reading steamy French novels: "[E]difying say you—Well I was sick I knew they could'nt hurt me." An additional rationale was her professional interest, for she contemplated writing a critique of Eugene Sue's novels: "They are powerful but *stiflingly* devoid of moral principle—Their atmosphere like the air of a forcing house at 90—or so—tho full of luscious blossom & fruit make you stagger & pant for the air—not the first discernment of any boundaries between right & wrong in them." If she wrote a "condemnatory article" she wondered, "will all the saints go & read them to see if it is true?"[39]

Before his breakdown Calvin collected $25 from the *Evangelist* for Harriet and arranged for it to be carried to her. She wrote back that they owed her closer to $35. "I think if you will take my letter I wrote giving a list & look over a file of papers you will find it so—better see to it."[40] Clearly, her system of accounting worked for *her*. Calvin Stowe got up from his sickbed, but remained "so nervous that any attempt to preach on the subject of raising money," he assured Harriet, "brings on neuralgic pains that are intolerable and lay me aside for a week or two."[41] He planned to return home after a College Board meeting in New York on September 25.

At the end of their five-month separation the Stowes took stock of their marriage and made plans for improvement. On September 29 Calvin wrote: "I know I appreciate all your excellencies, that I love you as much as I am capable of loving a fellow creature, and that you are the wife of my choice if the whole world were open before me now to choose from. My only wish is that I had an income sufficient for your comfort and that I might be permitted to live with you without interruption."[42] Harriet viewed their reunion with a mixture of desire and dread. "My dear husband," she wrote to him,

> As the time draws near for you to return again to your home I am often made sensible how warmly & fervently my heart still clings to you—Tho by hard endurance I have learnt a degree of self control which sometimes makes me doubt whether I have any feeling yet there are times when the old fountain rises again warm, fresh & full & I feel myself as of olden times
>
> I have had such a delightful visit with Henry this summer such warm full confiding outpouring of soul to soul—I love him so much—you dont know how much—it really makes me cry to think of it—Oh this love—if we only could have enough of it—I could be any thing or do any thing for & by love—but without how desolate & waste & cheerless—You will love me very much at first when you come home & then, will it be as before all faded off into months of cold indifference—I do not know as this can be helped—but it seems to me as if my mind was like one of those plants which can very well bear a long steady winter but is killed by occasional warm spells forcing out all the little blossom buds, to be nipped by succeeding frosts.[43]

A woman who found it difficult to parcel herself out in little bits, who gave herself totally to the moment, and who was exquisitely sensitive to criticism, Harriet was at particular risk in a marriage to such a volatile man as Calvin Stowe. At the same time, he judged his ultimate success not on the basis of his performance in the marketplace, but in his own home. "Pray for me that I may not be deceived, and that I may stand the test of domestic cares and temptations," he wrote Harriet. "I must be a different man in my family than I have ever been before, and by God's help I will be."[44] As September drew to an end, he renewed his promise to Harriet that, with the help of God, he would become "a consistent, steady, affectionate house-father."[45] She continued to "feel strangely—wishing yet dreading your return—hoping to find you indeed renewed in spirit yet fearing that it may not be so, & that we may again draw each other earthward." Her hopes and fears were shot through with a millennial expectation of "some more perfect state," a longing, as she confessed, that made for "the success of the Oberlin papers & doctrines."[46] This perfectionist strain made it less likely that Harriet's hopes would be realized on earth.

Harriet had often complained that Calvin did not permit her opportunities to develop her "business talents."[47] Having had the responsibility for the boardinghouse venture on her shoulders without any financial control of the outcome, she found the contradictions of her position intensified by Calvin's breakdown and total abdication of domestic responsibilities. Perhaps emboldened by these developments, in 1844 she requested control of their domestic finances. Calvin had laid down an ultimatum at the end of July: "[Y]ou have made up your mind that you cannot take boarders, and I have made up my mind that I cannot be an agent. Unless, then, we can live at Walnut Hills without taking boarders or going on agency, we must leave. Now fix that definitely in your mind." His recipe for staying was not likely to appeal to Harriet: "I am willing to live on the coarsest and plainest food, to dress in the coarsest and plainest manner, to own the cheapest kind of furniture, to cease entirely the purchase of books, to dispense with a room by myself and study with my family—to do anything except run in debt for my living—and that I will not do—so help me God."[48] Harriet wrote back that were he dead, were she a widow with five children, "I would not doubt nor despond nor expect to starve. . . . I know God would give me and my children passage in such fashion as suited him." She added, "If you will put the affairs all into my hands & let me manage them my own way . . . *I'l engage* to bring things out right in the spring."[49]

Calvin acceded to her request, but not without an admonitory sermon on her propensity to be "thoughtless of expence and inclined to purchase whatever [struck her] eye," a propensity "indulged and greatly increased," in his view, by her relations with her sister Kate. He bought the seeds and manure she requested for her garden, grumbling, "I hope you will be content this winter with keeping a very few choice plants—for *labor* is a great article in our family; and we must adopt some plan to save labor and fuel." He could not say no to her, but he could point out the lack of proportion with which she and her family approached all schemes earthly and divine:

> [Y]ou seldom hesitate to make a promise, whether you have ability to perform it or not, like your father and Kate, only not quite so bad; and promises so easily made are very easily broken. On this point Kate has no conscience at all, your father very little; and you have enough to keep you from making some promises, if you would only think beforehand whether you could fulfil them

or not. . . . Do you remember last winter telling your father you would help him copy his sermons, when you could n't write five minutes at a time without bringing on neuralgia? And if I had wished, you would have promised in the same breath to do all my writing into the bargain; and your father would have promised me a salary of $1200 a year punctually paid; and Kate would have added her promise to any account that might have been required by the circumstances; and not one of them, except yourself, would ever have thought it was wrong to promise beyond one's ability to perform.[50]

Since she had had no part in setting up the arrangements, Harriet refused to settle accounts with Mr. Boardman, insisting that Calvin see that duty through. Whether or not they earned anything from this revolution of their household is not clear, but they remained at the end of it in debt. That October Harriet thanked Sarah Beecher for her willingness to lend them a sum of money "which will very materially aid us in our present embarrassments." In the same letter she told Sarah that her baby Georgy had come home from the wet nurse ("she is the sweetest loveliest quietest little creature you ever saw,—tho still a little baby who cannot even crawl") and that Calvin, whom she had expected home from his ill-fated eastern tour the day before, still had not arrived. "I suspect he has been entrapped by this good for nothing river & is now lying cooling his impatience on some sand bar—comfortable, that—for a man who has been away from home six months."[51] In addition to the $100 she borrowed from Sarah, Harriet borrowed another $100 from her father.[52]

Material aid came from another quarter as well. The ladies of Park Street Church in Boston, Edward Beecher's old pulpit, desired to buy a cloak for Professor Stowe's wife so that he could bring back from the East a token of their esteem; after inquiries failed to clarify what style she might prefer ("whatever would be proper & suitable for a clergyman's wife in Boston would be equally so for me," Harriet told Calvin, adding that "Boston sends *us* the fashions and not we Boston"), they sent her $40 rather than risk a cloak and bonnet that might not suit her taste.[53]

This was not the only recognition that Calvin Stowe's wife received while he was on agency. In Pittsburgh, while Calvin was the guest of the Rev. Albert Barnes—a colleague of Lyman Beecher in his battles with the Old School Presbyterians—he heard the first of many laudatory reviews of her writing. "Mrs. B[arnes] inquired after you with great interest," Calvin told Harriet:

They both told me that they devoured everything of your writing they could get hold of, and wished you would write more and oftener &c. &c. As to my own writings, br[other] B[arnes] evidently seemed to think he would just allude to them, but evidently it was your pen that *put in the flourishes, te he he!* Very well—let it be so; I'll take it all out in nodding at you when I get vexed: Take your advisement of that.[54]

A few days after this incident Calvin wrote to Lyman Beecher, "Harriet quite beams away the pale sun rise in the literary world, and I mean she shall call *herself Mrs. C. E. Stowe*, for this very day I was asked by a *young gentleman* 'if Mrs. *H. B. Stowe* was any connexion of mine?' Considerable of a connexion, I guess he would think, if he could see all that has come of it."[55] Calvin's reference to the progeny he had fathered gained back a measure of masculine pride, but it was clear that already Calvin was shining in his wife's reflected light. At the end of his eastern tour Calvin told Harriet, "I cannot tell you what admiration I have heard expressed of you wherever I have been, & not always in a way at all calculated to soothe my vanity."[56] Nonetheless, his strong support of the literary woman he had baptized "Harriet Beecher Stowe" did not waver.

She had need of his more single-minded focus in the year ahead, as she again allowed herself to be drawn into the orbit of Beecher family projects for saving the West. In 1842 Lyman Beecher, realizing that concerted action was required upon the part of Christian civilization in order to counter "the infinitude of depraved mind here bursting forth, and rolling in from abroad upon us like a flood," formed the Society for the Promotion of Collegiate and Theological Education at the West and set about raising money for it. By such national organizations as this and the American Home Missionary Society, the evangelical Protestants hoped to counter both a growing secularism and the highly organized, authoritarian structures of Roman Catholicism. "[I]f we fail to hold our own in our own land," Lyman Beecher appealed to a potential supporter, "how shall we lead in the aggressive movement for the conversion of the whole world? I am on the field. The battle is begun. We give notice of it to our fathers, and mothers, and brothers, and sisters, and children at the East, and call for help. Who is on the Lord's side—who?"[57] Harriet found it hard to resist such trumpet calls, notwithstanding the tolerant view of Catholics she had espoused in the 1830s. Neither had she forgotten the young women of Indiana. Unable to educate them herself, she recommended to Henry Ward Beecher a Miss Boyes, who professed to be adept in all the English branches as well as French, Latin, vocal music, and drawing: "She is not what may be called a *marrying* young lady at all—her present idea is to devote her whole life to this enterprise—you can attach what value you think proper to this consideration." Single women like Miss Boyes were Catharine Beecher's answer to the Roman Catholic nuns whose self-denying devotion to their vocation provided a cheap and efficient means of promoting their religion and worldview. Adopting Catharine's strategy and Lyman Beecher's rhetoric, Harriet challenged Henry Ward: "[W]ho will educate the Indiana mothers if you do not—meet these Jesuits by Yankee women—I'll risk the combat—one bright well trained free born Yankee girl is worth two dozen of your nuns who have grown up like potatoe sprouts in the shades of a convent." She laid out a plan for a school, urging Henry to begin small, "make no fuss work along till you see how things will develop themselves & act accordingly—This is the way to begin any enterprise."[58]

Her efforts on behalf of the women of Indiana were interrupted that winter by ill health, probably compounded by a miscarriage.[59] By June she was still frail and suffering increasingly from a mental disorganization that made their household a "helter skelter" affair. On some days she was unable to formulate plans or to remember them when she had. While Calvin complained of "the restless, unsettled condition of the family,"[60] she lost her appetite and grew "quite ethereal." She was at one of her low points when she wrote the following to Calvin while he was away at a ministerial convention in Detroit.

June 16, 1845

My Dear Husband,
It is a dark, sloppy, rainy, muddy, disagreeable day, and I have been working hard (for me) all day in the kitchen, washing dishes, looking into closets, and seeing a great deal of that dark side of domestic life which a housekeeper may who will investigate too curiously into minutiae in warm, damp weather, especially after a girl who keeps all clean on the *outside* of the cup and platter, and is very apt to make good the rest of the text in the *inside* of things.

I am sick of the smell of sour milk, and sour meat, and sour everything, and then the clothes *will* not dry, and no wet thing does, and everything smells mouldy; and altogether I feel as if I never wanted to eat again.[61]

The warm, damp days of June not only depressed the spirits of housekeepers, they also provided a perfect breeding ground for cholera. As the hot, sticky weather of July moved toward the even more intense heat of August, Harriet, her body weakened by the illnesses of the previous winter, suddenly succumbed to the deadly disease. The doctor was called for, but he was delayed an hour by his difficulty in finding a horse. For three hours Harriet lay without medical aid while the cholera ran its violent course of diarrhea, fever, spasms, and cramps. When the doctor arrived he was "thunderstruck" to learn that it was cholera and feared he had come too late. He "made some medicale prescriptions but without any expectation she would live," Lyman Beecher told his wife. After the administration of some brandy Harriet began to sing and called "in a wandering way" for others to join her. Two women stayed up with her throughout the night, her father slept in the next room, and the doctor stayed in case an emergency required his assistance. But the "night of suspense" passed, and in the morning Harriet was better. She was not out of danger, but clearly her strong constitution was resisting the disease.[62]

"As to a journey, I need not ask a physician to see that it is needful to me as far as health is concerned," Harriet observed to Calvin that summer.[63] Traveling was a common prescription for ill health; the tonic it provided was especially needful to women beset with small children. As Samuel Foote explained to relatives in Nutplains who wondered that they did not plan to bring their children with them on their visit, "You Eastern Barbarians do not appear to have any true understanding of the principal motives for our coming amongst you this summer—It is that Elizabeth may be relieved from the Care of Housekeeping—the care of Children & the care of matters & things in general."[64] Travel was especially needful to Harriet Beecher Stowe, judging from the astonishing number of trips she took during her early marriage. She made regular visits to her brothers in Putnam, Lawrenceburg, Chillicothe, and Indianapolis. Calvin complained to Lyman Beecher, "It was quite characteristic for Harriet to go fooling things the bottom up road of Indiana *for the benefit of her health*," offering the opinion that the next time she wanted such a benefit she might as well saddle one of their horses "and roll over & over down hill into the gully. . . . Nevertheless, she will be just as earnest to go again next spring, and just as sure that the roads are in the best of order, as if she had never seen to the contrary."[65] In addition to such western jaunts, Harriet made the 900-mile journey by canal, steamboat, and stage to the East in 1834, 1839, 1842, and 1844—riding the railroad for the first time on the latter trip. Thus it was not surprising that in August 1845, when Calvin went East on business, which included a meeting of the Foreign Missionary Society in Boston, Harriet accompanied him.[66]

While she was in Hartford her mind turned to the issue that had preoccupied her before she became ill the previous winter: saving the beautiful young women in the West through education. Since 1843 Catharine Beecher's energies had been devoted to establishing a national organization for the training of teachers, for, like her father, she recognized that only through concerted action could the West be saved from the heterogeneous cultures that were pouring in. Harriet took up her pen to appeal to Zilpah Grant (now Banister), an experienced teacher who had refused Catharine Beecher's invitation sixteen years earlier to come to the Hartford Female Seminary:

September 23, 1845

Dear Mrs. Bannister
    As my health will not permit my doing much writing I send you the enclosed that you may see my Sister's plans—You perceive that the whole is now reduced to the practical issues of finding thirty teachers to come on as soon as possible, whose successful location will demonstrate the practicality of the whole move. All the means are provided—board, support, places, protection. We want now *the women*. I am in N[ew] England, comparatively a stranger an *invalid*—& very much of one—You have the most experience on this subject of any person I know of except Miss Lyons & I am very desirous of having a personal interview with you on this subject. Mr. Stowe & myself will be in Boston Thursday the 9th of October & shall remain there until Monday the 13, when we start for the West—Will it be possible for you to meet us there at that time.[67]

Catharine Beecher even succeeded in drawing the reluctant Calvin Stowe into her scheme. She got him to agree to be the figurehead of her national organization, believing that it would have more credibility with a man at the helm. Calvin was to have many opportunities to regret his involvement.[68]

A two-part series Harriet wrote for the *New-York Evangelist* the following winter at Catharine's urging demonstrates the extent to which she had taken up the Beecher family causes, with all their associated provincialisms and nativistic assumptions. Entitled "What Will the American People Do?," this series was a plea for Protestant education in the West to counter the well-organized efforts of the Jesuits and the Roman Catholic nuns. Situating herself at her writing desk purportedly with letters from women in Indiana and other parts of the country in front of her, all lamenting the shortage of competent and cultivated teachers, Harriet took up a letter from "a lady in the State of New York" who pointed out the low social class and training of Irish Catholic teachers: one young woman "recently was a chambermaid at an inn in the place. Another in this vicinity is taught by a young man, an Irish Catholic—who, just before, was the keeper of a nine-pin alley." Middle-class Protestant women readers were supposed to draw back their skirts in horror from this lower-class lot of Irish teachers and pack their bags for the West. To galvanize them into action, Harriet cited some ominous statistics from the Catholic Almanac of 1844, which listed all the various orders of Catholic nuns and their numbers. Reminding her readers of the deference to human authority taught by Catholicism and the zealous proselytizing in which the religion engaged, she concluded, "If then Protestants, knowing all this, will not provide schools of their own, what should they expect?"[69]

The ease with which Harriet was pulled back into the religiocultural chauvinism that had drawn Lyman Beecher to the Mississippi Valley thirteen years earlier is a reminder of just how strong the family culture was. It is also a measure of how much more evangelical Harriet had become during this period of her life, in contrast to the cosmopolitan posture she adopted as a young unmarried woman. The acceptance of a wide variety of cultures and regions that her western experience encouraged in Semi-Colon parties was, in the 1840s, overshadowed by the hope and fear that the Lord would come at any time. "Who is on the Lord's side?" Such questions did not allow of inclusive answers, nor did they make easier the search for a voice that might speak nationally.

At the same time, Stowe's understanding of the Bible as a literary as well as a religious resource provided the groundwork for a national literature. In true Protestant style, she viewed the Bible as a book of the people. In an essay in the *New-York Evangelist* she went even further, characterizing the Bible in a homely way that made it the apotheosis of parlor literature. The touchstone of the family room, it contained "stories of human love and hate, of births, and marriages, and deaths"; in the oral tradition of fireside chats, these stories "are poured into our ears with a simple-hearted, motherly minuteness, a full explicitness as to all the little undignified how, why and wherefore, which makes the old Hebrew legend the one universal legend of every home and fireside, wherever there live human creatures with human hearts."[70] In this description the Bible is similar to a series of "motherly" women's letters read with great appreciation of their trifling detail to the assembled family in the parlor. Seen in this homely light, the Bible was not above imitation. As Stowe strove for "a state of mind . . . in which the high devotional language of the Bible becomes the spontaneous and habitual language of the soul,"[71] she rehearsed for the epic recasting of the life of Christ she would write six years later in *Uncle Tom's Cabin*.

A sketch entitled "Immediate Emancipation," published in January 1845, also shows her moving in with deftness on the dialect, moral principles, and plot that would bring her international fame. A slave named Sam has been sent by his southern master on an errand. When he does not return, the master investigates and learns that he has run away, aided by a Quaker. This is the plot that Cincinnatians had seen played out many times, as slaves hired out from Kentucky masters used the opportunity to escape. But this "true story" "occurring in the city of Cincinnati" takes a different turn. The master goes to the Quaker's house intent on recovering his property, but finds himself instead persuaded by the Quaker that any man in Sam's condition would want to be a free man. Although the slave was well cared for, the Quaker reminds the owner that through debt and resale his slave "may come to be a field hand, under hard masters, starved, beaten, overworked— such things do happen sometimes, do they not?" This is, in a nutshell, the story of Uncle Tom. But unlike Mr. Shelby, this master, not being embarrassed financially, accedes to the likelihood of this scenario and frees his slave. Stowe concludes her sketch by introducing what she claims is an actual letter that she has before her, in which the former master wishes his slave well—a touch that links her sketch to the realism of the epistolary tradition.

In this sketch not only does Stowe make excellent use of dialect and dialogue, she also adopts the strategy that would make *Uncle Tom's Cabin* effective with a wide audience. She deliberately attacks slavery *as a system*, thus avoiding what she calls "[t]he great error of controversy," its readiness "to assail *persons* rather than *principles*." "The slave system as a system, perhaps, concentrates more wrong than any other now existing, and yet those who live under and in it may be, as we see, enlightened, generous, and amenable to reason."[72] Later recognizing the lineaments of Auguste St. Clare in the reasonable master of this story, Stowe cited this incident in her "Concluding Remarks" to *Uncle Tom's Cabin* to show the reader that she had based her story on truth. Forrest Wilson observed that in spite of the eighteen years Stowe lived in Cincinnati, it "made but the faintest of impressions upon her as a literary woman," adding that "one can read through from beginning to end the score and more of her principal works and never find a reference to Cincinnati or any use of the city as a background."[73] Yet, as this sketch demonstrates, Harriet did write a "true story" of Cincinnati, one that formed the germ of her masterpiece. In ways subtle and pervasive, the bordertown of Cincinnati, with its race riots, commercial trading, runaway slaves, disease, and death, and Walnut Hills, with its gardens, nurseries, and parlors, its poverty and its hopes for a better world, formed the tide-mud of "the Real" out of which emerged Stowe's most powerful work of fiction.

CHAPTER SIXTEEN

The Water Cure:
1846–1848

*H*arriet's religious conversion of 1843 was paralleled in 1846 by a secular conversion to the water cure. Both were informed by the millennial hope of a perfect world, and both placed a baptism and a crisis at the heart of the cure. "Wash and Be Healed," proclaimed the banner of the *Water-Cure Journal*, unabashedly appealing to millennial hopes. Hydropathy promised to do for the body what religious conversion had done for the soul. "We labor for the Physical Regeneration of the Race" announced the *Water-Cure Journal*'s frontispiece. "It is the appointed and glorious mission of the *Water-Cure Journal* to proclaim and hasten the advent of UNIVERSAL HEALTH, VIRTUE, AND HAPPINESS." Appealing to the reformist striving of the age, hydropathy's goals were framed in specific, this-worldly terms that siphoned off religious energies into secular channels; in this respect the water cure was a harbinger of late-Victorian culture. "We shall never look for 'perfection' either in man or woman, yet we may hope for a high state of physical and mental cultures," wrote the editor of the *Water-Cure Journal*.[1] One historian characterized hydropathic physicians as "secular saviors attempting to lead the medically unregenerate toward 'the great hygienic revival.' "[2] Like religious perfectionists, water-cure enthusiasts were narrowly focused on the self.[3]

Advocating noninterventionist, natural methods of cure, hydropathy emphasized temperate eating, abstinence from all drugs (including alcohol), abundant fresh air and exercise, and—its centerpiece—liberal internal and external applications of water. Water-cure patients douched, splashed, show-ered, soaked, and sweated. Hydropathy taught that hygienic living was the best prevention of illness, and that through self-care one could enjoy good health and freedom from drugs and doctors. An alternative to allopathy, the medical orthodoxy, hydropathy had strong links with homeopathy, which advocated the use of miniscule doses of medicine. Both the water cure and homeopathy were a reaction against the often brutal interventions of allopathic medicine.

Many were drawn to the water cure after near-death experiences—some at the hands of allopathic physicians.[4] It may well have been Harriet's brush with cholera in the summer of 1845 that drew her to the waters of Brattleboro, Vermont. As her life hung in the balance, she was given a traditional allopathic treatment, brandy, for such "stimulants" were prescribed for virtually every ailment, sometimes in doses of up to five shots a day.[5] This was only the last and certainly not the most damaging treatment she received at the hands of allopathic medicine. Organized around the ancient notion of "humors," allopathic medicine used bleeding, blistering, and purging to adjust the body's balance of blood, phlegm and bile. When Harriet became ill while in the East in 1839, the doctor had recommended the application of leeches to her head[6]—a standard remedy at a time when leeches were applied to virtually every part of the body, including the womb and the inside of the nostrils.

While leeches caused excruciating pain when placed on delicate tissues, this allopathic intervention was not as damaging as the universal prescription of "blue pills," or calomel. Calomel is mercurous chloride, an organic compound of mercury the toxic effects of which are potentially lethal. One nineteenth-century historian reported the instance of a three-year-old child whose ailment was treated by twice-daily administrations of calomel as an expectorant. The child developed very bad breath; upon inspection it was discovered that he had lost all his lower teeth and gums through gangrene.[7] Yet most households used such drastic "remedies" on a routine basis. When Calvin Stowe was ill in the winter of 1841, Harriet described for the Beecher family the course of treatment. At its center were the infamous blue pills:

> Just at this moment my spouse the gracious Doctor Calvin is sick & I have been most of the day "messing" & fussing roasting apples & making some of that "ineffable trash" commonly denominated water gruel, making pills (blue of course, or *azure* if you want to be genteel) & doing them up in invisable shapes for him to swallow & now having soaked his feet & tucked him safe away with the other children for the night I catch a moment to speed this circular.[8]

Harriet herself ingested a significant quantity of calomel during her young womanhood. "Dr Drake gave me blue pill enough to last one life time," she told her brother Henry, "in consequence whereof I have been four or five times saturated."[9] Her most serious disabilities bear a striking resemblance to the symptoms of chronic mercury poisoning: headache or "neuralgia," loss of control of the hands, lassitude, and mental disorganization. Organic mercury compounds attack the central nervous system, producing a blurring of vision, an inability to concentrate, and ataxia—the loss of coordination of the limbs.[10] This last symptom both she and her sister Catharine experienced in 1842, when neither was able to knit or write or do anything with their hands. Industrial workers exposed to mercury developed tremors in their hands and curious mental eccentricities—Lewis Carroll's "Mad Hatter" is an example, for hatters handled felt treated with mercury. Harriet's lack of domestic system, a temperamental preference, was surely aggravated by the effects of chronic mercury poisoning. "When the brain gives out, as mine often does," Harriet had written to Calvin in the miserable summer of 1845, "and one cannot think or remember anything, then what is to be done? All common fatigue, sickness, and exhaustion is nothing to this distress."[11] The water cure, if it did nothing else, delivered its practitioners from the rigors of allopathic treatment.

When Harriet went to the Brattleboro Water Cure in 1846 it had been open for just one year; indeed, the water-cure idea had been imported from Europe just a few years earlier. Her eager consumption of this new therapy is characteristic of her openness to the popular culture. It is one of the ironies of her marriage that she *paid money* to adopt the simple life that Calvin Stowe had always advocated. A self-help scheme that was theoretically available to Americans of all classes and races, the water cure was packaged in a way that made it the preserve of the middle- and upper-middle-class white patrons of water-cure establishments who paid an average of $7.50 a week to come to bathe and drink water.[12] Historians have contrasted the water-cure establishments to the fashionable spas, known chiefly for their cotillions, races, champagne suppers, and the marriage market.[13] The water cure reinvented for the middle class—around pure, not mineral water—a social gathering place adapted to the self-help values of this class. Their activities were more energetic and less aristocratic, but the water-cure establishments were inexorably drawn toward the upper-class culture they professed to disdain. The Brattleboro Water Cure was among the most expensive and exclusive of the water cures. Its "spacious building, with billiard-rooms, bowling alleys, parlors for music and conversation, and an open piazza three hundred feet in length," drew "some of the best and most refined people of this and other lands," wrote one observer. " 'Hydropathic Balls' became a fashionable function to which society was attracted from afar."[14] Its European origin and flavor—it brought "the art of life lived in the open air as practiced by Europeans" to urban-born Americans—gave the water cure an aristocratic aura. Some said it was a poor man's substitute for the European tour.[15]

But in America the water cure was also an institutional response to what had become a popular expectation: that married women's health would rapidly decline. "[I]s not the ill health of women in these days proverbial?," asks one of Harriet Beecher Stowe's characters in an 1843 story. "Where is there one girl in ten, whose constitution is not almost entirely shattered, in two or three years after her marriage?"[16] Eunice Beecher was married with a flower in her hair in 1837; nine years later, broken by malaria, tuberculosis, child-bearing, and the care of sick children, she wrote to Harriet, "I think you would have some trouble to recognise your sister in the thin faced—grey headed—toothless old woman you would find here."[17] Catharine Beecher talked to women all over the country and documented their poor health in her *Letters to the American People on Health and Happiness* (1855). During this period there was a great disparity between ideologies of women's improving status—whether propounded in the companionate marriage, the feminization of teaching, or the more-radical Seneca Falls "Declaration of Sentiments"—and the reality of women's biological lives. Popular between 1843 and 1900, and reaching a peak before the Civil War, the water cure functioned for women as a kind of halfway house during a period of transition when middle-class women desired a wider sphere yet were still tied to reproductive and domestic roles. By taking them away from their husbands and children, the water cure gave them respite from both.[18] As Dr. Silas O. Gleason of the Elmira Water Cure explained, "there was a large class of patients for whom physicians could do little in their home environment. They needed change of scene, systematic and constant oversight and the most healthful of mental, moral and physical aid, free from the cares and despondency that came of routine that had grown depressing."[19]

Harriet distributed her children with various friends and relatives: Eliza went to Mrs. Vale's, Fred to Joanna Smith's, Henry ("Howie") accompanied Calvin to his summer preaching post in New York City, and Hatty and Georgie went with Anna to Hartford for the summer. One of the last things Harriet did before she left was to write to Henry and Eunice Beecher, who had just lost their fifteen-month-old son, Georgie. Ordinarily such a distressing loss would have prompted many pages from her pen, but she explained, "I am not well enough to write you a letter, for I am very feeble & nothing hurts me like writing—my hands have again been almost useless."[20] By March she was on her way to Brattleboro.

Harriet had not been well since her physical and spiritual breakdown after her brother George's death in 1843. The cumulative effects of chronic mercury poisoning, cholera, and miscarriages—another in the fall of 1845—reduced Harriet to a state of "uselessness." Yet soon after her arrival in Brattleboro she was pursuing the rigorous regimen prescribed by hydropathy. "I walk habitually five miles a day—at intervals between my baths," she told Calvin, "never in my poorest days less than three—in some *good* days I have walked 7—& not suffered for it."[21] As a girl, Harriet had enjoyed the outdoor life in Litchfield. Horseback riding and required calisthenics punctuated her days at the Hartford Female Seminary. As a married woman, however, her orbit had been insular and indoors, limited to the desultory movements of a housewife: descending and climbing stairs, bending to lift a child, walking from the kitchen to the parlor to the nursery. Seven pregnancies and five confinements had further limited her mobility. "One of the reasons nine-teenth-century women thought themselves frail and weak," Kathryn Sklar has observed, "was that they *became* frail and weak during the protracted convalescence that orthodox medicine prescribed after childbirth. Most women remained in bed for several weeks and grew progressively enfeebled."[22]

Probably nothing at Brattleboro so invigorated Harriet's body and spirit as did hydropathy's program of regular exercise. Situated on the Connecticut River where it met the Whetstone Brook and the West River, with views alternating between mountain and forest, the Brattleboro Water Cure returned Harriet to the New England of her girlhood and gave her an oppor-tunity to wander through woods and streams with a poignant awareness of the luxury of such idle hours. The hills surrounding the town were full of freshwater springs. The year Harriet was there the patients constructed sev-eral walking paths that meandered from Elliot Street, where the buildings of the Water Cure were located, to Centerville and back again, past a woolen mill and an aqueduct, along shaded roads, fields of trailing arbutus, and cool trout brooks whose banks were dotted by fern and maidenhair. A summer house known as the "Eagle's Nest" was a favorite point of refuge.[23]

The indoor regimen of the water cure was something else. Progressive in its advocacy of exercise and its avoidance of drugs, hydropathy had not moved far from the ancient notion of humors on which allopathic medicine was based. It merely substituted showers, douches, sitz baths, and other watery rituals to draw out the noxious humors that allopathic physicians chased with drugs and leeches. Patients were stripped, bathed, and then rubbed with wet sheets. This water treatment, described as a sensuous and exhilarating experience by some historians, had unpleasant aspects as well.[24] A "crisis"—an irruption of fluids usually in the form of boils on the skin— was de rigueur and patients submitted to great discomforts in order to secure one. The founder of the Brattleboro Water Cure, Dr. Richard Wesselhoeft, whose authoritarian style and willingness to use small amounts of drugs set him apart from strict hydropaths, described his method:

> The patient is waked about four o'clock in the morning, and wrapped in thick woollen blankets almost hermetically; only the face and sometimes the whole head remains free; all other contact of the body with the air being carefully prevented. . . . After a while he begins to perspire, and he must continue to perspire till his covering itself becomes wet. . . . As soon as the attendant observes that there has been perspiration enough, he dips the patient into a cold bath, which is ready in the neighborhood of the bed. As soon as the first shock is over he feels a sense of comfort, and the surface of the water becomes covered with clammy matter, which perspiration has driven out from him. The pores, which have been opened by the process of perspiration, suck up the moisture with avidity, and, according to all observations, this is the moment when the wholesome change of matter takes place, by which the whole system gradually becomes purified.[25]

The emergence of such "clammy matter" was highly prized as evidence of the body's purification: the more noxious the discharge, the more effective supposedly the cure. But one historian has pointed out that the boils and pus that were taken as evidence of a cure were likely caused by infections brought on by the wet, unclean linen.[26] When Calvin Stowe took the cure the following year he marveled at the "quagmire of pus interspersed with hummocks of hard red blotches" that appeared on his abdomen. "[I]f it has not been *created* rather than brought out by the water," he mused, it was a wonder that he was not "long ago consigned to the grave or a mad house."[27] The unpleasant smell of the wet bandages—like sauerkraut, he complained—was further evidence of unsanitary conditions and local infections.[28] The numerous glasses of water that hydropathic patients were directed to drink were more beneficial than the constant soaking of the skin. Certainly, for those like Harriet who had been "saturated" with calomel and other toxins, the drinking of large quantities of water helped to purify their blood.

Harriet became an almost instant convert to hydropathy, renouncing allopathy and all its pomps and works. She consulted Dr. Wesselhoeft about Calvin's nervous symptoms and urged him to come and join her. He could leave Henry with Mrs. Fowler or Mrs. Blackwell, and the expenses for the two of them would not be that excessive because Dr. Wesselhoeft would give them a special rate. Calvin could rent out the house in the meantime and count on that income. He was tempted, but he decided that his conscience would not permit him to forsake his preaching duties and incur more expenses. (Harriet suggested he preach a sermon on the relationship between bodily health and religion.) He gave Harriet his prescription for his cure: "If your health were so far restored that you could take me again to *your bed and board*, that would be the surest, and safest, and indeed the only infallible way."[29] He complained volubly about the sexual restraint his wife's health imposed on their marriage.

During the summer Calvin traveled from New York to Brattleboro to visit Harriet. There he was met by an affectionate but physically inaccessible wife. Swathed in strips of linen tightly bound around her skin and kept wet through regular ablutions—the "wet bandage" that was intended to facilitate the exchange of fluids[30]—Harriet was as securely locked away if she had donned a chastity belt. Upon his return to New York Calvin wrote to her:

> It is a satisfaction to see that you do love me after all. Were it not for this miserable wet rag matter, and the mean business of sleeping in another bed, another room, and even another house, and being with you as if you were a withered-up old maid sister instead of the wife of my bosom, I believe I should run the risk as to expense and start off next Monday to spend another week with you. But this *having the form of marriage and denying the power therof* is, to my mind, of all contemptible things the most unutterably contemptible; and I shall not go 200 miles to put myself into it again.[31]

Cut loose from husband, children, and home cares, Harriet was not without society in Brattleboro. The water cure took a distinctly communal approach to health, and the social benefits of daily association with pleasant companions in a scenic rural area were a self-conscious part of the cure. Not by accident, her sister Catharine was also taking the cure. Samuel Foote, with characteristic pithiness and spirit, urged his wife, who went to Brattleboro with her daughter the following summer, to avail herself of this social benefit: "I was very glad to hear you were getting so many acquaintances & people that you *knew of* around you & have no doubt it will be of service to you—cheerfulness & gaiety are much better medicine than Hydropathy— Homeopathy or Allopathy & I hope you will use it largely."[32] Moreover, it was mainly a woman's world at Brattleboro. While men did take the water cure, Kathryn Sklar has estimated that two-thirds of the residents at Brattleboro were women, and many of the outdoor activities were particularly adapted to their tastes: " 'Breakfast and luncheon on the veranda, needlework and reading aloud by groups in sequestered nooks, walking at all times and in all directions, archery and picnics in favoring weather were features of the curriculum,' wrote one observer."[33] This "curriculum" re-created many of the long-lost pleasures of a female seminary: an orderly structure built around female camaraderie, reading, exercise, and socializing, the water cure gave women a space in which their physical and intellectual autonomy was secure. Sklar points out that the water cure provided women with a communal experience at a time when such were not readily available.[34] Certainly the women gathered at Brattleboro were more congenial, more homogeneous, and in Harriet's eyes more fit for companionship than the ragtag crew Mrs. Boardman had let into Harriet's boardinghouse. Among the 392 patients who took the cure with Harriet in 1846, for example, were Julia Ward Howe and her husband, Samuel Gridley Howe. Another literary woman who frequented Brattleboro was Harriet's former pupil, Fanny Fern. Interestingly, many of the guests were from the South.[35] Thus, like a female seminary, the water cure afforded a national social experience. The second summer that Calvin Stowe was there, he was joined by Horace Greeley, one son of Martin Van Buren, and two sons of John C. Calhoun—an unlikely set of political bedfellows who gathered to hear Greeley make a speech. "Such combinations (or reunions as the French call them) are brought together by the water-cure," Calvin commented.[36]

The women lived together in a building called "Paradise Row," where they enjoyed "long long talks lingering in each others rooms," as Harriet remembered. Just as at a female seminary the bonds of sisterhood were strengthened during a time of revival as students encouraged and supported one another in their spiritual life, so at Brattleboro the women spent their evenings "comforting one another with hope of crisis."[37] Harriet was a "general favorite" at Brattleboro.[38] While she was there she clipped a lock of her rich, auburn brown hair as a rememberance; she perhaps exchanged it with a new acquaintance in a ritual reminiscent of schoolgirl romances.[39] "Not for years, have I enjoyed life as I have here," Harriet admitted, "real keen enjoyment—everything agrees with me—& tho my right hand has not yet found her cunning I think it cannot but come right when health rises in every other respect."[40]

At the end of the summer, having completed his interim preaching duties at his Bleeker Street parish, Calvin traveled to Hartford to retrieve Anna and the children, preparatory to returning to Cincinnati, where they would set the house in readiness for Harriet's return. Harriet, however, convinced Calvin that she had not yet received the full benefit of the water cure and that she should stay through the winter. The letter she wrote him on August 14 marches in her characteristically strong, evenly slanted hand, showing no evidence of a tremor; still, she was saving herself by having her sister write part of the letter to her dictation. "For ought I know, my *hands* are so that I could write a quire, but my eyes are so weak I cannot write two lines without their giving out," she explained to Calvin.[41] "I feel as if I should come home well," she told him, "& if I do it will be with firmer health than I have had these ten years—comfort your heart with this—weeks fly fast—March will soon be here & we will come together again."[42] Calvin agreed to this plan, believing that to secure his wife's health would return her to his bed. "Much as I suffer from your absence," he told her, "I should suffer still more from you presence, unless you can be in a better condition than you have been for a year past. It is now a full year since your last miscarriage, and you well know what has been the state of things both in regard to yourself & me ever since."[43] As the winter months stretched his patience, he reported to her what Walnut Hills thought of her extended absence—as embodied in the views of a Mrs. Overacre. Harriet responded that it was not as if she were *enjoying* herself, and she wondered at the curious view of old Lady Overacre that wives could "be better dispensed with in summer than in winter." It was trying that people did not understand the sacrifice she was making in order to restore her health.[44] Calvin reminded her that it was "almost 18 months since I have had a wife to sleep with me. It is enough to kill any man, especially such a man as I am," and neither did people appreciate "the real and hard sacrifices I make, and the purpose for which I make them."[45] In a passage that exhibits the nineteenth century's easy acceptance of same-sex physical intimacy (later termed "deviant" by the sexologists), Calvin told her, "When I get desperate, & cannot stand it any longer, I get dear, good kind hearted Br[other] Stagg to come and sleep with me, and he puts his arms round me & hugs me to my hearts' content."[46]

That physical intimacies flourished in the dormitories of Brattleboro is likely. Harriet's letters are silent on this point, but Calvin, much more forthright about such matters, told Harriet of his innocent affair with a total stranger, a Mr. Farber of Newton, Massachusetts. His engagement to be married postponed by a disease of the eyes, Mr. Farber came to the water cure and "[took] it into his little black-curly pate to fall desperately in love with me," Calvin told Harriet; "and he kisses and kisses upon my rough old face, as if I were a most beautiful young lady instead of a musty old man. The Lord sent him here to be my comfort. . . . He will have me sleep with him once in a while, and he says, *that is almost as good as being married*—the dear little innocent ignorant soul."[47] For the Stowes, such same-sex physical intimacies allayed the deprivations of their voluntary celibacy and bore no hazards of reproduction.

Harriet's hands and eyes were well enough on January 1 for her to write a very long letter to Calvin in which she assessed their marriage. She was moved by the fact "that the seventh of January now coming is the anniversary of our wedding some eleven years ago," adding, "I am not precisely sure that I have got the date of the thing exactly right but that is no particular matter as you know that my forte is not in remembering dates" (their anniversary was the sixth of January). Acknowledging their temperamental differences and her own lack of sensitivity to his needs for order, she suggested that they not dwell on past mistakes but rather build on their "mutual respect & affection" for one another and use their differences to lead one another to mutual improvement. Harriet named as one of three reasons for their marital problems "the want of any definite plan of mutual watchfulness, with regard to each others improvement of a definite time & place for doing it with a firm determination to improve & be improved by each other—to confess our faults one to another—pray one for another that we may be healed—If we are only faithful & constant in this I am *sure* that we shall find no trouble in any thing else." Such a scheme would, Harriet knew, be a brake on Calvin's impulsive and often overly harsh criticisms. He was quite capable of using strong language when he was angry—such as telling her to "go to grass"—and while he forgot his words as soon as he uttered them, for Harriet they conjured up vivid pictures that she could not dispel. "[Y]ou are willing *general* to admit that you are often hasty & unjust but very seldom—almost never to admit it in any particular case—you leave the poisoned arrow in the wound—Now my nature is such that I *cannot* forget such words,—if they are only taken back I get over them directly but if not they remain for months." A scheme of criticism and self-criticism—which in fact they regularly engaged in in letters such as this—would make for calmer assessments. "Did you ever speak to me in a considerate careful affectionate manner of my faults," Harriet asked him, "[and] find me unwilling to listen?" On the other hand,

> when a wife is daily & hourly tried by a careless servant who leaves undone half she tells her & spoils her best plans & arrangements yet in spite of all this difficulty has by great effort been punctual in her hours for four or five days of the week—at last comes a day when she fails—if then her husband tells her that its always just so—things *never* are regular—is it likely to make her confess her faults—What he accuses her of is not true—tho it *is* true that she has failed that time.

Harriet observed, "This fault my dear is not peculiar to you but is I believe very general among your sex in their efforts for domestic reform."[48]

One historian of the family cites this letter as an example of the way in which Victorians used marriage as a vehicle for sanctification;[49] it could as easily be cited as an example of the way in which the drive for perfection shaped the institution of the companionate marriage. While social reformers founded utopian communities such as Brook Farm and Oneida, the Stowes struggled to put their marriage on a proper footing, engaging in a private way in the search for a new order. The scheme of mutual criticism Harriet suggested in this letter was in fact an institution at Oneida, and one that surely contributed to the long life of that perfectionist communal experiment. John Humphrey Noyes instituted a community ritual whereby anyone who had a complaint about anyone else in the community spoke it freely and publicly— a necessary safety valve in a tightly knit group experimenting with new sexual arrangements.[50] Perfectionism melded the religious and the secular in a volatile mix, threatening to create all things new.

For his part, Calvin Stowe traced the source of his domestic troubles to what he called the "Beecher buzz." He told Harriet, "you are good, and kind, and devotional, with a rich and glowing soul—but you are not one of the *resting sort*—some wheel must be buzzing where you are—and this breaks up all my resolutions and endeavors." He came to understand the Beecher buzz by observing the negative effect of visits from Catharine Beecher. "Whenever Kate makes her appearance in the house all my distresses are multiplied a million fold, because she has a million times more buz than you have, and in addition to that, a most total incapacity for perceiving or even imagining that anything which she does can possibly be in the least annoying or disagreeable to any one of God's rational offspring."[51] He recalled with horror the previous February, "when Cate was ke-crutcheting round here like a streak of forked lightning."[52] He told Harriet, "I seriously think it to be just as much your duty to renounce Cate Beecher and all her schoolmarms, as it is to renounce the devil and all his work," adding, "[s]he would kill off a whole regiment like you & me in three days."[53] The scheme with which Catharine was currently bedeviling Calvin was her Central Committee for Promoting National Education, which in a moment of weakness he had agreed to head. At Stowe's urging the task had been taken from his shoulders by Governor Slade of Vermont, but he could not escape hearing about Catharine's work—which easily slipped into her assuming that he would perform time-consuming tasks. Harriet wrote back to him, "As to Kate & Gov Slade it is all a mere nervous fidget on your part. Nothing will come on you that I know of & she expects nothing of you—you seem some how to connect very terrible ideas with poor Katy as if she was going to carry you off bodily one of these days but I think on this point you may set your heart at rest."[54]

In mid-January Harriet wrote, "We still splash on here & it grows colder & colder." The bar she held on to during her ten-minute douche was covered with a half-inch of ice, but she endured five or six of these "srubbings & dashings" each day and walked eight to ten miles in the crisp Vermont air. "After tea in the evening we have a reading circle or else act proverbs & charades & play games till eight." She ate "like a judgement" and had no difficulty sleeping. "The fact is that by night every thought feeling or emotion is pretty thoroughly washed out of me as you may see by this letter."[55] At the end of February she delayed her return once again. There were eruptions starting on her back and she wanted the benefit of this final crisis. They felt like "nettles" and were coming "exactly over the place where so much tartar emetic ointment has been rubbed in."[56] She did not draw the conclusion that this irritation of the skin might have been caused by the tartar emetic. She was a believer.

Harriet planned to return as soon as possible after the canals reopened in early March. Calvin hoped that she would come home in "tolerable health" and in a frame of mind to be "contented with things as they are about home, and not fretting me in everlasting torture with projects of improvement." Time and money were both tight. He was involved in an ecclesiastical lawsuit that promised to be harrassing and time consuming; moreover, her father had asked for the return of the $100 they had borrowed two years ago and it had to be paid out of this quarter's salary. If they stayed at Lane for two more years, they would then be in a situation to go ahead,[57] but in the meantime, he begged her, "make up your mind to be quiet and easy with things as they are" and not injure herself and him with her "incessant schemes and plans."[58] In a more positive and less self-protective mood he encouraged her, "I want you to learn just what it is that God made you for, and just try to be that and nothing more nor different. You are capable of great things, but you have been worn out and disabled by very little things."[59] Harriet was disposed to go along with his prescription for domestic peace, only worrying that people would expect too much of her. She described herself as "a broken pitcher that had been boiled in milk, that needs very careful handling, or it will come in pieces again."[60] She planned to "keep up hydropathic rules" when she returned home, particularly outdoor walking.[61] She wrote confidentially to her husband, "Let us you & I stroll together through the woods as we used to & go to our tulip tree once more."[62]

But Calvin and Harriet were not the only ones who determined the rhythms of their household. Soon after her return in early April there descended on Walnut Hills the avatar of Catharine Beecher—in the form of thirty-five of her missionary schoolteachers enroute to points west. Catharine had made no arrangements for board and room for the young women in Cincinnati, perhaps assuming that her family would take care of them. The women were unceremoniously left without baggage in the middle of the road, with no sense of where to go or to whom to apply. As soon as Calvin Stowe heard of it, Samuel Foote reported, "he fell sick & took to his bed and left the management of the whole troop to Harriet." She distributed the women around in small clumps—leaving some at her house with Calvin and then retreating to her Uncle Samuel's house where they placed another group. The teachers stayed for two days, after which, Samuel Foote observed, they left for "the uttermost parts of the Earth—determined, as I inferred from some casual remarks, to root up the weeds of Popery which have been springing up in our land—whilst we slept—and to drive the Scarlet Woman & all her dreadful praying beyond the Rocky Mountains & into the great Pacific Ocean."[63] Uncle Samuel's skeptical, cosmopolitan voice rang in Harriet's ears as it had from early childhood. When at the end of her career, long after she had adopted the Episcopalianism of her mother's family, she wrote her fictionalized reminiscence of growing up in Litchfield, it was this voice that gave a satirical edge to her portrait of the ladies of the town as they reacted to one of her father's antipapist sermons:

> Old ladies in their tea-drinkings talked about the danger of making a right-eousness of forms and rites and ceremonies, and seemed of the opinion that the proceedings of the Episcopal church, however attractive, were only an insidious putting forth of one paw of the Scarlet Beast of Rome, and that if not vigorously opposed the whole quadruped, tooth and claw, would yet be upon their backs. (PP, 55)

The comic overstatement—a staple of western fiction and a device well-worked by Mark Twain—suggested a doubleness of vision, the worldliness of a traveler who could compare contrasting beliefs and mores. It was not the voice of an evangelical missionary.

Harriet had not written anything except a few letters while she was at the water cure. Her last publications had come out early in 1846; one of them was the series that sounded the alarm for teachers in the West. Calvin scolded Catharine Beecher for putting her up to this expenditure of her limited energy, but Catharine defended herself by saying that Harriet had always been a partner in her enterprises and it was only fair to have her so represented in public. She shrewdly observed, "that I should not have asked her to do had I not known that you wished her to write & she had determined to do so—& I knew she could get more money at less expence of nerves by this, than any other piece she would write."[64] It was a well placed shot, for in his worry over their debts Calvin put considerable pressure on Harriet to keep her pen moving. While she was still recuperating at Brattleboro, Calvin was remembering fondly the $15 a page she earned at the Lady's Book and looking forward to the time when "she will be able to write again and pick up a little pocket money."[65] Harriet spent the fall after her return from Brattleboro sewing rather than writing. Nothing appeared under her name the following year except one short piece in the New-York Evangelist and a reprints of two pieces published earlier.[66]

Nine months after her return from Brattleboro Harriet gave birth to her sixth child, Samuel Charles. Born in January 1848, he bore testimony to the salubrious effects of the water cure, for he was the healthiest, happiest baby Harriet had ever had. In contrast to the sickly, fussy infants who refused to nurse, "Charley" was a rosy bud of baby flesh who eagerly took the breast. He acted, Harriet told Calvin, as if "women were made for his especial convenience."[67] The physical and emotional delight Harriet took in this baby, intensified by her ability to nurse him, reminded her of the empty arms and aching heart of her sister-in-law, Eunice, who had lost yet another of her children, Katy, aged sixteen months:

> "I . . . have thought even in your sorrow that it would give you pleasure to know that after ten years of trial God at length has given me a baby that I can *nurse myself*—My little Charlie is larger & more thriving than any child I ever had— I nurse him exclusively & use both breasts (one you know I never used before with any of my other children) & have an abundance for him & I have thought often when I felt what a comfort it was to have him by my side at night & in my arms by day how greatly you were tried dear sister in losing what you had thus watched & cherished."[68]

Four and a half years had elapsed since Harriet had last given birth, the longest respite from reproduction that she had ever had. If Charley's health owed something to this spacing, it owed more to hydropathy. Her previous baby, Georgiana—irritable and high-strung—may have been adversely affected in utero by the large amounts of mercurous chloride in her system. Harriet conceived Charley with her body cleansed of poisons and strenthened by exercise, plain food, and plain living. Just as significant were the psychological benefits of hydropathy's approach to the body as an animal system that would follow a natural course if only the laws of health were respected—an approach that had particular significance for pregnancy, which regular physicians treated as a disease. Moreover, a number of hydropathic physicians made the physiology of women a particular specialty and developed approaches to birthing that eased women's anxiety and discomfort. Instead of using drugs, hydropathic physicians prescribed gentle sitz baths for women in labor; the soothing water and the control the woman took of the process—she was encouraged to move around as much as she wished—provided a supportive atmosphere. Hydropathy brought birthing— fraught with terror in a period when puerperal fever and other iatrogenic diseases were common—back into the ordinary processes of life.[69] There is no evidence that Dr. Wesselhoeft made parturant women his special objects of care, but Harriet could have read about these new methods in the *Water-Cure Journal.* Even if she did not, the water cure's unabashed focus on the nude body, communal bathing, and daily sharing of symptoms helped Victorian women to repossess their bodies. Harriet's easy ability to nurse Charley was continuous with the water cure's expectations. The fat, healthy baby who smiled up at her was tangible proof of hydropathy's claim to Regenerate the Race.

CHAPTER SEVENTEEN

Crossing the River:
1849–1850

*I*n a small, gilt frame rests a daguerreotype of Harriet's baby Charley. He is a year and a half old—that magical age when even the homeliest child takes on a glow of irresistible wonder. Charley is exceptionally handsome. His head, resting on a large, white pillow, is turned slightly to the left, facing the viewer. His regular features are set with an eye to classical proportions. The broad, high forehead suggests a generous inheritance of intelligence from both his Beecher and Stowe ancestors. Calvin called him "my pride and my hope, my Martin Luther boy." He is wearing a white gown, which shows up against the dark comforter on which he lies. His hands, resting on his stomach, are gently curled around a sprig of holly. He appears to be sleeping; his eyes are closed and his expression is serene. But Charley would wake no more. He had been struck by the dreaded cholera. The pure water of Brattleboro bore little relationship to what Cincinnatians drank in the hog capital of the world; there the liquid that purportedly brought health was the bearer of a deadly contagious disease.

In March 1849 Harriet wrote to Sarah Beecher, "It is all shoreless tideless hopeless unmitigated mud here—mud without hope or end—dreadful to look upon & like the Egyptian frogs it comes into our houses to our bed chambers & kneading troughs—& still the weather is cross & sour & doleful & every one is sleepy & has the head ache my own poor self among the number—I long now for spring—this betwixt & betweenity I dont admire." Harriet Beecher Stowe stood on the edge of changes that would totally transform herself, her family, and her career. When she emerged on the other side of them, she was a bereaved mother, her western career was over, and she was internationally famous. Now her concerns, as reflected in her letter to Sarah, were more quotidian: Charley might have the measles, Mr. Stowe was going to Brattleboro again that summer, she hoped to secure the services of Aunt Esther for a few months, she might come East in July or August, and she was "driving hard" on the spring sewing and had "bought & cut & fitted dresses aprons sacks jackets pantaloons double gowns aprons and all sorts of matters" till her "head ached again"; in a postscript she asked if Sarah had read Thomas B. Macauley's *History of England,* the first two volumes of which had been published the previous year.[1]

From the watery depths of Brattleboro where he spent the summers of 1848 and 1849, Calvin scolded Harriet for what he perceived was the state of "utter exhaustion" in which her letters were written, worrying that she would quickly reduce herself to the condition from which she had so recently recovered. "What right have you to be preparing Charles's papers for publication, or taking care of Miss K. to your own destruction, or the neglect of your family?," he demanded. Harriet had allowed herself to be drawn into the project of editing a series of lectures her brother Charles was about to publish. Charles Beecher, who was struggling to emerge from an adolescence protracted by an aversion to the ministry and a near-fatal attraction to romantic poetry, adopted in his letters the bracing tone of an Old Testament prophet and wrote jeremiads calling down doom on "the *democratic body politic.*" Increasingly involved in abolitionist activity after his sojourn in New Orleans, he told Harriet, "This guilty land will not escape." Dipping his pen in the imagery of the Book of Revelation, he poured out several vials:

> The Woman will first ride the Democratic beast & become drunk with blood. Then she herself will be destroyed. Democracy become Anarchy, & universal confederacy against God. Antichrist will rise to the surface, & ride on the foam-wave, & then will come the End.—Father may not live to see it. But I for one expect either to die by violence or to live in the fastnesses & retreats of the forest.—The plot is laid. The explosion will come soon.[2]

Such looking toward Armageddon on the part of pietistic perfectionists helped set the stage for the Civil War. The first battles were fought in the Protestant churches, many of which split into northern and southern factions over the issue of slavery when, in their assemblies and general meetings, they found themselves confronted with resolutions condemning slavery and slaveholders. The proslavery factions argued that the Bible sanctioned slavery; that it was a political institution with which the church had no business meddling; that slavery had always existed. But what to do when a Christian slave brought accusations of unchristian behavior against a Christian master? The New School Presbyterian Church in Petersburg, Virginia, resolved the matter by declaring that, "as slave-holders, we cannot consent longer to remain in connection with any church where there exists a statute conferring the right upon slaves to arraign their masters before the judicatory of the church." This included cases in which a Presbyterian slave charged that a fellow church member was selling him against his will.[3] When Charles Beecher was called to a new Congregational church in Washington, D.C., he was assured that he would be able to preach the "whole gospel," that is, to exclude slaveholders from membership and communion. One of his colleagues encouraged him to take this post in "the centre of the field of Armageddon," assuring him that he would "be respectably sustained by the Sacramental host that will gather with you to the battle of God Almighty."[4]

Harriet edited Charles's book as he requested, even contributing an introduction and a page on the infant Jesus. Harpers published it in 1849 under the title *The Incarnation; or, Pictures of the Virgin and Her Son.* The aim of the book was to provide a fictionalized biography of Christ, or, as Harriet expressed it in her introduction, "to reproduce the Sacred Narratives, under the aspects which it presents to an imaginative mind, with the appliances of geographical, historical, and critical knowledge." In a passage that could be compared to Nathaniel Hawthorne's prefaces to his romances, Stowe addressed skeptical readers: "There may be some who at first would feel a prejudice against this species of composition, as so blending together the outlines of truth and fiction as to spread a doubtful hue of romance over the whole. They wish to know that what they are reading is true. They dislike to have their sympathies enlisted and their feelings carried away by what, after all, may never have happened." She answered this objection by pointing out that readers always form *some* conceptions, however hazy, from their reading, and that the narrative of a scholar is at least as good as the impressions one has "borrowed from some antiquated engraving or old church painting, the fruit of monkish revery or of artistic inspiration." In "this hard and utilitarian age" there were imaginative minds yearning for aliment; if the godly Protestants supplied the need, these fervent spirits would be spared the need for "the strains of a Byron, or the glowing pictures of a Bulwer or a Sue." Thus did Harriet help in a Beecher family project to fend off Romanism and secular decadence.[5]

As for the page she wrote for Charles on the infancy of Jesus, which he incorporated,[6] Harriet drew inspiration from the reigning baby in the Stowe household. Calvin wrote to her when Charley was six months old, "You are so proud of your baby, one would think you never saw a baby before. Well, you had trouble enough with the infancy of the others—I am right glad you can take comfort with this one."[7] Several months later he wrote in another key, "You almost alarm me with your constant eulogies of Charlie. You set your heart upon him so much, I fear the Lord will find it necessary to take him away from us. Hold him loosely and at the Divine disposal, as you do all other blessings, or you may have a heart-break."[8] Harriet had given this child to God by naming him Samuel Charles—"Samuel in remembrance of the beautiful story of Hannah in the old Testament—'Long as he liveth he shall be lent to the Lord.' "[9] She did not expect, however, that God would require his services so soon.

When cholera broke out in June 1849, Cincinnati, used to these summer scourges, continued as usual. Most assumed that it would be confined to the poor sections of the city where the Irish and the Negroes lived. Statistical probability was on their side: in almost every epidemic for which figures are available, cholera fell on the poor in disproportionate numbers, a fact easily explained by the crowded and often unsanitary conditions in which they lived.[10] By the end of the month, however, it was clear that this was a particularly malignant and virulent epidemic. On June 29 Harriet wrote to Calvin that 116 had been reported dead in one day; "Hearse drivers have scarce been allowed to unharness their horses, while furniture carts and common vehicles are often employed for the removal of the dead." She reported that a "universal panic" had begun to take hold in the city. "[T]hose who had talked confidently of the cholera being confined to the lower classes and those who were imprudent began to feel as did the magicians of old, 'This is the finger of God.'" The mayor proclaimed a day of fasting, humiliation, and prayer. As wagons and carts rumbled past her window, their fearful burden arranged for burial with obvious marks of haste, Harriet and her family strove to keep up calm and cheerful dispositions. She advised against Calvin's return: "To exchange the salubrious air of Brattleboro for the pestilent atmosphere of this place with your system rendered sensitive by water-cure treatment would be extremely dangerous."[11] Calvin advised her, "don't go to the city very often (you have had cholera once & that increases your liability to it)."[12] He gave vent to the distressing thought that in the haste of burials, "many a poor creature has probably been buried alive."[13] When such reflections were not contained by a religious frame of reference, they slid uneasily toward the gothic horrors of a Charles Brockden Brown or an Edgar Allan Poe.[14]

On July 4 the usual Independence Day celebrations with their full complement of drunken patriots took to the streets, heedless of whether Death was one of the uninvited guests. This careless revelry—reminiscent of Poe's tale of pestilence, "The Masque of the Red Death"—led Harriet to reflect:

> One hundred and twenty burials from cholera alone yesterday, yet to-day we see parties bent on pleasure or senseless carousing, while to-morrow and next day will witness a fresh harvest of death from them. How we can become accustomed to anything! A while ago ten a day dying of cholera struck terror to all hearts; but now the tide has surged up gradually until the deaths average over a hundred daily, and everybody is getting accustomed to it. Gentlemen make themselves agreeble to ladies by reciting the number of deaths in this house or that. This together with talk of funerals, cholera medicines, cholera dietetics, and chloride of lime form the ordinary staple of conversation. Serious persons of course throw in moral reflections to their taste.[15]

Even as she was writing, the cholera had made its way into Walnut Hills. Professor Allen wrote on July 6 to Lyman Beecher—who like Calvin Stowe was out of town—that a recent meeting of the Lane board of trustees had failed to gather a quorum as some people were away and "Burroughs *dead—*of cholera."[16] Professor Allen and his wife Sarah were themselves recovering from dysentery, often the first symptom of the disease. A rural paradise two miles outside the city, Walnut Hills inadvertently was laid open to the spread of cholera by a decision of the Lane board of trustees. Under the pressure of a declining financial base and in accordance with Lane's social principles, the board had divided a parcel of the campus into small lots and rented them at a low price to a number of poor families, including a dozen families of freed slaves. Black women from "shacktown" entered the houses of the white professors as servants—they were Harriet's "favorite resorts in cases of emergency."[17] It is likely that cholera plucked off the most vulnerable in shacktown and then spread to the rest of the neighborhood by the coming and going of these domestic servants.

On July 10 Harriet wrote to Calvin, "Yesterday little Charley was taken ill, not seriously, and at any other season I should not be alarmed. Now, however, a slight illness seems like a death sentence, and I will not dissemble that I feel from the outset very little hope." The doctors were all overworked, but Harriet managed to carry Charley to one of them, who so discouraged her with his prognosis that she was frightened and wished for the support of her absent husband and father. At one o'clock in the morning on July 12 Harriet was awakened by the shouts of a servant, who told her that eleven-year-old Henry had been seized by vomiting. She sprang out of bed, calling on God for help, tended Henry, who was soon relieved, and turned her attention to Charley. She applied hydropathic remedies—a wet sheet rather than the calomel that was liberally dispensed for cholera. He appeared to be improving, as measured by his increased crankiness. "Never was crossness in a baby more admired," she told Calvin.[18] For the next week he continued to improve. Calvin stood in admiration of his wife's strength: "In a day of calamity you are worth having, yours is a heart that never fails."[19] He praised her handling of Henry's case—"a very bad one to manage, he had had the diarrhea so long; and you took the best course possible. It was better than all the Doctors."[20]

On July 15 an old black woman who did washing in the neighborhood was taken ill over her tubs and died the next day. Anna, Harriet, and her daughters made a shroud for Aunt Frankie, who had been one of Harriet's stays in emergencies; after perhaps helping to prepare the body of this "good, honest, trustful old soul," they went to her funeral.[21] The next day Charley came down with what was unmistakably cholera. For five days Harriet watched helplessly as his small body was wracked by the disease. On July 23 Harriet wrote to Calvin, "At last, my dear, the hand of the Lord hath touched us. We have been watching all day by the dying bed of little Charley, who is gradually sinking." She did not expect him to survive the night. There was no point in Calvin returning: "All will be over before you could possibly get here, and the epidemic is now said by the physicians to prove fatal to every new case."[22] Charley lasted three more days, his healthy constitution now only an instrument of prolonging his end.

On July 26 Harriet went wearily upstairs. In the parlor down below lay

Charley, pale and cold, dressed in a much smaller shroud than Harriet had made for Aunt Frankie. As Harriet reached for paper and pen to tell her husband "At last it is over," her heart was still full of the scenes of suffering to which she had been an unwilling witness. That such befell the child who of all her children caused her the least trouble made her grief keen and her own responsibility to Charley sadly incomplete:

> Never was he anything to me but a comfort. He has been my pride and joy. Many a heartache has he cured for me. Many an anxious night have I held him to my bosom and felt the sorrow and loneliness pass out of me with the touch of his little warm hands. Yet I have just seen him in his death agony, looked on his imploring face when I could not help nor soothe nor do one thing, not one, to mitigate his cruel suffering, do nothing but pray in my anguish that he might die soon.[23]

With the death of Charley, Stowe experienced one of the most common and profound events of nineteenth-century family life. Certainly the death of a child is among the most difficult of all deaths to come to terms with, for it so upsets what we think of as the natural order of things. In the mid-nineteenth century, such feelings were intensified in the popular culture by a historical shift underway that elevated the status of the middle-class child. In contrast to the prosaic eighteenth-century view in which children were seen as little adults whose labor power should be utilized as soon as humanly possible, the nineteenth- century middle-class child was increasingly viewed as an object of special care whose nurture became central to the elaboration of the bourgeois home. In an inverse equation Thorstein Veblen would later explain, the child's symbolic value increased as his direct contribution to the domestic economy diminished. This is one meaning of the daguerreotype that Harriet had made of Charley before he was buried. This new way of emotionally investing in children grew at a pace that outstripped the harsh demographic reality. Although infant mortality among their class was declining—a contributing factor in this new evaluation of children—the investment of the middle class in a more sentimental approach to childhood was growing even faster. Parents engaged in a delicate balancing act as they attempted to hold their children loosely and at God's disposal. In 1831 Elizabeth Foote wrote of her son, "I never have thought much of George until this winter, but now my admiration is as unqualified as any other persons— I think he is one of the prettiest little fellows that I ever saw yet I am almost afraid to rejoice in him—I am afraid it is not true that he is to remain with us and grow to be a healthy and intelligent child it seems too much like a miracle to be true."[24] This child died three years later. The notion of the "special child"—of whom Little Eva was the apotheosis—grew out of this historical shift. "Is there a peculiar love given us for those that God wills to take from us," Harriet wondered after Charley's death. "Is there not something brighter & better around them than around those who live—Why else in so many households is there a tradition of one brighter more beautiful more promising than all the rest, laid early low."[25] The notion that God had appointed these special children had, as Nina Baym has observed, "immense reconciling power in an era when many children did in fact die young."[26]

The distance between this "special child" enshrined in nineteenth-century literature and daguerreotypes and the slave child removed from parents as soon as profitable was as vast as it was unremarked upon. After the external slave trade was abolished, the South depended on reproduction to replenish the ranks of cotton pickers and hoe wielders and plow handlers. Indeed, Deborah Gray White notes that "some masters figured that at least 5 to 6 percent of their profit would accrue from natural increase."[27] When slave women did not readily find a mate of their own, they were crudely bred with mates of the master's choosing, or impregnated by the master himself. Under these oppressive circumstances, refusing to have a child was sometimes a form of resistance. While the fertility of slave women was nevertheless double that of the white population, there were stories of bondwomen who aborted pregnancies rather than bring another child into slavery. There were also stories of bondwomen who gave their children poison rather than see them sold away from them into a life of degradation, pain, and oppression. "I just decided I'm not going to let Old Master sell this baby; he just ain't going to do it," a slave mother was reported to say. "She got up and give it something out of a bottle, and pretty soon it was dead."[28] Although such behavior was not typical, Harriet Beecher Stowe included several references to infanticide among bondwomen in *Uncle Tom's Cabin*, one in her "Concluding Remarks," and more prominently, in the story of Cassy, who took her child in her arms, gave him laudanum, and held him "while he slept to death," declaring this the best death she could have given him, for "he, at least, is out of pain" (UTC, 2:145). Stowe's sensitivity to circumstances that could drive a mother to such acts, in the name of maternal love, was surely heightened by watching at the bedside of Charley as the Calvinist God, for reasons best known to himself, extracted a full toll of suffering before releasing her baby. "There were circumstances about his death of such peculiar bitterness," she later wrote, "of what might seem almost cruel suffering, that I felt that I could never be consoled for it, unless it should appear that this crushing of my own heart might enable me to work out some great good to others."[29]

The capriciousness of a Calvinist God, to whom there was no recourse but submission to his disciplinary rod, was monstrously paralleled by the cruelty of an overseerer who held the human destiny of slaves under his whip. Infant mortality among slaves was twice that among the white population and slaves possessed their own children only at the whim of the master, who often sold them into distant bondages.[30] To escape this fate, a slave woman and her child fled across the Ohio River in a celebrated story.[31] Thus slave parents experienced in extreme form the contradictions of middle-class parenting. Stowe turned the distance between the "special child" of bereaved middle-class parents and the exploited slave child into a source of political energy. By focusing in *Uncle Tom's Cabin* on the separation of children from parents, Stowe tapped the overwrought feelings of white, middle-class parents and enlisted their sympathies for slave parents through the powerful metaphors of an evangelical religion shaped by both loss and bondage. "It was at *his* dying bed, and at *his* grave," she later wrote of Charley, "that I learnt what a poor slave mother may feel when her child is torn away from her."[32]

Harriet laid her baby in a grave close by her house in Walnut Hills, perhaps with the thought that she would be able to visit it regularly and tend to the flowers she planted there. Such was not to be the case. Before the dreadful summer of 1849 had turned into fall, Harriet and Calvin turned their faces eastward. Her family had already begun their retreat from the West—a tacit admission that the Mississippi Valley was lost. In 1846 Calvin Stowe remarked that although Lyman Beecher was in fine health, "[h]e thinks . . . that he can't govern the world much longer, and that he will have to leave it to God after all."[33] In 1847 Henry Ward Beecher accepted a call to Plymouth Church in Brooklyn. The next year Samuel Foote, conceding that the western climate was too "debilitating" for his wife, declared his intent to take his family back to Connecticut.[34] In 1850 Calvin Stowe finally felt justified in laying down the labor that had consumed the prime years of his professional life between age thirty and forty-eight. The nine thousand who lay dead of cholera within three miles of his house were a strong inducement to leave Lane Seminary and to remove his family to the brisker air of New England.[35] He accepted a call to Bowdoin College, his alma mater and first teaching post. Harriet's departure from Walnut Hills before she had grieved for Charley through a complete change of seasons meant that nostalgia for her home blended indiscriminately with nostalgia for Charley. In the process, Walnut Hills became a memory and a myth, a home that reverberated with strains earthly and celestial.

While Calvin taught at Lane through the fall term of 1850, Harriet went on ahead to Brunswick, Maine, to set up housekeeping. In April 1850, reversing the patriarchal trek of Lyman Beecher and his sons and daughters westward eighteen years earlier, Harriet set out. She was six months pregnant and she traveled without benefit of male escort, accompanied by her three oldest children and Aunt Esther. "There is to be no gentleman in our party," Esther remarked, "but as I told Eunice an *Old Maid* at the head of a party of females will be as efisicent to keep off all intruders as half a dozen mastiffs."[36] As their canal boat passed through the center of Pennsylvania, the children exclaimed over the mountains that rose so much more steeply than the Kentucky hills across the river from Cincinnati. When they passed through locks, Harriet skipped out of the boat and walked to the next elevation. Removed from the humidity of the Mississippi Valley, Harriet's pursuit of hydropathic health might have a better result. Indeed, she declared that the two years she spent in Brunswick were the healthiest and happiest years of her life.[37]

After stops in Brooklyn to see Henry and Eunice and Hartford to see Mary and Thomas and Isabella and John, she went to Boston to buy furniture and to visit Edward and Isabella Beecher. Edward had been in the vanguard of the Beecher family on abolition in the 1830s, and now he and Isabella had heated talks with Harriet about the Fugitive Slave Law, which Congress was debating. Part of the package known as the Compromise of 1850 after it was adopted in September of that year, the Fugitive Slave Law brought to a boil the regional tensions that had been simmering since the Missouri Compromise of 1820. By admitting one free state (Maine) and one slave state (Missouri) and barring slavery north of the latitude 36° 30′, the Missouri Compromise maintained a precarious nationhood cobbled together around the contradiction of slavery in a democratic country. The rapid annexation of new territories, under the pressure of war fever and manifest destiny, not only made the mission of the Beecher family in the West a drop in the bucket against the tides of cultural change, it exceeded the political abilities of statesmen charged with papering over deep sectional rivalries that threatened the Union. The Compromise of 1850 admitted California as a free state, organized the Utah and New Mexico territories on the basis of popular sovereignty, abolished the slave trade in the District of Columbia after January 1, 1851, and, to allay southern feelings, put teeth in the 1793 fugitive slave law. This new Fugitive Slave Law, by requiring northerners to assist in the capture and return of human property, brought "the abomination of slavery to our very door," as Henry Ward Beecher observed with some satisfaction.[38] While making it impossible to ignore the issue, the Fugitive Slave Law further stretched the delicate fabric of the Union. "[O]ne thing is *certain*," thundered the New York *Independent*, "[T]his Union will NOT be permanent, if its Government is to carry out this enslavement of black men in the free cities and towns of the North."[39]

In Brunswick, the Bowdoin professors and their wives did everything they could to welcome and assist Harriet. Professor Uphams's wife engaged a woman to make carpets and to stay with her until her confinement. Harriet found a wonderful old house to rent—the Titcomb homestead, formerly occupied by Henry Wadsworth Longfellow while he was a student at Bowdoin with Calvin Stowe. The rent was high; Calvin had expected when he negotiated his salary that $75 would suffice for housing, but this house cost $125. Harriet was undeterred, however. She planned to pay the rent with money earned from her writing, and she would need only to write "an extra piece or two" to meet this price.[40] Taking deep breaths of the Maine air into her lungs, she set about making good on this promise. After five years of virtual silence Harriet began writing again, and writing with an ease and facility that suggested much benefit from her time of lying fallow.

Harriet's optimistic plans met their first challenge in the Titcomb house. It was light and airy, but the sunshine revealed a damp, old house in desperate need of repair. Much of the work of painting rooms, revarnishing and upholstering furniture, and making bedspreads, bosters, and pillowcases fell to Harriet, who organized teams of quilters and needleworkers from the area. With the major repairs like plumbing, she acted as general contractor, which required the patience of Job and the tact of a diplomat. For weeks she had to run her large household with neither a sink nor water privileges. She bought two large hogshead to serve as cisterns, but found that they would not fit down the cellar stairs. Not to be deterred, she hired a cooper to take the hogshead apart in staves and to reassemble them in the cellar. Then she set about cajoling the plumber to set up her sink. The man who acted in capacity of plumber was none other than John Titcomb, part owner of the house she rented and related to all the "best families" in town, so it was clear that she could not easily presume on his time and talent. In a letter to Sarah Beecher she described the delicate "negotiations" that extended from the first of June until the first of July:

> How many times I have been in & seated myself in one of the old rocking chairs & talked first of the news of the day—the railroad—the last proceedings in Congress—the probabilities about the Millennium & thus brought the conversation by little & little round to my sink! . . . Sometimes my courage would quite fail me to introduce the delicate subject & I would talk of every thing else—turn & get out of the shop—& then turn back as if a thought had just struck my mind & say
> Oh Mr. Titcomb about that sink?

In the midst of this tearing down and setting up came a letter from Calvin Stowe, "saying he is sick a bed—& all but dead," Harriet told Sarah; "don't ever expect to see his family again wants to know how I shall manage in case I am left a widow—knows we shall get in debt and never get out—wonders at my courage—thinks I am very sanguine—warns me to be prudent as there won't be much to live on in case of his death, &c &c. I read the letter and poke it into the stove, and proceed."

Just as coming away from New England eighteen years earlier had given rise to her first burst of literary creativity, so this move unleashed a pent-up rush of words evident in the flurry of letters that she sent in all directions— witty, eloquent, whimsical, detailed letters that brought back the voice of the domestic letter writer, the voice of parlor literature. The letter to Sarah Beecher from which the above is taken is a choice example. She drew swift sketches of the Yankee, John Titcomb, his lineaments more strongly marked by the contrast they presented to her western experience. She threw in large swatches of dialogue. She wrote in the midst of every domestic distraction:

> Since I began this note I have been called off at least a dozen times—once for the fish-man, to buy a codfish—once to see a man who had brought me some barrels of apples—once to see a book man—then to Mrs. Upham to see about a drawing I promised to make for her—then to nurse the baby—then into the kitchen to make a chowder for dinner & now I am at it again for nothing but deadly determination enables me ever to write—it is rowing against wind and tide.[41]

Even before arriving, while she was enroute from Boston, she re-established her bond to her dear schoolmate, Georgiana May, now Sykes, urging her to come and visit: "[W]e will have a long talk in the pine woods, and knit up the whole history from the place where we left it."[42] Georgiana wrote back that she had given herself permission "to *long* after" her because she had good expectation "to *have*" her. She urged Harriet to write—not just to her, but to all the readers who, according to a recent notice in the New York *Pathfinder,* were clamoring for more from her pen and regretting that she should be "putting her light under a bushel." "[R]eally, Hatty," she urged her, "why not publish a "*Second Series* of your scatterings?" Ralph Waldo Emerson's *Essays, First Series* (1841) and *Essays, Second Series* (1844), published just before and just after *The Mayflower,* suggested the pattern for such a two-volume gathering. Georgiana teased that she should call this one "the Passion-Flower," but she was serious: "Your *girls* are large enough to copy and arrange them for you—and the thing must be done."[43]

Harriet was seated at her writing desk on the morning of July 8, about to begin a letter to Eunice Beecher when, as she wrote Eunice a few days later, she was "obliged to give previous attention to some other affairs—about noon the household were thrown into commotion by the arrival of a young stranger in these parts—said to be a great beauty—to have excellent lungs & to look just like his pa, three very important items in his condition."[44] Just as her mother had named her Harriet after the little Harriet who had died, so she named her newest baby Charles Edward, and he grew fat and healthy like his namesake.

As Harriet watched the New England summer turn into fall and the leaves drop from the trees, she harvested her memories. She remembered the luxuriant vegetation of Cincinnati, watered by the Ohio River, drenching her summers in intoxicating smells and vivid colors of mignonette and geranium and hydrangea. She remembered Charley, her "summer child," whose golden hair caught the sun. She remembered what she had taken for granted: the richness of her relationships with other women. Informal bonds of "kinship" developed among women engaged in the common task of tending children: they delivered one another's babies, suckled them, sewed for them, and passed on clothes that their children had outgrown. They tended them together in leisurely times and became surrogate mothers in difficult times. The meaning of her experience rose up before her as she sat at her writing desk communing with her Walnut Hills neighbor, Sarah Allen. She confided, "Do you know what I count the happiest years of my married life—those just after you came to the hills when our children were all babies and we raised flowers together & discoursed of roses callas & geraniums & babies between whiles—that was the Indian Summer of my life."[45] This eulogistic rendering of her experience bears little relationship to the record of domestic trials strewn behind her. Just four years earlier Harriet had recalled the early years of her marriage as a time of "sickness pain perplexity, constant discouragement—wearing wasting days & nights," concluding, "Ah how little comfort had I in being a mother—how was all that I proposed met & crossed & my way ever hedged up!"[46] Had Harriet forgotten this?

Both accounts were true. Like swamp grass lit by a lowering sun, her trials were shot through with tenderness, compassion, and joy—a mixture of intense and often contradictory feelings suggested by the nineteenth-century phrase "the bonds of womanhood."[47] When she wrote to Calvin, she made the most of her domestic difficulties; but when she was writing to a woman she often threw in touching details, vivid and spirited descriptions, and a generally optimistic view of her domestic situation. As she wrote to Sarah Allen, she may have remembered the night she was awakened at half past two and called to her side to act as midwife. After a baby daughter made her appearance, Harriet "washed & dressed & humanised her," and, as she later wrote, "of course feel quite a tenderness for her."[48] Viewing motherhood from within the institution, Harriet elaborated it in its own cultural terms and found much to delight in. Viewed from without, however, the duties seemed mean and harrassing.

This makes all the more significant the cornucopia of letters that Harriet wrote to sisters, sisters-in-law, and women friends. Through them she explored the meaning of her domestic experience. She gathered up the tattered ends of days interrupted by a thousand small cares and cast them in a pattern, a shape of words. The contradiction between the fullness of her days and her seeming lack of accomplishment—a central contradiction for a woman with small children— she expressed with clarity and vividness in the memorable letter to Sarah Beecher. After her detailed description of the heroics of setting up housekeeping in Brunswick and the birth of her seventh baby, Stowe added, "[d]uring this time I have employed my liesure in making up my engagements with newspaper editors—I have written more than anybody or I myself would have thought—I have taught an hour a day in our school—& I have read two hours every evening to the children. . . . yet I am constantly pursued & haunted by the idea that I dont do anything.[49] One reason that her accomplishments seemed so negligible is that, as a domestic worker, she did not have formal, important-sounding titles to put on her activities. If performed in the public world, the work she did setting up housekeeping would have earned her the titles Seamstress, Upholsterer, and more significantly, Diplomat. But as she was, in the modern phrase, "just a housewife," her work remained invisible and unrecognized. By expressing the discrepancy between the private reality and the public perception, Harriet took a step toward a powerful melding of the private and the public realms. When these poles met, the fusion released energies she had not dreamed of.

If the writing of domestic letters primed the pump, the parlor activity in which Stowe surrounded herself in Brunswick further set the stage for the literary renaissance she was about to experience. She was every day involved for two hours in teaching school in her house; she and Anna Smith (who, treated to classes in drawing and piano playing in exchange for part of her

services, had come a long way under her tutelage) joined with Catharine
Beecher to set up what was to be a short-lived venture into a neighborhood
school. This didactic activity carried over in the evening to several hours of
reading aloud. At seven o'clock Harriet gathered her children and servants
about her in the parlor, one of two rooms warmed by the stove, and read the
historical novels of Sir Walter Scott, in order. By December she had read
The Talisman, The Abbot, and *Ivanhoe* and was about to start *Kenilworth.*
Scott celebrated the particularity of local dialects and translated love of place
into a national literary movement. Not only did this reading put in Stowe's
mouth and ears the rhythms of a popular writer and the narrative strategies
of the historical novel, it put her in touch with an immediate audience whose
reactions, from anticipation to delight and tears, showed her what moved
people.[50] These domestic gatherings also reminded her of those who were
absent. To Aunt Esther, Harriet wrote that she missed her presence at their
readings: "I dont know any body in the states that I would so willingly have
for a listener as yourself Aunt E—because you enter so heartily into it that
it comforts & encourages my heart."[51] Gathering this audience was as important as gathering her experiences.

Around this time Sarah Josepha Hale, who had not forgotten that Harriet
Beecher Stowe had been a valued contributor to the *Lady's Book,* wrote to
Stowe to request a biographical sketch. Hale was compiling material for her
monumental *Woman's Record; or, Sketches of all Distinguished Women, from
"The Beginning" till A. D. 1850.* One of the many reminders of her literary
life that women put before her during this period, Hale's request inspired
genuine astonishment on Stowe's part, for she had grown accustomed in the
past five years to thinking of herself primarily as a wife and mother. During
this time she had written nothing, her energies totally consumed in trying
to keep her head above water. She told Sarah Hale how she had amused
herself by telling her children of "the unexpected honor that had befallen
their mamma." She continued,

> The idea of the daguerroetype especially was quite droll—& I diverted myself
> somewhat with figuring the astonishment of the children should the well
> known visage of their mother loom out of the pages of a book before their
> astonished eyes—But in sober sadness,—having reflected duly & truly on my
> past life, it is so uneventful & uninteresting that I do not see how any thing
> can be done for me in the way of a sketch. My sister Catherine has lived much
> more of a life—& done more that can be told of than I whose course & employ-
> ments have always been retired & domestic—The most I can think of is that I
> was born in Litchfield Conn—was a teacher from my fifteenth year till my
> marriage that I have been mother to seven children—six of whom are now
> living—& that the greater portion of my time & strength has been spent in the
> necessary but unpoetic duties of the family—These details you can throw into
> two or three lines—as great a space as I should have any claim to occupy in
> such company[52]

These modest remarks form the substance of the biographical sketch Hale
published in her encyclopedic rendering of about 2,500 distinguished

women, arranged in "Four Eras," from Julia Agrippina in the First Era to Emma Willard in the Fourth Era. For each, Hale published an excerpt of her writing. Stowe was represented by a patch of dialogue from one of her frequently reprinted stories, "The Tea Rose." Stowe declared herself "well pleased" with the selection.[53] In her critical remarks Hale observed Stowe's light touch: she "makes wisdom seem like a pleasant friend, instead of a grave Mentor. None of our female writers excel Mrs. Stowe in the art of entertaining her readers; the only regret is, that she does not write more."[54] Similar tribute was paid her in *Female Prose Writers of America,* a "new, eloquent, six dollar volume," as Calvin proudly wrote Harriet: "*Mrs. H. B. Stowe* figures next after Miss Marg. Fuller, Countess What's-her-name— Mrs. Stowe has written but little, but has made a deep impression—inherits the splendid talents of her father— particularly distinguished for clearness & force—exuberant wit— wonderful play of fancy etc- etc—On the whole pretty fair." He could not resist adding, "Cate is not mentioned at all—Sarah Greeley says it must be because *she is a class by herself, and will be discussed in a separate volume.*"[55]

That winter in Brunswick was one of the coldest in fifteen years. The Titcomb house proved to be drafty and difficult to heat. Water left in pails froze solid; biscuit dough froze to the board before it could be rolled out. The most comfortable members of the household were the cats, who spent the night in the stove near the burned-out embers of the day.[56] As the holidays approached both Harriet's homesickness and her letter writing increased. (In *Uncle Tom's Cabin* Stowe pointed out that illiterate slaves forcibly separated from kin had not even this comfort of writing and receiving letters. (UTC, 1:189). Using the dialect of her wet nurse, Harriet told her husband, "I feel very *lonesome* after you as Irish Catharine says."[57] She told her father's wife, "I miss the old study fire with the sofa in front of it & you & Father cosily seated in either corner—Our thanksgiving & Christmas will be lonely without you & I am quite inclined to join in the homesick regrets of the children."[58] Her daughter Eliza, who had heretofore been a rather flighty and thoughtless child, cried bitterly over the loss of her home and the loss of her brother Charley, declaring it was no good to love anything if it were just going to be taken away.[59]

With the birth of the second Charley, Harriet took up the mourning process where she had abruptly broken it off by moving East. "I often think of what you said to me," she told Sarah Allen, who had also lost a child, "that another child would not fill the place of the old one that it would be another interest and another love." She continued, "so I find it—for tho he is so like I do not feel him the same nor do I feel for him that same love which I felt for Charley—It is a different kind—I shall never love another as I did him— he was my '*summer child.*'" She described feelings she would soon attribute to the character of Mrs. Bird in *Uncle Tom's Cabin:* "I cannot open his little drawer of clothes now without feeling it thro my very heart," and she asked Sarah, "How is it with you in your heart of hearts when you think of the past—I often wonder how your feelings correspond with mine."[60] Her new baby was a source of both comfort and anxiety. He grew more beautiful every day, but "every line of his face in its likeness, warns me not to love him too well.[61] The November nights were long, and as she sat alone in the darkened house her thoughts turned to the past. She admitted to Calvin, "I am lonesome nights in this rattletrap house where every wind shakes out as many noises as there are ghosts in Hades—screeching snapping cracking groaning."[62] The baby in her arms eased her heartache but gave rise to a fear she hardly dared acknowledge. Would this one too be taken away? First she worried that he was too thin, then that he was too fat. She had a breast infection that kept him from thriving for the first six weeks. Then she engaged an Irish woman who had plentiful milk, and together they supplied Charley so well that by age three months he weighed nineteen pounds! Harriet feared that if he were to catch the croup, his weight would make it hard for him. In November he developed an infection of the tonsils that caused violent coughing. Harriet slept fitfully during this period. "When I did sleep," she told her sisters, "it was to dream that he was dying of the croup & to wake to hear his hard breathing."[63]

That she was revisiting the scenes of Charley's death is evident. If more proof is needed, the review she wrote of the autobiography of Heinrich Stilling for the *New-York Evangelist* provides it. In the midst of this review she produces, as an example of the need to trust in God, the example of a mother nursing her dying baby. Fueled by her own preoccupations, the passage jumps out and is developed beyond the purposes of her essay.

> Let us suppose a case. A mother sits holding her sick infant, and watching, as only a mother can, the changes of its suffering face. A deadly disease is hurrying it with irresistible force to death, and all human means and appliances bend before it as a reed before a torrent. In such anguish the heart, untaught, instinctively cries out to God for help. . . .
>
> How distracting the responsibility thus thrown on the helpless, short-sighted parent. "Have I chosen the right physician? Has he gained a right view of the case? Perhaps I am doing in my anxiety the very worst thing—perhaps he, sincerely and honestly, is pursuing a course that leads to death and not to life," and while time is flying and a precious life is ebbing with each moment, how worthless seems human knowledge and human aid.[64]

Memories of Charley's death may have been intensified by the presence of her wet nurse. "Irish Catharine" gets little mention in Harriet's letters and is sent away as soon as her function is past, yet in the absence of husband, father, and sisters, Harriet was inevitably thrown on the companionship of her help. What must it have been like to see this woman take Charley to her breast, knowing that he was a temporary replacement for her own child? Slave mothers similarly took to their breasts the babies of their white masters. Did Catharine talk with Harriet about her little one? It is suggestive that "lonesome" is the one word of Catharine's that made its way from her speech into Harriet's letters, first self-consciously, then without remark. Perhaps like Harriet she was mourning both the loss of fireside and friends and the loss of a baby. It would not have been surprising if, as they sat by the stove in the darkened house, they shared heart secrets.

Harriet's removal from the West and her painful tendering of Charley from this world to the next marked an epoch in her consciousness. She had piloted one of her children through the breakers of life, and at the age of eighteen months he was safely on the other side of the river. When she looked across the miles from Brunswick to Walnut Hills, her nostalgia was intensified by her awareness that there was a little grave there that she would visit no more. All the longing for a more perfect world that drove her first to a second baptism, then to schemes of domestic reform and the waters of Brattleboro, were, after her abrupt separation from Charley and Walnut Hills, stretched taut in a keen pang of homesickness. The pain of this double loss was one of the twin engines of *Uncle Tom's Cabin.* The other was a white anger. Virginia Woolf, well schooled by the angel in the house whom she rejected, took Charlotte Brontë to task for the anger that, in *Jane Eyre,* "tamper[ed] with the integrity of Charlotte Brontë the novelist."[65] How creative and transformative anger could be was a great discovery for Harriet Beecher Stowe. The anger that she could not direct to a Calvinist God she heaped upon the patriarchal institution of slavery. That it was anger *for others* went a long way toward excusing this breach of proper womanhood.

CHAPTER EIGHTEEN

A Rush of Mighty Wind:
1850–1851

*I*n *Uncle Tom's Cabin* Stowe *describes* Mrs. Bird as a small, gentle, and timid woman who ruled her domestic flock by "entreaty and persuasion." There was but one exception to her placid chirruping: "[A]nything in the shape of cruelty would throw her into a passion, which was the more alarming and inexplicable in proportion to the general softness of her nature" (UTC, 1:103). The author, a woman who disliked confrontations, who rode over unpleasantness with optimistic goodwill and turned aside anger with humor, found herself, as public opinion brewed over the Fugitive Slave Law, consumed with a rage unlike anything she had ever experienced. The mealy-mouthed postures of editorialists and clergymen who hemmed and hawed and attempted "to hush up and salve over such an outrage on common humanity" infuriated her.[1] It was as if, she said, "a man should get up and with great parade and begging a thousand pardons tell us that *he* really as an individual could not see his way clear to murder his father and mother in bed even tho required to do it by the laws of his country."[2]

Her intense feelings were the more oppressive for having no outlet. Male professors, male clergy, male politicians made the laws and shaped the public opinion of the land, and women who found themselves morally repelled by their work had little recourse. The political impotence Stowe felt in the face of unjust laws was building up like water behind a dam for many middle-class women. During the decade of the 1850s women engaged in rather extraordinary acts of civil disobedience, provoked by laws that they themselves had had no part in making. As the temperance crusade moved from

202

the podium to the ballot box with the passage of the first legal constraint on the liquor trade, the "Maine Law" of 1851, women who had been active in temperance societies keenly felt their disfranchisement. Not able to cast a vote against the liquor trade, women "openly engaged in illegal acts of massive violence." In dozens of communities across the nation respectable women formed themselves into bands, armed themselves, marched into saloons, and destroyed the stock. "In a political system that gave them no legal redress for the encroachments of the liquor trade on the stability of the family," observed Jed Dannenbaum, "women adopted vigilante justice." The civil disobedience advocated and practiced by many nineteenth-century women went well beyond Thoreau's refusal to pay his poll tax. During this turbulent decade when "women first found their own voice, developed their own perspective, and exercised their own power in the battle against the drink trade,"[3] Harriet Beecher Stowe found her voice as well.

Passed by Congress and signed by President Fillmore in September 1850, the Fugitive Slave Law had, as Henry Ward Beecher observed, provisions odious enough "to render an infamous thing consistently infamous throughout." Section five commanded citizens "to aid and assist in the prompt and efficient execution of this law, whenever their services may be required." Under section seven persons who gave shelter, food, or assistance to an escaping slave were liable to a fine of $1000 and six months in prison. The Fugitive Slave Law effectively abrogated individual rights such as habeas corpus and the right of trial by jury and provided what abolitionists called bribes to commissioners by awarding them $10 for every alleged fugitive they remanded to slavery, but only $5 for every one they determined to be free.[4]

Soon after its adoption the papers were full of reports of outrages against blacks, particularly in urban centers. The first case to be tried under the new law took place in Washington, D. C. James Hamlet, claimed by Mary Brown of Baltimore, was captured, tried, and remanded to slavery on September 7, 1850. The north went into a frenzy of political organizing. Abolitionist papers carried stories on the most effective way to resist the law.[5] In New York $800 was raised for the purchase of James Hamlet and turned over to his claimants in exchange for his liberty. In Massachusetts meetings were called all over the state to protest the "terrible decree."[6] In Chicago no one could be found to serve as commissioner under the new law, and in Philadelphia the commissioner resigned rather than put the law in force.[7] Free blacks everywhere took up arms and "enter[ed] into a solemn covenant to defend each other's liberty," emptying ammunition stores of their revolvers and prompting editorials on "The Mob Spirit."[8] Dr. Leonard Bacon declared that the fugitive slave was "a prisoner of war" and "that the escape of the slave was on his part 'nothing more than *a legal act of hostility against a government to which he* OWES NO ALLEGIANCE.' "[9]

Boston, where many fugitives had found work, was the center of much of the "catching business" and of strenuous resistance to the law. In the cradle of liberty where the colonists had dumped tea into the harbor rather

than obey an unjust law, the businesses of blacks were broken up and pil-
laged, families were torn apart, and terror painted with a broad brush on all
black people living in the city. One man left his prosperous crockery business
and fled to Canada on foot in midwinter, not daring to risk a public convey-
ance. Both his feet froze and had to be amputated.[10] In a highly publicized
case Frederick Wilkins ("Shadrach"), a fugitive slave from Norfolk, Virginia,
was apprehended at Taft's Cornhill Coffee House where he had been
employed for almost a year. He was carried, with his apron still on, to the
nearby courthouse, but before his case could be heard he was rescued by "a
throng of colored persons whose united momentum proved a little too much
for the doors," and spirited away to Canada.[11] Henry Clay fulminated on the
floor of the Senate against this breach of law and order committed by "Africans and the descendants of Africans," declaring that the question of the
day was "whether the government of white men is to be yielded to a government of blacks."[12] President Fillmore threatened to send federal troops to
Boston "to teach Bostonians to obey the laws, and to put down riot."[13] Theodore Parker, who was at that time harboring in his home fugitive slave Ellen
Craft, responded with patriotic defiance: "The Bostonians remember how
that business of quartering soldiers on us in time of peace worked in the last
century!"[14] Even Catharine Beecher was radicalized by the Fugitive Slave
Law. "Dear Sister," Harriet wrote to her, "Your last letter was a real good
one, it did my heart good to find somebody in as indignant a state as I am
about this miserable wicked fugitive slave business—Why I have felt almost
choked sometimes with pent up wrath that does no good."[15]

During the free speech battles of the 1830s Harriet Beecher had helped
her brother Henry buckle on his armor; she had written pseudonymously in
defense of abolitionists and slipped these notices into the *Cincinnati Journal,*
then under Henry Ward Beecher's temporary editorship; she had stood by
and cheered as he poured bullets into molds and prepared to defend Lane
Seminary. Now, after just three years in New York, Henry Ward Beecher
was a media phenomenon; his lectures, accompanied by "unreportable pyro-
technic splendors," enthralled "jammed audiences" at the Tremont Temple.[16] He was a regular contributer to the New York *Independent,* where his
editorials appeared under the sign "*", and the "asteroidal observer" had
already penned a strong protest against the Fugitive Slave Act. On February
1, 1851, Harriet wrote him to strengthen him in his resistance.

Her letter makes it clear, however, that vicarious access to the organs of
public opinion was too attenuated a channel for the mighty rush of indignation she felt. "You don't know how my heart burns within me at the blindness and obtuseness of good people on so very simple a point of morality as
this," she told him. "Some of the defenses of these principles are so very
guarded and candid and cautious and sweet and explanatory that they put
me in mind of little Dr. Chillip laying his head on one side and saying 'Do
you know Mr. Copperfield—that I *don't* find Mr. and Miss Murdstone in
the New Testament?' " She was a regular reader of the religious press, and

the namby-pamby postures of "good people"—so disproportionately reasonable and scripture-quoting and full of lengthy, dull, and tedious explanations that lost their audience and left them wondering what all the fuss was about—made Harriet feel as though she would explode:

> Must we forever keep calm and smile and smile when every sentiment of manliness and humanity is kicked and rolled in the dust and lies trampled and bleeding and make it a merit to be exceedingly cool—I feel as if my heart would burn itself out in grief and shame that such things are—I wish I had your chance—but next best to that it is to have you have it—so fire away—give them no rest day or night.[17]

The number of kidnappings and forcible re-enslavements of black people was growing almost daily. Henry Long, a waiter at the Pacific Hotel in New York, was violently seized while waiting on table and taken to the U. S. Clerk's office, where he learned that he was claimed by one John T. Smith. In spite of evidence that he was in New York months before he was supposed to have fled from Richmond, Virginia, Long was sent South to his claimant. His case proved, in the words of the New York *Independent*, "that almost no colored man is safe in our streets."[18] "Is it possible that Henry Long is hopelessly sold," Harriet expostulated to Henry, "and in all this nation of freemen there is not one deliverer brave enough and strong enough to recover him." While the regularity of such incidents had a numbing effect on certain portions of public opinion, Harriet found that each case intensified the pain of the last. She dropped hot tears on her pillow and raged against the "cool way" the press and the public lumped together "all the woes and crimes the hearbreaks the bitter untold agonies of thousand poor bleeding helpless heartwrung creatures with the bland expression its very sad to be sure—very dreadful—but we mustn't allow our feelings to run away with us we must consider &c, &c, &c." She longed to "do something even the humblest in this cause."[19] When she found her way, she would paint graphic pictures that brought the sufferings of individual bondmen and bondwomen into the parlors of white America. When she finished with her readers, many would be weeping, and none would be cool.

Her friendship with Professor and Mrs. Upham was tried by the rapidly politicizing climate of opinion. In her indignation over the treatment of fugitive slaves, Harriet was ready to throw law and even the Union to the winds. "The union!," she burst out in a letter to Catharine Beecher, "Some unions I think are better broken than kept," especially one "cemented on such terms." Professor Upham was more cautious. Espousing a colonizationist position, he believed the slaves should be educated, purchased, and then sent back to Africa. "[U]ntil that is done he is for bearing every thing in silence & stroking & saying 'pussy pussy'—so as to allay all prejudice & avoid all agitation," Harriet fumed. She went on, "He and I had over the tea table the other night that sort of an argument which consists in both sides saying over & over just what they said before, for any length of time—but when I asked him flatly if he would obey the law supposing a fugitive came to him Mrs Upham laughed & he hemmed & hawed & little Mary Upham broke out 'I wouldnt I know.'" Women and children—who could not vote—debated the laws of the United States in that domestic sphere of power, the parlor, and found them wanting. And just as the resolve of Senator Bird would be tested in the lovely chapter in *Uncle Tom's Cabin* entitled "In Which It Appears that a Senator Is but a Man," the very next day after this tea-table exchange a fugitive slave came to Brunwsick and knocked on Professor Upham's door. After hearing his story the professor gave him money, looked on as his wife supplied him with provisions, and then bade him godspeed to Canada. Harriet had the opportunity to crow over this evidence of Professor Upham's humanity, for she heard the whole story when the fugitive next stopped at her house for refuge overnight. "Now our beds were all full," she told her sister, "& before this law passed I might have tried to send him somewhere else—As it was all hands in the house united in making him up a bed." As northerners had their resolve tested by such direct appeals, many found, as Harriet observed, "their hearts are better on this point than their heads."[20] She knew where to aim her arrows.

As it happened, Stowe had just received $100 from Gamaliel Bailey, editor of the *National Era,* with a note urging her to continue supplying his magazine with material.[21] Bailey had a long association with abolition, having taken over the editorship of the *Philanthropist* in 1838 when James G. Birney gave it up. His moderate approach reached a wider audience than the fiery denunciations of William Lloyd Garrison. Having lived in Cincinnati, Washington, D.C., and Baltimore, he shared with Stowe what his biographer calls a "border state perspective" that made him more sensitive to the feelings of the South than abolitionists from the Northeast.[22] Since removing to Brunswick Harriet had published four pieces in his paper, including, on August 1, 1850, a response to the Fugitive Slave Act. In that piece, "The Freeman's Dream," Stowe employed a parable. A family of fugitive slaves asks food of a farmer, who, mindful of the law, refuses to give it; soon after the fugitives are overtaken and captured. Suggesting that the man refused out of fear, Stowe mobilizes a greater terror than that of the state: "And after these things the man dreamed, and it seemed to him that the sky grew dark, and the earth rocked to and fro, and the heavens flashed with strange light, and a distant rush, as of wings, was heard, and suddenly, in mid heavens, appeared the sign of the Son of Man, with his mighty angels." The man is borne upward to the Seat of Judgment and a voice thunders, "Depart from me ye accursed! for I was an hungered, and ye gave me no meat."[23] In January 1851, in a more practical and secular frame of mind, Stowe was "projecting a sketch for the Era of the capabilities of liberated blacks to take care of themselves." She asked her husband, "Cant you find for me how much Willie Watson has paid for the redemption of his friends—& get me any items in figures of that kind that you can pick up in Cincinnati."[24] Meanwhile, Isabella Beecher wrote her letter after letter from Boston detailing the latest outrages wreaked by the Fugitive Slave Law. In one of them she urged Harriet to buckle on *her* armor: "Now, Hattie, if I could use a pen as you can, I would write something that would make this whole nation feel what an accursed thing slavery is." One of the Stowe children remembered that when this letter was read aloud in the parlor, Harriet "rose up from her chair" and declared "I will write something. I will if I live."[25] She wrote to Calvin in December 1850, "[a]s long as the baby sleeps with me nights I can't do much at any thing—but I shall *do it at last.* I shall write that thing if I live."[26]

There is a great deal of confusion as to where Calvin Stowe was during this period, owing largely to the confusion the professor himself was experiencing. When the Lane board of trustees were unable to find a replacement for him, they prevailed upon Calvin to seek leave from Bowdoin in order to continue at Lane during the winter term, 1850–1851. The Bowdoin faculty had just agreed to this arrangement when another complication arose. Andover Theological Seminary in Andover, Mass., offered Calvin the chair of sacred literature, a plum carrying with it both a handsome salary and a house. Even more appealing to one of Calvin Stowe's temperament was the promise of living a quiet, scholarly life surrounded by advanced students. It would be a fitting place to end his career. At Andover the humiliations of poverty, institutional fundraising, and shrinking classes that had wearied him at Lane Seminary would be be forgotten and his original aim, to live and die a "literary man," could be fulfilled. Whatever he told to Professor Edwards A. Park in response to this offer was sufficiently encouraging for Andover to announce his appointment. Forrest Wilson describes the result:

> Lane Seminary had already announced that Professor Stowe was remaining on its faculty for another year. Bowdoin had announced his election to the Collins Professorship, and the invitations for his induction were out. A correspondent of the New York *Independent* commented sarcastically: "How far Dr. Stowe approximates to the faculty of omnipresence, we are not informed; but if, as the papers have stated, he is to have an actual and effectual connection with one college and two theological seminaries at the same time, he must stand in need of something like it."[27]

Harriet was furious. Not only had she barely settled in Brunswick, but the ridiculous figure that her husband cut in the press through this confusion was doubtless a source of humiliation to her Beecher blood. After discussing the matter with Professor and Mrs. Upham, she wrote to him in no uncertain terms that it was his duty to stay at Bowdoin. She reminded him that he was called there specifically to counteract Unitarianism and "neologism"; that two previous attempts to fill the Collins Professorship had failed; in Professor Uphams's view, if Stowe withdrew, it would be tantamount to giving up the project and turning over the field to the Unitarians. "Some like you for your literary reputation," Harriet told him, "some because of your old school orthodoxy—some because of your liberality of opinions & all because you are a creditable addition to the college." If God had wanted them to go to

Andover, he would have done it without these embarrassments. Calvin would not be able to accomplish anything if it was known he planned to leave. He should publicly decline the Andover offer.[28]

But Calvin, having made a disastrous decision eighteen years earlier when he cast his lot with Lane Seminary, was not about to make another mistake. He accepted the position at Andover. He could not get out of his commitment to Lane and taught there for the winter term, which ran from November 1850 to March 1851. He persuaded the Bowdoin faculty to give him leave so that the following winter term he could make an appearance at Andover. In the two summer terms (May to September) he honored his commitment to Bowdoin. Harriet, who found the society in Brunswick more agreeable than any she had ever known, prepared to leave it. But the move to Andover was the last significant decision that Calvin Stowe made as head of the family.

While her patriarch was in this confusion, Harriet was moving ahead with her determination to speak out on slavery. On March 9 Harriet wrote to Gamaliel Bailey that she had embarked on a story that she thought would run "through three or four numbers." She projected "a series of sketches which give the lights and shadows of the 'patriarchal institution'":

> Up to this year I have always felt that I had no particular call to meddle with this subject, and I dreaded to expose even my own mind to the full force of its exciting power. But I feel now that the time is come when even a woman or a child who can speak a word for freedom and humanity is bound to speak. The Carthagenian women in the last peril of their state cut off their hair for bowstrings to give to the defenders of their country; and such peril and shame as now hangs over this country is worse than Roman slavery, and I hope every woman who can write will not be silent.

Having written only short sketches, she knew that this story would "be a much longer one than any I have ever written," but she had no notion of the sprawling novel that would run in weekly installments from June 5, 1851 until April 1, 1852 in the *National Era.* What was absolutely clear, however, was the fact that she was entering the national debate with women's weapons. The hair that the Carthagenian women cut for bowstrings was paralleled by her selection of rhetorical tools: "My vocation is simply that of a painter, and my object will be to hold up in the most lifelike and graphic manner possible Slavery, its reverses, changes, and the negro character, which I have had ample opportunities for studying. There is no arguing with *pictures,* and everybody is impressed by them, whether they mean to be or not." The "graphic sketches" that made women's letters come alive with distant people and events were to be employed in the highly political arena of sectional strife; the intimate narrative voice that melded region to region in domestic letters would now speak to a nation deeply divided; the pleasures that this national narrative voice afforded to a nation eager to see pictures of itself would lure the reader into a dark tale of freedom and bondage. "I shall show the *best side* of the thing," Stowe told Bailey, "and something *faintly approaching the worst.*"[29]

Her intention to study "the negro character"—probably in her mind an undertaking similar to her shrewd sketches of regional types—embroiled her in racial politics that continue today. It is true, as she told Bailey, that she had "had ample opportunities for studying" African Americans; she did not consider, however, that her evidence was garnered mainly in domestic settings in which her position as white mistress to black servants radically compromised her perceptions. Her generalizations about African Americans repeatedly assume their childlike dependence—a posture or "mask" that could be accounted for by the economic and psychological exigencies of the mistress–servant relationship. At the same time, however, mistress and servant shared the bonds of womanhood. When it came to sexuality, reproduction, and motherhood, white mistress and black servant were in parallel situations—though the bondwoman's lot was much more severe and she had fewer recourses. Resisting the political and biological raids on their bodies as best they could, neither had the legal right to resist the sexual advances of her master; the often plentiful number of children that resulted from these unions were a mixed blessing, for the emotional comfort they provided was a thorn to mothers who could not, as Stowe knew too well, expect to keep them.

The complicated relation in which Stowe stood to her domestic servants is reflected in her contradictory consciousness. While she overidentified with them as women, she distanced herself from their race and class. One could say that she used them to carry her own burden of loss and anger. But she also transformed those feelings into an engine of social change; pursuing the Calvinist injunction to "improve the affliction" and reap "the peaceable fruits of righteousness" in the wake of Charley's death, she stirred up the nation to an awareness of its sin. "You see . . . how this subject has laid hold of me," she wrote to her brother Henry,

> but I have known a great many slaves—had them in my family known their history & feelings and seen how alike their heart beats to any other throbbing heart & above all what woman deepest feels I have seen the strength of their instinctive and domestic attachments in which *as a race* they excel the anglo saxon. The poor slave on whom the burden of domestic bereavement falls heaviest is precisely the creature of all Gods creatures that feels it deepest.[30]

Stowe's attribution of deeper feeling to African Americans "as a race" was consistent with what George Fredrickson has called "romantic racialism," a blend of philanthropic and paternalistic attitudes toward blacks. One of the earliest formulators of this ideology was Alexander Kinmont, who, in his 1837–1838 lectures in Cincinnati, proclaimed the moral superiority of African Americans: "All the sweeter graces of the Christian religion appear almost too tropical and tender plants to grow in the Caucasian mind; they require a character of human nature which you can see in the rude lineaments of the Ethiopian." It is highly likely that Harriet Beecher Stowe, living in Cincinnati at the time Kinmont delivered his lectures, was exposed to his ideas. The likelihood is increased by the fact that his lectures were published in Cincinnati in 1839. Such romantic racialism was widespread by 1851.[31]

Drawing on such views and on her own experience with domestics, Stowe drew a highly colored portrait of the slave's humanity, inflected by a sense of "otherness" not unlike the exotic image of woman created by man, through a similar hierarchical perception of a social inferior. Stowe cared enough about her washerwoman, Aunt Frankie, to make her shroud and attend her funeral, but the limitations of her response are painfully evident in this confession:

> If any body wants to have a black face look handsome, let them be left as I have been, in feeble health, in oppressive, hot weather, with a sick baby in arms, & two or three other little ones in the nursery, & not a servant in the whole house to do a single turn: & then if they should see my good, old Aunt Frankie, coming in, with her honest, bluff, black face, her long, strong arms, her chest as big & stout as a barrel & her hilarious hearty laugh, perfectly delighted to take one's washing, & do it at a fair price, they would appreciate the beauty of black people.[32]

In *Uncle Tom's Cabin* she holds up for our scrutiny the businesslike slavetrader, Haley, who thinks of "Tom's length, and breadth, and height and what he would sell for" (UTC, 1:153), but her functional assessment of black beauty is not so very different. Stowe's political achievement was to make a national audience see the subjectivity of black people, but what she herself saw was filtered through a white woman's consciousness.

For all the limitations of her point of view, Stowe's attempt to put the *voices* of the oppressed into her tale went a long way toward reconstructing the subjectivity that her white-mistress consciousness brought to the tale. Just the mere act of carefully listening to and recording the voices of a colonized people acknowledges their presence and their self-created subjectivity. People who have their own speech have the potential for "resistant orality" and a "fugitive tongue."[33] They have the power to get away—even from their creator who may put rather conventional views in their mouths. Stowe had pioneered the use of dialect eighteen years earlier in her prizewinning characterization of "Uncle Lot"; her ear for dialogue, her awareness of regional speech, her delight in the particularity of local accents—now intensified by her move back to New England—all of these were well established in 1851. As she put these in the service of a silenced people, her model, insofar as she had a literary one, was probably Maria Edgeworth, whose novels were part of the literary culture into which Harriet Beecher was born. Read by her mother, read aloud by Sarah Pierce to the students at the Litchfield Female Academy, even cast in a play by Catharine Beecher for home consumption, the stories of Maria Edgeworth made prominent use of dialect. Born in England to a father who was a landlord in Ireland, Edgeworth satirized the decadence of this colonial society in *Castle Rackrent*, a tale that makes political use of domestic sketches and records the accents of the oppressed Irish people. In *Uncle Tom's Cabin*, Stowe's tale of American-style feudalism, it is pre-eminently the voices of Stowe's characters that demand our attention. As Edmund Wilson observed, "They come before us arguing and struggling, like real people who cannot be quiet. We feel that the dams of discretion of which Mrs. Stowe has spoken have been burst by a passionate force that, compressed, has been mounting behind them, and which, liberated, has taken the form of a flock of lamenting and ranting, prattling and preaching characters, in a drama that demands to be played to the end."[34] The freshness of Stowe's characterization of black voices is what caught the attention of the reviewer in the *New York Daily Times:* "The slang of 'Ethiopian Serenaders' for once gives place to thoughts and language racy of the soil, and we need not say how refreshing it is to be separated for a season from the conventional Sambo of the modern stage."[35]

It is well known that for her plot Stowe drew on the narratives of escaped slaves, particularly those of Josiah Henson and Henry Bibb, both of whose adventures took them to Cincinnati.[36] The slave narrative—more properly called the "freedom narrative," as Toni Cade Bambara has pointed out[37]—is a highly exciting genre focused on escape. That all of the energies of this genre are focused on the point at which, to invoke one of Stowe's chapter headings, "Property Gets into an Improper State of Mind," highlights the agency of the teller of the tale. Property that has a will of its own demonstrates self-ownership. It was precisely this will to be free that Stowe had argued for in her early sketch for *Uncle Tom's Cabin*, "Immediate Emancipation." The act of escape and the life-imperiling risks that flight entailed impressed a populace that had not, until the Fugitive Slave Law, given a lot of thought to the subjectivity of the oppressed, assuming in many cases that the slave was better off under slavery than freedom. One cannot read Henry Bibb's tale of Indian captivity, attack by wolves, and desperate fording of rivers without developing a deep appreciation of his longing for "the blessings of Liberty."[38] In 1850–1851, as the newspapers carried stories of the enforcement of the Fugitive Slave Law, similar morals emerged from the resistance of "property." In Pennsylvania six white men burst in on a black family in the middle of the night in an attempt to capture a fugitive. In the story printed in the *Pennsylvania Freeman* and reprinted in the New York *Independent,* one of the deputy marshalls reported "that the slaveholder was so impressed by the heroism displayed by these brave colored people that he remarked:—'Well, if this is a specimen of the pluck of the Pennsylvania negroes I don't want my slaves back.' "[39] In *Uncle Tom's Cabin* the man who helps Eliza up the bank of the Ohio River after her heroic crossing has a similar response: "You're a right brave gal. I like grit, wherever I see it" (UTC, 1:78). But seeing heroism in black slaves was a new experience for the nation. Commenting on the resistance of the black family in Pennsylvania, the *Independent* correspondent wrote, "If the occupants of the house thus broken into at dead of night had been Italian or Hungarian refugees, the country would have rung with acclamations of their bravery. But with some the fact that they were only negroes will make quite a difference."[40] This must have lodged in Stowe's memory, for in "The Freeman's Defence," the chapter of Uncle Tom's Cabin in which George Harris defends his liberty against the slave catchers, she uses the same editorial line: "If it had been only a Hungarian youth, now, bravely defending in some mountain fastness the retreat of fugitives escaping from Austria into America, this would have been sublime heroism; but as it was a youth of African descent, defending the retreat of fugitives through America into Canada, of course we are too well instructed and patriotic to see any heroism in it" (UTC, 1:260).

The use Stowe made of selected incidents from press accounts and slave narratives is immediately evident when one reads these stories side by side. But even more striking is how Stowe transformed the genre of the escape narrative. By linking the story of Eliza and George Harris with that of Uncle Tom, she yoked the freedom narrative to a bondage narrative. While this considerably reduced the sense of black agency, it had the political virtue of directing the reader's attention away from escape and back to the enduring realities of slavery. While the Harrises flee north to Canada and a new life, Tom is taken south to the Red River plantation and death.

Twentieth-century critics have objected to the Christian script of passivity and sacrifice into which Stowe cast Tom. In Hortense Spillers's words, Uncle Tom is a victim in "a thematics of sacrifice" which Stowe "orchestrates" in a Christian drama that has a Calvinist "theological terror" at its heart. That the Christian message can also, as Spillers observes, be read "in a subversive way, in a way that does *not mandate* the sacrifice of children, the crucifixion of black bodies, male or female" is certainly true—as the story of Eliza suggests. But Stowe was dealing not only with the politics of Christianity; she was attempting to show the reality of slavery, which *did* mandate the crucifixion of black bodies.[41] By casting a male in the bondage plot, however, she did something new.

The freedom narrative, like the resistance to the Fugitive Slave Law, was primarily a male plot; male slaves escaped, men organized into armed groups, men exchanged pistol fire as carriages containing fugitives careened through the cities of the North. The bondage narrative was the pre-eminent female plot, as the women, like Henry Bibb's Malinda, were left behind. Male slaves, regularly hired out and sent on errands, had more opportunities to escape than bondwomen who had children to think of; to leave them was in many cases unthinkable; to take them made escape even more difficult. Some bondwomen did escape, but the literary genre of freedom narratives had gender markings: Josiah Henson's wife and child accompanied him, but he tells the story; Ellen Craft's escape was one of the most remarkable, yet she disguised herself as a man and her husband tells the tale.[42] With Eliza Harris's miraculous escape, Stowe feminized the freedom narrative; with Uncle Tom's death she recast the sex roles in the bondage narrative.

To do this she had to depart explicitly from the male literary models she worked with. In Cincinnati Josiah Henson had a chance to run away, but he honored his master's trust; later, however, he regretted this decision and determined to escape, which he did. As for Henry Bibb, who observed the effort of his master to get more money for him by making it appear that he "was so pious and honest" that he "would not run away for ill treatment," Bibb commented tersely, "a gross mistake, for I never had religion enough to keep me from running away from slavery in my life."[43] Stowe shaped her material to fit the notions of romantic racialism that her character Tom embodied.[44]

His story of bondage is packaged between two heroic and ingenious stories of female liberation. Balancing Eliza's escape in the early pages of the novel is Cassy's brilliant stratagem of "haunting" Legree's house and so unbalancing his superstitious mind that she and Emmeline escape and effect their eventual reunion with their families. As Gilbert and Gubar point out, Stowe transformed the gothic story of women's entrapment in a decaying mansion by having her characters *employ* the plot that had been used against governesses and other dependent women; the attic of Bertha Mason's bondage in *Jane Eyre* becomes in Stowe's hands the means of Emmeline's and Cassy's freedom.[45] Tom, on the other hand, is cast in the role of the angel in the house, the martyr, the perfect Christian, the Roxana Beecher. While he bore the sins of all, and particularly the burdens of perfection in both its patriarchal Calvinist and domestic ideologies, these women escape from slavery, and through their activism challenge the cult of true womanhood.[46] Insofar as they *could* be seen as falling into that construct, "woman," their heroic example could be a source of liberatory energy for all women, white as well as black. Their escape presages the transformations that Stowe's literary fame would effect in her own life.

The July 10, 1851 edition of the *National Era* carried the most memorable episode of *Uncle Tom's Cabin*. Eliza's crossing of the Ohio River with the slave catchers in close pursuit of her little Harry takes just two paragraphs to recount, yet it came for many to symbolize the movement of the entire liberation epic. When the novel was put on stage, a hush fell on the audience at the National Theatre in New York as Eliza escaped from her pursuers and reached the northern side of the river. An observer who turned to look was astonished to see that the entire audience, from the gentlemen and ladies in the balconies to the rough-shirted men in the galleries, was in tears.[47] The centerpiece of the popular "Tom shows" that made the rounds, later exaggerated in vaudeville skits and invoked in films such as Rogers and Hammerstein's *The King and I,* Eliza's flight across the river draws its power not only from its dramatic, visual character, but from the intensity of maternal feeling Stowe brought to it and the layers of Christian and pre-Christian myth that the imagery plumbed. The Ohio River, whose "sullen, surging waters . . . lay between [Eliza] and liberty" (UTC 1:69), was both the River Jordan and the River Styx. On the other side was the country where departed spirits were united, where burdens were put down and sorrows ended. As Mrs. Shelby's slave, Sam, explained about Eliza, "she's clar 'cross Jordan. As a body may say, in the land o' Canaan" (UTC, 1:93). As Stowe transformed her loss of Charley into Eliza's gain, she wielded powerful metaphors and tapped deep strains in nineteenth-century culture.

In the rhetoric of evangelical religion, "crossing the river" was a common metaphor for death. This imagery was well established in Christian hymns, where the saints on earth and the saints in heaven were "divided by the stream, / The narrow stream of death." The last three verses of Charles Wesley's 1759 hymn follows the imagery of Exodus:

> One army of the living God,
>   To his command we bow;
> Part of the host have crossed the flood,
>   And part are crossing now.
>
> E'en now by faith we join our hands
>   With those that went before,
> And greet the ever-living bands
>   On the eternal shore.
>
> Jesus, be thou our constant Guide;
>   Then, when the word is given,
> Bid Jordan's narrow stream divide,
>   And bring us safe to heaven.[48]

Eliza's miraculous crossing of the river was part and parcel of the miracle of crossing from this world to the next. Through this story Harriet accomplished the grief work of carrying Charley tenderly and lovingly to that shore where his sufferings were ended.

Stowe's transformation of her own bereavement into this mythic drama is well disguised under a surface texture of convincing realism. The cracking of the ice floes under Eliza's weight, the swearing of the slave catchers Loker and Marks, the careful articulation of their lower-class voices and those of Sam and Andy, the Shelbys's slaves, and the skillful narrative pacing in which the reader's attention is shifted between the Shelbys's house and Eliza's flight—these details keep the reader fixed on the story at hand. In no other single episode of her fiction does Stowe more effectively blend realism, high purpose, and mythic power.

In this she was aided by what Albert Raboteau has called the "reciprocity" between evangelical religion and slave religion, a condition that made for a two-way cultural transference.[49] In *Uncle Tom's Cabin* Stowe notes that in the "meetin" held in the Negro cabin, the hymns sung "made incessant mention of 'Jordan's banks,' and 'Canaan's fields,' and the 'New Jerusalem,'" and that the slaves clapped and cried "or shook hands rejoicingly with each other, as if they had fairly gained the other side of the river" (UTC, 1:37). As the geography of the holy land was laid over the geography of slavery, the Ohio River, separating the free state of Ohio from the slave state of Kentucky, became fraught with moral significance. Certainly the parallels between the Hebrew exodus from the land of Pharoah and the desire of Africans to escape from southern slavery made hymns about crossing the River Jordan into the land of Canaan a powerful form of expression and of political organizing in slave communities. "Preachings" or religious meetings were sometimes the setting for conspiracies. In 1800 Gabriel's Rebellion in Richmond, Virginia, had the assistance of Gabriel's brother, a preacher who in one discussion of the rebellion "contended that 'their cause was similar to the Israelites', and that in the Bible God had promised 'five of you shall conquer a hundred and a hundred a thousand of our enemies.' "[50] By incorporating their own historical reality into Protestant evangelical religion, black Christian slaves brought the other world back to earth and interpreted the Scriptures in a fashion perhaps more in keeping with the original Hebrew experience. It was precisely this insistence on uniting the secular and the religious realms that, as Eric Sundquist has observed, made Stowe's novel so radical.[51]

In some crucial respects the emphasis of slave religion closely approximated that of the German pietistic theologians whom Calvin Stowe admired. Both focused on the historical Jesus and the Bible as a record of God's acts in history.[52] In her house in Walnut Hills Harriet was privy to both the burrowings of her husband into German texts and the powerful faith of black women like Aunt Frankie, "who hungered and thirsted for righteousness."[53] In one ear she heard Mr. Stowe's translations from the German; in the other she heard the accents of an oppressed people. She concluded that "bleeding Africa" was the incarnation of Christ in nineteenth-century America.[54] The immense social, spiritual, and political power that the death of a lowly carpenter released two thousand years ago, Stowe attempted to release again in a liturgical re-creation. *Uncle Tom's Cabin* was the Protestant equivalent of the Roman Catholic mass, a dramatic re-enactment of the Crucifixion. Tom's body, given for others, was to be the bread and wine of a social revolution that would bring the kingdom of heaven.[55]

This was no tea party. The awful millennial hopes and fears of the 1840s were still burning in Stowe's breast. "O, Church of Christ, read the signs of the times!," she apostrophied in her "Concluding Remarks." Just as she had portrayed in "The Freeman's Dream" the damnation of the man who turned away a fugitive slave, now she prophecied a *"day of vengeance"* for the Union: "Not by combining together, to protect injustice and cruelty, and making a common capital of sin, is this Union to be saved,—but by repentance, justice and mercy; for, not surer is the eternal law by which the millstone sinks in the ocean, than that stronger law by which injustice and cruelty shall bring on nations the wrath of Almighty God!" (UTC, 2:250–51). This is, as Jane Tompkins has pointed out, a classic example of the jeremiad, a political sermon well known in New England history;[56] appropriate to this genre, Stowe speaks in the voice of an Old Testament prophet, modulated by the "theological terror" of the Calvinism in which she had been raised. She had not yet distanced herself from the patriarchal structures of religion, though her respect for the moral power of the clergy was fast crumbling in the wake of the Fugitive Slave Law crisis.

Stowe's inchoate politics and her tangled race, class, and sexual allegiances account for the complexity and contradiction of *Uncle Tom's Cabin*. But it was precisely her stirring of these deep currents that created the volatile narrative that moved so many people. And while she remained unselfconscious about some of her own social and political attitudes, she nevertheless skillfully manipulated those of her readers at various points in her narrative. Her story opens with a vignette that paints stark class contrasts between slave owner Shelby and slave trader Haley:

> For convenience sake, we have said, hitherto, two *gentlemen*. One of the parties, however, when critically examined, did not seem, strictly speaking, to come under the species. He was a short, thick-set man, with coarse, commonplace features, and that swaggering air of pretension which marks a low man who is trying to elbow his way upward in the world. He was much overdressed, in a gaudy vest of many colors, a blue neckerchief, bedropped gayly with yellow spots, and arranged with a flaunting tie, quite in keeping with the general air of the man. His hands, large and coarse, were plentifully bedecked with rings; and he wore a heavy gold watch-chain, with a bundle of seals of portentous size, and a great variety of colors, attached to it,—which, in the ardor of conversation, he was in the habit of flourishing and jingling with evident satisfaction. His conversation was in free and easy defiance of Murray's Grammar, and was garnished at convenient intervals with various profane expressions, which not even the desire to be graphic in our account shall induce us to transcribe. (UTC, 1:1–2).

In her parting sally, Stowe allies her narrative voice with the disdain she has gone to some pains to evoke toward the slavetrader. She masterfully builds on this in page after page of brilliant satire of this "Man of Humanity" whose concern for the slaves he buys and sells extends only to what might "damage the article"—satire almost exclusively conveyed through Haley's own words. As Haley incriminates himself, he puts before the reader the commercial realities of slavery, including the sexual degradation of "the fancy trade" and the routine separation of parents and children. All of this takes place in the words of a character whom so far we have been allowed to despise, a low-down slave trader. But then Stowe gathers up the reader's disdain and turns it back, with a vengeance:

> Are you educated and he ignorant, you high and he low, you refined and he coarse, you talented and he simple?
>
> In the day of a future Judgment, these very considerations may make it more tolerable for him than for you. (UTC, 1:173).

Readers who have heard much about Stowe's use of "sentiment" will be surprised by the highly refined and pointed anger that charges Stowe's narrative, particularly in the first section where her focus is on the Fugitive

Slave Law. Punctuating her narrative is a polemical, editorial voice commonly found in slave narratives. As she combined the whimsy and detail of the epistolary tradition with pointed assaults on public opinion, she created a highly effective medium that combined literary realism, political satire, and sermonic power.

CHAPTER NINETEEN

Cato's Daughter:
1851–1853

In Chapter 12, Stowe put Uncle Tom on a steamboat headed for New Orleans, a part of the country she had never seen. Foreseeing her need for information, she wrote to Frederick Douglass in July 1851 (with what Robert Stepto has called "a remarkable admixture of civility and imperiousness"[1] seeking his help. "You may perhaps have noticed in your editorial readings a series of articles that I am furnishing for the Era under the title of 'Uncle Tom's Cabin or Life among the lowly,'" she wrote to Douglass, whom she had not met. She continued:

> In the course of my story, the scene will fall upon a cotton plantation—I am very desirous to gain information from one who has been an actual labourer on one—& it occured to me that in the circle of your acquaintance there might be one who would be able to communicate to me some such information as I desire—I have before me an able paper written by a southern planter in which the details & modus operandi are given from *his* point of sight—I am anxious now to have some now from another stand point—I wish to be able to make a picture that shall be graphic & true to nature in its details—Such a person as Henry Bibb, if in this country might give me just the kind of information I desire.[2]

Having chosen to persuade not by argument but by pictures, Stowe's rhetorical power depended on having at hand details about slavery that were "graphic and true to nature." This was a formidable task for a northerner, and an even greater one for a woman. Stowe had been south only once, and this trip had occurred seventeen years earlier; in 1834 she had spent several days on a plantation in Kentucky. She had never been to the deep South, where she placed her hero first in the lackadaisical St. Clare household, and then in the remote Red River plantation under the cruel Simon Legree. On August 21 Stowe missed the *Era*'s deadline, and instead of Chapter 12 there appeared a brief notice that it had arrived too late for inclusion. Her uncertain grasp of the material reality of her story may have accounted for her delay. From this point until her publication of *A Key to Uncle Tom's Cabin* (1853) Stowe's access to information was as important as her ability to cast details in an imaginative frame.

Lamenting the nineteenth-century woman novelist's limited knowledge of the world, Virginia Woolf observed, "we must accept the fact that all those good novels, *Villette, Emma, Wuthering Heights, Middlemarch,* were written by women without more experience of life than could enter the house of a respectable clergyman; written too in the common sitting-room of that respectable house."[3] How was Harriet Beecher Stowe—the daughter and wife of clergymen—to extend her reach to embrace scenes of oppression and degradation on which her story depended? The answer lay in the "invisible" network of servingwomen whose stories passed from woman to woman in an oral tradition. Through her domestic servants, the shadow of the patriarchal institution fell aslant her own parlor floor. Her cook, Eliza Buck, raised in Virginia and abruptly sold to a plantation owner in Louisiana, told "of scenes on the Louisiana plantations," Stowe recalled, "& how she has often been out in the night by stealth, ministering to poor slaves, who had been mangled & lacerated by the whip." Later sold to a Kentucky slave master who became the father of all her children, Eliza Buck summed up the sexual reality of a slave woman's life: "You know, Mrs. Stowe, slave women can't help themselves."[4] Through Eliza Buck and many other cooks, washerwomen, and servants the private sphere that Virginia Woolf imagined to be so respectable was awash in stories of bondage, whippings, and the moral corruption that absolute power breeds.[5] A southern planter's wife experienced, in the words of Mary Boykin Chesnut, the double standard of life with "[a] magnate who runs a hideous black harem with its consequences under the same roof with his lovely white wife, and his beautiful and accomplished daughters."[6] The cult of true womanhood elevated the sexual purity of the white woman to "protect" her from what she knew too well. These facts were available to a clergyman's daughter in the sanctity of her own home. In the end Stowe's problem was not just knowledge, but an ideology of womanhood that decreed that some knowledge was inadmissable. Writing from her "retired closet," Stowe dragged out the hidden things of darkness into the light of day, insisting that the private relations between master and slave be subjected to the scrutiny of public opinion. This broke down the ideological barriers between the public and the private sphere, a revolutionary act that had the potential to free white women as well as male and female slaves.

That respectable sitting room in which Stowe had grown up was also populated by a large family of scholars and preachers and reformers known for their propensity to pull together in times of emergency; they possessed, singly and collectively, a vast reservoir of information. Harriet called to her side her brother Charles, who in 1839–1840 had worked in a countinghouse in New Orleans; as he traveled by boat through the bayous of Louisiana tracking down delinquent debtors he had hobnobbed with wealthy planters, gaining an inside view of their lavish life-styles, their shaky finances, and their strenuous defenses of "the domestic institution of the South." "[T]ruly these planters be excellent people to spend a night with talking & laughing & performing the mutualities of hospitality, whatever they may be to live with," Charles had written at the time.[7] When he received Harriet's letter "saying she was sick and unable to do any thing and he must come on instan-tur and help her about her book and no one but he could help her," he "started up instantly." She offered to "pay for a supply to his pulpit if need be," but Lyman Beecher, who was in the East visiting, took over his Newark pulpit to enable him to go to his sister's aid.[8]

The rallying of the family also included a four-month visit from Catharine Beecher, a woman whose help never came without complications. At Cathar-ine's urging, Harriet had agreed to found in concert with her yet another school. This one was to be small, to be housed on the premises of Harriet and Calvin's domicile, and to include mainly Harriet's children and various relatives. "We want *our own blood*," Catharine explained to querulous family members who were slow to give up their daughters—though kinship extended, it seems, to the children of well-to-do friends such as Susan and John Tasker Howard, wealthy parishioners of Henry Ward Beecher. Harriet was to teach composition and Catharine history.[9] Anna Smith, who had run a school in Walnut Hills, was also on the payroll of this latest venture. In January 1851 it was but a small affair—only two scholars besides the Stowe children. They met in a back room of the rambling Titcomb house, and all the comings and goings of little feet were confined to the woodhouse stairs, Harriet explained to Calvin, who lacked enthusiasm for the project. She assured him that when he returned the school would be arranged "just as you think best."[10]

In September, besides worrying about her story, Harriet made a big push to interest the influential members of the family in Catharine's educational schemes. Having recently read her sister's last book—*True Remedy for the Wrongs of Women*—Harriet urged it upon her father and brother Henry. "Until I read it I had no proper appreciation of her character motives of action for this eight or ten years past—I considered her strange nervous visionary & to a certain extent unstable—I see now that she has been busy for eight years about one thing . . . this plan of educating our country by means of its women." If they would garner financial support for Catharine's far-flung schemes, then her mind would be free to engage the task at hand; as Harriet explained, "She has agreed to give me a year of her time to act conjointly with me in taking a class of our young relations & carrying on their education with that of my own children."[11] This plan necessitated alterations to the house, new carpet, school furniture, dry goods, and larger heating bills. The educational philosophy Catharine articulated—to teach her charges *"how to acquire & how to communicate knowledge . . . that they will go forward henceforth & educate themselves & in due time educate others"*[12]—was designed to create independent young women who could pass on the torch. With unusual vision, Catharine Beecher labored all of her life to extend the reach of the women of her class; no longer would such a woman claim that her stock of knowledge simply "walked into her head," as she herself had experienced education. However, unable to attract a sufficient number of paying scholars, this venture soon ended as had the Western Female Institute—with both sisters in debt. Harriet toted up the expenses she had incurred, including four months' room and board for Catharine Beecher. [13]

While she was in residence in the fall and winter Catharine assisted by relieving Harriet of household supervision so that she could get on with her book. "I am trying to get Uncle Tom out of the way," Catharine explained at the end of September. "At 8 o clock we are thro' with breakfast & prayers & then we send off Mr. Stowe & Harriet both to *his room at the college.* There was no other way to keep her out of family cares & quietly at work & since this plan is adopted she goes ahead finely." She added that she hoped that the book would be finished before the schoolchildren arrived, arrangements for which would be in place for an October 15 opening. But Harriet had more than half of the book ahead of her and would be writing into the spring. At the end of October and again in December Stowe missed her deadlines. Bailey inserted the following notice in the October 30 *National Era:* "MRS. STOWE'S STORY—We regret exceedingly that the nineteenth chapter of Mrs. Stowe's Story did not reach us till the morning of the day on which the *Era* goes to press, and after all its matter, except one column, was set up. It shall appear next week." [14] In February 1852 she went to Andover with Calvin, where she planned to stay until the book was finished. She left behind her under Catharine's care her own children and her nieces Fanny Foote and Catherine Beecher Perkins, the latter of whom described how things went on at home under Catharine's leadership: "Aunt Kate's head is in a very precarious state so she can't bear any noise"—of which there was a considerable amount: the baby had "extensive endowments" in this line, Georgie was "ten times worse than the baby," Georgie and Freddy kept up "a constant light fire of quarrel," and then there were "four girls, none of us remarkable for quietness." Catharine maintained her distance in the upper regions of the house, appearing "once in a while like a comet" and never missing meals, at which she sat "with a very martyrized air until she has piled up a plate of provisions abundant enough for even *my* appetite," her niece observed, "and then declares she *can't* stand so much noise & departs."[15] Isabella Beecher Hooker, who brought her daughter Mary to visit a few months later while she helped Harriet with her correspondence, confirmed that there was "no lack of noise all over the house" and feared that her

daughter would become "wild as a hawk," especially under the influence of
Georgie, whom she described as "a real romp."[16] While Catharine provided
sisterly support by keeping Harriet away from the clatter and bang of domestic cares, Isabella acted as amanuensis, a laborious chore when documents
had to be copied by hand to preserve a record. Aunt Esther's arrival soon
after Isabella's completed the rallying of the Beecher women.[17]

In the meantime, in Andover, Harriet worked the details of Charles
Beecher's New Orleans experience into her story. The steamboat he had
taken down the Mississippi—*La Belle Riviere*[18]—bore Tom toward his new
master. Louisiana made Charles think of Spain and Italy (which he had never
seen)[19]; so it was the "Spanish" and "Moorish" quality of the St. Clare mansion that Harriet emphasized (UTC, 1:213). Charles had met an overseer
who boasted of his fist, hard from "knockin' down niggers"; around this
kernel grew up Stowe's characterization of Simon Legree.[20] Even southern
critics did not guess how slim was Stowe's firsthand knowledge of the
South,[21] yet the quality of her writing changed perceptibly when her story
moved to terra incognita. Just a glance at chapters 14 and 15 reveals part of
the reason. Whereas the first thirteen chapters of *Uncle Tom's Cabin* are
peppered with dialogue, these stand as almost unbroken blocks of narration.
Stowe wasn't sure what people sounded like; she was easing her way into
this unfamiliar country, and as she did so she cast about for props. Instead
of letting the members of the St. Clare household reveal themselves, she
provided stock histories of their past and, for little Eva, relied on her nineteenth-century audience's experience with "perfect" children who died young
to supply the credibility that her narrative lacked.

Yet Stowe's lack of realism was more than made up for by her ability to
manipulate cultural icons. Little Eva aroused sympathy even among southern readers.[22] They objected to many of the other characters but found in
Eva a domestic saint they recognized from the incomplete lives of the children they had buried. "Has there ever been a child like Eva?," Stowe asked
her readers. "Yes, there have been; but their names are always on grave-
stones" (UTC, 2:6). In February 1852, while Stowe's story was reaching its
climax in the pages of the *National Era, Godey's Lady's Book* published the
words and music to a parlor song entitled "Ye Come to Me in Dreams." The
singer of the song dreams of a baby nestled against her breast, only to wake
and remember he is dead. The song concludes:

> Yet I am happy even now—
>   This thought my grief disarms—
> A few short months I fondly clasp'd
>   An angel in my arms
> . . . .
> Thou wert my blessing here on earth,
>   And though tears dim my eyes,
> I feel that I am richer far
>   To have thee in the skies![23]

The reservoir of grief tapped by such sentiments and the compensatory images of heaven that grew up to soften it explain the popularity of Little Eva. One popular stage version of *Uncle Tom's Cabin* concluded with Eva, now transformed into an angel, appearing high over the heads of the other characters. *"Gorgeous clouds, tinted with sunlight,"* say the stage directions. *"EVA, robed in white, is discovered on the back of a milk-white dove, with expanded wings, as if just soaring upwards."*[24] The Cleveland *Plain Dealer* called Evangeline "one of the most perfect creations of the mind."[25] While Stowe's dialogue and most of her shrewd characterizations live on for readers today, Little Eva is a period piece—and one that contributed to the novel's extraordinary contemporary success. The portrait she drew of Eva in her white shroud, with her "head turned a little to one side, as if in natural sleep," was strikingly like the daguerreotype of her baby Charley (UTC, 2:53). How many of her readers had on the parlor table a similar daguerreotype?

In March 1852 Stowe entered into a contract with John P. Jewett, who had published books by other family members. Catharine Beecher had offered the book to her publisher, Phillips, Sampson, & Co., but they had turned it down on the grounds that a novel by a woman on an unpopular subject was too risky. According to an account Jewett later wrote, his wife, who had been following *Uncle Tom's Cabin* in the *National Era*, sat by his side "[o]n a cold morning in January, 1852 . . . reading from the last number of the *Era* the touching death scene of Little Eva, having more than once urged me to write Mrs. Stowe soliciting the story for publication in book form."[26] Published on March 20, 1852, *Uncle Tom's Cabin* sold 10,000 copies within the first week and 300,000 by the end of the first year. Just three weeks after the book's publication Calvin Stowe wrote sanguinely that "[t]he very great success of my wife's book, and the probably not much inferior success of another of the same size, which will be published in the autumn, (to be followed also in due time by two others,) has so changed my prospects in respect to Seminary matters, that another professorship with higher salary is not necessary to myself personally, as it was a year ago."[27] The contract that Harriet and Calvin had agreed to gave them 10 percent of the sales—not an unusual agreement for the time and one that netted $10,000 in the first three months of sales—the largest sum of money ever received by any author, either American or European, from the sale of a single work in so short a period of time," the press noted.[28]

When the extent of the novel's success became evident, the Stowes regretted that they had not taken up Jewett's offer to split both the profit and the risk equally—a proposal they with their straitened circumstances and family responsibilities had not been in a position to accept. As she talked with other businesspeople in America and England, Stowe began to think that Jewett had taken advantage of their ignorance. Calvin, who had handled the negotiations, had less practical sense than Harriet, and he had let Jewett talk him out of his original proposal—20 percent of the sales—by arguing that they would *make more* by taking 10 percent and allowing Jewett to invest the difference in advertising. Stowe later wrote Jewett that she did not dispute his making more than they did on the book, nor did she want him to "pay back any part of the proceeds of Uncle Tom." She merely wanted him to reply to her question, "Were you correct in persuading me & Mr Stowe that a ten percent contract on books that sell as mine have is better for us than a twenty percent one?" She also asked him for a business reference that would corroborate his 10 percent theory.[29] Jewett, a man whom Stowe described as "positive—overbearing—uneasy if crossed," responded angrily and broke off with her.[30] Catharine Beecher was outraged on behalf of the sister whose career she had supported through poverty and struggle; she planned a public exposé of Jewett. The other Beechers trembled at this news, for they remembered too well the embarrassing furor raised by Catharine's last crusade on behalf of a wronged woman. Delia Bacon, whose engagement was abruptly and humiliatingly terminated, found her situation exposed to public scrutiny in a book by Catharine Beecher entitled *Truth Stranger than Fiction*; undertaken out of sympathy and concern for Bacon, it may have contributed to this unstable woman's collapse into insanity and death. Isabella Beecher Hooker, who thought it too bad that "with all her good traits [Catharine] should be so meddlesome" recognized her good motive: "[S]he is so anxious that Hatty should have the means of educating her three million children she wont rest till she has made trouble somewhere."[31]

Harriet declined to press the matter with Jewett; she had another book under contract with him on the same terms and decided to go ahead rather than to risk a public airing of the dispute. She may have had glimmerings of the figure she would cut in the press, and her public image was worth more to her than she stood to gain from Jewett. Moreover, Jewett may have been right in presenting the 10 percent royalty as more advantageous, for he had agreed in return to "employ agents every where" and "spare no pains nor expense nor effort to push the book into an unparalled circulation."[32] The cultural elaborations of this publishing event are owing partly to his efforts. "The theatres have it," wrote Francis Lieber. "It will enter largely into exhibitions of paintings and possibly statuary. It will have its music."[33] Jewett helped this process along by paying John Greenleaf Whittier $50 to write a poem about Little Eva and getting someone else to set the words to music.[34] The poem was published in the *Independent* and circulated hand to hand. Whittier's New England ear rhymed "Eva" with a series of words ending in "r" in three stanzas that had little to do with the main burden of *Uncle Tom's Cabin*.

> Dry the tears for holy Eva
> With the blessed angels leave her,
> Of the form so sweet and fair,
> Give to earth the tender care.
> For the golden locks of Eva
> Let the sunny south land give her
> Flowery pillow of repose,
> Orange bloom and budding rose.

All is light and peace with Eva,
There the darkness cometh never,
Tears are wiped and fetters fall,
And the Lord is all in all.
Weep no more for happy Eva,
Wrong and sin no more shall grieve her,
Care and pain and weariness
Lost in love so measureless.

Gentle Eva, loving Eva,
Child confessor, true believer,
Listener at the Master's knee,
"Suffer such to come to me,"
Oh, for faith like thine, sweet Eva,
Lighting all the solemn river,
And the blessing of the poor
Wafting to the heavenly shore.[35]

"[T]hey are beautiful," Isabella Beecher Hooker wrote of these verses, "but you should hear Charles [Beecher] sing them, in his clear, rich voice, to know their full power."[36] In October Jewett & Co. announced a lavish gift edition of *Uncle Tom's Cabin* that would be out in time for the holidays. One hundred engravings by prominent engravers were part of their plan to make it "one of the most splendid books ever published in America."[37] By such means Jewett spread the popularity of the book and the fame of Harriet Beecher Stowe, and she stood to gain "as much more in time" as the $10,000 Jewett paid her in cash at the end of June 1852, as well as "something more from other things yet unwritten." [38]

It was well Harriet declined to sue Jewett, for she soon found herself threatened with legal action from another quarter. In the twelfth chapter of *Uncle Tom's Cabin* Stowe let loose her fury against the American clergy whose pronouncements in press, pulpit, and annual meeting supported the abomination of slavery. In the process she singled out for notice Joel Parker, a Presbyterian minister personally known to Lyman Beecher and Calvin Stowe, who threatened her with a $20,000 libel suit if she did not retract her words. The passage in question occurs in Chapter 12, "Select Incident of Lawful Trade," in which Tom witnesses a slave auction:

Tom had watched the whole transaction from first to last, and had a perfect understanding of its results. To him, it looked like something unutterably horrible and cruel, because, poor, ignorant black soul! he had not learned to generalize, and to take enlarged views. If he had only been instructed by certain ministers of Christianity, he might have thought better of it, and seen in it an every-day incident of a lawful trade; a trade which is the vital suport of an institution which an American divine tells us has *"no evils but such as are inseparable from any other relations in social and domestic life."* (UTC, 1:170)

A footnote attributed this quotation to Dr. Joel Parker of Philadelphia. "After painting a scene of shocking inhumanity," Parker complained to her, "you hold me up to the public, in an odious light, by representing me as uttering sentiments that seem to justify or, at least to palliate the cruelties which you have described."[39] Since Stowe was quoting from a newspaper account in which Parker had been quoted to this effect—without producing any challenge from him—she thought his indignation odd. In her reply she reminded him of this and said that if she had taken his sentiments to be proslavery, the reading public had doubtless formed a similar view and it was to them that he owed an explanation. "In the chapter in which your remark occurs I considered myself as the advocate of the poor & uneducated against the educated & the powerful," she told him, articulating a stance that was increasingly to take her into anticlerical positions.[40] Throughout this exchange, which extended from May to November 1852 in private correspondence, publicly printed letters, editorial attacks and documentary replies, the larger issue was slavery, but an underlying source of irritation to Parker and to his defenders in the pages of the *New York Observer* was the audacity of a *woman* daring to publicly challenge a man and a minister. Without having a clear political consciousness of the implications, Stowe was shaking the foundations of patriarchy. She was also beginning to see some crucial links between slavery and clerical structures.

What Parker had actually said in the *Christian Observer* of December 25, 1846, was, "What then are the evils inseparable from slavery? There is not one that is not equally inseparable from depraved human nature in other lawful relations."[41] Although the words were different, the sentiment of this syntactically treacherous sentence was the one Harriet had attributed to Parker: hold the double negatives still, and slavery is equated with other legal institutions, such as marriage. Now it is true that there were certain correspondences between the legal status of slaves and that of married women: neither had a civil voice or could hold property. It was this correspondence that led Angelina Grimké to declare, "The investigation of the rights of the slave has led me to a better understanding of my own." Stowe challenged Parker's words with no acknowledgment that they had any bearing at all on the situation of white, married women; whether she reflected on her own lack of rights, we do not know. The danger of this analogy is nowhere better illustrated than in the use Parker made of it; if it could be used to alert white women to their yoke, it could also be used to dismiss the oppression of the slave. Moreover, it rendered invisible the situation of bondwomen, who bore the rigors of slavery and reproduction with neither the right of legal marriage nor the institutions of motherhood and womanhood.

Although apparently Parker had not uttered the exact words quoted in *Uncle Tom's Cabin*, that statement was widely attributed to him in published documents illustrative of proslavery views, including, as Henry Ward Beecher pointed out to him, "in the annual report of the Anti-Slavery Society, which . . . is made up of facts and documents which are supposed to have a permanent and historical importance." Why, if the words were so offensive to his honor and character, had he not objected to these attributions? Parker's reply was "that he did not think, when standing in connection with such names, that it could produce an unfavorable impression on the public mind, but that it was very different when he alone was singled out by Mrs. Stowe."[42] Parker's willingness to be guided not by his own convictions but by whatever made a favorable impression on the public mind confirms Stowe's impression of him as "a weak vain man" easily influenced by others.[43]

The dispute might have been quickly settled—in spite of a series of delayed, misaddressed, and miscopied letters that, even for Harriet, was extraordinary[44]—if it had not become the shuttlecock in other political rivalries and jealousies. The chief of these was a long-standing rivalry between two New York religious papers, the antislavery *Independent* and the proslavery *Observer*. On May 20, just as the dispute between Parker and Stowe was breaking, the *Independent* announced a new contributor: Harriet Beecher Stowe would make "frequent and perhaps weekly contributions" to its pages, "sometimes an essay, sometimes a story, sometimes a graphic picture of home-life, or a sketch of the olden time."[45] No more would Harriet have to rely on secondhand access to one of the most powerful organs of religious opinion in the country, one that "silently preach[ed] to a larger and more confiding audience, every week, than any hundred clergymen together."[46] Her first contribution appeared simultaneously with this announcement and showed, as the *Independent* noted, "that Mrs. S. will not want for topics even outside the pale of lighter literature." Her maiden essay was an impassioned defense of Kossuth, the leader of the Hungarian revolution of 1848. Kossuth was currently on tour in the United States, where he was being received with great acclaim as a liberator of his people. Stowe's point of departure was an article in the *New York Observer* that sought to diminish this reputation by producing Kossuth's tavern bills. Stowe leaped to the defense of that "great apostle and martyr of *Liberty* and *Christianity*" in a brief column that simultaneously held to scorn the petty scandalmongering of a supposedly high-toned religious publication.[47] The *New York Observer* retaliated by devoting regular space to the controversy with Joel Parker, which became public on June 24 when Henry Ward Beecher published letters that were meant to settle the matter but only gave rise to the *Observer*'s charge that Beecher had forged the documents. (The *Observer* had a battle going against Henry Ward Beecher for his liberal views of evangelicalism, and it was not loathe to engage him on another front.) Its editor called attention to the "decidedly anti-ministerial" impression made by *Uncle Tom's Cabin,* a stance he found strange for an author with "a father, a husband, and half a dozen brothers in the ministry." His charges against Stowe were specifically framed in gender terms. Parker had been "gibbeted as a monster by the pen of a lady philanthropist." Moreover, he characterized Stowe's defense of Kossuth as "coarse" and "unladylike."[48]

Acknowledging that her attack on the *Observer* provoked the editor, S. Irenaeus Prime, to come to the defense of Joel Parker, Stowe reaffirmed her actions in a letter to her brother Henry:

There is nothing in this whole affair that has the power to stir my blood that
that bitter taunt on Kossuth had—It was the answer to *that* slander that
brought this on me—& so far I rejoice that I am worthy to suffer something
in defence of so noble a heart & noble a cause. . . . Did he [the editor of the
New York Observer] mean to poison the air around the mother & sister of
Kossuth just landing on our shores—& to profane the sacred name of religion
by taking *that* for his shield—then for the mother & sister who cannot speak,
a woman *shall* speak,—so help me God—If Christ has a follower on earth it is
Kossuth—if there is a holy cause it is that of *Liberty!*[49]

Stowe answered the *New York Observer*'s charge in a letter to the editor
in which she simultaneously wrapped herself in the cloak of true womanhood
and took the wraps off:

Sir. After reading as I did by mere accident, the first number of the recent
articles in the NYork Observer relating to myself & brother, I came to the
conclusion that the attack was commenced in a style & spirit with which self
respect & christian principle would alike forbid me to intermingle. I therefore
have read none of the succeeding articles & have taken refuge in that sanctuary
of silence which is the most proper resort of a christian woman when assailed
by abuse of any kind.

The "sanctuary of silence" was not congenial for a Beecher, however, and
Stowe did not stay long on this high ground. Taking up the *Observer*'s challenge, she framed her defense of Kossuth in terms consonant with yet transformative of the bounds of true womanhood:

You have spoken of my article as *unladylike*. There are some occasions when
a true woman must and will be unladylike. If a ruffian attacks her children,
she will defend them even at a risk of appearing unladylike & you may be sure
that whenever a poisoned dagger is lifted to stab the nobly unfortunate *in the
back* that some woman's hand will *always* be found between its point & his
heart, tho the act be unladylike, & the touch poison to her. We women are
naturally retiring fearful shrinking from the coarse abuse of life, but when we
once truly believe in the honor & worth of man [or woman—crossed out] or
cause we follow them thro good report & evil report, into prison & unto death.[50]

It was the same rationale that moved the timid Mrs. Bird in *Uncle Tom's
Cabin*. Women could act and speak—but only for others. Just as Harriet
could not be angry for *herself*, Eliza Harris fled to protect her child, not
because she longed for liberty. This simultaneous granting and muting of
agency to women was a reflection of the muffled voices of nineteenth-century women and of the contradictions held together by the ideology of "true
womanhood." Chief among these was the entwining of (white) women's
empowerment with the needs of "the nobly unfortunate." In the historical
moment in which Stowe spoke for the slaves, they could not readily be heard;
yet in the political economy Stowe articulated, women's empowerment
depended on the continued presence of the needy. In this sense the critics
of Stowe's "thematics of sacrifice" are right: she needed Uncle Tom's martyrdom. Yet Stowe was moving toward the assertion of a group conscious-

ness, albeit a consciousness not tested by group activity. "I speak not alone for myself but for the women of my country."[51]

The Joel Parker affair revealed the fighting spirit of Lyman Beecher's daughter in another letter to the editor of the *New York Observer* that never appeared in its pages, but was destined to have a longer life in a publication of its own. In the *Observer* Joel Parker foolishly challenged Stowe to document her charge that the proslavery sentiment she had attributed to him was common in clerical circles. She exulted over this challenge in a letter to Henry: "The man has no kind of idea what he has brought upon himself nor of the tremendous antislavery battery that he has pledged himself to erect in the sacred limits of the Observer if I only will be so good as to furnish him materials." Materials she had—drawn from the stock of her own memory and supplemented by the research assistance of her brothers, whose polemical talents had been honed in clerical disputes, heresy trials, and antislavery activity. "Edward who in his way is no fool particularly in exhuming all sorts of inconvenient declarations & arranging them in most uncomfortable proximities is already up to his chin in documents which he reads & makes notes of with that grave thoughtful smile peculiar to him," she told Henry. She went on to note:

> [W]e have a great abundance of declarations of Synods, Presbyteries & Ecclesiastical bodies of all denominations which are in their way considerably striking. All I want is a few declarations selected from the back files of the N. Y. Observer—I am very sure that that sentiment has been asserted there—also the back files of the Philadelphia Observer—I think the sentiment that slavery stands on the same ground with other lawful relations was pretty broadly asserted in a review of Uncle Tom in that paper. Ask Lewis Tappan "that very active & persevering secretary" (N. Y. O.) if he has any thing on his shelves. Let him write & tell us *what he has* & if we have n't got it, he can send it to us. Documentary reports of Ecclesiastical bodies are the thing. Back numbers of the Princeton Repertory—during the time of the controversy with Albert Barnes are specially requisite.

Harriet crowed to Henry, "I will write an article that shall cite the delinquents on this subject at the bar of public opinion every where from here to Leipsic. . . . Can't you come & see us—Things are getting decidedly interesting."[52] If Parker thought that as a woman Harriet Beecher Stowe would shrink from this public battle, he was about to find out, as she told him in her first letter to him, that he had more to fear from this than she. The clerical disputation that had been the meat and drink of Lyman Beecher's ministry was ordinarily not Harriet's cup of tea, but the epigraph she affixed to the beginning of her "antislavery battery" displayed both her relish of the battle and her family pride. Taking the words of Portia in Shakespeare's *The Merchant of Venice*, she wrote:

> I grant I am a woman—but withal
> A woman well reputed, Catos daughter
> Think you I am no stronger than my sex
> Being so fathered.[53]

As "Cato's daughter," Stowe's reliance on male institutions of power to which she had always had some access kept her from affirming a more radical consciousness of her sex. Yet she skillfully used the male forms of clerical disputation in her letter to the editor of the *New York Observer*. Having cited page after page of proslavery resolutions passed by clerical bodies, such as the resolution of the Georgia Annual Conference of the Methodist Church "that slavery *as it exists, in these United States is not a moral evil*," she concluded,

> "Thus—Mr Editor, in answer to your request,—or perhaps—more properly— your demand, the above facts have been laid before you.—Now—if you think, as you say, that the sentiment attributed to Mr Parker in Uncle Tom's Cabin, was an atrocious sentiment,—what will you say of these enlargments & defences of that same sentiment?—Some of the most striking of them are from individual & ecclesiastical bodies in full communion with the part of the Presbyterian Church to which you belong."

Her parting sally was superb: "When clergymen are guilty of any prominent heresy . . . it is customary for the remainder of the Church to clear themselves from complicity with such heresy by some public act," she said sweetly, "and the author asks simply, for information, whether anything of the kind has been done in this case." Now it was up to Joel Parker and Irenaeus Prime to demonstrate that their churches had denounced the heresy of slavery. "Dont you admire the closing request in my letter," Harriet asked Henry, fully aware of the twist she had put on her knife.[54]

The editor of the *New York Observer* was not foolish enough to print Stowe's reply to his challenge, and so her antislavery battery found another avenue to her audience. The documents that she and her brothers assembled were ultimately published in *A Key to Uncle Tom's Cabin*.[55] Although this book was written to meet a vast array of objections made about the truth of her depiction of slavery as the South rose in angry denunciation of the novel that was sweeping the land, the initial impetus may have come from this battle with Joel Parker. Nothing is mentioned of the *Key* until November 1852, at which point Stowe envisioned an "appendix" of one hundred pages.[56] In fact the book grew to 259 closely printed pages in four parts, with ten to fourteen chapters to each part. It was carved out of "a mountain of materials" that poured in in quantities much larger than she could use.[57] The aim of the book, Stowe joked to her brother Henry, was to dissolve the Union: "[I]f you have any plans or arrangements that would be affected by such an event get 'em all settled within four weeks."[58]

A difficult book to read, *A Key to Uncle Tom's Cabin* puts before the reader in shocking detail the legal status of the slave, the abuses to which this led in specific cases, and the defenses of slavery by the Protestant churches. It was in many respects a reprise of Theodore Weld's *American Slavery as It Is* (1839), a book Stowe drew on for factual detail in *Uncle Tom's Cabin* and which, like her *Key*, assembled documentary evidence from the slaveholders themselves.[59] In some cases this material illuminates the actual sources she drew upon for her novel; in many more cases the material corroborates her portraits after the fact. "I must confess, that, until I commenced the examination necessary to write this," she told Eliza Cabot Follen, "much as I thought I knew before, I had not *begun* to measure the depth of the abyss." She was particularly affected by reading the legal cases: "The laws, records of courts, & judicial proceedings are so incredible, as to fill me with amazement whenever I think of them."[60] She mentioned this material again in another letter, commenting, "It is worse than I supposed or dreamed."[61] Stowe's critics had pounced on Legree's murder of his own slave as a totally unrealistic event; it was a crime expressly forbidden by slave law, as decided in *Souther v. The Commonwealth.* In Part II of the *Key* Stowe responded by presenting case after case of slave justice, including *Souther v. The Commonwealth,* the details of which were more graphic than anything she had put in her book, confirming, as she told a correspondent, that "if my representations have erred anywhere, it is by being under rather than overcolored."[62] The court record told of a slave in Virginia who was tied to a tree for twelve hours and tortured with every conceivable means at hand, from whipping and kicking to burning with fire; when his body was fully open with wounds, the master made a solution from pods of red pepper and poured it over his body. Wearying of his efforts, the master forced two of his other slaves to continue the punishment. In the trial for murder that ensued when the slave died, the defense coolly argued that at worst the master's crime was only manslaughter, for he had not meant to kill the slave. Holding up this case as illustrative of "the ne plus ultra of legal humanity," Stowe commented: "Any one who reads the indictment will certainly think that, if this be murder in the *second degree,* in Virginia, one might earnestly pray to be murdered in the first degree, to begin with."[63] Southern reviewers who complained that they could not refute a novel because the incidents in it had not really happened had some hard facts to confront,[64] and Joel Parker and the *New York Observer* had the antislavery battery they asked for.

If it required moral hardihood and a strong stomach to read the material in the *Key,* much more of these qualities was required to sift through the documents and select the most telling ones. "I suffer excessively in writing these things," Stowe told Eliza Cabot Follen. "It may be truly said I write with *heart's blood.*"[65] Besides opening her mind and heart to this painful material, Stowe in writing both *Uncle Tom's Cabin* and the *Key* had to face down the conventional proscriptions on women's speech. A true woman would not acknowledge that slaves were stripped and beaten, that bond-women were the sexual as well as the legal slaves of their masters, that slave masters fathered children of all colors. As in so many cases of abuse, the defenders of the status quo cried out that the crime was not that of slavery, or of rape, or of incest, but rather lay in the *speaking* of such atrocities. "Grant that every accusation brought by Mrs. Stowe is perfectly true, that every vice alleged occurs as she has represented," wrote a southern critic, "the pollution of such literature to the heart and mind of woman is not less." He implied that this "Cincinnati schoolmistress" showed herself "much more conversant than the majority of Southern gentleman" with moral corruption. Louis S. McCord, reviewing *Uncle Tom's Cabin* in the *Southern Quarterly Review*, said it represented "the loathsome rakings of a foul fancy." William Gilmore Simms was even more intemperate in his review of the *Key*. "Mrs. Stowe betrays a malignity so remarkable," he said, "that the petticoat lifts of itself, and we see the hoof of the beast under the table."[66]

The risk that a woman author took in identifying herself with the cause of the slave was considerable. Stowe placed her own womanhood on the line. Either her reputation would be blasted, or she would transform the meaning of womanhood. Her very conventionality, her insistence on the forms of "true womanhood," was her armor in the battle to transform the meaning of the term. That she was the wife of a clergyman and the mother of seven children gave her some latitude in following out the implications of unconventional ideas—more than, for example, a single woman like Catharine Beecher. The southern outcry against Stowe's breach of decorum was the same public response she would meet with when she published *Lady Byron Vindicated*, except that in the latter case the North joined the South in its condemnation of her coarse and unladylike knowledge. In 1853 such caviling was drowned out by the voices of Stowe's fans. "[S]he has learnt to perfection the craft of the advocate," wrote a reviewer in the *New York Daily Times*. "*Euclid*, she well knows, is no child for effecting social revolutions, but an impassioned song may set a world in conflagration. Who shall deny to a true woman the use of her true weapons?"[67] True womanhood and social revolution now marched hand in hand. Stowe was soon joined in her crusade by over a half a million women in England, Ireland, and Scotland who, in response to *Uncle Tom's Cabin*, affixed their signatures to a petition on behalf of the slave. Stowe saw the *Key* through the press, and then, on April 1, 1853, she sailed for England to receive this petition.

CHAPTER TWENTY

Antislavery Activist:
1853–1854

O n April 10, 1853, after a ten-day voyage, the *Canada* made its
approach to Liverpool. On the deck with Harriet were her husband,
her brother Charles, her sister-in-law Sarah Buckingham Beecher,
and Sarah's brother, William, and son, George. This was the first transat-
lantic trip for everyone save Calvin. As they watched the skyline of this great
commercial city loom closer, they discerned on the dock a curious sight.
Amassed as far as the eye could see was a crowd of English men, women,
and children who were straining for their first glimpse of the author of *Uncle
Tom's Cabin*. They were quiet, respectful, eager, wondering what Mrs. Stowe
looked like. As Stowe was whisked into a cab sent by their host, John Cropper, a small boy climbed up on the wheel to look in. Lining the street as the
cab pulled away were smiling, nodding, welcoming faces.[1] Such receptions
swelled in size and enthusiasm as Stowe made her triumphant tour of Great
Britain, where the sales of *Uncle Tom's Cabin* were more than triple the
already phenomenal figures of the United States, reaching a million and a
half in the first year.

In this highly literate kingdom, British citizens young and old, from lords
and ladies to bakers and candlemakers, read *Uncle Tom*. It was in the the-
aters and the dance halls, at every railway bookstall and in every third traveler's hand. An immense Sunday-school edition priced at one shilling
ensured that the first views British schoolchildren would have of the American republic would be stamped by Eliza, Tom, Eva, Topsy, Dinah, Miss
Ophelia, Augustine St. Clare, and Simon Legree.[2] In a public meeting in

Scotland one of the testimonial speakers credited Stowe with having revo-
lutionized the British view of American literature:

> We have long been accustomed to despise American literature—I mean as
> compared with our own. I have heard eminent *litterateurs* say, "Pshaw! the
> Americans have no national literature." It was thought that they lived entirely
> on plunder—the plunder of poor slaves, and of poor British authors. [Loud
> cheers.] Their own works, when they came among us, were treated either with
> contempt or with patronizing wonder—yes, the "Sketch Book" was a very good
> book to be an American's. To parody two lines of Pope, we
>
> > "Admired such wisdom in a Yankee shape,
> > And showed an Irving as they show an ape."
>
> [Loud cheers.] . . . Let us hear no more of the poverty of American brains,
> or the barrenness of American literature. Had it produced only Uncle Tom's
> Cabin, it had evaded contempt just as certainly as Don Quixote, had there
> been no other product of the Spanish mind, would have rendered it forever
> illustrious. (SM, 1:xxxviii)

In a similar vein, Charles Kingsley called the book "a really healthy indigenous growth, autochthonous, & free from all that hapless second & third-
hand Germanism, & Italianism, & all other unreal-isms which make me sigh
over almost every American book I open." Kingsley quoted a critic who found
Uncle Tom "the greatest novel ever written," reminiscent "in a lower sphere"
of Shakespeare "in that marvellous clearness of insight and outsight, which
makes it seemingly impossible for her to see any one of her characters without shewing him or her at once as a distinct individual man or woman,
different from all others."[3] The British saw that the originality of the book
sprang from Stowe's grasp of the nationality of her material: an epic theme—
republican ideals in conflict with a feudal institution—was enshrined in a
narrative bristling with regional types. Moreover, British readers could
embrace *Uncle Tom's Cabin* with unalloyed enthusiasm, secure in the knowledge that the last vestiges of black slavery had been abolished in their colonies. At the same time, the resonances between race and class operated
powerfully on British readers to tap a sympathy with the poor and oppressed,
a sympathy that connected broadly with concerns that had been swelling in
England under the Reform Act of 1832, the Chartist movement, and the
novels of Elizabeth Gaskell, Charles Dickens, and Charles Kingsley. Harriet
Beecher Stowe spoke for the lowly, and for this, she found herself lifted
high.

Like the fabled Dick Wittington, Stowe woke up one morning to find
herself being received by the Lord Mayor of London—and all the nobility of
England. Just as dramatically, she found herself thrust into the center of
antislavery politics. The literary success of *Uncle Tom's Cabin* made Harriet
Beecher Stowe's the single most powerful voice on behalf of the slave. Her
preparation for this political role had been virtually nil. She had never been
a member of an antislavery society, much less an officer in one. The only

organizations she had ever been a part of were her sister's schools and the free and easy Semi-Colon Club—both of them family projects. Added to her lack of experience was a singular contradiction: although hers was the most powerful voice on behalf of the slave, by the canons of nineteenth-century womanhood she could not speak in public. With varying degrees of grace and success, Stowe applied herself between 1853 and 1854 to fulfilling the expectations of her new role as antislavery activist.

Stowe's previous lack of thought on the matter of antislavery politics was the subject of smug self-congratulation on the part of Isabella Beecher Hooker, who was struggling in this family of preachers and prophets to find her own niche. The summer after the publication of *Uncle Tom's Cabin* she wrote to her husband,

> It is amusing almost to see how Hatty is coming strait onto our Anti slavery platform—she has been you know a father & Mr Stowe abolitionist hereto-fore—but she said to me here, the other day, when some little talk about politics had been going on, "Bell, what do you think, or what does John do about this matter"—I smiled & said, why just as he always has done, votes for nobody who is in any wise committed to slavery—"Well said she, so shd I.—there is no other way—" & yet she was so absorbed in the dawn of her own ideas, she did not once remember that in common with others of our family she *had* doubted the wisdom of such practice.[4]

Had Stowe been politically attuned, it is unlikely she would have whole-heartedly embraced Kossuth, who drew the wrath of the abolitionists for his refusal to speak out on behalf of the slave during his American tour. The colonizationist position she advocated at the conclusion of *Uncle Tom's Cabin*—to which Frederick Douglass retorted, "The truth is, dear madam, we are *here*, & here we are likely to remain"[5]—was similarly the product of a certain lack of attention; she was swayed by the forces nearest her, and she was, indeed, "a father and Mr Stowe abolitionist" before the Fugitive Slave Act politicized her and led her to write a book much more radical than its colonizationist valedictory.

Antislavery politics was a minefield even for a seasoned activist. Full of visionaries, anarchists, antisabbatarians, millennialists, malcontents, and free-lovers, the antislavery movement reserved its most venomous attacks for fellow reformers whose ideological purity was suspect. Sectarianism was rife. There were colonizationists, gradualists, and immediatists; those who advo-cated compensating the slave owner for his slaves and those who held that if anyone was due recompense it was the slave whose labor had been appro-priated. The American Anti-Slavery Society split in 1840 when Lewis Tappan led a walkout over the issue of women's role, forming the American and Foreign Anti-Slavery Society. A more radical group supporting women's right to participate in antislavery politics coalesced around the dynamic William Lloyd Garrison, who had already formed the New England Non-Resistance Society. For those who could not embrace Garrison's uncompromising pacifism and iconoclasm, a third option was James Birney's Liberty party, which worked for the abolition of slavery through the political process. After the abolition of slavery in the West Indies in 1833, the British anti-slavery movement focused on American slavery and followed the split into Garrisonian and anti-Garrisonian factions. Somewhat paradoxically, Stowe's lack of experience with abolitionist politics enabled her to act as a unifying force. Precisely because she was unaffiliated, she could be claimed by all. Knowing "next to nothing of the abolition movement," she was, as one partisan observed, "a type of back number in the United States who are hardly touched by the turmoil of the Abolition warfare."[6] The antislavery movement in Great Britain drew strength from the overwhelming and undivided response Harriet Beecher Stowe called forth, and Stowe managed to maintain sufficient neutrality so as not to disarm this unity.[7]

Antislavery activists waged a behind-the-scenes struggle to ensure that Stowe's influence would be weighed in on their side. "Mrs. Stowe seems the general pivot of effort at present," wrote Scottish activist Eliza Wigham, "& I do not regret it at all, although to honour her is small anti slavery—yet to get the public enthusiastic on the A. S. question of which she for the present appears the impersonation is a great matter."[8] The invitation to visit Great Britain had issued from two groups in Glasgow acting in concert: the Glasgow Ladies' Anti-Slavery Society and the Glasgow Female New Association for the Abolition of Slavery. The New Association was less radical than the original Anti-Slavery Society and was viewed with suspicion by Garrisonians. Garrison, anticipating the political skirmishing that awaited Stowe on the other side of the Atlantic, wrote Stowe a letter before her departure warning her against certain factions of Glasgow ladies and suggesting that she read the pamphlets he enclosed.[9] Although she claimed not to have read his letter until after she sailed,[10] her landing in Liverpool rather than Glasgow established some distance from the Glasgow organizations. Understanding that she was a de facto ambassador of American culture, she had carefully informed herself before she arrived in England: she had met with Garrison, acquainted herself with his American Anti-Slavery Society, and studied the *Liberator*. Whether she had read Garrison's outspoken paper before is not clear, but by February 1853 she was reading it closely enough to challenge a statement Wendell Phillips made about her father's role in the Lane Debates. Exonerating the aging Lyman Beecher against the charge that "the weight of his heavy hand had always been felt against the slave" was to be part of her antislavery agenda. But the tone of conciliation she adopted in her letter to Phillips, which began by praising his article, suggests that she already had in view an interdenominational antislavery coalition that, to Lyman Beecher, would have been inconceivable.[11]

She may have initially approached Garrison as she did Henry Wadsworth Longfellow, "so that," she told the poet, "I shall be able to say in England that I have seen Longfellow!"[12] Her meeting with Garrison, however, had a profound effect on her view of the man. She would still be wrestling with the question of Garrison's "infidelism" after she returned from England, but

Harriet Beecher Stowe's birthplace, Litchfield, Connecticut. (*Stowe-Day Foundation, Hartford, Connecticut*)

Grandmother Foote, from a miniature painted on ivory by Roxana Foote Beecher. (*Stowe-Day Foundation, Hartford, Connecticut*)

The Hartford Female Seminary. (*Stowe-Day Foundation, Hartford, Connecticut*)

Samuel Foote's house, Cincinnati, Ohio, frequent meeting place of the Semi-Colon Club. (*Stowe-Day Foundation, Hartford, Connecticut*)

Catharine Beecher, educator, c. 1860. (*The Schlesinger Library, Radcliffe College*)

Stowe around the time of writing *Uncle Tom's Cabin*. (*The Schlesinger Library, Radcliffe College*)

Calvin Stowe, Professor of Biblical Literature, Lane Seminary, c. 1845. (*The Schlesinger Library, Radcliffe College*)

Samuel Charles Stowe, b. 1848, d. 1849. (*The Schlesinger Library, Radcliffe College*)

"Cato's Daughter." Lyman Beecher and Harriet Beecher Stowe, c. 1853. (*Stowe-Day Foundation, Hartford, Connecticut*)

Harriet and Calvin, 1853. (*The Schlesinger Library, Radcliffe College*)

The Beecher Family, c. 1859. Photograph by Mathew Brady. *Standing, left to right*: Thomas, William Edward, Charles, Henry Ward. *Seated, left to right*: Isabella, Catharine, Lyman Beecher, Mary, Harriet. *Insets*: James *(left)*, George. *(Stowe-Day Foundation, Hartford, Connecticut)*

Henry Ellis Stowe, c. 1857. (*The Schlesinger Library, Radcliffe College*)

Frederick Stowe, volunteer in the Union Army. (*The Schlesinger Library, Radcliffe College*)

Harriet and one of her dogs during the Andover years. (*Stowe-Day Foundation, Hartford, Connecticut*)

Oakholm, 1865–1870. (*Stowe-Day Foundation, Hartford, Connecticut*)

Eliza Stowe, 1854.
(*The Schlesinger Library,
Radcliffe College*)

Hatty Stowe, 1854.
(*Stowe-Day Foundation,
Hartford, Connecticut*)

Georgiana May Stowe, 1865. *(Stowe-Day Foundation, Hartford, Connecticut)*

Calvin Stowe and son Charley, 1860. *(The Schlesinger Library, Radcliffe College)*

"My Rabbi." Calvin Stowe in retirement. (*The Schlesinger Library, Radcliffe College*)

Stowe with her first grandchild, Freeman Allen, 1870. *(The Schlesinger Library, Radcliffe College)*

Calvin and Harriet at Mandarin, Florida, c. 1880. (*Stowe-Day Foundation, Hartford, Connecticut*)

Stowe with grandchildren Lyman Beecher Stowe and Leslie Stowe, c. 1886.
(*Stowe-Day Foundation, Hartford, Connecticut*)

she seems to have felt an almost instant rapport with Garrison personally. "You have," she told him, "a remarkable tact for conversation."[13] His uncompromising commitment to open discussion and his millennial politics appealed to the same instincts in Stowe. A man whose "countenance call[ed] to mind the pictures of the prophet Isaiah in a rapt mood,"[14] he was well equipped to be the Martin Luther of slavery whom Harriet had longed for. She spoke about Garrison "with great affection," asserting that "[n]o one . . . could know him & not love him—love him personally love him for his earnestness & his faithfulness."[15] The propinquity of Andover to Boston, the home of Garrison's Anti-Slavery Society, made this radical group easily accessible to Stowe and enabled her to draw on it for information and support. Still, she was careful not to align herself; it was the view of Ann Warren Weston, who observed Mrs. Stowe's frequent visits to the Anti-Slavery Society office, that she was "quite willing to get all she can out of us, but means to be very careful how she mixes up herself with the Old org[anization]s."[16]

In Liverpool Stowe's party stayed at the home of John Cropper, who lived a mile and a half out from the city in the "Dingle," a secluded retreat on the banks of the Mersey River. The day after their arrival Stowe was surprised to find that a breakfast arranged in her honor included upwards of forty people. She sat next to the Rev. Dr. McNeile, whom Stowe described as "one of the most celebrated clergymen of the established church in Liverpool (SM, 1:24). In his opening remarks Dr. McNeile sympathized with what "she must feel, and, as a lady, more peculiarly feel, in passing through that ordeal of gratulation which is sure to attend her steps in every part of our country." Instructing her on the script she was expected to follow, he prayed that "in the midst of the most flattering commendations" she would say and feel " 'Not unto me, O Lord, not unto me, but unto thy name be the praise, for thy mercy, and for they truth's sake.' "(SM, 1:xiv). The circumstances under which Stowe had written *Uncle Tom's Cabin* were conducive to the posture McNeile urged upon her. The powerful meshing of Stowe's private and public experience, through the close coincidence of her baby's death and the Fugitive Slave Law, must have made her feel as though she were taken over by a higher power. She wrote in this vein to Lord Denman before her voyage:

Could anything flatter me into an unwarrantable estimate of my self, it would be commendation from such sources as your Lordship—But I am utterly incredulous of all that is said, it passes by me like a dream I can only see that when a Higher Being has purposes to be accomplished, he can make even "a grain of mustard seed" the means—

I wrote what I did because as a woman, as a mother I was oppressed & broken-hearted, with the sorrows & injustice I saw, because as a Christian I felt the dishonor to Christianity—because as a lover of my country I trembled at the coming day of wrath.—

It is no merit in the sorrowful that they weep, or to the oppressed & smothering that they gasp & struggle, nor to me, that I *must* speak for the oppressed—who cannot speak for themselves.[17]

That she wrote as a woman, a mother, a Christian, and a lover of her country is an accurate summary of the four most important rhetorical strategies in *Uncle Tom's Cabin*, and equally accurate is the picture she drew of her emotional, visceral, *necessary* speaking out. However, under the pressure of remarks like Dr. McNeile's—which were stock inscriptions of the moral superiority of true womanhood[18]—the political meaning of such statements subtly changed. What Stowe had experienced as an inspiration to speech was portrayed as retirement from the world. Enabling this slippage was the crucial fact that Stowe's "vocation," as she had said to her brother in 1830, was "to preach on paper" rather than "viva voce."[19] Acting privately and properly, she was nevertheless speaking publicly. Stowe was careful in her outward behavior to do nothing that would upset this delicate standoff between ideology and reality, for it allowed her to move back and forth between the private and the public realms and to have an influence in both. In particular she was careful to do nothing that would set her apart, in word or deed, from her natural power base: the women.

"You have rightly guessed my feelings with regard to any thing of the nature of public demonstration," Harriet had written before she left to Edward Baines, the abolitionist editor of the *Leeds Mercury*. "I hope by such means as a lady may use, to do something to promote a good understanding among all the enemies of slavery."[20] In spite of her wishes, large public meetings—"soirees"—were held in her honor in Glasgow, Edinburgh, Dundee, and London. Women's roles were encoded in the architecture of the public halls in England, where the "ladies' gallery," separated from the main hall by a lattice, enabled ladies to "see and not be seen." Charles Beecher called this arrangement in the House of Commons an "oriental rookery"; it was the architectural version of the veils that covered women in Islamic cultures.[21] During the public meetings held in her honor Stowe sat in side galleries and respected the convention that forbade women from speaking in public. In Glasgow, where Stowe's party went from Liverpool, two thousand people gathered on the evening of April 16 to sing the hymn "Old Hundredth" and listen to seven hours of speeches. When Harriet entered the hall the enthusiasm surpassed even the receptions in America of Kossuth and Jenny Lind. "When they welcomed her," Charles Beecher reported, "they first clapped and stomped, then shouted, then waved their hands and handkerchiefs, then stood up—and to look down from above, it looked like *waves* rising and the foam dashing up in spray."[22] When she reached her seat, Harriet sat quietly while her husband rose to read her speech. More often at such gatherings Calvin Stowe and Charles Beecher made speeches of their own.[23]

Nor could the ladies who had been active in Stowe's behalf speak directly to her. At a public meeting held in Liverpool on April 13 the two hundred women gathered in a small room heard a man explain to Stowe that "[t]he modesty of our English ladies, which, like your own, shrinks instinctively from unnecessary publicity," had made his presence necessary. It was hoped

that at the last minute Mrs. John Cropper might summon sufficient courage
to act in the leadership position which she had, in fact, pursued as organizer
of this event. "But," as Mr. Hodgson explained to Stowe, "she has felt with
you that the path most grateful and most congenial to female exertion, even
in its widest and most elevated range, is still a retired and a shady path; and
you have taught us that the voice which most effectually kindles enthusiasm
in millions is the still small voice which comes forth from the sanctuary of
a woman's breast, and from the retirement of a woman's closet" (SM, 1:xvi).
It was "in the closet" that the horrors of slavery transpired, and woman's
"retirement" in that dark quarter gave her ready knowledge of its abuses;
Stowe's attack on the patriarchal institution radically undermined the ideology of separate spheres, yet her public behavior supported the fiction of
woman's separation from the world.

After the publication of *Uncle Tom's Cabin* Stowe became highly sensitive to her public image and did much to cultivate an outward posture of
true womanhood. One of the most polished examples of this retired and
womanly species of self-promotion was the famous letter she wrote to Eliza
Cabot Follen in response to her request for some information about the
author of *Uncle Tom's Cabin*. Follen, a writer of children's stories, was a
Boston abolitionist of the Garrisonian persuasion; cut loose after her husband's death, she was now in London, where she met with Harriet in her
West End apartment and acted as an informal ambassador between Harriet
and the British antislavery women. In an often quoted passage, Stowe told
Mrs. Follen,

> So you want to know something about what sort of a woman I am—well, if
> this is any object, you shall have statistics free of charge.
>
> To begin, then I am a little bit of a woman—somewhat more than 40—
> about as thin & dry as a pinch of snuff never very much to look at in my best
> days—& looking like a used-up article now. I was married when I was 25 years
> old to a man rich in Greek & Hebrew, Latin & Arabic, & alas! rich in nothing
> else. . . .
>
> During these long years of struggling with poverty & sickness & a hot debil-
> itating climate, my children grew up around me. The nursery & the kitchen
> were my principal fields of labour.
>
> Some of my friends pitying my toils, copied & sent some of my little
> sketches to certain liberally paying annuals, with my name. With the first
> money I earned in this way, I bought a *feather-bed* ! . . . After this, I thought I
> had discovered the philosopher's stone, & when a new carpet, or a mattress
> was going to be needed, or when at the close of the year, it began to be evident
> that my accounts, like poor Dora's, *"wouldn't add up,"* then I used to say to my
> faithful friend & factotum Anna, who shared all my joys & sorrows, "Now, if
> you'll keep the babies, & attend to all the things in the house for one day, I'll
> write a piece, & then we shall be out of the scrape," and so I became an
> authoress Very modest, at first I do assure you, & remonstrating very seriously
> with the friends who had thought it best to put my name to the pieces, by way
> of getting up a reputation, & if you ever get to see a wood cut of me, with an
> inordinately long nose, on the cover of all the Anti Slavery almanacs, I wish

you to take notice that I have been forced into it, contrary to my natural modesty by the imperative solicitations of my dear 5000 friends & the public generally.[24]

While the facts were more or less true, the retiring posture she assumed did
not acknowledge the determination with which she had arranged her household service so that she would *regularly* have three hours a day to write; and
arranged to have a room of her own; and declared to her husband that if she
chose to be a "literary woman" she had a good chance to succeed. This "little
bit of a woman" insisted on full payment from editors, demanded an accounting from J. P. Jewett of his business methods, and faced down the Rev. Joel
Parker and the *New York Observer*. But her letter to Mrs. Follen, copied and
passed from hand to hand, won the hearts of the British antislavery women.[25]
By reassuring them that she was not going to be carried away by her own
importance, she affirmed her bond with them as women and maximized her
ability to act as a channel of public opinion. She *used* modesty very much as
Benjamin Franklin did, as an efficient means to community action that
would ultimately redound to her credit.[26]

From Glasgow Stowe went to Edinburgh, Aberdeen, and Dundee. "At
every place where the cars stop," recorded her brother, "crowds are waiting.
She cannot go out to ride nor show her face without crowds & hurrahs." At
Dundee the streets were "all the way alive, with workingmen and women,
boys and girls, a perfect ovation."[27] In each place subscriptions were taken
up. The ladies of Liverpool presented Harriet with an embossed gold purse
engraved with her name and the date; inside was 130 pounds in English
banknotes, the equivalent of $650.[28] In the same city the Negroes' Friend
Society Meeting presented her with "a sum to be appropriated for the benefit
of the slave" (SM, 1:39). In Aberdeen a purse of 150 pounds for the Underground Railway was pressed upon her; at the Edinburgh soiree Stowe took
home a silver salver covered with 1000 pounds; part of the "Penny Offering"
that was taken up all over the British Isles, this fund originated out of the
idea that because Stowe reaped no English royalties from *Uncle Tom's Cabin*,
each reader should contribute one penny to the author. Ultimately Stowe
took home upwards of $20,000, which led one cynic to observe, "Garrison
has made a living and Mrs. Stowe a fortune out of the cause of the colored
race."[29] People who wanted the immediate sense of "doing something" for
the cause of the slave reached into their pockets. While some of these testimonials were designated for specific work such as redeeming slaves, most
of the money was given to Stowe with a general understanding that she would
use it as she saw fit. A deputation from Ireland presented her with a bog oak
casket carved with national symbols containing "an offering for the cause of
the oppressed" (SM, 2:431). The Quaker women in Edinburgh took Harriet
aside and presented her with work of their own hands: a beautiful papier
mâché box that contained "all ladies' working articles and a beautiful *agate
cup*" cut out of Scotch pebble. The wine-colored cup contained 100 gold
sovereigns that were reserved for the use of "Mrs. Stowe *herself*."[30] Most of
the money given to Stowe was not so clearly designated.

Throughout Scotland Stowe urged cooperation between all factions of abolitionists and spread good reports of William Lloyd Garrison (causing "a few inward groans," but also "a great deal of satisfaction").[31] "We are all well satisfied with what we hear she has said in Glasgow, Edinburgh & elsewhere of him & of us," wrote a Garrisonian. "The 'Glasgow Muses' have not received any especial 'aid and comfort' at her hands."[32] The split in British antislavery ranks between Garrisonian and anti-Garrisonian parties was also a split between the provinces and the center; Scotland, Ireland, and the English provinces were heavily represented by the more radical, old Garrisonian party while the London-based British and Foreign Anti-Slavery Society spoke for the newer, more-conservative group.[33] The neutral course Stowe steered in Scotland was imperiled when she turned south and entered the orbit of the conservative London abolitionists. There she was taken in by Joseph Sturge of Birmingham, a long-time Quaker activist who—in spite of the fact that Garrison was "almost a Quaker" and Sturge was an immediatist—was counted in the anti-Garrisonian camp. A wealthy and somewhat humorless man, Sturge's philanthropy issued both from Quaker principles and guilt over his prosperity. He had strong links with American antislavery forces and in particular with the *National Era*, a publication he had provided with generous financial support. During the struggle to abolish slavery in the West Indies the Society of Friends had organized a boycott of slave-grown sugar; in the 1850s a similar movement was gaining strength to boycott slave-grown cotton. Sturge was a strong proponent of the view that if the markets for slave cotton disappeared, so too would slavery.[34]

Not having any formulated antislavery platform to stand on, the Beechers were readily susceptible to the plan presented them by their Birmingham hosts. After a meeting arranged by Sturge with Elihu Burritt, Harriet's party agreed to work with the Quakers in promoting "free-labour."[35] This quick, easy victory for the non-Garrisonian antislavery camp must have delighted Sturge and Burritt. Calvin Stowe and Charles Beecher—to whom fell the burden of making public speeches on Harriet's behalf—were no doubt relieved to have something to say. At a huge meeting at Exeter Hall on May 16 Calvin Stowe put forward a wordy resolution the substance of which was to urge "the development of the natural resources of countries where slavery does not exist, and the soil of which is adapted to the growth of products—especially of cotton" (SM, 1:lv). This speech, widely reported on both sides of the Atlantic, brought immediate rejoinders and attacks. Cobden and Bright's paper came out "fiery against it," Cobden objecting on the practical grounds that it was hard to distinguish slave cotton from free.[36] Isabella Massie, writing to another Garrisonian, dismissed the "twaddle" of Calvin Stowe's "Cotton plaister": "We are *likely* to sit down in shiftless idleness till the Chinese shall have peopled the state with free labourers!"[37] William Wells Brown, in England, sent Garrison reports of the Exeter Hall meeting and observed, "I look upon this cotton question as nothing more than to divert the public from the main subject itself. Mr. Stowe is not very young, yet he is only a child in the anti-slavery movement. He is now lisping his

A. B. C., and if his wife succeeds in making him a good scholar, she will find it no easy thing."[38] Although Harriet had supported the same position in a speech to a "Quaker Ladies meeting for free-labor,"[39] her speaking in this retired nook spared her public notice and reaction. Her fans vilified her husband but attributed a nobler and broader view to her. One advantage of woman's enforced retirement from public speech was that the public could attribute its most cherished views to her without any evidence to contradict them.

Throughout her tour poor Calvin Stowe acted as a lightning rod for negative reactions while Harriet escaped not only unscathed, but with her reputation enhanced by her modesty and good sense. After his speech at the Glasgow soiree, Charles Beecher remarked several times that Calvin had "never appeared so to advantage," but the view of the Scottish Quaker women was considerably less charitable. Eliza Wigham, their Edinburgh hostess, reported that both Harriet's husband and her brother "left a very unfavorable impression on many minds partly by their American manners, partly by their not speaking out explicitly against the sin of the churches in countenancing this iniquity." While Harriet had no conscious intention to rattle the bars of her own cage when she attacked the patriarchal institution, the anticlerical animus aroused by *Uncle Tom's Cabin* landed squarely on her ministerial husband and brother. At the Exeter Hall meeting the Rev. Samuel Ward, a black clergyman from Canada, in what William Wells Brown called "the best speech of the evening," "exposed the hypocrisy of the American pro-slavery churches in a way that caused Professor Stowe to turn more than once upon his seat."[40] As for "American manners," Calvin's tendency to patronize his hosts by alluding to the great progress the British had made did not enhance his standing. By contrast, Mrs. Wigham found Harriet "a very sweet person—with most unassuming deportment, unselfish— thinking of the Cause, ascribing the success of her book to the blessing upon it not to herself."[41] After his cotton speech at Exeter Hall, the contrast between Calvin and Harriet provoked Isabella Massie to "pity poor Mrs Stowe": "I can fancy no misery more supreme than for a Mind of such delicate texture to be bound in the bundle of this life at least with such a Man—Chagrin & wrath were on his lips—a thorn on his tongue and I fear that she poor thing would find his heart was a tinderbox that night."[42] The position he was put in by virtue of his wife's fame was sorely trying to a man not overly able to absorb insult. Subjected to humiliating representations in the press and private jibes at "the husband of Harriet Beecher Stowe," Calvin cut short his trip; instead of accompanying the party to the Continent, he returned home at the end of May. The British antislavery women were relieved that Harriet's "bungling husband" was out of the way. With that irritation removed and Harriet safe in the hands of Maria Weston Chapman and family (described by Charles Beecher as "high-church Abolitionists" of the Garrison school), the Garrisonians relaxed their vigilance.[43]

On May 2 Harriet dined with the Lord Mayor of London, where she was seated across from Charles Dickens. In a toast, the two authors were held up "as having employed fiction as a means of awakening the attention of the respective countries to the condition of the oppressed and suffering classes."[44] If Stowe's visit united the antislavery movement, it also gave a boost to the claims of the poor and working class for social justice.[45] As Josephine Donovan has pointed out, Stowe wrote *Uncle Tom's Cabin* during a period of "revolutionary ferment."[46] In 1848 kings were falling like rotten pears. Stowe put in the mouth of Augustine St. Clare a prediction that the present "mustering among the masses, the world over" would lead to a millennial day of wrath (UTC, 1: 305). The analogy between black slavery and white slavery was a standard ingredient in labor rhetoric.[47] Like the analogy between slavery and other "domestic institutions," however, it was fraught with contradictory political implications. In *Cannibals, All!*, a book whose title suggests the author's conservative interpretation of the analogy, the most outspoken defender of southern slavery cited the same statistics on the working class that Karl Marx used in *Capital*; but while Marx used the figures to show the oppression of wage slavery, George Fitzhugh used them to argue that black slavery was more humanitarian than capitalism.[48]

In an article in *Fraser's Magazine* Arthur Helps, a British essayist and historian about Stowe's age, attempted to correct Stowe's "exaggeration . . . respecting the condition of the English labourer." Defending the Poor Laws and recent improvements in the condition of the laboring classes, he disputed "the idea that the English labourer is the least like a slave."[49] Stowe replied that she had put those words in the mouth of St. Clare precisely because this sentiment was commonly invoked by slaveholders in defense of slavery and she had taken pains to portray their position in as fair a light as she could.[50] But she also challenged Arthur Helps to bring forward statistics that proved his point about the improvements in the lives of his country's poor. She had trouble reconciling the impression of his article "with those I have received from much current English literature," citing in addition to the works of Charles Dickens and Charles Kingsley, several by Charlotte Elizabeth (Mrs. Charlotte Elizabeth Tonna Brown), a prolific writer of evangelical tracts and stories whose *Helen Fleetwood* called attention to England's child labor laws—which at that time allowed children as young as thirteen to work in factories.[51] When Stowe broached this subject with Richard Whately, the English Archbishop of Dublin, he assured her that her literary evidence was suspect, especially her use of Charles Kingsley: "He, & a Profr Maurice, & some others, are what are called Christian Socialists; giving such a representation of Christianity as would have justified the Roman Emperors in putting it down by force, as leading straight to anarchy."[52] Between Garrison and Kingsley, the company Harriet found congenial suggested her radical affinities, and Archbishop Whately's invocation of "anarchy" is germane: Stowe's visceral and largely unsystematic responses to injustice had the weaknesses as well as the strengths of anarchistic political thought. Like Garrison, she took careful aim at fundamental props to church and state, but these radical impulses more often held sway in her fiction—a ground that could absorb millennial and visionary thought—than in her explicitly held political positions. In England she backed away from the radical implications of the race–class analogy, asserting that the present state of the working class had much to do with habits of intemperance.[53] In *Sunny Memories* she took her readers on a tour of model tenements in England and concluded of the English poor, "one can see that their case is essentially different from that of plantation slaves" (SM, 1:68).[54]

The English–American rivalry over issues of social justice was repeated in much-less-civil tones in the proslavery American press. Stung by the extraordinary popularity of *Uncle Tom's Cabin* in England, the proslavery forces became apoplectic when the Duchess of Sutherland, along with the Earl of Shaftesbury and the Earl of Carlisle, drew up a petition that instructed Americans on their Christian duty in regard to the slave. Like *Uncle Tom's Cabin*, "An Affectionate and Christian Address of Many Thousands of Women of Great Britain and Ireland to Their Sisters the Women of the United States of America" appealed to "sisters," "wives," and "mothers" to protest slavery's outrages on the Christian family. The text of the "Affectionate and Christian Address," drawn up by the Earl of Shaftesbury, singled out the laws that "deny in effect to the slave the sanctity of marriage, with all its joys, rights, and obligations; which separate, at the will of the master, the wife from the husband, and the children from parents." It also objected to the practice of denying the slave "education in the truths of the Gospel and the ordinances of Christianity."[55] Women circulated this petition in their networks and carried it door to door, ultimately collecting over half a million signatures. In neither the United States nor the British Isles could women vote; petitions were one of the few ways in which they were able to have a political voice.

The reaction to this unwelcome example of women's speech was swift. While it was still being circulated, the text of the "Affectionate and Christian Address" was passed to proslavery papers in America, who variously parodied it, lambasted the British women as busybodies, and suggested they attend to the complaints of their own poor. The *New York Observer* made the latter point by reprinting the address with references to America's black slavery changed to refer to England's white slavery.[56] The Duchess of Sutherland was taken to task for her treatment of her tenants on her highland estates, charges Stowe took pains to refute in *Sunny Memories of Foreign Lands*.[57] The *British Army Dispatch* printed a vicious attack on the women who dared to organize the petition drive, prompting Stowe to reiterate her view of embattled womanhood. "It is an exceedingly annoying & disagreeable thing for pure womanhood to come in contact with unscrupulous scurrility & vulgarity," she told a British organizer of the petition. "There is about our sex—(perhaps its greatest fault) a sensitiveness to what exposes to ridicule which often leads us to shrink from a right cause, with undue fastidiousness—but if there is any cause under heaven that needs the support of pious womanhood it is that of the poor slave." She knew from her own experience with southern reviewers what vulgarity her sisters in England might be subject to. "Christianly & gently as they have spoken," the ladies of England "lay their hand on a terrible—a *mortal* wound—and not the softest hand in England can touch that place without exciting convulsions."[58]

When the canvassers finished their work, the signatures to the "Affectionate and Christian Address" filled twenty-six thick volumes. It is still a moving experience to read the individual names and the occupations of these women, from every walk of life, who read *Uncle Tom's Cabin* and united with Stowe in her woman's outrage against the treatment of the lowly.[59] The petition and the signatures were presented to Stowe at the social and symbolic climax of Stowe's British tour: a meeting on May 7 at Stafford House, the palatial residence of the Duchess of Sutherland. Harriet was met at the door by two Highlanders in full dress. Liveried servants with powdered wigs and sonorous voices called out "Mrs. Harriet Beecher Stowe"; as her name was passed from archway to archway down long corridors of marble floors, pillars, statuary, and paintings, she took in the splendid decor, "more perfectly suited my eye and taste than any I had ever seen before" (SM, 1:287). Here she was received by the Duchess of Sutherland, the Earl and Countess of Shaftesbury, the Duke and Duchess of Argyll, Lord and Lady Palmerston, the Earl of Carlisle, Lord John Russell, William Gladstone, Thomas B. Macaulay, the Archbishop of Dublin, and virtually every person of rank and prominence except Queen Victoria. The Duchess of Sutherland, a tall, handsome woman who had immediately taken to Stowe, presented her with a gold bracelet formed like a slave's shackle; on one of the links was inscribed the date of the abolition of slavery in the British colonies. A space was reserved on another link for inscription of the date on which American slavery would be abolished. In a note of thanks Harriet told the duchess, "The memorial you placed on my wrist will ever be dear to me—mournfully dear— I may not live to have engraved there the glorious date of emancipation in America but my *children will* if I do not—& I trust *that date* shall yet be added to this chain."[60]

When Stowe had agreed to receive the "Affectionate and Christian Address," she promised to establish in America a women's committee that would be the counterpart of the one that carried the movement in the British Isles. In the winter before her trip she had begun writing to prominent American women in order to enlist a committee comparable in republican America to the distinguished group of earls and duchesses in England. Aristocratic privilege gave English women entitlement to speak, but it is revealing that in America Stowe turned on the one hand to women novelists, and on the other to Quakers. "I intend to apply to Miss C M Sedgewick, Mrs. [Caroline] Kirkland and to some leading lady in the Quaker denomination," she wrote in February 1853.[61] She also wrote to Henry Wadsworth Longfellow enlisting his wife's support, and at the meeting at Stafford House a letter from Cassius M. Clay, a prominent abolitionist from Kentucky, announced his wife's acceptance of a place on this committee.[62] Harriet planned to put her sister, Catharine Beecher, at the helm of this organization—a dubious choice that reflected Stowe's perception of reform as a Beecher family project.[63] Nothing ever came of this American women's committee. No reply to the "Affectionate and Christian Address" issued from Stowe's pen until 1862. While the women in England managed, using antislavery organizations and neighborhood networks, to involve half a million women in a political activity, Stowe was unable—partly because she was unconnected to either women's organizations or antislavery groups—to mount a comparable response. In this sense she failed to capitalize politically on the extraordinary response her novel evoked among women.

With the $20,000 of the Penny Offering in her possession, Stowe was bound by the dictates of conscience and public opinion to carry forward the antislavery sentiments that her novel had aroused. Calvin Stowe, foreseeing trouble, told her, "[t]here will be the greatest pulling & clawing for that money when you get home, and for your own too, so that there will be no end to the vexation. It would be well if you could have your mind pretty fully made up what to do with it before you get home." Knowing her free and easy approach to managing money, he trembled at the confusion she could wreak with the $60,000 that had flowed in in eighteen months.[64] "[Y]ou owe it to yourself & your family, to your God and to your fellow man to keep a book of accurate statements of incomes and out goes every day, or you will soon find yourself in the swamp and your family in wretchedness. I give you warning."[65] Within a few months of the publication of *Uncle Tom's Cabin* Harriet's sister Isabella observed that Harriet was "already besieged with applications for pecuniary assistance."[66] Her large family stood by to help her dispose of her windfall. Many of them had provided material aid during the writing of the book, and Harriet was disposed to be generous; she intended to give the lion's share of such family charities to her brother Charles, who acted as her secretary and travel agent in Europe; he was struggling to establish himself in Newark against the odds of miserable health, five children, and no money. Catharine Beecher, who ran Stowe's household while she was in Europe, made claim for $1,500, which included a gold chain that Calvin called "Cate's swindle"; James Beecher was given or loaned $1,811.[67] Harriet's twin daughters, now seventeen, were at an age when spectacular sums could be spent on education, dancing lessons, and dress. "[T]he money is melting away like snow before the summer's sun," Calvin told her.[68] Harriet did her part as a tourist, purchasing souvenirs at every point in her trip and buying whatever struck her. In London she acquired a steam-operated device for drawing pictures.[69]

Harriet did have some preliminary plans for employing funds for the cause. Before she undertook her trip to England she had written to Mrs. Follen of her intent to "erect in some of the Northern States a normal school, for the education of *coloured* teachers in the United States & Canada. I have very much wished that some permanent memorial of good to the Coloured race, might be erected out of the proceeds of a work which has had so unprecedented a sale."[70] When antislavery activists raised objections to this plan, first because it would found a segregated institution and second because it was a "lateral object" to "the annihilation of the system of slavery," Stowe pulled back, advocated mixed schools, but still urged support of a highly successful, all-black school in Washington, D. C. known as Miss Miner's School. Founded by Myrtilla Miner, a white woman called the Prudence Crandall of her day, it had persisted, like Crandall's school in Canterbury, Connecticut, in the face of threats and attacks by whites. Stowe meant to make it a showcase of what free black women could attain, and choosing a school "under the immediate eye of a slave-holding population" was part of her calculation. It cannot be said to have been an especially radical or egalitarian institutution, however. While African-American women received a good education there, they also resented Myrtilla Miner's attitude of white superiority.[71]

Another educational scheme, championed by Frederick Douglass, was the establishment of an industrial school for black men. Douglass had met with Stowe before her voyage and presented this plan to her. Having the experience of Lane Seminary behind her, Stowe knew the difficulties of manual labor schools and was not sanguine about the practicality of this idea. Douglass persisted, using his antislavery paper to keep the scheme alive, and others began to wonder aloud why Mrs. Stowe, with all the money she had reaped from *Uncle Tom's Cabin*, was not backing it. Stung by this public criticism, Stowe burst out to Wendell Phillips, "Of all vague unbased fabrics of a vision this floating idea of a colored industrial school is the most illusive. If they want one why dont they *have* one—many men among the colored people are richer than I am—& better able to help such an object—Will they *ever* learn to walk?" Douglass's plan met with objections by both black and white abolitionists; after several years of discussion the committee on the manual labor school recommended that the Colored National Convention drop the idea.[72]

No "permanent memorial" to the cause of the slave issued from the Penny Offering. Forrest Wilson says that Stowe's disposition of this money "remains a mystery," "[n]or did she ever render any account of her stewardship." He supposes that she simply mixed the Penny Offering in with her other earnings and let them all slip through her fingers.[73] In fact, however, Stowe did make a formal accounting of the monies given her in the British Isles—moved, clearly, by the public criticism she had received. In 1856 she wrote a long letter to the Earl of Carlisle, the Earl of Shaftesbury, Joseph Sturge, and G. W. Alexander, who formed the committee that formally tendered the Penny Offering to her. Before she laid out the particulars, she reminded these men that she had not solicited these funds; at the time the money was "providentially" given her, she had specified that "it was to be with the understanding that it was to be strictly *mine* as much as any portion of my private property & that I should be subject to account to no one but to God and my conscience." She gave two reasons for this insistence. In the first place, accounting was "onerous." Second, the schisms in the antislavery movement would make it impossible to please anyone "if any one of them felt *that they had the slightest right to be consulted.*" She had "maintained strict neutrality as to all their personal feuds and bitternesses," giving, for example, to both *Frederick Douglass' Paper* and to the *Anti-Slavery Standard*, "notwithstanding the unhappy difference which has arisen between the society of which the Standard is the organ & Mr. Douglass." She went into some detail on this item because one of Douglass's friends, a woman, was now traveling in England and spreading dissatisfaction on this subject. "The aid which we given to Mr. Douglas has been considerably *more* than that afforded to the Standard, because as a coloured man he has the peculiar disabilities we thought it no more than right that he should have also peculiar encouragements." She listed the disbursements she had made: for books and tracts, $1,566; for papers and periodicals, $745; for ransoming slaves, $611; for aiding fugitives, $411; for the free labor movement, which she expected to "prove one of the most powerful" influences on slavery, $615; for [t]he promotion of education among the coloured people," $2,370. No sum was listed next to her largest project: Miss Miner's School. "It is to this school that I shall look as the most conspicuous monument of what has been effected by this fund," she wrote, yet she put that expenditure (for "a large & elegant building") in the future tense and provided no estimate of expenses.[74] In all, Stowe accounted for $6,318. The rest of the money (she gave no figure) had been loaned to individuals or invested at a rate of return of between 9 and 12 percent interest. The Earl of Shaftesbury found her accounting "satisfactory"; to the Earl of Carlisle her letter was a source of "gratification." When the letter made its way to America a year and a half later, the Garrisonians noted with satisfaction Stowe's praise of their activities. No one complained that only a third of the money had been accounted for. Philanthropy was a long way from being professionalized. Even a generation later temperance reformer Frances Willard, until she was put on a straight salary by the Women's Christian Temperance Union, "considered money contributed to her personally as subject to any use she saw fit to make of it, including supporting her mother and paying household bills."[75]

Publicly successful, Stowe was not as skillful and sensitive in a private antislavery matter. Before her trip she had received a letter on behalf of Harriet Jacobs, a former slave. At the time she sought Stowe's help, Jacobs was living in Baltimore as a domestic in the home of Nathaniel and Cornelia Willis and struggling to rear her children. Unlike many of the appeals Stowe received, Jacobs's request was not for money but for literary advice and support. Jacobs wanted to tell her story, and she asked Mrs. Stowe to help her. She knew that the materials of her life were quite dramatic; they provided vivid testimony that if slavery was terrible for men, it was "far more terrible for women."[76] Pursued by her master, Dr. Norcom, who was determined to make her his mistress, Jacobs formed a liaison with a white man of her own choosing—a Whig candidate for Congress—by whom she had two children. Hiding for seven years in an attic crawl space in which she could not stand up, she managed to elude both Dr. Norcom and the bonds of slavery. The current excitement about the Fugitive Slave Law made the time propitious to tell her story. Overcoming her embarrassment about her sexual history, Jacobs permitted Amy Post to write frankly to Mrs. Stowe about her life—a personal risk, for not even her employer knew the truth about the alliance that had produced her children. Stowe's response mortified Jacobs. She sent Amy Post's letter to Mrs. Willis, inquiring whether this extraordinary story were true, and if so, whether she might use it in her *Key*. Jacobs's strategy of hiding in the attic was strikingly similar to the ruse Cassy devised to elude Legree, and Stowe hoped to use it to corroborate her fiction.

Both Harriet Jacobs and Mrs. Willis were stunned by this precipitous revelation of Jacobs's history. As Jacobs wrote to Amy Post, "[Mrs. Willis] knew it embarrassed me at first but I told her the truth but we both thought it was wrong in Mrs. Stowe to have sent your letter. She might have written to enquire." When Stowe discovered that Jacobs wanted to tell her own story, that she would supply her "some facts for her book" but not her narrative, Stowe answered none of her four succeeding letters.[77] Stowe's behavior—an extreme example of insensitivity bred by class and skin privilege—was probably exacerbated by her sense of literary "ownership" of the tale of the fugitive slave. Wedded to the notion that she "spoke for the oppressed, who cannot speak for themselves," she tried in this instance to appropriate the story of a former slave who could—and eventually did—speak for herself. Had Stowe been able to penetrate the contradictions of womanhood instead of merely manipulating them, had she cast off the indirection of private speech and the subterfuge of speaking for others and found her own voice for her own womanhood, she perhaps would not have needed to exercise power over a black woman, who by any measure was at the very bottom of the patriarchy.

Stowe did act in the role of patroness to a number of former slaves—but none of them were literary women. Among those whom she took under her wing were the Edmondson family. During the summer of 1852 she had raised money at antislavery bazaars to redeem their children from slavery; later the Edmondson sisters studied at Oberlin at Harriet's expense. But unlike Harriet Jacobs, the Edmondsons yielded their story to Stowe for publication in the *Key*, and in 1856 it was published as an antislavery tract. Milly Edmondson, who told Stowe the tale, could "not read a letter of a book, nor write her own name."[78] In England Stowe supported the theatrical talents of Mary Webb, for whom she wrote a dramatization of *Uncle Tom's Cabin*, and the musical aspirations of Miss Greenfield, a singer whose extraordinary range was the marvel of audiences at Stafford House. For such individual women of talent Stowe paid for lessons, arranged introductions, bought dresses, and sponsored events that would help them establish themselves.[79] When her role was clearly that of patroness of the arts and of "the race,"

Stowe functioned comfortably—though the difficulties of guiding the Webbs through the intricacies of English society led Stowe to admit "how shallow my benevolence was—& how soon one grows weary of doing what one *writes* about."[80]

On June 4, 1853, Harriet left England for the Continent. After a stay in Paris with Maria Chapman, Stowe's party traveled to the Swiss Alps and thence to Germany. Exhausted from the crowds and the soirees, Stowe retreated to the anonymity of a tourist. They stopped in Basel, Heidelberg, Cologne, and Erfurt, engaged in a pilgrimage to shrines of Martin Luther. Aside from Lyman Beecher, Luther was Harriet's strongest model. They saw his letters and the church where he was buried. In Erfurt they visited Luther's cell. Charles Beecher recorded, "We breathed where he had breathed. We sat where he had sat. And we handled the familiar objects of his toil, the weapons of his warfare." These were not lance and broadsword, but "only a pocket testament and an inkstand."[81] These were Harriet's weapons as well. From Germany they circled back to Paris and crossed the English Channel in rough water, reaching the English shore "crest fallen, half drowned, shivering—profoundly miserable," Harriet wrote to the Duke and Duchess of Argyle. "With such an initiation into a country who can wonder that parties on both sides land in no delightful humor!"[82] She had planned to visit with the duke and duchess at their estate in Inverera, and then tour Ireland, but Calvin Stowe was getting increasingly impatient for her return. "It seems a long, long time to wait till November before seeing you," he wrote. "And then it is so uncertain, you are so habitually and exceedingly unpunctual; and always, no doubt, for the very best of reasons. My only hope is that Charles will get so impatient to be with his wife and children again that he will not stay beyond the time. His wife talks about his being at home in Sept. If he comes without you, I shall never expect to see you again."[83] At the end of August, moved by the news that one of her daughters had developed a lung complaint, Harriet cancelled her engagements and cut short her trip.

She boarded a steamer on September 7, laden with a number of antislavery talismans through which her labors were linked with those of the great emancipators of English history: a large cameo of Wilberforce, made by the sculptor Nevill Northey Burnard, and a gold brooch containing a lock of Thomas Clarkson's hair, presented to her by the Great Emancipator's wife. From the ladies of Surrey chapel had come a large silver inkstand on which were represented three figures: a slave breaking his shackles and another slave accepting a Bible from a woman meant to represent Stowe.[84]

Unsuccessful in either raising a "permanent memorial" from the Penny Offering or engendering a mass political movement among American women, Stowe upon her return did, on a modest scale, continue her antislavery efforts. She remained sporadically active in antislavery bazaars, an activity through which women were highly successful in raising money.[85] She also continued her efforts to promote unity in the antislavery movement, believing "that the great humanities of the present day are a proper ground on which all sects can unite" (SM, 1:38). First, however, she had to make her own peace with the issue that most often divided Garrisonians and anti-Garrisonians: "infidelism."

In November 1853 she wrote Garrison of her reservations about endorsing his party and his paper. Her comments are deeply revealing of the limits of her radicalism:

> I am a constant reader of your paper & an admirer of much that is in it. I like its frankness fearlessness—truthfulness & independence—at the same time I regard with apprehension & sorrow much that is in it Were it circulated only among intelligent well balanced minds able to discriminate between good & evil I should not feel so much apprehension. To *me* the paper is decidedly valuable as a frank & able expose of the ultra progressive element in our times. What I fear is that it will take from poor Uncle Tom his bible & give him nothing in its place—you understand me—do you not?[86]

In fiction she trusted Uncle Tom to remain true to his Christian principles under the extremest torment; in real life her elitist sense of mission, a heritage of Lyman Beecher, undercut her faith in the lowly. Throughout her career she would read radical materials but insist that they were dangerous for the masses. In a long and masterfully argued reply, Garrison pointed out to her that she was betraying a lack of faith—and a selective one, for while she professed no difficulty with the airing of proslavery views in the *Liberator*, she was less confident that religion could survive free discussion. Her position was like that of "the Romish Church in regard to the indiscriminate circulation of the Bible among the laity," he taunted her. He disagreed that Garrisonians believed that the Bible sanctioned slavery, observing that even if they did, this was the view of "nine-tenths of the evangelical clergy in the United States" with whom she sat at the communion table. "How marvellously inconsistent is your conduct, as between these parties!"[87]

Stowe admitted the force of his arguments, believed he hadn't fully comprehended her position, and repeated her request for a meeting at which they could talk freely; she asked that he return her letter "of which your beautifully written epistle makes me sufficiently ashamed." She had written hers when she was ill and had let it go simply because she did not have strength to rewrite it.[88] But Garrison had other plans. "He snuffs the prey like a vulture," wrote Bronson Alcott of Garrison, "nor will he rest till his beak and talons are fast in the eagle's breast and the lion has seen him torn in pieces. He has perfect skill in the use of his own weapons, nor has he ever lost a battle. He cannot give quarter even, and is as unrelenting to friends as enemies."[89] Garrison printed his letter to Stowe in the December 23, 1853, edition of the *Liberator*. Although she was not named, her reservations and Garrison's demolition of her logic were spread across the pages of his paper. Stowe declined to engage him in a public debate, believing, as she told him, "a more private discussion of the matter likely to prove more useful."[90]

Having humbly submitted to Garrison's discipline, she reproached him for his continuing feud with Frederick Douglass. She had met with Douglass and formed an impression "far more satisfactory than I had imagined," she hastened to tell Garrison. "You speak of him as an apostate," she chided him. "Where is this work of excommunication to end—Is there but one true anti slavery church & all others infidels? & who shall declare which it is?"[91] In February 1854 she wrote Garrison, "I am increasingly anxious that all who hate slavery be united if *not*, in form, at least *in fact*.—Unity in difference. Our field lies in the church as yet. I differ from you as to what *may* be done & hoped there."[92]

In the winter of 1853–1854 she organized, in concert with Garrison, a Boston antislavery lecture series, believing that this was an effective way to cultivate into convictions "the popular impressions . . . produced by the reading and acting of Uncle Tom's Cabin."[93] She proposed to pay an honorarium of $25 for each speaker and to support the series up to the amount of $200. She hoped to involve speakers of "catholic" views "so far as shades of antislavery sentiment are concerned, embracing such as are willing to take the ground that slavery is a sin," but she admitted that her list was heavy on orthodox clergymen "who had not spoken before in public on the subject." It was also weighted with two names whose antislavery reputations needed polishing: Calvin Stowe and Lyman Beecher. Her intentions were good, but her antislavery activity never moved far from the status of a family project.[94] She invested time as well as money in this scheme, writing to speakers and making sure that the Anti-Slavery Office was doing its part to publicize the lectures. By the spring of 1854, however, the excitement over the Kansas-Nebraska Act eclipsed this rather mild enterprise, and attendance at the lectures was sparse.[95] As the events of "bleeding Kansas" and John Brown's raid moved the nation closer to civil war, both Stowe's patience with the Protestant clergy and Garrison's pacifism were sorely tested.

CHAPTER TWENTY-ONE

Andover, Kansas, and Europe:
1854–1857

*H*arriet had used the first check from *Uncle Tom's Cabin* to renovate an old stone structure in Andover for use as the Stowe family residence. The "Stone Cabin" stood between Andover Theological Seminary and Phillips Andover Academy. It had been used in former times as a carpentry shop for the manual-labor students at the seminary; in more recent years it had been converted to a gymnasium. Harriet transformed this shell into a domestic space that satisfied her taste for light and beauty. The centerpiece was a long parlor that ran the width of the house. Elizabeth Stuart Phelps, a child of eight when the Stowes came to Andover, remembered with special delight the deeply recessed window seats of this parlor and the "brightly-colored, rather worldly-looking pillows" with which they were generously supplied. Tables and sideboards sported fresh flowers, even in winter, and Harriet coaxed an ivy to grow up and around in a bower of summerlike foliage. To Phelps, "[i]t was an open, hospitable house, human and hearty and happy," teeming with visitors, children, and every species of dog life. "Mrs. Stowe was the most unselfish and loving of mothers," remembered Phelps, "and there were always dogs; big and little, curly and strait."[1]

The pressure of writing *Uncle Tom's Cabin*, followed closely by the *Key* and then her English trip, had kept Harriet busy for two and a half years. Now she turned her attention to her children. Charley, the baby, had just had his third birthday. Georgie and Fred likewise had had birthdays that summer while she was in England—Georgie turned ten, and Fred thirteen. Henry Ellis was almost sixteen and the twins turned eighteen the month she returned. All but Charley were in school. Eliza, Hatty, and Georgie attended the Abbot Academy, a distinguished school for girls in Andover. There were still no colleges for women, although the first—Elmira Female College— would be founded in 1855. Women's education still entailed great expenditures of women's time and effort; in the fall of 1854 Harriet initiated and helped to organize a fundraising bazaar to furnish the new boardinghouse for Abbot Academy students. Moved by a "telling speech" delivered by Mrs. Stowe to a "meeting for ladies," the women of Andover raised $2000 by selling coffee, tea, ice cream, oysters, and other delicacies at a gala social event. The women then "resolved themselves into a sewing-society" to supply the boardinghouse with curtains, bedspreads, and bolsters. Harriet's daughters benefited from the intelligent leadership of the academy by Nancy J. Hasseltine, but after two years of shouldering "too heavy burdens" Miss Hasseltine developed "alarming symptoms" and left after the winter term of 1855–1856.[2]

Henry was preparing for Dartmouth, which he would enter in the fall of 1856. A portrait of him that hangs in the Stowe house in Hartford shows a handsome youth with the full, sensuous lips of his mother and something of her dreamy expression. Very little record exists of his character and relationships. In an ink-blotted note to his parents, Henry wonders why they have not answered his last letter and requests they send the $10 entrance fee so that he might begin his studies at Dartmouth.[3] Calvin thought him "indolent and self indulgent," while Harriet found in him "sympathy of nature" and "mutual understanding."[4] Isabella Beecher said he was the "best beloved" of the Stowe children.[5]

Although he was an ordained minister, Calvin had long ago relinquished responsibility for his children's spiritual lives to Harriet and Anna Smith, declaring himself "abundantly satisfied" with the instruction they provided. "If they grow up unconverted," he once remarked, "I shall feel very differently."[6] Harriet appears to have put little pressure on her children to convert, being free and easy in her approach to most things and in this instance reacting against the example of her father, who made his children's lives miserable with his constant scrutiny. The death of Aunt Esther in 1855, however, turned her thoughts forcibly to the state of her son Henry's soul: "Henry death is a *great experience*—we cant tell what we are ourselves till a friend dies & then we see a great deal," she wrote to the son whose death nineteen months later would strike iron into her heart. "I *do love you* Henry, & I know you do love me— but oh my darling, I want you to choose my Redeemer—your Father's & mother's God for your own."[7]

Fred was enrolled at Phillips Andover Academy. Harriet described this son as "a smart bright lively boy—full of all manner of fun & mischief fond of reading more than of hard study." To her old neighbor and confidant Sarah Allen, Harriet admitted, "[T]o say the truth tho Fred gives me twice the anxiety & uneasiness that Henry does." Exposed to the temptations of bad company at Phillips Andover, Fred was picking up some dangerous habits: "There are some southern boys here all *dash* who are very captivating inspiring restless desires for pistols & cigars—& breathing an atmosphere of Devil-may care & I have had great pains to combat various passions of Fred's inspired by such company."[8] This was the first of many letters Harriet would write about this son, letters in which she would use "tobacco" as a euphemism for alcohol. In the years ahead Harriet would be torn by the conflicting demands of a career that required a constant stream of literary productions and a flock of children who were more restless and certainly less disciplined than their mother. "Sister Hattie has a very hard lot in many respects," observed her sister Mary in a letter to Isabella; "I would not take her burden with all her trials even if the money & the fame came too—If she could only know what was the best way to manage it would be comparitively easy, but we can only grope about in the dark."[9]

The death of Aunt Esther deprived Harriet of an important source of support, and caused her to reflect on the meaning of this single woman's life. At a time when marriage was the expected portion for women, Esther Beecher had employed her singlehood in constant productive activity in the homes of her nephews and nieces. While she remained independent of marriage, she was largely dependent for her social and her financial status on the households she served. "[S]he was a great sufferer," Harriet eulogized her. "She had high feelings a proud nature—great intensity of feeling—& all these had to be made subject to Christ No nun in a convent ever lived a more self denying life." Remembering the many ways in which Aunt Esther had stitched her life into the fabric of her own, Harriet longed "to speak to her & to have her *speak* to me once more."[10] Unable to make the night journey to her funeral, Harriet planned to make some moss garlands to send to her grave.

Esther had bequeathed to Harriet an exquisite vase, knowing well her love for beautiful things; but when Harriet heard this, she thought she would rather have had something that Aunt Esther had passed through her fingers in daily use, such as her workbasket.[11] The prosperity brought on by the success of *Uncle Tom's Cabin* coincided with and was part of the vast increase in consumer goods that began in the 1850s and would swell to excessive proportions in the decades ahead. As Harriet was borne along on this wave of prosperity, she increasingly looked back to simpler times and to self-denying lives like Aunt Esther's. The nostalgia of her New England novels would speak to a nation similarly transported from republican simplicity to the ornateness of high Victorian culture. Whereas the middle-class woman's emerging role as consumer at this bazaar of national prosperity was increasingly associating woman with the material excesses of the Gilded Age, Stowe in her New England novels eulogized women as exemplars of simplicity, frugality, and "faculty." *The Minister's Wooing*, published at the end of this decade, was the first, and one of the most important, of these forays into this arena of cultural myth.

Social life in Andover was dominated by the theological seminary, which meant that a male tone prevailed. Women were so outnumbered that Elizabeth Stuart Phelps compared the demography of Andover to that of western towns. "Theological teas" gave the professors and young men from the seminary opportunities to sharpen their wits and display their talents for splitting theological hairs. Women were expected to be silent listeners at these social occasions; presumably they had nothing to say about foreordination, predestination, and all the other "ation" words that buzzed like mosquitoes during these informal theological conventions. How different this presumption of superior male knowledge from the western equality that prevailed between men and women in the Semi-Colon Club! Stowe would have been struck too by the exclusion of women from debate, so different from the way she had been included, in a family of ministers, in every discussion that she had cared to enter. Coming to Andover now after achieving international fame, she was acutely aware of the pretensions, posturings, and academic politics of reputedly the best theological seminary in the land.[12]

While the ministers sipped their tea and decided the fates of millions of souls, the politicians in Washington were carving up a territory half as large as the Mississippi Valley and deciding whether its inhabitants should be slave or free. "The whole nation lies spread out like a gambler's table," wrote Henry Ward Beecher in the pages of the *Independent*.[13] Stephen Douglas, the senator from Illinois, in an attempt to ensure that the transcontinental railroad would run through his state, introduced in January 1854 a bill effectively repealing the Missouri Compromise of 1820. Those who had argued against appeasing the South with the Fugitive Slave Law now saw their worst fears confirmed: the slave power, emboldened by a sympathetic president, the self-interest of politicians like Douglas, and the craving of the country for more land, argued that the time had come to do away with the compromise that had kept slavery out of all territories to the north of latitude 36° 30'. As the country expanded, the demand for labor intensified and the price of slaves skyrocketed. While abolitionists fumed, the economics of slaveholding tightened the noose on the slave population.

The "Nebraska Bill," as it was called, proposed to let popular sovereignty decide whether Kansas and Nebraska should be free or slave soil. In a move clearly modeled on the "Affectionate and Christian Address," Stowe published in the *Independent* "An Appeal to the Women of the Free States of America, On the Present Crisis in Our Country." On the eve of the Senate vote on the Nebraska Bill, she urged women to action: "Women of the free States! the question is not, shall we remonstrate with slavery on its own soil? but are we willing to receive slavery into the free States and territories of the Union?" She urged women to petition, to organize lectures, and to pray, citing the example of the British women's organization to outlaw the slave trade. "Seventy thousand families refused the use of sugar, as a testimony to their abhorrence of the manner in which it was produced. At that time women were unwearied in passing from house to house, distributing tracts and books, and presenting the subject in families. . . . The women all over

England were associated in corresponding circles for prayer and for labor."[14] Stowe had seen the effectiveness of such women's circles, not only in the huge success of the "Affectionate and Christian Address," but also in the peace organizing undertaken by the Society of Friends. She remarked several times on the "Olive Leaf Circles" organized by Elihu Burritt: "[His] mode of operation has been by the silent organization of circles of ladies in all the different towns of the United Kingdom, who raise a certain sum for the diffusion of the principles of peace on earth and good will to men" (SM, 1: 248, 251). She may have remembered long ago when the students at the Hartford Female Seminary organized in "circles" to govern the school in Catharine Beecher's absence. She had a vision of women's decentralized power uniting in a coordinated wave against the slave power, but she had no sense of how to bring this movement about.

Nor was there time to discover it. After a brief debate the Senate passed the Nebraska Bill early in March and sent it to the House. At this point Stowe engaged in direct action. Using money from the Penny Offering, she financed a signature-gathering blitz in the Northeast. "We are starting two petitions from Andover," she wrote Garrison, "one for men & the other for women."[15] In less than two weeks the signatures of 3,050 clergymen were collected and sent to Congress. In their "remonstrances" against the bill, the clergymen were joined by other petitioners: the students of Hamilton College sent a petition, as did the Philadelphia Female Anti-Slavery Society and 3,000 persons in Brooklyn (perhaps members of Henry Ward Beecher's Plymouth Church). Senator Edward Everett of Massachusetts submitted the signatures of the 3,050 clergymen on March 14, prompting Stephen Douglas to take the floor to denounce the signatories and impugn their motives. But the agitation appeared to have an effect: on March 26 the House voted to send the Nebraska Bill to the Committee of the Whole, in effect consigning it to the bottom of the docket of bills. Stowe wrote to the Duchess of Sutherland explaining "in strictest confidance" that it was money from the Penny Offering that allowed for such swift organizing to block the bill.[16]

The bill, however, was not defeated but only deferred; at the beginning of May there were rumblings that it would be resurrected. By various machinations, a way was cleared for the bill to come again before the House. After just four days of debate (compared to *nine months* on the admission of California as a state) the Kansas-Nebraska Act passed in the wee hours of the morning on May 26, 1854. As the *Independent* editorialized, "This measure passed to its place on the statute-book from out of the darkness of midnight sessions in both branches of Congress, rendered lurid by the glow of human passions, and made memorable by bitter feuds and implacable heats these engendered."[17]

The stage was now set for the bloody struggles in Kansas that were the first battles of the Civil War. "Popular sovereignty" meant letting the settlers in Kansas fight among themselves to determine whether the territory should be free or slave. Antislavery voices called for emigrants from the free states to settle in Kansas and declare it free soil. The "Emigrant Aid Society" was formed and sent settlers to establish antislavery communities, including a significant one in Lawrence, Kansas. But every time an election was held in Kansas "Border Ruffians" poured in from Missouri and put proslavery men in power. Henry Ward Beecher's Plymouth Church sent boxes of Sharpe's rifles, known as "Beecher's Bibles," to help the antislavery settlers protect themselves from proslavery focus. The sectional warfare that prevailed in Kansas between 1854 and 1858 was most intense between December 1855 and September 1856—the period during which Harriet Beecher Stowe wrote her second antislavery novel, *Dred: A Tale of the Great Dismal Swamp*.[18]

Stowe had toyed with the idea of calling her novel "Canema" after the plantation belonging to her southern heroine, but the events of the summer of 1856 convinced her that a more terrific-sounding title would strike the right chord.[19] On May 21, 1856, proslavery men raided Lawrence, Kansas, seizing and torching property and destroying the presses of two antislavery newspapers. In retaliation, John Brown and his sons murdered five proslavery men in a night massacre at Pottawotamie Creek. Just a few days earlier the eloquent antislavery senator from Massachusetts, Charles Sumner, had been attacked by a southern colleague on the floor of the Senate and beaten so badly that it took him three years to recover. "The book is written under the impulse of our stormy times," Stowe wrote the Duchess of Argyle; "how the blood & insults of Sumner and the sack of Lawrence burn within us I hope to make a voice to say."[20]

The escalating violence of the 1850s led her to choose a hero very different from Uncle Tom: Dred is presented as the son of Denmark Vesey, the historical figure hanged in South Carolina for fomenting rebellion among the slaves, allegedly through his work with the African Methodist Church. Like Uncle Tom, Dred's identity is defined by religion; but Tom's New Testament Christian pacifism is replaced in *Dred* by a militant invocation of the Old Testament prophets who called for "a day of vengeance." The insurrectionary purpose to which the Bible was put in "secret meetings of conspirators" bore out the worst fears of slave owners who believed that liberating a slave's mind was the first step toward liberating his body. Having "heard of prophets and deliverers, armed with supernatural powers, raised up for oppressed people,"[21] Dred imagines himself the Moses of his people. The Garrisonian nonresistance movement was plagued by the question, "Was the Negro who epitomized the doctrine [of nonresistance] bereft of means to liberate himself?"[22] In this novel Stowe tentatively approached this question, imbued with a much stronger sense than *Uncle Tom's Cabin* conveyed of a slave culture of resistance.

In *Dred* Stowe understands slavery as a form of colonial imperialism; this radical analysis penetrates the "mask" of the oppressed: "In all despotic countries . . . it will be found that the oppressed party become expert in the means of secrecy" (D, 2:140). In one of the most daring examples of the cunning and double meanings that a culture of oppression gives rise to, Tom

Gordon's personal servant explains that he has been at a religious "meeting." In reality he had been plotting his escape at a rendezvous in the woods. When the master challenges him to produce the text preached on, the slave replies "ye shall sarch fur me in de mornin' and ye won't find me" (D, 2: 175–76). Dred, Stowe's hero, lives in a maroon community in the swamp known to the slaves on the surrounding plantations but never mentioned in the presence of the masters. Stowe adorns her hero in symbols of his own culture: "a fantastic sort of turban," a garment of "negro-cloth" bound around the waist with a strip of scarlet flannel, though which was stuck a bowie knife and hatchet. A rifle and a "rude game-bag" which "hung upon his arm" complete the equipment of this man described as "intensely black" and of "herculean strength" (D, 1:247–48). The generalizations about the African race that Stowe freely sprinkled throughout *Uncle Tom's Cabin* are, with a few exceptions, replaced in *Dred* by more particular attention to African ancestry; Dred is part Mandingo, "one of the finest of African tribes, distinguished for intelligence, beauty of form, and an indomitable pride and energy of nature" (D, 1:260). Stowe incorporates in her narrative long passages from the printed reports of Denmark Vesey's conspiracy, including a description of Gullah Jack, a coconspirator with enormous power over his fellow Africans by virtue of his sorcery and charms. The Denmark Vesey story assumes but inverts the story of the faithful Uncle Tom, for all the leaders of the conspiracy, except Gullah Jack, enjoyed the "highest confidence" of their owners (D, 1:258). Stowe prints as an appendix to *Dred* "Nat Turner's Confessions," in which Turner, like Dred, reads insurrectionary signs in the heavens and in the Old Testament prophets.

In spite of the rich possibilities of this culture of resistance, *Dred* is neither an incendiary tract nor a good novel. Stowe rushed into print with insufficiently imagined characters, stilted dialogue, and a novel much too long for the action it sustains. Dred, an initially mysterious and appealing character, soon makes the reader sigh over turgid passages in which he speaks not in dialect but in the accents of an Old Testament prophet who is getting paid by the page. Stowe's plot was severely constrained by her gender and racial politics. As Charles Foster observed, *Dred* "leave[s] us approximately where it found us."[23] Having created a hero seemingly more militant and radical than Uncle Tom, she stifled the insurrectionary impulse of her novel by encasing the action in a typical romance plot. In tediously drawn-out scenes, Nina Gordon chooses among several lovers and undergoes a kind of moral education that makes her fit to be the heroine of Stowe's story. When her evolution is complete, Stowe accords her the ultimate reward of the sentimental heroine: death. As feminist critics have observed, plots present particular problems for women writers because there is so little that women characters can *do*.[24] Just as Uncle Tom was assimilated to a feminine ethos of Christian suffering, so is Dred assimilated to the sentimental heroine's fate. His Old Testament militancy is stilled by the words of Milly, a female slave imbued with New Testament pacifism, and then he too is killed. It is a measure of Stowe's failure to make him come alive for the reader that we do not care when he dies.

Stowe wrote the entire two-volume novel in about three months (as compared to more than a year for *Uncle Tom's Cabin*), and this haste surely contributed to its weakness. On June 11, 1856, Calvin Stowe wrote to her publisher, "Mrs. Stowe thinks the printers now have in hand about one hundred pages of ms. She engages to finish every day steadily, on an average, enough for twelve pages. She is tolerably well, we shall do every thing in our power to lighten her domestic cares, & I think she will reach the mark, or nearly so."[25] The "mark" was a publication date in late August, which she did indeed meet. "Aunt Hattie is writing about 16 pages a day," wrote Isabella Beecher Hooker to her children on June 16; "she goes to her study, with Mrs Dagon who is her *amanuensis* (this is for you Mary) at ten o'clock & is not disturbed by anyone till dinner time at one. Then she reads aloud, (after dinner,) what she had written to the whole family & they make their respective comments." Eliza and Hatty, with the bloodthirsty tastes of teenagers, applauded the "tragic" parts and were "so glad when she makes somebody die."[26] On July 13 Stowe wrote to her publisher requesting that he send a half a dozen more bottles of Catawba wine "to support the hot weather & the long pull." She was now writing twenty pages a day; as the deadline loomed she wrote even faster. Calvin recommended that publication be delayed so that the ending "not be *hurried* or *botched*," but Harriet plowed ahead.[27] "I wrote 25 pages ms, yesterday & 20 day before & send herewith 45. Shall write fifty more to day & to morrow," she told Mr. Phillips. "Mr. Stowe says I am writing better now than in any past—*There will be a cracking* among people when they come to these last chapters, which contain the winding up & result of the whole train I have laid thro the book."[28]

With allusions to the sacking of Lawrence and the assault on Sumner, the final chapters demonstrate that the South (portrayed so reasonably in *Uncle Tom's Cabin*) would terminate by lynch mob any attempts to reform the institution of slavery. Edward and Anne Clayton, a brother and sister team, run a model plantation in which they teach the slaves to read and write. These didactic activities, undertaken expressly to empower slaves to cast off slavery in a bloodless evolution, take place in an edifice that sounds like a cross between the Hartford Female Seminary and the "elegant building" Stowe promised to erect for Miss Miner's School: it has "the external appearance of a small Grecian temple, the pillars of which were festooned with jessamine." There slaves were inspired with "ideas of taste, refinement, and self-respect" in an environment in which "learning [was] associated with the idea of elegance and beauty" (D, 1:394). But the Claytons are forced by their neighbors to abandon this project and flee to the North. Stowe resurrects a minor character and hastily arranges her marriage to create the illusion of closure, and *Dred* totters to a merciful conclusion. In the hardening climate of the 1850s neither evolutionary reform nor slave rebellion appeared a feasible solution to Stowe, and the failure of her plot reflected a failure of her political imagination. So murky was her purpose that Nathan Hale, Jr., concluded from his reading of the novel that it established "beyond doubt, that the exertions of the abolitionists have been the great obstacle to the amelioration of the condition of the slave."[29]

If *Dred* was Stowe's response to the sectional warfare in Kansas and the increasingly open political struggle between proslavery and antislavery forces, it was just as much a sharp response to the male culture of Andover and its theological teas. Indeed, the most fully realized scenes in the book depict the clerical hypocrisy of characters such as Mr. Titmarsh, "a theological dictionary with a cravat on" who staunchly defends slavery, and Father Bonnie, who bargains to buy a slave in between sermons at a camp meeting (D, 1:360, 322). Through the character of Dr. Shubael Packthread, Stowe had her revenge on the Rev. Joel Parker. "While other people look upon words as as vehicles for conveying ideas, Dr. Packthread regarded them only as mediums for concealment. His constant study, on every controverted topic, was to adjust language that, with the appearance of the utmost precision, it should always be capable of a double interpretation. He was a cunning master of all forms of indirection; of all phrases by which people appear to say what they do not say, and not to say what they do say" (D, 2:41).

If most of the reprehensible characters in *Uncle Tom's Cabin* are male, in *Dred* most of the villains are, in one way or another, Calvinist theologians. The rigid and unfeeling Aunt Nesbit disapproves of "countenancing Episcopal errors" and uses the "ation" words—"justification" and "sanctification"—as a test of orthodoxy (D, 1:152, 319). Abijah Skinflint, who would sell his own wife and children to make money, has "a turn for theology, and could number off the five points of Calvinism on his five long fingers with unfailing accuracy" (D, 1:290). In the character of Mr. Jekyl, a lawyer whose skillful arguments result in the appropriation into slavery of a woman, her children, and their plantation, Stowe presents a man whose "belief in slavery was founded on his theology" (D, 1:209). He is immune to pity, for too much theological tea has made the blood run cold in his veins:

> Mr. Jekyl, though a coarse-grained man, had started from the hands of nature no more hard hearted or unfeeling than many others; but his mind, having for years been immersed in the waters of law and theology, had slowly petrified into such a steady consideration of the greatest general good, that he was wholly inaccessible to any emotion of particular humanity. . . . What considerations of temporal loss and misery can shake the constancy of the theologian who has accustomed himself to contemplate and discuss, as a cool intellectual exercise, the eternal misery of generations?—who worships a God that creates myriads only to glorify himself in their eternal torments? (D, 1:210)

Like the politicians in Washington and the theologians in Andover, Mr. Jekyl casually assigned the vast mass of humanity to slavery on earth and to hell in the afterlife. What particularly enraged Stowe was the *coolness* with which all this "disinterested benevolence" transpired.

Stowe was working out an analysis of patriarchal power embodied in the male professions of law, theology, and politics and rehearsing for her next novel, *The Minister's Wooing* (1859). In a passage that simultaneously recalls Thomas Jefferson, Karl Marx, and the Old Testament prophets, Stowe analyzed the way in which institutions could become an end in themselves. The makers of these idolatrous structures were explicitly *men*:

> There is a power in men of a certain class of making an organization of any kind, whether it be political or ecclesiastical, an object of absorbing and individual devotion . . . as the idolater worships the infinite and unseen under a visible symbol till it effaces the memory of what is signified, so men begin by loving institutions for God's sake, which come at last to stand with them in the place of God. (D, 2:46)

Stowe went to England to establish international copyright for *Dred* while still writing the last pages of the novel on board ship. Her publisher, Seth Low, met her party in Liverpool and expedited them through customs. Harriet had persuaded her sister Mary to accompany her and enjoy the perquisites of life with a literary lion. By her side was a less enthusiastic Calvin Stowe, who would soon develop hypochondriacal symptoms and return to America. Son Henry and daughters Eliza and Hatty completed the party. After a brief visit with John Cropper and family in the Dingle, they went to London, where Mr. Low established them in the Adelphi Hotel on Montagu Street, right across from the British Museum. There the final services were performed on *Dred*. "We have all taken hold with all our might to help Hatty get the book done," wrote Mary to her husband. "I write to her dictation & the girls make another copy—we hope to finish tomorrow (Friday) *15th* so as to send a copy back by the Niagara which sails Saturday—Miss Low has also been here all day assisting us—& Mr. Stowe is making the appendix."[30] On August 20 Mary got up at six in the morning to write, at Harriet's dictation, the preface. Three days later they had copies of the book in hand, another testimony to the effective cottage industry that the Beechers made together.

Unlike *Uncle Tom's Cabin*, *Dred* sold better in the United States than in the United Kingdom. The *Edinburgh Review* came down hard on the book, insinuating that the gauche evangelical circles in which the author traveled had not prepared her to write of the Southern aristocracy; with a condescending reference to "the provincial patois of Connecticut," the reviewer called her southern heroine Nina Gordon "a nondescript combination of the Parisian lorette with the Yankee factory-girl."[31] Stung by this review and convinced that it was motivated by sympathy for the South, Stowe wrote to Lady Byron to ascertain the most effective vehicle in which to answer this attack. "The Edinburgh is an important paper & I do not like to have such statements go in it uncontradicted but I hardly know how to reach them. What would you advise?"[32] Lady Byron recommended a notice in the *Times*, but urged Harriet, "O do not be susceptible to these 'darts,' my dear friend.

No one can tell you better than I that there is an invisible shield which turns them away."[33] Harriet had met Lady Byron on her first trip to England at a lunch where many people were present. Now she arranged several private meetings with her, cementing their relationship at a time when Lady Byron was in frail health and Harriet was increasingly drawn to the image of woman's self-denying power—a role the maligned and long-suffering widow of Lord Byron played well.[34]

Lady Byron's advice that Harriet put on an invisible shield was apt, in that *Dred* was the target of other arrows. A male reviewer suggested in all seriousness that Harriet Beecher Stowe had not written the book by herself; the "trifling parts" he was willing to attribute to her, "but [he] says that some parts are so far above the ordinary range of us women," Harriet wrote to the Duchess of Argyle, "that some of the earnest *men* spirits of America must have chosen me as their Pythones to hand their oracles to the public." Harriet cast this off with humor. "Think of my being made a myth of while alive & walking—I really begin to think of pluming myself on this."[35] Yet the tenor of this review reflects the growing resistance to the success of women writers in a field that had previously been left wide open to their campaign. Nathaniel Hawthorne, whose *Scarlet Letter* had been an immediate popular and critical success, was writing ill-tempered attacks on women who had forsaken the needle for the pen, suggesting that these "ink-stained Amazons" were modern-day Anne Hutchinsons who deserved similar banishment.[36] With characteristic optimism, Harriet soon forgot her outrage at the *Edinburgh Review* and noted that *Dred* sold well in America, where its topical references to burning political issues were better understood. Calvin wrote to her that "Dred . . . is marching on triumphantly. . . . 'Mrs. Stowe' is aparently an '*Institution*'—and people must be cautious how they meddle with her."[37]

But Harriet overestimated by more than half the profits she would reap from the book. As the national election approached in November, sales fell off. "The Fremonters eulogize it, the Buchaners curse and damn it, and the Fillmorites moan and whine and deprecate its injurious tendencies," Calvin told her, but he believed that no matter which way the election went, sales would revive after it passed. When the news of Buchanan's election crossed the Atlantic, Harriet and her party were glum. Frémont, their Free Soil hope, was vanquished, *"owing to the unscrupulous use of bribery & illegal voting among the foreign population,"* Harriet wrote to the Duke of Sutherland.[38] Sales of *Dred* did revive, but it was a "gradual sale, some 500 a week," not the spectacular success of *Uncle Tom's Cabin*.[39] Having learned from her experience with Jewett, she had this time negotiated with Sampson and Low a contract that gave her half the profits, and she confidently estimated she would make between $30,000 and $50,000 on the American sales alone. When the payment fell due on March 20, 1857, she learned that Low's half profits were considerably below Jewett's 10 percent. The combined sales on both sides of the Atlantic gave her just $20,000, and she had already spent

$8,000 of it in travel, education, and family support by the time the money arrived.[40]

Harriet made immediate plans to write another book to replenish her supply of cash. Having written *Dred* in the summer of 1856, she calculated on the spring of 1857 for her next book, to be on the British aristocracy. Calvin registered a strong objection to her plan "to hurry a book through the press this spring," as he did to the idea of Hatty and Eliza remaining in Paris through the summer. He reminded her of the haste that left its marks on the pages of *Dred:* "Your next book ought to be carefully written, the MS deliberately revised by yourself before it goes into the printer's hands, and then carried through the press at such a moderate rate of speed as will give the proof reader a fair chance to do his duty. Dred, what with a very bungling amanuensis, and the furious haste with which it was written & driven through the press, has too many pimples on its face." If she must write another book now, she should at least set aside June and July to finish it properly. "It is a pity you should be made a slave to your pen; but till some means can be devised to *save* as well as to *get*, I fear it will be your doom."[41]

Calvin also had severe doubts about the topic that she proposed, rightly perceiving that a book on the British aristocracy would compromise her ability to speak for "the lowly." "As you stand before this country you must not *even seem* to countenance any kind of wrong, oppression or hardship on the poor abroad which you would condemn at home, and the oppressive institutions of the old world should meet with no more quarter at your hand than the oppressive institutions of the new."[42] While his decision-making power was sharply curtailed by Harriet's financial and geographical independence, Calvin retained the power to enter into contracts. He had "no fancy" for going to London in April to establish copyright; it was "no use" for her to expect it. In the face of Calvin's resistance, Harriet dropped her plans to produce a book that spring.[43]

Harriet enjoyed this quiet trip to England more than her first one; with greater control of her itinerary and energies, she spent much of her time with artists and writers. She visited Harriet Martineau, to whom she had been compared when she was a young woman in Cincinnati.[44] She went out of her way to arrange a visit with Charles Kingsley, whom she had apparently not met on her first trip. "You promised us the last time you were in England!," wrote Fanny Kingsley to her. "We long to see you—& I long too that you sh$\underline{d}$ see my dearest Husband in his work among his poor—& if you could give us a Sunday & hear him preach, it would be perfect."[45] They made a four-day visit and found the Kingsleys so "intelligent" and "frank" and "wide awake" that their ready conversation left Mary and Harriet "entirely *used up* and tired out." Except for his pronounced stutter, the tall and thin Charles Kingsley reminded them forcibly in manner and appearance of Edward Hale, who had married Mary Beecher Perkins's daughter Emily. "Hatty said she expected every moment to hear him call her 'Aunt Harriet.' "[46] They also had lunch with Mary Webb and her husband; she was well established with her dramatic readings and he had just written a story he hoped to publish. They paid an evening visit to Mr. and Mrs. S. C. Hall—he was the editor of an art journal and she the writer of "very pretty Irish stories."[47]

Calvin Stowe "gave out" several weeks after their arrival and returned home, but Mary Beecher Perkins, who had lived her adult life within the range of Litchfield and Hartford, found it "very convenient to be in the train of a lion."[48] With her family very supportive of her trip, Mary opened herself to a European education. As she met the queen, strolled on the spacious estate of Lady Mary Labouchere, and attended religious services at the cathedral in Durham, this provincial Protestant found that Europe required a certain readjustment in her standards and tastes. On the grounds of Stoke Park, the estate of Lady Mary ("sister of the Duchess of Southerland—& daughter of the Earl of Carlisle—sister of the present Earl who is viceroy of Ireland," Mary wrote breathlessly to her family), she was met at every turn by nude statuary. She supposed the statues "very good" art, but she had the impulse to dress them. "So much for my American education," she remarked. Harriet and her daughters were "quite enchanted" with the intoning and singing at the cathedral in Durham, but Mary was less enthusiastic: "As it was meant for the worship of God—I could not help trying to worship—but found it hard work—It seemed much more like an opera than any thing else."[49] Eliza and Hatty, who were made quite miserable in the United States by Calvin Stowe's refusal to let them attend the opera, greedily drank in the sensuous service.[50]

At the same time these elaborate cultural expressions were making their way into Mary's consciousness, Harriet wrote to the publisher of a new magazine devoted to the simplicities of home life: "The effort to exalt and beautify home & common life, to render ordinary existence beautiful," she told him, "is one with which I deeply sympathise & one which is now called for by the advancing spirit of the age."[51] In the 1840s Harriet had praised Dickens's celebration of "our coarse, common world," identifying out of her daily work and struggle in a women's culture. In the increasingly secular and complex culture of consumption that was emerging in the 1850s, Stowe was well positioned to capitalize on what had recently been only an imperative of her gender role. Women's culture now made good copy. Just as the hard edges of "regionalism" were discovered at the moment when regions were passing into an emerging national culture, the celebration of the "age of homespun" signified its demise. With it went the rigors of evangelical religion. Perhaps nothing so succinctly suggests the increasing secularization of American culture than Stowe's depiction in *Dred* of Nina Gordon's conversion experience: "I feel, sometimes, as I did when I first heard a full orchestra play some of Mozart's divine harmonies" (D, 1:436). The cultural gulf that was opening in the 1850s between the age of homespun and the Gilded Age that was to emerge full-blown after the Civil War is the context for both *Sunny Memories of Foreign Lands* and *The Minister's Wooing*, two very different works that nevertheless share a common purpose. In a seemingly artless and effortless style, Stowe spoke to a nation in the throes of a vast cultural transformation, reassuring them, pointing out new roads, criticizing the past so as to help ease them into the future. In the process she achieved an effective voice and role as shaper of the emerging secular culture.

Whereas her father had lived to see his evangelical campaign falter against the forces of pluralism and cosmopolitanism, Harriet understood that in order to maintain cultural power she had to speak in the terms of the emerging culture of consumption. European travel was an increasingly common symbol of the growing surplus of the American middle class. Harriet's three trips to Europe in 1853, 1856, and 1859 put her in the vanguard of this movement, just as in the 1840s she had converted to the water cure almost as soon as it had crossed the Atlantic. Her *Sunny Memories of Foreign Lands* (1854), a travel guide that tourists carried under their arms as they would later carry Baedecker's and Fodor's, interpreted the European experience to innocent Americans.

Harriet's first experiences of European art had left her with some of Mary's shocked sensibilities. Upon seeing her first paintings by Rubens, Harriet declared them "carnal, fleshly, fat."[52] Advised by Maria Weston Chapman that *Consuelo* was "the most unexceptionable" of the works of the scandalous George Sand, Harriet sent her brother out to buy the novel in Paris; as he read it aloud, she marvelled "that so corrupt a woman could describe so beautiful a character."[53] But the success of *Uncle Tom's Cabin* had made Harriet the heroine of her own life; she soon overcame her scruples and drank in the beauties of Rubens's flesh tones, her own face "flushed" with pleasure as she stood in the halls of the Louvre, and she eventually read everything that George Sand wrote. By the time she wrote *Sunny Memories*, she had readjusted her American sights sufficiently to provide her wary countrymen and countrywomen an introduction to the cultural richness that awaited them on the other side of the Atlantic. At the same time, she remained in touch with her folksy innocence in a move calculated to reach and reassure her audience of recently arrived consumers of culture. The "fall" into high culture of an American innocent—a literary theme that was to attract Mark Twain, Henry James, and Harold Frederick—was anticipated by Stowe in her travel book.[54]

Her first calculation was casting *Sunny Memories* in the form of travel letters. This common journalistic technique (used by Calvin Stowe on his first European tour and later employed to good effect by Samuel Clemens in his travel letters in the *Alta California*) linked Stowe's foray into what was already becoming "high" culture with the familiar forms of parlor literature.[55] It is noteworthy that many of the letters were addressed to "Aunt E," that paragon of order and virtue from an earlier age. Stowe also employed "markers" of women's epistolary style: in a letter describing a visit to Sir Walter Scott's grave, she picked daisies and moss "which, with some sprigs of ivy from the walls, I send you," she told "Aunt E" (SM, 1:142). Just as these epistolary rituals had linked family members scattered from the East to the

West in the 1830s, now, inscribed in a travel guide, they made the terra incognita of Europe seem familiar. They also embroidered cultural shrines like the graves of Scott and Shakespeare with homely allusions. This was all the more needful at a time when these artists of the folk were rapidly being appropriated by the keepers of high culture. Lawrence Levine has shown how Shakespeare's plays, familiar to a wide audience of urban and rural Americans in the pre–Civil War period, were "sacralized" and reserved for an elite audience as a "cultural hierarchy" emerged in the latter half of the century.[56] Stowe mediated between folk art and high art during this period of transition. Her visit to Shakespeare's house in Stratford is narrated by her brother with a self-consciousness reflective of this coming change. As she looked around the plain, low-ceilinged room, Harriet fell into a dreamy trance, wondering "what Willy's mother used to say. 'Why' said Stowe, she used to say— 'Bill, come in & eat your supper'—and in he came out of the street, then crept in here to the chimney corner, took his porringer, ate his bread and milk, and looked in the fire to see the figures."[57]

While such homely allusions claimed culture for the folk, Harriet also used the pages of her travel book to impart useful information and to instruct her readers on the etiquette of travel. Just as her early sketch "The Canal Boat" had introduced her readers to a new form of national transportation, her first letter in *Sunny Memories* now introduced them to the mysteries of international travel via an Atlantic steamship. And just as her *Primary Geography* had introduced schoolchildren to the sprawling lands west of the Hudson River, so her travel book introduced the affluent middle class to the geography of Europe: "Roseneath occupies the ground beneath the Gare Loch and Loch Long," Harriet explained. "The Gare Loch is the name given to a bay formed by the River Clyde, here stretching itself out like a lake." Like a schoolteacher, she cited the population and chief manufactures of the towns she passed through (SM, 1:74, 123–24). Indeed, there were many similarities in voice and role between her first occupation and her emerging role as folk guide to the grand tour. "I may as well stop here," she says in the Swiss Alps, "and explain to you, once for all, what a glacier is" (SM, 2: 213). She also instructed her readers against such thoughtless behavior as scrawling names on the side of Shakespeare's house (SM, 1:202). If her brother Charles's behavior is any indication, such caveats were not superfluous. In the Alps he insisted on throwing stones to dislodge the glaciers so that he could "hear it smash" (SM, 2:292–93). On one occasion he was so successful that a large ice chunk careened dangerously down the hillside where shepherds grazed their livestock, leading Harriet to joke that she would be presented with a bill for "one shepherd and six cows."[58]

We can infer from such passages the process through which travelers were taught how to respond to foreign travel and to "culture." The most important lesson that many had imbibed from guidebooks was that they were not to give free rein to their own spontaneous responses. This restraint applied not just to destructive and boorish acts such as defacing property and landscape; the voices of cultural "authorities" also shut down the inner emotions the traveler brought to historical sites, for, as Stowe remarked on approaching Melrose Abbey, "all your raptures are spoken for and expected at the door" (SM, 1:150). The codification of culture thus undermined the traveler's trust in her own taste. Stowe includes in *Sunny Memories* a telling anecdote in which she was chastised by an "artist" for her raptures over a "melodramatic" Victorian sculpture. The sculpture, which Stowe describes in detail, was a typical didactic piece depicting a popular nineteenth-century theme, death—in this case, the death of Princess Charlotte, the daughter of King George IV. A female figure lies in the listless posture of one who has just succumbed. Around her are four figures with their heads bowed in "mute despair." "Above this group rises the form of the princess, springing buoyant and elastic, on angel wings, a smile of triumph and aspiration lighting up her countenance. Her drapery floats behind her as she rises. Two angels, one carrying her infant child and the other with clasped hands of exultant joy, are rising with her, in serene and solemn triumph." This is of a piece with the vastly popular iconography of Little Eva's death. "I ask any one who has a heart, if there is not pathos in it," Stowe addresses the reader, admitting that she and her whole company cried over it —"a fact of which I am not ashamed, yet." Now enter the artist, "who is one of the authorities, and knows all that is proper to be admired." He tells her the statue is in "miserable taste." " 'Dear me,' said I, with apprehension, 'what is the matter with it?' " " 'Oh,' said he, 'melodramatic, melodramatic—terribly so!' " Stowe reports herself "so appalled by this word, of whose meaning I had not a very clear idea, that I dropped the defence at once, and determined to reconsider my tears. To have been actually made to cry by a thing that was melodramatic, was a distressing consideration" (SM, 2:45–47).

This story illustrates the process through which *Uncle Tom's Cabin* would be relegated to that same category beneath contempt, "melodrama," and the book's power to evoke a powerful emotional response from the reader would become a reason to despise it as unartistic. When the authority to judge passed from the people to the artists and critics, a cultural divide opened between popular entertainment and high art. Before this time works such as *Uncle Tom's Cabin* were read with appreciation, pleasure, and instruction by mechanics and bakers as well as by ministers and lords. Shakespeare and Stowe were read together, and critics of *Uncle Tom's Cabin* did not think they were stretching the critical fabric to compare them.[59]

In *Sunny Memories* Stowe both observes the increasing codification of high culture and takes steps to undercut it. In the process she attempts to empower both the unsophisticated traveler and her humble self. The posture that she adopts is of a naif appoaching high culture with a guidebook in hand, but determined, as she says as she prepares to view the Old Masters in the Dulwich Gallery, that she "will not get up any raptures that do not arise of themselves" (SM, 1:279). She is determined, that is, to resist the voice of the "artist," the "expert," the keeper of culture. That she herself is speaking in a guidebook, of course, is a potential source of self-parody and irony. Stowe recognizes this in a good-humored fashion that simultaneously undercuts her pretensions to high culture and maintains her foothold in it. She pokes fun at herself and her party as they work hard at the job of being tourists. In Switzerland, as she and her party make their way toward Mont St. Bernard shut in "a crab-like, sideway carriage" with the blinds pulled against a broiling sun, "as uncognizant of the scenery we passed through as if we had been nailed up in a box," Stowe remarks, "Nothing but the consideration that we were traveling for pleasure could for a moment have reconciled us to such inconveniences" (SM, 2:259). By such ironic deflations, she maintained an intimacy with her audience even as she instructed them in the intricacies and absurdities of high culture. The irony that she was able to encompass in her own voice, Samuel Clemens often employed two characters to achieve: a genteel traveler and a boorish American.[60] Only when he created an imaginary folk character like Huckleberry Finn would he have the ironic range of Stowe's narrative voice.

By speaking in a colloquial, "folksy" voice about what was increasingly becoming high, inaccessible art, Stowe's intent was not to debunk the art but rather to encourage a "spontaneous" response to it—although in this increasingly self-conscious cultural encounter, it is hard to know what spontaneity might look like. Her agenda in this regard was similar to the one she pursued in *The Minister's Wooing*. Just as Calvinist theology had paralyzed its practitioners by its formalist demands, so had the guidebooks frozen spontaneous response to culture. Stowe in her capacity as low-key, garrulous guide lightened the weight of these cultural expectations even as she genuflected at the shrine of culture. In 1854, it was a highly successful strategy. "We went over, in great part, the same ground as Mrs Stowe & her husband & party, with her book (Sunny Memories) in hand," reported a traveler that year, "& can bear our testimony to the beauty & fidelity of her descriptions, expressed with no less truth than gracefulness." He noted that the book had been reprinted in the United Kingdom in two cheap editions "& is to be seen at every rail way S[t]ation for sale, & in the hands of every traveler."[61]

Mary wrote to her husband at the beginning of November, "Can you realize that we really are in Paris—the city of pleasure for all the world [?]" They had planned to go directly on to Florence but ended up staying three months in Paris "because Harriet & the girls wish to get the best French accent," and "there is more to see & enjoy here than any where else." They went regularly to the famous salons of Madame Mohl and Madame de Stael, where they encountered such luminaries as a granddaughter and great granddaughter of Lafayette, a daughter of Fanny Wright, and the former ambassador to England, Francois Guizot. Harriet quickly acquired enough facility in the language to carry on long conversations. They visited Madame Belloc, the translator of both Maria Edgeworth's novels and *Uncle Tom's Cabin*. A visit to Rosa Bonheur in her studio found her in her usual attire, a petticoat of thick cloth and a jacket with a linen collar and large pockets

for her artist's tools. Her short, curling hair was a decided innovation in
women's fashion, and with her "bright dark & very intelligent" eyes she had
the look of "a resolute decided original person."[62] Harriet's European education extended her notion of both "woman" and "artist."

In the meantime, in Andover, Calvin had closed off the dining room to
save fuel; he reported with some complacency the order that had descended
on his household: meals were simple and punctual "and every body punctual
at them—We have plenty of time and all get though at the same time." With
the mistress of the household gone, very little breakage of crockery occurred
that winter. Nor were there "old shoes nor old bonnets, nor old petticoats
nor cast off dresses, nor papers, nor books, nor letters taped here & there
and every where," Calvin wrote, and "no mob in the kitchen or dining room,
and no expenses except what I am consulted about before hand & approve."
Fully able to exercise his tastes and prerogatives, he didn't "have the blues
at all."[63]

By mid-January Mary was tired of the social whirl in Paris, but Harriet
and her daughters were still going out every night. Mary reported that Harriet
had decided to put the girls into Madame Coulons's boardingschool. "They
are reconciled to their fate but do not expect any great happiness.—They
have had a very nice time jaunting about & visiting & now they ought to
study but I never saw girls who were so bright & intelligent who so hated to
study & apply themselves." In fact Harriet left her daughters under the care
of Madame Borione while she went on to Italy where she continued her
pleasant visits with artists.[65] The sculptor William Wetmore Story was settled
in Italy and acted as a kind of magnet for other Americans. At one of his
breakfasts in Rome, Stowe met Elizabeth Gaskell and entertained the group
with what Mary called a "sermon" on Sojourner Truth. Based on Sojourner
Truth's visit to the Stone Cabin in Andover, Harriet's account, in dialect,
commanded the full attention of the company. When Harriet later wrote this
up for the *Atlantic Monthly*, Sojourner Truth complained that Mrs. Stowe
had laid it on thick, for she never called people "honey."[65]

When they were not visiting they took in the famous sights, including
Guido's celebrated Beatrice Cenci, the Coliseum by moonlight, and the
Venus de Medici. These evangelical Protestants planned to stay in Rome
until Holy Week so that they could see the full pomp and splendor of the
Roman liturgy, but a letter from Calvin Stowe urging a speedy return trun-
cated their trip, which had already extended eight months, and would stretch
to almost a year before their feet touched American soil again. "As you &
your family friends seem so little aware of the amount of time you spend
away from your home," Calvin told Harriet, "I have, for more than a year
past . . . kept a regular account of every day's absence, & shall continue to
do so."[66] They traveled to Lucerne, Switzerland, taking a bottle of champagne
"to keep up our spirits" as they passed through cold mountain passes "&
found it a great comfort." From Lucerne they journeyed by rail and diligence
to Strasburg and then on to Paris. Harriet and Mary traveled first class even

though "Mr Whitney said none but Princes rode first class." Mary explained to her husband, "we felt the necessity of making ourselves as comfortable as possible—& I think a little saved in this way is poor economy." Her education had taken. Mary had the comfort also of attending a Roman Catholic service in Strasbourg that had her in tears moments after the organ began to play. On June 6, laden with trunks of treasures and sated with experience, they sailed for home.[67]

CHAPTER TWENTY-TWO

Her Father's and Her Mother's God:
1857–1859

O*n the afternoon of June 17, 1857,* an expectant group filled the long parlor of the Stone Cabin. Calvin Stowe, Fred, Georgie, and little Charley, who thought of his Mama as an "invisible fairy princess," were awaiting her return from Europe. Isabella Beecher Hooker and her children had already arrived from Hartford with Georgie, who had boarded with them for part of the year. Isabella had promised her children the treat of seeing their aunt unpack her Italian treasures. Missing from the family group were Eliza and Hatty, still in Europe, and Henry, at Dartmouth. Harriet arrived looking "very fat & well" and "very glad to get home." After tea came "the *great* unpacking" which Isabella's daughter Mary reported "even more entertaining than we had expected." Isabella noted that one of the vases Harriet had brought her had been broken en route: "Hers were not Bohemian—& were very cheap—as were most of her purchases."[1]

During the year that Harriet was abroad Fred's drinking had increased to alarming proportions. Calvin, "in despair," had sent Fred during the winter to stay under the care of Harriet's brother, Thomas. Thomas Kinnicut Beecher was engaged in a rather unconventional ministry in Elmira, New York, where he took as his charges the castaways of society—prostitutes, drunkards, and street people—who frequented his storefront church. He was sympathetic to Fred's drinking problem because, as he told Calvin, he for "so many years . . . fought the same fight." Fred dried out at the Elmira Water Cure, where Thomas paid his $10-a-week board and promised to take him in "just as soon as he is *four weeks old* as a victorious abstinent."[2] That was in February. Now Isabella reported that he was still "very feeble" though "wonderfully improved—by intercourse with Tom, who has gained (all unconsciously it would seem) a great ascendency over him."[3]

After a week or so in Andover, Harriet and Fred went to Hartford to visit Isabella's family. Urged by Isabella and John Hooker, Harriet and Calvin were seriously considering a move to Hartford. Georgie was delighted at the thought of being near her cousins and living in "that pretty spot," a lot in Nook Farm that lay along the river. After Isabella and John invited Calvin to stay with them for a part of the spring, he declared that "Hartford looked so pleasant and the folks seemed so kind & obliging, that I thought I should like very well to live & die there when I get too old to work." Calvin, whose professional ambitions had once been so high, was now looking forward to nothing so much as retirement. "My seminary work is very hard, & I feel that adverse current which so often before has oppressed me," he had written to Harriet in Europe. "If I could live without the salary, I should think seriously of giving up."[4]

Andover had been the setting for Calvin Stowe's youthful triumphs. There as a brilliant seminarian he had mastered five biblical languages and translated from the German Johann Jahn's *History of the Hebrew Commonwealth*. Returned to the scene of his young career, Calvin, now in his fifties, blew feeble breaths on the remnants of his once passionate literary ambition. But the bright light of his wife's fame made his flickering candle all but disappear. "That is the plague of my life, to work so hard & suffer so much, and have only a horrible little mean scrawl to show for it when I have done," he told Harriet. "If I could only *do* what you have done, I should be glad enough to suffer all that you have suffered or are likely to suffer."[5] "I suffer & have nothing. Your birth pangs bring living, immortal children, Uncle Tom & Dred—mine, long continued, agonizing, never ceasing, all end in abortions."[6] In spite of these powerful feelings, Calvin took immense pride and delight in Harriet's accomplishments and remained her strongest supporter and most judicious literary adviser. "On the whole I am always happy with you alone," he told her, "but when there are others on the carpet with us, I am often quite sensible of a jar in my feelings." When she scolded him for his churlishness, he reminded her that he had cause: "You must take into consideration your celebrity and my obscurity, & the fact that I have ambition as well as other people; and that if my love for you were not very deep & sincere & wholehearted, our relative positions acting on my sensitive, irritable & hypochondriach nature, might be productive of still more offensive & painful results."[7] Burden though he could be to her, he was not as bad as Henry Ward Beecher's wife: "[Y]our affliction is the lightest—Don't you think so?"[8] Celebrity took a toll on a marriage, and Eunice Beecher was currently feuding with almost every member of the Beecher family. Some scholars have surmised that if indeed Henry Ward Beecher did stray into greener pastures, he was in part driven out by his mate. Harriet and Calvin remained faithful to one another to the end, struggling "as well as we can," Calvin said, "till *this corruptible shall have put on incorruption*."[9]

At the Hooker home in Nook Farm, Harriet and Isabella had long, confidential talks. In previous years, watching her older sister struggle with poverty and more children than she could manage, Isabella had questioned her own comfortable estate. Harriet had reassured Isabella, "the Lord truely loves you dear sister, & would have you lay aside that anxiety with which you seem to regard the prosperity he sends you."[10] Just as Harriet had acted effectively in a pastoral role at the Hartford Female Seminary, so she functioned within her network of sisters and sisters-in-law. They turned to her with their troubles and doubts, trusting that as she herself had suffered, she would know how to comfort them. Now Isabella felt "nearer to her than ever" and confident of her love. "She is very lovely—& were it not that her children must bring sorrow & anxiety deep & ever present, I should hope her days of prosperity & happiness were already come—as the fruit of a long discipline of suffering—I fear however that the worst is not yet." While Fred had taken steps toward recovery, his weak will and lack of a fixed purpose cast the outcome in serious doubt. Harriet and Fred left after a week for Elmira, where Fred wanted to stay until "his health & habits are confirmed."[11]

Harriet's six children were so many hostages to fate, and while she was preoccupied with Fred, tragedy struck from a different quarter. On July 9 as she was returning from Elmira, Henry Ellis Stowe went swimming in the Connecticut River with his roommate and several other Dartmouth students. Caught in a current too strong for him, he drowned. On the day the news reached Hartford, Isabella feared that Harriet would arrive on the noon train without having heard it. As it happened, Harriet had stopped the previous day in New York City to visit her brother Henry and his parisishioners, John and Susan Howard, with whom she had become close friends. At ten o'clock that evening she was seated with her brother Henry at John and Susan Howard's house when a telegram was handed in. As Susy Howard approached Harriet with the fearsome news, hesitating to speak, Harriet guessed from Susy's pale lips that something was wrong. " '[I]s it my husband'?—Susy shook her head—'is it Charley' . . ." Finding the suspense "worse than anything," Harriet reeled off the names of each of her children, reaching Henry last. "Drowned," gasped Susy. Harriet sat "perfectly still for some moments." Then she quickly took paper and wrote a "comforting letter" to Fred and the following note to Lyman Beecher.[12]

My dearest Father

    Lest your kind heart should be too much distressed for me I write one word. This affliction comes from One nearer & dearer than all earthly friends who loves us far better than we love ourselves—This may suffice—

    In regard to Henry's eternal estate I have good hope—The *lamb* of my flock he was I *rested* on him as on no other & He who has taken will care for him.

He who spared not his *own son*—how shall he not with him freely give us all things—

    Pray for my *other children*.

HB Stowe

The next morning Harriet took the train to Andover, accompanied by Henry Ward Beecher as far as Hartford. When she got off to change trains she was met by Isabella and her daughter Alice. Isabella reported that she "looked calm—almost saintly—more like an inspired prophetess looking far into the future—with keen upward vision." When they were in the ladies' room together, Isabella offered to travel on with her. Harriet made no reply. When they emerged, Harriet greeted Isabella's daughter with a kiss, and as she embraced this living child she broke into tears. She tried to tell Isabella that she would like her to go with her. On the train she talked about Henry "with great feeling." She reviewed his life, his character, his prospects, and her hopes for his eternal salvation, later putting many of her remarks into a eulogy read at his funeral and circulated to the family. "Henry was the only one of our children that we had begun not to feel anxious for & to hope to rely on him ourselves," she told Isabella. "Poor mother," wrote Isabella in the privacy of a letter to John, "I cannot but feel, that had his life been spared, her disappointment might have been greater than now—but we will hope for him—even as she does."[13] When Harriet arrived in Andover she found her house filled with Henry's grieving classmates, who had accompanied his body home. Arrangements were made for his burial in Andover, and then Harriet and Calvin went to Dartmouth to visit the relics of their son's life. Harriet had never seen his college or his room, decorated with memorials he had brought home from Europe.

Faced with the finality of death just days before she expected to be reunited with Henry, Harriet took comfort in the fact that between them "there was little . . . unspoken." Her last talk with Henry before he left their party in England nine months earlier was a "full overflowing of heart to each other." They had made their farewells with an intensity of love, "as if we had known that the ocean he was about to cross were indeed that solemn one from whose shore no traveler returns." In the days ahead as she yearned for just one more look, one more embrace, she thought about the first of her children who had crossed to the other side. She opened the drawer where she kept the "little old brown hat" and "the soiled gingham dress" that her baby Charley wore the last time she saw him healthy and happy. As she handled these tiny memorials, she "saw how much heavier blow may strike us than the loss of the dearest infant that ever nestled to our bosom."[14] When Charley died, Calvin had reminded his remaining children that "Charlie had never grown old enough to be disobedient to God—he knew no sin—he was innocent and pure. If he had lived he would have been a sinner, and felt the agonies of remorse and perhaps died unconverted. . . . Suppose he had taken any of you instead of Charlie, could we have been comforted with the same confidence of hope?"[15]

Now this question came back to haunt their sorrow. The grief that oppressed Henry's bereaved parents was shaped by the culture of Calvinism in which they grew up. Did Henry die "unregenerate?" He was moving in a hopeful direction, but the day of reckoning had come like a thief in the night. What if the work of salvation was not in his case complete? Harriet wrote a long, searching letter to Catharine, scrupulously turning over evidence:

> My hope for Henry is founded on this basis—in the knowledge I have had of his mental history for the greater part of his life—He has lived in more intimacy in his interior life with me than any child—there has been a more tender sympathy we have felt and prayed together & tho his piety did not assume always the technical approved form & tho it had the variations and inconsistencies incident to a developing & unsettled period of mind & body yet I think the evidence was of the best kind—viz great self mastery attained thro religious principle in those points where he felt he was most dificient—His mind had become fully settled on the subject of the Bible & the christian system as he told his Aunt in his last visit at Natick some months ago & in a letter to Freddy he said that tho perhaps he might not be what the world would call a christian yet it was his intention to lead such a life as christians *ought* to lead—such as every real man ought to lead.[16]

Of course, Harriet knew that her desperate search for "evidences" was the same kind of grief work that Catharine Beecher had engaged in almost forty years earlier when she learned that her fiancé—just a few years older than Henry—had been drowned off the coast of Ireland. Helping to organize materials for Lyman Beecher's *Autobiography*, Harriet had recently read Catharine's early letters. In 1823 Catharine had pored over Alexander Fisher's diary and his papers, searching for seeds of hope. Evangelical Christians who could work through the "evidences" and come to a comfortable faith that their departed were with God had a means of comforting their bleeding hearts. The theology of Calvinism was, in this sense, the form in which they poured their suffocating feelings of loss; like ritual in other religions, it provided a structured response to insupportable feelings that, without outlet, might prove overwhelming.

But Calvinism had long been institutionalized in a clerical structure presided over by men. In sermons and volumes of systematic theology male ministers elaborated a rigid structure that significantly enhanced their earthly power and diminished that of their flock. Like the institutions Stowe described in *Dred*, which "men begin by loving . . . for God's sake," Calvinism had come "to stand . . . in the place of God" (D, 2:46). As the system became more important than the divine principle it was meant to express, it likewise became more and more divorced from the bereavement it was meant to structure. What comfort could a bereaved mother find in the dry preaching of Professor Edwards A. Park, who held forth each Sunday in the chapel at Andover? Park's scholarly publications were on Samuel Hopkins, an eighteenth-century Calvinist theologian who espoused the theory of "disinterested benevolence"; Park was known in Andover for his "hard" preaching in the Hopkinsian mold. "Disinterested benevolence" reduced the mystery of death and salvation to a mathematical formula in which the sufferings of a few were justified by the greater good that came from it—the same instrumental thinking that Mr. Jekyl invoked in *Dred* to justify slavery. While mothers mourned the loss of children, Park performed his pastoral duty by explaining in a "dry heartless unfeeling cold manner" "that by using up three million in this way thirty three million times more happiness can be made to exist in the end."[17] This theology created a God as cold and intellectual as the Andover theologians themselves.

The intensity of Stowe's physical and emotional response to her son's death was in marked contrast to this detachment. When she thought of Henry's "so very hopeful & beautiful development" cut off so abruptly, her regrets cut through her "with a dagger thrust." The controlled response with which she initially met the news at Susy Howard's gave way to "a state of great physical weakness" during which "the most agonizing doubts of Henrys state were thrown into my mind—as if it had been said to me—You trusted in God did you?—you believed that he loved you—you had perfect confidance that he would never take your child till the work of grace was mature—& now he has hurried him out without warning without a moments preparation—& where is he."[18] Shortly after Henry's death Harriet wrote to Eunice, "These two weeks I have thought sometimes I must sink—if a portion of my heart had been really torn away I could not have felt more utterly prostrate."[19] Nearly two years later her grief held her in a state of deep depression. She explained to her daughter Georgie why she had neglected writing to her:

> Because, dear Georgie, I am like the dry, dead, leafless tree, and have only cold, dead, slumbering buds of hope on the end of stiff, hard, frozen twigs of thought, but no leaves, no blossoms; nothing to send to a little girl who does n't know what to do with herself any more than a kitten. I am cold, weary, dead; everything is a burden to me.
>
> I let my plants die by inches before my eyes, and do not water them, and I dread everything I do, and wish it was not to be done, and so when I get a letter from my little girl I smile and say, "Dear little puss, I will answer it;" and I sit hour after hour with folded hands, looking at the inkstand and dreading to begin. The fact is, pussy, mamma is tired.[20]

The codification and decadence of Calvinism, a once-vital religious expression, occurred at the historical moment when the emotional investment of bourgeois parents in their children was increasing—a development that contributed to the decline of Calvinism. This created a growing contradiction between ideology and experience, a contradiction felt most keenly by those entrusted with the care and Christian education of children. "As to this theological question," Catharine Beecher wrote to Leonard Bacon, "it is to me now not a *theory* alone—it is practical. I cannot go forward with any more education plans till it is settled whether I may train teachers to educate as I suppose common sense & the Bible requires or not. The whole operation I have been carrying on the last seven years is stopping to have this question settled."[21] Catharine had just published the first of three volumes articulating her theological beliefs. Entitled *Common Sense Applied to Religion, or the Bible and the People* (1857), it "attacked the Calvinist notions of original sin, conversion, and God's grace" as aberrations introduced by Saint Augustine.[22] While Catharine thus explicitly embraced what was called "the Pelagian heresy," she claimed that she was only stating what "the New Haven Divines" had taught for years. To verify this, she sent her manuscript to a spokesman of this school, Nathaniel Taylor, to see if she had accurately represented him. "He said *no*—objected—& put in his views." Catharine adopted Taylor's revisions *"exactly in his own words."* When they were published under Catharine's theological authority in her *Common Sense*, however, he complained that she had "done him an injustice." Catharine wrote to Leonard Bacon to discover how she could "get right" on this issue.[23] In all likelihood the real issue was Catharine's usurpation of the male ministerial role by writing a volume of systematic theology. The only way she could "get right" was by retreating into silence and letting male speech prevail. Catharine Beecher's theology was not a radical departure; as Kathryn Sklar has shown, in many ways it replicated her father's system against which her young heart had dashed itself with such a fearsome struggle.[24] But for a woman to assume the role of cultural authority in such a male-dominated genre as theology was to invite attack. Women weren't even supposed to speak up at Andover's "theological teas."

It was to circumvent these strictures on women's speech that the novel, as Elaine Showalter has pointed out, became "the essential instrument of female participation in the male monopoly on theological debate."[25] While British women novelists created clerical heroes whom they used as their mouthpieces, American women novelists (and notably also Nathaniel Hawthorne) created male clergy figures only to subject them to devastating scrutiny. Real spiritual power is clearly lodged in women characters. This reflected the realities of the women's culture in which Stowe herself had been an informal minister. Though not ordained or formally called, women carried out the functions of the ministerial office, preaching the gospel, comforting the afflicted, and burying the dead. Their spiritual power to comfort and counsel came not from a course of study at Andover or Yale, but from the power of sympathy born of experience. Exalted by their clerical role, male ministers were perceived to be "mathematical," abstract, and doctrinal, more inclined to tell a grieving parishioner how she *should* feel than to sympathize with her distress. Sara Parton ("Fanny Fern") put it succinctly in "Notes on Preachers and Preaching": "I don't believe in a person's eyes being so fixed on heaven that he goes blundering over everybody's corns on the way there."[26]

Clergymen came under direct fire for their callous treatment of women in mourning, a subject treated at length in novels by Harriet Beecher Stowe and Elizabeth Stuart Phelps. In Stowe's *The Minister's Wooing* Candace, a black woman, provides a bereaved mother with the comfort that her very abstruse and abstracted minister is incapable of giving; in Phelps's *The Gates Ajar* a woman comforts her bereaved niece by providing her with an image of heaven in lavish domestic contrast to the sterile heaven of the Rev. Dr. Bland. In both cases men are criticized for their pedantry and shallowness of experience.[27] Like Stowe, Phelps—the daughter and granddaughter of Andover professors—was reacting to an academic theology that had no place for human feelings.

The Minister's Wooing, written in the year following Henry's death, was Stowe's answer to Professor Park's theology. Writing in a more acceptably female genre, Harriet produced a much more radical work than her sister's systematic theology. Charles Foster is right in saying that Stowe reconstrued rather than rejected the theory of "disinterested benevolence" and that she said both "yes" and "no" to Calvinism;[28] but Stowe's challenge to the male clergy was unmistakable. While Catharine Beecher presumed to put on the cloak of male authority, Harriet set about undermining the ranks of privilege on which the men stood. Her elevation of a lay ministry of women and her pervasive anarchism toward theologicial structures puts the radicalism of this book in the same tradition as *Uncle Tom's Cabin*.

As she did in *Uncle Tom's Cabin*, Stowe drew on the values and experience of a women's culture to pose a radically democratic alternative to feudal and clerical structures. The hierarchical institutions Stowe attacked depended on separations between the public and the private, head and heart, the system makers and the victims of systems. In *Uncle Tom's Cabin* and *The Minister's Wooing* Stowe simultaneously invokes these separations and undercuts them through satiric juxtapositions of "high" and "low" culture designed to reveal the arrogance, posturing, and mendacity of such disjunctions. The high, abstract, male world of the lawmakers and theologians is revealed as humanly oppressive—built on the labor of women and blacks who then bear the added burden of the ideologies such lofty thinkers pass down. By valuing the human experience of "lowly" characters, Stowe forces a reevaluation of white, male systems of thought and, as feminist critics have pointed out, depicts women and blacks as instruments of salvation history.[29]

Both stories pit abstract systems of civil and religious justice (created by men) against the concrete realities of human life (which women were assigned the task of nurturing). In *The Minister's Wooing* men make theological systems—abstractly—but women, Stowe suggests, must deal with the emotional reality behind them:

> These hard old New England divines were the poets of metaphysical philosophy, who built systems in an artistic fervor, and felt self exhale from beneath them as they rose into the higher regions of thought. But where theorists and philosophers tread with sublime assurance, woman often follows with bleeding footsteps;—women are always turning from the abstract to the individual, and feeling where the philosopher only thinks. (MW, 19)

Like *Uncle Tom's Cabin*, *The Minister's Wooing* attacks patriarchal institutions for the violence they do to a bereaved mother's heart. In it she takes aim at two influential Calvinist preachers, Jonathan Edwards and Samuel Hopkins, who were skilled in painting vivid pictures of the sufferings of the damned. Dr. Hopkins was fond of explaining that "[o]ne way in which God will show His power in punishing the wicked will be in strengthening and upholding their bodies and souls in torments which otherwise would be intolerable." As for the sermons of Jonathan Edwards on this subject, Stowe remarks that they "are so terrific in their refined poetry of torture, that very few persons of quick sensibility could read them through without agony" (MW, 245). Edwards's best-known example of what Stowe calls his "refined poetry of torture" is "Sinners in the Hands of an Angry God," in which he likens the sinner to a spider suspended over the pit of hell by a slender thread. At any moment God can loose his hold and the spider will fall to destruction.[30] Stowe notes that people often observed the discrepancy between the terrible groans and shrieks produced by his preaching and the cool, reserved demeanor maintained by Edwards himself as he preached. The reason for his calm is not far to seek: while his congregation identified with the spider, Jonathan Edwards identified with God. Stowe's reworking of Calvinism makes the spider the heroine of the salvation drama. For the terrifying individualistic vision of Edwards she substitutes a communal vision in which women are spinners and weavers—knitters-up of the social fabric. They create webs of relationships that securely hold the lonely sinner whom Edwards trifled with. One of the important minor characters in *The Minister's Wooing* is Miss Prissy, the dressmaker. She makes the garments for all the ceremonial occasions—the baptisms, the weddings, and the funerals—and her work takes her continually into the homes of the townsfolk, where through her friendly gossip she functions as the "binding force" of the community.[31] In this women's world the "high" and the "low" are replaced by a complex set of peer relationships.

Stowe's assumptions about the relationship between this world and the next, between the "low" and the "high," are explicitly voiced in a passage in which Miss Prissy has been discussing Dr. Hopkins's treatise on the Millennium. Suddenly she exclaims, " 'Take care, Miss Scudder!—that silk must be cut exactly on the bias!' and Miss Prissy, hastily finishing her last quaver, caught the silk and the scissors out of Mrs. Scudder's hand, and fell down at once from the Millennium into a discourse on her own particular way of covering piping cord" (MW, 149). This mixing of the "high" and the "low"— a product of women's experience—is in Stowe's hands a subtle and deliberate way of erasing hierarchies of privilege. In another place Mrs. Marvyn discusses a treatise on optics while in the same breath giving precise instructions to the maid: "take care, that wood is hickory, and it takes only seven sticks of that size to heat the oven" (MW, 77). Referring to Miss Prissy's fall from the Millennium, Stowe comments "So we go, dear reader,—so long as we have a body and a soul. Two worlds must mingle,—the great and the little, the solemn and the trivial, wreathing in and out, like the grotesque carvings on a Gothic shrine" (MW, 149). Stowe consistently juxtaposes the high, disinterested theology of the Andover theologians to very concrete images of "perfection" in a woman's world: "faultless" loaves of cake and perfectly turned dresses.

In *The Minister's Wooing* Stowe both undercuts ministerial detachment and elevates the informal "priesthood" of women who suffer. The plot turns on the supposed death at sea of James Marvyn, a dashing young man who like Henry Stowe was in an "unsettled" spiritual state. The conflict between Stowe's vision of human connectedness and the male logic of Calvinism comes to a crisis through the character of Mrs. Marvyn, who is unable to reconcile herself to her son's death and everlasting damnation. Having invested years in his care and nurture, she finds it hard to believe that he has been thrown on the trash heap of eternity. The thought that all of God's power is now directed to torturing him causes her to question the God of her fathers—and what Stowe in another place called "the Hopkinsian arithmetical method of disposing the great majority of the human race."[32] She exclaims to Mary, the young woman in love with James:

> Think what noble minds, what warm, generous hearts, what splendid natures are wrecked and thrown away by thousands and tens of thousands! How we love each other! how our hearts weave into each other! how more than glad we should be to die for each other! And all this ends— . . . Brides should wear mourning,—the bells should toll for every wedding; every new family is built over this awful pit of despair, and only one in a thousand escapes! (MW, 250–51)

That "awful pit of despair" is Jonathan Edwards's famous pit, which stands in contrast to the woman's image introduced before it: "how our hearts weave into each other"—an image of human connectedness, of people, like spiders, weaving webs out of their very inner life. In her "ecstasy of despair" Mrs. Marvyn declares that she can never love the God who has severed these threads—"it is contrary to my nature!" Mary, distraught and unable to answer the contradiction between Mrs. Marvyn's impeccable Calvinist logic and her mother's heart, calls in Mr. Marvyn, who is likewise helpless to comfort her. At this moment Candace, the Marvyns's former slave, chances by. Perceiving that Mrs. Marvyn's extreme distress threatens her sanity, she talks "gospel" to her, comforting her the way in which women had learned to comfort children:

> "Come, ye poor little lamb," she said, walking straight up to Mrs. Marvyn, "come to ole Candace!"—and with that she gathered the pale form to her bosom, and sat down and began rocking her, as if she had been a babe. "Honey, darlin', ye ain't right,—dar's a drefful mistake somewhar," she said. "Why, de Lord ain't like what ye tink—He *loves* ye, honey! Why, jes' feel how I loves ye,—poor ole black Candace,—an' I ain't better'n Him as made me! (MW, 253)

Under Candace's preaching, Mrs. Marvyn is able to cry for the first time since her son's death, and as her "healing sobs" fill the room all cry with her. Candace urges her to descend from the superhuman heights of Dr. Hopkins's preaching and come to Jesus: "Jes' come right down to whar poor ole black Candace has to stay allers,—it's a good place, darlin'! Look right at Jesus. Tell ye, honey, ye can't live no other way now. Don't ye 'member how He looked on his mother, when she stood faintin' an' trembling' under de cross, jes' like you? He knows all about mothers' hearts; He wont break yours" (MW, 253–54). Candace reasons from this world to the next, and her logic has immediate verification in the maternal love she extends: "jes feel how I loves ye . . . an I ain't better'n Him as made me!"

It is remarkable that in the figures of Mrs. Marvyn and Candace, Stowe split herself into two mothers, a white mother who sorrowed and a black mother who comforted. Making Candace the high priest of suffering was consistent with Stowe's view of the outrages slave mothers had experienced and with her view, articulated in *The Minister's Wooing*, that only those who had experienced "a great affliction" were fit to "guide those who are struggling in it" (MW, 260).

Three years after the death of Henry, Stowe learned that her friend Susan Howard, who had been with her when the news of Henry's death arrived, had just received similar news. In the summer of 1860 Susan Howard's daughter Annie, a young woman, died suddenly in Italy. Upon hearing the news Stowe wrote to her friend:

> Ah! Susie, I who have walked in this dark valley for now three years, what can I say to you who are entering it? One thing I can say—be not afraid and confounded if you find no apparent religious support at first. When the heartstrings are all suddenly cut, it is, I believe, a physical impossibility to feel faith or resignation; there is a revolt of the instinctive and animal system, and though we may submit to God it is rather by a constant painful effort than by a sweet attraction.

Although she was still working within the Calvinist injunction to "improve the affliction," Stowe's emphasis was not on Christian duty but on the almost unbearable pain of that submission.

> Since that fearful night at your home every hour of life has been to me with an upper and an under current, and every day I have been making again and again that hard sacrifice, and it is a submission now as painful as at first.
>
> > "Time but the impression stronger makes
> > As streams their channels deeper wear."
>
> and I know all the strange ways in which this anguish will reveal itself,—the prick, the thrust, the stab, the wearing pain, the poison that is mingled with every bright remembrance of the past,—I have felt them all,—and all I can say is that, though "faint," I am "pursuing," although the crown of thorns secretly pressed to one's heart never ceases to pain.[33]

Her language evoked the physical pain—"the prick, the thrust, the stab"— and put off until a later day the spiritual submission, which Stowe implied would never come easily, nor perfectly.

In her advice to troubled and grieving women, Stowe's efforts were repeatedly focused on removing from their shoulders the added burden of feeling that they should not feel the way they did, a burden that was largely the result of Calvinist preaching by male ministers. "The things I said to you in parting," she wrote to Martha Wetherill, "I said hoping perhaps they might have at least some influence in relieving your good heart of a burden which our dear father never meant us to carry—the awful burden of thinking that every person who does not believe certain things and is not regenerated in a certain way *in this life* is lost forever."[34] Women turned to Stowe for relief from a particular kind of religious scruple that they would not have been able to express to their ministers. Her sister Mary wrote to her, "I wish you were here dear Harriet I want you to help me, for I am tempest-tost and not comforted & no one feels as I do or sees things as I do, & God does not speak to me & I am at times most unhappy most completely wretched."[35] Her son Frederick, then in college, had not only been insubordinate to the faculty but had been arrested for fighting with a policeman.[36] But Mary's distress was not so much for Frederick as for her resulting spriritual crisis. She had labored for years under the assumption that "[i]f I truly desire my child's salvation more than anything else & consecrate him to God, & bring him up accordingly, I have the promise that God will give his spirit to aid me & will regenerate my child." Now she was *"heart sick"* with "hope deferred": "If I had been told—you must do the best you can for your children & perhaps they will be saved & perhaps not I should not now feel so bitterly disappointed. . . . Now what does the bible promise to those who truly desire to train their children aright? Tell me what you think of the subject & what you thing of *my feelings* are they wrong?"

Stowe answered this mother's cry in a book she thought of as a series of "household sermons." To the mother "who has consciously no power, whose children are often turbulent and unmanageable," she counseled, "let her not be discouraged, if she seem often to accomplish but little in that arduous work of forming human character wherein the great Creator of the world has declared Himself at times baffled" (LF, 213). And she cited the Old Testament parable of the vineyard: "Wherefore, when I looked that it should bring forth grapes, brought it forth wild grapes?" (LF, 208–9). Once again Stowe ministered to troubled women by understanding and accepting their feelings—and telling them that God does the same. Her image of God was based on her own understanding of a mother's love, and she repeatedly counseled that, in the words of Candace in *The Minister's Wooing*, "I ain't better'n Him as made me" (MW, 253). Isabella Beecher Hooker, who often turned to her sister for advice on matters maternal and religious, summed up Harriet's pastoral style: "She . . . has no temptation to form or to adhere to theories merely—& she has the largest charity."[37]

Mothers stood as the type of "disinterested benevolence." "He who made me capable of such an absorbing unselfish devotion as I feel for my children so that I could willingly sacrifice my eternal salvation for theirs," wrote Harriet to her sister, "he certainly did not make me capable of more disinterestedness than he has himself—He invented mothers hearts—& he certainly has the pattern in his own."[38] By contrast with a mother's engagement, Dr. Hopkins's "disinterested benevolence" looked more like lack of interest. In Stowe's novel, only when he put himself on the line and had something at stake could he claim the same moral ground. When he showed himself willing to sacrifice his ministerial reputation and personal happiness by preaching against slavery and releasing Mary from her vow to marry him, he demonstrated true "disinterested benevolence." As in *Uncle Tom's Cabin*, the radicalism of Stowe's Christianity came not from the boldness of her ideas but from her insistence that Christians must live out the practical consequences of their beliefs. *The Minister's Wooing* was in an important sense an undoing of theology, an antisystem that worked by putting ideas in practice and so exploding neat systems.

The nimbleness with which Stowe negotiated the boundaries of women's sphere is suggested by the fact that she invited Professor Park to tea to read him her version of Samuel Hopkins. A quiet mutiny was brewing at this time among Park's seminarians, the brightest of whom were restlessly "push[ing] theological inquiries in [his] classes." While Park himself had been an intellectual rebel in his youth, he had been "pecked and pursued as a heretic" until, as Harriet explained to her brother Henry, "he is cowardly and dares not allow his young men to go one step beyond his lectures for fear they will implicate him & Andover." Harriet was quietly supplying such eager young men with introductions to her liberal brother, whose mellow, Christocentric preaching reached a much wider audience than Park's "dry, shingle palace of Hopkinsian theology." So threatened was Park that he had declared that all students who "could not fully come into [the faculty's] views" by the end of their second year must leave the seminary. Calvin Stowe found this blatantly unconstitutional and threatened to resign if free inquiry were not allowed.[39] In the midst of this simmering controversy Professor Park came to tea at Mrs. Stowe's and listened to her read the latest installment of *The Minister's Wooing*—many details of which she had drawn from Park's *Memoir* of Hopkins. Harriet, who warned her children against the "system" Park preached in the Andover chapel, now had him as a captive audience. What could he say to his hostess? This was, after all, *her* theological tea.[40]

Setting *The Minister's Wooing* in the 1790s, close to the birth pangs of the new American republic, Stowe suggests that Dr. Hopkins is a representative of the old order that will have to pass away before the promise of democracy can be realized. "For although he, like other ministers, took an active part as a patriot in the Revolution, still he was brought up under the shadow of a throne, and a man cannot ravel out the stitches in which early days have knit him" (MW, 18). In contrast to Dr. Hopkins's "monarchical" thought, Stowe projects a radically egalitarian vision of America in which the "high" and the "low" are only different-colored threads woven into the woof of our common humanity.[41]

In spite of the radical egalitarianism shot through it, *The Minister's Wooing* is also a nostalgic homage to New England and the Beecher family. Through the project of Lyman Beecher's *Autobiography*, which the aging patriarch now relied on his children to excavate from a lifetime of papers, Harriet was immersed in family letters and reminiscences, reading them perhaps for the first time. She made generous use of these materials in her novel, even quoting directly from an early letter from Roxana Foote to Lyman Beecher.[42]

The Autobiography of Lyman Beecher resembles what one imagines Lyman Beecher's study to have looked like. Correspondence, reminiscences, sermons, and history are all jumbled together with only a passing nod at chronology. Catharine Beecher's reminiscences of Litchfield are separated by hundreds of pages from Harriet's. The material is rich, but badly in need of an Aunt Esther to put each article in its own proper cubbyhole. Yet this cacaphony of voices, clamoring, contradicting, interrupting, modifying, elaborating, all charged with what Harriet called "moral oxygen" and "intellectual electricity," accurately conveys the Beecher family culture. "It was a kind of moral heaven," reminisced Harriet, "the purity, vivacity, inspiration, and enthusiasm of which those only can appreciate who have lost it, and feel that in this world there is, there can be 'no place like home.'"[43] Stirred by nostalgia, Stowe penned a narrative that spoke to Americans similarly cast adrift from their moorings.

At the beginning of a period of the most conspicuous consumption in American history, Stowe wrote a paean to domestic simplicity. In the first chapter of *The Minister's Wooing* Stowe invokes the high society of Newport, which already in the 1850s was blooming "like a flower-garden with young ladies of the best *ton*" who were "capable of sporting ninety changes of raiment in thirty days, and otherwise rapidly emptying the purses of distressed fathers" (MW, 15). Upon this material excess she superimposes like a palimpset the pre-industrial life her mother led in Nutplains, calling this chapter, "Pre-Railroad Times." Stowe locates her nostalgia in the New England kitchen of yesteryear, breaking into her narrative to address the reader familiarly, as she did in her Semi-Colon papers:

> The floor,—perhaps, Sir, you remember your grandmother's floor, of snowy boards sanded with whitest sand; you remember the ancient fireplace stretching quite across one end. . . . Oh, that kitchen of the olden times, the old, clean roomy New England kitchen!—who that has breakfasted, dined, and supped in one has not cheery visions of its thrift, its warmth, its coolness? The noon-mark on its floor was a dial that told off some of the happiest days; thereby did we right up the shortcomings of the solemn old clock that tick-tacked in the corner, and whose ticks seemed mysterious prophecies of unknown good yet to arise out of the hours of life. (MW, 13)

While the slip into panegyric mars the tone of her narrative, the image of the "noon-mark" on the floor is a powerful reminder of days when local time was told by the sun casting shadows on familiar objects. Time itself was to become more abstract in the decades ahead. On November 18, 1883, the American Railway Association with a stroke of the pen reduced the more than fifty time zones of the nation into just four; while this helped the trains run "on time," it also removed time from the local specificity of the "noon-mark" on the kitchen floor. As a national culture shaped by such corporate entities removed people from the concrete realities of time and place, the nostalgia of Stowe's New England novels depicted an appealing world of clear and straightforward relations between people and things. As custodians of household economy in a preindustrial age, women and women's work were endowed with value, importance, and centrality. As Judith Fetterley has observed, "[m]uch of the pleasure that the contemporary reader takes in this literature stems from its ratification of women as significant subjects."[44]

By contrast with the yardages of dresses churned out by textile mills in the 1850s, Stowe's heroine (like her mother Roxana in Nutplains) spins her own flax and has in her possession only special objects with family histories. She is innocent of worldly things like Italian paintings and the French language.[45] Yet Stowe embroiders her narrative with her newly acquired French vocabulary, stitching her New England girlhood neatly together with her proto-Gilded Age sophistication by telling her readers that "faculty"—that mysterious quality that enabled New England women to have work "always done and never doing"—was "Yankee for *savoir faire*" (MW, 2). When she introduces Virginie de Frotignac she moves from dropping French words in her narrative voice to allowing her character to speak brief passages in French. *The Minister's Wooing* simultaneously validates the provincial past and the cosmopolitan present, and the vehicle is the Beecher family history. Reading Catharine Beecher's reminiscences of life in Nutplains, Harriet learned that this mercantile town had been connected via sea routes to distant lands, that her mother had learned French from a political exile, that she read the latest novels from England while sitting at her spinning wheel. Supplying her heroine with a similar education, Harriet consolidated her European present with her Nutplains past. Just as Uncle Samuel brought to Nutplains Turkish slippers and turbans from Mogadore, as well as beliefs that challenged the provincial Protestantism of his village, so James Marvyn brings "a flaming red and yellow turban of Moorish stuff, from Mogodore" as well as "new modes of speech" and challenges to "received opinions and established things, which so often shock established prejudices" (MW, 20). Stowe invites the reader to see James Marvyn–Henry Stowe as no reprobate but a man of the world like maritime Uncle Samuel—a cosmopolitan like Harriet's well-traveled self. Harriet, however, brought back from Europe no radical challenges to the status quo, but only rather commonplace middle-class reactions to the culture of Europe; her most radical ideas were those that sprung from her immersion in her native culture.

In spite of her lyrical apostrophe to "grandmother's kitchen," with its cosy settle by the fire and its sanded floors, Stowe's novel works hard to reconcile newly rich Americans to the comforts of their luxurious lives. Stowe's growing comfort with prosperity is suggested by her story's ending. After James Marvyn comes back from the sea, quite alive, he marries Mary Scudder, who then undergoes a somewhat startling transformation: "The fair poetic maiden, the seeress, the saint, has passed into that appointed shrine for woman, more holy than cloister, more saintly and pure than church or altar, a Christian home" (MW, 410). That this "Christian home" is "a fair and stately mansion"—a monument to the extraordinary wealth amassed in nineteenth-century Newport—dramatizes the transformation taking place in the informal women's culture that Stowe's novel celebrates. When women's informal ministry was enshrined in Victorian parlors swathed with tapestries and filled with worldly goods, its radical challenge to male structures of power was sharply curtailed. Likewise, the conferring of honorific titles— "seeress" and "saint"—indicated that women's culture was itself not immune to codification and hierarchy.[46]

A more complex and successful integration of materials than *Dred, The Minister's Wooing* similarly packaged radical materials in a conservative frame. Stowe achieved significant cultural power through her skillful synthesis of New England's past and present—a cultural power dramatized by the serialization of her story in the most prestigious literary magazine to emerge in the nineteenth century: the *Atlantic Monthly*.

CHAPTER TWENTY-THREE

The *Atlantic* and the Ship of State: 1859–1864

*T*he Atlantic Monthly *was formed in 1857* by a group of New England brahmins who intended it to be a beacon of culture to the masses. According to Ralph Waldo Emerson, who met at the Parker House with James Russell Lowell and Francis Underwood to plan this new literary magazine, the *Atlantic*'s cultural mission was "to guide the age." Thomas Wentworth Higginson, another of the *Atlantic*'s founders, recalled that the *Atlantic* writers "were teachers, educators, and bringers of the light with a deep and affectionate feeling of obligation towards the young republic their fathers had brought into being. That New England was appointed to guide the nation, to civilize it, to humanize it, none of them doubted."[1] This was precisely the agenda Lyman Beecher had taken to the West twenty-five years earlier, with, of course, the very significant difference that winning souls to Christ was no longer germane; the religion of Christianity had, by 1857, been superseded by the religion of Culture. Carrying on the conservative Beecher family mission in a secular, literary venue, the *Atlantic Monthly* gave "culture" a new meaning: no longer an everyday process continuous with knitting and sewing, by the end of the century it would be "sacralized" in museums and explained in literary critical texts. "Here at mid-nineteenth century in America," observed Ann Douglas, "we see the beginnings of the split between elite and mass cultures so familiar today."[2] One literary historian argues that with the creation of the *Atlantic Monthly*, a formerly undifferentiated market split into "high" and "popular" culture, with the *Atlantic* skimming off the cream.[3]

"Phillips's project for a Magazine, a New England Blackwood of the right stamp, will certainly succeed," Calvin wrote Harriet on May 4, 1857. "In addition to the names I sent you last week, Mr Prescott comes heartily into it. It will speak a bold, manly, fearless, free word. Motley is one of the noblest men of the time, decided, unequivocal, enthusiastic for the right, a host in himself He goes into it heart & soul. They all say 'Mrs Stowe must begin with a serial and give us her wings for the first year, and Hawthorne shall follow in the second.'"[4] The serial she gave them, *The Minister's Wooing*, itself participated in the mythification of New England so central to the *Atlantic*'s mission. Yet Stowe would live to see herself and other women writers left behind by the cultural hierarchy she participated in establishing. If she knocked down the male clerical authorities in *The Minister's Wooing*, her support of the *Atlantic Monthly* helped to elevate a new priesthood of cultural authorities. The *Atlantic*'s first editor, James Russell Lowell, born "within the sound of the college bell at Cambridge," was a professor at Harvard.[5] As male institutions of cultural power began to define the terms in which literature would be read and to select which books were worthy to be read, the wide access to readers that had made *Uncle Tom's Cabin* an international phenomenon was obstructed by a cadre of experts who recommended only the most highly refined cultural productions. The broad canvasses that depicted a range of "high" and "lowly" characters would likewise be replaced by much narrower "slices of life." Popular novels by women who used literature to pursue social and political agendas would be demoted to "low" literature, commonly recognized by their "sentimentality" and "melodrama." But before this stratification was complete, Stowe enjoyed a decade that was in many respects the high tide of her career. She became a professional writer, and jumping aboard the *Atlantic* gave her her passage.

From the beginning, however, women were not full-fledged members of the *Atlantic* club. Boston society was organized around a series of overlapping men's clubs, and the *Atlantic* was grafted onto this structure.[6] A literary historian observed what a "genial circumstance" it was "that most of the decisions regarding the early courses of the *Atlantic* were taken at dinner-tables."[7] However genial these gatherings, the removal of literary business from the parlor to the rooms of the Parker House had the effect of excluding women writers. As a prime mover in the founding of the *Atlantic*, Harriet Beecher Stowe should have been included in these social business meetings. In fact, she was invited to just one of these dinners, and it proved awkward and embarrassing. In July 1859 the *Atlantic* circle planned a dinner meeting at the Revere House in Boston, to which they invited a number of their women writers as well as their usual circle of men. The latter regularly included Thomas Wentworth Higginson, J. Elliot Cabot, James Russell Lowell, Henry Wadsworth Longfellow, John Lothrop Motley, Oliver Wendell Holmes, Frances Underwood, and Ralph Waldo Emerson, many of whom were accustomed to dining together once a month as a self-styled "Saturday Club."[8] The mixed-sex gathering at the Revere House was to be a sendoff for Harriet Beecher Stowe, who was about to depart for her third trip to Europe.

Even though she was invited as honored quest, Stowe responded by circumspectly inquiring whether wine would be served with the meal. If so, she would not attend. Stowe was not a particularly ardent advocate of temperance. She took wine with her meals in Europe—much to the consternation of her teetotaling brother Charles—and sipped glasses of Catawba wine while she finished work on *Dred*. Her concern was not with the wine per se but with the character of the gathering. She may have heard rumors that flip, a punch laced with rum, was so liberally dispensed at these literary gatherings that poets zigzagged through the streets of Boston on their way home.[9] In order to secure her participation, the men assured her that no wine would be served.

On the appointed evening Harriet and Calvin Stowe appeared at the Revere House. Harriet wore a plain silk dress with a garland of artificial grape leaves in her hair. They had high expectations of the conversation, for Lowell and Holmes were fabled talkers; the reputation of their Saturday Club led one member to expect that it would go down in history with Samuel Johnson's circle. Although many invitations had gone out, only one other woman came; this was Harriet Prescott (later Spofford), a very young and shy writer. Julia Ward Howe was detained by another engagement and Rose Terry was at Saratoga. Women who declined the invitation may have feared that this *Atlantic* club was too decidedly male in tone. While the dinner was delayed in the vain hope that more women would arrive, the two Harriets waited in an upper chamber for forty-five minutes, speaking only when Mrs. Stowe asked Miss Prescott for the time. Calvin was waiting in a separate parlor with the men. When the dinner was finally announced, the men hesitated to send one of their members to fetch the women for fear that the chamber in which they were ensconced was not a parlor but a bedroom. Finally Lowell and Higginson overcame this Victorian scruple and knocked on the door of the women's room, which was indeed a parlor, and escorted them downstairs. Harriet Beecher Stowe was placed at one end of the table at Lowell's right; Harriet Prescott was seated at the other end of the table at Holmes' right. In between stretched a gauntlet of men: Thomas Wentworth Higginson, Calvin Stowe, Edmund Quincy, Edwin Whipple, Horatio Woodman, William Stillman, the publishers Francis Underwood and John Wyman, and the bashful John Greenleaf Whittier, who had to be strongarmed into this mixed-sex gathering. No sooner were the men and the two women seated at the table when an awkward silence descended. The men began exchanging doleful looks and whispering to one another. There was no wine. Jokes about wine began to circulate sotto voce, and soon one man handed his water glass to the waiter. When it reappeared, the "water" had a distinct hue. Others followed suit. The men became more jovial. Holmes took it upon himself to persuade Calvin Stowe that the practice of swearing had originated in the pulpit. In the meantime, the women sat in virtual silence. This was the last time women were invited to a meeting of the *Atlantic.*[10]

The awkwardness of this mixed-sex gathering stands in stark contrast to the literary meetings of the Semi-Colon Club, whose male and female members had joined on the gender-neutral turf of the parlor to talk, read, debate, dance, and drink madeira. The difference between these two literary parties may reflect the difference between the more established social structures of the East and the less structured society of the West. All-male literary clubs were a feature of the eastern seaboard during the 1830s and 40s—and similarly functioned around alcoholic beverages. Edgar Allan Poe's "Seven Stars" club met in a tavern of that name. While men's clubs were well established in the East by the 1860s, they became more self-consciously exclusive as their membership rebuffed challenges from men of color and white women. (Women of color were not even standing on the sill looking in.) These clubs were explicitly restrictive; members paid a fee to join and new members had to be voted in by the existing membership. The Town and Country Club, founded by Emerson, refused admittance to Frederick Douglass; that Douglass was one of the most eloquent men of his age was not enough to overcome Emerson's "mild instinctive colorphobia."[11] As Harvard opened its doors to students of more democratic backgrounds and the classical gentleman's curriculum gave way to an elective system more responsive to the needs of an open society, "Old" Harvard responded by withdrawing more and more into gentlemen's clubs. The Porcellian Club became the last vestige of what Harvard used to be before Italians and Jews were admitted. The establishment of the white male canon of American literature began in these Cambridge men's clubs, whose members supported one another's literary reputations, taught the first American literature courses, and wrote the first literary histories of the United States.[12]

The growing prominence of all-male clubs was also a defensive reaction to the changing nature of the parlor. No longer a common room in which all ages and sexes met for family entertainments, the Victorian parlor had become a cold, ostentatious room into which no one went for comfort and sociability. It was also increasingly associated with women, who were in charge of turning it into a shrine of conspicuous consumption.[13] The man who wanted a comfortable leather chair, a pipe, and a fire had to seek these in a men's club. But when the middle-class women were left in the parlor and the men withdrew to the club, cultural power went with the men. Women chose the curtains and the furniture, but men decided what Americans would read.

The *Atlantic* needed Harriet Beecher Stowe, however, for she had a genius for falling into trends before they had caught on with the general populace; any magazine that aspired to cultural leadership needed someone with her nose for the new. Was she not about to embark on her third trip to Europe? Her second serial for the *Atlantic*, in fact, helped establish what would be an increasingly popular genre: the international novel.

Agnes of Sorrento, which ran in the *Atlantic* from May 1861 to April 1862, is no more unreadable today than Hawthorne's *The Marble Faun* (1860) and shares with it a lush Italian setting, a virginal young heroine, and a brooding atmosphere of Catholicism and decadence.[14] None of this is likely to appeal to contemporary readers, but *Agnes of Sorrento* like Stowe's *Sunny Memories of Foreign Lands* introduced her readers to foreign climes and cultures at a time when the American nouveaux riches were eagerly looking toward a European tour to solidify their new class position. If all of this links Stowe's novel to the high culture of the Gilded Age, the circumstances under which the novel was conceived link it to an earlier tradition of parlor literature.

Stowe and her entire family, except Charley, departed for Europe on August 3, 1859. Once again the occasion was to establish international copyright, this time for *The Minister's Wooing*. Calvin and Georgie returned home when that business was completed. Fred and his cousin, Sam Scoville, set out for a walking tour of Italy. A lively and thoroughly engaging young man of twenty-one, Fred was trying desperately to recoup his life. He was painfully aware that for four years he had been nothing but a burden to his family. Determined to stand on his own, he undertook the walking tour to clear his head and strengthen his body through clean living.[15] After joining Fred in Florence, Stowe and her party toured southern Italy, passing through Naples, Sorrento, Salerno, Paestum, and Pompeii. In Salerno they were detained for a day and a night by a storm. That evening as the storm made the outdoors gloomy and impassable, the travelers contrived parlor amusements to make the time pass agreeably. "Songs and stories were the fashion of the day," Stowe remembered. She wrote the first chapter of *Agnes of Sorrento* for this spontaneous literary club. As Stowe later told her editor, her story met the approval of the gathering and was "voted into existence," much as her stories for the Semi-Colon Club had been. Stowe drew for inspiration on two figures she had observed in Sorrento, a beautiful young girl ("Agnes") and a silver-haired woman with a sharp glance ("Elsie"). Her story having been ratified by the group, Stowe "expanded & narrated as we went on to Rome," writing in a commonplace book which she "used as a diary and sketch book combined, jotting down in it, our daily songs & sketching whatever caught my eye or took my fancy." The weaknesses of *Agnes of Sorrento* owe much to this picaresque mode of composition. "I have it still," Stowe remarked in later years of the book in which she began writing her novel; "it is an odd little affair part story, part journal interspersed with sketches an old gateway here, a moss grown fountain there—trees rocks and flowers."[16] Too much of *Agnes of Sorrento* reads exactly like this— "an old gateway here, a moss grown fountain there." *Sunny Memories* had been constructed in much the same way, using Charles Beecher's journal as a reminder of their itinerary; toward the end of that book Stowe had even resorted to using passages from his journal in lieu of chapters she worked up herself—but what worked for a travel book did not work as well for a novel.

Her audience at Salerno and the readership of the *Atlantic Monthly*, however, had more patience with this desultory story than readers today, judging by the number of international novels that ran in its pages.[17] Hawthorne's *Marble Faun* was judged by his contemporaries to be his finest work.[18] A book "steeped in Italian atmosphere," it drew praise from a reviewer in the *Atlantic* for its "many landscapes . . . full of breadth and power, and criticisms of pictures and statues always delicate, often profound."[19] Eager for information, Gilded Age readers were less particular about form than a later generation of novel readers would be. Just the description of the gorge at Sorrento was worth the price of the magazine for many erstwhile European travelers. Many of Samuel Clemens's longer works are similarly picaresque, shapeless amalgams of travel experiences. The international novel that Henry James turned into an art form, Stowe and Hawthorne pioneered in their Italian stories. James's notion of an architecturally contructed novel was a long way in the future. "We can write only as we are driven," Stowe told her readers at the beginning of *The Minister's Wooing*, "and never know exactly where we will land" (MW, 21). The narrative license she claimed is echoed by Clemens's most famous picaresque hero, Huck Finn, who explained his method: "I went right along, not fixing up any particular plan, but just trusting to Providence to put the right words in my mouth when the time come; for I'd noticed that Providence always did put the right words in my mouth, if I left it alone."[20] This is the voice of the genteel amateur, transformed by Clemens into a folk hero. In the hands of Henry James all traces of personality would be expunged from the narrative voice and a professional, omniscient narrator would be established as the proper voice of the novelist.[21]

What sets *Agnes of Sorrento* apart from the writing Stowe did for the Semi-Colon Club is the more elite nature of her audience. While her Semi-Colon papers addressed an audience of emigrants from the East distinguished more for their wit and education than for their wealth, the international novel presupposed access to a very expensive experience: European travel.[22] The audience in Salerno who listened to Stowe's reading of the first chapter of *Agnes of Sorrento* included Susan and John Tasker Howard and their daughter Annie. John Howard had been one of four men who had put up the money to buy the building in Brooklyn that became Henry Ward Beecher's Plymouth Church. (His son Joseph was imprisoned in the 1860s for bribery and forgery in connection with a scheme to influence the stock market.[23]) Increasingly, American culture would be defined by men who had money, rather than simply education and family connections, just as Gilded Age culture itself was founded on the surplus generated from the industrial boom. Thus Stowe's second serial in the *Atlantic Monthly* bespoke the transition from parlor literature to a literary business: linked in conception and form to the earlier tradition, in its appeal to an elite audience it reflected the cultural hierarchy that emerged as literature was professionalized.

In Italy Stowe made the acquaintance of James T. Fields and his wife,

Annie Adams Fields. James Fields had just succeeded Lowell as editor of the *Atlantic*, and Stowe wasted no time in cementing this relationship, destined to be one of the most important of her career. She changed her sailing plans so that she would return on the same ship with James and Annie on June 16, 1860. Nathaniel Hawthorne and his wife were also on board, but Hawthorne stayed closeted in his cabin; he was temperamentally reserved and had no particular need to seek out the company of James Fields, having regular opportunities to meet him socially.[24] For Stowe, however, this represented a rare and lucky chance, and she improved upon it by arranging a meeting with the Fieldses in London before departure. "Apart from pleasure," she wrote Annie Fields, "I have some particular *business* to arrange with your husband—I have begun a story for the Atlantic & want to talk with him about it."[25]

James T. Fields had begun his career as a bookseller in the hospitable Old Corner Bookstore in Boston. Before assuming his post at the *Atlantic* he had been a partner in the publishing house of Ticknor and Fields. He enjoyed an advantage over Lowell, who held the editorship of the *Atlantic* from 1857 to 1859, in that he had a free hand in setting the terms of payment, for he was publisher as well as editor. He adopted the practice of paying authors on acceptance and was known for his generosity, particularly to struggling women writers. He was well connected to the Boston men's clubs, but unlike most of the men in his circle he supported women's suffrage. Elizabeth Stuart Phelps, who herself was the recipient of Fields's literary support, left this description of him:

> Mr. Fields was a man of marked chivalry of nature, and, at a time when it was not fashionable to help the movements for the elevation of women, his sympathy was distinct, fearless, and faithful. In a few instances we knew and he knew that this fact deprived him of the possession of certain public honors which would otherwise have been offered him.
>
> He advocated the political advancement of our sex, coeducation, and kindred movements, without any of that apologetic murmur so common among the half-hearted or the timid. His fastidious and cultivated literary taste was sensitive to the position of women in letters. He was incapable of that literary snobbishness which undervalues a woman's work because it is a woman's. A certain publishing enterprise which threatened to treat of eminent men came to his notice. He quickly said: "The time has gone by for that! Men and women! Men and *women!*"[26]

Fields believed in mixing men and women socially as well. Largely owing to the energy and intelligence of his beautiful young wife, Annie, their house at 148 Charles Street became an oasis in the middle of what Julia Ward Howe called the "frozen ocean" of Cambridge social life.[27] It was the one place that women writers, excluded from the network of male clubs, could meet on an equal footing with male writers and publishers. The congenial breakfasts and dinners at James and Annie Fields's house, orchestrated with Annie's consummate skill, became a familiar routine for Harriet Beecher

Stowe, Oliver Wendell Holmes, Nathaniel Hawthorne, Mary Abigail Dodge ("Gail Hamilton"), James Russell Lowell, Elizabeth Stuart Phelps, William Dean Howells, Lucy Larcom, Celia Thaxter, and John Greenleaf Whittier. Annie's self-effacing and somewhat worshipful attitude toward literary personalities and her instinctive tact provided an irresistible atmosphere that considerably enhanced her husband's publishing business. Charles Dickens stayed with the Fieldses during his long visit to America in 1867–1868. For a later generation of women writers, including Sarah Orne Jewett, who became Annie's companion after James Fields's death in 1881, the salon at 148 Charles Street provided important comradeship and professional support.[28] At a time when literature and society were becoming sexually segregated, the evenings in James and Annie Fields's parlor were a throwback to an earlier age. But these carefully constructed events were hardly spontaneous parlor games. In Richard Brodhead's words, they provided James Fields "a scene where he could both produce his authors as a kind of sacred cultural elite and win new recruits to the spreading of their fame."[29]

James Fields was somewhat given to flattery, but his taste in literature was universally admired. Higginson called it "very good and far less crotchety than Lowell's." In addition, Fields was "always casting about for good things, while Lowell is rather disposed to sit still and let them come." Ten years earlier Fields had stopped by Hawthorne's house to see whether he had anything that might be ready for publication; he was rewarded with the manuscript of *The Scarlet Letter*. Fields was also more professional than Lowell, who had the reputation of burying manuscripts in a heap of unread papers on his desk. Punctilious about the smallest matters of business, Fields organized his life by means of an annotated appointment book to which he referred continually in the course of a day. He was the essence of reliability and punctuality. As Stowe was neither predictable nor punctual, she valued these qualities exceedingly in others, particularly in publishers.[30]

Fields was not certain about Stowe's story, it appears, for she went to some lengths to reassure him about *Agnes*. Fortified by the approval of her children and husband, she wrote to Fields that she meant to "go on" with her Italian story. In its favor was its foreign setting, a change from the Yankee stories currently getting much play. "Eliza suggests that the Novo-Anglo dialect as represented by Homes & Rose Terry & Miss Prescott in her last story is in danger of being run into the ground in the Atlantic Monthly—& that therefore a story of another class might be desirable as a change," she wrote Fields. Calvin Stowe had assured her that *Agnes* was "as good as anything I ever wrote and advises me to finish it for all the reasons I have stated." She swept away Fields's reservations: "Therefore let us cross the Rubicon—The story will not discredit your paper & if it be not immediately ad captandum has in it materials of great power—At any rate it must be written."[31]

The strongest reason not to write a story in "Novo-Anglo dialect" was the fact that Stowe was already engaged in one for the *Independent*. When that paper's managing editor, Theodore Tilton, had approached her for a story, she had initially resisted his entreaties on the grounds that writing *Agnes of Sorrento* would take all her time and strength. Tilton assured her that a short story, to run through four numbers, would be finished and done with before the *Atlantic* and the London *Cornhill Magazine* began serializing *Agnes of Sorrento*.[32] Against her better judgment, Stowe agreed; the first chapter of *The Pearl of Orr's Island* appeared in the *Independent* on January 3, 1861. Calvin's fears that Harriet would become a slave to her pen were borne out during the 1860s. Her need for money would balloon to new heights when she undertook to build a many-gabled house in Hartford during the inflationary war years. Opportunities to write, in the meantime, escalated rapidly as the publishing business expanded. Between 1860 and 1880 the compensation an author could expect for literary journalism tripled.[33] For the first time in the United States it became possible to support oneself solely through authorship, and many periodicals wanted to list Harriet Beecher Stowe on their masthead. Stowe retained her easy optimism and reluctance to say no. One of the casualties of her overextended commitments was *The Pearl of Orr's Island*, which might have been one of her masterpieces.

By the middle of December 1860, when she sent Tilton her second installment of *Pearl*, Stowe realized that she was in for a long story. "Of course, you wicked magician, you saw in the coals what was coming & I see in the coals that I am in for it, for the thing begins to stir & feel round & the children like it—& the likelihood is that it will run thro as many more numbers—woe is me."[34] She had begun this novel in the summer of 1852 under the influence of the salty air of the Maine coast and the confidence that came in the wake of her enormous success. That this was a total departure from *Uncle Tom's Cabin* augured well. The springs would fill from a new source. Calvin had told her that she had yet to write her best work, and urged her to write a novel of New England.[35]

The Pearl of Orr's Island begins in a style more textured and psychological than anything she had ever written. Its contemplative, metaphoric language probes the inner lives of her characters in a style reminiscent of Hawthorne's works. In addition, Stowe's novel is enlivened by garrulous characters who come on stage with distinctive voices. The practical Miss Roxy Toothacre undercuts the sentimentality of the opening scene, in which Mara Lincoln's mother dies shortly after giving birth to her, by remarking "She'll make a beautiful corpse." At the end of Chapter 2, Stowe describes Mara as having struck her roots "in the salt, bitter waters of our mortal life," a phrase that concisely recalls the shipwreck of her parents and her own orphaning at the moment of her birth. Spare, crisp descriptions of the wild and bare scenery of coastal Maine create an island apart.[36]

It has often been remarked that some of America's classic books are children's stories.[37] Usually this curious fact is linked to the nature of the nineteenth-century family audience, which encouraged authors to censor from their books inadmissable topics such as sexuality. It has been less noticed that these stories—for example, *The Adventures of Huckleberry Finn* and *The Call of the Wild*—are about the psychic trauma of growing up, and particularly about the damage inflicted by the gender, race, and class roles that had to be embraced in order to enter adulthood on society's terms.[38] *The Pearl of Orr's Island* was Stowe's story of what it meant to a young girl to grow up in a society that prescribed sharply curtailed possibilities for women. Written at the same time that she was reading *Jane Eyre*, it is as close as Stowe ever came to writing a fictionalized autobiography.[39] Unlike *Poganuc People*, her reminiscences of her youth, it sprang from her inner life and longings. The failure of this broken-backed book in part reflects the failure of her society to grant full humanity to women; its structural flaws point toward a deep fissure in American republican ideals, just as the declension in power that critics have noticed in the last part of *Huckleberry Finn* is related to the political realities of Reconstruction America into which Clemens projected his liberated slave and his boy hero.

Stowe's personal investment in her heroine is evident from parallels between herself and Mara Lincoln. Both are slight of build with dreamy, heavy-lidded eyes that look as though they are longing for something they will never find. In deep feeling they are silent, repressing the reservoirs of emotion that wash over them. Miss Ruey Toothacre says that Mara is longing for her mother; in truth, the ghost of Roxana Beecher haunts the pages of *The Pearl of Orr's Island*, from the opening scene in which the heroine is orphaned soon after birth to the closing scenes in which Mara Lincoln follows in her mother's footsteps by dying young. But what Mara Lincoln longs for is not just her mother. She longs for a wider sphere in a world in which men represent ambition and adventure. When Moses, her male counterpart, goes on his first fishing expedition, Mara is left at home to dream dreams for him, her "glorious knight" (POI, 124). Moses comes back full of his own importance, and Mara's response is to resent "the continual disparaging tone in which Moses spoke of her girlhood."

Mara's adventures are all inward; like the young Harriet Beecher, she finds a fragmentary copy of Shakespeare's *The Tempest* and reads it with the conviction that it transpired in a place much like Orr's Island.[40] While Moses has the advantage in outdoor exploits, Mara surpasses him in imagination and learning. The readiness with which she acquires Latin by overhearing Moses struggling unsuccessfully with it leads the minister, Mr. Sewall, to teach her along with him. This strange, sensitive, extraordinary young girl, all nerve and spirit, causes Mr. Sewall to reflect, " 'If she were a boy, and you would take her away cod-fishing, as you have Moses, the sea-winds would blow away some of the thinking, and her little body would grow stout, and her mind less delicate and sensitive. But she's a woman,' he said, with a sigh, 'and they are all alike. We can't do much for them, but let them come up as they will and make the best of it' " (POI, 153).

At the time she was writing *The Pearl of Orr's Island* Stowe's own daughters Eliza and Hatty were entering the rocky coast of young womanhood. They were twenty-four years old. Hatty had had a complicated and unhappy love affair that ended when the man in question announced his engagement to someone else. Like most of the girls of their period, the twins had been trained for nothing in particular. Hatty was now nursing her wounded feelings at the Clifton Springs Water Cure where she would remain for five months. Her mother urged her to stay "till you have really firm good health," inquired about her French class and reading club, and told her she was "writing now full steam seventeen or eighteen pages a day to get ahead of my Independent story."[41] Trained by her sister Catharine to assume an independent life, Harriet Beecher Stowe was too distracted by her large family, dyspeptic husband, demanding career, and temperamental lack of system to pass on this heritage to her daughters. With indifferent educations, some literary talent but no ambition to compete with their mother, Eliza and Hatty Stowe seemed content to enjoy the comfortable life made possible by their mother's literary success.

Having satisfied Tilton with the first numbers of *The Pearl of Orr's Island*, Stowe in the middle of January 1861 sent her first installment of *Agnes of Sorrento* to James Fields, apologizing for the delay by explaining that she held up her "little darling" so that she might read it through again. "Authors are apt I suppose like parents to have their unreasonable partialities Every body has—& I have a pleasure in writing this that gilds this icy winter weather—I write my Maine story with a shiver & come back to this as to a flowery house where I love to rest."[42] Stowe's preference for *Agnes* over *Pearl* was in part psychological. Her Maine story recalled her to the pain of loss and the limits of a woman's circumscribed life. Her Italian story set her loose on an ocean of possibility. In *Pearl* Mara and Moses float out to sea in a small boat, unaware of danger as they embrace life's adventure (POI, 104–5); this sharply etched vignette of childhood's heroic ambition—from which Mara would be abruptly awakened by the exigencies of gender—had a different outcome in Stowe's life. The success of *Uncle Tom's Cabin* allowed Stowe in her adult life to live out this fantasy of sailing toward a distant horizon, and the writing of *Agnes of Sorrento* was a testament to the expanded possibilities of her international literary personality.

While she was balancing the writing of these two stories, Stowe also participated in a literary club that considerably enlivened the social life of Andover. Called the "Pic Nic" or the "Pic," this club met during the academic year. Stowe was delighted to have, once again, a literary club. The Pics were entertaining and would perhaps function for her daughters as they had for her in Cincinnati: to introduce them simultaneously to polite society and a literary life. She wrote to Hatty,

> I do wish my dear child we might hope to have you with us by the first of May because all our home pleasures begin then—the pic's begin their meetings of which every one has been pleasanter than the last—Before we had them Andover rivalled Clifton in dullness but since, there has been a perceptible rising social enthusiasm & the last two or three times there has been such an impulse & perfect wave of enjoyment that we have come almost to twelve oclock without the fact being percieved by the most steady.[43]

Like the Semi-Colons, the Pics freely mixed forms, engaging in "farewell communications in poetry and prose," songs, plays, games, and charades. The expense and ornateness of these parlor games, however, was specific to the Gilded Age. The meeting of February 20, 1861, featured a tableau of Madame Pompadour's salon in which the Pics donned elaborate period costumes. When the American parlor imitated the salon of the mistress of King Louis XV, it had truly entered its decadence.[44]

As the time neared for *Agnes of Sorrento* to begin its serialization, Stowe brought *The Pearl of Orr's Island* to a halt. She could not keep two serials going simultaneously, particularly when one of them demanded that she thread her way through psychically perilous waters. At the end of Chapter 17 of *The Pearl of Orr's Island* Stowe perfunctorily added ten years to the lives of her charges, throwing into this paragraph hints of an education very like Harriet Beecher's: Mara reads Virgil and learns "to paint partridge, and checkerberry, and trailing arbutus." That is to say, Stowe launched her heroine on the ocean of womanhood prepared with the education of a young man and the "accomplishments" of a young woman. At this critical juncture in her story, Stowe brought Part I to a close and explained to Tilton that she would not be able to continue her story until the fall. A card inserted in the April 4, 1861, issue of the *Independent* explained this situation to her readers.

A week later, on April 12, the Civil War began. The confusion into which the nation was plunged with the attack on Fort Sumter was enacted in the Stowe household through the drama of Fred Stowe, who immediately responded to President Lincoln's call for 75,000 volunteers by dropping out of medical school and enlisting in the Union army. His parents, wanting the best for him, had set him on a slow and uncongenial course of study. In the course of walking up and down the hills of northern Italy Fred had come to the decision that he should learn a trade rather than go to medical school. He was not sure he had the head for medicine, and if he studied to become a doctor, he would be twenty-eight years old before he would be independent. An apprenticeship, on the other hand, took only four years. Had he been encouraged to act on this plan he might have been rooted in productive activity. As it was, Fred rushed off to redeem a life that he could not seem to get launched. Harriet spent three days getting him outfitted and then engaged in the first of many interventions on his behalf. He had applied to be a surgeon's aide, but with less than a year of medical school behind him he lost out to more qualified men. Stowe applied to Annie Adams Fields, whose brother was a surgeon in the First Massachusetts Regiment. Dr. Adams agreed that if Fred would apply to his regiment, he would immediately choose him for hospital steward. For three weeks Stowe struggled in a "nightmare dream," at any moment expecting that Fred's regiment would be called away. Three times it was ordered to march, and three times his family went to see him off, only to find that the regiment had been delayed. Publicly Stowe rejoiced that the young men "embrace [the cause] as a bride, and are ready to die [for it]"; privately she prayed with Fred and tried to prepare herself for the worst. In her vivid imagination Stowe pictured her son in army camp, subject to the temptations of a soldier's life; there were some things worse than death.[45]

Soon after the stars and stripes of the United States had been replaced at Fort Sumter by the palmetto of South Carolina, Stowe urged the readers of the *Independent* to prepare for "a long pull." The war had come like a whirlwind, amazing even those who had foretold a bitter harvest of violence. Many thought it would be over quickly, but Stowe foresaw "a long, grave period of severe self-denial . . . which will *task* the resources, physical, mental and moral, of our Northern states." The title of her column, "Getting Ready for a Gale," reflected her recent immersion in her Maine story, but her dominant metaphors were evangelical: this was a millennial war, "the *last* struggle for liberty" that would precede the coming of the Lord. "Yet God's just wrath shall be wreaked on a giant wrong," she proclaimed in the nine-line verse with which she concluded her column.[46] She and Henry Ward Beecher were out in front of the editorial position of the *Independent*, which praised Wendell Phillips and William Lloyd Garrison for not mixing the slavery question in with the present crisis. Although everyone knew that the sectional struggles over the extension of slavery had been the most obvious precipitating cause of secession, most northerners carefully avoided the issue of slavery, agreeing with President Lincoln that to do otherwise would undercut his call for volunteers and provoke several more states to secede. Officially, this was a war to preserve the Union.[47] The sermon that Henry Ward Beecher preached at Plymouth Church two days after the war broke out was much less circumspect. After retelling the epic struggle of Moses leading his people out of pharoah's land, he thundered, "And now our turn has come. Right before us lies the Red Sea of War." There was blood in the sea and it was a bloody struggle over slavery to which the Lord had called his people, against their wishes.[48] "The innocent for the guilty!," Harriet Beecher Stowe echoed. The blood of innocent victims now "is the dreadful ransom of our guilt being extracted." Invoking both the Four Horsemen of the Apocalypse and the redemptive Blood of the Lamb, Harriet Beecher Stowe beat out the theme that Julia Ward Howe would immortalize in "The Battle Hymn of the Republic": "That awful wine-press of the Wrath of Almighty God; what is it? who can measure it?" The sacrifice of 620,000 men in the fiery furnace of war was the final payment the nation made to the God of the Old Testament.[49]

In Andover the seminarians organized themselves into a company of ninety men called the Havelock Grays. Even the boys at Phillips Academy were in uniform. The steady tramp, tramp, of their drilling and the sound of the fife and drum floated above the peaceful summer days. A flag-raising ceremony presided over by professors Phelps and Stowe included speeches, the singing of a "banner hymn" written for the occasion, and "coffee and a collation" at Professor and Mrs. Stowe's "cabin." Harriet rejoiced that the seminarians were becoming healthier and more "manly" in response to the war: "We venture to say if this state of things prevails, there will be no dyspeptic views of theology so far as this generation of ministers is concerned."[50]

In mid-June Harriet retreated to Brooklyn to the cool study of a friend and applied herself to her writing. Besides her columns for the *Independent*, she was working on the last chapter of *Agnes of Sorrento* and hoping to get ahead on her Maine story. "At home I have so many other cares on my mind that I cant think of it," she told her daughter; "the train of thought & feeling gets tangled up with bills butchers garden pea vines & Joe Pearson [the gardener] so that I cant smooth it out—My writing is the least of my cares & takes probably the least time."[51] When the fall came, Stowe was not ready to resume *The Pearl of Orr's Island*. Perceiving that readers of the *Independent* might feel she was unfairly neglecting them, she told Tilton to explain the truth—that he had persuaded her into this commitment against her better judgment and that the rest of the mischief was effected by her garrulous characters who would not get to the point. And then, "Who could write stories, that had a son to send to battle, with Washington beleaguered, and the whole country shaken as with an earthquake?" Tilton printed her letter in the November 21, 1861, issue of the *Independent*. On December 5 she resumed her tale, apologizing to readers who had been misled by the advertisements of "Mrs. So-and-so's *great* romance," for her story was "pale and colorless as real life and sad as truth." She also apologized to the children in her audience for making her characters grow up.[52] Her story was indeed a sad commentary on growing up female.

After drawing a radical portrait of a woman's life, Stowe provided her tale with a conventional ending. Instead of the wider sphere that Mara so clearly longs for in the first part of the novel, Stowe accords her heroine a sublimely sentimental death. This is Mara's revenge on the insensitive and insistently male Moses, who, being dull but not dead, is made to realize her worth only when it is too late. He marries instead the sprightly Sally Kittridge while Mara is transformed into what Stowe calls the "angel in the house" (POI, 392). One of Mara's last acts is to request that Sally take good care of Moses; the two women friends are joined by their mutual love of a man, just as Eliza Tyler and Harriet Beecher were, and Mara ascends to heaven trailing the halos of Roxana Beecher. The woman who lived out the plot of her famous father paid homage in *The Pearl of Orr's Island* to the shadow of her vanished mother.[53]

"What started out as a Maine idyl," Bruce Kirkham observes, "degenerates into a second-rate potboiler." Sarah Orne Jewett praised the originality and strength of the beginning and lamented "that she couldn't finish it in the same noble key of simplicity and harmony; but a poor writer is at the mercy of much unconscious opposition. You must throw everything and everybody aside at times, but a woman made like Mrs. Stowe cannot bring herself to that cold selfishness of the moment for one's work's sake."[54] In fact, Stowe had a great deal of the artist's capacity to "throw everything and everybody aside" while she drove on a tale; she wrote *Uncle Tom's Cabin* under the pressure of a new baby, running a school, and presiding over two moves. *The Pearl of Orr's Island* was the most personally challenging story of her life, and Stowe was either unwilling or unable to give it the attention necessary to work through the implications of her womanhood. She was at a disadvantage in trying to come to terms with her gender while remaining loyal to a mother who was more a myth than a reality.

In March 1862 Stowe wrote to her daughter Hatty that it was time she chose "a definite and settled religion." She continued, "you need to cast down an anchor somewhere that shall keep you from endless & aimless turnings."[55] Endowed with the undemonstrative temperament of the Foote family, Hatty Beecher was "fastidiously averse" to displays of strong feeling and to the "*emotive* experience toward Christ" that came so naturally to Harriet Beecher Stowe and Henry Ward Beecher.[56] It was unlikely that she would ever be subject to the throes of a religious conversion. She had often expressed a desire to join the Episcopal Church, and now her mother not only consented, she offered to "remove any obstacles in your way." She told her daughter that she would buy a pew in her church and sometimes come with her, "always to sacrament because I find that service is more beneficial to me than ours."[57] In advanced age, Lyman Beecher was in a childlike state that precluded his knowing about this apostasy.

It is not coincidental that Harriet's permission to her daughter coincided with a long visit from Catharine Beecher, who was herself planning to join the Episcopal Church that spring. As usual, Catharine had a carefully thought-out educational philosophy behind her change of religious affiliation. The Congregational churches of New England, she complained, had "shut the little children out of the fold of Christ" by telling them that if they were unregenerate, their prayers were worthless. As a result, the children ceased to pray. Catharine pointed out that not one of Lyman Beecher's children entered the church until "grown up or nearly so." The Episcopal churches, by contrast, "take the children into the church to be trained & in England & in this country *childhood piety* is found in that communion more than anywhere else." The Episcopal Church's emphasis on a gradual development of Christian character in many ways made it a congenial home for Harriet, given the intellectual and spiritual battles she had engaged in with the Calvinist God of her father. It also represented a link with her mother at a time when she was reasserting those bonds. "As for me," said Catharine Beecher, "I have only stepped from my fathers house into my mothers—& did it by a public act to take with me some lambs that I could not draw into the fold any other way within my reach."[58] That spring Harriet's three daughters were confirmed—along with their aunt—in the Episcopal Church. Henry Ward Beecher, knowing that they feared his disapproval, assured them they had his blessing "just as freely & willingly as if you had been about to unite with Plymouth Church instead. I have *no* feeling in regard to denomination"; the main thing was that "they found it an easier or more luminous way to Christ."[59] The following year Lyman Beecher died at age eighty-five. An epoch had come to an end.

In July 1862, unbeknownst to the public, Abraham Lincoln met with his cabinet and proposed to free the slaves. His Emancipation Proclamation would be kept secret for several more months as he waited for a Union victory before unveiling it. In the meantime pressure mounted to push the president in this direction, and Harriet Beecher Stowe added her voice. "The time has come when the nation has a RIGHT to demand, and the President of the United States a right to decree, their freedom; and there should go up petitions from all the land that he should do it," she urged in the *Independent* on July 31. "How many plagues must come on us before we will hear the evident voice, 'Let this people go, that they may serve me?,'" demanded Stowe.[60]

On August 20 Horace Greeley's "The Prayer of Twenty Millions" editorial in the influential *New York Tribune* urged emancipation.[61] Lincoln held fast. He responded to Greeley's editorial by announcing, "My paramount object in this struggle *is* to save the Union, and is *not* either to save or destroy Slavery. If I could save the Union without freeing *any* slave, I would do it; . . . What I do about slavery and the colored race, I do because I believe it helps to save the Union; and what I forbear I forbear because I do *not* believe it would help to save the Union." Stowe publicly challenged Lincoln on this famous utterance. In a passage that displays to advantage the anarchic impulse of her best social and political thought, she rewrote Lincoln's words to reflect the priorities of "the King of kings":

> My paramount object in this struggle is to set at liberty them that are bruised, and *not* either to save or destroy the Union. What I do in favor of the Union, I do because it helps to free the oppressed; what I forbear, I forbear because it does not help to free the oppressed. I shall do less for the Union whenever it would hurt the cause of the slave, and more when I believe it would help the cause of the slave.[62]

On September 23, five days after the battle of Antietam in which McClellan repelled the advance of Robert E. Lee into the North, the papers published the president's preliminary Emancipation Proclamation, which he planned to make final on January 1, 1863. A military measure that freed slaves only in those states that were in rebellion, the president's proclamation nevertheless moved in the direction of Stowe's hopes. Emancipation! She had not expected to live to see this day. The Congress had already voted to abolish slavery in the District of Columbia, an entity over which it had full control. As Stowe made plans to inscribe the date of this emancipation on the gold-link bracelet given her by the Duchess of Sutherland, she remembered the generous enthusiasm of the English people for the cause of the slave, embodied in the twenty-six volumes of signatures that accompanied the "Affectionate and Christian Address of the Women of Great Britain to the Women of America." The contrast between that outpouring of humanitarian concern and England's current sympathy for the cotton interests of the South could not be more striking. In an effort to influence public opinion in Great Britain, Stowe took up her pen to write a reply to the "Affectionate and Christian Address."

Eight years had passed since the women of Great Britain had pressed their concern on her. On the eve of emancipation Stowe explained that "the women of our country, feeling that the great anti-slavery work to which their English sisters exhorted them is almost done, may properly and naturally feel moved to reply to their appeal." She claimed to speak on "behalf of many thousands of American women," and doubtless she did; but she was directly privy only to her own thoughts and those of her immediate family members. Her reply would be unaccompanied by signatures and would be transmitted through the pages of the *Atlantic Monthly*. The periodical press was, after all, her best pulpit and most effective organizing tool.

England's sympathy for the South was widely attributed to the economic dependence of England on southern cotton. Calvin Stowe came out of scholarly seclusion to point out in the pages of the *Independent* that his much-reviled cotton speech at Exeter Hall eight years earlier had been right on target. Throughout the summer of 1861 Harriet's columns in the *Independent* had followed closely the reaction of England to America's crisis. At first she excused the failure of the English to rally to the side of the antislavery forces; they could have been misled by the caution with which the administration had sidestepped this issue. Proclaimed as a war for the Union, the battle between the North and the South was no different in many English eyes than the American Revolution. Stowe sought to counteract this impression, fostered on all sides in the North, by pointing to the bald declarations of the vice president of the Confederacy, Alexander Stephens. In a speech at Savannah, Georgia, on March 21, 1861, Stephens revealed the cornerstone of the Confederacy: the "great truth that the negro is NOT equal to the white man." To this statement, Stowe juxtaposed England's eagerness to recognize the Confederacy. "O England! England!" she apostrophized. "What! could ye not watch with us one hour?"[63]

Her "Reply" to the "Affectionate and Christian Address" likewise chastised England for her inconstancy, while taking pains to show the steps that had been made in the United States toward abolishing slavery. The most significant of these, of course, was the president's proclamation. Stowe had written eighteen pages—about two-thirds of her "Reply"—when she decided that it would be prudent to find out whether Lincoln was serious about his intent before she publicly put her voice behind his proclamation. "I am going to Washington to see the heads of department myself & to satisfy myself that I may refer to the Emancipation Proclamation as a reality & a substance not to fizzle out at the little end of the horn," she told James Fields on November 13. She planned to talk with " 'Father Abraham' himself." Her other reason to make this trip was that her son's regiment was in Washington. "I *must* see Fred," she told her daughter. "[S]ince I heard that his physician was prescribing whiskey for his ague I have had no rest—god only knows what the temptations of soldiers are in so cold & comfortless a life as theirs."[64]

She tried to persuade Henry Ward Beecher to go with her. If he could glean some encouraging news in Washington, he might moderate his attacks on the Lincoln administration, which Harriet thought dangerously demoralizing. "As you say in your last leader he is to be our President for these two years and had he better have a nation and army who trust him or a nation and army who think him a well meaning imbecile?"[65] Henry declined to come, and Harriet took with her her daughter Hatty and her sister Isabella. She left in mid-November, spent a week in Brooklyn with the Howards, and then pressed on to Washington. Her first act was to visit Fred at Fort Runyan and to arrange for him to leave camp with them. After an interview with Brigadier General Steinwahr—a great admirer of hers—she announced to the delighted Fred that Steinwahr proposed to take him on his staff.[66] Harriet visited the Capitol and called on Lincoln's secretary of the treasury, her old acquaintance from Cincinnati, Salmon P. Chase. On the streets of Washington Harriet and her party caught a glimpse of the handsome James Beecher riding by at the head of his black regiment. The following September James led his brigade against Charleston, carrying the banner that Harriet had devised: a rising sun with the word LIBERTY above it in immense crimson and black letters and below it the inscription "The Lord Is Our Sun & Shield." When Harriet imagined her brother's black regiment planting this banner under the eyes of the Charlestonians, she was sure that the spirit of Denmark Vesey strengthened their arms and helped them wing the bombs.[67]

The high point of her Washington expedition was a visit, on Thanksgiving Day, to the barracks of the "contrabands," fugitive slaves who had come over to the Union side during the war. They were enjoying their first Thanksgiving on free soil. The blessing before the Thanksgiving meal was invoked by an old man called by his fellows John the Baptist. Then the contraband choir sang what Isabella Beecher Hooker referred to as "a negro Marseillaise," "forbidden to them down South—but which they shouted in triumph now." The song was "Go Down, Moses," sung in call-and-response style, with hundreds of voices in every imaginable harmony joining in on the chorus, "Let my people go." Harriet found this "a strange and moving sight." Whereas Lincoln had initially said he would not interfere with southern property relations, here was living proof that the northern army was not respecting the Fugitive Slave Law. Moved by that experience or by intelligence gathered in her movements around the Capitol, Stowe completed her "Reply" that day and sent it to James Fields. "It seems to be the opinion here that the president will stand up to his Proclamation," she told Fields. "I have noted the thing as a glorious expectancy."[68]

Her "Reply" was dated and mailed a week before she and her party were invited to the White House to meet President and Mrs. Lincoln. On her stopover in Brooklyn she had called on Mrs. Lincoln, who promised to invite her to tea at the White House. They went on December 2, accompanied by

Senator and Mrs. Henry Wilson of Massachusetts. Wilson was a long-time abolitionist and presently chairman of the Senate Military Affairs Committee, in which capacity he had kept before Lincoln the idea of emancipation as a war measure. One would give a good deal to know the details of this meeting between Harriet Beecher Stowe and Abraham Lincoln, but the accounts leave almost everything unsaid. "It was a very droll time that we had at the White house I assure you," Hatty Stowe wrote her twin sister. "I will tell you all about it when I get home. I will only say now that it was all very funny—and we were ready to explode with laughter all the while . . . but we succeeded in getting through it without disgracing ourselves." When they got back to their rooms, she reported, "we perfectly screamed and held our sides while we relieved ourselves of the pent up laughter that had almost been the cause of death." Harriet's report to Calvin is likewise elliptic: "I had a real funny interview with the President introduced by Henry Wilson the particulars of which I will tell you."[69]

On January 1, 1863, Harriet went to the Boston Music Hall to be with others who had worked and written and struggled for the abolition of slavery. The Emancipation Proclamation began the process of dismantling the system of laws that had created a separate nation within the republic, a nation of people who were declared to have no legal identity, no soul, no purpose but to work for others, no stake in the republican experiment. The crowd assembled there was joyous, triumphant, celebratory. They chanted "Harriet Beecher Stowe, Harriet Beecher Stowe!" until the author of *Uncle Tom's Cabin* stood up and, with tears in her eyes, silently acknowledged the tribute.[70]

While mothers thanked God that their sons were spared the perils of the war, the young men who had volunteered impatiently pushed to get into battle. Henry Ward Beecher's son begged Theodore Tilton to get him a transfer into a company that would see action; Tilton complied, and Eunice Beecher never forgave him. Fred Stowe likewise champed at the bit. He wrote to his parents, "My regt will *neaver* go into action and so long as I remain here I shall neaver be advanced."[71] He had an opportunity to transfer into the Seventy-Third Ohio Regiment and he asked his parents to use their influence with Senator Charles Sumner to effect it. Whether his mother interceded on his behalf is unclear, but by March 1863 he had been transferred and was in the front ranks of the war; it is possible that Harriet feared the dullness of camp life and the lure of the bottle more than the dangers of battle.

"I know not what day the news may come to my house which has come to so many noble families of one more empty saddle & broken sword," Harriet wrote to the Duchess of Argyle on June 1, 1863. "I look for it in every battle & wonder as yet that amid the perfect rain of shell & shot in a recent battle my boy as yet lives." One month later Fred saw action at Gettysburg in one of the costliest battles of the war. When the guns stopped after three days of shooting, the carnage was almost inconceivable: 51,000 men were dead, wounded, or missing. Fred Stowe had been in the cemetery, "the very central point of the battle when fifty two shells a minute exploded around them." A piece of shell struck him and entered his ear. When his parents saw his name in the long list of casualties published in the paper, Calvin Stowe immediately set off by train to see him. He got no farther than Baltimore, where his pocket was picked of $130 and all the letters that his wife and daughters had written to Fred. Typically, he then became ill, sent for a doctor, and was ordered to return home where he could be cared for.[72]

In the meantime, on July 13, in response to the draft that had been imposed to bolster the volunteer army, riots broke out in many cities of the North. The mails were disrupted for a week and the Stowes heard nothing from Fred. Under the impression that her son was on his way home, Harriet feared that he had been "torn limb from limb" by the "wild beasts" who were destroying property and lynching blacks in the streets of New York. When it became clear that Fred was not en route home, Harriet wrote to Secretary of War Stanton requesting a three-month medical furlough for him. Stanton replied in his own hand. He arranged for Fred to continue on nominal duty but to convalesce in New York City where he could obtain medical attention. When Fred arrived in New York on November 26, his mother, who had "been bearing a burden heavier than all my others together for him," was there to meet him. Fred was effectively disabled by the war. A year later the wound in his ear, which gave him headaches and intense pain, had still not healed.[73] The experience of terrific and deadly warfare did nothing to stabilize this vulnerable young man. At Harriet's request, Henry Ward Beecher went to Washington to intercede on Fred's behalf with Secretary of War Stanton and obtain a discharge.[74]

In the meantime, Stowe fretted over her other children. She could look ahead and see that her gay, sparkling daughters who were the delight of parties would be on her hands if she did not push them toward adult responsibilities. "Hatty & Eliza grow more & more so, as they grow older," remarked a relative. "They are dressed as usual in expense of the worst & most exagerated fashion." Calvin thought their education had been "too worldly."[75] Harriet worried about their lack of earnestness and warned them against living for "outward show." But she also bought them silk dresses whenever she had a windfall of money and delighted like a schoolgirl in the fashions.[76] In this age of hoopskirts and crinolines, Harriet and her daughters wore skirt supporters to take the weight of their clothing off their bodies. To a levee at Professor Park's house, Harriet told Hatty, "I dressed in my low necked green with gold band & wheat—Didnt I feel Roman? I thought I would dawn on the natives. . . . Eliza wore her new dress with a low neck & berthe of black puffed tulle with little velvet bows of ribbon to match dress. . . . Georgy splurged in the blue you gave her."[77]

While she delighted in displaying her daughters in company, Harriet was uneasy about Georgie, who "seems to turn out under excitement like phosphoros" and who was given to manic-depressive turns, "a poor drooping bird half the time & then *too* excited & too frolicsome the rest."[78] When Stowe wrote this description of Georgie, her daughter was sixteen and may already have been exhibiting symptoms of the morphine addiction that would plague her for the rest of her life. Like calomel, morphine was routinely prescibed by doctors. Stowe's response to the ills and ailments of her pampered daughters was to urge them to partake of the smorgasbord of "cures" that her money put within reach: besides the water cure, she urged upon them electrical treatments, pills to help them sleep, and Dr. Taylor's "movement cure." She herself had gotten relief from headaches through Dr. Massey's electrical treatments; his office was beseiged by fashionable young women suffering from lameness, eye problems, and less-specific complaints. "My hopes are strongly excited for myself and for you," she told Hatty after she had taken the liberty of making an appointment for her.[79]

Even more than the other children, Charley had been petted and indulged to the point that Calvin admitted he could do nothing with him. When he was eleven years old his parents sent him to a boardingschool in Washington, Connecticut. At The Gunnery the boys wore cadet cloth uniforms, engaged in military drill twice a day, and went hunting in their leisure hours.[80] Calvin and Harriet hoped that Mr. Gunn would succeed with their son where they had failed. Charley's especial fault was his habit of lying. His mother attributed it to the system of secret police employed at Phillips Andover Academy—a good preparatory school for the college-bound but a terrible influence on young boys, she felt—and to Charley's "excessive approbativeness." He was inclined to say whatever would gain him the approval of his listeners, a trait that grew under the influence of his father's "uncommon development of philoprogenitiveness." Mr. Gunn's methods were far removed from the language of phrenology in which Harriet described Charley's faults, or from the romantic notions that underlay Catharine Beecher's system of "moral influence" at the Hartford Female Seminary. "Mr. gunn has some very queer kinds of punnish-ments," Charley reported to his parents. "If a boy wis-pers he puts a corn-cob in his mouth and makes him hold it there for an hour." His treatment for lying consisted of tying a handkerchief around the mouth of the boy in question and making him stand in public with this humiliation as "a lesson to the other boys."[81] After eighteen months under Mr. Gunn's strict regimen, Charley ran away. He made his way to Bridgeport and signed up to be a sailor. The letter of farewell he sent his parents reached them, with the name of the ship, before the date of sailing, and his parents retrieved him before he embarked. Recognizing the hypos of young manhood, Harriet sympathically recalled her younger brothers' experiences. "Henry and Charles came near to shipwreck in the Boston latin school at this age," she told Mr. Gunn. She remembered Lyman Beecher telling her "that that period in the life of all his boys was one when he 'cast out the anchors & wished for day.'" Calvin and Harriet persuaded Charley he would not rise to be a shipowner, as he imagined, unless he prepared by taking some courses in bookkeeping and accounting. Harriet set him to a year-long course of study at a commercial school in Hartford, but Charley could not be kept from the sea. In July 1864, just weeks after he had been apprehended, Harriet took him to New York where he shipped a sailor before the mast on the *Monitor*, bound for Spain and Italy. "Unfortunate is the hen who hatches a duck," Harriet wrote to Annie Fields, "but she must make the best of it."[82]

CHAPTER TWENTY-FOUR

Professional Writer:
1863–1867

*I*n 1863 *Calvin, now sixty-one,* retired from Andover. Harriet was fifty-two. For the next sixteen years she was the sole breadwinner, the head of the household, and a very determined professional writer. Her first step in arranging her life around this new reality was to impress her twin daughters into household service. They were now twenty-seven years old and the likelihood that they would marry was slim. If they were to be dependent on their mother, like Fred and Calvin and everyone else, it was imperative that they contribute something toward supporting *her* or else she would go under. "[I]f my health fails *all will fail,*" she warned them. The twins were reluctant to give up their lives of leisure. "[T]he energy with which you often say that you detest housekeeping," Stowe complained, "that you hate accounts & cant keep them that you dont like to write letters & cant write them—that you hate sewing—that you cant take care of sick people all these leave a load upon me which if you were differently inclined you might take off." She reminded them that if she were to die, there would be little for them to live on; she even threatened them with the specter of "*another mother*"; if they did not develop household competence, remarriage would be Calvin's only alternative in the event of her death. She urged, "There comes a time when girlhood must end & womanhood must begin." But the womanhood to which she bent their reluctant hands bore little resemblance to the independent life she herself had achieved.[1]

The immediate cause of this revolution in her household was the very sobering fact that Calvin's two-thousand-dollar-salary would soon cease.

They would have to cut back on help and Harriet would have to write more to make up the difference. Their household service had never been the same since Anna Smith left them after the move to Andover. A series of gossiping, inefficient servants who quarreled among themselves would plague their domestic peace. Harriet, who dreaded such domestic skirmishing and had no skill in cutting through it, proposed that they dismiss the two servants they now had and find a young girl of twelve whom they could have bound to them: "A stout well grown girl whom we would get bound to us would cost just her board & clothing but as she could be clothed in great measure from our cast off clothing it would not be a heavy bill & we might also be doing some good by giving some poor orphan a home—& she might gradually grow up to be valuable steady help." It is striking that in the year Lincoln signed the Emancipation Proclamation, the practice of indenturing servants could be a mainstay of Harriet Beecher Stowe's domestic arrangements. Harriet did not pause to remark upon this striking fact as she made her calculations. Their annual household expenses were $2,890. Their investments yielded about $1,500 a year and she usually brought in another $500 through her writing. Harpers had offered her $400 a number for a serial story. If Hatty and Eliza could take some of the home cares from her shoulders, she would be at liberty to take advantage of this offer, coming just at that time when the expense of moving into their new house was coinciding with Calvin's retirement. "Now it is very easy for me to write," she told her daughters; "writing is my element as much as sailing is to a duck. But keeping accounts, making contracts & settling bargains especially the little household economics and matters are *not* natural to me." She meant that it should become so to them. "You cannot make money—but you can set my mind free to make it for you."[2]

Much of the money that she had already earned from her writing went into building "Oakholm," her first house in Hartford. Having purchased the lot along the Park River in 1860, in the fall of 1862 she contracted with the man who had built Isabella and John Hooker's house—a man "so perfectly honest & faithful that he almost cheated himself," Harriet assured Calvin. They would save on lumber because the chestnut and oak trees on the lot were so plentiful that the carpenter could work some of them up for use in the house, "and still leave all we want for shade & beauty."[3] She supervised the opening of the street, the digging of the drains, and the details of the architect's plans, putting off her family, who were impatient for her return to Andover. "[I]t is a heavy responsibility for a woman like me in delicate health to prepare a home & move a family," she told them, "& however pleasant it may be to have your mother at home—you will soon have no home at all if I do not now make the preparations of it an immediate object."[4] In fact, she relished domestic convulsions and threw herself into this project whole hog. She wrote to James Fields, "Tell Mrs. Fields that my house with *eight* gables is growing wonderfully and that I go every day to see it—I am busy with drains sewers sinks digging trenching—& above all with manure!—

You should see the joy with which I gaze on manure heaps in which the eye of faith sees Deleware grapes & D'Angouleme pears & all sorts of roses & posies."[5] The trouble and fuss of building a house was considerable, but it had the advantage of taking her mind off the war. It also gave her the idea for her most successful wartime series, the "House and Home Papers."

In July 1863 the bloody battle at Gettysburg was followed by Colonel Robert Gould Shaw's attack on Fort Wagner. Shaw, from a prominent Massachusetts family of abolitionists, led an all-black regiment, the Fifty-Fourth Massachusetts. Harriet had visited their camp in Boston and was impressed by their "true soldierly bearing." She noted, "they are full blacks—most of them fugitive slaves—and as they moved with a sturdy strong tramp in heavy columns marching & wheeling they seemed grand & solemn."[6] Shaw begged for the opportunity to put his soldiers to the test. After being ordered to charge across a spit of sand that led up to a heavily fortified hill, Shaw was shot through the heart and nearly half his regiment was killed. The heroism of the black troops moved many, including a writer in the *Atlantic Monthly*: "Through the cannon smoke of that dark night the manhood of the colored race shines before many eyes that would not see."[7]

In the fall of 1863 Stowe wrote to James Fields "in great haste & housebuilding" to tell him that she had about "half finished the beginning of a set of articles to be called 'House & home papers.'" She described her projected series of household papers as

> a sort of spicy sprightly writing that I feel I need to write in these days to keep from thinking of things that make me dizzy & blind & fill my eyes with tears so that I cant see the paper I mean such things as are being done where our heroes are dying as Shaw died—It is not wise that all our literature should run in a rut cut thro our hearts & red with our blood—I feel the need of a little gentle household merriment & talk of common things—to indulge which I have devised this.[8]

It just happened that what Stowe needed to write about was exactly what the public needed to read about. In a reply that illustrates the comfortable partnership and informal contracts that characterized their early relationship, James Fields wrote back to her:

> Capital idea of yours, and I adopt your title of "House and Home Papers" as a good one.
> Let this be understood then between Mrs. Stowe & T[icknor] & F[ields]. They are to pay $100 for each no. of these papers on receipt of the document. Enclosed therefore in accordance with this understanding please find then cheque for $100 being in payment for no 1 which will offer in our January no.Let the others follow by all means in ample time.[9]

From January to December 1864, during some of the darkest days for the Union army, Stowe's essays on carpets, household economy, servants, cooking, and sundry other domestic topics appeared in the *Atlantic Monthly*. With the genius of the popular writer, Stowe accurately predicted that the horrors of war would create a reaction toward the comfort of home things. And yet her *House and Home Papers* were intimately connected to the transformation in American life that the war helped to bring about.

Her first number, "Ravages of a Carpet," told of the seemingly innocent introduction of a new carpet into the modest home of Christopher Crowfield. "My dear, it's so cheap!," his wife had told him, and so it was. As the demand for arms, ammunition, uniforms, shoes, and rations for the hundreds of thousands of Union troops stimulated the foundries, textile mills, armament factories, and meat-packing industries, the most massive mobilization in the country's history created an economic boom. The groundwork had been laid during decades marked by transportation improvements and a flowering of inventions such as the power loom, which turned out a volume of carpets that drastically reduced their price. But it became increasingly difficult to live simply and economically in the midst of the plethora of consumer goods being pumped into the market. Christopher Crowfield watches in horror as his comfortable and unassuming parlor, filled with serviceable but well-worn furniture, goes the way of the old carpet. When the new Brussels carpet arrives and is universally admired, a watchful eye notices the sun striking it. Blinds are declared necessary. By degrees the sunny parlor flourishing with children, dogs, plants, and good cheer is turned into "a cold, correct, accomplished fact."[10] In the meantime their friends, children, and dogs gravitate to Mr. Crowfield's library, furnished with the old mahogany furniture and ingrain carpet rejected from the parlor. The new parlor sits in state, shut up like a mausoleum.

Realizing that she had hit upon a powerful symbol of the increasing wealth and complexity of American life, Stowe continued in her next three papers to ring the changes taking place in the American parlor. In "Homekeeping vs Housekeeping," a young couple embark upon married life in an elaborately equipped home set up by the bride's family. (A few years later Olivia Langdon's family would give her and her new husband, Samuel Clemens, a small mansion as a wedding present.) While the bridegroom imagines sociable dinners with his male friends in his new house, the narrator has "an oppressive presentiment that social freedom would expire in that house, crushed under a weight of upholstery" (HP, 23). Stowe perceived that the new parlor of the 1850s and 60s was an uncongenial place for bachelors and boys, and in her *House and Home Papers* she repeatedly warns that if they are not made to feel at home, they will run away to sea or seek out other haunts on land. (Melville's *Typee* and *Moby-Dick* had already anticipated this flight, and Huck Finn would light out for the territories twenty years later.) The accuracy of this presentiment is confirmed when the husband of the newly married couple invites his cronies to dine with him at Delmonico's, defending this domestic betrayal with the words, "hang it, a fellow wants a home somewhere!" (HP, 27). The American parlor of the 1830s—the setting for Harriet Beecher's literary apprenticeship and a center of women's cultural power—was a multipurpose room; the new parlor of the 1860s—"a museum of elegant and costly gewgaws" (HP, 43)—betrayed not a trace of human activity. "Do they write letters, sew, embroider, crochet? Do they ever romp and frolic? What books do they read? Do they sketch or paint? Of all these possibilities the mute and muffled room says nothing" (HP, 83).

As the oldtime parlor became "mute and muffled," literary women lost their voices. Stowe chose to narrate these domestic talks in the voice of a man, "Christopher Crowfield." Stowe had chosen a male pseudonym— "Franklin"—for her first editorial back in the 1830s when she spoke out in the midst of the free speech battles. At that time she was an unknown female author for whom a subterfuge was prudent given the controversial nature of her topic. If there were rhetorical advantages to be gained in 1864 by her choice of a male persona to speak on domestic topics, it is hard to discern them. Rather, speaking in a male voice was the price of admission to the *Atlantic* club. Stowe chose a voice very like that of Oliver Wendell Holmes in *The Autocrat of the Breakfast Table*, which had appeared in the *Atlantic* to great acclaim.[11] The rise of a masculine literary establishment, intimately connected with the decline of the parlor, meant that even parlor talk was now to be filtered through a male voice. From there it would be a small step to devaluing women's culture and women's literary achievement during what had been the formative years of American literature, 1830–1860.[12]

Stowe's intense participation in the society she lived in and wrote about meant, inevitably, that at this point in history she would be an accomplice to her own declension in cultural power. At several points in her essays on the best way to arrange one's parlor, "Christopher Crowfield" recommends the decorative power of books. Invoked as a part of the decor, like the statuary, books now exist "as completed artifact, something already made and already designated as of classic value."[13] Moreover, all of the books "he" mentions were written by male authors. In these domestic talks in the *Atlantic Monthly* Stowe repeatedly enshrines the male authors who were in the process of elevation to high culture, such as "Hawthorne and Emerson and Holmes" (HP, 89). When she had heard in 1863 that Hawthorne's preface to *Our Old Home* praised proslavery Franklin Pierce, she had written angrily to James Fields, "Do tell me if our friend Hawthorne praises that arch traitor Pierce in his preface & your loyal firm publishes it. . . . I regret that I went to see him last summer—what! patronize such a traitor to our faces!"[14] But for Christopher Crowfield, Hawthorne is explicitly associated with a kind of escapism. Crowfield tells of reading "for the two-hundredth time Hawthorne's 'Mosses from an Old Manse,' or his 'Twice-Told Tales,' I forget which,—I only know that these books constitute my cloud-land, where I love to sail away in dreamy quietude, forgetting the war, the price of coal & flour, the rates of exchange, and the rise and fall of gold" (HP, 85). Stowe, who had insisted that the nation look at the unspeakable horrors of slavery and who made the hard edges of social realism a trademark of her fiction, now capitulated to the strongest forces in her culture. It is quite a bit like the capitulation Samuel Clemens made in the last part of *Huckleberry Finn*, in which Huck Finn bows to the cultural authority of Tom Sawyer and "the books." Crowfield's daughter plans to put in her parlor "uniform editions of Scott and Thackeray and Macaulay and Prescott and Irving and Longfellow and Lowell and Hawthorne and Holmes and a host more" (HP, 78). All of the American writers named, with the exception of Irving, who had died in 1859, were members of the Saturday Club. They represented the very best cultural authorities, the same kinds of white, male authorities—like Sir Walter Scott—whom Tom Sawyer invoked whenever he planned a foolhardy adventure. The uniform editions of their work aided the formation of the first canon of American literature, and Stowe's mention of them used the pages of the *Atlantic* reflexively to enshrine male *Atlantic* writers who would later effect her eclipse; she made no mention of Rebecca Harding Davis, whose *Life in the Iron Mills* had appeared in the *Atlantic* in 1861; or of Harriet Prescott or Rose Terry or Julia Ward Howe or Celia Thaxter. Her canon was male.

Stowe's friendship with Oliver Wendell Holmes grew naturally out of her association with the *Atlantic* and her closeness to James and Annie Fields. Holmes bought a house just down the street from the Fields's townhouse on Charles Street and was a frequent guest at their breakfast table, along with, as a rule, several other prominent authors. Holmes was a man of many parts, a wide frame of reference, and a ready wit. His sympathetic nature and ebullient sense of humor would have appealed to these traits in Stowe. But he was also arrogant and egotistical. His insistence on being the center of attention was widely tolerated because he was such a brilliant conversationalist. A story told by Thomas Wentworth Higginson suggests the lengths to which Holmes would go:

> There was a legend that he once met in the street the late Tom Appleton, at that time the second best talker in Boston, who told him a capital story. It turned out they they were going to the same dinner party, and Holmes said to himself, "That story will be Appleton's *piece de resistance*; it will be good fun to circumvent him." Accordingly, before they had begun upon their soup, Holmes burst out with the story. It won immense success, and Appleton sat glum and silent through the rest of the dinner. There was nothing really malicious about it; it was simply a joke, although, it must be confessed, a little cruel.[15]

Stowe's looking to Holmes for literary approval was a lot like Huckleberry Finn's looking to the arrogant Tom Sawyer, who played humiliating tricks on Jim, the fugitive slave, just for the fun of it.

Under the spell of Holmes, the *Atlantic Monthly*, and the masculine culture of wartime, Stowe contracted with the *Watchman & Reflector*, a leading Baptist weekly, to write a set of sketches about eminent men. This was strictly a money-making project, one of many such she undertook in the decade of the 1860s. Stowe described it to William Lloyd Garrison, whom she included in her *Men of Our Times*, as "the lives of the men who have fought this battle both in a physical & a moral sense."[16] In private letters

Stowe praised the courage and resourcefulness of women like Elizabeth Comstock, who, like Clara Barton, created new and useful spheres for women during the war years. But her public representation of heroism contained only men. "It will be a good thing for young men to read & young women too," she told Annie Fields.[17]

In her male persona, Stowe urged women to confine their heroism to the home. "We have heard much lately of the restricted sphere of woman," pontificates Christopher Crowfield in *House and Home Papers*: "We have been told how many spirits among women are of a wider, stronger, more heroic mould than befits the mere routine of housekeeping. It may be true that there are many women far too great, too wise, too high, for mere housekeeping. But where is the woman in any way too great, or too high, or too wise, to spend herself in creating a home?" Reworking the ideology of Republican Motherhood to fit the Civil War, Crowfield continues, "From such homes go forth all heroisms, all inspirations, all great deeds. Such mothers and such homes have made the heroes and martyrs, faithful unto death, who have given their precious lives to us during these three years of our agony!" (HP, 52–53).

Stowe elevated home and simplicity while in the throes of building what one historian called "a gorgeous Italianate mansion."[18] While it was ornate and would prove expensive to run, her new house paid tribute to her love for sunlight and plants in a semicircular glass conservatory that she designed and later popularized among her Nook Farm neighbors, including Samuel Clemens.[19] In April 1864 Stowe went to Hartford to oversee the final stages of construction. "The confusion at present grows wilder every day," she wrote her daughter, "but it is the confusion of activity & I am driving at every body's heels."[20] Soon she was flat on her back, exhausted by her efforts. "Dr. Wells came this morning & gave me electricity & I am better, tho weak," she wrote Hatty. "My brain is sore from the number of things I have been thinking of." And she reminded Hatty to pack carefully the "*tumbler* of *nice candytuft seed*" that she had taken some pains to save and to have Miss Greene pack up her papers "herself so that she may be sure no papers are lost."[21] By May the furniture was in but much of the finishing and trimming still remained to be done. She wrote Annie Fields from "Oakwold"—she was still experimenting with the name—to see if "pr accident any money should be standing due to me on account," for "now would be a most welcome time to receive it."[22] A month later she was still in an unfinished house, "dependent on a carpenter a plumber, a mason, a bell hanger who come and go at their own sweet will breaking in making all sorts of chips dust dirt—going off in the midst leaving all standing—reappearing at uncertain intervals and making more dust chips and dirt," she wrote James Fields; "our parlor & my library have thus risen piece meal by disturbance & convulsions." She thought that in another month she might "get my brains right side up."[23]

As her *House and Home Papers* drew to an end, Stowe took stock of her literary prospects. Some months back she had promised the *Atlantic* a romance, to run concurrently in the British *Cornhill Magazine*. The serial was to begin in January 1865, the month after her domestic series concluded.[24] Moved by the great success of the *House and Home Papers* and by a proposal made to her by Madame Demorest, Stowe reconsidered. Ellen Louise Demorest was the managing editor of the *Mirror of Fashions*, founded in 1860. She and her husband, William Jennings Demorest, the publisher, were about to transform this fashion quarterly into *Demorest's Illustrated Monthly and Mme Demorest's Mirror of Fashions*. They planned to add serial fiction, music, poetry, and miscellany to their colored fashion plates. Madame Demorest asked Stowe if she would aid her in this expansion by becoming a contributor. As Stowe looked over her prospectus, it became clear to her that Madame Demorest had the makings of a huge list of subscribers. "You see," she wrote to James Fields, "whoever can write on home & family matters, on what people think of & are anxious about, & what to hear from has an immense advantage." She laid out her plan:

> The success of the H & H papers has shown me how much people want this sort of thing, & now I am bring the series to a close—I find I have ever so much more to say—In fact, the idea has come in this shape. How much easier to keep up a domestic & family department in the Atlantic than to try to add a literary department to Madame Demarest. Now I have projected the plan of a set of papers for the next year to be called Christophers Evenings—which will allow great freedom, & latitude—a capacity of striking any where when a topic seems to be on the public mind & that will comprise a little series of sketches or rather little groups of sketches out of which books may be made.

In her choice of a format that would allow her to strike "any where when a topic seems to be on the public mind," Stowe made her calculations with an eye to the market and public opinion. Writing sketches "out of which books may be made," she would reap a handsome monetary reward. Her final touch was in casting her sketches in the form of parlor literature. "You understand Christopher writes these for the winter evening amusement of his family," she explained to Fields. This framing device, in which Crowfield's papers are introduced via casual discussions with his wife and children, mimics and capitalizes on parlor literature even while it points toward the professionalization of letters that was occurring. "Now I could prepare my story for your magazine," Stowe conceded, "but I do not feel that the public mind is just now in a state for a story—It is troubled, unsettled, burdened with the *real*. . . . *Home* is the thing we must strike for now it is here we must strengthen the things that remain."[25]

Not the least remarkable part of her proposal was her suggestion that she contract to write only for the *Atlantic* instead of getting her topics off her mind "piece meal for this & that paper." She had already broken with the *Independent*. Concluding that she could not afford to write for it on their terms, she requested in 1862 that the editors withdraw her name from their list of contributors. When a year later her name was still on their masthead, she wrote angrily to her brother, who had assumed the editorship, "My name belongs to those papers who pay me for the use of it."[26] Having cleared the decks of her commitment to a religious weekly and held off an offer from a fashion magazine, she now zeroed in on the most prestigious cultural organ emerging. She proposed "to keep up a Domestic Department" in the *Atlantic* "—for the same price which I should want for a romance—two hundred a month." She explained that she had made about that much in 1864 "by dividing my forces here & there—on different papers but I would greatly prefer to spend all my time & strength on one thing and I am pretty sure that I could make this thing more popular just now than the others." This was a shrewd and self-protective move on Stowe's part. Consolidating her contracts with one magazine not only simplified her professional life, it gave her better control over the amount of work she contracted for. The bind she had put herself in by contracting for *Agnes of Sorrento* and *The Pearl of Orr's Island* with two different magazines had produced neuralgia, headaches, and a rather embarrassing disappointment of her public. She would have only one very affable and supportive publisher with whom to deal, and if he accepted her proposal, she would *double* the pay she received for the first series of *House and Home Papers*. When Fields did not immediately reply, she prodded him with another letter reminding him that she had an application from another magazine in front of her. "I had rather write for the Atlantic sole & only than to write for several if I can do as well by it you understand."[27] Fields agreed to her plan, and she launched *The Chimney-Corner* papers for 1865. At Stowe's urging these sketches were made up in a handsome book for the Christmas trade under the title *Little Foxes*. It appeared in three English editions the following year. In the United States it went through seven more editions between 1866 and 1875 and by 1893 it had appeared in twenty-five editions. At the end of 1865, as *The Chimney-Corner* series was drawing to an end, Stowe renewed her financial agreement with Fields and wrote *The Chimney Corner for 1866*. It was likewise issued in book form, and Calvin Stowe reported in 1868 that "S. Low in his Publisher's Circular announces the 10th thousand of your Chimney Corner in London."[28] Thus Stowe's domestic series and the arrangement she secured with the *Atlantic* were enormously profitable. For two years running she secured a steady annual income of $2,400, exclusive of the hefty 45 to 55 percent royalties she earned on the Ticknor and Fields's book sales and her income from Sampson and Low's sales in Great Britain.[29]

Stowe thought of *Little Foxes* as "a course of household sermons." In them she preached not on the seven deadly sins, but on the little annoyances that "nibble away domestic happiness, and make home less than so noble an institution should be" (LF, 7–8). Fault-finding, Irritability, Repression, Persistence, Intolerance, Discourtesy, and Exactingness each come in for a chapter in which she used her narrative skill to sketch domestic scenes that, like examples in a preacher's sermon, illustrate her points. These sketches are particularly sensitive to the jarring of temperaments that occurs within the home as people of very different disposition are thrown together in daily intercourse. Indeed, in their psychological realism they are much more revealing of the home than her idealization of that institution in her first set of papers. The voice of Christopher Crowfield is also less obtrusive; Stowe appears to forget for long stretches that he is the narrator and her own voice assumes its characteristic turns. She describes the home as "a place not only of strong affections, but of entire unreserves; it is life's undress rehearsal, its backroom, its dressing-room, from which we go forth to more careful and guarded intercourse, leaving behind us much *debris* of cast-off and every-day clothing" (LF, 9).

At a time when the high Victorian culture was producing the home as a haven from the heartless world, Stowe insisted—as she had in her most radical novels—that the separation between the private and the public sphere was meretricious. She provides for the reader's edification a certain Mr. X, a clergyman who sounds a bit like Hawthorne's Arthur Dimmesdale. By overtaxing his strength and living on coffee, Mr. X "has preached or exhorted every night, and conversed with religious inquirers every day, seeming to himself to become stronger and stronger, because every day more and more excitable and excited. To his hearers, with his flushed sunken cheek and his glittering eye, he looks like some spiritual being just trembling on his flight for upper worlds; but to poor Mrs. X., whose husband he is, things wear a very different aspect." Having witnessed this chain of events before, Mrs. X foresees the inevitable reaction that will take place in the home:

> He who spoke so beautifully of the peace of a soul made perfect will not be able to bear the cry of his baby or the pattering feet of any of the poor little X's who must be sent
>
> > "Anywhere, anywhere,
> > Out of his sight";
>
> he who discoursed so devoutly of perfect trust in God will be nervous about the butcher's bill, sure of going to ruin because both ends of the salary don't meet; and he who could so admiringly tell of the silence of Jesus under provocation will but too often speak unadvisedly with his lips. Poor Mr. X will be morally insane for days or weeks, and absolutely incapable of preaching Christ in the way that is the most effective, by setting Him forth in his own daily example. (LF, 79–81)

Of course, insisting that a preacher live the ideals he preaches has the effect of whittling down grand schemes to human proportions. Drawing on homely metaphors that were the staple of Lyman Beecher's speech, Harriet contrasted "ideal gardens" and "book-children" and "book-servants" with the reality of cutworms and squash bugs and real children and real servants. She drily remarked, "A husband is another absolute fact, of whose conformity to any ideal conceptions no positive account can be given" (LF, 266–68). While Nathaniel Hawthorne wrote stories about self-deluded men who rigidly stuck to a perfectionist track, Harriet Beecher Stowe did her best to unsettle patterns and humanize stereotypes.

Like Henry Ward Beecher, Harriet preached to a newly affluent class uneasy about their station, unsure how to manage servants and the array of expensive wedding gifts with which they started their life together. But whereas her brother tried to make his Plymouth Church congregation comfortable with their wealth, Harriet preached simplicity and common sense. In *Norwood*, Henry Ward Beecher's popular novel of 1867, Dr. Wentworth commends the family table as "a kind of altar, a place sacred and so to be made as complete in its furnishings as may be." As William McLoughlin points out, this is a rationale for godly extravagance: "As God's altar, the Victorian dinner table could freely indulge in the most extravagant display of heavy silverware, fine china plates, ornate condiment servers, rich cut-glass bowls, magnificent crystal goblets, double-damask table clothes and napkins, curiously worked salt cellars, and all the other expensive accessories of dining that were to make Tiffany's famous."[30] While Henry Ward Beecher worked out a justification for Victorian excess, Harriet Beecher Stowe preached to the same families, understanding that their anxiety came not from guilt over their wealth but from a restless striving. They did not know how much was enough. In *Little Foxes* Stowe speaks to them through a fictional family whom she aptly names the Mores.

The Mores have the best of everything and are perfectly miserable. Mrs. More sits in her "elegant, well-regulated house" with her mind clouded by regrets:

> You compliment her on her cook, and she responds, in plaintive accents, "She can do a few things decently, but she is nothing of a cook." You refer with enthusiasm to her bread, her coffee, her muffins and hot rolls, and she listens and sighs. "Yes," she admits, "these are eatable,—not bad; but you should have seen the rolls at a certain *cafe* in Paris, and the bread at a certain nobleman's in England, where they had a bakery in the castle, and a French baker, who did nothing all the while but to refine and perfect the idea of bread." (LF, 258)

The More daughters take singing and drawing lessons with celebrated teachers, but soon give up in disgust: "If they could draw like Signor Scratchalini, if they could hope to become perfect artists, they tell you, they would have persevered; but they have taken lessons enough to learn that drawing is the labor of a lifetime, and, not having a lifetime to give to it, they resolve to do nothing at all" (LF, 257). It is striking that perfection has become emptied of all Christian associations and is now simply a secular ideal.

Stowe contrasts the Mores with a good-natured family she calls the Daytons. The Daytons are an average family who are mediocre housekeepers, tolerable singers, indifferent sketchers of pictures; they contentedly gather around the piano for amateur recitals, while the Mores sit in perfectly repressed silence, afraid of discord or of sounds that fall short of the music of the spheres. The Daytons are reflective of an earlier style in which home entertainments were sought as a means of amusement, not as a badge of cultural achievement. It is worth observing that this less demanding and more social approach to creativity was likely to draw out women more readily than the professional model that was emerging. How many women in 1865 were sufficiently immune to gender roles that they could determine to devote a lifetime to perfecting an art form?[31] Rather than point this moral, Stowe urged a healthy balance; the Mores would gain in happiness by developing some of the Daytons's self-contentment, and the Daytons would be stimulated by incorporating some of the Mores's standards of achievement. She helped the middle class find the middle ground.

In her literary career Stowe herself pursued a hybrid model. A professional writer, her voice was as distinct from that of the parlor amateur as it was from that of the cultural aesthete of the latter part of the nineteenth century, yet it would always betray its origins in the parlor. Her colloquial style and her indifference to punctuation grew out of her rootedness in an oral tradition. Stories told in the parlor carried their point by the rhythms and inflections of the language, not by marks on a page. "My printers always inform me that I know nothing of punctuation & I give thanks that I have no responsibility for any of its absurdities," she told Annie Fields. "Further than beginning my sentence with a capital I go not." She relied on George Nichols, a legendary proofreader at Ticknor and Fields, and later on a Mr. Bigelow, whom she described as "a direct & lineal descendent of 'my Grandmother'" to "put those things all right."[32] Her casualness extended to her manuscripts, which she sometimes mislaid, misaddressed, or subjected to domestic vagaries. She sent a sticky mass of papers to her amanuensis, explaining that she had left the manuscript on her table while she went for a ride: "A sudden storm came up entered blew down the writing stand upset an inkstand & broke a tumbler of sugar & water upon it—out of which chaos I drew it when I came in wet with rain." She concluded, "I hope it will not stick to yr fingers inconveniently."[33]

As a literary journalist, she was more interested in making a point than in creating an object of art. In her magazine writing she made compromises with her material in the interests of striking while a topic was still hot; a perfect article published a month after the public had ceased to wonder about the subject of the piece was of infinitely less value than an approximation that struck at the right moment. Yet she was not casual in her approach to her writing, even of such journalistic pieces as *The Chimney-Corner* papers. She reported to James Fields, "I have read & reread my chimney corner articles & at every reading see that they touch on subjects which are treated in a very imperfect & fragmentary manner—I would not be willing to put them out in book form without thorough rewriting & the addition of many collateral topics."[34] While she revised her serials when they came out in book form, the finished product often bore the stamp of the periodical press. They were, in a sense, performance pieces, outlines of what would occur when they were read aloud—like musical notes that are then inflected, embellished, and improvised upon. When an Arnoldian idea of culture and an aesthetic ideal of "art for art's sake" took hold, her work was divorced from its audience and judged by standards of formal unity; then, not surprisingly, imperfections in Stowe's art loomed larger than the social and political purposes that had moved her to pick up her pen.

If Stowe's canny relationship to the literary marketplace set her apart from both the parlor amateur and the cultural aesthete, so did the unabashed fact that she wrote for money. From the $50 prize she received for her story of "Uncle Lot" to the astounding profits that followed *Uncle Tom's Cabin* to the more modest but regular income that her writing yielded in the 1860s, money was always a concern. Her unrelenting need for that article drew her into a thicket of commitments that effectively undid the agreement she had reached with Fields to devote herself solely to the *Atlantic*. During 1865 she in fact wrote for two other magazines as well, although one of them was a Ticknor and Fields publication. Like Hawthorne, she used her literary talent to write children's stories, for which there was a growing market. Beginning in February 1865 and continuing for the next three years she contributed almost on a monthly basis to Ticknor and Fields's *Our Young Folks*, one of the specialized publications for children that arose as the market became increasingly differentiated. Besides a number of individual stories, she launched two serials—"Pussy Willow" and "Our Dogs"; like "Our Charley," which had appeared in the *Independent* in 1858, these sketches drew on Stowe's everyday domestic experiences and turned them into magazine copy. In addition, Stowe contributed a series of Italian sketches to the *New York Ledger*. Under Robert Bonner's flamboyant leadership, the *Ledger* grew to a circulation of 350,000, enabling him to pay his authors exceedingly well.[35]

At the end of 1865 Stowe wrote to James Fields, "The time has come in which I must look ahead & make my arrangements for next year—I have applications on hand from other papers, & first, I wish to know whether you wish to make the same arrangement with me as last year."[36] Knowing well that she had not exactly kept to the letter of her bargain, she suggested a change of terms:

> This year I shall feel obliged to ask you to remit that portion of our contract, in respect of this one fact, that the high prices make the liberal terms you offer in fact less than I used to have, as a hundred dollars buys only fifty dollars' worth of anything. I do not ask, however, any increase from you, only to allow me to make use of what time remains over and above the supply of my agreement with you, to gain something from other papers.
>
> The Watchman & Reflector have been always remarkably honorable and gentlemanly in their treatment of me, and are anxious to have six pieces for the coming year, for which they offer so good a sum that I would like to accept.[37]

Besides feeling the effects of wartime inflation and the expenses of her new house, Stowe had a wedding to pay for. In June 1865 Georgiana Stowe married Henry Allen, a recently ordained Episcopal priest. In preparation, the landscaping of Oakholm was zealously pushed ahead and spring cleaning accelerated, in the midst of which Stowe misplaced a $250 check from Ticknor and Fields. Writing to request a replacement check, Stowe explained to Fields that the commotion in which she existed included "dress making for one bride and three ordinary females—also Fred Charleys & Mr Stowes wardrobe to be overlooked also carpets to be made & put down—also a revolution in the kitchen cabinet threatening for a time to blow up the whole establishment altogether also lists of invitation to be made out cards written in the family—also articles for Atlantic & what not so that at this time writing I am reduced to a condition bordering on idiocy."[38] James Fields sent as a wedding present to Stowe's daughter a complete set of Hawthorne's works, uniformly bound in white leather. "Nothing could be prettier, more lastingly beautiful," Harriet wrote Fields in response, "the first adjective belonging you observe to the getting up,—the second to the contents." (The following month, for a wedding gift to her niece, Katy Foote, Stowe requested that Fields "have a set of my works immediately bound in a style like the Hawthornes you sent to Georgie." She too could become an institution.)[39] After assuring Fields she would send the next issue of *The Chimney-Corner* in good time in spite of the wedding, she reminded him of the expense of the dressmakers and asked, since her account had not been rendered since January, that he let her know what she might hope for "in the present crisis."[40]

Driven by her need for money, Stowe began to turn out books faster than James Fields felt the market could absorb them. All that was necessary was that she stop and collect in one place the pieces that she had done for magazines. Ticknor and Fields had announced early in the 1860s that they were to publish a volume of Harriet Beecher Stowe's religious poetry. The preparation of *Little Foxes* had intervened, and when Stowe returned to this project she realized she did not have the poems at hand to look them over. She told Fields, "if I only were in your store I could get them for they are like leaves blown in the hollows in autumn & the hollow in which they lie are mostly on your bookshelves."[41] She asked him to send her proof sheets of them so that she could look them over and revise them in her spare moments. When in October 1866 Fields explained that her poems, announced for that September, had been delayed so as not to saturate the market with her work, Harriet wrote back that she was disappointed and could not see how the publication would hurt the sale of the other books, as *Little Foxes* had only revived the sales of its predecessor, *House and Home Papers*.[42] She kept constant pressure on Ticknor and Fields about this volume of poetry, and the following year saw the simultaneous publication in England and America of both her religious poems and a volume of children's stories. She had a long-standing relationship with the London publisher, Sampson, Lowe and Son, and she arranged for James Fields to send them advance sheets of whatever works Ticknor and Fields was about to publish, for, as she told Fields, "Sampson Lowe has always done well & liberally by me."[43]

Over the years Stowe had become experienced at money management. The Stowes's investment portfolio was managed by their friend and Henry

Ward Beecher's parishioner in Brooklyn, John Howard, but Stowe exercised oversight of the cash flow. Here is a typical business letter to Calvin on money matters:

> My dear Husband
>   I understand Wrights letter to ask 1st on Woods behalf, will we have the whole 5000 or a part of it now. To which as you see I answer "The whole if you please"—
> 2d—Will we invest 200 of the 500 on 6/o int[erest] with mortgage—To which I answer that government sixes paying in gold are better & quite as sure & much easier to come at than any mortgage—Am I not right If so you will forward my letter.[44]

While she nominally deferred to Calvin's judgment, it was she who managed the money, made wills, and paid contractors. She was effectively the head of the household.

In spite of her conscious effort to keep the suffering of the war from overwhelming her, Stowe's defenses were overcome at various points during the war by the steadily mounting casualties. In November 1864 as she sat down to write one of the "sprightly" domestic pieces that served this work so well, she found her paper swimming before her eyes as she saw in her mind's eye all the homes and firesides laid waste by the war. Writing about the comfortable homes of Gilded Age America in this instance only served to remind her of this dreary contrasting set of images. She followed in the direction this vision led, and wrote a New Year's piece that spoke to those bereaved households.[45] Her readiness to trust her own responses allowed her to reflect, like a barometer, the flux of national feeling in troubled times.

On the domestic front, the cost of the war was before her daily in the spectacle of her poor, shattered son. In January 1864 Fred took a positive step toward reconstructing his life. He decided to be confirmed in the Episcopal Church, moved not by "great ecstatic joy" but by "a quiet belief theat there is a God & that he is taking care of me." He told his mother, "I am afraid sometimes that this is all false but I shall believe it real until I fail in my reform—all my leaving off of these things I have put into other hands than mine."[46] Harriet took great comfort in having four of her children confirmed, and in Fred's evident desire to quit drinking. Yet it was to prove a hard course. On a rainy Wednesday evening in October of that year, as she planned to leave for Brooklyn to visit the Howards and hear her brother's Sunday evening "political sermon," Fred walked out in the rain and disappeared. Harriet immediately canceled her trip but was unable to locate her son. As speculation and gossip flew, she was finally persuaded to confide in family members who then made discreet inquiries. A young man in their circle had seen Fred the following morning at the Allyn House "apparently just getting over a spree." "Poor Hattie—& poor sisters," commiserated Isabella, "they are all heart broken—it seems to have come to them at last, that he is hopelessly bound to this habit & they are in despair."[47]

Eliza and Hatty found the public shame that Fred's drinking reflected on them almost more than they could bear, and reacted judgmentally. Harriet reminded them that they had faults that seemed just as amenable to reform, and yet it proved no easy task for them to break these habits. "He is no weaker, no more unsuccessful against his beseting sin than you against yours—only the consequences to him are more fatal & dreadful." She begged them not to draw back from Fred: "If poor Fred fails in one respect, he is *exemplary* in others, where many find self control is difficult—He is gentle & patient, forbearing—unapt to judge harshly or speak evil of others—& this is the more affecting as his brain & nerves are so shattered that it is difficult for him to steady himself at all."[48]

The healing of the nation began with the conclusion of the Civil War in the spring of 1865. By way of allowing herself to realize both the cost and the victory, Stowe reread *Uncle Tom's Cabin*. She told the Duchess of Argyle, "when I read that book scarred & seared & burned into with the memories of an anguish & horror that can never be forgotten & think it is all over now!—all past!—& that now the questions debated are simply of more or less time before granting legal suffrage to these who so lately were held only as articles of dead merchandise—When this comes over me—I think no private or individual sorrow, can ever make me wholly without comfort."[49]

While legal suffrage for black men did follow in short order, the "more or less time" that was to elapse before African Americans enjoyed full civil rights was to stretch well beyond the ninety years the American republic had already been in existence, into the indefinite future. From Stowe's perspective, however, there was a huge difference between the working out of the problems of freedom and the existence of a legal code of slavery. She saluted William Lloyd Garrison's dissolution of his Anti-Slavery Society—a move criticized by Wendell Phillips, who preferred to stay organized for political action until the civil rights of the African American were guaranteed. "Garrison's attitude is far more great than that of Wendall Phillips," she wrote to the Duchess of Argyle. "He acknowledges the great deed done—He suspends his Liberator with words of devout thanksgiving & devotes himself unobtrusively to the work yet to be done for the freedman—While Phillips seems resolved to ignore the mighty work that has been done, because of the inevitable short comings and imperfections that beset it still.[50] Stowe wrote to Garrison that God would finish the "great work [of Liberty] he has begun among us," concluding, "With warmest congratulation I therefore stretch to you the right hand of fellowship."[51] Garrison responded with warm regards to Mrs. Stowe, who, he marveled, had remained simple and unassuming in her manners in spite of her celebrity.[52] But subsequent events were to bear out Wendell Phillips's prescience. When the South moved swiftly to reestablish white dominance through the establishment of Black Codes and the creation of the Ku Klux Klan, Stowe turned, with the tide of the country, toward a more grudging and guarded view of the victory. The work of reconstruction was neither easy nor politically clean.

Henry Ward Beecher had been invited to make the address at the ceremony in which the Union forces formally reoccupied Fort Sumter, a highly
charged national event. In the heady circles in which Henry now moved, he
had the ear of powerful men, including President Andrew Johnson. Harriet
reported to the Duchess of Argyle that her brother had "talked with [the
president] earnestly and confidentially, & has faith in him as an earnest good
man seeking to do right."[53] Johnson, a southerner and a slaveowner who had
ascended to the presidency upon the assassination of Lincoln, adopted a
lenient approach to the defeated South. His policy of "restoration" was
designed to quickly integrate the rebels back into the Union. In the meantime, the South demonstrated its unreconstructed character by the nature
of the delegations it sent to Congress. To the Thirty-Ninth Congress that
convened in December 1865 the South sent four Confederate generals,
many colonels, and even the Confederacy's former vice-president, Alexander
Stephens. In response to this arrogance, Congress refused to seat the southern delegates and began to override Johnson's moderate policy of "restoration" with more punitive policies of "reconstruction." Henry Ward Beecher
remained a public advocate of Johnson and his policies, and so came in for
his share of bruising as the reaction set in. Harriet, who was more in step
with public opinion, told him that it appeared "that you have received your
impression of the South & its needs from the former aristocracy the men
who have heretofore governed her & want to govern her again." She also
thought that "it may be the design of God to set aside this old aristocracy in
the reorganization of society at the south and to bring up the *common people*
as in New England."[54] Neither had Henry taken into account the feelings of
the northerners, as they silently counted over in their hearts the cost of
victory. "*The conquerors are sore with suffering*—too sore to be quite reasonable—you did not know quite how sore."[55] The summer after the conclusion
of hostilities she published in the *Atlantic* a piece on the North's war martyrs
deigned to counter the "pseudo talk of humanity & magnanimity to these
cruel assasins [Jefferson] Davis and others" by dramatizing "the more legit-
imate objects of pity," the Union men who had died in southern prisons.[56]

The drive and determination that Harriet brought to her gardens, her
books, and her houses, she directed at this time toward supporting her husband's lagging literary ambition. Several years after his retirement Calvin
Stowe undertook, with Harriet's encouragement, a book on the history of
the Bible. It was important to his self-esteem and to their marriage that
Calvin have something to show for his life. Whether she made the initial
overture to James Fields is not clear, but Calvin attributed the interest of
Ticknor and Fields in his work to "personal regard, especially for my wife."[57]
He sent Fields the title in February 1866 and promised that an outline would
follow shortly. But Calvin's gloomy temperament often undercut his ambitions and made the completion of a long project a shaky proposition; always
disposed to see obstacles and to let other things come in the way of his goal,
he dragged down with one hand what he put up with the other. Corey,

Fairbanks, and Webster had published his *Introduction to the Criticism and Interpretation of the Bible* in 1835, announcing it as a two-volume work, but he had never completed the second volume. His lectures on the New Testament still lay in manuscript. Harriet was determined that it would be different with this project. By October 1866, when he had written a good portion of the book, she wrote to James Fields, "In regard to Mr Stowe you must not scare him off by grimly declaring that you want *the whole manuscript complete* before you set the printer to work—You must take the three quarters he brings you and at least make believe begin printing & he will immediately go to work & finish up the whole—otherwise what with lectures & the original sin of laziness it will all be indefinitely postponed." She continued, "I want to make a crisis that he shall feel that *now* is the accepted time & that this must be finished first & foremost."[58] She followed this letter with another urging them to start the presses:

> I have feared this book would follow the fate of two others which he got almost ready to publish—fell back upon—waited & finally gave up altogether
>
> This book I am sure will be a success only get it into print as fast as you can & the spell will be broken & the volume on the Old Testament will follow next year As to the title of this volume you can modify it if you please only get the matter into print so as to save & make it sure.[59]

Harriet accurately predicted the book's success, but Ticknor and Fields was not to be the publisher. The Hartford Publishing Company, which was one of several large publishing houses in Hartford that were "driving their presses & making their fortunes," agreed to take Calvin's book on the New Testament. It sold books on agency, which ensured a large sale of any book it took on. Having taken Calvin's book, it now wanted a book from Mrs. Stowe to sell along with it, "justly thinking," Stowe told Fields, "that an agent could just as well talk a fellow up to buying two books as one." His book would be out in the spring of 1867 so she would have to move quickly. She asked Fields if she could let them have her *Chimney-Corner Papers* for 1866, which she had held back from publication in book form until such time as she could revise them. Her reasoning mixed mutual self-interest with a modicum of what she called patriotism:

> This agency business after all will play into your hands for they go out into the high ways & hedges & compel men to buy books & thus create a love of reading which will double and treble your market—I have been looking into it lately and see that as a patriot I have reason to rejoice in their success—They make immense sales. They tell Mr. Stowe they shall sell a hundred thousand of his book the first two years & if mine goes with it you see they will do the same for me.[60]

The next day she sent Fields another letter countermanding the first. "I have concluded on talking with the Hartford Firm not to take the Chimney Corner for them. They had rather wait till next fall & have men of the Times—as they have engravings ready for that."[61] Her commitment to turn into a book

the sketches of eminent men she had done for the *Watchman & Reflector*
would complicate her writing life in the years to come, but she needed the
money.

Calvin never wrote the Old Testament volume that Stowe had promised
Fields would follow in short order if they began printing, but it did not matter. His volume on the New Testament, entitled *The Origin and History of
the Books of the Bible*, was a hit. At the beginning of August 1867 Stowe
reported, "Mr Stowes book is selling at the rate of 400 pr day three presses
working at it as hard as they can—of course he likes that."[62] Within six
months it had sold 25,000 copies and earned him $3,000.[63] The recognition
that came from the public and the scholarly community was even sweeter.
His position was being taken up and debated by other scholars and even
merited a lampoon by one of the radical Unitarian papers. "So you see I am
coming up," Calvin wrote Harriet. On the strength of the book, Calvin was
asked to deliver a course of lectures in Boston. His booming voice and
sledgehammer delivery made him an effective speaker, and by "special
request" the lectures were extended into the summer of 1868. "They are
drawing more & more," Calvin told Harriet, "especially among the Unitarian
elite of Beacon street, more particularly of the honorable women not a few."
After one of the lectures, Dr. Andrew Peabody, the Plummer Professor of
Christian Morals at Harvard, thanked him "most cordially" for his book and
told him "that he had read it over & over again, and recommended it most
warmly to the Harvard boys. So I seem to be doing something in my old age.
This Boston lecture has been a real God send to me."[64]

While Calvin's success adjusted the conjugal equilibrium, it was less
clear what should be done about Fred. A return to medical school was out
of the question. In 1866 Stowe put up the money for him to go in with
several other young men to lease a cotton plantation in northern Florida.
"Two of the young men have been a year on the place & raised one crop,"
she told James Fields, "but it is so large they are glad to take in more hands
to work it." Immersed in the responsibility of healthful, outdoor work, Fred
would be removed from the temptations of city life. He would also be in-
sulated from the gossiping tongues and social obloquy that were quick to
descend in Hartford. Harriet made plans to go to Florida herself at the end
of February to preside over housekeeping. She had always found it difficult
to write in the cold weather, and the indeterminate days of the late winter
were particularly doleful. Now she had "a refuge from these March horrors
which always make my life a burden."[65]

CHAPTER TWENTY-FIVE

Florida and *Oldtown Folks*:
1867–1869

"*The American is a migratory animal*," wrote an observer in 1865. The vastness of the country so habituated the American to travel "that he packs his portmanteau, and starts on a journey of hundreds of miles, as readily as he puts on his coat and comes down to breakfast."[1] With her discovery of Florida, Stowe and her husband became what Gail Hamilton called "birds of passage flitting North & South on the slightest change of air."[2] On her first trip she took with her her brother Charles and her nephew Spencer Foote, his wife Hannah, and their baby. Spencer Foote was one of the partners in the leased plantation, the others, besides Fred, being two Connecticut farmers, Messrs. Kinney and Chamberlin, whom Harriet described as "two fine Yankee ex officers."[3] The passage from New York to Savannah was exceedingly rough, and Stowe was seasick much of the time. In spite of her discomfort, she was struck by the changing look of the land as they passed deeper and deeper into the South. She planned "to write an article for the Watchman describing this strange beautiful sea island country more particularly." The seas had calmed by the time they reached the mouth of the St. Johns River, by which they entered Florida. "In all my foreign experience & travels I never saw such a scene," Stowe wrote to her family. "The fog was just up as we came in—the river broad as the Connecticut in its broadest parts. . . . The shores white and dazzling like driven snow & out of this dazzling white rises groves of palmetto pine."[4] When they arrived at their destination the air was fragrant with orange blossoms. Harriet went to her room, "stripped off the woolen garments of my winter captivity put on a thin dress white skirt & white saque & then came & sat down to enjoy the view of the river & the soft summer air." When she broke a sprig from an orange tree and put a blossom in her hair, "feeling quite young & frisky," her rebirth was complete: "I feel as if I had wings—Every thing is so bright & the air is so soft."[5]

Florida in 1867 was a frontier country. Harriet immediately set to work creating a home in the wilderness. "You would hardly recognize this place now," wrote Arthur Foote to his sister less than a month after Stowe's arrival. "In stead of that miserable little whitewashed shanty which was here when you was she has quite a large & handsome house with gables or dormer windows in all directions." The dining room was turned half round and moved, a shed adjoining the house was connected to the main house, a stairway was thrown up and rooms built overhead, and all was lathed and plastered. Stowe was in her element.[6] She had planned to return by April 1, but on April 17 she was still in Florida. "We have been going upward & onward since you left, slowly emerging from barbarism," she wrote her brother Charles. "Hannah & I have extended the dominion of law & order over [the front veranda]. . . . We no longer bolt the door by drawing a sack of sweet potatoes in front of it—but some kind of arrangement has been made so that in a windy night it will hold together."[7] Calvin told James Fields that Harriet had found "the Paradise described in the last chapters of Revelation, banning the alligators."[8]

Almost immediately Harriet began to look for a place to buy.[9] She cast her eye on the east side of the river, in Mandarin, an even prettier spot than the one they were in. "It is a wild uncultured country forest all around the sea on one side & the broad St Johns five miles wide on the other," Harriet wrote.[10] Northerners had begun to discover this paradise, and Stowe meant to secure her piece of it. She wrote a letter in great urgency to Calvin, telling him that she had found a place she could have for $5,000. Prices were rising rapidly as more and more northerners came down and it was imperative that they buy immediately. "I want you to send [Spencer Foote] the 5000 at once—either by selling any of our stock—or borrowing on our house—or placing our Panama stock as collateral in Geo Bissels hands as Mr Perkins may advise. Only send it."[11] With this money, she bought a parcel of land containing a cottage, five large date palms, an olive tree, and an orange grove warranted to produce 75,000 oranges. Barely settled into Oakholm, Stowe had acquired another house and joined the mass hegira of northerners who came to Florida every winter.

Stowe hoped that the Florida air would thaw out her romance, still unwritten. With the exception of the interrupted *Pearl of Orr's Island*, this would have the longest gestation of any of her books. She had a clear view of its subject back in February 1864, at which time she was planning to have it ready for serialization the following year: "It is to be of New England life in the age after the revolutionary war & before rail roads had destroyed the primitive flavor of our life—the rough kindly simple religious life of a Massachusetts town in those days when the weekly mail stage was the only excitement." She continued to Fields, "It is something I have been skimming & saving cream for many years & I have a choice lot of actors ready to come onto the boards."[12] Three years later on the eve of her departure for Florida she told Fields that her story "is all created but writing—& that moves heavily." Attributing her difficulties to the "winter weather and cold," she invoked the similar resistance Henry Ward Beecher was encountering with *Norwood*:

> Henry says to me the other day—My thoughts never run free till the sap begins to rise in the trees—winter months freeze me—He has been tugging along thro the sand hills like me neither of us showing our work to the other—But I am going to take my writing desk & go down to Florida to Freds plantation where we have now a house. . . . & then I doubt not I can write my three hours a day—. . . Cold weather really seems to torpify my brain—I write with a heavy numbness—I have not had yet one *good* spell of writing tho I have had all thro the story abundant clairvoyance & see just how it must be written—but for writing some parts I want *warm* weather & not to be in the state of a "froze and thawed apple."[13]

Harriet, whose slight build gave her little insulation against cold, had long been on record as despising in between weather; successive freezings and thawings did not suit her temperament. And yet there were other problems complicating the writing of this book, and they had to do less with the weather than with the climate of public opinion and the changing role of the novelist.

"I dont satisfy myself," Stowe complained to Fields as she attempted to write her romance, "even tho when I read it aloud to my critics it seems to take hold of them."[14] As recently as the writing of *Agnes of Sorrento* in 1860 the acclaim of her family and friends had been all she needed to steam full speed ahead. Between that time and the present, she had been engaged in journalistic writing and children's stories, all of which she found easy to turn out on cue. Now when she took up her pen as novelist, she did so with the sense that it was a more momentous undertaking than she had previously realized. She revealed some of her awe of the creative process in her response to receiving from Fields the contract for this book, which would eventually be published under the title *Oldtown Folks*.

> My Dear Mr. Fields
>   I have this day received the contract. There are two things in it which I am averse to confirming with my signature
>   First I am so constituted that it is absolutely fatal to me to agree to have any literary work done at certain date.—I *mean* to have this story done by the first of September It would be greatly for my pecuniary interest to get it done before that because I have the offer of eight thousand dollars for the newspaper use of the story I am planning to write after it.
>   But I am bound by the laws of art. Sermons essays lives of distinguished people I can write to order of times & seasons A story *comes*—grows like a flower—sometimes will & sometimes wont—like a pretty woman—when the

spirits will help I can write—When they grin, flout, make faces & otherwise maltreat me I can only wait humbly at their gates watch at the posts of their doors.[15]

This talk of "the laws of art" was a new note in her business correspondence. In the past all she needed was a clear view of her audience and something to tell them. Now Stowe was listening to the voices of "the critic" and "the artist" who were busily creating an aura of cultural holiness around high-culture productions. Like the Victorian parlor, art had become a more complex cultural production.

In her magazine writing Stowe had met the monthly deadlines of her serials, driven by what she had already written and sustained by the audience response it evoked. Once a chapter was printed and into the hands of her readers, there was no going back to change a scene or recast a character. The writing of *Oldtown Folks* was to be different. The story would be entirely framed, written, and revised within Stowe's own head before any of it saw print. She would write the whole with only her imagined audience in front of her. Not even her family heard much of it in advance; while she did read the beginning section to Calvin, he was reduced to pulling proof sheets out of the waste bin to see what she was up to in the rest.[16] In her distance from her audience, the writing of *Oldtown Folks* was a more abstract undertaking than any of her other novels and moved decisively away from the tradition of parlor literature. It was a magnum opus, her claim to being a "classic" writer. "It will answer my purpose better to be read at once in a book," she told Fields, who had urged serial publication. "To spend two years in getting my story before the world before half of my friends will read or judge would not suit my views."[17]

Nor had she ever written with so many sets of male eyes looking over her shoulder, figuratively speaking. While she sat at her writing desk, Henry Ward Beecher was at his writing *Norwood*, for which Robert Bonner had given him a $25,000 advance. In spite of the fact that this was Henry's first novel, Bonner rightly predicted that the name recognition of America's most famous clergyman would carry the sales. As Harriet started to bring her characters onto the boards, Oliver Wendell Holmes's "The Guardian Angel" was being serialized in the *Atlantic*. Having some awareness of the power he held for her and also of the readiness with which she assimilated literary influences, she told Fields, "I do not read Holmes' story—purposely I deny myself because he is so fine & subtle that I might imbibe & absorb influences from his that I am not aware of."[18] Judging from her ready absorption of Hawthorne's style and even his themes, her caution was in order. Her short story "The Mourning Veil," published in the first issue of the *Atlantic*, drew so obviously on Hawthorne's "The Minister's Black Veil" that a writer of a later generation might have been inclined to sue for breach of copyright.[19] But Stowe was writing before the establishment of international copyright, during the end of that period in which piracy was normal and ownership of literary goods was in the hands of the printer. In 1853 she had lost a civil suit against a man who had translated *Uncle Tom's Cabin* into German and then kept all of the proceeds from the books and pamphlets he sold to the German-speaking population of Pennsylvania; the judge in that case had declared that an author's copyright extended only to "a right to multiply copies of his book, and enjoy the profits therefrom, and not in an exclusive right to his conceptions and inventions, which may be termed the essence of his composition."[20] Clearly, however, the professionalization of publishing that was creating classic literary writers was also forging a more individualistic and possessive sense of literary goods, and Stowe's circumspection reflected that. The fact that Holmes, Beecher, and Stowe were all writing New England stories made it all the more imperative that they write in isolation from one another, sharing "only dim outlines of what we are trying to do."[21] The growing importance of originality further distanced literary production from the oral tradition of the parlor fireside.

In this era of uniform editions and prestigious literary magazines and James Fields's assiduous promotion of his stable of authors, it was not so easy for Stowe to find the right voice in which to begin. Somehow it would not do to talk so familiarly with the reader as she had in her previous novels. To do so might undercut the pretensions to literary authority and cultural leadership that the *Atlantic* writers were claiming. In the end Stowe chose a male narrator, "Horace Holyoke," alphabetical successor to Christopher Crowfield. The beginning of *Oldtown Folks* is far less engaging than that of the chatty gossip who tells *The Minister's Wooing* or the ruminative narrator of *The Pearl of Orr's Island*. Horace Holyoke's resolve to be a passive mirror, a mere "observer and reporter," is a step toward the objective, omniscient narrative voice of the late-nineteenth-century novel that Henry James perfected. This checking of Stowe's opinionated, funny, whimsical, narrative voice considerably narrowed the register of expressiveness available to her, and the beginning of *Oldtown Folks* reads as if she is casting about in a tight place.

The difficulties Stowe had with voice were to prove incapacitating for Nathaniel Hawthorne in his late career. Initially prized for his literary rendition of the common and everyday in sketches such as "Little Annie's Ramble" and "A Rill from the Town Pump,"[22] in the 1860s his name was on every one's lips, and his work had achieved a celebrated status in American letters, largely through the efforts of James T. Fields. From his discovery of the manuscript of *The Scarlet Letter* to his clever marketing strategies and constant puffing of Ticknor and Fields's authors to his gathering together of Hawthorne's works in a uniform edition, Fields "created" Hawthorne the classic writer. Richard Brodhead describes the cost to Hawthorne of becoming a literary celebrity:

> [T]he more he accepted his place as classic author, the harder he found it to make his own work. When Hawthorne returned to America in 1860 he built a tower onto his house with a writing-room on its top floor. But after he got himself (in Fields's words) "fitly enshrined" at this Hilda-like elevation, nothing

came out. "I spend two or three hours a day in my sky-parlor, and duly spread
a quire of paper on my desk," he wrote Ticknor in early 1861, "but no very
important result has followed, thus far."[23]

The "sky-parlor" of high culture was a less congenial setting for storytelling
than the more familiar antebellum parlor. Hawthorne died a few years later,
a gloomy and downcast man. He left behind four unfinished romances.

While Hawthorne fell into silence, Stowe struggled to bring to fruition
the novel she thought to be the culmination of her career. She had a different
problem, in a way. Whereas Melville was discovering in Hawthorne a "black-
ness" and a countercultural, "prophetic" voice that said "No! in thunder,"
Stowe had already exercised with unparalleled success the voice of the
prophet. Her evangelical voice had marshalled the prophetic fire and thunder
of the Old Testament prophets and directed it at the institution of slavery.
At a time when "religion" and "culture" were increasingly distinct, she
needed to reinvent herself as a cultural prophet of the ilk that the *Atlantic
Monthly* sent into the homes of all the aspiring consumers of Gilded Age
culture.[24] But if this book were truly to reflect the range and depth of her
career, she needed to encompass not only this secular and consumption-
oriented audience, but also her earlier audience, the orthodox religious folk
who supported her when she was writing for the *New-York Evangelist* and
the *National Era*. Consideration for this original audience led her to decline
serial publication of the novel in the *Atlantic*. The reputation of that journal
was so clearly secular and associated with casual, humorous sendups of
orthodox religion such as Holmes's "One-Hoss Shay" that she thought religiously inclined folk would be prejudiced against the book if it appeared in
the *Atlantic*'s covers. "[T]he Atlantic has on the part of my people—(ie the
orthodoxy) prejudices to encounter which would *predispose* them to look
suspiciously on it more than even the fact of its being by a Beecher," she
told Fields. "Dr Holmes has stung & irritated them by his sharp scathing
irony & keen ridicule—& after all, they are *not* ridiculous."[25]

Another difficulty was that in this age of railroad and steam, the reading
public did not have the same leisure to bestow on books that they had during
the heyday of the triple-decker romance. "[I]f I must be confined to one
volume as seems best now a days," she wrote Fields, "still it will be best to
choose that type & getting up which will enable me to put as much into the
volume as in the two volumes of Nina Gordon [Dred] or Uncle Toms Cabin
To play off my characters as I want to I *want room*—& have so many of them
that I want to show off & I can have any amount of fun with them."[26] The
narrowing of the broad canvases of the great nineteenth-century novels to
what would become by the end of the century a "slice of life" meant, for one
thing, that the range of contrasting classes and social types that gave Stowe's
novels such kinetic energy would be sharply curtailed.

Balanced against this formidable array of problems with voice, audience,
and form was Stowe's elastic and exuberant confidence. She was not stopped
by these difficulties, but, combined with her domestic complications, they

did slow her down. It would take her several more years to write her romance. "Here goes the first of my nameless story," wrote Stowe to Annie Fields in August 1867, "of which I can only say it is as unlike every thing else, as it is like the strange world of folk I took it from."[27] *Oldtown Folks* was a chronicle of Natick, Massachusetts, Calvin's hometown, and much of the material had come from Calvin's stories, just as her prizewinning story "Uncle Lot" had drawn on stories she had heard her father's generation tell. She did not want to be held to writing a strictly accurate account, nor did she "wish to direct attention to real characters." Therefore, in her original title she changed Natick to Shawmut, thinking to take for her title "Old Times in Shawmut" or perhaps "Our Folks & their ways."[28] When she learned that Shawmut was the Indian name for Boston, she changed again to Waban, thinking now to title her story "Chronicles of Waban," or "Old times in Massachusetts by Horace Holyoke," or perhaps "My Grandmother & her times." Stowe wrote to Fields that Gail Hamilton—another *Atlantic* author— was coming to visit in a week, and if he and Annie were to come and visit at the same time they could settle the matter of the title "in a twinkling."[29] Of the 440 pages she had written, she sent about 130 on. "I partake in Mr Fields disappointment that it is not done," she told Annie, "but it is of that class of things that cannot be commanded as my friend Sam Lawson (vide ms) says—'theres things that can be druv & then agin theres things that cant & this is that kind'—its had to be humored—instead of rushing on, I have often turned back & written over with care—that no thing that I wanted to say might be omitted—it has cost me a good deal of labor to elaborate this first part namely to build my theatre and to introduce my actors."[30]

A year later she sent to Fields instead of the last chapter of her romance, in Annie Fields's words, "a chapter of excuses":[31]

> I have a long story to tell you of *what* has prevented my going on with my story which you must see would so occupy all the nerve & brain force I have that I have not been able to write a word, except to my own children. To them in their needs I *must* write *chapters* which would otherwise go into my novel. But if Mr Fields will have patience I want to have time to write it *when* I can write well—& without my head distracted with something else & when the burden of the hottest weather is over I hope that time may come.[32]

It is unlikely that Stowe told the Fieldses the nature of her domestic difficulties, for at the heart of them was Fred's drinking problem. In July 1867, just months after Stowe had returned from Florida, Fred unexpectedly left the plantation and appeared in Hartford. Calvin and Harriet were not home, having gone to Stockbridge, Massachusetts, where Georgiana and Henry Allen settled after their wedding. Stowe not only gained a son-in-law but added to her list of visiting places an exceptionally congenial country town. "Stockbridge is one of those lovely shady wide streeted green turfed quiet country places known only under the stars & stripes," she wrote the twins after her first visit. "The house plain red brick with green blinds but looking cozy & pretty as possible inside—Georgie seems as happy as possible in her miniature little dominion."[33] When Calvin and Harriet learned of Fred's unexpected return, they "were loth to leave," but immediately returned to Hartford, no doubt fearing the worst. In Isabella Beecher Hooker's circumspect words, Fred was "ill" and had "come north to recruit."[34] Subsequent events make it clear that Fred's drinking was again out of control.

After a month or two of what must have been an emotionally taxing time, Calvin and Harriet resolved to institutionalize Fred. He had dried out at the Elmira Water Cure years ago. Now Catharine Beecher made inquiries for him at a mental institution. "God *will* hear my prayer and open some way of escape I know," Harriet wrote to Eliza and Hatty, explaining that Fred "must go into an asylum & be under medical care for a year or so."[35] At an institution in Binghamton, New York, Fred voluntarily submitted to the discipline of a Dr. Butler, who locked him in his room while he went through the initial stages of withdrawal from nicotine and alcohol. His first three months there were "months of prostration gloom & despair." He asked Dr. Butler to tell him "whether he was insane or not." Dr. Butler told him that his head wound had affected his brain, but that months of repose would settle him; he advised Fred's family that they "ought to expect him to recover & encourage him to expect it—but that he must take *time* to do it."[36] In December 1867 Fred wrote to his sisters begging them not to be ashamed of him and to forgive him for his "course of life." "Do not let the feeling of shame bear too heavily on you at the thought of my being here," he told Hatty and Eliza, "it is better far better that I should be here than out in the world disgracing the name you bear it is fare more honorable to have it said that he is here than to have it said that he has gone to the bad."[37]

The following summer Calvin took Fred on an ocean voyage to the Mediterranean to consolidate his cure. Fred's addiction sorely tried Harriet's optimism, but she continued to hope for his recovery. Poignant evidence of her sometimes fragile faith is contained in a letter she wrote to Rebecca Harding Davis in January 1869. She had never met Davis, but she had defended her against an ill-tempered attack in the the *Nation* the previous year. Now she wrote to her about Davis's latest serial, "The Tembroke Legacy," a temperance tale running in *Hearth and Home*. She told her that she had been following the story "with intense and painful interest." Nothing so concisely suggests the power of narrative to affect states of feeling and belief as Stowe's pathetic request to Davis to refrain from making "a whole tragedy of this thing." To demonstrate that a happy ending would not betray her commitment to realism, Stowe told Davis stories of miraculous cures: "Dr Day has saved men whom drink had reduced to maundering idiocy whom he picked up frozen in the streets and they are leading temperance men in Boston." She continued, "When I was at Dr Days I examined piles of papers & letters from redeemed men now holding station & conducting business every where who had been wallowing brutes with this curse." She urged Rebecca Harding Davis, "Frighten us dreadfully but dont quite kill us."[38]

While Fred's difficulties occupied a great deal of Stowe's time between 1867 and 1868, her writing life was complicated by her commitment to supply the Hartford Publishing Company with *Men of Our Times*. She had written the sketches of eminent men for the *Watchman & Reflector* from an assortment of miscellaneous documents she was able to assemble by writing to the principals and ransacking the shelves of Ticknor and Fields. For the rest, she had relied on anecdotes picked up at parties and her own narrative skill. The result, predictably, was less than finished. John Andrew, the much celebrated antislavery governor of Massachusetts, wrote to her protesting that her sketch of him was riddled with errors. When she wrote back requesting he supply her with a list of corrections so that she could get the story right for the book, he unhelpfully replied that there were too many of them to count.[39] Harriet did what she customarily did when she needed documentation: she called on her family for help. This time she reached down into the next generation for her literary support, enlisting her nephew, Frederick Perkins. Stowe planned to get the work out of the way in two weeks. She apologized to Fields for stopping her story, explaining, "one cant always tell in driving such horses as we drive *where* they are going to bring us."[40] "*My own book* instead of cooling boils & bubbles daily & nightly and I am pushing and spurring like fury to get to it I work like a dray horse—& I'l *never* get in such a scrape again—It isn't my business to *make* up books but to make them—I have lots to say."[41] Even with Fred Perkins's help, Stowe was forced to stop work on *Oldtown Folks* in October 1867 and devote the next several months to the lives of eminent men.

Perhaps reasoning that as long as Stowe was out of the storytelling trim and into another mode, she might as well set herself to the task of revising the *Chimney-Corner* papers that had been awaiting her attention for a year, Fields urged this task upon her. "Behold the results of your insistance," Stowe wrote to him around Thanksgiving. "I have looked over & prepared this. To it I should add by way of enlarging the book the New Years Story in the Atlantic which has the same general drift & mood." She assured him that she was "steaming away on the obstacle that stands between me & my story which I long to be at," adding, "Please remind your sovereign of her promise to get me some taking anecdotes [about Governor Andrew]."[42] Stowe often enlisted Annie Fields in her literary labors, and Annie complied out of friendship to her and loyalty to her husband's publishing house.

In December Stowe was still checking facts and writing to her subjects to request further documentation. When she finished *Men of Our Times* in early 1868, she was brought up short by the realization that she had spent many months on a project that she really didn't give a fig for. She had undertaken it for the money, but at that, as she calculated her time, it was rather poor pay. Immediately upon the heels of the eminent men came a proposal from the same publishing house that she write a series of sketches of eminent women, in collaboration with Charles Beecher and the noted biographer and popular writer, James Parton (who was married to Harriet's former pupil,

Fanny Fern). Mr. Betts of the Hartford Publishing Company asked the authors to name their terms, and Stowe took this offer under advisement. After mulling the matter over, she wrote to James Parton a letter extraordinary in its clearheaded view of authors' interests and exhibiting an incipient trade-union consciousness. After telling Parton she felt that they ought to reach a "common understanding" as to price, she continued,

I live in a great centre where I see immense fortunes being daily & constantly made *out of us*, in which *we* have scarcely any share. There are four or five houses here with their agents who choose some subject, of deep common interest—hire well known authors who ask them only ordinary magazine prices for their work & then *make* for themselves a clear profit of fifty or a hundred thousand dollars. The first work of the kind whose career I noticed was a very inferior one got up by a non descript woman called the "Nurse & Spy"—It sold two hundred thousand copies—it traded on the sympathies of the war The next was women of the war—got up as I think without payment by the contributions of friends arranged & corrected by an editor—I know I wrote one sketch without out money or price.—This has had a great sale also My husbands book on the Bible was now bargained by these adventurers—He was as literary men generally are timid & modest & unfit to make a bargain—They have sold in six months 25000 copies—Made 40,000 dollars & he has made about 3000—

They also engaged me to prepare for them sketches of "Men of the Times"—& I assented to the same bargain of 12 pr cents on a copy without much reflection—I had certain sketches which I had prepared for newspapers and I thought carelessly that it was all they were worth.

When however I come now to see what the revising & getting up of this work has cost me I take a widely different view of it & of what I ought to have for my share—Meanwhile I have not the smallest doubt that my assenting to these terms and my husbands doing the same has led Henry Wilson to let them have a book on the same understanding & thus the injustice grows But I have made a stand—Mr Stowe & I have told them that we will not allow them another work without more equal division Mr Stowes second volume on the Old Testament he will make altogether another arrangement for—When this Betts wrote to me to furnish a sketch of Queen Victoria & Mrs Fremont—I said that I could not do it under six hundred dollars—Am I extravagant Let us consider that this person skims the cream off the leading American writers & sells it—& when he has paid us magazine prices he has copy right clear of our ideas & style &c.

Stowe hoped to enlist Parton in a collaboration much more significant than the one proposed by the Hartford Publishing House: "I wish that somehow, we writers could form a sort of guild of mutual protection."[43]

James Parton told her she was "partly right and partly wrong." Unless she knew for a fact that the publishers had made $40,000 on Calvin's book, he thought this was highly unlikely. He pointed out that their big sales were made possible only through the vast amount of money that agents put into promotion, and all of these costs had to be reckoned before their profits could be calculated. Calvin had made a bad bargain, he admitted, a much worse bargain than she had made for her book because his material was new and also it could have been predicted that a book on the Bible would have a smaller sale than a work of entertainment like *Men of Our Times*. Therefore he should have had fifty cents, or at least thirty, on every copy, whereas her bargain was closer to the fifteen cents per copy that he thought she should have had. He countered her proposal for an author's guild with the classic American response to trade unionism: laissez-faire individualism:

> No "Guild," I fear, is possible, because no two authors have, or can ever have, the same rank or value. You, standing at the head of literature, should never put pen to paper under $500: nor sell an article outright for less than $1000. Those people *must* have had you, either as writer, or subject, or both. An article by Mrs. Stowe on Queen Victoria, written in part from original material, would be well worth $1000 to them. They seem good people: they have got hold of a good idea, and they will make money.

The $1,000 valuation he put on Stowe's work compared to $1,250 that he had just secured for a single article. He described this potboiler as "Horrid work," but necessary if he were to write his heart's desire, a life of Voltaire. "I am trying desperately to get a little money ahead before plunging into that wide, wide sea of material."[44]

While it was too bad that the proposal to write on eminent women had not come before she had written on eminent men, Stowe made the sensible decision not to supply these additional sketches. This kept the decks clear for her story but it did not entirely solve her difficulties. The economics of the "classic" story favored those who were independently wealthy and did not rely on a steady income from their writing. No doubt the uncertainties she faced in writing her romance made distractions more tempting, but her need for ready cash built up to momentous proportions while she delayed and revised her magnum opus. She interrupted her story several times to supply the *Atlantic* with material that would yield immediate cash. These included a tribute to the Duchess of Sutherland and a domestic piece on the doings and sayings of toddlers entitled "Little Captain Trott." Probably referring to this last piece, Stowe wrote to Fields, "If it suits you you can have it for the usual price you have paid for my monthly articles—I write it just now because I want a little of the ready."[45] In the meantime she was gathering materials for an article on Planchette, a ouija board that was transforming the parlor into a spiritualist séance. She told Fields that her materials for the Planchette article were "really very extraordinary" but that she didn't want to write it while she was "driving so hard upon my book."[46] She threw herself on James Fields's mercies in a letter marked "Private":

> I am going in heart and soul on my story & I think doing well on it but the fact is I am constantly tempted to swerve aside for it for the need of a hundred or two dollars here & there that I could make by stopping to write this or that article—I want therefor to get together all that is fairly mine from all sources & wish you would see if any thing is due me on your account as I have at this moment an especial pressure & it worries me Then think how quickly I could

earn a thousand dollars if I were not daring & ought not to bring myself in this—

The thing has been an awful tax & labor for I have tried to do it well—I say also to you confidentially that it has seemed as if every private care that could hinder me as woman & mother has been crowded into just this year that I have had this to do.

Probably to encourage Fields to add an advance to what was due her, Stowe told him she was "in sight of the end" and predicted that *Oldtown Folks* would do twice as well as *Norwood*, which had sold 25,000 copies after appearing in the *Ledger*. "But mean while see if there is nt some money that I can have to keep matters strait at home."[47] No doubt Fred's residential treatment under Dr. Butler set her back considerably.

To all of her domestic and professional difficulties must be added the ones of her own making. By purchasing a house in Florida Stowe secured a piece of paradise at the cost of a semiannual convulsion. "Fold we tents like Arabs," Stowe joked to James Fields, but the movement of the Stowe household to Florida bore a closer resemblance to Grant's army marching to Vicksburg. Provisions, clothing, and all of the materials Harriet would need for her writing and professional correspondence had to be selected and prepared to ship via steamer. To these were added a bushel of books to content the omnivorous Calvin. The large Hartford house had to be prepared for the winter, plants dug up and packed, carpets shipped south. Setting up at Mandarin meant marshalling a whole host of domestic equipment and required heroic economies. They broke down chairs, shipped them to Mandarin, and reglued them upon arrival. Harriet was the general in charge of this campaign, enlisting servants to accompany them and issuing directives to Hatty and Eliza: "I wish to take our plaited teapot sugar & creamer and little tea-kettle our knives & forks & spoons. . . . I want the little stove in the spare room boxed up & sent south with the smallest pair of and irons."[48] When all the dogs, people, and goods were accounted for and aimed in the right direction, the Stowe household boarded either a steamer or a train, along with a crush of other sunshine seekers. On the train to Savannah they opened their lunches of fruit, crackers, and canned tongue and helped themselves to hot coffee and fried chicken hawked in the aisles at regular intervals by "old mammies."[49] "[A]ll the north seemed moving down on the South as usual," Stowe wrote from the sleeping cars to Jacksonville, "a great deal of genteel well dressed appearing folk They say all the hotels are overflowing & full."[50]

Harriet was too much of a Beecher to settle in paradise without first improving it. She conceived a plan to establish on the banks of the St. Johns River a New England mission. Her fullest statement of this project occurs in a letter to her brother Charles, whom she tried to enlist in her Reconstruction army of missionaries. After urging him to buy the property next to theirs in Mandarin, she continued,

I am now in correspondence with the Bishop of Florida, with a view to establishing a line of churches along the St. John's River, and if I settle at Mandarin, it will be one of my stations. Will you consent to enter the Episcopal Church and be our clergyman? You are just the man we want. If my tasks and feelings did not incline me toward the Church, I should still choose it as the best system for training immature minds such as those of our negroes. The system was composed with reference to the wants of the laboring class of England, at a time when they were as ignorant as our negroes now are.

I long to be at this work, and cannot think of it without my heart burning within me. Still I leave all with my God, and only hope He will open the way for me to do all that I want to for this poor people.[51]

Together they would carry Lyman Beecher's New England mission into the South, planting schools and churches as they went. "I wish you could know of the sorrow & suffering I see—among people that one cannot help pitying," Harriet wrote en route to Florida, "Yet a brighter day is breaking both for *white* & black."[52] When Charles declined her invitation to join the Episcopal Church, Harriet enlisted her husband. "Papa has consented to go south with me this winter and act as Missionary in our parish," she wrote in 1869 to Eliza and Hatty, whom she also tried to recruit. "If you could help teach these poor neglected children you would be making an offering to the Savior in whose church you have been received."[53] Harriet became, in Marie Caskey's words, "a self-appointed home missionary to Mandarin and its vicinity."[54] Harriet and Calvin held Sunday services in their parlor and dining room, and in spite of the fact that the locals were "jealous that we want to make Episcopalians of them," the rooms were full.[55] Harriet set about getting a subscription for a church that would be "free to religious services of all denominations," meanwhile musing that "a good zealous Episcopal missionary" might easily draw into union members of both the Roman Catholic and the Methodist Episcopal churches.[56]

Harriet still believed in education as the key to social change; now it represented an important element in Reconstruction. In 1866 she had urged Henry Ward Beecher to enlist Plymouth Church in the support of free, integrated schools in the South.[57] One of her first steps upon arrival in Florida in 1867 was to visit the teachers of the black school in Jacksonville, four of whom lived together with a married couple "in a primitive white washed building with next to no furniture."[58] In the North she began interviewing potential teachers, including an Alice Dike, who hoped to be able to join Stowe in Florida so she could "form an intelligent and comprehensive judgment of the work of education at the South."[59] When the Freedman's Bureau began to build a school within sight of her house, Harriet wrote to Annie Fields, who was moving into a volunteer career in charity work, requesting "help from your northern education funds to sustain a teacher."[60] She wrote as well to William Lloyd Garrison to request $300 from the Anti-Slavery Society, telling him that "with it, I can not only keep up a school in my own district, where there are now, forty colored children without any means of instruction—but can also keep up a school in a negro settlement four miles off, where there are thirty families settled on Government land."[61] To Henry Ward Beecher she wrote in the rhetoric of the 1840s,

"The Jesuits said nothing but they half undid the reformation by schools—we can do the same for good: They have free schools in Wilmington & Richmond—now—let us have them every where."[62]

Like her father, she believed that New England was the blueprint for the nation—"the seed-bed of democracy," as she expressed it in *Oldtown Folks*—and her Florida mission depended upon founding a New England colony there. On board a steamer en route to Florida she took paper and pen and wrote to a prospective buyer of the lot next to hers, "we are very anxious for New England men to come among us. Ours is a sort of colony there are six or eight young men who have come in and are trying experiments in agriculture with promising success but we hail every accession from the North."[63] Those most susceptible to recruiting were family members. Her nephew, Christopher Spencer Foote, took up land adjacent to hers; Charles Beecher bought a lot on the Gulf Coast.[64]

In spite of these time-consuming distractions, Stowe managed to write *Oldtown Folks*, which would be published in 1869. The resistance she experienced in writing it was overcome by the fact that she still had a political message to parlay. Ostensibly a novel of post–Revolutionary War Massachusetts, *Oldtown Folks* was directly influenced by Reconstruction politics. In it she criticized northern-style capitalism, now rampant, and began to retreat into the past. Like so many of her novels, it had a radical, millennial vision held in check by conservative political impulses.

The beginning of *Oldtown Folks* reads like a series of digressions, as if Stowe the storyteller is in a frame of mind like that of Sam Lawson, the village do-nothing of Oldtown, who, when he is supposed to be repairing a clock, "would roost over it in endless incubation, telling stories."[65] In Chapter 5 she drew on a piece she had written years ago for the *Lady's Book* , a description of a New England Sunday meeting. While this rendition of local eccentrics is not without interest, as a description of the funeral of Horace Holyoke's father it is inappropriate—unless the reader is to believe that Horace's grief was easily displaced by his bemused appraisal of fellow townsfolk. This points toward Stowe's largest miscalculation: putting the story in Horace Holyoke's mouth. He is a colorless character given to feckless exclamations such as "Poor dear souls all of us!" and "Such is life!" (OTF, 2:130) Not until Chapter 7, in which Stowe drops into her own voice and relates the history of Tina and Harry, two orphans who fall under the care of Old Crab Smith and Miss Asphyxia, does Stowe's story fully engage the reader. These chapters also reveal the development of her thinking under the pressure of Reconstruction politics.

When Stowe was in the first flush of optimism following the conclusion of the war, she wrote "A Family Talk on Reconstruction" for one of her papers in *The Chimney-Corner*. In it she created as a foil to the optimistic views of her spokesman, Christopher Crowfield, the darker predictions of one Theophilus Thoro. Theophilus foresees Black Codes, turbulent uprisings of the Irish, and a "headlong chase after *money*" in the North. He rejects

Crowfield's rosy picture of a steadily democratizing South in favor of a more Hobbesian view of human nature: "The desire to monopolize and dominate is the most rooted form of human selfishness; it is the hydra with many heads, and, cut off in one place, it puts out another" (HP, 284). By the time she wrote *Oldtown Folks* Stowe had adopted a more darkly colored picture of the future. The work ethic, a cornerstone of the New England women of "faculty" in *The Minister's Wooing*, is taken to its extreme by Miss Asphyxia, whom Stowe repeatedly compares to locomotive engines and industrial machinery: "As related to her fellow-creatures, she was neither passionate nor cruel. We have before described her as a working machine, forever wound up to high-pressure working-point; and this being her nature, she trod down and crushed whatever stood in the way of her work, with as little compunction as if she had been a steam-engine or a powerloom" (OTF, 1:121). Upon assuming the care of the orphan, Tina, Miss Asphyxia's first act is to regard her abundant, curly hair as an affront: "Apparently she was somewhat puzzled, and rather scandalized, that Nature should evidently have expended so much in a merely ornamental way on an article which ought to have been made simply for service" (OTF, 1:113). She cuts off the child's curls and sets her to stints of sewing, regarding her "exactly as she did her broom and her rolling-pin and her spinning-wheel,—as an implement or instrument which she was to fashion for her uses" (OTF, 1:139). Stowe's prophetic eye was now trained on what she called the "golden calf" before which New England had "fallen down and worshipped" (OTF, 1:126): efficiency. It was northern industrial efficiency, in large part, that had won the war, and efficiency was to be the byword of Frederick Winslow Taylor, the father of "scientific management" who devised ways to screw industrial productivity to greater and greater heights. By setting her story in the late eighteenth century Stowe blunted the political force of her remarks, but there is no mistaking the fact that she wanted her readers to draw analogies between black slavery and white slavery. When Tina's brother Harry, under the watchful eye of Old Crab Smith, is told he cannot visit his sister, "Something stirred within him, such as makes slavery bitter" (OTF, 1:129). Tina and Harry run away from their cruel taskmasters as if they are fugitive slaves.

From this point on, *Oldtown Folks* might be read as a search for the perfect form of family or human community. After the hell of Miss Asphyxia and Crab Smith, Tina and Harry take to the forest, where they encounter a seemingly idyllic Indian camp. Here the children are welcomed and fed and sheltered. But Stowe quickly reveals this idyll to be an illusion when the Indian husband returns the next morning, beats his wife, and scatters the puppies and children. Tina and Harry move on to Oldtown, where they are taken in by the kindly Deacon Badger and Miss Mehitable. Much of the rest of Stowe's story is taken up with describing manners and mores in Oldtown, but the real millennial community of her story lies elsewhere. When the children come of a certain age they are sent to be educated at a celebrated academy in Cloudland, under the care of Miss Mehitable's brother, Jonathan

Rossiter. Cloudland is clearly the mountain town of Litchfield and Rossiter is Harriet's favorite teacher at the Litchfield Female Academy, John Pierce Brace. In short, Stowe found the millennial community in the Litchfield of her youth. While she was never as bitter and dark about the industrial future as Mark Twain would be in *A Connecticut Yankee in King Arthur's Court*, like Twain she drew back from the corruption and greed and power-mongering of Reconstruction America and retreated to the past.

Like *Dred*, the only other novel that Stowe had published in book form without previous serialization, *Oldtown Folks* totters on and on long past the time it should have been ended. It is as if Stowe needed the check of an actual audience to shape her story. "Dont chop it off like a log, but let it taper out gracefully like a tree," Henry Ward Beecher advised her, and she determined that she would conscientiously abide by the advice of her brother, suddenly elevated to literary heights.[66] She wrote regularly to James Fields to allay his impatience. "I am almost through but am stopped a little in revising—trying to write over & satisfy myself better in a certain spot where I have not pleased myself as yet—as soon as I get past this place I have a cartload prepared (so to speak)." Stowe clapped onto her story a stock romantic plot, telling Fields, "I have a denoument & a villain and a tragedy but shall end well at last—You shall see."[67] Many of the scenes and characters in *Oldtown Folks* are, in Henry May's words, "warmed over from previous use."[68] It is almost as if she is producing her familiar characters and scenes in a musical revue. Her villain is the stock Byronic seducer who reads French novels and leads girls astray, and like Aaron Burr of *The Minister's Wooing* he is the grandson of Jonathan Edwards gone to seed. This Ellery Davenport is "deep, artful, and to be unmasked" (OTF, 2:183). He marries Tina, makes her unhappy in unspecified ways, and dies in a duel. Readers who are still awake will learn that Tina then marries the feckless narrator, Horace Holyoke.

Of course, plot summaries do little justice to the kind of writing in which Stowe was engaged. "[W]ill foolish people here & there persist in judging it as a novel?—& talk about *plot* etc. etc.," wrote Maria Weston Chapman to Stowe. "They themselves are marplots,—doing what they can to misrepresent one of the most charming Idylls (or succession of them) that was ever said or sung."[69] But even as a New England idyll, *Oldtown Folks* is labored. Lydia Maria Child found it tedious and "liked it less than anything she ever wrote."[70] Stowe had a lighter touch in *The Minister's Wooing* when she wasn't so self-consciously set on preserving New England as a museum piece. Sam Lawson is a wonderful creation, but Stowe overworks his "Lordy massy's" as she did the dark predictions of her black prophet in *Dred*. Lawson is most effective when played off against his mate, Hepsy, "a gnarly, compact, efficient little pepper-box of a woman" who contrives to do her work and Sam's too while he is out gossiping and attending to other people's business. Stowe comments,

This might do very well; but when Sam, who believed with all his heart in the modern doctrines of woman's rights so far as to have no sort of objection to Hepsy's sawing wood or hoeing potatoes if she chose, would make the small degree of decency and prosperity the family had attained by these means as a text on which to preach resignation, cheerfulness, and submission, then Hepsy's last cobweb of patience gave out, and she often became, for the moment, really dangerous, so that Sam would be obliged to plunge hastily out of doors to avoid a strictly personal encounter. (OTF, 1:37)

This beautifully sustained sentence draws out the subordinate clauses of eighteenth-century prose stylists to intensify the western understatement of her final phrase, "a strictly personal encounter." While there is some very good writing and good dialect in *Oldtown Folks*, Stowe's distance from her audience dulled her ear and her awareness of how far she could stretch the reader's tolerance. "It is clear," Henry May writes, "that Mrs. Stowe intended this book, for which she ransacked so ruthlessly her own and her husband's memories and her own earlier works, to be a masterpiece."[71] If a "masterpiece," like a "classic," is one of those intellectually uplifting but ponderous books that one *should* read, in company with the other impressive books one keeps prominently displayed on the bookshelf, then she succeeded. But as a whole it lacked the energy and life of her best work.

Oldtown Folks was published on May 15, 1869. By May 6 Stowe was en route to Canada to establish British copyright, a precaution she insisted upon to Fields. "It is not for profit but protection I say it. It is of the last importance that all the publishing houses in England shall *not* have the power to print *garbled copies*."[72] In Montreal she and Calvin stayed on Notre Dame Street in a room with a fire, where she caught a cold. After three days they started back to Hartford by way of Boston and Andover.[73] Upon arriving home she read her mail, which included a dismissive review of *Oldtown Folks* in the *Nation*, a weekly newspaper that grew up after the Civil War under the editorship of E. L. Godkin. The *Nation*, as Stowe had told Rebecca Harding Davis after its attack on Davis's *Waiting for the Verdict*, had "no sympathy with any deep & high moral movement."[74] It had already begun carrying in its pages articles on the decline of New England, and now it took the publication of *Oldtown Folks* to be the last nail in the coffin of this once vital region. The reviewer offered the opinion that "it is some years since our New Englanders have even been a little tedious," with their "Puritan parson, and the Puritan deacon, and the Puritan tithing-man; and the Puritan Thanksgiving, and 'Lection cake, and May Training; and the Puritan 'revivals,' and 'doctrines,' and donation parties."[75] Stowe was as outraged as she had been when the *Edinburgh Review* made snide comments about *Dred*. She wrote to Annie Fields, "The Nation has come out with a wild mad *rave* about Old Town folks the general drift of which is that there is nothing in it—not a character & never was in any thing I ever wrote & that they are tired & sick of it & vote it a bore—There is criticism for you!"[76]

This was not the only review that indicated that a change was in the air so far as Stowe's literary reputation was concerned. From the West came Bret Harte's review in the *Overland Monthly*, declaring that "Mrs. Stowe's treatment of 'Oldtown Folks' is even more provincial than her subject." His objection was not to the "much-used stock of New England provincials" but to Stowe's producing them "with the provincial satisfaction of a village gossip recalling village worthies." When Harte's *The Luck of Roaring Camp, and Other Stories* was published the following year, they delighted Stowe's "unsanctified hankering for 'slang,'" but Harte did not recognize in Stowe a fellow wordsmith and dialectician.[77] His review of *Oldtown Folks* concluded by suggesting that it was time for Stowe and all she had stood for to exit the scene. He looked forward to "that time [when] we shall lose, for obvious reasons, the 'negro bondman,' whom Mrs. Stowe seems to find as difficult to keep out of her writing as 'Mr. Dick' did the head of Charles I from his. And in this view of the case it behooves Mrs. Stowe to consider whether we may not lose her with the rest."[78]

Sensitive to public opinion and her own reputation, Stowe knew how to fight back. She spurred her publishers to greater and greater heights of promotion, suggesting to them likely venues for advertisements, such as the *Banner of Light*, a spiritualist publication. Referring to the "visions" that arose unbidden to her narrator, Horace Holyoke, Stowe explained to Osgood, "It is calculated that there are between *four & five million* of *spiritualists* in this country—and I want to get their ear—Purposely I inserted that element into the story—not only because it actually *was* there, but because I wanted to get the ear & attention of so many who are of that way of thinking and feeling."[79] In another note she urged Osgood that the *Banner of Light* "commands an immense circulation & influence and a notice of the 'spiritualistic features' of the book in it would ensure a sale of many copies." She pointed out that they carried ads for Elizabeth Stuart Phelps runaway best-seller, *The Gates Ajar*, a book that promised more than a peep into the world beyond.[80]

Stowe attempted to do single-handedly what Hawthorne had a whole network of college friends, editors, and literary associates to do: keep her fame alive. It is not coincidental that her reputation began to falter in the year that James Fields fell into the depression that would lead to his retirement from Fields, Osgood & Co. in 1870 and from the *Atlantic* in 1871. His energies had been divided since 1864 when he undertook, in addition to his other duties, the editorship of the *North American Review*. "Can he steer such a flotilla?," Stowe had asked Annie Fields in disbelief when she heard of this new responsibility. The answer, apparently, was no, for Fields withdrew from his compulsive overwork into a mysterious illness that Annie referred to in elliptical diary entries about her "silent and sad" Jamie. Stowe corresponded increasingly with Fields's partner, whom she addressed as "Mr. Osgood" in curt, businesslike notes that contain none of the whimsy of her letters to James Fields. She was losing her most influential and enthusiastic supporter.[81]

Stowe was relentless in promoting her work. "Have you noticed Lowes Publishers Circular this month," she asked Osgood. "It contains some extracts from the Examiner on Old Town folks that I think you could use with advantage here."[82] She wrote Fields that Natick, Massachusetts, planned a celebration of its history and "all the old traditions are to be hawked up & Mr Stowe is to go & make a speech & all the places celebrated in Old Town folkes are to be visited & you and Annie must not fail to be there." Like *Oldtown Folks,* her new series of Sam Lawson stories, eventually published under the title *Oldtown Fireside Stories,* exploited the lucrative market for New England nostalgia. Stowe predicted that the latter, appropriately got up and illustrated, "will make a book that will sell immensely on the cars and every where & combined with authentic New England traditions will make quite a rush—Moreover it will keep 'Old Town folks' afloat & going."[83] She suggested he publish an illustrated edition of *Oldtown Folks* to capitalize on the historical interest it had aroused. This idea led to another, fueled by her regular trips to the South: Fields should "get up a new illustrated Edition of Uncle Tom to be sold by agents for the southern market." She laid out the cash advantages of this plan:

In this consider It was for years a forbidden book here. Many have heard of but never seen it. A whole generation of reading & writing colored people have come up and I think the pictorial edition now might be sold to thousands of colored families—Think of that too—

It would however need to be an *agency* book. Books to do any thing here in these southern states must be sold by agents. The population is sparse and they are engrossed in worldly cares and need to be put up to read—Yet *there is money* on hand even down to the colored families and an attractive book would have a history You own the illustrations of Uncle Tom—-Why not try it?[84]

Her indomitable energies and the manifest strengths of *Oldtown Folks* carried the day. By August the book had sold 25,000 copies in the face of the carping reviews—a fact that in itself suggests the growing gap between what the public was reading and what the critics were recommending.[85]

In order to protect her reputation, Stowe also went on the counterattack. She responded to the review in the *Nation* with a long letter to editor E. L. Godkin in which she instructed his reviewers on "literary good breeding." "Rudeness & heedless discourtesy, an assumption of supercillious contempt I think are just as much out of place in literary criticism as in a private parlor," she told him.[86] Godkin, who had a family connection to Stowe by virtue of having married a Foote, occasionally visited at her home. He had dropped her a note of apology as soon as the review appeared, explaining that he had not seen it until it was too late. Stowe accepted his apology with the comment, "Accidents will happen you know in the best regulated fam[ilie]s,"[87] but the dismissive tone of the review rankled and stirred up old resentments she had against the *Nation* for its abuse of Rebecca Harding

Davis and Anna Dickinson. It was becoming clear that family connections were insufficient protection against the assault on women writers that issued from high culture journals.

The *Nation* was a hard case, for it was founded on many of the Reconstruction principles that Stowe supported, including the elevation of the Negro, popular education, democratic principles, and the equality of "the laboring class at the South." It was commonly viewed as having inherited the mantle of the *Liberator,* a perception reinforced by the fact that in its employ was William Garrison's son, Wendell Phillips Garrison. While the *Nation* also supported political rights for women, its democratic principles did not embrace literary women or women who presumed to speak for themselves. Like many of the prestigious journals emerging in post–Civil War America, the *Nation* was an institution of male literary power. The first issue contained no articles by women, prompting Henry Clapp of the *Saturday Press*, whose contributors included Harriet Prescott and Mary S. Gove Nichols of water-cure fame, to suggest that "for this and other reasons its name be changed to the Stag-Nation."[88] In fact, the *Nation* took the lead in the backlash against women's cultural power.

Stowe had first experienced its particular combination of critical expertise, political savvy, and condescension toward women in its review of *The Chimney-Corner*, in which the reviewer had made it clear that he considered Stowe's domestic feminism tiresome. "She discusses the woman question at length and under various aspects, but by whatever road she travels she reaches in the end one constant bourne. The delights of a well-kept house, the lively comfort of seeing one's face reflected in a series of well-scoured pans—this or something essentially like this forms the endless refrain of her song." While the reviewer professed to have a higher view of woman's intellectual capacities than Mrs. Stowe, behind his remarks stalked a reaction to the decades-long dominance of women in the parlor and the press, a reaction that hints of misogyny:

> One may be permitted, after studying life in this chimney corner, to turn, not without a feeling of relief, to Thoreau's counter-irritant Walden housekeeping, and sympathize with him in his rejection of the foot-mat because it would waste precious time to shake it; to pick up Montaigne and perhaps find his easy contempt for woman healthier than the feeling which enthrones her as the goddess of the kitchen and the sitting room, the highly cultivated nymph of the innocent greenhouse.[89]

Combining praise for Thoreau with "easy contempt for women," the "Stag-Nation" led the way toward the establishment of the male literary canon.

The *Nation's* power came not from its circulation, which never reached more than 12,000 in its first fifty years, but from the frequency with which it was quoted as a cultural authority.[90] Between 1830 and 1860, by which time male ministers had lost their cultural authority, the power to shape public opinion had passed to the periodical press, in which women writers had a significant voice; now the new ministers of culture were taking back the power. At a time when women lacked the vote, the *Nation* insisted that the important issues of Reconstruction should be decided in the political arena and literary women should give up their pulpits, pens, and podiums. The *Nation's* method was to attack the literary excellence of women writers in the name of "art." Stowe complained to Godkin that women writers, and especially those who wrote on domestic subjects, came in for a species of broadax criticism in the pages of the *Nation.*[91] She had in mind not only its negative reviews of *The Chimney-Corner* and *Oldtown Folks*, but its even more savage attacks on Rebecca Harding Davis and Anna Dickinson.

Anna Dickinson, the famous nineteen-year-old orator who held audiences spellbound, had so irrevocably broken down the barriers to women's public speaking that even Harriet Beecher Stowe would go on the lecture circuit in 1872. Educated only until age fourteen, when she went to work to support her fatherless family, Anna Dickinson was known for her fearless honesty and flaming eloquence. Dismissed from a well-paying job at the United States Mint for publicly calling General McClellan a traitor, she won public acclaim for her speeches on behalf of civil rights for blacks and women. In 1868 she published her first novel, *What Answer?* This fictional defense of interracial marriage showed Dickinson to be as fearless in print as she was on the podium.

Dickinson's *What Answer?* had been published amid loud acclaim from, among others, Lydia Maria Child and Harriet Beecher Stowe. Stowe was drawn into Anna Dickinson's orbit through her sister Isabella, who described her novel as "the most emphatic protest against the spirit of caste that has appeared in American literature." Having read *What Answer?* in one absorbed sitting the night before Dickinson had come to visit Isabella, Harriet, at Isabella's urging, dropped Dickinson a note of encouragement. Stowe, now fifty-seven, in effect passed on the mantle of reform to this nineteen-year-old prodigy. Sending greetings from her "grandmother in the good old cause," Stowe bade Anna be of good cheer and not mind what the papers might say of her novel. Not willing to leave the latter entirely to chance, Stowe also enclosed a laudatory paragraph about *What Answer?* that she had sent to the *Hartford Courant*. In it she called Dickinson's novel "a brave, noble book."[92] In contrast to her male-identified writing for the *Atlantic*, Stowe was gravitating toward a women's network.

The *Nation* reviewer perceived in the acclaim of Stowe and Child for *What Answer?* a cabal of women. He was right, in that Stowe and other women writers were beginning to recognize the necessity of clubbing together in order to counter the clubbiness of literary men. In this year, 1868, Jane Cunningham Croly founded the Sorosis Club in response to the exclusion of women from a reception for Charles Dickens by the New York Press Club. At this same time Julia Ward Howe and other Boston women created the New England Women's Club.[93] Ignoring the fact that male reviewers regularly puffed male writers, the *Nation* complained that "Mrs.

H. B. Stowe comes promptly to the front, and allows her name to be printed in large characters in the publishers' advertisements as authority for the assertion that Miss Dickinson's novel is 'a brave, noble book.'" Observing that "[t]his is in no sense the language of criticism," the *Nation* reviewer patronized Stowe while elevating "the critic" to a position above the vox populi. "And yet we scarcely find it in our heart to condemn Mrs. Stowe. It is just these vague random utterances and all this counterfeit criticism that make the rational critic the more confident of his own duties." He cooly observed that "the mere fact that many people habitually say a certain thing is not always conclusive proof of its entire or even of its partial falsity." Not always, he smugly implied, but usually.[94]

The *Nation* prided itself on its professional approach to book reviewing. Instead of assigning one reviewer the task of commenting on the whole range of literary, scientific, and historical publications, the *Nation* instituted what was then the new practice of "matching" reviewers to books.[95] Because its staff was all male, this practice reached a predictable impasse when it came to the fiction of women writers. It addressed this deficiency by heaping hostility, vitriol, and contempt on the writings of women. In its attack on Anna Dickinson it included, by implication, Rebecca Harding Davis, Lydia Maria Child, and Harriet Beecher Stowe who, it claimed, thought that all that was necessary to write a good novel was to have a good cause. The work of women was labeled "earnest," "sentimental," "didactic," and bad art. These remarks appeared in a review that was ostensibly on Rebecca Harding Davis's novel, *Dallas Galbraith* (Philadelphia: J. B. Lippincott, 1868), and the reviewer admitted that he had not yet read Dickinson's novel. This did not stop him from dismissing it. It was a woman's book and he knew the type. "When the best thing that can be said of a novel is that it is brave or noble or honest or earnest, you may be sure that although it may be, as Mrs. Stowe pronounces Miss Dickinson's tale, a very good deed, it is a very bad book." He extended this highly refined species of criticism to Rebecca Harding Davis's work:

> Mrs. Davis's stories are habitually spoken of as "earnest" works, and it is not hard to detect in reading them a constant effort to deserve the epithet. Their pretensions are something very different from those of the simple novel of entertainment, of character, and of incident. The writer takes life desperately hard and looks upon the world with a sentimental—we may even say, a tearful—eye. The other novel—the objective novel, as we may call it, for convenience—appeals to the reader's sense of beauty, his idea of form and proportion, his humanity, in the broadest sense. Mrs. Davis's tales and those of her school appeal, we may say—to the conscience, to the sense of right and wrong, to the instincts of charity and patronage.

Urging Davis to "abjure her ultra-sentimentalism" and her "moralism," he suggests she study "the objective novel" in the works of Alexandre Dumas. Apparently he found stories of three male musketeers more interesting than the stories of social and political protest that engaged Davis's pen. Admitting that "life is a very serious business," he priggishly countered, "Art, too, is a very serious business."[96] When Elizabeth Stuart Phelps published *Hedged In*, her novel about a fallen woman, the *Nation* used the occasion to bemoan the "uncontrolled tendency" of "American authoresses" and "songsters" "to dwell upon what is morbid and painful in life."[97]

The agenda of the New Criticism that would dominate twentieth-century academic reading tastes was hammered out in such reviews. The reviewer of Davis's *Dallas Galbraith* was none other than Henry James, then in his early twenties.[98] While claiming objectivity and a dispassionate regard for the truth, he pronounced on books he had not read and countered the dominance of women in the field of letters by an aggressively gendered criticism. Whenever the *Nation*'s reviewer declared, "There isn't a character in it," he invariably meant there were no (to him) credible male characters. James criticized Davis's hero, Dallas Galbraith, as "a vapid sentimentalist. He is worse than a woman's man—a woman's boy. Active and passive, he is equally unnatural, irrational, and factitious." Galbraith's self-sacrificing gesture of bearing the guilt of a business partner and submitting to five years in prison discredits him as a real man, in the eyes of Henry James. And yet such was the character that Stowe, exporting women's values to her hero, Tom, created in *Uncle Tom's Cabin*. James snorts that Dallas Galbraith is "like nothing in trousers," and conducts himself "like a hysterical school-girl." When women characters step out of his notion of gender roles he criticizes them for "indelicacy." There were many things wrong with Stowe's choice of Horace Holyoke to narrate *Oldtown Folks*, but the *Nation*'s reviewer chose to complain that "[w]hile he is young he is not a boy but a little dreamy female" and when he grows up "he becomes a more or less unsuccessful simulacrum of a man, except when he is a more or less unfeminine woman."[99]

Anna Dickinson's novel of interracial marriage challenged the sexual politics of the *Nation* even more strenuously, but instead of admitting this truth, James made her defense of miscegenation secondary to her betrayal of "art," which he declared to be best served not by passionate conviction but by objectivity. Anna Dickinson had written "a thoroughly bad novel" with no plot and no characters, a declaration that considerably eased the task of the reviewer. Claiming to be interested only in knowledge, beauty, and truth, he advised Anna Dickinson that she had spoken rashly on a subject she knew nothing about. There were cadres of experts diligently researching this question of the sexual relationship of the races—"laborious ethnologists and physiologists"—and until they rendered their verdict, Miss Dickinson should keep silent.[100] (How well such explosive social issues were served by leaving them to the experts was already manifest in the scientific racism of those who produced cranial measurements that allegedly proved the inferiority of Africans.) While professing Reconstruction democracy, the *Nation* insisted that only experts (who were incidentally white and male) were qualified to speak. Responding to their attack on Dickinson, Isabella Beecher Hooker objected that the "whole drift of your criticism is, 'Thou shouldst never have spoken a word, young woman, till thou hadst mastered all things; let us hear no more from thee till thine eyes are turned from the vanity of making a living, and thy lips, in perfected utterance, drop only wisdom for the multitude.' "[101] Theodore Tilton pointed out that "[a] great moral reform elicits many books and speeches—the best of which are seldom faultless in artistic structure or literary finish." Citing *Uncle Tom's Cabin* as an example, he put both Dickinson's and Stowe's novels in the tradition not of the novel but of political speech:

> Does anybody ever stop to ask whether or not the Declaration of Independence is in good English? . . . Did not our whole nation recognize that Abraham Lincoln's homespun words at Gettysburg were greater than Edward Everett's gilded oration? Once when Father Taylor, in preaching to his audience of seamen, found himself entangled suddenly in a thicket of accumulated clauses, he extricated himself by exclaiming, "I have lost track of the nominative to my verb, but my brethren, one thing I know—*I am bound for the Kingdom of Heaven!*" That was oratory superior to rhetoric! It was getting the wine of eloquence by crushing the grapes of style.[102]

Pointing out that few Harvard men of age twenty-five could sway an audience as effectively as Anna Dickinson, Elizabeth Cady Stanton suggested that the "cultivated, carping men of letters, who are all the time criticising the women of this country who do write and speak," could better employ their time by working "to open the doors of Harvard to both sexes."[103] Stowe characterized Henry James as "an insolent man who is unable to comprehend [Dickinson's] goodness or greatness."[104] The *Nation*'s concerted attack against literary women was a measure of how much social and political power women exercised through their pens. Stowe's response to the regiment of men lining up against women writers was to fire the most sensational shot of her career.

CHAPTER TWENTY-SIX

Woman's Rights and Woman's Wrongs:
1869–1872

"I *have read the Nations very uncivil* criticism on Mrs. Davis its unmannerly & brutal attack on Anna Dickinson with astonishment," Stowe wrote to James Fields on November 6, 1868. She enclosed a reply that she asked him to send to the Boston *Advertiser* or some other paper as he saw fit, only making sure that her authorship of it was kept secret. Prominently implicated in the attack, Stowe was constrained by her family ties to Godkin.[1] Her sister Isabella, who would soon demonstrate in her response to the adultery trial of her brother that family loyalty did not outweigh loyalty to her sex, was less circumspect. She sent a full and well-argued reply to the *Nation* under her initials, privately calling its attack "ugly—narrow and badly written." Isabella, who described herself as "deep in reform matters," had just attended the Boston Woman's Rights Convention, for which she had written the call. There she responded powerfully to the oratory of Lucy Stone, whom she thought to be a better speaker even than Anna Dickinson. Her own need to speak out was rising like a wave under the pressure of such eloquent models: "Sister Hattie says when she had finished Uncle Tom she was at rest—but she nearly died with the pent up feeling before that—So I—on this Woman question—see & feel so clearly the truth. . . . I can hardly breath[e] till I have borne my testimony."[2] Isabella went on to become prominently involved in the struggle for suffrage and other civil rights for women. Harriet's response was to be less direct.

In the same month in which Stowe read the *Nation*'s review of *Oldtown Folks*, she began designing a public defense of a wronged woman, a woman whose very silence was now being used against her. On Stowe's second trip to England in 1856 she had become the confidant of Lady Byron, who had revealed to her the sordid sexual history of her estrangement from Lord Byron. Publicly, Lady Byron had maintained a stoic silence, believing it to be the best defense of true womanhood. Privately, she told Stowe the whole story, seeking her advice as to whether it might be better to break her silence. At the time Stowe counseled silence, reminding Lady Byron of the pain that public exposure would entail. Lady Byron died a few years later, taking to her grave the knowledge of Byron's incestuous liaison with his half-sister, Augusta Leigh. Now, in the aftermath of the *Nation's* attack on Dickinson, Davis, herself, and her masterpiece, *Oldtown Folks*, Stowe determined to tell the tale. Three months later "The True Story of Lady Byron's Life" was spread across the pages of the sedate *Atlantic Monthly*. Those who had enjoined women to keep silent would see just how loud a noise she could make.

The fury that had driven Stowe to move the nation to tears in *Uncle Tom's Cabin* was now tapping secret places in her heart while responding more directly to the attacks that she and other literary women were experiencing. "The True Story of Lady Byron's Life" was, appropriately enough, a battle of the books, a literary protest against a literary man. Countess Guiccioli, Byron's mistress, had just published a memoir that resurrected the story that Stowe remembered hearing as a young girl in Litchfield when Lord and Lady Byron had separated; painted in pathetic tones and told from the man's point of view, the public, male version of the story of their failed marriage dwelt on the heroism and genius of Byron and cast Lady Byron in the role of the cold and calculating wife. Because Lady Byron had chosen to keep silent, her side of the story had never been told, while Byron's, incorporated into his poetry, had been sung from the rooftops of Italy. Stowe, still working from the assumption that a woman could speak only on behalf of some other wronged person, now took the crucial step of speaking for a wronged *woman*.

Though she wrote about British, aristocratic subjects, Stowe's story of marital betrayal and incest reverberated powerfully within the political culture of the American woman's movement, and particularly the wing led by Elizabeth Cady Stanton and Susan B. Anthony, who had made marriage, divorce, and sexuality prominent topics of debate. As Stowe read the flurry of newspapers that crossed her writing desk, she began for the first time to think systematically about the issue of women's rights. She may have had a glimmering notion that no woman alone, not even Lyman Beecher's daughter, could stem the cultural tide that was threatening to swamp her literary reputation. At the same time Stanton and Anthony began assiduously courting Harriet Beecher Stowe and Isabella Beecher Hooker. They hoped to list them as "editor" and "associate editor" of their new paper, the *Revolution*. For a brief few months in 1869, a powerful alliance between the heavy artillery of the women's rights movement and the queen bee of American letters hung in the balance.

Stowe's decision to take up Lady Byron's cause took place at a crucial moment in the development of the woman's movement. The American Equal Rights Association had just split over the Fourteenth Amendment, which for the first time introduced the word "male" into the Constitution as a qualification for citizenship. The faction led by Stanton and Anthony took the ground that to give the vote to black men while withholding it from women of all colors was only to raise more masters above women. On the other side, many supporters felt that to link woman suffrage to the enfranchisement of black men was to imperil a measure essential to the freedman's emancipation. Frederick Douglass's refrain, "This is the Negro's hour," carried the day, and he provided a powerful rhetorical justification for black male suffrage:

> When women, because they are women, are dragged from their homes and hung upon lamp-posts; when their children are torn from their arms and their brains dashed upon the pavement, when they are the objects of insult and outrage at every turn; when they are in danger of having their homes burnt down over their heads, when their children are not allowed to enter schools; then they will have [the same] urgency to obtain the ballot.[3]

To this argument Stanton replied, "Do you believe the African race is composed entirely of males?"[4] Douglass's rationale ignored the fact that black women and children were also attacked and killed in the aftermath of emancipation. "When women are dragged through the streets," Douglass had said, it will be time enough to give them the vote. That white women were subject to sexual humiliations in the privacy of their own bedrooms, that men's conjugal rights gave them unrestricted sexual access, kept them politically in their places too, but it was a problem too trivial, too invisible to merit public attention. As Stanton told her abolitionist cousin, Gerritt Smith, "Tyranny on a southern plantation is far more easily seen by white men in the North than the wrongs of women in their own households."[5] Determined to bring white women's vulnerability and dependency into the spotlight, Stanton and Anthony broke with the Equal Rights Association, founded an all-woman's group, the National Woman Suffrage Association, and engaged in a highly public campaign to dramatize the sexual politics of the home. Beginning in 1868 and extending through 1871, they organized mass meetings around sexual scandals to popularize their message about the necessity of changing the marriage and divorce laws.

In a celebrated case Abby McFarland, estranged from her abusive husband, was accused by Mr. McFarland of engaging in an affair with Albert Richardson. In the meantime, Mrs. McFarland secured a divorce. The jealous Mr. McFarland took matters into his own hands by shooting Richardson, who clung to life by a thread, but just long enough for Henry Ward Beecher to come to the dying Richardson's bedside and join him in marriage to Abby McFarland. To supporters of the status quo, this represented a shocking lack of taste; to woman's rights agitators, it became a cause célèbre, particularly after McFarland was declared innocent by virtue of insanity and given custody of his child. While the *Nation* thought it strange that Mrs. McFarland could transfer her affections so abruptly, Elizabeth Cady Stanton compared her to a fugitive slave who had "escaped from a discordant marriage."[6] The propaganda value of this case and that of Hester Vaughn, an immigrant domestic servant who was convicted of infanticide after having been raped by her employer, was immense.[7] Stowe's literary attempt to exonerate Lady Byron and put Lord Byron on trial was of a piece with these and other sexual scandals and was her maiden attempt at sexual speech. "The True Story of Lady Byron's Life" would be the *Uncle Tom's Cabin* of woman's sexual slavery.

"No one in England would dare to do it," she told James Parton on June 1, 1869, as she prepared to tell all. "I shall have to take the responsibility on my sole & single self—& think I am adequate to it, on the whole."[8] As she put herself in fighting trim, she may have recalled how thoroughly "Cato's daughter" had vanquished the Rev. Joel Parker in a highly public battle. She might also have remembered a less flattering parallel, Catharine Beecher's publication of *Truth Stranger than Fiction*, in which, against the wishes of the principals, Catharine told in great detail the story of a woman's sexual humiliation at the hands of a man. "I never in all my life saw such mulish obstinacy & fixedness of purpose," wrote Mary Beecher at the time that Catharine had resolved on exposing Delia Bacon's plight. "She thinks also that she has a *divine commission*—she seems to feel all a martyrs spirit—so far as self sacrifice is concerned—to me she seems a real *fanatic* & if she had lived in olden times would have been one who had a divine commission to kill the oppressors of the church."[9] The courage it took to expose someone else's sexual peccadilloes could always be questioned—and this was one of the risks of speaking for another instead of standing on the platform of one's own experience.

Byron's incestuous relationship with Augusta Leigh was actually rather common knowledge, for Lady Byron had confided in others besides Stowe. She told the same story to Mrs. Follen, who had told a friend, who told a foreign correspondent in Manchester, who admitted this to the *Independent* after the story broke.[10] Gail Hamilton mentioned it in her letters in 1867, having heard the story, it would seem, from Professor and Mrs. Stowe.[11] James Parton, writing to Osgood to encourage publication of the story in the *Atlantic*, assumed that he might know the outline of the tale. In England, particularly, the circumstances surrounding the breakup of Lord and Lady Byron's marriage were well known. It had not, however, been talked about publicly. Everyone agreed that, as James Parton told Osgood, "it will make the greatest sensation."[12]

By the third week in June 1869 Stowe had written "The True Story of Lady Byron's Life" and sent it to Osgood. "I think on the whole," she told him, "as this article is very important, & will probably make a good deal of sensation, that I should have time quietly to revise the proof sheets—& therefore we had better calculate it for the September number. In that case it will come out in the middle of August, which will be a good time for the reading public."[13] When the proof sheets arrived she sent them to Oliver Wendell Holmes. If she had said anything that overstepped the bounds of taste, he would tell her. The uncharacteristically flat and factual style Stowe adopts in this piece suggests that she was taking care to reveal a sensational story in a highly proper manner. Walking a line between truth and taste, she tells the reader that Lady Byron discovered "in a manner which left no kind of room for doubt" the nature of "the abyss of infamy which her marriage was expected to cover." She labels this infamy "incest."[14]

On July 4 Holmes returned her manuscript accompanied by a very careful critique that included corrections of grammar, overstatement, and error. Stowe had quoted long passages from Byron's poetry to illustrate how he had alternately confessed and justified his guilty secret; Holmes verified the quotations, remarking that they must have been copied in haste for they "swarm with errors." For the piece as a whole, however, he had the highest admiration:

> I need not say that the story is one of surpassing interest, and that you have told it in a clear and admirable manner. If I had found any fault which seemed to me serious, I would have told you unsparingly, for the world will settle on this paper like three clouds of pigeons that break the haunches of the trees.— When has anything ever appeared in any periodical so like to attract universal attention and comment?[15]

While Stowe was preparing her exposé of Byron, Elizabeth Cady Stanton and Susan B. Anthony were determined that the *Revolution*, their weekly cannonade against male privilege, should begin its third year of publication with a story from the pen of Mrs. Stowe. The early issues of the *Revolution* had serialized Mary Wollstonecraft's *The Rights of Women*; Stanton and Anthony used their paper to popularize the arguments on behalf of women's political rights, just as during the 1867 petition drive for woman suffrage they had circulated 10,000 copies of John Stuart Mill's parliamentary speech in support of the vote for women.[16] But the most effective way to popularize a political issue, as *Uncle Tom's Cabin* had demonstrated, was to treat it in fiction. In its second year of publication the *Revolution* serialized *Up Broadway* by Eleanor Kirk. Now Anthony set her sights on Stowe. "Alice Cary wants I should take [a story] from her," Anthony wrote Paulina Wright Davis,

> her *name is good* but of course Mrs. *Stowe's* is the *Queen Bee* in that hive— And if she will do so much for *The Rev.*, we can at once set it on its own *splendid feet*—And if *Cash will bring Mrs Stowe* to The Rev. with her *deepest holiest Woman, Wife & Mother Soul struggle*—clothed in her *inimitable story garb*—then *it is cash that must be*—Mrs. Stowe—even—has never *yet given to the world her very best*—for she nor any other woman can, until she *writes direct out of her own souls experiences*.[17]

Stanton and Anthony had launched the *Revolution* in 1868 with money provided by George Francis Train, a wealthy Irish Fenian with whom they had teamed up in the Kansas campaign of 1867. Undertaken for purely pragmatic reasons, their alliance with Train became to many the symbol of Stanton and Anthony's questionable judgment, for Train was considered a lunatic given to extreme statements and racist rhetoric. "He may be of use in drawing an audience," remarked William Lloyd Garrison, "but so would a kangaroo, a gorilla or a hippopatamus."[18] Before Stowe could consider an alliance with the *Revolution*, she needed reassurance about Train. "Dear Hattie," wrote Isabella to Harriet at the beginning of their negotiations, "I wrote Mrs. Stanton about Train's coarseness, sympathising however with her desire to have an organ at whatever cost." She told Harriet that she had invited Stanton to come visit them, and she enclosed for Harriet the reply she had received. In it Stanton claimed to have little knowledge of Train's writings, assuring Hooker, "We can throw Train overboard the moment we can find friends enough who will give their money to support a paper that is bound to unveil the abominations in high and low places." She expressed eagerness to meet Mrs. Hooker and Mrs. Stowe.[19] To Paulina Wright Davis, who arranged the historic meeting of Hooker, Stowe, Stanton, and Anthony at her house, Stanton wrote, "I think she will find us reasonable women."[20]

Not long before this meeting in August 1869, Stowe had written to Anthony that she was "not quite ready to join the Woman's Rights Church." Anthony wrote Isabella Hooker, "when she does enter it—I can tell you there will be *rejoicing* in our heaven not less than that we read about." Probably referring to Stowe's column on "The Woman Question," which had just appeared in *Hearth and Home*, Anthony observed that Stowe "is not only studying up our question, but actually writing it in *her own* splendid way. . . . What our Movement now needs is an accession to our numbers of *The Literary Women*—of the Country—And so fast as I come to know them— they, one & all, *believe in our Gospel*—and wait only the revival forces to bring them into line of actual members."[21] Stanton, who had been under increasing attack from within and without the movement for her radical views, was willing to retire from the front lines of battle and turn over the leadership to women who were more likely to attract a wide following. "We are through the wilderness," she wrote Davis, "and now if Mrs. Hooker and Mrs. Stowe will take it up, and one of them be President of the National Association and one editor of 'The Revolution' no one would rejoice more than I."[22]

That this proposal could in all seriousness be put to Stowe demonstrates how thoroughly the Civil War and Reconstruction had changed the political climate. Woman suffrage, though far from won, was no longer the ridiculous proposal it had been in 1848 when the women at Seneca Falls had inititally balked at including it in their "Declaration of Sentiments." Stowe's own mind was changing rapidly, in large part due to her reading. It was a measure of the changing times that a number of men felt called upon to defend what had once been commonly assumed, the doctrine that women should remain in their "sphere." A conservative pamphlet on "Women's Rights" by Dr. John

Todd provoked a witty and able reply by Mary A. Dodge, one of Ticknor and Fields's authors who wrote under the name of Gail Hamilton. In *Woman's Wrongs: A Counter-Irritant* (Boston: Ticknor and Fields, 1868), Hamilton skewered Todd on his own logical and grammatical infelicities. It was doubtless through their common publisher that Stowe and Hamilton became correspondents and friends during this period, visiting one another's houses and keeping in touch through Annie Fields. Stowe wrote to Fanny Fern, "Have you read Gail Hamiltons Woman's Wrongs—If you havent *read it*, before you are a day older—Its decidedly the brightest, cleanest healthiest noblest kind of a book—Do you know her? She is a trump—a real original—healthy—largehearted & simple minded & good as she can be."[23]

Although Hamilton supported woman suffrage, she argued that too much had been made of it, "as if the ballot were a sort of talisman, with a power to ward off all harm from its possessor." Taking a literary woman's point of view, she argued that suffrage was a "clumsy contrivance for bringing opinion to bear on government,—fine, delicate, precise, as compared with the old-time method of the sword; but coarse, blundering, and insufficient when compared with the pen, the fireside, and the thousand subtle social influences, penetrating, pervasive, purifying."[24] Her view that suffrage was a blunter instrument than the pen not only suggests the power of literary women during this period; it suggests how consciously nineteenth-century writers merged literature and politics. While advocates of woman suffrage echoed the cry of the colonists, "No taxation without representation," women writers had access to tens of thousands of voters through *literary* representation.

The year after Hamilton's *Woman's Wrongs* appeared both Horace Bushnell and John Stuart Mill stirred the pot by their respective defense of and attack upon the orthodoxy of separate spheres. Stowe delighted in the "roasting" that Bushnell received in the columns of *Hearth and Home* and she read Mill's *On The Subjection of Women* as soon as the American edition appeared. She wrote Fanny Fern, "It has wholly converted me—I was only right *in spots* before now I am all clear."[25] Mill's arguments fit neatly with the problems that Stowe was wrestling with in Reconstruction America. In one of her *Chimney-Corner* papers she put in the mouth of Christopher Crowfield these sentiments:

> This question of Woman and her Sphere is now, perhaps, the greatest of the age. We have put Slavery under foot, and with the downfall of Slavery the only obstacle to the success of our great democratic experiment is overthrown, and there seems no limit to the splendid possibilities which it may open before the human race.
>
> In the reconstruction that is now coming there lies more than the reconstruction of States and the arrangement of the machinery of government. We need to know and feel, all of us, that, from the moment of the death of Slavery, we parted finally from the régime and control of all the old ideas forced under the old oppressive systems of society, and came upon a new plane of life. (HP, 250–51)

Mill's appeal to progress and the enlightenment of the age fell on fertile Reconstruction soil in America. Even more apt was his insistence that the private sphere of the family needed radical reconstruction before individual liberty could be guaranteed. While contemporary political theory assumed that the family was the training ground for liberty, in fact, Mill pointed out, the patriarchal family was a "school of tyranny." Mill shined the bright light of logic into corners heretofore hidden from view, and although his upper-class bias led him to attribute domestic violence to the lower orders of society, one could read his message as confirmation of the desecration of marriage vows that went on in all orders of society, even the highest.

Stowe told her readers in *Hearth and Home*, "John Stuart Mill says all popular reforms have to go through three stages—Ridicule, Discussion, Acceptance. The question of Woman's Rights is just passing out of the stage of ridicule into that of fair, respectful discussion."[26] She meant to help it along, using the pages of *Hearth and Home*, a magazine that she coedited with Donald G. Mitchell (Ik Marvell) from December 1868 to December 1869. Although this agricultural and domestic weekly was a far cry from the *Revolution*, it gave Stowe a podium on which to speak out on domestic issues, animal rights, and woman's rights. How far she had moved from the domestic feminism of her *House and Home Papers* may be seen in her column, "The Woman Question," which appeared in *Hearth and Home* the same month that her story of Lady Byron's life ran in the *Atlantic*. Stowe told her readers, "You will see that the position of a married woman, under English common law, is, in many respects, precisely similar to that of the negro slave." After enumerating the married woman's lack of civil rights, she pointedly alluded to the sexual implications of her yoke: "The common law, while it allows to a husband the free privilege of living apart from his wife, if he does not choose to be with her, allows to the wife neither privacy nor retreat from her husband if he proves disagreeable to her."[27] Although Stowe was fortunate to have a husband who was willing to check his sexual impulses for the sake of her autonomy and health, she nevertheless had borne seven children and endured several miscarriages; she knew enough about the tensions and difficulties of woman's conjugal duties to imagine how desperate a woman could become. As for woman suffrage, she urged upon her readers a strategy that Susan B. Anthony would soon test at the polls. Appealing to the Declaration of Independence, Stowe argued that women already were entitled to vote. "Now, the question arises, which is in fault, the Declaration of Independence, or the customs and laws of America as to women? *Is* taxation without representation tyranny or not?" That summer she watched with anticipation as the Connecticut state legislature prepared to debate amendments drafted by John Hooker that would revise the marriage and property laws. If adopted, the amendments, in Stowe's words, would "set [woman] free." Only if the legislators were willing "to recognise *the absolute equality of woman in the marriage relation*" would she "be willing to claim Connecticut as my mother," Stowe told George Eliot.[28]

As coeditor of *Hearth and Home*, Stowe also exercised for the first time a shaping power over columns other than her own, a power she used not only to promote women writers such as Lucy Larcom, but issues such as woman suffrage.[29] Indeed, as Gail Hamilton had suggested, the pen and the ballot were but different modes of enfranchising women's voices. Knowing well the weight that respectability gave to opinions, she tried to persuade Ralph Waldo Emerson to write a two-column article on woman suffrage for which she was prepared to pay $50. She told him that his name and philosophical balance might win the ear of "fastidious circles" and "take [suffrage] out of the sphere of ridicule into that of rational consideration." Citing the diplomacy of his letter to the Boston Woman's Rights Convention in November, 1868, she told him:

> You might with perhaps less offence and with more profit than any one give a little *well timed advice* to the zealous earnest leaders of this movement to avoid shocking the *public taste* by a too prominent urging of extreme views, which are not essential to the main point & by an ungraceful and ungracious manner of presenting the truth—and at the same time give to the cause the support of a respectful and delicate consideration.[30]

The cloak of respectability that Stowe urged Emerson to throw over woman's rights was precisely what Stanton and Anthony hoped to gain by enlisting Hooker and Stowe at the head of their movement, but neither of Lyman Beecher's daughters could see themselves on the masthead of a journal called the *Revolution*. They inquired of Stanton and Anthony whether the name might be changed to something a trifle less shocking to public taste. Stanton and Anthony, who had already invested two years of hard work and writing to launch the *Revolution*, were not prepared to rename it. "The establishing of woman on her rightful throne is the greatest revolution the world has ever known or will know," replied Stanton. "A journal called the *Rosebud* might answer for those who come with kid gloves and perfumes to lay immortal wreaths on the monuments which in sweat and tears others have hewn and built; but for us . . . there is no name like the *Revolution*."[31] Clearly their differences over the name covered less tangible issues of style, stance, and politics. While Stanton continued through December 1869 to hope that the third year of the *Revolution* would issue under the names of Hooker and Stowe, the Beecher sisters were loath to assume editorial responsibility for the wide range of socially explosive material discussed in its pages. They told Stanton they would be more comfortable as occasional contributors. As the year 1870 approached, Stanton finally admitted defeat by announcing a new story by Alice Cary, "The Born Thrall, or Woman's Life and Experience," claiming, "What 'Uncle Tom's Cabin' was to the Anti-Slavery movement, this work will be to the cause of Woman." Isabella Beecher Hooker wrote a New Year's piece for the January 6, 1870 issue, but Stowe, already up to her ears in controversy over the Byron case, had enough trouble on her hands.[32]

After she had returned the corrected proof sheets of "The True Story of

Lady Byron's Life" to the offices of the *Atlantic Monthly*, she had time to reflect. "I tremble at what I am doing & saying but I feel that justice demands it of me & I *must* not fail," she told William Dean Howells, a new *Atlantic* editor. On July 25 she wrote to Fanny Fern that she was "scared" and "ready to run behind a door," but her letter displayed the confident striding of a mind on the move and a woman ready to challenge the aristocracy of sex. "Yes I do believe in Female Suffrage," she told Fern, "The more I think of it the more absurd this whole government of men over women looks." She continued,

> A friend of mine put it rather nicely the other night—"I dont much care about voting she said the other day—but I feel as the girl did who was offended when the cake plate was nt passed her
>> Why I thought you did nt love cake
>> But I do like to have the chance of refusing it, says she
> This agreement of Tom Dick & Harry not to pass the cake plate lest we make ourselves sick with cake seems absurd Dare not trust us with suffrage lest we become unwomanly. Let them try it Unsexed?—I should like to see what could make women other than women & men than men—The colors we are died in are warranted to wash.[33]

Within days of writing this arch and confident letter, Stowe suffered a physical collapse. As she awaited the arrival of the September *Atlantic Monthly* bearing her sensational story, she had what she termed a "sinking turn" that took all her strength. She went to Stockbridge to recuperate. "When I first came," she told Hatty and Eliza, "I could not walk down into the garden without my limbs & knees trembling under me and a feeling all the while in my head as if I were going to fall." Her defense of Lady Byron was a calculated risk, but nevertheless a very daring one. As in her revelations of the sexual debasement licensed by chattel slavery, Stowe hoped to transform the nature of womanhood by speaking the unspeakable. The risk to her own reputation was great, and now riding on the latter were the fortunes of her entire family. "[A]ll the income that supports the family comes from my ability to labor at my pen," she told her daughters, "and I feel as a sailor does who knows that if he can *only* row to a certain point he will be in smooth water—If I only can keep up for a few years longer the ability to write and lay by the money I make I can get to a point where there will not need to be such constant effort." She took peruvian bark, quinine, and iron, but most effective was the cure that Calvin hit upon. Every day he rented a carriage and took her "into the mountains round here to breathe the fresh mountain air" and, she told her daughters, "it has sensibly restored me."[34] In mid-August as the September *Atlantic Monthly* began arriving at households across the nation Harriet wrote a clear, dark postscript along the side of her letter to Hatty: "Please mail to me my copy of John Stuart Mill."[35]

While Stowe's defense of wronged womanhood was clearly motivated by her burgeoning political consciousness, her politics were still fairly inchoate. Stanton and Anthony had a highly refined political consciousness but wrote for a magazine with a circulation of 3,000; Stowe had access to tens of thousands of readers, but her consciousness was clouded by notions of male chivalry and noble womanhood. Her motives were also mixed. It is likely that she took up Lady Byron's case out of her desire to regain the attention of a modern audience bored with her stories of New England life.[36] Indeed, it is hard to disentangle this motive from her outrage over the treatment of literary women. To all of this must be added the electric bond that Stowe felt with Lady Byron from the first time she met her. Like Stowe, Lady Byron was a woman of slight build and vast intellect. Stowe praised Lady Byron as a suppressed woman of genius. "She kept a journal She corresponded with most of the distinguished persons in England & Europe she was a splendid writer—she had more mind on all subjects & more knowledge than any person I met in England & all this has been locked away from the world because this guilty secret was the key of all."[37] Alice Crozier has suggested that the two women were "kindred spirits in righteousness."[38] After their last interview Stowe wrote to her, "I left you with a strange sort of yearning throbbing feeling—you make me feel quite as I did years ago a sort of girlishness quite odd for me."[39] Stowe's identification with Lady Byron may have caused her to read into Lady Byron's life a dynamic from her own. Writing of Lady Byron's early days of marriage with Lord Byron, Stowe voiced a sentiment she had expressed in less extreme form to the volatile Calvin Stowe: "The most dreadful men to live with are those who thus alternate between angel and devil. The buds of hope and love called by a day or two of sunshine are frozen again and again till the tree is killed."[40]

Stowe expected an outcry in response to her revelations about Byron, but she was not prepared for the storm of abuse that broke on her. She was accused of sensationalism and prurience and told that even if the story were true, she "should not have stained herself" by revealing it.[41] The most virulent criticism came from the *Independent*, which, like much of the religious press, had become increasingly secular in recent years. Henry Ward Beecher, who had long used the pulpit and the religious press to preach avowedly political sermons, inadvertently contributed to this development, which was effective as long as one could rely on a religious tone in one's audience. In the highly secular culture emerging in post–Civil War America, however, there was no longer a strong counterpull. Stowe, who viewed Lady Byron as a long-suffering Christ figure much like her hero, Tom, was astounded at attacks such as this one written by Justin McCarthy and published in the *Independent*:

> An authoress of reputation gets hold of a disgusting story about Byron—a story which, true or false, is revolting and obscene. She sells it to a publisher; and for weeks before its appearance the press is inundated with little preliminary puffs, whetting and goading on the meanest curiosity on the part of the public. The coming disclosures are advertised, announced, heralded, trumpeted everywhere; and, of course, the result is a splendid success. A story which would have suited and delighted the taste of a Borgia family-circle is sent into every

household in the United States; and the circulation of the magazine is thereby made enormous.[42]

When they were not impugning her motives, the male press attacked the credibility of Lady Byron. Stowe, relying on her subject's "pure venerable and religious" character, never thought "that Lady Byrons testimony to direct facts that she had personal opportunity of knowing could be doubted."[43] Instead, the cry went up that Lady Byron was insane. A writer in the Cologne *Gazette* concluded "that the tale arose from a delusion of Lady Byron's mind during her last illness."[44] The *London Times* agreed it was "probable that the wife was a victim of delusion. . . . It would only be what thousands of unhappy wives have done before, to have suspicions of exceptional enormity."[45]

Stowe wrote to Osgood, "The course the American papers takes is trying. As my health is not good & I am trying to avoid all excitement I do not read at all upon the subject."[46] The failure of the American papers to rally behind Lady Byron reflected badly, Stowe thought, on her countrymen:

> I had a high idea of the chivalry of America for women & therefore took from my bosom a name dear to me as that of my own mother & cast it down before them. It appears it was casting pearls before swine—Of course the poor pigs know not what they do but the discovery of so many of that class is painful to me—
> Never again shall I say as I did before that America is a land where a woman is sure of defenders![47]

As the men rose in concert against Stowe's exposé of Lord Byron, Elizabeth Cady Stanton came to Stowe's defense, suggesting that the bluster of the press came not from any sympathy with the Byrons but from a reaction against Stowe's "unveiling of man as woman's natural protector," a "blow . . . that will . . . hasten the day when the worst form of slavery, that of woman to man. . . . shall be no more."[48] Stanton wrote to Isabella at the beginning of September, "Next week I shall have an editorial on Mrs. Stowe & Byron. Is there anything you would like to have me say."[49] In "The Moral of the Byron Case" Stanton predicted that "Mrs. Stowe's fearful picture of the abominations of our social life, coming out simultaneously with John Stuart Mill's philosophy of the degradation of woman, will do much to rouse wise men to new thought on the social wrongs of the race, for whatever enslaves woman debases man; together we must rise or fall." Instead of attacking Stowe, Stanton urged women to examine "the real position of woman today" and to ask, have the men in your lives "helped you to develop all the powers of your whole nature, ever subordinating their grosser appetites to your highest health and happiness?"[50]

In the growing movement for "voluntary motherhood," more and more women were coming forward with stories of male sexual abuse within marriage and arguing that men should control their sexuality in the interests of both women and the race. Angela Heywood's advice to men captures the intensity of the sexual politics of this period: "Man so lost to himself and woman as to invoke legal *violence* in these sacred nearings, *should have solemn meeting with, and look serious at his own penis until he is able to be lord and master of it, rather than it should longer rule, lord and master, of him and of the victims he deflowers.*"[51] While Stowe's exposé of Lord Byron met a ready audience in women whose own experiences had made them the victims of male sexuality, a serious problem with the case Stowe had undertaken was that Byron had not forced himself on either Lady Byron or Augusta Leigh. True, he had deceived Lady Byron by proposing to her for ulterior motives, but then so, perhaps, had she accepted for less-than-laudable reasons. Marriages of convenience were commonplace among the aristocracy. As for the charge of incest, it reflected just as badly on Augusta Leigh, who was apparently a willing partner. Stowe might have argued that the marriage laws were so weighted in favor of the man that a woman had little recourse in the event of postnuptial revelations of infamy. But Stowe did not use the case to argue for a change in the marriage laws; her purpose was much more personal and limited: to readjust Lady Byron's reputation in the scale of public opinion.[52]

Having brought a truth too painful for utterance before the public, Stowe prepared to weather this backlash of anger and disbelief, just as she had ridden out the storm over *Uncle Tom's Cabin.* "Such a scoffing at Christs spirit in a professed Christian country I have not seen since I saw half the professed Christians of America on their knees before the fugitive slave law," she wrote to a supporter.[53] Just as the publication of *Uncle Tom's Cabin* had given rise to demands for documentation, so her story of Lady Byron drew forth strenuous demands for proof. "[T]he very fact that it is a crime against nature ought to be *prima facie* evidence against its commission," argued the *Independent.* "If proof is needed to convict of any crime under heaven, proof ought to be demanded to convict of this."[54] James Russell Lowell disbelieved her story because it defied conventional wisdom: "Incest when it does happen (and it is rare enough) is not the fruit of perverted lust but of thwarted animal passion. It occurs in lonely farmhouses and not in cities swarming with public women."[55] Henry Ward Beecher, acknowledging that his sister had "stirred up the annual family row," remarked to her,

> The papers are certainly excited—the N. Y. Sun, the Times—the World—the Tribune, half & half—The fact is, that in all our great Dailies we have Englishmen & Irish writers, & I suspect them of being the vindicators of the dirty Byron, in this case—But—it will compell, now, a *full discussion in England,*— and I suppose that there is proof enough. Had not Lady Byron *documents* which establish the facts beyond all controversy?[56]

Stowe wrote to Osgood that it would be better if someone else supplied the proof. But she also wrote to Charles Follen to follow up on a remark she remembered him making years ago "that there were documents in chancery that proved the paternity" of Medora Leigh, the child of the incestuous union of Byron and Augusta Leigh.[57] Soon she was deep into documents. "Macmillan has sent me all on the subject in the English papers," she wrote Fields and Osgood, "& the communication of Lord Lindsay is an unhoped for accession of strength." She found among her papers "three letters from and to Lady Byron on this subject, returned by her executors," as well as other letters written around the time of her confidence to Stowe that demonstrated the clarity of her mind.[58] Resigning her editorship of *Hearth and Home* effective the 31st of October, Stowe threw herself into writing *Lady Byron Vindicated*. She called her sisters Isabella and Catharine to her side and devoted several intense months to expanding her eighteen-page article into a book. She instructed Osgood to "choose plain type for the *documents* so that *nobody may skip them as fine print*." As she prepared to write the first part of the book she told Osgood, "It will come like an avalanche I *feel* how it is coming."[59]

In important respects, however, *Lady Bryon Vindicated* was different from *A Key to Uncle Tom's Cabin*. First, the latter had provided documents to support Stowe's fictional treatment of an institution that affected four million African Americans, but *Lady Byron Vindicated* focused narrowly on the facts in the case of Lord and Lady Byron and provided no comparable documentation of the abuses of the institution of marriage. Second, Stowe's *Key* had followed a book that had brought graphically before the reader's imagination characters and scenes that were their own proof. "There is no arguing with *pictures*," Stowe had said at the time. Now, constrained by the canons of taste and propriety, writing about real people and facts that could be disputed, Stowe could make no use of her most powerful tools, her ability to create realistic dialogue and a texture of presumed fact. *Lady Byron Vindicated* drew her into a morass of conflicting accounts, dates that had to be verified, new revelations that had to be taken into account. When the *London Quarterly* published correspondence between Lord Byron and Mrs. Leigh, Harriet, suspecting the authenticity of the letters, instructed Calvin to have printed in the papers a notice requesting that the public "suspend their judgment" in regard to these letters "until they appear in their proper historical connection in her forthcoming volume."[60] She urged Osgood to be "up & doing" to help her gather authentic material. "This is *war* to the knife—& the enemy are perfectly unscrupulous."[61]

Stowe's "proof" depended in the first part of her book on her showing a pattern of intent in Lord Byron's conduct, which in turn depended on a careful reconstruction of dates and events. "This thing has got to be done carefully" she told Osgood, "this investigation of Lord Byrons plot, cost me an intense amount of study & rummaging and comparing dates."[62] It was a kind of detailed research for which Stowe, who created enormous work for her biographers by not dating her letters, was not temperamentally suited. Once she had assembled the facts in a chronology that satisfied her, she was reluctant to commit her manuscript to the mails for fear if it were lost she would not be able to reconstruct it. Then she waited impatiently for Osgood to send the proof sheets. "I assure you you risk losing the proper time for the book to appear by letting things go on so," she told him. "You must let me have *proofs faster* or this will never be out or the shape of things will alter so it will not *fit* which it does now exactly."[63] Her worst fears materialized when parts of the manuscript *were* lost and had to be reconstructed. "The disturbance that this is to her may be readily imagined," Isabella wrote Fields and Osgood, adding, "the state of her health & the great nervous exhaustion she daily suffers are causes of great anxiety to her friends."[64]

In order to keep up her strength, Harriet went to New York and put herself under the regimen of Dr. Taylor's Swedish Movement Cure, a kind of urban variant of the water cure. Substituting massage and a gymnasium full of equipment for showers and baths, Dr. Taylor's movement cure, located on the corner of 38th Street and Sixth Avenue, had facilities for boarders and was a decidedly social gathering place for those who could afford such treatment. George Taylor was also a spiritualist, and Harriet took part in at least four séances presided over by medium Kate Fox Jencken.[65] Harriet was joined at Dr. Taylor's by her husband, who lost two inches around his ample waist under his care; Susan Howard, who had been sent to Dr. Taylor's for treatment of "a sort of gastralgia"; and Catharine Beecher, who acted as mother and nurse to Harriet so she could devote all her energies to laying to rest the demons of Lord Byron.[66] Harriet explained her routine to her daughters, whom she urged to come and try the cure:

> I work hard all the morning & then try to throw all off—ride or walk in the Park go to the Movement room at 4—& am ribbed & stretched & otherwise operated on till I feel calm & collected—& in the evening talk or make calls till 10—then sleep well till morning The printing is begun & is going on rapidly. Dudley Fields has promised to read all & be my lawyer—& the world will see by & by what they shall see Till I began the investigation I had no idea of the strength of the case. Lady Byrons voice will rise, clear as the sun fair as the moon, & terrible as an army with banners.[67]

It is notoriously difficult to establish the truth in cases of sexual misconduct because the only witnesses, as a rule, are the accuser and the accused. The credibility of each depends heavily on the credibility of their sex, for in a sexual crime sexual stereotypes are often more powerful lenses than individual characters. Stowe's depiction of Lady Byron as an "angel," a type of the suffering Christ, suggests that she was seeing her as an idealization of Victorian womanhood, invested with all the power and nobility of that type. When skeptics asked why Lady Byron would stay with Lord Byron long after her discovery that her husband was regularly committing incest, Stowe responded that she did so out of concern for the state of Lord Byron's soul: she martyred herself in the hope of reclaiming him. To the *Nation*, this explanation made Lady Byron appear ridiculous. Stowe responded, "What would Christ say to that? Did not Christ for three years bear daily contact with what he calls an evil and adulterous generation?"[68] To claim that Lady

Byron would have fled in horror from the crime is to expect, said Stowe, that she would act like a "common correct English wife," an expectation which "does no justice to her."[69] Stowe's elevation of Lady Byron above self-interest, moral outrage, and jealousy was of a piece with the Victorian strategy of "passionlessness," a strategy that increased nineteenth-century woman's power by insulating her from her husband's sexual demands. But Stowe was inadvertently confirming the very portrait of Lady Byron she aimed to combat: that of the cold and aloof wife who drove her husband into the arms of others. From the point of view of the woman's movement, Stowe's strategy was also seriously flawed; she could not simultaneously hold up Lady Byron as a type of universal womanhood and yet make that womanhood dependent on her superiority to the common English wife. Stowe's maiden attempt at sexual speech was riven by deeply held class assumptions.

The contradictions covered by the stereotype of the Victorian angel were soon to break forth in the "free love" movement, at the helm of which was Victoria Woodhull. Woodhull was married at age fourteen to a drunkard and gave birth to a retarded son.[70] Her unfortunate experiences led her to the radical position that marriage was sexual slavery, that wives were raped by their husbands, and that sexual relations ought to be regulated by love alone. In "Tried as by Fire," a speech that she estimated a quarter of a million people had heard, Woodhull expostulated, "Prate of the abolition of slavery! There was never servitude in the world like this one of marriage." Her rhetoric and politics were a highly colored extension of the analysis encouraged by Stanton and Anthony in their mass meetings on sexual scandals, but for most women there was a vast difference between reforming the marriage laws and abolishing marriage. Here is where the analogy between marriage and slavery—widely invoked by Stanton, Stowe, and Woodhull—fell into confusion.[71] If marriage were truly like slavery, there would be no more point in reforming it than there would be in reforming slavery. Abolition of marriage was the only logical position to take if the analogy were an accurate one. Victoria Woodhull rushed to this precipice and threw herself over the edge, attempting to take with her the unwary women, like Stowe, who had invoked the metaphor of slavery without thinking through the implications. The result, predictably, was that Stowe dug in her heels and reversed her direction.

Lady Byron Vindicated was published, after great effort on Stowe's part, in January 1870. In order to "prevent its being garbled, misprinted and otherwise abused," she planned to go to Canada to establish copyright, but changed her mind when she realized that this trip would delay the publication.[72] It was almost impossible to make her book respond exactly to the state of public opinion, for new articles and books were appearing every day. Just as she was going to press, Medora Leigh, the child of the incestuous union, published her version of the story. Her purpose was to exonerate her father, but Calvin Stowe said it was a "most wonderful instance . . . of 'judicial blindness,'" for her story corroborated everything Stowe had said. Stowe considered stopping the presses and adding a reference to this new evidence, but finally let the book go as it was.[73] She sent back the last proof sheet on December 13, but did not return immediately from New York, explaining to her daughters that she wanted to give herself several more days at Dr. Taylor's: "I think that if I suddenly break off *both* writing and treatment after working so hard there may be a great reaction."[74] To Annie Fields she explained another motive for staying in New York: "I have access here to many who are influential with the *Press* and by staying another week I think I may have some influence to prevent that violent prejudgement and opposition that my friends cause has hitherto met." In order to get the right people "to look on the subject in a new point of view," she planned to use her "social & personal influence."[75] She wrote to Horace Greeley asking "as a favor" that he read her book and "write *yourself* whatever may be said of it in your paper," appealing to his "deep feeling for woman:" She told him, "I consider Lady Byron's story as a type of the old idea of woman: that is, a creature to be crushed and trodden under foot whenever her fate and that of a man come in conflict."[76]

Narrowly cast, *Lady Byron Vindicated* vindicated neither Lady Byron, the cause of woman's rights, nor Stowe's reputation. The *Nation*, which had corroborated Stowe's version of the facts if not her interpretation of them, observed that for all the new material *Lady Byron Vindicated* brought forth, "the only additional proof" Stowe offered was "more extended and explicit reports of the conversation in which Lady Byron revealed the secret; . . . this conversation will help to confirm the impression of many people that she was not sound in her mind on this subject in later years." Typically dismissing rather than engaging women's issues, the *Nation* concluded, "We sincerely hope if anybody else has any dirty particulars about the Byron family or its branches in his possession, he will keep them to himself."[77] George Eliot, with whom Stowe had recently opened a correspondence, told her that she "should have preferred that the 'Byron question' should not be brought before the public, because I think the discussion of such subjects is injurious socially."[78] Perhaps the most telling comment on the whole affair was a cartoon that pictured Stowe clambering up a statue of Lord Byron; he is striking a noble pose while she is hunched in a suggestive posture, leaving dirty footprints as she pulls herself up.[79] In the eyes of public opinion, Stowe had lost. She had not shaken the power of woman's "natural protectors," who assumed as part of the masculine role a certain level of sexual indiscretion. While she had dirtied herself, she had left untouched the stereotype of the Victorian angel in the house, above passion and self-interest. Villified for stepping outside the bounds of true womanhood by stooping to scandal, Stowe experienced the double jeopardy of that Victorian ideology. If one had no self-interest, one could not be wronged; the price of purity was silence.

Stowe's bold attempt to recoup her international readership had the opposite effect, and the circulation of the *Atlantic* went down with her, suffering "so serious a blow that the recovery from it was not accomplished for many years."[80] It would be a mistake, however, to view the Lady Byron mis-calculation as the "cause" of Stowe's declining reputation. It was itself a symptom of the polarization of literature along gender lines that was such a striking feature of the post–Civil War period. The masculinization of liter-ature, rather than the Byron affair, brought down not only Stowe but a whole generation of women writers who used literature to advance political issues.

Stowe was never again to attempt such direct sexual speech. Having gotten severely burned in this early attempt to speak of woman's wrongs, Stowe retreated to her earlier posture of speaking indirectly and attempting to wield her influence behind the scenes. She had already declined taking up the banner of woman's rights at public conventions and at the helm of the *Revolution*. In 1870–1871, as the issues of marriage and sexuality which she herself had raised in the Byron case came more and more to dominate discussions of woman's rights, Stowe became more circumspect yet. She wrote editorials that she urged her brother to publish under his name. It was safer and perhaps more effective to be a *femme couverte*. Stowe was in a good position to pursue this strategy, for Henry Ward Beecher had just acquired a new newspaper.

With the help of money from John Howard, Beecher bought out the *Church Union* and set about creating a rival religious organ to the *Indepen-dent*, still under the editorship of his old partner, Theodore Tilton. Effective with the first number that issued under his name in January 1870, Beecher changed the name to the *Christian Union*. Elizabeth Cady Stanton praised not only the change of name "but the enlargement of the paper, with much additional artistic beauty." She called Beecher's inaugural article "a model of newspaper excellence" and expected that the new magazine's "success and prosperity" would be "well deserved."[81] Although Stanton listed both Isabella Beecher Hooker and Harriet Beecher Stowe as "principal contrib-utors" to the 1870 *Revolution*, Harriet's lukewarm support of Stanton's paper could not withstand the appeal of a Beecher family paper. Stowe hailed her brother's acquisition of the *Christian Union* as an opportunity to have the pulpit she had always desired. "I have all my life but especially lately gone with a gospel burning in my bosom which I longed to preach but could not because I was a woman," she told Henry; "[I] have had to sit under preaching that did nt hit & did nt warm & did nt comfort." She hoped together they could make the *Christian Union* "so distinctively a gospel that seekers & enquirers shall come to it as their natural food."[82] When Harriet had sat in the chapel at Andover under the dry preaching of Professor Parks, she had dreamed of a kind of Beecher family college: "Edward on systematic theology and Ch[urch] History—Mr Stowe Biblical Criticism Revd HWB on home-letics & Pastoral Theology Revd Charles sacred Music Rhetoric & Oratory—There's a faculty for you."[83] Here at last was the medium for such a distin-guished Beecher family curriculum. She and Calvin agreed to supply the *Union* with three columns a week, he from his studies on the New Testa-ment, she from her lore of travel, current events, and scriptural meditations.[84] Catharine Beecher contributed occasional articles on education, Edward Beecher articles on theology, and Thomas Beecher articles on current topics. Eunice Beecher kept up a column on "Motherly Talks with Young Housekeepers" and Henry resumed the position he had had at the *Independent* of writing editorials.[85] "What I want is that the paper be a *power*—and a distinctively *Christian* power," Harriet wrote Henry; "Keep strong hold & *Beecherism* and the paper will be all right."[86] After her maiden attempt at sexual speech, Stowe beat a hasty retreat into "Beecherism," made possible by the *Christian Union*, which was in every sense a family organ.

Stowe soon had need of Henry's editorial power. In the summer of 1870 Justin McCarthy in the *Galaxy* and Eugene Benson in the *Revolution* published articles extolling George Sand's liberated views of "the Marriage Question." Benson quoted approvingly the following passage from Sand's *Jacques*: "[M]arriage is always, in my idea, one of the most barbarous institutions which society has sketched. I do not doubt it will be abolished some day, if the human species makes any progress toward justice and reason." Benson observed, "This was written thirty-five years ago. Today, John Stuart Mill in England and Henry James in our own country, have dared only incidently to put forth an analogous conception of the relation of the sexes."[87]

Stowe was appalled by this equation of the women's movement with "French" ideas. George Sand's sexual adventures had been the topic of discussion when Stowe was in Paris, and the sensation she created had led Stowe, ever attentive to public opinion, to investigate. She discovered that no French woman could visit Sand without fear of "lost caste."[88] Here was a woman who was "nearly a female Lovelace, misusing and abandoning men,"[89] who compounded her indiscretions by boldly writing about them in her books. As Stowe explained to her brother,

> She lived with Alfred De Musset & after he was dead published all the particulars of her adultery with him and his grossness to her under the title of "Elle et Lui"—a novel which I have read Then his brother Paul published *his* side & called it lui et Elle which I have read also & between the two it was *about* as vile a slough as I ever saw—Those two novels had just appeared when I was in Paris & I heard the discussions on them among the Literati of the time. *Lelia* was so bad a book that Beranger reproved her for publishing it. It *shocked* Beranger and if you consider what Beranger has published you may imagine *what Lelia* is—I have read that too.

Describing *Lelia* as the experience of a French prostitute—"the lustful despair of a worn out female debauchee"—Stowe explained to her brother,

> I read that too for at the time I was investigating French literature Now you see George Sand writes exquisite french—her style is something wonderful & *utterly untranslatable* so that we get none of that & *can* get none in a translation but she is as utterly without just moral training as it is possible to be. She is the animalism & atheism of this century impersonated.[90]

Nothing if not thorough, Stowe went to the very bottom of this slough of immorality and even read Sand's many-volumed autobiography, a project that greatly extended her vocabulary and education. Such debauched reading held no dangers for her but she was convinced it would mislead the masses.

Eugene Benson, the author of the article on Sand that appeared in the *Revolution*, was "said to be living in free love bonds with Mrs Fletcher," and as Harriet explained to Henry Ward Beecher, such people "[n]aturally . . . want to use the woman movement for establishing a new order of things in which men & women shall be free to choose over & over as often as they are tiring of a former love." Stowe feared that the "simple American women" were likely to follow down this dangerous path out of sexual ignorance—or to put it in Stowe's terms, ignorance of things *"French."* She noted, "Susan Anthony & other honest old maids who know no more evil than an old country ministers horse will suppose of course that Lelia is a womans right tract & bye & bye when Virginia Vaughn translates it we shall have the literary editor of the Watchman & Reflector & perhaps Times Herald giving it a lift."[91]

Stowe sent Henry an article she had written in reply to Benson, urging him to run it "as editorial in which case it will have the sanction of your authority." Acknowledging that they were both committed to the woman movement, she warned, "But if it gets under the generalship of Madame George Sand *we* can do nothing—It will be such a devils mess as we can have nothing to do with."[92] Although her thorough knowledge of George Sand's life and work made her the likely person to quell "this *French* movement which threatens the whole of the woman movement," she told Henry, "the things to be said are such as a *man* can far better say & such as would only draw malignant reaction on me. For if a woman undertakes to utter a protest when licentiousness is concerned she is overwhelmed with a deluge of filth."[93]

The Byron affair, while it constrained her public speech, raised her consciousness of the sexual double standard. Several weeks after her letter to Henry about George Sand an editorial in the *Nation* attempted to cast doubt on the reputations of the leaders of the woman's rights movement.[94] Harriet was outraged. She told Henry, "Mr. Godkins attack on the *character* of all the women of the movement by throwing broadcast among them in coarse terms the statement that *some* of them are abandoned characters, is one of the most brutal things I ever read . . . [and] ought not to be suffered to go."[95] She sent him yet another editorial. This one retreated from the bold declarations she had recently made in the pages of the *Hearth and Home* and in her personal correspondence. "The womans right folks are wrong on one point," she wrote. "The man *is* & ought to be the head of the woman he ought to be her head morally as well as physically and intellectually." Elevating man above woman was the only way Stowe could counter the double standard without giving up the fiction of the sexless Victorian angel, and the vicious response of the press to the Byron scandal convinced her that to do this would throw women into the slough of licentiousness with men. Thus she concluded that man should be even more pure than woman. His sin was made worse by his "sexual preeminence . . . as being the source of generative creative power."[96] The double standard she was attempting to reverse was embodied in the *Nation's* position that "any interference with men's established rights of licentiousness on womens part is indelicate." Harriet explained to Henry,

> [The *Nation*] has all along taken the ground that of course men are to know the ropes, to sow the oats to be comparatively "gross and low" & its standard is below—immeasurably below even that of modern English literature as expressed by Charles Dickens Thackeray & Trollop all of whom are writers that would elevate the sense of responsibility in young men on this subject
>
> I therefore have prepared an Editorial to meet the Nation on the religious ground
>
> The New Testament is the only ground on which we can fight both sides— The free lovers who claim licence for women instead of liberty & the Major Pendennises who claim licence for men & slavery for women
>
> But I must have liberty to fight this battle under your shield. You have seen how they can insult a woman that has a word to say. Give me the right of an editorial now & then & we will fire shots from the Christian Union on both sides.[97]

Henry, however, was preoccupied with other battles. When Harriet saw that her editorials had not appeared, she told him to send them back if he did not plan to use them. Worried about the dangers the topic of sexuality posed for the woman's movement and viewing Stanton as "dreadfully unfit to open such a subject,"[98] Stowe placed an item in the *Woman's Journal*, the well-financed organ of the American Woman's Suffrage Association (AWSA), the conservative, rival organization to Stanton's National Woman's Suffrage Association (NWSA). As the *Nation* noted, "Mrs. Stowe has written to the *Woman's Journal* warning the friends of suffrage against meddling with marriage and divorce, of which they are unjustly accused by the public."[99] When Stanton got wind of this and of Stowe's position on George Sand, all the disappointment that she felt over not landing Stowe for the *Revolution* was mixed with her disdain for Stowe's conservative betrayal, and she reacted. "You see, what an envenomed response has come from Mrs. Stanton [at] the mere glimpse of my sentiments on George Sand," Stowe wrote to Mary A. Livermore, editor of the *Woman's Journal*; "I was blank with astonishment." The contradictions held together by the ideology of true womanhood and the sexual double standard were about to break into full bloom and divide the woman's movement. "If it be free divorce & free love that is wanted & if Madame Sand is on the banner," she wrote to Livermore, "there will come a return wave whose strength you have no idea—I for one shall go with all my might and strength against such a movement."[100]

Attempting to head off the takeover of woman's rights by "free divorce and free love," Stowe reverted to her most effective medium, serial fiction. Stowe's *My Wife and I*, serialized in the *Christian Union* between November 12, 1870, and November 8, 1871, contained an extended portrait of Victoria

Woodhull, dubbed by Stowe "Miss Audacia Dangyereyes." A bold woman who walks with impunity into bachelor quarters and bullies men into taking her newspaper, which the narrator describes as "an exposition of all the wildest principles of modern French communism," Audacia Dangyereyes is condemned by Stowe for imperiling the post–Civil War movement of women toward independence. Her insistence on acting "like a man" and "claiming a right to dispense with womanly decorums" will "destroy the feeling of chivalry and delicacy on the part of men" and throw the republic into confusion as such mischief did "in France before the Revolution."[101] Lydia Maria Child shared Stowe's view of Woodhull, calling her and her associates "a great blister to my spirit. They are doing immense harm to the real progress of women."[102]

Almost simultaneously with *My Wife and I*, Stowe began another serial in *Old and New*, a journal edited by her nephew, Edward Everett Hale. In *Pink and White Tyranny*, as she explained to Henry, she "baited [her] trap" to capture women who "wont *read* an article on that subject."[103] Conceived in the spring of 1869 before her reading of Mill and her involvement with the Byron case, this story was designed, as Stowe explained to Hale,

> to show the domestic oppression practiced by a gentle pretty pink & white doll on a strong minded generous gentleman who has married her in a fit of poetical romance because she looks pretty It will be in a quiet way an offset to a class of writings which I am sorry to see which represent men as in most cases oppressors & women as sufferers in domestic life.
>
> This is my plan & being *to some extent* a woman's rights woman, as I am *to some extent*, something of almost every thing that goes—I shall have a right to say a word or two on the other side.[104]

By the time *Old and New* began serializing *Pink and White Tyranny* in August 1870, Stowe had the benefit of her experience with the Byron affair and the attempted takeover of woman's rights by advocates of free love. Both of these reinforced the more characteristic conservativism of her story as it was originally conceived. She used *Pink and White Tyranny* to have her say about woman's true role and took swipes at free love and French novels, whose invariable plot was "a young wife, tired of domestic monotony, with an unappreciative husband, solacing herself with the devotion of a lover."[105]

Stowe little dreamed that the free lovers would attack, as their first citadel to be stormed, Beecherism itself. In 1872 Victoria Woodhull used one of her well-attended public lectures to accuse Henry Ward Beecher of having committed adultery with Theodore Tilton's wife. As Woodhull explained in "Tried as by Fire,"

> It was not that I desired or had any right to personally attack this individual; but something had to be done to break down the partition walls of prejudice that prevented public consideration of the sexual problem, and fully to launch it upon the tide of popular discussion. . . . It was necessary that somebody should be hurt. I cast the thunderbolt into the very centre of the socio-religio-

moral camp of the enemy and struck their chieftain, and the world trembled at the blow. In twenty years not anybody will say that I was wrong, any more than anybody now says that the old leaders of the anti-slavery revolution were wrong in attacking slavery in the concrete.[106]

Perhaps because she bore some responsibility for provoking Woodhull, Harriet Beecher Stowe's response to this "thunderbolt" was more envenomed than anything in her entire career.

Within the Beecher family, the passions Woodhull's charge aroused were the more intense for being simultaneously alloyed with family honor, sibling rivalries, and conflicting positions on woman's rights. Isabella Beecher Hooker, having allied herself more publicly than Harriet with the sexual radicals of Stanton's NWSA (who in turn had embraced Woodhull), did not immediately rush to Henry's defense. Her skepticism about male sexual virtue and her belief that the sexual double standard must be done away with shaped her response. Her careful positioning of herself on these matters is evident in a letter she wrote to Anthony the preceding year. Referring to material she had read in Woodhull's newspaper, *Woodhull & Claflin's Weekly*, she wrote:

> One article in her paper in favor of licensing prostitution & one hateful one in favor of Black Crook have displeased me much—I wrote a reply to the first which may be published & may not—but any woman who allows her paper to go for that business will not long find herself at home in our company I think—I am keeping quiet however—still praising & defending her though my sisters, all three, staying at Dr Taylor's have nearly crazed me with letters imploring me to have nothing to do with her.

In spite of the fact that Harriet sent Isabella information implicating Woodhull in a sexual scandal with one of Henry's parishioners, Isabella took the position that she would "not denounce her publicaly, however guilty till the time when men guilty of the same crimes are avoided and denounced."[107] While Isabella moved toward Stanton's NWSA and Harriet toward the more conservative AWSA, Catharine Beecher bemoaned "the ignorance & mistaken zeal of my poor sister Bell & her coagitators" who did not understand "how much *moral* power [woman] gained by taking a subordinate place—as the Bible & Nature both teach is her true position."[108]

Woodhull's countercharge that Henry Beecher himself had committed adultery with one of his parishioners played beautifully on the sexual politics of the double standard. If Woodhull could bring down the major spokesman of religion, the fabric of Victorian deceptions and sexual stereotypes would be irreparably rent asunder. The fact that he might not be guilty of the particular crime she charged him with did not matter as much as the fact that many men were and that he might be. Then again, the truth or falsity of such charges could not be determined in any impartial court of public opinion as long as the double standard prevailed. Woodhull herself had suffered harassment, contumely, and eviction from her apartment in response to her attempt to form a radical third party to challenge the Republicans.[109] She had been put in jail for violating the Comstock Law, a broad piece of legislation passed in 1872 that, by outlawing the distribution through the mails of all material deemed obscene, effectively capped the fledgling attempts of the woman's movement to engage sexual issues. If the Comstock Law had been in effect in 1869 it would have made Stowe and the *Atlantic Monthly* liable to prosecution for "The True Story of Lady Byron's Life." It would be invoked in 1916 when Margaret Sanger was jailed for distributing information on birth control. Fairness, under the present unequal positions of men and women, was impossible, and Woodhull meant to right the scales of justice by storming what she took to be a bastion of male Victorian righteousness.

In December 1872, several months after her notorious attack on Beecher, Woodhull planned a public lecture in Boston, under the very noses of the American Woman's Suffrage Association of which Henry Ward Beecher was the president. Harriet, whose whispering campaign against Woodhull seems to have been in part the motivation for Woodhull's counter-charges against her brother, flew into action to prevent the lecture. She met with James and Annie Fields at the Osgoods and explained the situation. At Annie's suggestion, James Fields met with the man who made the arrangements with Woodhull for use of the Boston Music Hall, a Mr. Peck, but discovered that he was only an agent in a money-making speculation. Harriet, in the meantime, applied to Kinnard, apparently a man who had an interest and influence in the lucrative lecture-circuit business. While they were talking, in burst the redoubtable James Redpath, founder of the Redpath Lyceum Bureau in Boston. He persuaded Kinnard that Woodhull's lecture, if allowed to occur, would be "an eternal disgrace to Boston." Beecherism, Brahminism and Boston were, after all, more than casually connected. Harriet also sought out her friend, Mary Claflin, the wife of the governor. She found her "all on fire with indignation" at Woodhull's proposed assault on Boston's decency; perhaps at Harriet's urging, Governor and Mrs. Claflin applied to the mayor and his wife to stop the lecture.[110] "Those vile women 'jailbirds['] had the impudence to undertake to advertise that they were going to give a lecture in the Music Hall," wrote Harriet to her daughters. "It appears that lectures cannot be given without a license from the city government which is not to be forthcoming."[111]

While Boston's best attempted to squelch free speech on sexual issues, the Beecher–Tilton affair smouldered on, providing a riveting soap opera of sexual intrigue and masculine rivalries that dominated the national press for over a year. Henry Ward Beecher was ultimately exonerated of all charges, but not before he endured both an ecclesiastical trial and a civil trial. The financial cost alone to Beecher totaled $118,000.[112] Just as Stanton's party had used the McFarland case and Stowe's implication of Lord Byron to publicize the wrongs of woman, so they milked the Beecher–Tilton trial for all it was worth. Harriet felt that the sexual roles were totally reversed, however, and with them, the wrongs. Just as Lady Byron had kept a noble silence that was used against her, so her brother Henry chose at first not to answer the charges. This stance led to an elaboration of the evidence against him, and his silence was taken for guilt. His Brooklyn parish stood solidly with him, but Harriet complained to Mrs. Claflin about "the cold indifference of much of the press." Worse was the perfidy of Tilton and his colluder, Frank Moulton. At the request of a parish committee charged with investigating the charge, Henry had turned over private correspondence to them. Harriet was outraged to learn that while Henry was respecting the pledge of silence he gave to Moulton and Tilton, "they were showing all his letters & notes & concessions to Mrs. Stanton & the free love roost of harpies generally who were exulting over the scrape he was being drawn into & meaning to use it to coerce him into favoring their unclear theories & unclear leader." Harriet told Mrs. Claflin, "Having been inside I know how false & devlish beyond all expression the whole crew are."[113] To Harriet, their publication of letters entrusted for safekeeping was an outrageous betrayal; to Stanton, it was a logical use of ammunition in the war of the sexes.

In her most passionate attacks on the apologists of slavery, Stowe had never demonized the slaveholders. Now Stowe labeled Woodhull a "witch" and explained her power over her sister Isabella as a form of demonic possession. Begging her to keep "strictly confidential the *talk I had with you the other night*," Stowe wrote to Mrs. Claflin,

> No one could understand the secret of her influence over my poor sister— incredible infatuation continuing even now. I trust that God will in some way deliver her for she was and is a lovely good woman & before this witch took possession of her we were all so happy together. I hope my sister going abroad & that this will break the spell. . . . I did want in case it should creep out & you should hear it that you should understand the whole story.[114]

Writing to Henry to support him in his struggle against "the powers of darkness," she warned him, "Fully do I believe that wretched woman to be under the agency of Satanic spirits—& I recognize that in this attack we wrestle not with flesh & blood."[115] When, in the 1840s, Calvin Stowe had written to Harriet about the sexual temptations to which male ministers were regularly exposed, she had had a vivid vision of her husband and her brothers falling. Now, she enshrined in her heart a sexless portrait of Henry as an "angel." Although he was fifty-eight years old, Stowe confessed to the Duchess of Argyle that to her he was still her baby brother: "I cannot feel him any thing else than young." To her cousin, Elizabeth Lyman, Harriet wrote, "he is more angel than brother—he is too good for me—I sit and think over all his sorrow, all the *injustice* that was at one time done him—& all his gentle childlike tenderness of heart."[116] Reconstructing Henry Ward Beecher as a sexless angel was consistent with her new policy of attacking the double standard by holding men to a standard even more virtuous than that of the Victorian woman.

Harriet refused to hear any discussion of the mere possibility that her brother might be guilty of adultery. This meant that she had, for the time being, to avoid seeing Isabella. "Your aunt is like many monomaniacs," Harriet explained to her daughter Eliza, "all right if the wrong string is not jarred but I fear that seeing me will jar it." She continued:

> I am not a person who takes offence easily—it is very difficult to offend me— but there are things which strike my *very life* and these accusations against my brother are among them. I cannot hear that subject discussed as a *possibility* open for inquiry without such an intense uprising of indignation & scorn & anger as very few have ever seen in me in these late years—but if ever I should hear those who ought to know better maundering out insinuations & doubts about him I think there will be the eruption of a volcano that has for years been supposed to be extinct—they will see *what* I am—when thoroughly roused.[117]

Knowing full well that this was a battle that would ultimately be decided in the court of public opinion, Harriet urged the editors of the *Christian Union* to be up and doing in defense of their standard-bearer. The paper had followed Henry's example by maintaining a discreet silence, but its subscribers, who wanted more than anything to read the latest episode in the melodrama, began falling off. Harriet urged that it was not too late: "[L]et the Union stand forth in a bold manly attitude of defence of Henry and the truth, & subscribers will come in fast enough—Give people what they want & they'l subscribe Boldness becomes truth & boldness boldness boldness is my crusade."[118] To the reluctant Henry she urged, "we need to thunder from Zion a little to clear the atmosphere."[119] She was even willing to cultivate an unsavory alliance with a Mr. Amos, "a little black haired black eyed sallow wirey man," because of his influence with the *Memphis Daily Appeal* and the *Louisville Courier*. Admitting that Mr. Amos was "sanctimonious" and "not really very engaging," she told Eunice Beecher, "but I think he has power at the south."[120]

Her work behind the scenes included her serial stories. In 1874 she wrote another, *We and Our Neighbors*, which, like *My Wife and I*, was serialized in the *Christian Union*. In these "society novels" Stowe wrote a kind of journalistic fiction, half editorial, half story. Loosely plotted and often carelessly constructed, these "society novels" still sparkle with Stowe's satirical asides and seemingly effortless metaphors. Here she is describing the social climbing of Mrs. Follingsbee in *Pink and White Tyranny*: "Now these Van Astrachans were one of those cold, glittering, inaccessible pinnacles in Mrs. Follingsbee's fashionable Alp-climbing which she would spare no expense to reach if possible. . . . It will be seen here that our friend, Mrs. Follingsbee, like all ladies whose watchword is 'Excelsior,' had a peculiar, difficult, and slippery path to climb."[121] Sometimes employing the male narrators and the family dialogues that were a feature of her *House and Home Papers*, Stowe attempted to regain control of the social issues and to speak on "hot" topics without getting burned herself. She used a medium that, in the words of her character, Henry Henderson, had "a power far outgoing that of the pulpit, and that of books. This constant daily self-asserting literature of newspapers and periodicals is acting on us tremendously for good or for ill. It has access to us at all hours and gets itself heard as a preacher cannot, and gets itself read as scarcely any book does."[122] With a circulation of 133,000, the *Christian Union* had a better chance of gaining the public ear than Woodhull, who had increasingly to rely on notoriety.[123] The Comstock Law effectively stemmed th e radical sexual utterances of the woman's rights folk, and Stowe did her best to corral the stray sheep of public opinion into the fold of Victorian respectability. The final phase of her career had begun.

CHAPTER TWENTY-SEVEN

Valedictory:
1870–1896

*I*n 1870, *in the midst of* the free love battles, Stowe became a grandmother. As she threw herself into the role of "first granny in waiting" to
Freeman Allen, Georgiana's son, a whimsical solution to the "woman
controversy" occurred to her. If all the women handed over the babies to the
men and refused to take them back until they had gained their rights, she
predicted that after a week the men would say, "Tell us what you want."[1]
Nevertheless, Stowe savored her new role. Increasingly she divided her time
between Georgie in Stockbridge and her winter home in Florida.

As she withdrew into family and friends, her children began once again
to feature prominently in the rhythms of her days. She had been with Georgiana when she gave birth and she stayed with her for several months afterward, attempting to lift her spirits and dispel a dangerous case of postpartum
depression. Stowe's efforts to create a cheerful atmosphere around the new
mother were checked at every turn by Mrs. Hatch, the nurse, who had had
ten children of her own and was incapable of the least movement without a
heavy sigh or a groan. As Stowe told her sister Mary, Mrs. Hatch's children
had had "every ailment under the sun" and consequently she took Freeman's
smallest cry or burp as evidence of the end. "[Y]esterday, [she] came croaking
to me because he started in his sleep & his face twitched & his eyes rolled
up—Twas a sign he was going to have fits she said—I told her I had had six
that twitched a good deal more & rolled up their eyes & had cholic every day
& they never any of them had fits."[2] When Mrs. Hatch wasn't fussing about
the baby, she was worrying Georgie about catching cold or bleeding to death

in five minutes. Stowe feared that she would fan one of Georgie's "flimsies" into full-fledged melancholia. "There never was a healthier woman in her circumstances nor a more perfectly quiet healthy baby," Stowe told Hatty; "The Doctor says he never saw any one get up better. But ever since that attack last summer Georgie has been liable to morbid fear—her situation seems to her full of unknown dangers."[3] Not perceiving this incipient paranoia as a symptom of morphine addiction, Stowe pitted her characteristic optimism against the dire predictions of Mrs. Hatch.

While she was attending Georgie, Stowe received news that Thomas Perkins was ill and dying. She wrote to Mary that she did not dare come to his deathbed, for this would mean leaving Georgie in the hands of the doleful Mrs. Hatch: "You know the danger with [Georgie] is not in the womb or the muscles or the want of physical strength but in that excitable state of the *brain* which came on before her confinement & which makes her extremely susceptible to fear & alarm."[4] While her concern for Georgie was real, Stowe increasingly protected herself from scenes of death and mourning.[5]

Freeman Allen was baptized later that month of October 1870. Stowe dwelled with satisfaction on the ceremonial details of the Episcopal service. The baptismal font was wreathed in evergreen ferns that Stowe herself arranged. Two-month-old Freeman Allen was layered in garments upon which women had bestowed many hours of stitching and ingenious design. His lace dress was topped by a richly embroidered white cashmere sack and "his best embroidered blanket and petticoat." The crowning touch was a pink afghan made by Eliza. When the baby and Georgie and Mrs. Hatch had been placed in a phaeton, Grandmother Stowe "ran with all [her] might" and managed to get to the church "by the time they were out of the carriage." Calvin Stowe, the godfather, cut a "venerable figure" and recited his part in the Episcopal ceremony, reported Harriet, "as if he had been born & brought up in the church."[6]

Thomas Perkins's death was the first since George Beecher's premature one in 1843 to strike within Harriet's generation. While she was still surrounded by a remarkably large group of siblings, headed by Edward, who would live into his nineties, Thomas Perkins's death shook her security. The family was beginning to break up. "I cannot describe how much this affects me," Harriet wrote to Mary after his death, "I cannot account for it—only ever since I felt that I no longer could go to my Father for advice & guidance & support I have always hurried to Mr Perkins He was always so cheerful so strong and so helpful and so willing to hear & advise & do that I never felt that I burdened him."[7] In some ways his death affected her more than her father's had, for Lyman Beecher had wandered mentally for many years before he died and Harriet had long ceased to lean upon him. In the midst of the quixotic Beecher family, Thomas Perkins had been a rock of predictability.

Although she had not been present at Perkins's deathbed, she received reports of his last hours. The groans he had made as he struggled to release

his soul from his body were very like, Harriet thought, the groans that Georgie had made as she delivered Freeman Allen into this world. Watching by
the bedside of death and life were remarkably similar experiences. Meditat-
ing on the similarity of these two great moments of transition, Stowe wrote
a piece for the *Christian Union* called "A Look Beyond the Veil." "It did me
good to write it and I hope it may do others good to read it," she told Mary.[8]
Describing heaven as a home "in a far country," Stowe drew together the
strands of what might be called an "emigrant's theology." As the large
Beecher family had spread itself geographically from the East Coast to the
far reaches of the Western Reserve, its members had frequent recourse to
the psalmist's lament, "here we have no continuing city but seek one to
come." In the 1830s family members viewed their geographical separation
as a removal almost like that effected by death. "Every day, & more & more
I look forward to our meeting in Heaven," Henry Ward Beecher had written
his father from Indianapolis. "On earth it hardly seems possible, that we can
be much together."[9] As family and friends were left behind—or sent ahead
to "my Father's house"—it was quite natural to speak of the treasures that
death was laying up in heaven and to think of heaven as home. "I feel like a
Stranger and a Pilgrim and wish to be content to travel the remainder of my
journey thro life like one who seeks in all humility for *a better country*," wrote
Harriet Foote from Cincinnati to her sister in Nutplains.[10] William Beecher
wrote from Putnam, Ohio, in 1841, "here we have very little company—&
really feel lonesome. . . . I do not expect to find a home or resting place
here."[11] The popular appeal of the domesticated heaven of Elizabeth Stuart
Phelp's *The Gates Ajar*, written in the aftermath of the tremendous losses of
the Civil War, tapped a pre-existing nostalgia for a home that never was.
Stowe's essay for the November 5, 1870, *Christian Union* reworked this
domesticated heaven with typical psychological realism:

> We are here upon this earth as a family of children, whose father has prepared
> for them a better home in a far country. We have not seen it, and so do not
> know exactly how it looks,—and the home where we at present sojourn is
> familiar and dear. When, therefore, one member after another is summoned
> to go forward—when the home is gradually being despoiled of this and that
> familiar belonging, sent forward to their future residence, there may come
> some dreary hours, and some natural sickness of heart.[12]

Stowe's most anguishing trial lay ahead of her, and it was not to be as
swift and sure as the stroke of death. She had long prayed that some "way
of escape" would open for her poor son Fred. In 1871, certain that he could
not overcome the temptation of drink and equally certain that his continued
presence was an insupportable burden to his family, Fred resolved to go to
sea. "[D]id I only think of my own comfort I would kill myself and end it
all," he told his mother, "but I know that you and all the family would feel
the disgrace such an end would bring upon you and the talk and scandle it
would give rise to."[13] He sailed around the Horn to San Francisco, but then

went ashore and simply disappeared. Whether he went on a waterfront drinking spree and then met with some untoward event or simply took his own life, his parents never learned. Even in his end, the unlucky Fred Stowe was unable to let his parents rest easy.

In Florida where Harriet and Calvin spent November through May of each year they escaped from the battles that raged in the press and often swirled around the Beechers. During Plymouth Church's investigation of the Beecher–Tilton affair, Harriet told Annie Fields that, "[f]ar from the centres and taking no New York paper we feel not the daily rockings & undulations of its life & know only in generals."[14] Her room opened on a veranda among the orange trees; from there she had a fine view of the St. Johns River. Sometimes she would move her writing desk outside so she could sit facing "the glorious blue river . . . with the cool air playing through the branches about me."[15] Here she and Calvin caught up on their reading. In his retirement Calvin had grown a long white beard and increased his weight to 210 pounds. Harriet called him her "Rabbi," an appellation that fit the biblical scholar; perhaps Harriet bestowed it with an awareness that she played the role of the Jewish wife supporting her scholarly husband.[16] When June came, Harriet was often reluctant to pack up and return to the North. "I hate to leave my calm isle of Patmos—where the world is not & I have such quiet long hours for writing," she told James Fields. "Hawthorne ought to have lived in an orange grove in Florida."[17] When the sun warmed the surface of her skin and the lizards darted in and out of the shingles of the roof and the mingled calls of the birds made the yard reverberate, then "merely to breathe and be is to be blest."[18]

Under the influence of her second season in Mandarin she opened a correspondence with George Eliot. Although the two were never to meet, Stowe poured out her heart in long, searching, reflective meditations on her past, her literary career, and their common interests as literary women.[19] She described for Eliot her life in Mandarin:

> It is like Sorrento—so like that I can quite dream of being there & when I get here I enter another life The world recedes—I am out of it—it ceaces to influence—its bustle & noise die away in the far distance—& here is no winter— an open air life a quaint rude wild wilderness sort of life both rude & rich— but when I am here I write more letters to friends than ever I do elsewhere. The mail comes only twice a week & then is the event of the day—
>
> My old Rabbi & I have set up our tent—He with German & Greek & Hebrew—devouring all sorts of black letter books—& I, spinning ideal webs out of bits that he lets fall here & there.[20]

While she was in Florida in the spring of 1872 Stowe received an inquiry from a Mr. Williams, who ran the American Literary Bureau of Boston. He wanted her to do a series of readings from her works. It would be a New England tour of the principal cities, perhaps beginning in Boston and moving in a circle through towns in Massachusetts, then moving into Rhode Island,

New Hampshire, and Maine. The value of such a tour in promoting her work was obvious, and to claim lecture-circuit status along with Emerson and Holmes and other luminaries of the Saturday Club had an equally obvious appeal. Mr. Williams offered liberal terms. Stowe worried about her health and whether she could fill such a vast space as Tremont Temple, but she did not once consider that to read in public might be unladylike. The Civil War and the outspokenness of woman's rights advocates had finally made the public sphere available to women of all classes.[21]

After spending the hottest weeks of the summer at Twin Mountain House, a resort in New Hampshire, Stowe opened her tour in Springfield on September 13, followed by engagements at Lynn and Salem on September 16 and 17. Before she had even started her tour she viewed it as a convenient way to visit friends en route. She made plans to stop at Nutplains to visit her cousin, Hannah Foote, and she hoped to stay with James and Annie Fields either in Boston, where she would be at the end of the month, or at their summer home in Manchester when she came to Salem.[22] Mrs. Claflin tried to enlist her to read at her North End Mission, a favorite charity, but Harriet had to tell her she was already booked.[23] She did read in Portland and Bangor, reporting to her husband that

> the latter, which I had dreaded as lonesome and far off, turned out the pleasantest of any place I have visited yet. I stayed at the Fays; he was one of the Andover students, you remember; and found a warm, cosy, social home. In the evening I met an appreciative audience, and had a delightful reading. I read Captain Kittridge, apparently to the great satisfaction of the people, who laughed heartily at his sea stories, and the "Minister's Housekeeper" with the usual success, also Eva and Topsy.[24]

In October all of her plans were jeopardized when she got word that Calvin Stowe had been stricken suddenly by paralysis. She wrote to Williams to see if she could be released from her contract, but the very next day after Calvin had had to be carried up the stairs he was able to ride horseback. The attack returned seven days later, and then seven days after that—the telltale sign of malaria.[25] Harriet arranged for the twins to make sure that Calvin did not skip any of his doses of quinine and she kept going; she read at Haverhill the next Tuesday night, then in Wakefield on Wednesday and North Bridgewater on Thursday. She spent the weekend with Charley, who was a student at Harvard. Then it was off to Peabody and Danbury, where she read November 20, and then north to Amherst, east to Andover, south to New London, east to Newport, finishing with engagements in two towns in southern New Hampshire. "Andover was quite a trump," she reported to Annie Fields. "I never spoke to so sympathetic an audience—it was an ovation."[26] She found that the traveling agreed with her. "So far, my health has been better than any autumn for several years," she told her daughters. "The fatigue of excitement & all lessens as I get accustomed to it & the fatigue of railroad travel seems to do me good I never sleep better than after a long days ride." Just to make sure, she doused her system with four bottles of cod liver oil and phosphate of lime.[27]

In the meantime Calvin Stowe convalesced at the home of the Eastmans in Boston, attended by the loyal twins. Harriet fussed long distance about his medication and his failure to follow instructions,[28] but the most awkward part of his illness was not that Harriet was away from home but that there was no home for him to go to. One of the motivations for buying a place in Florida had been to escape from the cost of Oakholm during the most expensive months of the winter. It had become apparent almost as soon as they moved into Harriet's dream house that it was not a practical choice; by 1867 they were looking for a way to lift "the great burden of that Hartford establishment . . . from [their] shoulders."[29] They sold Oakholm in 1870. For the next two years they would have no home except Mandarin; when they were in the North they either vacationed in New Hampshire, visited Georgie, or boarded. As Harriet prepared to buy presents for the Eastmans as a token of her appreciation of their kind hospitality to her husband, whose illness precipitated a stay of three weeks, she wrote to her daughters, "[M]y first object now is to secure a peaceable & quiet *home* where he may have all his things about him & not be in danger of becoming a burden in other families than his own." She recalled how harassed Lyman Beecher had been in his old age by the domestic upsets and shiftings that poverty and circumstance imposed on him, to the detriment of his mental health, in Harriet's view. Expressing great relief that Calvin Stowe had escaped this crisis with his mental faculties intact, and perhaps feeling some accumulated guilt for the lack of order in which he had lived most of his life with her, Harriet determined to settle down.[30] She told her children, "I am so grateful to God that he is spared to me a little longer for I am so dependent on his superior knowledge & judgement in my profession, that I hardly feel that I could ever be much without him."[31] Conventional patriarchal pieties regularly appear in Stowe's letters to her children, as if she were protecting them from the independence she herself had achieved and shoring up Calvin's status as head of the house. Yet her reliance on Calvin's literary and scholarly judgment was real; moreover, their long life together had forged a deep loyalty.

In December 1872, as she sent her children Christmas presents from where she was staying in Framingham, Massachusetts, she wrote

> If it please God this shall be the last season that my family shall be scattered wanderers sick in hotels & boarding houses & other people's families—it is not respectable & there must be an end to this. I have about concluded to buy Mr Chamberlain's house possession given the middle of April. Every body says it is a valuable property & rising in value & it is a lovely beautiful house & the terms are quite within my means.[32]

With the purchase of this house on Forest Street in Hartford, Stowe acquired a comfortable home next door to which Samuel Clemens would soon rear a red-brick mansion designed to look like the Mississippi steamboats of his youth. Here she and Calvin settled into the final years of their life together.

Not, however, before Harriet took on another lecture tour, this time in the West. in 1873 she made a circuit of the Western Reserve that forty years earlier Lyman Beecher had vowed to save for godly New Englandism. The tour opened in the Opera House at Reading, Pennsylvania, on September 30, where she drew an appreciative but moderate-size audience. She read from eight to ten o'clock in the evening. Then her daughter Hatty, who accompanied her, packed their trunks and they took the night train for the next stop, Williamsport, where she read the next evening, followed by a stop in Elmira, where they stayed with Thomas Beecher. On October 2 she read in Oswego, on October 3 in Syracuse. Then it was the sleeping cars to Buffalo for a reading on October 7. She was in Cleveland on October 8, in Toledo on October 9, and Detroit on October 10. Then it was off to Indianapolis.[33] Her agent, Mr. Williams, had sent a man ahead of her to clock the times so that she had no more than a half day's travel and several hours of rest before each reading. "Hattie goes with me & takes all the care of packing & every thing of this kind & a lively sprightly young Mr. Saunders is deputed to wait on us as valet de voyage," Stowe told her son Charles, "so that it really amounts to a journey in the pleasantest month in the year with all attendence & expenses paid."[34] She rode trains from central Pennsylvania to upper New York State into Ohio and Michigan; from Michigan she dipped down into Indiana, Kentucky, Illinois, and Missouri before heading back by way of Cincinnati and Pittsburgh to New York.

As she ranged into the West of her young womanhood, the audiences grew larger; moreover, she was greeted at every stop by former neighbors, friends, and domestic servants. In Toledo it was a schoolmate from the Litchfield Female Academy.[35] In Bloomington, Indiana, reported Hatty, "Who do you think came to see us there but Mary Magham who married Sarah White's brother She seemed overjoyed to see us and gave ma on parting a patch work bed quilt which she had made and a picture of her little boy." In Chicago they were united with William Beecher and family, who Hatty reported "look much as they used to," as well as "a Mrs Merriam and her daughter that we used to know as Laura Parkhurst on Walnut Hills." Uncle William drove them around the city so that they could see how splendidly it had been rebuilt after the Great Fire. Hatty, who objected to the coal smoke in St. Louis and Cincinnati, found Chicago "by far the finest and most attractive city that I have seen at the West."[36]

These reunions grew more frequent in Ohio. In Columbus, Stowe was met by a man who represented a Mrs. Neil, who "wished to have Mrs Stowe stay with her while in town." Upon arriving at her house, they discovered that Mrs. Neil was none other than "Mrs Ely that we used to know in Cincinnati—she is married for the *third* time," Hatty reported to her sister.[37] Often after a reading Harriet found herself looking into the eyes of a former domestic servant eager to renew her ties with her mistress. In Cleveland Stowe was greeted by "a woman named Ellen who used to live with us in Brunwsick," reported Hatty; "she was living with us at the time we left there but did not go with us to Andover I dont know as you remember her I had forgotten her entirely until I saw her."[38] Many of these former help were

Irish. In Detroit a Miss O'Chahan hailed them. In Chicago, wrote Hatty to her sister, "who should come to see us looking as fresh and rosy and natural as possible but *Mary Neugent* who used to live with us so long ago at Andover." Betraying the prejudices of her Beecher kin, Hatty continued, "She brought her oldest boy with her to see us—And you have no idea what a nice pretty refined looking little fellow he is—you would never in the world take him to be the child of Irish parents."[39]

After a fourteen-hour journey from Chicago over three hundred miles of extremely rough railroad track they arrived in Cincinnati, "shaken almost to pieces." Hatty told Eliza, "I don't know that I ever saw Ma so utterly used up worn out and exhausted as she was by that days journey." They had left Chicago at eight o'clock in the morning and arrived in Cincinnati at nine-thirty that evening. Harriet was to read the following night at Pike's Opera House. By keeping perfectly quiet all the next day and fortifying herself by "being rubbed with bay rum and cloroform liniment and taking fresh raw eggs beaten up with sherry," she got through the reading creditably. According to Hatty's account, "the people all seemed perfectly delighted and came around her like bees after it was over shaking hands kissing and congratulating her."[40]

The next day, squired about by Sarah Beecher's son, George, they visited Walnut Hills. They found familiar landmarks, though the seminary buildings had been much glorified and the surrounding area built up. Splendid mansions lined the streets, and Walnut Hills was now within the city limits. They visited Lyman Beecher's house and the house they had lived in, next door to which sat the home of Professor and Mrs. Allen, looking very much the same. Here Harriet got out of the carriage and walked all around the yard of her former home, allowing memory to mix with long-buried feelings. Going into the house, they found it "very little changed and . . . very natural." After visiting with old friends and neighbors—the Wrights, Mrs. Perry, and Mrs. Bates—they continued on to Zanesville, Ohio ("a dark gloomy and smutty town"), and to Pittsburgh ("black and full of smoke"). At the hotel in Pittsburgh, Hatty reported, "a very nice neat looking colored woman came to see ma." She was Eliza Cox, who as a little girl had lived with them in Cincinnati.[41] The reading in Pittsburgh was quite successful; Stowe described the audience as "one of the largest & most important of any," and she was glad that her engagement in Steubenville, Ohio, had been canceled so that she was able to do Pittsburgh justice.[42] "Her performance could hardly be called a reading," reported the Pittsburgh *Gazette*. "It was recitative and she seldom glanced at the book. Her voice betrayed the veritable Yankee twang. . . . Her voice is low, just tinged in the slightest with huskiness, but is quite musical. In manner she was vivacious and gave life to many of the pages, more by suggestive action than by utterances. . . . She seemed perfectly possessed on the stage, and read with easy grace."[43]

On November 6 she wrote to Mrs. Claflin that she planned "to cast myself into your friendly arms—'all that is left of me' on monday the 10th."

Mr. Williams was talking about extending the eastern end of her tour by adding engagements in Lawrence and Boston, but Stowe was determined at any event to have a week at home with Georgie and her baby, who were arriving November 10 or 11. She had been on the road for five weeks. She told her son Charles that a lecture tour "was one of those things that have to be done once, to learn not to do it again."[44]

Yet a year later she was recommending it to James Fields. Urging him to "try a southern tour," she continued to Annie, "Ask him to get laid out for him one in Richmond one in Baltimore one in Washington one in Savannah two or three in Jacksonville which in March is *full* of idle company one in Magnolia—Green Cove Springs—& one or two in St. Augustine. These places are *full* of thousands of idle rich people panting for some new thing and with money in their pockets.[45] The thousand-dollar check she deposited to her account at the end of her 1873 tour was proof of the fact that there was good money to be made from the lecture circuit.[46] She considered undertaking a Canadian tour in 1874, attracted by the thought of being in cooler climes for the summer, but somewhat daunted by the prospect of reading to the stiff-necked John Bulls whom she described to James Redpath as "inclined to look down on anybody that does any thing to please them for money."[47] In the end she declined, claiming "many engagements domestic and literary."[48] Among these, in addition to her society novels and her writing for the *Christian Union*, were *Palmetto Leaves*, a collection of Florida sketches originally published in the *Christian Union* and brought out by Osgood and Fields in 1873, and *Woman in Sacred History*, a series of sketches of biblical heroines, published by J. B. Ford & Co. in 1874. In 1877 J. B. Ford and Co. brought out a series of her religious studies entitled *Footsteps of the Master*.

For *Woman in Sacred History* Stowe drew upon her husband's vast knowledge, her own reading of the Old and New Testament, and her research. "The studies on the Patriarchal women I think the best," she told her son Charles. "The study of Delilah I am indebted for to Mr Manricis lectures on the O[ld T[estament] which he gave to The Working Men's College in London."[49] In *Woman in Sacred History* Stowe fictionalized the Bible much as she had biblicized her most famous fiction, *Uncle Tom's Cabin*. She used generous amounts of description and dialogue to remind her readers "that these men and women of the Bible were really flesh and blood, of the same human nature with ourselves."[50] Yet *Woman in Sacred History* was as much an art book as it was a religious study. Jewel-toned chromo-lithographs of famous paintings by Raphael, Batoni, Boulanger, and other artists brought European culture into the parlors of America. Readers who had yet to face nude statuary were gently led down the paths of Culture, past a languorous Jeptha's daughter, a Delilah in a low-necked gown, and a Miriam in the bullrushes with one of her breasts in full view. Through these illustrations, painstakingly reproduced, Stowe popularized high art just as she secularized her biblical subjects. Stowe continued to play the role of mediator between high and low culture, but now the balance of power was clearly on the side of high culture.[51]

Between her new writing, royalties received from books in print, and her investments, Stowe had supported her family comfortably since Calvin's retirement in 1863. But beginning with the failure of Jay Cooke's brokerage firm in 1873, the speculative bubble that had been expanding since the beginning of the Civil War burst and the economy went into a decline for the rest of the decade. In the first year of the depression alone, five thousand businesses failed. Another panic hit in 1877. "What a year this is," Stowe wrote to Susie Munroe, the young woman her son Charles was to marry. "Who is not losing—who is not being straitened in income—As to my own little income which for many years has been as certain & regular as any thing could be about one third now has become non productive & I am only thankful that the principle is not lost—But we are all sailing close to the wind & making our expenses as small as possible."[52] Her sister Mary, who had watched as her piano and all of her parlor furnishings were auctioned off after the Panic of 1837, was now forced to witness a different kind of tragedy. Her daughter Katy's husband, caught short by the panic, altered a $3,000 certificate to $30,000. When the forgery was discovered, Mr. Gilman was bankrupt and his reputation blasted. "Your Aunt Mary is terribly overcome," Harriet wrote to her son. "Katy was her darling—she never really liked her husband—& now she finds no comfort."[53] Gilman himself had been sentenced to prison. Eunice Beecher reported that Henry was more "dreadfully depressed" over this than he had been over tragedies in his own life.[54] Katy Gilman appeared to make a quick recovery from the nervous state into which the scandal had plunged her, but two years later she was dead at age forty-four.[55] She had paid the price of her generation, who, raised amid the material plenty of the Gilded Age, had no concept of retrenchment.

Harriet instructed Spencer Foote to manage her affairs in Florida so as to economize expenses. "I think if I can just keep things from going back, it is all I can do—& the orange trees *will* go forward now & take care of themselves."[56] She wanted to contribute to the household expenses of Charley and Susie, but in February 1879 she told him she would not be certain until spring of "what I can do for you. This is the very hardest year I have had in respect to investments since that year in Stockbridge when you fitted for college."[57] She urged them to marry before the hot weather set in so that she and Calvin would be able to come. To Susie she wrote, "As to running down one day marrying you & running back the next—I for one dont think that is making enough of marriage—I believe in a reasonable share of consideration and external demonstration in such an event & in giving friends an opportunity to show their sympathy & rejoice with one."[58] She did not tell Susie that when she married Calvin Stowe forty-three years earlier, not even all of her brothers and sisters knew about the quiet ceremony.

After a long career promoting and founding educational institutions for women, Catharine Beecher returned to Hartford in 1870 and took up her old post at the Hartford Female Seminary. It soon became apparent that neither she nor the institution was now what they had been in the 1820s, and she left the following year amid squabbles with the trustees over money.[59] Looking around for a retirement home, Catharine decided against living with Harriet, who never stayed long enough in one place. In 1877 Catharine settled in Elmira with Thomas Beecher. Harriet wrote her that she was happy and relieved that she had a home: "Too many years have passed over your head for you to be wandering like a trunk without a label," she told the sister who had been mother and mentor to her.[60] A year later Catharine Beecher died of a stroke in her sleep.

The comparative objectivity that Stowe had maintained in her relationship with her son Charley, even in his most troublesome seagoing years, was richly rewarded in his adulthood. He gratified his parents by becoming a minister—though not without detours into science and rationalistic unbelief—and took a hard assignment in Saco, Maine, where the parish had a rear guard of old-style Calvinists. Stowe was pleased that her son was heading to a brisk climate she herself had so enjoyed, and even more pleased that he appeared to approach the ministry as a calling rather than, like many of the young ministers in the 1870s, seeking out the highest salaries and the best berths. To his fiancée's mother, who may have had some hesitations about the missionary life her daughter was entering, Stowe wrote, "I have seen the beginning of seven brothers in the ministry—Henry & Charles & George all began in little obscure western villages far from the refinements of life and on missionary salaries. . . . My brother Edward who began by taking Park St was nearly broken down in health & had to resign—It is best to begin small & grow—My own father began at Easthampton on a salary of $200."[61] Still, Charlie and Susie shared their generation's expectation of a high level of material comfort. Hoping to sustain them in what she believed was a good beginning in the ministry, Stowe supplemented Charley's salary by a handsome $600 a year.[62] The November after their marriage Stowe wrote to Susie that she would not be able to send them $200 for a piano until the spring. "I understand Charley has $1400 pr ann your expenses at present are small. I have at present only $1370 to depend on from investments & another thousand from plantation & books.—so that *for you two* your *income* is about equal to mine—I can make something over this by occasional writing."[63]

She offered to make lounges and ottomans for their new house,[64] and when their first baby was born Stowe was there to greet him. "I got in just in time to take the new comer from the Doctor," Stowe exulted; "he looked out of his blanket with large bright eyes & with apparent curiousity to know where he had got to & who I was."[65] The baby was named Lyman Beecher Stowe. Remembering her own experience, she instructed Susie, "[K]eep him as Christs own—we are not sure how long these dear ones may be spared to us."[66]

Charley had settled down some since his seafaring years, but his youth and his Beecher blood were still much in evidence. Harriet sent him long, closely written letters of advice as he pursued what became a very contentious ministry in Maine. She told him, "[w]hen a young man of original mind begins to preach truth as he sees it & *to adapt* truth to the wants of the men he meets—he immediately steps out of formulas & in that way excites the fears of good men, who are accustomed to the sound of certain formulas. This was your grandfathers experience—it was your uncle Henrys—& I apprehend it will be yours." Urging him to be "prudent," she told him, "I hope you will never say or do any thing to express a young mans self esteem & that might look like want of reverence for the hardy old christian soldiers who have been bearing the burden of the day in Maine—Never preach *against* old formulas—quietly substitute truth for error."[67] When she calculated that his troubles with his parish had grown to serious proportions, she asked Henry Ward Beecher to go and help him out with one of his famous irresistible sermons that doubled as fundraisers. She told Henry that Charley, having had the disadvantages of being his nephew "and a pestilent young sprig of Beecherdom," now deserved some of the advantages of the connection.[68]

Charley was now her only son—nothing had been heard from Fred save what his mother called "the supposed communication" from him through a spiritualist medium. Although she asked for a copy of this message, Stowe "committed Fred to my Savior,"[69] and redoubled her investment in Charley. "I give you to Christ as all I have left—my only son my hope & He will do for you more than I can ask or think."[70] While she had strength left, she did not leave the process entirely in God's hands. She sent Charley outlines of sermons, "remembering how often I have found your mind working over and adding to suggestions of mine."[71] His flirtation with universalism and rationalism called forth a torrent of agitated letters from his mother, and it is clear that Charley was still extracting the young man's pound of flesh from his parents. In February 1881 Stowe wrote to him:

> As to saying that you despise Liberal Orthodoxy for its [']slovenly inconsistency & its dishonesty'—I cannot imagine what you mean. What I, and your Uncle Henry believe & teach is not either slovenly or inconsistent & we are neither of us dishonest Your uncle is precicely the model I would hold up to you, of how a manly & honest man should guide himself in the ministry in an age when God is shedding new light on religion thro the development of his own natural laws in science.[72]

Charley survived what Stowe characterized as "the chicken pox and measles of philosophy"[73] and remained an extraordinarily loyal son. Stowe was distressed when she heard that he was looking to leave his post in Maine—having had enough of the narrow and bigoted opposition that blocked his every move. She reminded him of the great opposition that his grandfather, Lyman Beecher, had ridden to victory. "My father used to say 'When things are so that you feel as if you couldnt hold on a minute longer—never give

up then—for the tide is sure to turn.' "[74] But Charley instead answered a call
to the Windsor Avenue Church in Hartford. Although she had opposed his
move, Stowe delighted in having him close at hand. He looked in on his
parents every day, oversaw the winterizing of their home, and brought
his children (a daughter, Leslie, was born after Lyman) to visit with their
grandparents and aunts Eliza and Hatty.[75]

"Mr Stowe and I lie on opposite sofas and doze & occasionally compare
notes like two old superannuated carriage horses," Harriet wrote to Mary
Claflin.[76] The last years of her life were filled with very small yet significant
gestures of human connectedness: writing notes to friends, fashioning home-
made wedding gifts, sending poems and flowers. She still enjoyed painting,
and when her friends' daughters married she would often send a fan covered
with black satin on which she had painted orange blossoms.[77] In May 1880
a group of Chicago women requested her signature to incorporate into an
"Autograph Silk Quilt" they were preparing as a benefit for the Illinois Industrial School for girls.[78] Through the exchange of small gifts—a rose pinned
to a satin pillow at Christmas, a collection of seeds, a book of hymns—she
kept in touch with a network of friends and family.[79] She shared a sense of
humor with her Nook Farm neighbor, Samuel Clemens. After Clemens's
wife had scolded him for coming to visit Stowe without the formalities of a
hat and tie, Clemens sent his butler over with those articles on a tray. Stowe
joked that he had "discovered a *principle* . . . that a man may call by installments."[80]

Even at the height of her fame as a writer she had maintained her ties
to the parlor culture that had fostered and sustained her literary writing. In
Andover she had participated in tableaux parties and literary picnics in
between her heavy writing schedule for magazines and publishers. In Hartford Stowe gathered around her a small group of neighbors and read aloud
Dickens's *Bleak House* while Calvin Stowe held a home study group which
read Faust.[81] At the sunset of her career as she retired from publishing she
was sustained by the theatricals and readings that went on in the community.
"We have a dramatic Club & had a play acted Christmas night & are going
to have another," she told Mary Claflin in 1880.[82] In the summer of 1882
she participated in a benefit arranged by Cecil Haven for the Gardner, Massachusetts, public library. "I read the Ministers Housekeeper with apparent
success," she told Hattie; "he read 'Laughing in Meeting' & read it well too
& they had a burlesque operetta & several songs & duetts."[83] By the end of
that summer she had read twice more: "Once at Old Orchard for the little
Episcopal Church there & last night over at our hotel at the request of the
boarders for their amusement." Sam Lawson, her garrulous New England
ne'er do well, "does duty on all these occasions."[84]

Her elegy to her New England childhood, *Poganuc People*, published in
1878, marked the end of the literary career she had begun forty-four years
earlier. Like her best work, it had its origins in the oral tradition of the parlor.
"I have a story under advisement to be called 'when I was young,' " she had

written James Fields in 1870. "It will be my own remembrances of life & times I have thought of calling it Early Days of an odd little girl— . . . I have so often made my family laught over these sketches that they insist that I shall write them."[85] *Poganuc People* revisits in detail the parsonage in Litchfield, the meetinghouse, and the local eccentrics. It is infused with a strain of gentle satire that gives the narrative an edge and keeps the eulogy and nostalgia in check. Here she describes Dolly's father's sermon as a "masterpiece." "Indeed, he had the success that a man has always when he proves to an audience that they are in the right in their previous opinions" (PP, 54). Strong and supple, Stowe's narrative voice alternates between that of chimney-corner gossip, opinionated grandmother, and newspaper columnist. Stowe, who all her life had been alert to the latest cultural fads, now criticized some of the changes that she did not like, such as the self-consciousness that the Gilded Age had brought to childrearing. "In those early times," she writes, "the life of childhood was much more in the imagination than now":

> Children were let alone, to think their own thoughts. There were no kindergartens to train the baby to play philosophically, and infuse a stealthy aroma of geometry and conic sections into the very toys of the nursery. Parents were not anxiously watching every dawning idea of the little mind to set it straight even before it was uttered; and there were no newspapers or magazines with a special corner for the bright sayings of children. (PP, 31)

Relieved of the didactic purpose of her *House and Home Papers,* she commented lightly and deftly on common domestic scenes, as in her description of the family cat, who must contend with a parsonage overrun with rats:

> The family cat in Dolly's day, having taken a dispassionate survey of the situation, had given up the matter in despair, and set herself quietly to attending to her own family concerns, as a sensible cat should. She selected the doctor's pamphlet closet as her special domestic retreat. Here she made her lair in a heap of old sermons, whence, from time to time, she led forth coveys of well-educated, theological kittens, who, like their mother, gazed on the rats with respectful curiosity, and ran no imprudent risks. (PP, 124)

As she surveyed the New England of her youth, Stowe exhibited flashes of the nativism that was so closely bound up with Lyman Beecher's evangelical mission: "Such were our New England villages in the days when its people were of our own blood and race, and the pauper population of Europe had not as yet been landed upon our shores" (PP, 226).

On the occasion of her seventy-first birthday in 1882 the *Atlantic Monthly* gave Stowe a garden party at the home of Mrs. Claflin. It was the first of these *Atlantic* gatherings since the disastrous dinner of 1859 to include women—though the all-male dinners had continued in grand style. On December 15, 1875, when the *Atlantic* passed into new ownership, twenty-eight men had gathered to hear speeches by William Dean Howells, John T. Trowbridge, and James Freeman Clarke. Oliver Wendell Holmes read a commemorative poem with outrageous rhymes, C. P. Cranch chanted one of his songs, W. F. Apthorpe sang an operatic air, and Thomas Bailey Aldrich propounded his theory of short stories. These literary exercises were not so very different from parlor amusements, but they took place in a segregated men's club. As if to call attention to the absence of the women, Samuel Clemens was called upon at this 1875 gathering to respond for "The President of the United States and the Female Contributors of the *Atlantic*." The newcomer from the West who liked to play the role of bad boy fleeing from the strictures of the Victorian parlor was well chosen to represent the absent women. After "[p]rofessing to be staggered by the greatness of the subject," he asked permission "to attack it in sections." Ripples of mirth met his deadpan statement. There were no women present to respond, nor were women present at the 1877 dinner in honor of Whittier, though after the meal when the men had been sated by six different wines, "a number of them were admitted, and some even sat at the devastated table." After their exclusion from the Whittier dinner, the women writers of the *Atlantic* devised a clever literary protest in which they threatened to found their own magazine.[86]

The celebration of Stowe's birthday "Under the Elms" at Mrs. Claflin's house in Newtonville gathered two hundred people under a festive tent. "The world & his wife came," Stowe told her daughters, "& I shook hands with each one."[87] Among the many guests were *Atlantic* authors Elizabeth Stuart Phelps, John Greenleaf Whittier, Rose Terry Cooke, Thomas Bailey Aldrich, William Dean Howells, and Lucy Larcom. *Atlantic* author Julia Ward Howe sent regrets, as did Thomas Wentworth Higginson, Mary Abigail Dodge, Rebecca Harding Davis, James Russell Lowell, and Samuel Clemens. Oliver Wendell Holmes read a long poem with clever rhymes. Whittier too had prepared a poem, as had Adeline Dutton T. Whitney, Elizabeth Stuart Phelps, Georgiana Stowe, and John T. Trowbridge.[88] Annie Fields, in London, sent a commemorative poem for the occasion, the last line of which was "Who loves much is forgiven."[89] At least one man who was present found the large, mixed-sex gathering not to his taste. "[I]t was like adding water to a cup of tea," complained Arthur Gilman, who preferred the *Atlantic* club's all-male dinners. "There was a suggestion of the old times, but the strength of comradeship had been weakened."[90]

If comradeship was becoming a distinctively male ritual, soon to be celebrated by Jack London and the naturalistic novelists in a visceral reaction to the Victorian culture they perceived to be feminized, Sarah Orne Jewett recognized in Stowe's New England novels the inspiration for her own. The death of James Fields in 1881 officially ended the era of the "gentleman publisher" so supportive to Stowe and other literary women, but Annie Fields carried on the tradition, together with Jewett, who became her companion. Together they continued the famous literary salon at 148 Charles Street, and together they came to visit Harriet Beecher Stowe in 1884, bringing her a copy of Jewett's latest novel, *The Country Doctor*. Stowe wrote to Annie to thank her for bringing Miss Jewett to visit: "I have just finished reading her book—having been delayed in indulgence to Mr Stowe's eagerness to read it It is not only interesting & bright, but full of strong & earnest thought."[91] Jewett's masterpiece, *The Country of the Pointed Firs*, published in the last year of Stowe's life, celebrated a women's culture in an elegiac tone that signaled the passing of the once vibrant world from which Stowe had drawn so much of her vision.

In the 1880s Stowe wrote little except occasional notes to friends. She did, however, attend to literary business. She suggested to Henry O. Houghton, who had taken over the publishing house of Ticknor and Fields, that he bring out an illustrated edition of *Agnes of Sorrento*. "There is a great field for illustration in that book and photographs are very easy to be obtained," she told him, imagining how it would look interleaved with photos of Capri, the Gorge of Sorrento, and the Milan cathedrals.[92] When Mr. Houghton asked her to donate a set of her works to support a circulating library she happily complied, observing, "It may even as policy be a good plan & extend the sale."[93] She readily agreed to send Julia Ward Howe, president of the Bureau of the Woman's Department of the 1885 World's Exposition, a set of her books for display in New Orleans.[94] She took *"great satisfaction"* in receiving a copy of the new, illustrated *Uncle Tom's Cabin* that Houghton Mifflin issued in 1885. "So pretty a book, at so cheap a price ought to command a sale & from the letters constantly coming to me in every mail I judge the interest in it is unabated."[95] The same year she agreed to re-edit *Men of Our Times*. "In regard to compensation what I received before was 10 pr ct on the retail price," she wrote to Estes & Lauriat, confidently relying on the prodigious memory that had served her well in conducting business. When they wrote back that she had received 12, not 10 percent, she admitted her error and accepted the higher terms.[96] In 1886 she proposed to write a piece for the *Atlantic*. Thomas Bailey Aldrich answered her inquiry with a discreet note that combined courtesy with caution. "We should be very glad to have you send us the paper you mention," he told her. "Nothing would please us more than to give it to the readers of the Atlantic, in case the article is in the line of the magazine."[97] It did not appear, and it is unlikely she wrote it.

Stowe found in the increasing helplessness of old age a Christian message: "I lean back & confide all to the Everlasting Arms which carry me," she told her sister Mary.[98] Her immediate attendants, however, were her daughters Eliza and Hatty, who for years had borne the burden of managing two houses. When the twins arrived in Mandarin in 1881 they found that the house had leaked and now smelled, in Hatty's words, "like an old toad stool." They aired out the house and made fires to dry it out so that when their parents arrived it was comfortable.[99] Calvin, in his eighties, was still able to sit on the veranda where, wrote Harriet, he "nibbles a bit here & there at his book & reads the Hartford Courant."[100] They continued the annual migration to Florida until 1884, when Calvin fell victim to Bright's disease and began seriously to fail. "Mr. Stowe has been more than ever an invalid," Harriet wrote to Mrs. Claflin, "he is no longer able to walk out, can do only a little reading & no writing. We have at last concluded to spend the coming winter in our northern house for the first time for fifteen years."[101]

Harriet curtailed her traveling and visiting so that she could nurse him, and while she looked after Calvin, the twins looked after her. "I have some pretty fair sherry which Hatty serves out to me a small wine glass full at dinnertime at tea time & again at bed time," she told Henry, "& if I fell on my knees to her I could not get it at any other time."[102] Faced with her husband's final illness, Harriet reasserted her bonds with her siblings. "I think more of my brothers & sisters than I ever have done before & have written to all & got replies from all but Henry," she told Isabella, with whom she had long ago reconciled. "Mr Stowe sinks gradually from week to week. Edward [Isabella's son and Calvin Stowe's doctor] thinks he may last months His mind is clear & he is free from pain. We have the best of nurses & in short we have *all* under the circumstances we could ask for."[103] On February 4, 1885, Calvin told Harriet "The river seems *very wide*, where I am—& I long to be across."[104] He lived eighteen more months, dying on August 6, 1886. Harriet laid her companion of fifty years to rest without trusting her responses to paper.

The following year Harriet suffered the double losses of her brother Henry and her daughter Georgiana, who was forty-four. During the seventies and eighties Georgiana had had a series of physical complaints that appeared to originate in her high-strung temperament. The beautiful and witty young woman who at sixteen had "turned out like phosphorous" in company suffered everything from indigestion, vomiting, and diarrhea to less tangible ills such as melancholy and weakness at the back of the head.[105] In 1876 she underwent Dr. S. Weir Mitchell's now notorious "rest cure," pilloried in Charlotte Perkins Gilman's gothic story, "The Yellow Wall Paper" (1892). Mitchell, a fashionable Philadelphia doctor who specialized in nervous diseases ("neurasthenia"), "cured" nervous women by sending them to bed, allowing them no reading matter or stimulation whatsoever, and force-feeding them until they grew enormously fat. Men too experienced neurasthenia, but Mitchell had a different prescription for them: he sent them West, and some of them, like Owen Wister, found a literary career there much as Harriet Beecher had in the 1830s. Ann Douglas has argued that Mitchell's rest cure was based on the assumption that many women suffering from "nerves" were simply evading their domestic duties; by giving them more than they wanted of their own medicine, his cure was designed to propel them out of bed and toward the broom.[106] In the 1870s, however, the rest cure was the latest health fad, and Stowe was receptive to the theory of turning Georgie into a "cabbage" or a "clam" for a season. "The difficulty seems to be *a leak* in the nervous force," she told Charles, drawing on the language of a popular medical authority, George M. Beard. "She uses more vital force than she makes." Dr. Mitchell's "plan for accumulating nervous force by rest" and "mak[ing] tissue," Stowe reported, seemed to be making Georgie more cheerful.[107] But Georgiana remained susceptible to illness and depression. In

1881 she almost died from scarlet fever while on a trip to London. Her mother was with her during the night in August 1887 when she succumbed to her last illness. No longer able to transmute her grief into literary memorials, Stowe left no record of this deep cut into her heart's quick. While she watched at Georgiana's bedside, however, a poem she had written for the *Independent* went through her head and she wrote it down. The last two lines expressed her wish for her daughter: "Your joy be the reality / Our suffering life the dream." She carefully dated the transcription "August 5, 1887, The daughter's room."[108]

In 1889 Stowe suffered a major decline that left her with diminished faculties. When an admirer wanted to send her a signed copy of the hymn "America," Hatty discouraged it, explaining, "she is not capable of appreciating it, as you will understand when you see her. Intellectually she is not now above a child of two or three years."[109] In a more extended description of her mother Hatty wrote, "Ma is very well and cheerful has not had a cold, or any thing the matter with her all winter. If her mental faculties were only as sound as is her physical health she would be in absolutely perfect condition. But her mind is in a strange state of childishness and forgetfulness, with momentary flashes of her old self that come and go like falling stars."[110] When she lifted her pen to write, it was often to copy a motto that Lyman Beecher had been fond of: "Trust in the Lord and Do Good." Having most of her life signed her letters with the short form of her name, H. B. Stowe, she now took to signing herself in full, Harriet Beecher Stowe, as if to let the euphony and resonance of that name flicker in the dying embers of her consciousness.[111]

Aware of her limited power of concentration, she declined a request to write a hymn for her grandnephew's high school graduation. At eighty-two, she explained, "few are equal to verse writing." Observing that her good friend Oliver Wendell Holmes was "a notable exception to this rule," she continued, "I do not pretend to keep pace with his brilliant mind & so must excuse myself on the score of inability."[112] Still under the spell of the egotistic doctor, she took his own estimate of his abilities for an accurate measure. In 1893 she wrote to him,

As to myself, there is not so much to tell, as of you. I am passing the last days of my life in the city where I passed my school-girl life. My physical health, since I recovered from the alarming illness, I had four years ago has been excellent, and I am almost always cheerful & happy. My mental condition might be called nomadic. I have no fixed thoughts or objects. I wander at will from one subject to another. In pleasant summer weather, I am out of doors most of my time, rambling about the neighborhood & calling upon my friends. I do not read much. Now & then I dip into a book, much as a humming-bird, poised in air on whirring wing, darts into the heart of a flower—now here—then there and away. Pictures delight me, and afford me infinite diversion and interest. I pass many pleasant hours looking over books of pictures.

Of *music* I also am very fond I could not have too much of it, and I never *do* have as much as I should like. The street bands even organs, give me great pleasure, but especially the singing and playing of my kind friends, who are willing to gratify me in this respect.

I make no mental effort of any sort my brain is tired out. It was a womans brain and not a mans & finally from sheer fatigue & exhaustion in the march & strife of life, gave out before the end was reached. And now I rest me, like a moored boat, rising & falling on the water, with loosened cordage and flapping sail.[113]

Surrounded by a large group of family, including her children Eliza, Hatty, and Charles, her sister Isabella, and her nephew Edward, she died on July 1, 1896, two weeks after her eighty-fifth birthday.[114] She had set up a trust for Eliza and Hatty, now sixty years old, but there was not enough money in it by 1896 to allow them more than $75 a month, not nearly enough to maintain the Forest Street house. Annie Fields and Charles Dudley Warner tried to rally friends to raise a sum on which they could draw the interest, but before this plan could be put into place the house was sold and Isabella Beecher Hooker had made a public plea for the Stowe daughters that Hatty and Eliza found quite humiliating.[115] At the close of the nineteenth century, there were no stations of dignity and honor for the Aunt Esthers of the world, and the useful aunts of Stowe's fiction faded into myth.

In her will, Stowe distributed to her surviving children her most valued possessions. To Charles she gave the silver inkstand given her by the women of England and the bound volumes of the half a million signatures collected by them for the "Affectionate and Christian Address." To Hatty she gave "the large server waiter given to me by the women of England" and to Eliza "the silver cake basket given me by the women of England." Had Georgiana lived, she would have inherited the gold bracelet given her mother by the Duchess of Sutherland, now inscribed with the date of the Emancipation Proclamation.[116] Eliza and Hatty sent Sarah Orne Jewett the mementoes that they knew their mother would have wanted her to have: a photograph and a small box in which she had kept postage stamps. Jewett thanked them heartily for sending her "a thing she used to handle and with which she must have had some pleasant associations."[117] Stowe's mightiest legacy was the one she inscribed on the flyleaf of Charles's *Life of Harriet Beecher Stowe*: taking the words of Valiant for Truth in *Pilgrim's Progress*, she wrote, "My sword I give to him that shall succeed me in my pilgrimage & my courage & skill to him that can get it."

Notes

Preface

1. Kate Brannon Knight, "The Harriet Beecher Stowe Collection," in *History of the Work of Connecticut Women at the World's Columbian Exposition, Chicago, 1893* (Hartford, Conn., 1898), 93–123, esp. 93, 105. I am grateful to Barbara Sicherman for this reference. Teachers used translations of *Uncle Tom's Cabin* in English-language instruction, for a student who could master that text, with its range of regional, racial, and class dialects, could truly be said to have learned the language. In a letter to Calvin Stowe, Thomas Watts, librarian of the British Museum, said of *Uncle Tom's Cabin*, "There is every variety of style, from that of animated narration and passionate wailing to that of the most familiar dialogue, and dialogue not only in the language of the upper classes but of the lowest. The student who has once mastered 'Uncle Tom' in Welsh or Wallachian, is not likely to meet any further difficulties in his progress through Welsh or Wallachian prose"; quoted in Florine Thayer McCray, *The Life-Work of the Author of "Uncle Tom's Cabin"* (New York: Funk & Wagnalls, 1889), 116.

2. Two stimulating monographs discuss the development in the latter half of the nineteenth century of what Lawrence Levine calls a "cultural hierarchy." Richard Brodhead, in *The School of Hawthorne* (New York: Oxford University Press, 1986), argues that with the creation of prestigious journals such as the *Atlantic Monthly* a formerly undifferentiated market split into "high" and "popular" cultures and that this split created a new authorial persona for writers such as Hawthorne, Howells, and James. Lawrence W. Levine, in *Highbrow/Lowbrow: The Emergence of Cultural Hierarchy in America* (Cambridge, Mass.: Harvard University Press, 1988) demonstrates in splendid detail the process through which Shakespeare's plays and the opera, once popular entertainments for all levels of society, were "sacralized" and reserved for an elite audience whose participation in the shaping of these performances was sharply curtailed. Neither Brodhead nor Levine considers the effect of this new cultural hierarchy on women writers.

3. HBS to George Eliot, April 15, 1869, Berg Collection of English and American Literature, NYPL.

4. Sarah Josepha Hale, *Woman's Record; or, Sketches of All Distinguished Women, from "The Beginning" till A. D. 1850. Arranged in Four Eras. With Selections from Female Writers in Every Age* (New York: Harper and Brothers, 1853), vii.

5. Nathaniel Parker Willis, *The Rag Bag. A Collection of Ephemera* (New York, 1859), 262, as quoted in Ann Douglas, *The Feminization of American Culture* (New York: Alfred A. Knopf, 1977), 103.

6. McCray, *Life-Work of the Author of "Uncle Tom's Cabin,"* 97, 99.

7. CES to HBS, March 11, 1868, Acquisitions, SD.

8. The Rev. E. P. Parker, "Harriet Beecher Stowe," in *Eminent Women of the Age: Being Narratives of the Lives and Deeds of the Most Prominent Women of the Present Generation,* ed. James Parton (Hartford, Conn., 1869), 296–331.

9. HBS to the Editor of the *Evening Post,* [no earlier than 1887], Katharine S. Day Collection, SD.

10. HBS to the Duke [of Argyle], January 21, 1889, Harriet Beecher Stowe Collection, UVa. "Dear Friend," Stowe had written McCray on December 11, 1889, "You are quite welcome to write the sketch you propose I believe that all the material for such an one is quite at hand & at your disposal. Yours Very truly HB Stowe." McCray published a photocopy of this note at the front of *Life-Work of the Author of "Uncle Tom's Cabin."*

11. David McCullough, "The Unexpected Mrs. Stowe," in his *Brave Companions: Portraits in History* (New York: Prentice Hall, 1992), 50; originally published in *American Heritage,* August 1973.

12. Charles Beecher to Isabella Beecher, July 14, 1839, Joseph K. Hooker Collection, SD.

13. HBS, *Little Foxes* (Boston: Ticknor and Fields, 1866), 217. Subsequent references to this edition, abbreviated as LF, will be provided parenthetically in the text.

Chapter 1

1. *The Autobiography of Lyman Beecher,* 2 vols., ed. Barbara M. Cross (Cambridge, Mass.: Harvard University Press, 1961), 1:36.

2. *Autobiography,* 1:46.

3. *Autobiography,* 1:36.

4. *Autobiography,* 1:40.

5. *Autobiography,* 1:85.

6. Roxana Foote Beecher to Harriet Foote, November 15, 1899, in *Autobiography,* 1:85.

7. *Autobiography,* 1:127.

8. HBS, *My Wife and I; or, Harry Henderson's History* (Boston: Houghton Mifflin, 1896), 9–10.

9. *Autobiography,* 1:159.

10. *Autobiography,* 1:168–69.

11. On the revival at the Litchfield Female Academy, see Lynn Brickley, "Sarah Pierce's Litchfield Female Academy, 1792–1833" (Ed. D. diss., Graduate School of Education, Harvard University, 1985), 323–28.

12. *Autobiography,* 1:252.

13. Forrest Wilson, *Crusader in Crinoline: The Life of Harriet Beecher Stowe* (Philadelphia: J.P. Lippincott, 1941), 32.

14. *Autobiography,* 1:220.

15. *Plymouth Collection of Hymns and Tunes* (New York: A. S. Barnes & Co., 1856), 398. Harriet Beecher Stowe presented a copy of this hymnal to the Duke of Sutherland and marked with a cross the hymns that were favorites in her circle. Most of the other favorites likewise invoked images of heaven and judgment. They are "That awful day will surely come," "Must Jesus bear the cross alone," "When shall we meet again?," and "Who are these in bright array." See copy of Plymouth hymnal presented by HBS to Duke of Sutherland, SD.

16. HBS, *My Wife and I,* 35–36.

Chapter 2

1. Virginia Woolf, *A Room of One's Own* (New York: Harcourt, Brace and Co., 1929), 101.

2. HBS, "Recollections of My Life," in Stowe family account book, 1878, Katharine S. Day Collection, SD.

3. *Autobiography*, 1:222.

4. *Autobiography* 1:226, 224.

5. *Autobiography*, 1:223.

6. Barbara Welter, "The Cult of True Womanhood: 1820–1860," *American Quarterly* 18, no. 2 (Summer 1966): 161.

7. *Autobiography*, 1:223–24.

8. O. Elizabeth McWhorter Harden, *Maria Edgeworth's Art of Prose Fiction* (The Hague, the Netherlands: Mouton, 1971), 36–37. Marilyn Butler, *Maria Edgeworth: A Literary Biography* (Oxford: Clarendon Press, 1972), 166.

9. In *Autobiography*, 1:37, the ages of the sons are given as sixteen and fourteen; according to Abram W. Foote (*Foote Family: Genealogy of Nathaniel Foote of Wethersfield* [Rutland, Vt.: Marble City Press, 1907], 1:89ff), Andrew Ward was born on November 9, 1776, and died on September 29, 1794, and William Henry was born September 8, 1778, and died on October 7, 1794.

10. Edward Beecher to Catharine Beecher, July 18, 1822, folder 21, Beecher-Stowe Collection, SchL.

11. HBS to Harriet Foote, January 9, 1841, Foote Collection, SD.

12. *Autobiography*, 1:228.

13. HBS to Lydia Jackson Beecher, October 29, [1850], folder 96, Beecher-Stowe Collection, SchL. *Autobiography*, 1:159, 228–33.

14. *Autobiography*, 1:207.

15. John P. Foote, *Memoirs of the Life of Samuel E. Foote* (Cincinnati, Ohio: Robert Clarke & Co, 1860), 28.

16. *Autobiography*, 1:230.

17. *Autobiography*, 1:229.

18. *Autobiography*, 1:229, 230.

19. Roxana Foote to Harriet Foote, February 8, 1794, Acquisitions, SD.

20. Harriet Foote to George Foote, June 9, 1815, Foote Collection, SD.

21. "Row boats can go as far as the residence of Mrs. A. W. Foote in Nut Plains." Bernard Christian Steiner, *History of the Plantation of Menunkatuck and of the Original Town of Guilford, Connecticut* (Baltimore: Author, 1897), 182. For a description and a sketch of the spinning mill, see the *Autobiography*, 1:38, 152 (opposite).

22. Harriet Foote to George Foote, June 9, 1815, Foote Collection, SD.

23. Victor S. Clark, *History of Manufactures in the U. S., 1607–1860* (Washington, D. C.: Carnegie Institution of Washington, 1916), 386–89.

24. Steiner, *History of Guilford*, 250–51.

25. *Autobiography*, 1:233.

26. *Autobiography*, 1:233.

27. *Autobiography*, 1:98–99.

28. *Autobiography*, 1:228–29.

29. *Autobiography*, 1:234.

30. HBS to Isabella Beecher Hooker, August 14, 1889, Foote Collection, SD.

31. *Autobiography*, 1:225.

32. *Autobiography* 1:225.

Chapter 3

1. HBS, *Poganuc People* (Boston: Houghton Mifflin,1896), 117. Subsequent references to this edition, abbreviated as PP, will be provided parenthetically in the text.

2. *Autobiography* 1:87, 225.

3. Charles Beecher to Hatty and Eliza Stowe, July 23, 1896, folder 30, Beecher-Stowe Collection, SchL.

4. *Autobiography*, 1:390.

5. *Autobiography*, 1:388.

6. *Autobiography*, 1:191; PP, 122–23.

7. Charles Edward Stowe and Lyman Beecher Stowe, *Harriet Beecher Stowe: The Story of Her Life* (Boston: Houghton Mifflin, 1911), 20.

8. *Autobiography*, 1:160–61.

9. *Autobiography*, 1:391.

10. Kathryn Kish Sklar, *Catharine Beecher: A Study in American Domesticity* (New York: W. W. Norton, & Co, 1976), 26. *Autobiography*, 1:396.

11. *Autobiography*, 1:391.

12. HBS to Eliza Stowe, July 6, 1880, folder 168, Beecher-Stowe Collection, SchL.

13. *Autobiography*, 1:394–95.

14. *Autobiography*, 1:391.

15. *Autobiography*, 1:338.

16. HBS to [Henry Ward Beecher?], first part of letter is missing, n.d., Beecher Family Papers, SML.

17. Edward Beecher to Catharine Beecher, March 29, 1822, and August, 1822, folder 21, Beecher-Stowe Collection, SchL.

18. Brickley, "Litchfield Female Academy," 336.

19. Lyman Beecher to Edward Beecher, March 28, 1822, in *Autobiography*, 1: 353.

20. *Autobiography*, 1:392.

21. Lyman Beecher to Catharine Beecher, January 27, 1825, folder 3, Beecher-Stowe Collection, SchL.

22. *Autobiography*, 1:392.

23. *Autobiography*, 1:235.

24. Charles Beecher to Lyman Beecher, December 4, 1833, folder 22, Beecher-Stowe Collection, SchL.

25. Edward Beecher to Catharine Beecher, April, 1821, folder 2, Beecher-Stowe Collection, SchL.

26. HBS to Mary Dutton, (postmarked May 25), 1830, Collection of American Literature, BL.

27. Lyman Beecher to Catharine, Edward, Mary, and George Beecher, July, 1823, folder 2, Beecher-Stowe Collection, SchL.

28. *Autobiography*, 1:261–62, 272.

29. *Autobiography*, 1:268.

30. *Autobiography*, 1:273.

31. Alain C. White, *The History of the Town of Litchfield, CT, 1790–1920* (Litchfield, Conn: Litchfield Historical Society, 1920), 93, 128; the quotation is on p. 92.

32. White, *Litchfield*, 122.

33. White, *Litchfield*, 98. Linda Kerber's phrase "Republican Motherhood" captures the combination of Enlightenment and traditional views that informed discus-

sions of women's education in the post–Revolutinary War era; see Linda Kerber, *Women of the Republic: Intellect and Ideology in Revolutionary America* (Chapel Hill: University of North Carolina Press, 1980), 11. For an excellent discussion of the dialectic between these progressive and regressive views, see Nancy F. Cott, *The Bonds of Womanhood: "Woman's Sphere" in New England, 1780–1830* (New Haven, Conn: Yale University Press, 1977), 104–25.

34. Emily Noyes Vanderpoel, *More Chronicles of a Pioneer School: From 1792 to 1833* (New York: Cadmus Book Shop, 1927), 202.

35. Cott, *Bonds of Womanhood,* 101. Cott's conclusion that literacy was virtually universal may have to be slightly modified in the light of E. Jennifer Monaghan's persuasive argument that many colonial women who could sign their names could not read, because writing was taught before reading; see E. Jennifer Monaghan, "Literacy Instruction and Gender in Colonial New England," *American Quarterly* 40, no. 1 (March 1988):18–41.

36. Brickley, "Litchfield Female Academy," 4.

37. White, *Litchfield,* 110. Brickley, "Litchfield Female Academy," 22–23.

38. Mary Beth Norton, *Liberty's Daughters: The Revolutionary Experience of American Women, 1750–1800* (Boston: Little Brown, 1980), 271, 272.

39. White, *Litchfield,* 113, 116.

40. Vanderpoel, *More Chronicles,* 204.

41. From a catalogue of the books in the Gilchrist library, in the possession of John Gilchrist, a descendant of John P. Brace. I am grateful for his assistance.

42. Catharine Beecher, "Reminiscences of Litchfield," in *Autobiography,* 1:164.

43. HBS to Sarah Beecher, September 27, [1845], Acquisitions, SD.

44. HBS, "Early Remembrances," in *Autobiography,* 1:397. "John P. Brace," in Allen Johnson, ed., *The Dictionary of American Biography* (New York: Scribners, 1957), 1:541.

45. As was the custom in all schools in the early republic, students ranged in age from six to the midtwenties, but Lynne Brickley has concluded that the "clear majority of the pupils were between the ages of thirteen and sixteen." Brickley was able to ascertain the ages of 95 of the 157 students who attended the Litchfield Female Academy in 1816; of these, only three were nine or younger. See Brickley, "Litchfield Female Academy," 81.

46. Edward Beecher to Roxana Foote, September 29, 1821, in *Autobiography* 1: 344. Catharine Beecher to _____, November 21, 1817, in *Autobiography,* 1:271.

47. *Autobiography,* 1:164.

48. Vanderpoel, *More Chronicles,* 10–52, includes the "catalogues" of the school terms listing the pupils enrolled. Harriet's name does not appear until the winter term of 1820, but a letter from John P. Brace to Catharine Beecher (July 20, 1819, Acquisitions, SD), indicates that Harriet and George were both attending school by this time.

49. *Autobiography,* 1:164.

50. Brickley, "Litchfield Female Academy," 263, 308.

51. Vanderpoel, *More Chronicles,* 9.

52. My discussion of moral philosophy is drawn from Brickley, "Litchfield Female Academy," 296, where the quotation, from Frederick Rudolph, *The American College and University* (New York: Alfred A Knopf, 1962), also appears.

53. *Autobiography,* 1:397.

54. HBS to Sarah Beecher, September 27 [1845], Acquisitions, SD.

55. HBS, "Early Remembrances," in *Autobiography,* 1:398.

56. See HBS to Mary Dutton, n.d. (postmarked May 25), [1830], Collection of American Literature, BL.

57. Brickley, "Litchfield Female Academy," 233.

58. Brickley, "Litchfield Female Academy," 204.

59. *Autobiography*, 1:399.

60. Brickley, "Litchfield Female Academy," 125.

61. Brickley, "Litchfield Female Academy," 576.

62. The class lists in Vanderpoel, *More Chronicles*, 10–52, note those who won prizes.

63. HBS to Eliza, Harriet, and Georgiana Stowe, October 5, 1863, folder 125, Beecher-Stowe Collection, SchL.

64. *Autobiography*, 1:398.

65. Catharine Beecher to Samuel Foote, April 13, 1819, Acquisitions, SD.

66. Edward Beecher to Mrs.[George?] Foote, in *Autobiography*, 1:344.

67. *Autobiography*, 1:397.

68. This gentleman harbored some resentment of Catharine's aggressive entrepreneurial spirit. Referring to her Indian ballad, he wrote in his journal that Catharine "has, all her life, thus taken my best ideas, and by her imitations run away with the credit"; See Vanderpoel, *More Chronicles*, 159, and Brickley, "Litchfield Female Academy," 213, 565.

69. Brickley, "Litchfield Female Academy," 147, 149.

70. Brickley, "Litchfield Female Academy," 525–26, 392–96.

71. *Autobiography*, 1:273–74.

72. Brickley, "Litchfield Female Academy," 390.

73. "Harriet makes just as many wry faces, is just as odd, and loves to be laughed at as much as ever." _____to Edward Beecher, February 4,1819, in *Autobiography*, 1:301.

74. *Autobiography*, 1:352.

75. Lyman Beecher to George Foote, January 24, 1819, Foote Collection, SD.

76. The story of her conversion is told in Charles Edward Stowe, *Life of Harriet Beecher Stowe, Compiled from Her Letters and Journals* (Boston: Houghton Mifflin, 1889), 33–35, in which he cites an 1886 letter she wrote to him, probably at his request. According to this narrative, she was converted the summer after she began school in Hartford, which indicates the summer of 1825, during which she turned fourteen. This is probably more accurate than her comment in an earlier letter to Charles and Susie Stowe (March 21, 1880, folder 216, Beecher-Stowe Collection, SchL), "I was only twelve years old when Christ first became real to me," for in this same letter she also says she is "now sixty-seven" when in fact she was almost sixty-nine.

Chapter 4

1. Cecilia Eckhardt, *Fanny Wright: Rebel in America* (Cambridge, Mass.; Harvard University Press, 1984), 79. In the context of Lafayette's relationship with Fanny Wright, Eckhardt provides a delightful description of his tour.

2. J. Hammond Trumbull, ed., *Memorial History of Hartford County, Connecticut, 1633–1844*, 2 vols. (Boston: Edward L. Osgood, 1886), 1:593–94. *The Pocket Register for the City of Hartford, to Which Is Added, a Brief Sketch of the Reception of General La Fayette* (Hartford, Conn: Benjamin H. Norton, 1825), 55.

3. *The Pocket Register for the City of Hartford*, 1825, 57–58.

4. Catharine Beecher to Lyman Beecher, February 15, 1823, Acquisitions, SD.

5. Catharine Beecher, *Educational Reminiscences and Suggestions* (New York: J. B. Ford and Co., 1874), 51.

6. Catharine Beecher to Lyman Beecher, February 15, 1823, Acquisitions, SD.

7. Lyman Beecher to Catharine Beecher, December 3, 1823, folder 2, and December 26, 1825, folder 3, Beecher-Stowe Collection, SchL.

8. Sklar, *Catharine Beecher*, 54. For more on Joseph Emerson and his influence on women's education, see Kathryn Kish Sklar, "The Founding of Mount Holyoke College," in *Women of America: A History*, ed. Carol Ruth Berkin and Mary Beth Norton (Boston: Houghton Mifflin, 1979), 183–86.

9. Brickley, "Litchfield Female Academy," 565. Among the methods that Brickley traces to the Litchfield Female Academy are Catharine's emphasis on exercise, her use of assistant pupils, and her "modern" method of discipline. See Brickley, "Litchfield Female Academy," 122, 143, 562.

10. Catharine Beecher to William and Louisa [Wait], June 1, 1824, folder 14, Beecher-Stowe Collection, SchL. The *Hartford Courant* announced the opening of Catharine's school with the caveat, "No scholar under twelve years of age need apply"; quoted in Trumbull, *Memorial History of Hartford County*, 1:648.

11. *Catalogue of Hartford Female Seminary Officers, Teachers, and Pupils, of the Hartford Female Seminary for the Summer Term of 1828* (Hartford, Conn: Published by the Seminary, 1828), 7. Publications relating to the Hartford Female Seminary are held by both the Stowe-Day Library and the Connecticut Historical Society.

12. Joan Burstyn, "Catharine Beecher and the Education of American Women," *New England Quarterly* 47, no. 3 (1974): 397–98, calls attention to Catharine's advocacy of collegial governance at the Western Female Institute, observing that "her ideas on the governance of colleges were formed while she was running the Hartford Female Seminary."

13. Catharine Beecher, *Educational Reminiscences*, 30–31. It was typical for female teachers to have only slightly more training than their pupils. See Louise L. Stevenson, "Sarah Porter Educates Useful Ladies, 1847–1900," *Winterthur Portfolio* 18, no. 1 (Spring, 1983): 50.

14. Stowe and Stowe, *Life*, 41.

15. HBS to "Dear Aunt and all other Friends," addressed to George Foote, Guilford, September 10, 1824, Beecher Family Papers, SML.

16. Catharine Beecher, *Educational Reminiscences*, 31.

17. Catharine Beecher, *Educational Reminiscences*, 31.

18. Sklar, *Catharine Beecher*, passim, documents the closeness of the relationship between Lyman and Catharine.

19. Anne Throne Margolis, "A Tempest Tossed Spirit: Isabella Beecher Hooker and Woman Suffrage," in *The Isabella Beecher Hooker Project*, ed. Anne Throne Margolis (Hartford, Conn: Stowe-Day Foundation, 1979), 10.

20. Ann D. Gordon points out the importance of Franklin's model in "The Young Ladies, Academy of Philadelphia," in *Women of America*, ed. Berkin and Norton, 72–73. For discussions of the curriculum at Emma Willard's and Sarah Porter's schools, see Anne Firor Scott, "The Ever-Widening Circle: The Diffusion of Feminist Values from the Troy Female Seminary, 1822–72," in her *Making the Invisible Woman Visible* (Urbana: University of Illinois Press, 1984), 69; and Stevenson, "Sarah Porter Educates Useful Ladies," 42.

21. James McLachlan, *American Boarding Schools: A Historical Study* (New York: Charles Scribner's Sons, 1970), 33, 44. Brickley, "Litchfield Female Academy," 155.

22. Brickley, "Litchfield Female Academy," 180, 189. For an excellent discussion of "The Ornamental Curriculum," see Brickley, 152–91.

23. Tuition between 1828 and 1831, during which years catalogues of the school are available, remained essentially the same: the charge was $12 per term for all of the "English branches," which included all of the subjects in the "English school" model. Additionally, music cost $20 per term; French, Italian, and Latin, $12; the tuition for drawing went from $8 in 1828 to $12 in 1831. Catharine claimed that her charges were substantially lower than those prevailing in other female seminaries in urban areas. See *Catalogue of the Hartford Female Seminary*, Summer Term, 1828, 15, and *Catalogue of the Hartford Female Seminary, Together with an Account of the Internal Arrangements, Course of Study, and Mode of Conducting the Same* (Hartford, Conn: George F. Olmsted, 1831), 32. Tuition at the Hartford Female Seminary was approximately the same as at the Litchfield Female Academy, where in 1826 students paid $6 per quarter. See Brickley, "Litchfield Female Academy," 117.

24. *Catalogue of the Hartford Female Seminary*, 1831, 9.

25. *Catalogue of the Hartford Female Seminary*, Summer Term, 1828, 7; *Catalogue of the Hartford Female Seminary*, 1831, 9. John Lee Comstock (1789–1858) was a prolific writer of textbooks. Catharine used his *Elements of Chemistry; in Which the Recent Discoveries in the Science are Included, and Its Doctrines Familiarly Explained* (Hartford: D. F. Robinson, 1831) and his *A System of Natural Philosophy, In Which the Principles of Mechanics, Hydrostatics, Hydraulics, Pneumatics, and Magnetism are Familiarly Explained* (Hartford: D. F. Robinson, 1830).

26. Scott, "The Ever-Widening Circle," 69.

27. Scott, "The Ever-Widening Circle," 69.

28. Scott, "The Ever-Widening Circle," 77.

29. Because many female academies did not offer Latin and Greek, they had room for history and geography, which they then approached as "solid" subjects that gave intellectual weight to the curriculum; see Brickley, "Litchfield Female Academy," 238–39, 241.

30. Catharine Beecher, *Suggestions Respecting Improvements in Education* (Hartford, Conn.: Packard & Butler, 1829), 62. "The fact is," Catharine wrote to her brother, "there is not a single school book *upon earth* made as it ought to be, & one of the best things in the millennium will be, school books that will not tire the patience of Job to look at them. I feel sometimes as if I could *make a bonfire* of many of them with as much complacency as Don Quixote's old housekeeper brought forth to the flames his most mischievous books of chivalry" (Catharine Beecher to Edward Beecher, August 23, 1828, copy, SD; original in the Williston Library, Mount Holyoke College).

31. White, *Litchfield*, 113.

32. C. E. Stowe, *Life*, 65. Wilson, *Crusader in Crinoline*, 111–12, 114.

33. Angelina Grimké, diary for July 4–July 20, 1831, Weld-Grimké Papers, UMi. See also *Catalogue of the Hartford Female Seminary*, 1831, 17.

34. LF, 206.

35. David F. Allmendinger, Jr., *Paupers and Scholars: The Transformation of Student Life in Nineteenth-Century New England* (New York: St. Martin's Press, 1975), 9, 81–82, 84.

36. Kathryn Sklar suggests that another motive was Catharine's desire to be free from housekeeping duties; see Sklar, *Catharine Beecher*, 91–92.

37. Allmendinger, *Paupers and Scholars*, 104. It is striking that the boarding-out system is viewed in opposite ways, depending on whether the boarders are male or

female students. While Allmendinger sees the boarding-out system as an arrange-
ment that gave more independence to older male students, Ann Gordon and Louise
Stevenson see it as a restraint that fostered women's domestic, dependent social roles.
In Gordon's words, "Family government and domestic life were the ends of a woman's
education and should, therefore, be its means"; see Gordon, "The Young Ladies'
Academy of Philadelphia," 77; also see Stevenson, "Sarah Porter Educates Useful
Ladies," 57.

38. Catharine Beecher, *Educational Reminiscences*, 77–78.

39. *Catalogue of the Hartford Female Seminary*, Summer Term, 1828, 12, 14,
15.

40. *Catalogue of the Hartford Female Seminary*, Summer Term, 1828, 14.

41. HBS to Sarah [Terry], n.d., Katharine S. Day Collection, SD. The extensive
contact between the sexes that Lynne Brickley documents in Litchfield between the
students at Sarah Pierce's and the young men of the law school, who often boarded
in the same homes and were included as a matter of course in family entertainments,
does not appear to have prevailed in Hartford, owing mainly to the absence of a
corresponding male institution; see Brickley, "Litchfield Female Academy," 402–3.

42. *Regulations of the Hartford Female Seminary* (Hartford, Conn.: Hudson &
Skinner, 1830) 7.

43. Brickley, "Litchfield Female Academy," 171.

44. *Regulations of the Hartford Female Seminary*, 1830, 7; *Catalogue of the Hartford Female Seminary*, 1831, 12–13.

45. Gordon, "The Young Ladies' Academy of Philadelphia," 79. Ann Shepard, a
student at the Litchfield Female Academy, wrote home in 1817, "Our school is very
interesting, all united like sisters"; quoted in Brickley, "Litchfield Female Academy,"
400.

46. HBS to Mary [Swift], n.d., Harriet Beecher Stowe Collection, UVa.

47. Mary Kingsbury Talcott to Harriet Grew, n.d., Mary K. Talcott Collection,
SD.

48. See HBS to Elisabeth Phoenix, n.d., Phoenix Papers, UMi.

49. Sklar, "Founding of Mount Holyoke College," 190.

50. Catharine Beecher, *Educational Reminiscences*, 48–49. On the 1826 revival,
see Sklar, *Catharine Beecher*, 63–72.

51. Lyman Beecher to Harriet Porter Beecher, June 19 and 22, n.y. [1825–26],
Katharine S. Day Collection, SD.

52. Clarissa _____ to Sarah [Terry], n.d., Katharine S. Day Collection, SD.

53. Mary K. Talcott to Harriet Grew, n.d., Mary K. Talcott Collection, SD. For
other letters on religion in which students exchange feeling and worry about one
another's souls, see the fourteen letters from anonymous schoolfriends to Sarah
Terry, Katharine S. Day Collection, SD; also see the letters from Elizabeth Davenport
to Mary Talcott, 1832–1834, Mary K. Talcott Collection, SD.

54. For example, the Elizabeth Davenport letters to Mary Talcott, (1832–1834,
Mary K. Talcott Collection, SD) are very concerned about Mary's unconverted state
and exhibit a somewhat browbeating tone.

55. Mary K. Kingsbury to Harriet Grew, n.d., Mary K. Talcott Collection, SD.

56. See in particular HBS to Sarah [Terry], [1826], four undated letters from
HBS to Mary Talcott, [1831–1832], and HBS to [Elizabeth Bates], December 12,
[1832], Katharine S. Day Collection and Acquisitions, SD. A number of additional
pastoral letters by Catharine and Harriet are quoted in Marian Murray, "Notes from
Harriet Beecher Stowe and Her Sister Catherine to Pupils in Their School," clipping,

SD. For an analysis of the alternative ministry Harriet Beecher Stowe pursued, see my " 'Peaceable Fruits': The Ministry of Harriet Beecher Stowe," *American Quarterly* 40, no.2 (September 1988):307–32.

57. Sklar brilliantly and with great sensitivity to Catharine's distress tells the story of Lyman Beecher's "doctrinal" approach to her bereavement; see her *Catharine Beecher*, 37–42.

58. Lyman Beecher to Catharine Beecher, November 5, 1822, folder 2, Beecher-Stowe Collection, SchL.

59. See especially Lyman Beecher to Catharine Beecher, November 5, 1822, and January 27, 1823, folder 2, Beecher-Stowe Collection, SchL.

60. HBS to Sarah [Terry], [1826], Katharine S. Day Collection, SD.

61. As quoted in Stowe and Stowe, *Harriet Beecher Stowe*, 56–57. Commenting on just such male interference with women's spiritual experience, Sarah Grimké observed that "more souls have probably been lost by going down to Egypt for help, and by trusting in man in the early stages of religious experience, than by any other error"; see Sarah Grimké, *Letter on the Equality of the Sexes and the Condition of Women* (1837), in *The Feminist Papers*, ed. Alice Rossi (New York: Columbia University Press, 1973), 311.

62. HBS to Sarah [Terry], [1826], Katharine S. Day Collection, SD.

63. HBS to [Elizabeth Bates], December 12, [1832], Acquisitions, SD.

64. HBS to Mary Kingsbury Talcott, n.d., Mary K. Talcott Collection, SD.

65. HBS to Sarah [Terry], [1826], Katharine S. Day Collection, SD.

66. HBS to Edward Beecher, August, 1828, as quoted in Stowe and Stowe, *Harriet Beecher Stowe*, 56.

67. HBS to George Beecher, July 21, 1830, Acquisitions, SD.

68. *School Gazette*, no. 1, p. 1, Katharine S. Day Collection, SD.

69. My analysis draws on Mary Kelley's examination of the double consciousness of the women writers whom she calls "literary domestics"; see her *Private Woman, Public Stage: Literary Domesticity in Nineteenth-Century America* (New York: Oxford University Press, 1984).

70. *School Gazette*, no. 1, p. 12, Katharine S. Day Collection, SD.

Chapter 5

1. Stevenson, "Sarah Porter Educates Useful Ladies," 41.

2. Gordon, "The Young Ladies' Academy of Philadelphia," 83.

3. Emma Willard's Troy Female Seminary, opened in 1821, likewise offered an education equivalent to a man's under the assumption that women "should prepare themselves for self-support, and that they should not seek marriage as an end in itself"; see Scott, "The Ever-Widening Circle," 70. Miss Porter's School, begun in 1843, would pursue a more conservative agenda than the seminaries of these early pioneers; see Stevenson, "Sarah Porter Educates Useful Ladies." Angelina Grimké recorded Catharine Beecher's philosophy in her diary: "[She] [r]emarked that her Scholars were taught to feel that they had no right to spend their time in idleness, fashion & folly, but they as individuals were bound to be useful in Society after they had finished their education, & that as teachers single women could be more useful in this than in any other way, so many of her pupils tho' quite independent had become teachers simply from the wish of being useful" (Angelina Grimké Diary, July 4–July 20, 1831, Weld-Grimké Papers, UMi.

4. Angelina Grimké visited the seminary in Springfield and described it as "a flourishing Seminary under the care of julia hawkes once a Teacher of C B's. she

opened this school with the assistance of two of C's scholars" (Diary of Angelina Grimké, July 4–July 28, 1831, Weld-Grimké Papers, UMi). In the *Catalogue of the Hartford Female Seminary*, 1831, pp. 28 and 31, Catharine Beecher mentions the "constant change of teachers" as one of her biggest difficulties. See also Catharine Beecher, *Educational Reminiscences*, 76–77. On Mary Dutton, see Wilson, *Crusader in Crinoline*, 80.

5. Emma Willard was at this same time scattering her students-become-teachers to the northwest, the southeast, and the southwest; see Scott, "The Ever-Widening Circle," 72–75.

6. C. E. Stowe, *Life*, 37. Annie Fields, *The Life and Letters of Harriet Beecher Stowe* (Boston: Houghton Mifflin, 1897), 63.

7. Norton, *Liberty's Daughters*, 257.

8. S. V. Talcott, *Talcott Pedigree in England and America from 1598 to 1876* (Albany, N.Y.: Weed, Parsons and Company, 1876), 255. Her Lafayette ribbon and two awards from Miss Rockwell's school are in the Mary Kingsbury Talcott Collection, SD. It is not clear precisely how long Mary Talcott attended the Hartford Female Seminary; she entered in 1831 but may have left before 1833; the first letter to Harriet Grew written after she was clearly no longer there is dated April 8, 1834.

9. Mary Kingsbury Talcott to Harriet Grew, n.d.("Saturday eve"), Mary K. Talcott Collection, SD.

10. Using data from alumnae questionnaires, Scott found that 38 percent of the graduates of the Troy Female Seminary took part in some kind of voluntary association; see Scott, "The Ever-Widening Circle," 81.

11. Mary Kingsbury Talcott to Harriet Grew, May 17, 1835, Mary K. Talcott Collection, SD.

12. Mary Kingsbury Talcott to Harriet Grew, April 8, 1834, Mary K. Talcott Collection, SD.

13. Mary Kingsbury Talcott to Harriet Grew, September 5, 1835, Mary K. Talcott Collection, SD.

14. Mary Kingsbury Talcott to Harriet Grew, December 19, 1835, Mary K. Talcott Collection, SD.

15. Mary Kingsbury Talcott to Harriet Grew, May 13, 1836, Mary K. Talcott Collection, SD. Compare her letter to Harriet Grew, September 20, 1836, Mary K. Talcott Collection, SD, where she praised the memoir of Mary Jane Graham: "There are, doubtless, many more such, 'all unknown to fame'—yet comparitively the number must be small—So few of us have the time to devote uninterruptedly to intellectual pursuits, that it is scarcely possible to attain so high an elevation in mental culture and acquirements—even where there is originally as much native strength of mind—which, I have the vanity (as some would call it) to think not *very* rare."

16. Mary Kingsbury Talcott to Harriet Grew, April 8, 1834, Mary K. Talcott Collection, SD.

17. Mary Kingsbury Talcott to Harriet Grew, March 14, 1837, Mary K. Talcott Collection, SD. For a stimulating and persuasive analysis of the conflict between ladyhood and authorship that in many ways parallels Mary Talcott's struggle, see Mary Poovey, *The Proper Lady and the Woman Writer: Ideology as Style in the Works of Mary Wollstonecraft, Mary Shelley, and Jane Austen* (Chicago: University of Chicago Press, 1984). Analyzing popular American novelists, Kelley's *Private Woman, Public Stage* likewise focuses on the contradictions of consciousness that women writers of this period experienced.

18. Julia Grew to Mary Kingsbury Talcott, July 27, [1837?], Mary K. Talcott Collection, SD. She writes to Julia Seymour, [c.1838], Mary K. Talcott Collection,

SD, "I hope I shall see you again soon. I enjoy the society of my friends even more than I did when in health, and it may not be long that I shall be able to see them."

19. C. E. Stowe, *Life*, 145. Such declarations of mortality were not unusual in the 1840s, when life was viewed as tentative and death certain. See Lewis O. Saum, "Death in the Popular Mind of Pre–Civil War America," in *Death in America*, ed. David E. Stannard (Philadelphia: University of Pennsylvania Press, 1975), 37.

20. Catharine Beecher to Lyman Beecher, Feburary 16, 1827, as quoted in C. E. Stowe, *Life*, 37.

21. Catharine Beecher to Edward Beecher, Winter, 1827, as quoted in C. E. Stowe, *Life,*, 38.

22. Description of HFS taken from Mary Kingsbury Talcott's Memorandum Book, 1830s, SD.

23. Lyman Beecher to "My Dear Children," February, 1827, folder 4, Beecher-Stowe Collection, SchL.

24. Lyman Beecher to Catharine Beecher, February 3, 1827, folder 4, Beecher-Stowe Collection, SchL. On Mary Beecher's health, see Catharine Beecher to Louisa Wait, January, 1822, folder 14, Beecher-Stowe Collection, SchL; and Lyman Beecher to Catharine Beecher, December 3,1823, folder 2, Beecher-Stowe Collection, SchL.

25. *Catalogue of the Hartford Female Seminary*, 1831, 8.

26. Sklar, *Catharine Beecher*, 63.

27. Catharine Beecher to Edward Beecher, March 3, [1827], Acquisitions, SD.

28. Lyman Beecher to Catharine Beecher, March 21, 1823, folder 2, Beecher-Stowe Collection, SchL.

29. Sklar, *Catharine Beecher*, 138–39.

30. HBS to George Beecher, February 20, [1830?], Acquisitions, SD.

31. She cites the melancholy example of Frances Strong, who "became principal of the Hartford Seminary" and "lost her life, a martyr to unhealthful and cruel exactions" and of Julia Hawkes, head of a female seminary in Philadelphia, who "lost her health, went abroad, and died on her travels"; see *Educational Reminiscences*, 76–77.

32. HBS to Roxana Foote, January 3, 1828, as quoted in C. E. Stowe, *Life*, 41.

33. HBS to Roxana Foote, January 3, 1828, as quoted in C. E. Stowe, *Life*, 41.

34. Diary of Angelina Grimké, July 4,–July 28, 1831, Weld-Grimké Papers, UMi; her description is dated July 8.

35. *Autobiography*, 1:225.

36. HBS to Roxana Foote, January 3, 1828, as quoted in C. E. Stowe, *Life*, 41–42.

37. Stevenson, "Sarah Porter Educates Useful Ladies," 51.

38. HBS to Mary Swift, n. d. (postmarked December 27), [1828], Harriet Beecher Stowe Collection, UVa.

39. HBS to Georgiana May, November, 1828, as quoted in C. E. Stowe, *Life*, 45.

40. HBS to Edward Beecher, February, 1829, in C. E. Stowe, *Life*, 46.

41. Catharine Beecher, *Educational Reminiscences*, 38.

42. *Catalogue of the Hartford Female Seminary*, Summer Term, 1828, 10.

43. Mary Kingsbury Talcott to Harriet Grew, November 15, 1833, Mary K. Talcott Collection, SD.

44. HBS to Edward Beecher, February, 1829, as quoted in C. E. Stowe, *Life*, 45–46.

45. See two undated letters from HBS to Elizabeth Lyman, HBS to Elizabeth Lyman, December 9, [1835], Sarah B. Strong to Elizabeth C. Lyman, January 19,

1835, copies, SD, originals in Connecticut State Library, Hartford, Conn. Carroll Smith-Rosenberg, pointing out this phenomenon, writes "Older girls in boarding school 'adopted' younger ones, who called them 'Mother.' Dear friends might indeed continue this pattern of adoption and mothering throughout their lives; one woman might routinely assume the nurturing role of the pseudomother, the other the dependency role of daughter"; see Carroll Smith-Rosenberg, "The Female World of Love and Ritual: Relationships between Women in Nineteenth-Century America," *Signs* 1 (Autumn 1975): 19.

46. C. E. Stowe, *Life*, 32.

47. Catharine Beecher to Mary Dutton, February 3, 1832, Collection of American Literature, BL.

48. See Joyce A. Warren, *Fanny Fern: An Independent Woman* (New Brunswick, N.J.: Rutgers University Press, 1992).

49. Ethel Parton, "Fanny Fern: An Informal Biography" (unpublished manuscript, Parton Papers, Smith College), 57–58.

50. Catharine Beecher to Mr. and Mrs. Willis, May 27, 1829, Parton Papers, Smith College.

51. Parton, "Fanny Fern," 62–63.

52. Parton, "Fanny Fern," 60.

53. HBS to James Parton, n. d., Parton Papers, Smith College. See also Sarah Payson Willis Parton to HBS, February 14, 1868, folder 255, Beecher-Stowe Collection, SchL.

54. Ethel Parton, "Fanny Fern," 57. For other evidence that Miss Harriet was well liked, see Mary K. Talcott to Harriet Grew, n.d. ("Monday p.m. Study Hall"), Mary K. Talcott Collection, SD.

Chapter 6

1. Parton, "Fanny Fern," 64. Sklar, *Catharine Beecher*, 90–91.

2. Sklar, *Catharine Beecher*, 90.

3. HBS to Catharine Beecher, December 11, 1829, in Catharine Beecher, *Educational Reminiscences*, 69–70.

4. Catharine Beecher, *Educational Reminiscences*, 65, 66.

5. HBS to Catharine Beecher, December 10, 1829, in Catharine Beecher, *Educational Reminiscences*, 66–67.

6. HBS to Catharine Beecher, December 10 and 11, 1829, in Catharine Beecher, *Educational Reminiscences*, 68–69.

7. HBS to Catharine Beecher, December 12 and 14, 1829, in Catharine Beecher, *Educational Reminiscences*, 70–71.

8. HBS to Catharine Beecher, December 16, 1829, in Catharine Beecher, *Educational Reminiscences*, 73–74.

9. *Catalogue of the Hartford Female Seminary*, 1831, 21.

10. McLachlan, *American Boarding Schools*, 84.

11. *Catalogue of the Hartford Female Seminary*, Summer Term, 1828, 13.

12. Gordon, "Young Ladies' Academy of Philadelphia," 80, 79, 81.

13. Stevenson, "Sarah Porter Educates Useful Ladies," 48.

14. *Catalogue of Hartford Female Seminary*, 1831, 21.

15. *Catalogue of Hartford Female Seminary*, 1831, 20.

16. *Catalogue of the Hartford Female Seminary*, Summer Term, 1828, 12.

17. McLachlan, *American Boarding Schools*, 132–33.

18. *Catalogue of the Hartford Female Seminary*, Summer Term, 1828, 12. Catharine Beecher, *Educational Reminiscences*, 46.

19. Richard H. Brodhead, "Sparing the Rod: Discipline and Fiction in Antebellum America," *Representations* 21 (Winter 1988):87. Following Foucault, Brodhead suggests that the movement away from corporal punishment to more internalized norms of behavior resulted in a less cruel but more controlling environment, one that involved "inward colonization, not outward coercion" (73). The apotheosis of this manipulative strategy, according to Brodhead, are the characters in women's fiction, like Little Eva, who threaten to die if their charges do not do what they request. While Brodhead makes some brilliant connections between discipline and fiction, I find myself somewhat skeptical. Feminists have wondered whether it was accidental that postmodernists declared subjectivity an illusion at the very moment when second-wave women had begun to assert themselves as subjects. I am similarly suspicious of an analysis that finds moral suasion dangerous at just the historical moment that women found their podiums and pulpits. Is it the mode or the messenger that is threatening?

20. Catharine Beecher, *Educational Reminiscences*, 75.

21. The *Regulations* for 1830 made a small concession to student desires by allowing food to be taken into the school, though students were specifically limited to crackers. The other changes in the rules concern *speaking*—which suggests that students, having found a voice in running the school, were not easily muted. Whereas the *Catalogue* of 1828 forbade students "to speak without liberty," and rested the issue with that phrase, the *Regulations* of 1830 delimited the use of speech in some detail. Rule 2 specified, "No scholar is to communicate any ideas to another, by the mouth, by fingers, or by writing, without leave from the Governess when in the Hall, or from the Teacher when in the Recitation room. No pupil is to speak to another during school hours in the *entries* or on the *stairs* without leave from a Teacher." Rules 4 and 5 forbade students from speaking to a teacher after class or in study hall without permission—unless the student were addressed first. Finally, the issue of speaking during the evening study hours was to be decided in a republican fashion. No one was to speak unless it was *"absolutely necessary,"* and "[i]f a young lady has spoken during study hours, she must ask the opinion of her companions as to whether it was necessary, and the question is decided by the majority"; see *Regulations of the Hartford Female Seminary*, 1830, 7. This sudden attention to speech suggests that the student body had found a greater voice. Catharine continued to find it necessary to add rules of this sort. "The young ladies are required to lean their heads upon their desk during prayer time and not to communicate even by looks to each other"—so runs a pencilled addition to the rules in Mary Seymour's copy of the 1831 *Catalogue* (in SD).

22. *Catalogue of the Hartford Female Seminary*, 1831, 2.

23. HBS to Mary Dutton, (postmarked May 25), 1830, Collection of American Literature, BL.

24. Forrest Wilson points out that Harriet's remark on "emulation" is an allusion to the educational debate in which the Hartford Female Seminary had taken the other side; see his *Crusader in Crinoline*, 81.

25. HBS to George Beecher, February 20, [1830?], Acquisitions, SD.

26. HBS to George Beecher, July 21, 1830, Acquisitions, SD.

27. Mary K. Talcott, "Historical Sketch of the Seminary," in *The Hartford Female Seminary Reunion* (Hartford, Conn.: Case, Lockwood & Brainard Company, 1892), 6.

28. Catharine Beecher to Mary Dutton, February 8, 1830, Collection of American Literature, BL.

29. Sklar, *Catharine Beecher*, 72.

30. Welter, "The Cult of True Womanhood."

31. Angelina Grimké diary, July 4–July 20, 1831, Weld-Grimké Papers, UMi. All of the material on Grimké's visit comes from this diary. See also Sklar, *Catharine Beecher*, 98–100.

32. Grimké spent July 11–July 15 going to the seminary every morning. One would give a great deal to know her reactions, but they are apparently lost. She records in her diary entry of July 11, "Accompanied Catharine Beecher to her School both morning & afternoon & as I have kept a particular account of it on a separate piece of paper shall pass it over here." She does mention, however, that she found the mapmaking exercises tedious.

33. Scott, "The Ever-Widening Circle," 64–88.

34. Mary Kingsbury Talcott to Harriet Grew, n.d., Mary K. Talcott Collection, SD.

35. HBS to Sarah Beecher, September 29, [1845], Acquisitions, SD.

36. Catharine Beecher, *Educational Reminiscences*, 75. By 1839 the curriculum reflected more attention to women's "accomplishments": courses in Japan work and making wax flowers were included, and children younger than twelve were admitted; see *The Annual Catalogue of the Hartford Female Seminary* (Hartford,Conn.: E. Gleason, Printer, 1839), 14.

Chapter 7

1. Charles Cist, *Cincinnati in 1841: Its Early Annals* (Cincinnati, Ohio: Author, 1841), 35. Population figures are rounded to the nearest thousand.

2. WPA, *Cincinnati: A Guide to the Queen City and Its Neighbors* (Cincinnati, Ohio: Wiesen-Hart Press, 1943), 30.

3. Daniel Hurley, *Cincinnati: The Queen City* (Cincinnati, Ohio: Cincinnati Historical Society, n. d. [c. 1983]), 35.

4. Quoted in Milton Rugoff, *The Beechers: An American Family in the Nineteenth Century* (New York: Harper & Row, 1981), 167.

5. Henry Ward Beecher to HBS, March 8, 1832, Beecher Family Papers, SML.

6. Lyman Beecher to Catharine Beecher, July 8, 1830, in *Autobiography*, 2: 167.

7. *Autobiography*, 2:181; Catharine Beecher to Mary Dutton, 1830, Collection of American Literature, BL.

8. HBS to Mary Beecher Perkins, October 6, 1832, in *Autobiography*, 2:207.

9. Elizabeth E. Foote to Eliza Foote, August 2, 1829, Foote Collection, SD.

10. HBS to Georgiana May, in C. E. Stowe, *Life*, 59.

11. HBS to Mary Beecher Perkins, October 18, 1832, in *Autobiography*, 2:208.

12. In an amateur production written for a Cincinnati literary club, James Albert Green writes of Harriet and Henry Ward, "They were New Englanders when they came, very sure Boston was the hub of the universe, but when they left . . . [they] had become great Americans in the broadest sense of the word. This to them was a school of thought and feeling, where they learned to ignore the narrow provincialism to which they were born"; see James Albert Green, "The Beecher Family of Cincinnati" (unpublished manuscript, Cincinnati Historical Society). It takes an Ohioan to give this perspective on New England provincialism.

13. Catharine Beecher to Mary Dutton, February 3, 1832, Collection of American Literature, BL.

14. C. and H. Beecher, *Primary Geography for Children, on an Improved Plan*

with Eleven Maps and Numerous Engravings (Cincinnati, Ohio: Corey & Fairbank, 1833). The quote from the *Western Monthly Magazine* is included in a list of testimonials printed on an unpaginated leaf at the end of this, the fourth, edition.

15. Harden, *Maria Edgeworth's Art*, 36–37.

16. HBS, *Primary Geography*, 104.

17. Frances Trollope, *The Domestic Manners of the Americans*, ed. Donald Smalley (1832; New York: Alfred A. Knopf, 1949), 36.

18. Trollope, *Domestic Manners*, 17.

19. WPA, *Cincinnati: A Guide*, 40.

20. HBS to Mary Beecher Perkins, [Fall, 1832], in C. E. Stowe, *Life*, 63.

21. HBS, *Primary Geography*, 101–2.

22. HBS to George Beecher, January [25], [1834], Acquisitions, SD.

23. Brickley, "Litchfield Female Academy," 541–47.

24. HBS, *Primary Geography*, 105. On Cincinnati's growth, see Hurley, *Cincinnati*, 33, 34, 37.

25. Trollope, *Domestic Manners*, 43.

26. HBS, *Primary Geography*, 47.

27. Information on John and Samuel Foote is taken from the "Calendar of Manuscripts," Cincinnati Historical Society, and Foote, *Foote Family: Comprising the Genealogy*, 201.

28. HBS to Georgiana May, Summer, 1832, in C. E. Stowe, *Life*, 50–51.

29. Samuel Foote to Roxana Foote, December 27 and 28, 1833, Foote Collection, SD. He had written from Cadiz, Spain, to Lyman Beecher that the Corpus Christi Day was "celebrated with a pomp & magnificence of which a man who has never been out of a protestant country can have little idea, indeed the Catholics are the only people whose processions are worth looking at"; see Samuel Foote to Lyman Beecher, May 28, 1812, Acquisitions, SD.

30. HBS to George Beecher, January 3 [and 6], 1834, Acquisitions, SD.

31. HBS to Georgiana May, May, 1833, as quoted in Stowe, C. E. *Life*, 66.

32. HBS to Georgiana May, May, 1833, in C. E. Stowe, *Life*, 66–67.

33. HBS to Georgiana May, May, 1833, in C. E. Stowe, *Life*, 66.

Chapter 8

1. The average price of a hardback book during the antebellum period was $1.00, "a full one-sixth of the male's weekly wages and well over half of that of the woman's—equivalent today to anywhere between $50 and $150, a price few, then and now, would be willing to pay for books"; see Ronald J. Zboray, "Antebellum Reading and the Ironies of Technological Innovation," *American Quarterly* 40, no. 1 (March 1988): 74–75.

2. *Autobiography*, 1:313.

3. *Autobiography*, 1:396.

4. *Autobiography* 1:396, 397.

5. Harriet Foote to "Brother, sister & mother," March 1, 5, and 7, 1837, Foote Collection, SD.

6. Brickley, "Litchfield Female Academy," 222.

7. Jed Dannenbaum, *Drink and Disorder: Temperance Reform in Cincinnati from the Washingtonian Revival to the WCTU* (Urbana: University of Illinois Press, 1984), 47–48.

8. C. E. Stowe, *Life*, 61–62.

9. HBS to Mary Swift, (postmarked December 27), [ca. 1828], Harriet Beecher

Stowe Collection, UVa. Isabella P. Beecher to Catharine Beecher, October 22, 1837, folder 17, Beecher-Stowe Collection, SchL.

10. HBS to George Beecher, January [25], [1834], Acquisitions, SD.

11. Roxana Beecher to Lyman Beecher, February 23, 1810, in *Autobiography,* 1:132.

12. Catharine Beecher to Louisa Waite, May 11, 1819, folder 14, Beecher-Stowe Collection, SchL.

13. HBS to Susie Munroe Stowe, October 17, 1879, folder 211, Beecher-Stowe Collection, SchL.

14. HBS to Charley [and Susie] Stowe, September 27, 1879, folder 209, Beecher-Stowe Collection, SchL.

15. HBS to Susie Munroe Stowe, March 30, 1881, folder 222, Beecher-Stowe Collection, SchL.

16. Catharine Beecher to Louisa Wait, November 8, n. y., folder 14, Beecher-Stowe Collection, SchL.

17. Esther Beecher to HBS, July 7, 1837, folder 10, Beecher-Stowe Collection, SchL.

18. Catharine Beecher to Mary Cogswell and Mary Weld, May 29, 1837, folder 15, Beecher-Stowe Collection, SchL.

19. HBS to George Beecher, January [25], [1834], Acquisitions, SD.

20. Harriet Porter Beecher to Catharine Beecher, September 1, 1823, folder 11, Beecher-Stowe Collection, SchL.

21. Catharine Beecher to Mary Cogswell and Mary Weld, May 20, 1837, folder 15, Beecher-Stowe Collection, SchL.

22. In her study of westering women, Annette Kolodny points out the importance women attached to the packets of seeds and dried root cuttings that enabled them to plant the familiar on the open prairie; see Annette Kolodny, *The Land Before Her: Fantasy and Experience of the American Frontiers, 1630–1860* (Chapel Hill: University of North Carolina Press, 1984), 146, 237. I would add that while women were more deeply involved in this process by virtue of their domestic roles, men too participated in these exchanges. Gardening was a passion for many middle-class men of this period, perhaps reflecting the transition that had already been made in their lifetimes from an agricultural to an urban existence. This hobby provided a way of asserting a material continuity as plants grown in the East were rooted in the new soil of the West. Samuel Foote described "visiting" his family in Connecticut "when we smell our sweet scented Honeysuckles at the Bedroom window or meet with any other plant or flower which we have been in the habit of seeing at Nutplains" (Samuel Foote to Roxana Foote and family, August 23, 1830, Foote Collection, SD). Certainly men were vulnerable to the same feelings of homesickness as women, and it was to domestic culture they looked to root themselves in a reality that was both old and new.

23. Elizabeth E. Foote to Eliza Foote, December 1 and 4, 1831, Foote Collection, SD.

24. Isabella P. Beecher to Beecher family, January 22, 1838, Acquisitions, Circular Letters, SD.

25. The first national Thanksgiving Day was proclaimed by George Washington on November 26, 1789. Abraham Lincoln revived it as a national holiday when he proclaimed Thanksgiving to be the third Thursday of November in 1863. In antebellum times November was the common time to celebrate Thanksgiving in New England, but December 24 was Thanksgiving in other places, as it was in Ohio. See Harriet Foote to George Foote, Eliza Foote, and Roxana Foote, March 1,5, and 7,

1837, Foote Collection, SD: "We all of us went the day before Christmas (which was appointed by the governor as a day of Thankgiving) to dine with brother John."

26. HBS to Mary Perkins, [after November 14], 1832, in C. E. Stowe, *Life*, 63.

27. Charles and Sarah Beecher to the Beecher family, December 19, 1840, Acquisitions, Circular Letters, SD. The male tradition has been characterized by its attention to myth and romance. For mythic definitions, see R.W.B. Lewis, *The American Adam: Innocence, Tragedy, and Tradition in the Nineteenth Century* (Chicago: University of Chicago Press, 1955), Henry Nash Smith, *Virgin Land : The American West as Symbol and Myth* (Cambridge, Mass.: Harvard University Press, 1950), and Richard Slotkin, *Regeneration through Violence* (Middletown, Conn.: Wesleyan University Press, 1973). Arguing for romance as characteristic of the [male] American novel, Richard Chase writes that it is characterized by "a willingness to abandon moral questions or to ignore the spectacle of man in society, or to consider these things only indirectly or abstractly"; see Richard Chase, *The American Novel and Its Tradition* (Garden City, N.Y.: Doubleday and Company, 1957), ix.

28. Kolodny, *The Land Before Her*, 133.

29. Harriet Beecher Stowe, *Uncle Tom's Cabin; or, Life Among the Lowly*, (Boston: Houghton Mifflin, 1896), 2 vols.,1:116–17; hereafter cited in text as UTC. Robyn Warhol, "Letters and Novels 'One Woman Wrote to Another': George Eliot's Responses to Elizabeth Gaskell," *Victorian Newsletter* 86 (Fall 1986): 8–14. The examples Warhol cites here and in her essay "Toward a Theory of the Engaging Narrator: Earnest Intervention in Gaskell, Stowe and Eliot" (PMLA 101, no. 5 [October 1986], 811–18), point toward a distinctive narrative tradition in nineteenth-century women's novels. I am grateful to Marianne L. Novy for calling my attention to these articles.

30. Zboray, "Antebellum Reading," 77.

31. Forrest Wilson writes that after the publication of the *Geography* Catharine and Harriet "were invited to join with the cultural elite of Cincinnati" in forming the Semi-Colon Club (*Crusader in Crinoline*, 122). In fact the Semi-Colons had been meeting at least since early 1831; see Papers of the Semi-Colon Club, Greene-Roelker Papers, Cincinnati Historical Society, which include a paper by Samuel [Foote] dated March 11, 1831. It is possible that the Semi-Colons formed shortly after the Foote mansion was completed in the fall of 1829, for Foote and his nextdoor neighbor, attorney William Greene, were the core of the club. Louis L. Tucker's "The Semi-Colon Club of Cincinnati" (*Ohio History* 73, no. 1 [1964]: 13–26, 57–58) puts the club in its local context, provides descriptions of the members and the activities, and includes some excerpts of the literary productions. Lynette Carpenter, in "S/he Who Discovers a New Pleasure: Cincinnati's Semi-Colon Club and the Woman Intellectual" (Paper presented at the National Women's Studies Association, Minneapolis, 1987), speculates about the role such clubs played in supporting women authors.

32. HBS to Mary Perkins, [Fall, 1832], in C. E. Stowe, *Life*, 63–64.

33. Catharine Beecher to HBS, April 17, 1832, in *Autobiography*, 2:200. Other members of the Semi-Colon Club included E. P. Cranch, Charles Beecher, James Handasyd Perkins, Benjamin Drake, Nathan Guilford, and Judge Timothy Walker.

34. Wilson, *Crusader in Crinoline*, 116; Edward D. Mansfield, *Memoirs of the Life and Services of Daniel Drake, M.D., Physician, Professor, and Author; With Notices of the Early Settlement of Cincinnati and Some of Its Pioneer Citizens* (Cincinnati, Ohio: Applegate, 1855), 229.

35. Sklar, *Catharine Beecher*, 116–121.

36. Samuel Foote to Roxana Foote, August 10, 1839, Foote Collection, SD.

37. HBS to Georgiana May, n. d. [c.1833], in C. E. Stowe, *Life*, 69–70.

38. Wilson, *Crusader in Crinoline*, 124.

39. Margaret [Rives] King, *Memoirs of the Life of Mrs. Sarah Peter* (Cincinnati, Ohio: Robert Clarke & Co., 1889), 38.

40. Foote, *Memoirs of the Life of Samuel E. Foote*, 242.

41. Papers of the Semi-Colon Club, Greene-Roelker Papers, Cincinnati Historical Society.

42. Several examples of Semi-Colon Club productions are included in an appendix to Foote's *Memoirs*; the "Petition" appears on pp. 258–61.

43. Parlor music, in its sixteenth-century Italian forms, likewise displayed "a tendency to parody even in expressions of pain"; see Joanne Riley, "Tarquinia Molza (1542–1616): A Case Study of Women, Music, and Society in the Renaissance," in *The Musical Woman: An International Perspective*, 2 vols., ed. Judith Lang Zaimont (New York: Greenwood Press, 1987), 2:473. My conceptualization of parlor literature was sparked by Riley's analysis of women and parlor music.

44. This unsigned note in Harriet's hand is in the William Greene Letters, box 5–753, Cincinnati Historical Society. I am grateful to Lynette Carpenter for this reference.

45. King, *Memoirs of Mrs. Sarah Peter*, 38.

46. HBS to Georgiana May, [1833], in C. E. Stowe, *Life*, 69.

47. Kelley, *Private Woman, Public Stage*, esp. Chapter 5, "Secret Writers," 111–37.

48. Woolf, *A Room of One's Own*, 79–80.

49. HBS to Georgiana May, [1833], in C. E. Stowe, *Life*, 69, 70.

50. HBS to Georgiana May, [1833], in C. E. Stowe, *Life*, 70–1.

51. HBS to George Beecher, January 3 and 6, 1834, Acquisitions, SD.

52. Wilson, *Crusader in Crinoline*, 126.

53. HBS, *May Flower and Miscellaneous Writings* (Boston: Phillips, Sampson, 1855), 4, 113, 106, 127–57, 15.

54. Louis Tucker remarks on the "wistful, nostalgic remembrances of the ordered life of the past" that characterized many of the Semi-Colon Club papers; see Tucker, "The Semi-Colon Club," 23–24.

Chapter 9

1. Charles Beecher to Lyman Beecher, December 4, 1833, folder 22, Beecher-Stowe Collection, SchL.

2. See HBS to George Beecher, n.d. [c. September, 1833], September [13–17], [1833], and January [25], [1834], Acquisitions, SD.

3. HBS, *Primary Geography*, 61.

4. Trollope, *Domestic Manners*, 75. On the custom of men doing the marketing, see Trollope, 85, and the picture facing page 41. Smith-Rosenberg comments on the separation of men's and women's spheres and the rigidity this introduced into their social relationships; see Smith-Rosenberg, "The Female World of Love and Ritual," 20–21, 28.

5. Trollope, *Domestic Manners*, 58–59.

6. HBS to George Beecher, January [25], [1834], Acquisitions, SD.

7. Mansfield, *Memoirs of Daniel Drake*, 223.

8. Mansfield, *Memoirs of Daniel Drake*, 224.

9. Woolf, *A Room of One's Own*, 73.

10. Mansfield, *Memoirs of Daniel Drake*, 224.

11. Mansfield, *Memoirs of Daniel Drake*, 226.

12. [Mrs.] A. J. Lyman to Mrs. [Abby Lyman] Greene, November 8, [1834], Greene-Roelker Papers, Cincinnati Historical Society.

13. WPA, *Cincinnati: A Guide*, 30.

14. Robert Bruce Warden, *An Account of the Private Life and Public Services of Salmon Portland Chase* (Cincinnati, Ohio: Wilstach, Baldwin & Co., 1874), 206, 230.

15. HBS, *Primary Geography*, 48–51. On Bishop Purcell, see HBS to Georgiana May, May, 1833, in C. E. Stowe, *Life*, 65.

16. HBS to Georgiana May, May, 1833, in C. E. Stowe, *Life*, 65.

17. HBS to Henry Ward Beecher, March 18, 1835, Beecher Family Papers, SML.

18. Mansfield, *Memoirs of Daniel Drake*, 241.

19. HBS to Elizabeth Lyman, Summer, 1834, in C. E. Stowe, *Life*, 74–75.

20. Catharine Beecher to the Beecher family, [between January 24 and February 18, 1838], Acquisitions, Circular Letters, SD.

21. Poem in HBS's hand, August 1, 1834, Helen D. Perkins Collection, SD. Roxana Foote died in November 1840 at age ninety.

22. CES to Catharine Hills Crosby, February 1, 1826, and [February 28 or March 1, 1827], Acquisitions, SD. During his senior year at Andover he translated from the German Johann Jahn's *History of the Hebrew Commonwealth* (Andover, 1828 London, 1829); he was editor of the *Boston Recorder* the following year and in 1829 he revised and edited with notes *Lectures on the Sacred Poetry of the Hebrews*, a translation from the Latin of Robert Lowth by G. Gregory.

23. CES to Eliza Tyler, n.d. [1832], Acquisitions, SD.

24. CES to Eliza Tyler, March 29, 1832, Acquisitions, SD.

25. CES to Eliza Tyler Stowe, April 7, 1833, Acquisitions, SD.

26. Harriet Foote to Roxana Foote and family, September 6, 1836, Foote Collection, SD. On the unhealthful conditions in Cincinnati, see Trollope, *Domestic Manners*, 38–39, 40, 83–84; and Edward D. Mansfield, *Personal Memories: Social, Political, and Literary, with Sketches of Many Noted People, 1803–1843* (Cincinnati, Ohio: Robert Clarke & Co, 1879), 193–95; for statistics on cholera and contemporary understandings of its etiology, see Mansfield, *Memoirs of Dr. Daniel Drake*, 216–22.

27. Harriet Porter Beecher to Lyman Beecher, Catharine, and Harriet, August 12, 1834, Joseph K. Hooker Collection, SD. For Theodore Weld's reminiscences about cholera at Lane Seminary, see Beecher, *Autobiography*, 2:236–38.

28. "Eliza E. Stowe," clipping, Cincinnati Historical Society.

29. Harriet Porter Beecher to Lyman Beecher, Catharine, and Harriet, August 12, 1834, Acquisitions, SD.

30. See Hedrick, "'Peaceable Fruits': The Ministry of Harriet Beecher Stowe," 307–32.

31. HBS to Susan Howard, June 10, 1860, quoted in Fields, *Life*, 280.

32. CES to HBS, [1835], Acquisitions, SD.

33. Elizabeth Lyman to [William Lyman and family], December 24, 1834, Middlesex County Historical Society, Middletown, Conn.

34. CES to HBS, May 4, [1835], Acquisitions, SD.

35. CES to HBS, May 24 [and 25], [1835], Acquisitions, SD.

36. Charles Beecher to Lyman Beecher, December 4, 1833, folder 22, Beecher-Stowe Collection, SchL.

37. Charles Beecher to Lyman Beecher and family, November 23, 1835, Acquisitions, Circular Letters, SD.

38. *Autobiography*, 2:313.

39. HBS to Catharine Beecher and family, [December c. 21, 1835], Acquisitions, Circular Letters, SD.

40. Mary Dutton to Catharine Beecher, [1835, between December 21 and 23], Acquisitions, Circular Letters, SD.

41. HBS to Catharine Beecher and family, [December c. 21, 1835], Acquisitions, Circular Letters, SD.

42. HBS to the Beecher family, May 14, [1836], Acquisitions, Circular Letters, SD. Her brother William wrote, "I desire to congratulate Harriet & Mr Stowe—I have seen no notice of the marriage in the papers—& if George had not told us sh^d have been ignorant"; see William Beecher to George Beecher and family, February 8, 1836, Acquisitions, Circular Letters, SD. While Harriet guarded her privacy to an unusual extent, in other ways her marriage was typical. Ellen K. Rothman writes, "Early nineteenth century weddings were generally simple, almost informal affairs, which required little planning and advance preparation. Arrangements for the wedding were not made until shortly before the appointed day. A week appears to have been the average length of time between the issuing of invitations and the wedding." Brides were usually married at home, with a small group of friends in attendance. See Ellen K. Rothman, *Hands and Hearts: A History of Courtship in America* (New York: Basic Books, 1984), 77, 78.

43. Catharine Beecher to the Beecher family, [c. May 14], [1836], Acquisitions, Circular Letters, SD.

44. Rothman, *Hands and Hearts*, 72.

45. HBS to Elizabeth C. Lyman, December 9, [1835], Copies, SD; original in Connecticut State Library, Hartford, Conn.

46. C. E. Stowe, *Life*, 76–77.

47. CES to HBS, June 7, 1836; June 20, 1836; and May 19, 1836—all in Acquisitions, SD. HBS to CES, [June, 1836] in C. E. Stowe, *Life*, 80–81.

48. CES to HBS, [either June or December, 1836]; and August 12, [1836], and July 20, 1836—all in Acquisitions, SD. For his notes on dialect, see CES to HBS, June 20, 1836, and July 2, 1836, both in Acquisitions, SD.

49. CES to HBS, August 14, 1836, Acquisitions, SD.

50. CES to HBS, June 15, 1836; and October 16, 1836, Acquisitions, SD.

51. CES to Hepzibah Stowe, January 25, 1836, Acquisitions, SD.

52. HBS to George Eliot, September 23, 1872, Berg Collection of English and American Literature, NYPL.

53. CES to HBS, September 11, 1836; September 20, 1836; and October 26, 1836—all in Acquisitions, SD.

Chapter 10

1. *Autobiography*, 2:244.

2. For a splendid narrative of these events, see Rugoff, *The Beechers*, 146–51. Rugoff comments, "[H]istories have not given [the Lane Debates] their due as a thorough and radical exploration of the slavery question long before it became a national issue" (146).

3. *Autobiography*, 2:242.

4. Robert Merideth, *The Politics of the Universe: Edward Beecher, Abolition, and Orthodoxy* (Nashville, Tenn.: Vanderbilt University Press, 1968), 85–86.

5. *Autobiography*, 2:243, 244, 245.

6. *Autobiography*, 2:245, 246.

7. Wilson, *Crusader in Crinoline*, 149.

8. Rugoff, *The Beechers*, 165.

9. Bertram Wyatt-Brown, *Lewis Tappan and the Evangelical War against Slavery* (Cleveland, Ohio: Case Western Reserve Press, 1969), 145, 117–18, 156–57.

10. Merideth, *The Politics of the Universe*, 93–94.

11. Edward Beecher to the Beecher family, November 4, 1835, Acquisitions, Circular Letters, SD.

12. Catharine Beecher to the Beecher family, [c. May 14], [1836], Acquisitions, Circular Letters, SD.

13. Rugoff, *The Beechers*, 194.

14. C. E. Stowe, *Life*, 84–85.

15. Harriet's responses are taken, unless otherwise indicated, from HBS to CES, in C. E. Stowe, *Life*, 82–87; the other quotations are from the account in Jacob William Schuckers, *The Life and Public Services of Salmon Portland Chase* (New York: D. Appleton and Company, 1874), 39–40. The Cincinnati mob, planned and orchestrated by the city's establishment, was characteristic of anti-abolition violence in this period, motivated by anti-Negro and anti-amalgamation fear. See Leonard L. Richards, *"Gentlemen of Property and Standing": Anti-Abolition Mobs in Jacksonian America* (New York: Oxford University Press, 1970).

16. Wilson, *Crusader in Crinoline*, 185.

17. These excerpts are taken from a longer passage quoted in Wilson, *Crusader in Crinoline*, 184–85.

18. C. E. Stowe, *Life*, 82.

19. Angelina Grimké, Letters to Catharine Beecher, in *Feminist Papers*, ed. Rossi, 320.

20. Rossi, *Feminist Papers*, 305.

21. HBS to CES, [July, 1836], in C. E. Stowe, *Life*, 82.

22. C. E. Stowe, *Life*, 84.

23. Merideth, *Politics of the Universe*, 3, 101–2.

24. Catharine Beecher, *Essay on Slavery and Abolitionism, with Reference to the Duty of American Females* (Philadelphia: Henry Perkins Boston: Perkins & Marvin, 1837). Isabella P. Beecher to the Beecher family, January 22, 1838, Acquisitions, Circular Letters, SD.

25. Katherine E. Beecher to the Beecher family, April 3, 1837, Acquisitions, Circular Letters, SD.

26. C. E. Stowe, *Life*, 88.

Chapter 11

1. For Rachel and Zillah, see *Autobiography*, 1:159, 169; for Candace, see *Autobiography*, 1:224–25; for Dine, see HBS to Isabella Beecher Hooker, August 14, 1889, Foote Collection SD; for the "black girl" at Uncle Samuel's, see Samuel E. Foote to Roxana Foote and family, December 27 and 28, 1833, Foote Collection, SD; for the former slave Harriet hired, see C. E. Stowe, *Life*, 93.

2. Henry Ward Beecher to William and Katherine Beecher, October 4, 1836, folder 40, Beecher-Stowe Collection, SchL.

3. Catharine Beecher to Beecher family, [c. April 16,1837], Acquisitions, Circular Letters, SD.

4. Henry Ward Beecher to William and Katherine Beecher, October 4, 1836, folder 40, Beecher-Stowe Collection, SchL.

5. Henry Ward Beecher to William and Katherine Beecher, October 4, 1836, folder 40, Beecher-Stowe Collection, SchL.

6. Katherine E. Beecher to Beecher family, April 3, 1837, Acquisitions, Circular Letters, SD.

7. The quotations are from CES to [Samuel Fowler] Dickinson, October 7, 1836, folder 59, Beecher-Stowe Collection, SchL. For a description of the 5,000 volumes, see Wilson, *Crusader in Crinoline*, 195. On Lane's manual labor plan, see Cist, *Cincinnati in 1841*, 124.

8. CES to HBS, June 20, 1836, Acquisitions, SD.

9. CES to HBS, [January 23, 1837], Acquisitions, SD.

10. HBS to the Beecher family, [c. April 16, 1837], Acquisitions, Circular Letters, SD.

11. HBS to Elizabeth Lyman, April 7–May 5, 1837, Copies, SD; original in Connecticut State Library, Hartford, Conn.

12. Catharine Beecher to the Beecher family, [c. April 16, 1837], Acquisitions, Circular Letters, SD.

13. HBS to the Beecher family, [c. April 16, 1837], Acquisitions, Circular Letters, SD.

14. CES to HBS, October 16, 1836, Acquisitions, SD.

15. CES to HBS, December 22, 1837, Acquisitions, SD.

16. CES to HBS, October 16, 1836, Acquisitions, SD.

17. CES to HBS, July 22, [1837], Acquisitions, SD.

18. Esther Beecher to HBS, July 7, 1837, folder 10, Beecher-Stowe Collection, SchL.

19. Harriet Foote to Roxana Foote and family, March 1, 5, and 7, 1837, Foote Collection, SD.

20. Catharine Beecher to Mary Dutton, March 11, 1839, Collection of American Literature, BL.

21. Catharine Beecher to Mary Beecher Perkins, Isabella Beecher, and Esther Beecher, October 22, 1837, folder 17, Beecher-Stowe Collection, SchL.

22. Catharine Beecher to Mary Dutton, February 13, 1839, and Catharine Beecher to Mary Dutton, May 21, 1838, Collection of American Literature, BL.

23. Catharine Beecher to Mary Dutton, May 21, 1838, Collection of American Literature, BL. Wilson, *Crusader in Crinoline*, 201, 206.

24. Sklar, *Catharine Beecher*, 139.

25. Sklar, *Catharine Beecher*, 116; see also pp.117–21.

26. Wilson, *Crusader in Crinoline*, 181.

27. Mary Coffin to Catharine Beecher, October 22, 1837, folder 17, Beecher-Stowe Collection, SchL.

28. Esther Beecher to HBS, July 7, 1837, folder 10, Beecher-Stowe Collection, SchL.

29. Harriet Foote to Eliza Foote, March 2[9] and 30, April 1, 6, and 7, 1837, Foote Collection, SD. For the wages of household help, see Daniel E. Sutherland, *Americans and Their Servants: Domestic Service in the United States from 1800 to 1920* (Baton Rouge: Louisiana State University Press, 1981), 104, 109–10. Sutherland remarks that less well-to-do families expended as much as one-third of their income in order to secure servants (14). See also Faye Dudden, *Serving Women: Household Service in Nineteenth-Century America* (Middletown, Conn.: Wesleyan University Press, 1983), 65, 66, 97, 220.

30. Sutherland, *Americans and Their Servants*, 10.

31. CES to HBS, July 20, [1844], folder 61, Beecher-Stowe Collection, SchL.

32. HBS to CES, February 20, [1847], folder 72, Beecher-Stowe Collection, SchL.

33. CES to HBS, July 22, [1837], Acquisitions, SD.

34. HBS to CES, n.d. (received September 24), [1844], folder 70, Beecher-Stowe Collection, SchL.

35. Catharine Beecher to Mary Cogswell and Mary Weld, May 29, 1837, folder 15, Beecher-Stowe Collection, SchL.

36. Harriet Foote to Eliza Foote, March 2[9] and 30, April 1, 6, and 7, 1837, Foote Collection, SD.

37. Catharine Beecher to Mary Beecher Perkins, Isabella Beecher, and Esther Beecher, October 22, 1837, folder 17, Beecher-Stowe Collection, SchL.

38. Catharine Beecher to Mary Beecher Perkins, Isabella Beecher, and Esther Beecher, October 22, 1837, folder 17, Beecher-Stowe Collection, SchL.

39. Although contraceptive foams and sponges were in use in the nineteenth century, many people considered them unnatural and eschewed them for "voluntary motherhood," a method of spacing children which advocated abstinence as a means. See Linda Gordon, "Voluntary Motherhood: The Beginnings of the Birth Control Movement," Chapter 5 of her *Woman's Body/Woman's Right: A Social History of the Birth Control Movement in America* (New York: Grossmen,1976). The tensions that grew up around sexuality and reproduction are discussed in Mary Kelley, "At War with Herself: Harriet Beecher Stowe as Woman in Conflict within the Home," *American Studies* 19 (Fall 1978): 23–40.

40. CES to HBS, June 18, 1837, Acquisitions, SD.

41. CES to HBS, July 3, 1837, Acquisitions, SD.

42. Elizabeth E. Foote to Eliza Foote, December 1 and 4, 1831, Foote Collection, SD.

43. Trollope, *Domestic Manners*, 52.

44. Sutherland, *Americans and Their Servants*, 125. See also Dudden, *Serving Women*, 33–34.

45. Sutherland, *Americans and Their Servants*, 6.

46. *Autobiography*, 1:87.

47. Dudden, *Serving Women*, 59.

48. Sutherland, *Americans and Their Servants*, 64.

49. HBS to Mary Dutton, December 8, 1838, Collection of American Literature, BL.

50. Elizabeth E. Foote to Harriet Foote, January 25 and 27, 1839, Foote Collection, SD.

51. Daniel Sutherland writes that, the Irish and the Chinese aside, "a generally recognized hierarchy in the order of English, Scots, Scandinavians, Germans, Welsh, and Swiss existed, but there was no clear preferance"; see Sutherland, *Americans and Their Servants*, 42.

52. Rugoff, *The Beechers*, 144.

53. C. E. Stowe, *Life*, 93.

54. HBS, "Trials of a Housekeeper," in *May Flower*, 98, 100, 101, 102–3.

55. Wilson, *Crusader in Crinoline*, 212.

56. Katherine E. Beecher to the Beecher family, [c. January 2, 1836], Acquisitions, Circular Letters, SD.

57. Warden, *Salmon Portland Chase* 283.

58. C. E. Stowe, *Life*, 93.

59. In a letter to her sister-in-law she urged Eunice Beecher to do more sewing, which was relatively lucrative, and to hire out the washing and the ironing, the meanest and most poorly paid job in the household; see HBS to [Eunice Beecher], [c. 1838], Beecher Family Papers, SML.

60. HBS, "Trials of a Housekeeper," 103.

Chapter 12

1. CES to HBS, April 30, 1842, Acquisitions, SD.

2. CES to HBS, August 20, 1836, Acquisitions, SD.

3. HBS to "Dear Friend" [Annie Fields], September 24, 1884, Fields Papers, HL.

4. Brickley, "Litchfield Female Academy," 449.

5. Sarah J. Hale, *The Ladies Wreath* (Boston, 1837), as quoted in Ruth E. Finley, *The Lady of Godey's: Sarah Josepha Hale* (Philadelphia: J. B. Lippincott, 1931), 35–36.

6. HBS to Mary Dutton, before December 8 to December 13, 1838, Collection of American Literature, BL.

7. CES to Catharine Hills Crosby, [February 28 or March 1, 1827], Acquisitions, SD.

8. Suzanne Lebsock, *The Free Women of Petersburg: Status and Culture in a Southern Town, 1784–1860* (New York: W. W. Norton, 1985), 28.

9. HBS, *Oldtown Folks*, (Boston: Houghton Mifflin, 1896), 48; hereafter cited in the text as OF.

10. CES to HBS, September 29, [1844], folder 61, Beecher-Stowe Collection, SchL.

11. HBS to CES, September, 1846, in C. E. Stowe, *Life*, 115.

12. CES to HBS, September 30, 1844, folder 61, Beecher-Stowe Collection, SchL.

13. CES to HBS, February 19 & [and 20], 1847, Acquisitions, SD.

14. CES to HBS, July 14, 1839, Acquisitions, SD.

15. HBS to Catharine Beecher [and George], [c. March 12, 1841], Acquisitions, Circular Letters, SD.

16. CES to HBS, February 14, 1847, Acquisitions, SD.

17. Lyman Beecher to Catharine Beecher, October 6, 1823, folder 2, Beecher-Stowe Collection, SchL.

18. HBS to CES, n.d. (postmarked September 3), [1844], folder 70, Beecher-Stowe Collection, SchL.

19. HBS to CES, n.d. (postmarked May 21), [1844], folder 68, Beecher-Stowe Collection, SchL.

20. CES to HBS, September 7, 1846, Acquisitions, SD.

21. CES to HBS, May 19, 1842, Acquisitions, SD.

22. HBS, "Mark Meriden," *Godey's Lady's Book,* June1841, pp. 242–44; quotations appear on pages 242 and 244.

23. HBS to Georgiana May, June 21, 1838, in C. E. Stowe, *Life*, 90–92.

24. Catharine Beecher to Mary Dutton, March 11, 1839, Collection of American Literature, BL.

25. Elizabeth E. Foote to Harriet Foote, n.d. [January], [c. 1840], Foote Collection, SD.

26. HBS to Eunice and Henry Beecher, n.d. [c. 1840], Beecher Family Papers, SML.

27. HBS to Susie Munroe Stowe, November 22, 1880, folder 219, Beecher-Stowe Collection, SchL. HBS to Georgiana May, December, 1840, in C. E. Stowe, *Life*, 101.

28. HBS to Charles Beecher, [1841, c. September 8], Acquisitions, Circular Letters, SD.

29. Anna Smith to HBS, Summer, 1839, folder 236, Beecher-Stowe Collection, SchL.

30. Anna Smith to HBS, July 26–August 1, 1841, folder 236, Beecher-Stowe Collection, SchL.

31. Anna Smith to HBS, Summer, 1839, folder 236, Beecher-Stowe Collection, SchL.

32. Anna Smith to HBS, Summer, 1839, folder 236, Beecher-Stowe Collection, SchL.

33. Anna Smith to HBS, September 5, [1841], folder 236, Beecher-Stowe Collection, SchL.

34. HBS to Harriet Foote, January 9, 1841, Foote Collection, SD.

35. HBS to the Beecher family, [c. January 25, 1841], Acquisitions, Circular Letters, SD. It is instructive to compare Harriet's account in 1841 to the one her mother wrote in 1811, above, pp. 6–7 (*Autobiography*, 1:169). It is striking that all three of these women's accounts of parlor education mention scientific works—the cutting edge of Enlightenment thought and a subject not easily available in female seminaries. But the differences between Roxana Beecher's account and the others are more striking. She describes her intellectual frustration; Sarah Hale and Harriet Beecher describe their opportunities for further education. Roxana turned to *women* for her stimulation, gleaning bits from "the conversation of others," learning of metallic oxides from her sister Mary and urging the sister-in-law to "pray let me reap the benefit" of whatever knowledge she might have acquired. There is no mention of Lyman Beecher's role in her education. Although Sarah Hale and Roxana Beecher were exact contemporaries, both born in 1775, Sarah enjoyed a companionate marriage whereas Roxana was clearly in a subordinate role.

36. Harriet wrote to her brother Henry of Calvin's "endless studying & reading": "I get out of patience that he wont write with all this reading—He is a cormorant & keeps all to himself—If I had it it wouldnt I make it flare & flame"; see HBS to Henry Ward Beecher, February 1, [1872 or after], Beecher Family Papers, SML.

Chapter 13

1. Advertisement, *Godey's Lady's Book,* April 1852, 300.

2. HBS, "Uncle Enoch," *New-York Evangelist,* May 30,1835, p. 88.

3. HBS, "Uncle Enoch," 88.

4. W. J. Rorabaugh, *The Alcoholic Republic: An American Tradition* (New York: Oxford University Press, 1979), appendix A1.1.

5. This interpretation of Lyman Beecher's temperance activities is dominant in the scholarly literature; see Joseph R. Gusfield, *Symbolic Crusade: Status Politics and the American Temperance Movement* (Urbana: University of Illinois Press, 1983), chap. 2; and Ian R. Tyrrell, *Sobering Up: From Temperance to Prohibition in Antebellum America, 1800–1860* (Westport, Conn: Greenwood Press, 1979), 33ff. For a critique of this position, see W. J. Rorabaugh, *The Alcoholic Republic,* 188. For temperance in Cincinnati and for an excellent discussion of the Washingtonians, see Dannenbaum, *Drink and Disorder.*

6. For Whitman's newspaper days, see Justin Kaplan, *Walt Whitman: A Life* (New York: Simon and Schuster, 1980). Kaplan emphasizes the ordinary boorishness of the pre-1855 Whitman. Given to flag-waving rhetoric, the free-soil position that the Negro was not assimilable, and mannered prose filled with "benign condescension," Walter Whitman was neither cosmic nor particularly admirable. As Kaplan writes, "the long foreground of *Leaves of Grass* had been dominated by an inconstant newspaper editor, a sometime demagogue, and a writer of imitative fiction" (105–6).

7. Finley, *The Lady of Godey's*, 22, 23.

8. As quoted in Finley, *The Lady of Godey's*, 27. My sketch of Sarah J. Hale is drawn from Finley's account; her interpretation pays particular attention to the feminist implications of Hale's work, though she observes that she worked through female influence and was careful not to overstep the bounds.

9. Finley, *The Lady of Godey's*, 43–47.

10. HBS to [Eunice Beecher], n.d. [c. 1838], Beecher Family Papers, SML.

11. HBS to Mary Dutton, before December 8 to December 13, 1838, Collection of American Literature, BL.

12. CES to Hepzibah Stowe, October 27, 1847, Acquisitions, SD.

13. See Charles Beecher, "Eoline, or the Wind Spirit," September 1840, pp. 116–24; T. S. Arthur, "Blessings in Disguise," July 1840, pp. 16–20; T. S. Arthur, "Paying the Doctor," July 1840, p. 230; James T. Fields, "Peasant Girl at a Well," (October 1840), p. 161; HBS, "The Only Daughter," March 1839, p. 117, all in *Godey's Lady's Book*. Edgar Allan Poe published several of his stories in *Godey's Lady's Book*. In her study of giftbooks Sherry Sullivan reached similar conclusions about the broad audience of men and women for whom they were intended; see Sherry Sullivan, "Strategies for Success: Gender and the Production of the American Giftbook" (Paper presented at the Eighth Berkshire Conference on the History of Women, Douglass College, June 10, 1990).

14. HBS, "Sketches from the Note Book of an Old Gentleman. No. l. The Old Meeting House," *Godey's Lady's Book*, August, 1840, pp. 61–63.

15. HBS, "The Canal Boat," *May Flower*, 300.

16. HBS, "The Coral Ring," *Godey's Lady's Book*, June 1848, pp.340–343.

17. HBS to CES, June 27 and 29, 1842, folder 67, Beecher-Stowe Collection, SchL.

18. C. E. Stowe, *Life*, 103–4.

19. CES to HBS, April 30, 1842, Acquisitions, SD.

20. CES to HBS, May 11, 1842, Acquisitions, SD.

21. CES to HBS, June 12 and 14, 1842, Acquisitions, SD.

22. C. E. Stowe, *Life*, 104.

23. CES to HBS, May 19, 1842, Acquisitions, SD.

24. "With the most diligent industry a woman could not earn more than 60c to a dollar a week," Sarah Josepha Hale observed of the "slop-shops" in Boston; see Finley, *The Lady of Godey's*, 76. A woman sewing in a home could do better. Writing of one "Martha" and her prospects, Eunice Beecher opined that she was not sure she had enough work for her but "if she is 'spry' with her needle" she could earn $1.50 per week "beside what I should expect her to do for her board" (Eunice Beecher to HBS, October 1, 183[8], Beecher Family Papers, SML).

25. CES to HBS, May 19, 1842, Acquisitions, SD.

26. HBS to Beecher family, [c. June 27, 1842], Aquisitions, Circular Letters, SD.

27. HBS to Beecher family, [c. June 27, 1842], Acquisitions, Circular Letters, SD.

28. George M. Beard, *American Nervousness: Its Causes and Consequences* (New York, 1881), vi.

29. Isabella Beecher Hooker to John Hooker, July 4, 1852, Isabella Hooker Collection, SD.

30. HBS, "Frankness," *May Flower*, 122.

31. HBS, "The Canal Boat," *May Flower*, 296.

Chapter 14

1. C. E.Stowe, *Life*, 36.

2. C. E. Stowe, *Life*, 35.

3. Charles Stowe, *Life*, 34–35.

4. Charles H. Foster, *The Rungless Ladder: Harriet Beecher Stowe and New England Puritanism* (Durham, N. C.: Duke University Press, 1954), 23–24 and 95, contrasts Harriet's "easy conversion" of 1825 with her "true" conversion of 1845.

5. C. E. Stowe, *Life*, 36.

6. Joan Jacobs Brumberg in *Fasting Girls* (Cambridge, Mass.: Harvard University Press, 1988), describes anorexia nervosa as "a secular addiction to a new kind of perfectionism, one that links personal salvation to the achievement of an external body configuration rather than an internal spiritual state" (7).

7. Welter, "The Cult of True Womanhood," 151–74.

8. HBS to CES, n.d. [after November 6, 1850], Acquisitions, SD.

9. HBS to Eliza and Hatty Stowe, n.d. [November 1865?], folder 135, Beecher-Stowe Collection, SchL.

10. The tensions that Calvin and Harriet experienced over sexuality and reproduction are discussed in Kelley, "At War with Herself: Harriet Beecher Stowe as Woman in Conflict Within the Home," 23–40.

11. Catharine Beecher to Mary Dutton, March 11, 1839, Collection of American Literature, BL.

12. Catharine E. Beecher, *A Treatise on Domestic Economy* (1841; reprint, New York: Schocken Books, 1977), 136.

13. Catharine E. Beecher, *Domestic Economy*, 136, 137. In her splendid analysis of "The Pastoralization of Housework," Jeanne Boydston shows how during this period women's work in the home was idealized and made to seem as if it did not exist; see Jeanne Boydston, *Home and Work: Housework, Wages, and the Ideology of Labor in the Early Republic* (New York: Oxford University Press, 1990), 142–63.

14. Isabella Beecher to John Hooker, January 22, 1840, Isabella Hooker Collection, SD.

15. Katharine E. Beecher to the Beecher family, January 30, 1843, Acquisitions, Circular Letters, SD.

16. Henry Ward Beecher to Lyman Beecher, March 18, 1843, folder 41, Beecher-Stowe Collection, SchL.

17. HBS to Beecher family, [c. January 10, 1842], Acquisitions, Circular Letters, SD.

18. Katharine E. Beecher to the Beecher family, January 30,1843, Acquisitions, Circular Letters, SD.

19. George Beecher to the Beecher family, January 10, 1843, Acquisitions, Circular Letters, SD.

20. Esther M. Beecher to the Beecher family, September 6, [1841], Acquisitions, Circular Letters, SD. See also Wilson, *Crusader in Crinoline*, 210.

21. As quoted in Alice Felt Tyler, *Freedom's Ferment: Phases of American Social History from the Colonial Period to the Outbreak of the Civil War* (New York: Harper & Row, 1962), 73.

22. Charles E. Rosenberg, *The Cholera Years : The United States in 1832, 1849, and 1866* (Chicago: University of Chicago Press, 1962), 40–54.

23. Tyler, *Freedom's Ferment*, 75.

24. HBS to CES, September 4, [1842], folder 67, Beecher-Stowe Collection, SchL.

25. HBS to CES, September 4, [1842], folder 67, Beecher-Stowe Collection, SchL.

26. HBS to Thomas K. Beecher, March 16, 1844, Park Church Archive, Elmira, New York.

27. HBS, "The Dancing School," *New-York Evangelist,* (April 6, 1843, p. 53.

28. HBS, "Old Testament Pictures—No. 1," *New-York Evangelist,* November 14, 1844, p. 18.

29. HBS, "The Interior Life; or, Primitive Christian Experience," *New-York Evangelist,* June 19, 1845, p. 97.

30. *Autobiography,* 2:309–10, 2:311.

31. Esther Beecher to Beecher family, September 8, [1842], Acquisitions, Circular Letters, SD.

32. George Beecher to Beecher family, September 2, 1842, Acquisitions, Circular Letters, SD.

33. Catharine Beecher to Beecher family, November 2, 1842, Acquisitions, Circular Letters, SD.

34. Catharine Beecher to Beecher family, December 30, [1842], Acquisitions, Circular Letters, SD.

35. HBS to Sarah Buckingham Beecher, April 15, [1843], Acquisitions, SD.

36. HBS to "Dear Brothers and Sisters All," July 4, [1843], Beecher Family Papers, SML.

37. *Autobiography,* 2:346.

38. George Beecher, "Views on Christian Perfection," in *The Biographical Remains of Rev. George Beecher, Late Pastor of a Church in Chillicothe, Ohio, and Former Pastor of a Church in Rochester, New York,* ed. Catharine Beecher (New York: Leavitt Trow, and Co., 1844), 167–89.

39. HBS to Thomas Beecher, March 16, 1844, Park Church Archive, Elmira, New York.

40. HBS to "Dear Brothers and Sisters All," July 4, [1843], Beecher Family Papers, SML.

41. Diary of Sally Squire, August 4, 1815, as quoted in Paul C. Rosenblatt, *Bitter, Bitter Tears: Nineteenth-Century Diarists and Twentieth-Century Grief Theories* (Minneapolis: University of Minnesota Press, 1983), 103. In his sample of fifty-six nineteenth-century diaries, Rosenblatt found that the two most common reasons for controlling grief were "to deal with problems that arose or intensified as a result of the death and to maintain a comfortable relation with God" (101).

42. Rosenblatt, *Bitter, Bitter Tears,* 61.

43. HBS to Sarah Buckingham Beecher, July 6, [1843], Acquisitions, SD.

44. HBS to "Dear Brothers and Sisters All," July 4, [1843], Beecher Family Papers, SML.

45. Charles Beecher to Isabella Beecher, July 14, 1839, Joseph K. Hooker Collection, SD.

46. HBS to Thomas Beecher, March 16, 1844, Park Church Archive, Elmira, New York.

47. HBS to Sarah Buckingham Beecher, September 23, [1843], Acquisitions, SD.

48. Catharine Beecher, *Biographical Remains of Rev. George Beecher,* 9–10.

49. HBS to Sarah Buckingham Beecher, September 23, [1843], Acquisitions, SD.

50. HBS to Sarah Buckingham Beecher, September 23, [1843]; HBS to Susie

Munroe Stowe, November 22, 1880, folder 219, Beecher-Stowe Collection, SchL.

51. HBS to Sarah Buckingham Beecher, September 23, [1843], Acquisitions, SD.

52. HBS to Eunice Beecher, n.d. [Fall, 1843], Beecher Family Papers, SML.

53. HBS to Thomas Beecher, March 16, 1844, Park Church Archive, Elmira, New York.

54. HBS to Thomas Beecher, March 16, 1844, Park Church Archive, Elmira, New York.

55. HBS, "Earthly Care a Heavenly Discipline" (Boston: American Tract Society, n.d.). Stowe sent a copy to the Duke and Duchess of Sutherland, describing it as an essay "written for my own benefit during a season of heavy trial & deprivation. It has found without my agency a wide circulation in England" (*Journal of Charles Beecher*, 89).

56. HBS, "Literary Epidemics—No. 2," *New-York Evangelist*, July 13, 1843, p. 109.

57. HBS, "Literary Epidemics—No. 2," *New-York Evangelist*, July 13, 1843, p. 109.

58. HBS to Eunice and Henry Beecher, n.d. [1840], Beecher Family Papers, SML.

59. HBS, "Jesus," *New-York Evangelist*, February 19, 1846, p. 29.

60. HBS, "Lord, If Thou Hadst Been There!," *New-York Evangelist*, September 11, 1845, p. 145.

61. HBS, "The Interior Life; or, Primitive Christian Experience," *New-York Evangelist*, June 19, 1845, p. 97.

62. HBS to Charles Stowe, October 8, 1877, folder 192, Beecher-Stowe Collection, SchL.

Chapter 15

1. HBS to CES, October, 1843, in C. E. Stowe, *Life*, 110.

2. Lyman Beecher to Catharine Beecher, December 3, 1823, folder 2, Beecher-Stowe Collection, SchL.

3. CES to HBS, May 5, 1844, folder 61, Beecher-Stowe Collection, SchL.

4. HBS to CES, n.d. (postmarked May 21), [1844], folder 68, Beecher-Stowe Collection, SchL.

5. HBS to CES, n.d. (postmarked July 16), [1844], folder 69, Beecher-Stowe Collection, SchL.

6. HBS to CES, May 23, [1844], folder 68, Beecher-Stowe Collection, SchL.

7. CES to HBS, June 30, 1844, folder 61, Beecher-Stowe Collection, SchL.

8. CES to HBS, May 5, 1844, folder 61, Beecher-Stowe Collection, SchL.

9. HBS to Sarah Buckingham Beecher, April 15, [1843], Acquisitions, SD.

10. HBS to CES, June 14, 1844, folder 68, Beecher-Stowe Collection, SchL.

11. CES to HBS, July 19, 1844, folder 61, Beecher-Stowe Collection, SchL.

12. "Thoughts and Things at the West" by "Novanglus Occidentalis," *New-York Evangelist*, July 24, 1845. Lyman Beecher to Esther Beecher and Mary Beecher, June 13, 1844, Acquisitions, Circular Letters, SD.

13. CES to Lyman Beecher, July 17, 1844, folder 60, Beecher-Stowe Collection, SchL.

14. CES to HBS, July 19, 1844, folder 61, Beecher-Stowe Collection, SchL.

15. HBS to CES, July (postmarked July 16), [1844], folder 69, Beecher-Stowe Collection, SchL.

16. HBS to CES, July (postmarked July 16), [1844], folder 69, Beecher-Stowe Collection, SchL.

17. HBS to CES, n.d. (postmarked July 9), [1844], folder 69, Beecher-Stowe Collection, SchL.

18. HBS to CES, n.d. (postmarked July 9), [1844], folder 69, Beecher-Stowe Collection, SchL.

19. HBS to CES, July (postmarked July 16), [1844], folder 69, Beecher-Stowe Collection, SchL.

20. HBS to Eunice and Henry Beecher, n.d. [1845], Beecher Family Papers, SML.

21. HBS to CES, August, 1844, folder 70, Beecher-Stowe Collection, SchL.

22. HBS to Eunice Beecher, n.d. [1844], Beecher Family Papers, SML.

23. HBS to CES, August, 1844, folder 70, Beecher-Stowe Collection, SchL.

24. Steven Mintz analyzes the emergence of the family as "an inward-turning, self-contained unit" and cites as evidence the lengthening residences of adolescent children and the decline of resident nonfamily members such as apprentices; see Steven Mintz, *A Prison of Expectations: The Family in Victorian Culture* (New York: New York University Press, 1983), 13–16.

25. HBS to CES, August, 1844, folder 70, Beecher-Stowe Collection, SchL.

26. HBS to Eunice and Henry Beecher, n.d. [1845], Beecher Family Papers, SML.

27. Catharine Beecher to HBS, November 22, 1844; Mary Beecher Perkins to Beecher family, [c. December 3, 1844],—both in Acquisitions, Circular Letters, SD.

28. HBS to Eunice Beecher, n.d. [1844], Beecher Family Papers, SML.

29. CES to Lyman Beecher, July 17, 1844, folder 60, Beecher-Stowe Collection, SchL.

30. CES to HBS, July 29, 1844, folder 61, Beecher-Stowe Collection, SchL.

31. Mary Beecher Perkins to HBS, note written on CES to HBS, July 7, 1844, folder 61, Beecher-Stowe Collection, SchL; Mary Beecher Perkins to Sarah Buckingham Beecher, [c. July 14, 1844], Acquisitions, Circular Letters, SD.

32. CES to Lyman Beecher, July 17, 1844, folder 60, Beecher-Stowe Collection, SchL.

33. CES to HBS, July 29, July 19, and July 20, 1844, folder 61, Beecher-Stowe Collection, SchL.

34. HBS to CES, August, 1844, folder 70, Beecher-Stowe Collection, Schl.

35. See William H. Beecher to Beecher family, August 21, 1841, Acquisitions, Circular Letters, SD, where he sends a sermon with the note, "I think it worthy of notice even from you divines & divinesses."

36. As quoted in Tyler, *Freedom's Ferment*, 193.

37. CES to HBS, June 30, 1844, folder 61, Beecher-Stowe Collection, SchL.

38. Nancy F. Cott, "Passionlessness: An Interpretation of Victorian Sexual Ideology, 1790–1850," *Signs* 4 (Winter 1978): 219–36.

39. HBS to CES, July 19, 1844, folder 69, Beecher-Stowe Collection, SchL.

40. CES to HBS, July 7, 1844, folder 61; and HBS to CES, n.d. (postmarked September 3), [1844], folder 70, Beecher-Stowe Collection, SchL.

41. CES to HBS, September 14, 1844, folder 61, Beecher-Stowe Collection, SchL.

42. CES to HBS, September 29, [1844], folder 61, Beecher-Stowe Collection, SchL.

43. HBS to CES, n.d. (postmarked September 3), [1844], folder 70, Beecher-Stowe Collection, SchL.

44. CES to HBS, September 14, 1844, folder 61, Beecher-Stowe Collection, SchL.

45. HBS to CES, September 29, [1844], folder 61, Beecher-Stowe Collection, SchL.

46. HBS to CES, n.d. (received September 25), [1844], folder 70, Beecher-Stowe Collection, SchL.

47. CES to HBS, July 19, 1844, folder 61, Beecher-Stowe Collection, SchL.

48. CES to HBS, July 29, 1844, folder 61, Beecher-Stowe Collection, SchL.

49. HBS to CES, n.d. (postmarked September 3), [1844], folder 70, Beecher-Stowe Collection, SchL.

50. CES to HBS, September 30, 1844, folder 61, Beecher-Stowe Collection, SchL.

51. HBS to Sarah Buckingham Beecher, October [6 or 7], [1844], Acquisitions, SD.

52. CES to HBS, March 31, 1847, Acquisitions, SD.

53. HBS to CES, June 14, 1844, folder 68, Beecher-Stowe Collection, SchL. CES to HBS, June 20, 1844, folder 61, Beecher-Stowe Collection, SchL.

54. CES to HBS, May 2, 1844, folder 61, Beecher-Stowe Collection, SchL.

55. CES to Lyman Beecher, May 6, 1844, folder 60, Beecher-Stowe Collection, SchL.

56. CES to HBS, September 30, 1844, folder 61, Beecher-Stowe Collection, SchL.

57. Lyman Beecher to Albert Barnes, July 11, 1842, in *Autobiography* 2:342, 343.

58. HBS to Henry Ward Beecher, January 29, [1845], Beecher Family Papers, SML. For Catharine Beecher's analogue to the Roman Catholic nuns, see Sklar, *Catharine Beecher*, 171–72.

59. By November 1845 Harriet had had at least two miscarriages; see CES to HBS, November 22, 1846, Acquisitions, SD.

60. CES to HBS, November 1, 1846, Acquisitions, SD.

61. HBS to CES, June 16, 1845, in C. E. Stowe, *Life*, 111–12.

62. Lyman Beecher to Lydia Beecher, July 28, 1845, White Collection, SD.

63. HBS to CES, June 16, 1845, in C. E. Stowe, *Life*, 112.

64. Samuel Foote to George Foote, May 2, 1849, Foote Collection, SD.

65. CES to Lyman Beecher, August 17, 1844, folder 60, Beecher-Stowe Collection, SchL.

66. HBS to Lydia Beecher, August 15, 1845, Acquisitions, SD.

67. HBS to Zilpah Polly [Grant] Banister, September 23, 1845, Collection of American Literature, BL.

68. See Sklar, *Catharine Beecher*, 168–83, for a discussion of Catharine's development of a national network of teachers.

69. HBS, "What Will the American People Do?," *New-York Evangelist*, January 29, 1846, p. 17 and February 5, 1846, p. 26.

70. HBS, "Old Testament Pictures—No. 1," *New-York Evangelist*, November 14, 1844, p. 18.

71 HBS, "The Interior Life; or Primitive Christian Experience," *New-York Evangelist*, June 19, 1845, p. 97.

72. HBS, "Immediate Emancipation: A Sketch," *New-York Evangelist*, January 2, 1845, p. 1.

73. Wilson, *Crusader in Crinoline*, 107.

Chapter 16

1. Quoted in Susan E. Cayleff, *"Wash and Be Healed": The Water-Cure Movement and Women's Health* (Philadelphia: Temple University Press, 1987), 109–10.

2. Jane B. Donegan, *"Hydropathic Highway to Health": Women and Water-Cure in Antebellum America* (New York: Greenwood Press, 1986), 59.

3. Susan Cayleff observes hydropathy's "relative detachment from larger political issues" like the Civil War; see *"Wash and Be Healed,"* 124–25.

4. Cayleff, *"Wash and Be Healed,"* 27.

5. Cayleff, *"Wash and Be Healed,"* 122.

6. CES to HBS, July 14, 1839, Acquisitions, SD.

7. John S. Haller, Jr., *American Medicine in Transition, 1840–1910* (Urbana: University of Illinois Press, 1981), 86. I am grateful to Patricia Hill for drawing my attention to the effects of calomel.

8. HBS to the Beecher family, [January c. 10, 1842], Acquisitions, Circular Letters, SD.

9. HBS to Henry Ward Beecher, n.d., Beecher Family Papers, SML.

10. P. Lesley Bidstrup, *Toxicity of Mercury and its Compounds* (New York: Elsevier, 1964), 14, 77–79; see also Table IV, "Occupational Organo-Mercury Poisoning," 88–109. Typical symptoms listed include "Difficulty in holding small objects and performing fine movements," "Gross constriction of visual fields" (95), "Tiredness, headaches, irritability," and "Impairment of memory and power of concentration" (105).

11. HBS to CES, June 16, 1845, in C. E. Stowe, *Life,* 112.

12. Donegan, *"Hydropathic Highway to Health,"* 86.

13. Cayleff, *"Wash and Be Healed,"* 28. "Our Home," a "Hygienic School" founded in 1858, was billed as not "a place of fashionable resort, where dissipation, folly, vanity and heedlessness prevailed"; see Donegan, *"Hydropathic Highway to Health,"* 57.

14. *Annals of Brattleboro, 1681–1895,* 2 vols., ed. Mary R. Cabot (Brattleboro, Vt., E. L. Hildreth & Co., 1922), 2:573. The usual cost was $10.00 per week, but they offered the Stowes a special clergyman's rate of $2.50. The money was provided by various donors.

15. *Annals of Brattleboro,* 2:572; Donegan, *"Hydropathic Highway to Health,"* 186.

16. HBS, "The Dancing School," 53.

17. Eunice Beecher to HBS, December 27, 1846, Beecher Family Papers, SML.

18. Sklar, "All Hail to Pure Cold Water," in *Women and Health in America,* ed. Judith Walzer Leavitt (Madison: University of Wisconsin Press, 1984), 248.

19. Cayleff, *"Wash and Be Healed,"* 28, 17, 77.

20. CES to HBS, April 26, 1846, Acquisitions, SD. HBS to HWB, n.d. [1846], Beecher Family Papers, SML.

21. HBS to CES, May 27, 1846, folder 71, Beecher-Stowe Collection, SchL.

22. Sklar, "All Hail to Pure Cold Water," 249.

23. *Annals of Brattleboro,* 2:566, 569, 578.

24. Sklar and Cayleff emphasize the sensuousness of this experience. The nudity, the "exhilaration" reported by patients plunged into cold water and then rubbed down with a wet sheet, and the opportunity to talk openly about physical ailments provided, they argue, a physical release.

25. *Annals of Brattleboro,* 2:571–72.

26. Donegan, *"Hydropathic Highway to Health,"* 185–86.

27. CES to HBS, August 20, 1848, Acquisitions, SD.

28. CES to HBS, July 24, 1848, Acquisitions, SD.

29. HBS to CES, May 27, 1846, folder 71, Beecher-Stowe Collection, SchL. CES to HBS, June 30, 1846, Acquisitions, SD.

30. Cayleff, *"Wash and Be Healed,"* 38.

31. CES to HBS, August 20, 1846, Acquistions, SD.

32. Samuel Foote to Elizabeth E. Foote [and daughter Fanny], May 23, 1847, Foote Collection, SD.

33. Sklar, "All Hail to Pure Cold Water," 248. Other historians have argued that men found hydropathy equally attractive; see Donegan, *"Hydropathic Highway to Health,"* xv. It may be that some establishments, like the Brattleboro Water Cure, catered particularly to women and over time developed a predominately female clientele.

34. Sklar, *Catharine Beecher,* 214. Sklar, "All Hail to Pure Cold Water," 253.

35. *Annals of Brattleboro,* 2:567, 578, 573.

36. CES to HBS, August 19, 1849, Acquisitions, SD.

37. HBS to Catharine Day Andrews, January 1, 1850, Acquisitions, SD.

38. CES to HBS, July 14, 1848, Acquisitions, SD.

39. See HBS, Lock of Hair, November, 1846, Acquisitions, SD.

40. HBS to CES, May 27, 1846, folder 71, Beecher-Stowe Collection, SchL.

41. HBS to CES, August 14, 1846, folder 71, Beecher-Stowe Collection, SchL.

42. HBS to CES, n.d. (postmarked December 5), [1846], folder 71, Beecher-Stowe Collection, SchL.

43. CES to HBS, November 22, 1846, Acquisitions, SD.

44. HBS to CES, January 1, 1847, folder 71, Beecher-Stowe Collection, SchL.

45. CES to HBS, n.d. [1847], Acquisitions, SD.

46. CES to HBS, February 14, 1847, Acquisitions, SD. Even though men were not linked by the life-cycle rituals of women's domestic lives, this passage suggests that their physical expressiveness with one another was as free and acceptable as that described in the nineteenth-century women's letters Carroll Smith-Rosenberg analyzes in "The Female World of Love and Ritual." More recently, E. Anthony Rotundo has used evidence from nineteenth-century men's diaries and letters to present a comparable case for men's passionate relationships, at least up until the point of marriage; see E. Anthony Rotundo, "Romantic Friendship: Male Intimacy and Middle-Class Youth in the Northern United States, 1800–1900," *Journal of Social History,* 23 (Fall 1989): 1–25.

47. CES to HBS, July 31, 1849, Acquisitions, SD. For reports of heterosexual philandering at Brattleboro, see Isabella Beecher Hooker to John Hooker, July 7, 1852, Isabella Hooker Collection, SD.

48. HBS to CES, January 1, 1847, folder 72, Beecher-Stowe Collection, SchL.

49. Steven Mintz, *A Prison of Expectations,* 129. Mintz suggests that this be understood "as a transfer, or displacement, of religious needs and aspirations onto other, secular objects. By transforming relations of love and marriage into means of absolution and redemption, Victorians such as Stevenson, Eliot, and Stowe sought to give tangible meaning to abstract theological doctrines" (145).

50. Tyler, *Freedom's Ferment,* 192.

51. CES to HBS, February 19 & [and 20], 1847, Acquisitions, SD.

52. CES to HBS, November 1, 1846, Acquisitions, SD.

53. CES to HBS, August 8, 1848, Acquisitions, SD.

54. HBS to CES, December 4, [1846], folder 71, Beecher-Stowe Collection, SchL.

55. HBS to Eunice [and Henry] Beecher, January 14, 1847, Beecher Family Papers, SML.

56. HBS to CES, February 20, [1847], folder 72, Beecher-Stowe Collection, SchL.

57. CES to HBS, March 31, 1847, Acquisitions, SD.

58. CES to HBS, February 14, 1847, Acquisitions, SD.

59. CES to HBS, n.d. [1846], Acquisitions, SD.

60. CES to Hepzibah Stowe, February 7, 1847, Acquisitions, SD.

61. HBS to CES, March 2, 1847, folder 72, Beecher-Stowe Collection, SchL.

62. HBS to CES, January 24, 1847, folder 72, Beecher-Stowe Collection, SchL.

63. Samuel Foote to Elizabeth E. Foote, June 19, 1847, Foote Collection, SD.

64. Catharine Beecher to CES, August 14, 1846, in letter from HBS to CES, August 14, 1846, folder 71, Beecher-Stowe Collection, SchL.

65. CES to Hepzibah Stowe, October 27, 1847, Acquisitions, SD.

66. HBS, "Atonement—A Historical Reverie," *New-York Evangelist*, December 28, 1848, p. 205; HBS, "Feeling," *Godey's Lady's Book*, February 1848, pp.102–4; HBS, "The Coral Ring," *Godey's Lady's Book*, June 1848, 340–43.

67. HBS to CES, August–September, (postmarked September 16), [1848], folder 73, Beecher-Stowe Collection, SchL.

68. HBS to Eunice Beecher, June 2, [1848], Beecher Family Papers, SML.

69. Sklar was the first to call attention to hydropathy's alternative approaches to pregnancy and women's diseases (Sklar, *Catharine Beecher*, 207); also see Donegan, *"Hydropathic Highway to Health,"* 65–133, for a very good discussion of allopathy's "scientific management" of childbirth and the methods introduced by hydropathy.

Chapter 17

1. CES to HBS, July 29, 1849, SD. HBS to Sarah Buckingham Beecher, n.d. [March 9, 1849], Acquisitions, SD.

2. Charles Beecher to HBS, May 1, 1848, folder 29, Beecher-Stowe Collection, SchL.

3. HBS, *A Key to Uncle Tom's Cabin; Presenting the Original Facts and Documents upon Which the Story Is Founded. Together with Corroborative Statements Verifying the Truth of the Work* (Boston: John P. Jewett and Co., 1853), 195.

4. Charles Beecher to Lyman Beecher, February 1, 1848, folder 24, Beecher-Stowe Collection, SchL.

5. HBS, "Introductory Essay" to Charles Beecher, *The Incarnation; or, Pictures of the Virgin and Her Son* (New York: Harper and Brothers, 1849), iv, iv–v, viii–ix.

6. Charles Beecher, *The Incarnation*, 141–42. This passage is bracketed and identified in a footnote as "from the pen of Mrs. H.E.B. Stowe." As Mary gazes on her child during the Flight into Egypt, Stowe comments, "Even over ordinary infancy often hovers, like a mist, an air of mysterious sacredness, and shadows of strange, unworldly meaning often seem to float far away down in the clear depths of an infant's eye."

7. CES to HBS, July 14, 1848, Acquisitions, SD.

8. CES to HBS, September 10, 1848, Acquisitions, SD.

9. HBS to Charles Stowe, October 3, 1877, folder 192, Beecher-Stowe Collection, SchL.

10. Rosenberg, *Cholera Years*, 57.

11. HBS to CES, June 29, 1849, and July 1, 1849, as quoted in C. E. Stowe, *Life*, 120–21.

12. CES to HBS, June 11 and 12, 1849, Acquisitions, SD.

13. CES to HBS, July 9 [and 10], 1849, Acquisitions, SD.

14. See Karen Halttunen, "Gothic Imaginations and Social Reform: The Haunted Houses of Lyman Beecher, Henry Ward Beecher, and Harriet Beecher Stowe," in *New Essays on "Uncle Tom's Cabin,"* ed. Eric J. Sundquist (Cambridge: Cambridge University Press, 1986), 107–34.

15. HBS to CES, June 29, 1849, July 1, 1849, and July 4, 1849,as quoted in C. E. Stowe, *Life*, 121–22.

16. Diarca Howe Allen to Lyman Beecher, July 6, 1849, folder 9, Beecher-Stowe Collection, SchL.

17. HBS to Eliza Cabot Follen, December 16, 1852, Dr. Williams's Library, London. This letter exists in four manuscript copies and is quoted in four biographies whose authors might have had access to the manuscript. The original is lost. I have cited the text established by E. Bruce Kirkham, Ball State University, Muncie, Indiana, for his forthcoming edition of Stowe's letters, in progress. I am grateful for his assistance. After her removal to Brunswick with the Stowe family, Anna Smith sent greetings back to Walnut Hills, including in her remembrance "all friends who remember me—not forgetting the colored people & those who live in shacktown"; see Anna Smith to CES, January 27, 1851, folder 263, Beecher-Stowe Collection, SchL.

18. HBS to CES, July 10 and 12, 1849, in C. E. Stowe, *Life*, 122–23. Also see Rosenberg, *Cholera Years*, 66.

19. CES to HBS, July 9 [and 10], 1849, Acquisitions, SD.

20. CES to HBS, July 21, 1849, Acquisitions, SD.

21. HBS to CES, July 17, 1849, in C. E. Stowe, *Life*, 123.

22. HBS to CES, July 23, 1849, in C. E. Stowe, *Life*, 123–24.

23. HBS to CES, July 26, 1849, in C. E. Stowe, *Life*, 124.

24. Elizabeth E. Foote to Eliza Foote, December 1 [and 4], 1831, Foote Collection, SD.

25. HBS to [Sarah] Allen, December 2, [1850], Harriet Beecher Stowe Collection, UVa.

26. Nina Baym, *Woman's Fiction: A Guide to Novels by and about Women in America, 1820–1870* (Ithaca, N.Y.: Cornell University Press, 1978), 16.

27. Deborah Gray White, *Ar'n't I a Woman? Female Slaves in the Plantation South* (New York: W. W. Norton, 1985), 98.

28. White, *Ar'n't I a Woman*, 88.

29. HBS to Eliza Cabot Follen, December 16, 1852, Dr. William's Library, London.

30. On infant mortality among slaves, see Jacqueline Jones, *Labor of Love, Labor of Sorrow: Black Women, Work and the Family from Slavery to the Present* (New York: Vintage Books, 1986), 35. For slave children under the age of five, Kenneth Stampp estimates the mortality rate was more than double that of whites; see Kenneth Stampp, *The Peculiar Institution: Slavery in the Ante-Bellum South* (New York: Alfred A. Knopf, 1956), 319–20.

31. The sources of this incident are discussed in E. Bruce Kirkham, *The Building of "Uncle Tom's Cabin"* (Knoxville: University of Tennessee Press, 1977), 104–9.

32. HBS to Eliza Lee Cabot Follen, December 16, 1852, Dr. William's Library, London.

33. CES to HBS, November 22, 1846, Acquisitions, SD.

34. Samuel Foote to George Foote, August 17, 1848, Foote Collection, SD.

35. CES to Hepzibah Stowe, February 6, 1850, Acquisitions, SD.

36. Esther Beecher to Isabella Beecher Hooker, March 30, 1850, Joseph K. Hooker Collection, SD.

37. HBS to Susie Munroe Stowe, January 5, 1879, folder 203, Beecher-Stowe Collection, SchL.

38. Henry Ward Beecher, "The Fugitive Slave Bill at Its Work," *Independent,* October 3, 1850, p. 162.

39. "The Slave-Law and the Union," *Independent,* January 16, 1851, p. 10.

40. HBS to CES, [May?], 1850, folder 74, Beecher-Stowe Collection, SchL.

41. HBS to Sarah Buckingham Beecher, December 17, [1850], folder 94, Beecher-Stowe Collection, SchL.

42. Stowe and Stowe, *Harriet Beecher Stowe,* 129.

43. Georgiana May Sykes to HBS, May 21, 1850, Acquisitions, SD.

44. HBS to Eunice Beecher, July 13, 1850, Beecher Family Papers, SML.

45. HBS to [Sarah] Allen, December 2, [1850], Harriet Beecher Stowe Collection, UVa.

46. HBS to CES, January 1, 1847, folder 72, Beecher-Stowe Collection, SchL.

47. "Thine in the bonds of womanhood," Angelina and Sarah Grimké signed their spirited letters to one another. Nancy Cott used this felicitous phrase to title her book, *The Bonds of Womanhood.*

48. HBS to Eunice Beecher, [1847], Beecher Family Papers, SML.

49. HBS to Sarah Buckingham Beecher, December 17, [1850], folder 94, Beecher-Stowe Collection, SchL.

50. Perhaps some readers are thinking (with a measure of condescension) that this trained her to write literature for *children*; while a specific class of literature designated for children was, indeed, coming into existence at this time (Nathaniel Hawthorne and Harriet Beecher Stowe both wrote many volumes of it), this was more common in post–Civil War America. In the 1840s and 50s children were more typically included in family readings of what we think of as classic literature, much of which, like Dickens and Scott, was also popular.

51. HBS to Eunice Beecher, [November, 1850], Beecher Family Papers, SML.

52. HBS to Sarah J. Hale, November 10, [1850 or 1851], Fields Papers, HL.

53. HBS to Sarah J. Hale, November 10, [1850 or 1851], Fields Papers, HL.

54. Hale, *Woman's Record,* 837; the entry on Stowe does not include a daguerreotype.

55. CES to HBS, December 15, 1851, Acquisitions, SD.

56. HBS to CES, February 3, [1851], Acquisitions, SD. Eliza Stowe to CES, January 16, 1851, folder 75, Beecher-Stowe Collection, SchL.

57. HBS to CES, n.d. [after November 6, 1850], Acquisitions, SD.

58. HBS to Lydia Jackson Beecher, October 29, [1850], folder 96, Beecher-Stowe Collection, SchL.

59. HBS to CES, February 14, [1851], Acquisitions, SD.

60. HBS to [Sarah] Allen, December 2, [1850], Harriet Beecher Stowe Collection, UVa.

61. HBS to Isabella Beecher Hooker, [November, 1850], folder 95, Beecher-Stowe Collection, SchL.

62. HBS to CES, n.d. [after November 6, 1850], Acquisitions, SD.

63. HBS to Isabella Beecher, [November, 1850], folder 95, Beecher-Stowe Collection, SchL. HBS to Sarah Buckingham Beecher, December 17, [1850], folder 94, Beecher-Stowe Collection, SchL.

64. HBS, "Heinrich Stilling," *New-York Evangelist,* February 6, 1851, p. 21.

65. Woolf, *A Room of One's Own,* 76.

Chapter 18

1. HBS to "Dear Sister" [Catharine Beecher], n.d. [1850 or 1851], Beecher Family Papers, SML.

2. HBS to Henry Ward Beecher, February 1, 1851, Beecher Family Papers, SML.

3. Dannenbaum, *Drink and Disorder*, 204–5, 196.

4. Henry Ward Beecher, "The Fugitive Slave Bill at Its Work," *Independent*, October 3, 1850, p. 162. The text of the bill may be found in the *National Era*, October 3, 1850, pp. 160, 158.

5. "How to Oppose the Fugitive Slave Law," *Independent*, October 24, 1850, p. 174.

6. "First Case under the Fugitive Slave Bill," *National Era*, October 10, 1850, p. l63. "Return of James Hamlet," *Independent*, October 10, 1850, p. 167.

7. "How to Oppose the Fugitive Slave Law," p. 174.

8. "The Mob Spirit," *Independent*, February 20, 1851, p. 26.

9. "Dr. Bacon on the Fugitive Law," *Independent*, February 13, 1851, p. 26.

10. C. E. Stowe, *Life*, 144.

11. "The Second Boston Slave Case," *Independent*, February 20, 1851, p. 31. *The Letters of William Lloyd Garrison*, 6 vols., ed. Walter M. Merrill and Louis Ruchames (Cambridge, Mass.: Belknap Press of Harvard University Press, 1975), 4: 49, n. 2.

12. "Congress," *Independent*, February 27, 1851, p. 35.

13. "From Our Boston Correspondent," *Independent*, February 27, 1851, p. 35.

14. Florence B. Freedman, "Introduction," to William Craft and Ellen Craft, *Running a Thousand Miles for Freedom* (New York: Arno Press/New York Times, 1969), ix.

15. HBS to "Dear Sister" [Catharine Beecher], n.d., [1850 or 1851], Beecher Family Papers, SML.

16. "Lecture by Henry Ward Beecher on 'Character,'" *Independent*, January 16, 1851, p. 9.

17. HBS to Henry Ward Beecher, February 1, 1851, Beecher Family Papers, SML. An example of this attenuated form of argument is "The Civil Law: Man's Obligation to Obey It," a sermon delivered by Richard S. Storrs, Jr., and reprinted in the *Independent*, January 2, 1851, p. 1.

18. "General News," *Independent*, January 2, 1851, p. 3. "The Slave-Law and the Union," *Independent*, January 16, 1851, p. 10.

19. HBS to Henry Ward Beecher, February 1, 1851, Beecher Family Papers, SML.

20. HBS to "Dear Sister" [Catharine Beecher], n.d., [1850 or 1851], Beecher Family Papers, SML.

21. HBS to CES, n. d. [January, 1851], Acquisitions, SD.

22. Stanley Harrold, *Gamaliel Bailey and Antislavery Union* (Kent, Ohio: The Kent State University Press, 1986), ix–x.

23. HBS, "The Freeman's Dream; A Parable," *National Era*, August 1, 1850, p. 121.

24. HBS to CES, January 27, [1851], Acquisitions, SD. This sketch appeared not in the *National Era* but in the *New-York Evangelist* on June 12 and 19, 1851, under the title "The Two Altars; or, Two Pictures in One"; see Kirkham, *The Building of "Uncle Tom's Cabin,"* 70. The other pieces she published in the itra are "A Scholar's Adventures in the Country" (November 7, 1850), "Christmas; or, The Good Fairy (December 26, 1850), and "Independence" (January 30, 1851).

25. C. E. Stowe, *Life*, 145.

26. HBS to CES, n.d. [December, 1850], Acquisitions, SD.

27. Wilson, *Crusader in Crinoline*, 244.

28. HBS to CES, n.d. [January, 1851], Acquisitions, SD.

29. HBS to Gamaliel Bailey, March 9, 1851, typescript, BPL; the original of this letter has been lost.

30. HBS to Henry Ward Beecher, February 1, 1851, Beecher Family Papers, SML.

31. George M. Fredrickson, *The Black Image in the White Mind: The Debate on Afro-American Character and Destiny, 1817–1914* (New York: Harper & Row, 1971), 97–129, esp. 104–5, 110. The quotation, from Kinmont's *Twelve Lectures on the Natural History of Man* (Cincinnati, Ohio, 1839), is on p. 105. Stowe remarks on Kinmont's death (HBS to Mary Dutton, before December 8 to December 13, 1838, Collection of American Literature, BL).

32. HBS to Eliza Cabot Follen, December 16, 1852, Dr. William's Library, London.

33. Harryette Mullen introduces these useful concepts in her splendid paper, "Runaway Tongue: Resistant Orality in *Uncle Tom's Cabin, Our Nig, Incidents in the Life of a Slave Girl*, and *Beloved*" (Paper presented at the American Studies Association annual meeting, New Orleans, November 1990).

34. Edmund Wilson, *Patriotic Gore: Studies in the Literature of the American Civil War* (New York: Oxford University Press, 1962), 6.

35. Review of *Uncle Tom's Cabin, New York Daily Times*, September 18, 1852 (clipping in the Huntington Library).

36. Opinions about Stowe's use of slave narratives range from the cautious view of Eric Sundquist that their influence is "open to question" to Ishmael Reed's claim that Mrs. Stowe stole Josiah Henson's story; see Sundquist, "Introduction," *New Essays on "Uncle Tom's Cabin,"* 16–17, and Ishmael Reed, *Flight to Canada* (New York: Random House, 1976), 7–11. In a contemporary response, Martin R. Delany attacked Stowe's colonizationist scheme but found "the chief value of the novel . . . in its use of slave narratives;" see Thomas F. Gossett, *"Uncle Tom's Cabin" and American Culture* (Dallas, Tex.: Southern Methodist University Press, 1985), 174. For an evenhanded discussion of textual parallels, see Robert B. Stepto, "Sharing the Thunder: The Literary Exchanges of Harriet Beecher Stowe, Henry Bibb, and Frederick Douglass," in *New Essays on "Uncle Tom's Cabin,"* 135–53.

37. Toni Cade Bambara, "The Emancipatory Impulse in American Literatures" (Lecture presented at the Center for the Humanities, Wesleyan University, September 17, 1990).

38. Henry Bibb, *The Narrative of the Life and Adventures of Henry Bibb, Written by Himself*, in *Puttin' on Ole Massa*, ed. Gilbert Osofsky (New York: Harper & Row, 1969), 53–171; the quote is on p. 63.

39. "Official Slave-Hunting," *Independent*, January 9, 1851, p. 6.

40. "Official Slave-Hunting," *Independent*, January 9, 1851, p. 6.

41. Hortense J. Spillers, "Changing the Letter: The Yokes, the Jokes of Discourse, or, Mrs. Stowe, Mr. Reed," in *Slavery and the Literary Imagination*, ed. Deborah E. McDowell and Arnold Rampersad (Baltimore: Johns Hopkins University Press, 1989), 35–36. Spillers is writing in the tradition of James Baldwin, who coined the phrase "theological terror" in "Everybody's Protest Novel," *Partisan Review* 16 (June, 1949): 578–85.

42. William Craft and Ellen Craft, *Running a Thousand Miles for Freedom*. It is certainly true, however, that "in the slave narratives written by black women the authors placed in the foreground their active roles as historical agents as opposed to

passive subjects; represented as acting their own visions, they are seen to take decisions over their own lives." See Hazel V. Carby, *Reconstructing Womanhood: The
Emergence of the Afro-American Woman Novelist* (New York: Oxford University Press,
1987), 36.

43. Bibb, *Narrative*, 114.

44. As critics have pointed out, there was a natural affinity between "romantic
racialism" and "the cult of true womanhood." Both women and blacks were char-
acterized as dependent, childlike, and yet morally superior and more aptly Christian.
See Fredrickson, *The Black Image in the White Mind*, 113, and Elizabeth Ammons,
"Heroines in *Uncle Tom's Cabin*" in *Critical Essays on Harriet Beecher Stowe*, ed.
Elizabeth Ammons (Boston: G. K. Hall, 1980), 152–65.

45. Sandra M. Gilbert and Susan Gubar, *The Madwoman in the Attic: The
Woman Writer and the Nineteenth-Century Literary Imagination* (New Haven, Conn.:
Yale University Press, 1979), 533–35.

46. Even though as black slaves they were not within the purview of this white,
middle-class ideology, the fact that they were mulattoes raised in the ladylike ways
of genteel mistresses allied them with white womanhood. This has been seen as a
weakness by critics, who have dismissed Stowe's mulattoes, quadroons, and octo-
roons as "white" negroes who were imbued not only with white blood but with white
social markings that made them laudable to the author. That Stowe exhibits attitudes
of white superiority at various points in her narrative is undeniable; yet the fact that
Eliza and Emily are of mixed blood makes them mediating figures in the ideological
drama in which Stowe is engaged. Carby's analysis of the interdependence of the
constructions of white and black womanhood has helped me to see how Stowe
employed her white and black characters; see Carby, *Reconstructing Womanhood*,
esp. chapters 1–3.

47. Gossett, *"Uncle Tom's Cabin" and American Culture*, 270.

48. Charles Wesley, "Let saints on earth in concert sing," in *The Hymnal of the
Protestant Episcopal Church in the United States of America* (New York: Church
Pension Fund, 1940), no. 397.

49. Albert J. Raboteau, *Slave Religion: The "Invisible Institution" in the Antebellum South* (New York: Oxford University Press, 1978), 148.

50. Raboteau, *Slave Religion*, 147.

51. Sundquist, "Introduction," *New Essays on "Uncle Tom's Cabin,"* 6.

52. The congruence between German pietism and slave Christianity is suggested
by the request Charles Beecher made of Calvin Stowe regarding his fictionalized life
of Christ: "I wish Prof. Stowe would have the kindness to translate for Harriet, & let
her write down those passages he read to us one day from the German touching the
knowledge had by Jews in time of Christ of a suffering messiah"; see Charles Beecher
to Lyman Beecher, June 24, 1847, folder 24, Beecher-Stowe Collection, SchL. Marie
Caskey argues that Calvin Stowe's biblical studies and pulpit views were "the single
most important influence on her theological development"; see her *Chariot of Fire:
Religion and the Beecher Family* (New Haven, Conn.: Yale University Press, 1978),
180–83.

53. HBS to CES, July 17, 1849, in C. E. Stowe, *Life*, 123.

54. Raboteau explains how the "egalitarianism" and "religious reciprocity" of
evangelical religion encouraged cultural exchange between white and black Christians: "The intense emphasis upon conversion, which was the primary characteristic
of evangelical, revivalistic Protestantism, tended to level all men before God as sinners in need of salvation. This tendency opened the way for black converts to participate actively in the religious culture of the new nation as exhorters, preachers, and

even founders of churches, and created occasions of mutual religious influence across racial boundaries whereby blacks converted whites and whites converted blacks in the heat of revival fervor." That new forms of worship, blending African with Christian liturgies, had an influence on evangelical religion is evident in the condemnation, descriptively entitled *Methodist Error or Friendly Advice to Those Methodists Who Indulge in Extravagant Religious Emotions and Bodily Exercises,* published in 1819 by John Watson to correct errors of enthusiasm in the Philadelphia Conference. The author described the way in which slaves at camp meetings sang and danced "in the merry chorus-manner of the southern harvest field, or husking-frolic method," a style "very greatly like the Indian dances." In the emotional abandon of revival camp meetings such singing and dancing was readily imitated. Because this behavior was "only occasionally condemned," Watson warned that "the example has already visibly affected the religious manners of some whites." He knew of some camp meetings where fifty or sixty people crowded into a tent would stay after the regular exercises were over and "there continue the whole night, singing tune after tune, . . . scarce one of which were in our hymn books" (See Raboteau, *Slave Religion,* 152, 67). If such "errors" had crept into the Philadelphia Conference, they must have abounded in Ohio, lying so much closer to Cane Ridge, Kentucky, where the Second Great Awakening had begun with a shout in 1800.

55. Jane Tompkins points out Stowe's deliberate Christian eschatology and re-creation of the Bible; see Jane P. Tompkins, "Sentimental Power: *Uncle Tom's Cabin* and the Politics of Literary History," in her *Sensational Designs: The Cultural Work of American Fiction, 1790–1850* (New York: Oxford University Press, 1985), 122–146, esp. 134–141. Twentieth-century readers may appreciate Stowe's intent by recalling the revolutionary power invoked in the name of South African martyr Stephen Biko.

56. Tompkins, *Sensational Designs,* 140.

Chapter 19

1. Robert Stepto, "Sharing the Thunder," 137.

2. HBS to Frederick Douglass, [July 9, 1851], Acquisitions, SD. There are no known responses to this letter (see Kirkham, *The Building of "Uncle Tom's Cabin,"* 100).

3. Woolf, *A Room of One's Own,* 73.

4. HBS to Eliza Cabot Follen, December 16, 1852, Dr. Williams's Library, London.

5. In *A Key to Uncle Tom's Cabin* Stowe cited as a model for Eliza another important source: the nameless fugitive slave from Kentucky who joined the Stowe household in 1839 and subsequently escaped, with the Stowes' help, along the Underground Railway. See HBS, *A Key to Uncle Tom's Cabin,* 22–23.

6. Gossett, *"Uncle Tom's Cabin" and American Culture,* 198.

7. Charles Beecher to Catharine A. Foote, May 8, 1839, folder 25, Beecher-Stowe Collection, SchL.

8. Esther Beecher to Isabella Beecher Hooker, May 19, [1851?], Joseph K. Hooker Collection, SD.

9. Catharine Beecher to Mary [Beecher Perkins], September 27, 1851, Beecher Family Papers, SML.

10. HBS to CES, [January?], 1851, folder 75, Beecher-Stowe Collection, SchL.

11. HBS to Henry Ward Beecher and Lyman Beecher, September 19, [1851], Beecher Family Papers, SML.

12. Catharine Beecher to Mary [Beecher Perkins], September 27, 1851, Beecher Family Papers, SML.

13. HBS to Catharine Beecher, n.d., folder 97, Beecher-Stowe Collection, SchL.

14. Catharine Beecher to Mary [Beecher Perkins], September 27, 1851, Beecher Family Paper, SML. Kirkham, *The Building of "Uncle Tom's Cabin,"* 127.

15. Catherine Perkins Gilman to Thomas Clap Perkins, February 29, 1852, Katharine S. Day Collection, SD.

16. Isabella Beecher Hooker to John Hooker, June 25, 1852, Isabella Hooker Collection, SD.

17. William A. White to Lucy Jackson White, June 22, 1852, White Collection, SD.

18. Caskey, *Chariot of Fire,* 151.

19. Charles Beecher to Catharine A. Foote, May 8, 1839, folder 25, Beecher-Stowe Collection, SchL.

20. Wilson, *Crusader in Crinoline,* 218.

21. Only one reviewer suspected the truth; see Gossett,*"Uncle Tom's Cabin" and American Culture,* 196.

22. Gossett, *"Uncle Tom's Cabin" and American Culture,* 201.

23. "Ye Come to Me in Dreams," words by "Nilla," music by E. C. Davis, *Godey's Lady's Book,* February 1852, following the plates that follow p. 170.

24. Gossett, *"Uncle Tom's Cabin" and American Culture,* 268.

25. "Mrs. Stowe's Epic," *Daily Plain Dealer,* newsclip, SD.

26. Kirkham, *The Building of "Uncle Tom's Cabin,"* 140–49; the quotation is on p. 143.

27. Calvin E. Stowe to the Rev. Justin Edwards, D. D., April 12, 1852, Acquisitions, SD.

28. Review of *Uncle Tom's Cabin, New York Daily Times,* September 18, 1852, newsclip, HL.

29. HBS to John P. Jewett, n.d., folder 261, Beecher-Stowe Collection, SchL.

30. HBS to Edward [Beecher?], n.d., folder 261, Beecher-Stowe Collection, SchL.

31. Isabella Beecher Hooker to John Hooker, July 7, 1852, and June 26, 1852, Isabella Hooker Collection, SD. See also Mary Beecher Perkins to Lyman Beecher, January 22, 1853, SD.

32. CES, "Statement of Facts, by C. E. Stowe, in regard to the publication of mrs Stowe's work entitled 'Uncle Tom's Cabin,'" June 21, 1852, Acquisitions, SD.

33. Francis Lieber, manuscript review of *Uncle Tom's Cabin,* February 1853, HL.

34. Isabella Beecher Hooker to John Hooker, June 26, 1852, Isabella Hooker Collection, SD.

35. John Greenleaf Whittier, "Little Eva," *Independent,* July 29, 1852, p. 124. Whittier's poem appeared above another by Mary H. Collier entitled "Eva's Parting," which concludes "I see the gates of glory, / Your Eva soars to rest!"

36. Isabella Beecher Hooker to John Hooker, June 26, 1852, Isabella Hooker Collection, SD.

37. "Illustrated Uncle Tom," *Independent,* October 21, 1852, p. 171.

38. Isabella Beecher Hooker to John Hooker, June 25, 1852, Isabella Hooker Collection, SD.

39. Joel Parker to HBS, May 19, 1852, Beecher Family Papers, SML.

40. HBS to Joel Parker, n.d. [May, 1852], Beecher Family Papers, SML.

41. "The Grounds of Offense in Uncle Tom's Cabin," by G., *Independent*, October 21, 1852, p. 171.

42. "Mr. Beecher's Reply to the New York Observer," *Independent*, October 7, 1852, p. 161.

43. HBS to Mr. Sumner [attorney], September 27, [1852], Harriet Beecher Stowe Collection, UVa.

44. Forrest Wilson narrates in detail this series of mishaps and delays in *Crusader in Crinoline*, 307–22. Most of the documentary evidence may be found in the history of the affair published in the New York *Independent*, October 7, 1852.

45. "Mrs. Harriet Beecher Stowe," *Independent*, May 20, 1852, p. 82.

46. Henry Ward Beecher, "Mr. Beecher's Reply to the *New York Observer*," *Independent*, October 7, 1852, p. 161.

47. HBS, "Religious Scoffers," *Independent*, May 20, 1852, p. 82.

48. "Extract from the *New York Observer*," New York *Independent*, October 7, 1852, p. 161.

49. HBS to Henry Ward Beecher, October 1, 1852, Beecher Family Papers, SML.

50. HBS to the Editor of the *New York Observer*, copy in her hand, n.d. [May, 1852], Beecher Family Papers, SML.

51. HBS to the Editor of the *New York Observer*, copy in her hand, n.d. [May, 1852], Beecher Family Papers, SML.

52. HBS to Henry Ward Beecher, November 1, 1852, Beecher Family Papers, SML.

53. HBS to the Editor of the *New York Observer*, copy in her hand, n.d. [October, 1852?], Beecher Family Papers, SML.

54. HBS to Henry Ward Beecher, November 1, 1852, Beecher Family Papers, SML.

55. See HBS, *A Key to Uncle Tom's Cabin*, 193–205, esp. 195, 198–200.

56. HBS to Richard Bentley, November 13, 1852, Harriet Beecher Stowe Collection, UVa.

57. HBS, "Preface," *A Key to Uncle Tom's Cabin*, iii.

58. HBS to Henry Ward Beecher, n. d. [1853], Beecher Family Papers, SML.

59. Weld's book was apparently out of print at this time; British antislavery activist H. Webb reported being unable to obtain copies of *American Slavery as it Is*, and that "Mrs. Stowes Key will probably take its place, & with a more popular prestige to carry it forward" (H. Webb to M. A. Estlin, April 1, 1853, BPL).

60. HBS to Eliza Cabot Follen, December 16, 1852, Dr. Williams's Library, London.

61. HBS to Lord Denman, January 20, 1853, HL.

62. HBS to Lord Denman, January 20, 1853, HL.

63. HBS, *A Key to Uncle Tom's Cabin*, 81.

64. Gossett, *"Uncle Tom's Cabin" and American Culture*, 195.

65. HBS to Eliza Cabot Follen, December 16, 1852, Dr. Williams's Library, London.

66. Gossett, *"Uncle Tom's Cabin" and American Culture*, 191, 190.

67. Review of *Uncle Tom's Cabin*, New York *Daily Times*, September 18, 1852, newsclip, HL.

Chapter 20

1. Joseph S. Van Why and Earl French, eds., *Harriet Beecher Stowe in Europe: The Journal of Charles Beecher* (Hartford, Conn.: Stowe-Day Foundation,1986), 20–22; hereafter referred to in notes as *Journal of Charles Beecher.*

2. In the Scottish villages Stowe noticed "how universally the people read"; HBS, *Sunny Memories of Foreign Lands,* 2 vols. (Boston: Phillips, Sampson, and Company, 1854), 1:76; hereafter cited parenthetically in the text and notes as SM. Review of *Uncle Tom's Cabin, New York Daily Times,* September 18, 1852, newsclip, HL. Advertisement from *Bent's Literary Advertiser,* pasted in Francis Lieber, manuscript review of *Uncle Tom's Cabin,* HL. Lieber thought no development "could be more striking" than this immense special edition; see Lieber to George S. Hillard, April, 1853, HL.

3. Charles Kingsley to HBS, August 12, 1852, folder 242, Beecher-Stowe Collection, SchL.

4. Isabella Beecher Hooker to John Hooker, June 20, 1852, Isabella Hooker Collection, SD.

5. Gossett, *"Uncle Tom's Cabin" and American Culture,* 172.

6. R[ichard] D. Webb to M. A. Estlin, July 11, 1853, BPL.

7. This is the conclusion of Klingberg and Fladeland, and I have found nothing in the primary sources to contradict it. See Frank J. Klingberg, "Harriet Beecher Stowe and Social Reform in England," *American Historical Review* 43 (1937–1938): 542–52, and Betty Fladeland, *Men and Brothers: Anglo-American Antislavery Cooperation* (Urbana: University of Illinois Press, 1972), 342–81. For background on American and English antislavery politics I have relied on Lewis Perry, *Radical Abolitionism: Anarchy and the Government of God in Antislavery Thought* (Ithaca, N.Y.: Cornell University Press, 1973), Betty Fladeland, *Abolitionists and Working-Class Problems in the Age of Industrialization* (Baton Rouge: Louisiana State University Press, 1984), esp. chap. 3, "Joseph Sturge," 49–73, and C. Duncan Rice, "Controversies over Slavery in Eighteenth and Nineteenth Century Scotland," in *Antislavery Reconsidered: New Perspectives on the Abolitionists,* ed. Lewis Perry and Michael Fellman (Baton Rouge: Louisiana State University Press, 1979), 24–48.

8. Mrs. Eliza Wigham to M. A. Estlin, March 22, 1853, BPL.

9. Fladeland, *Men and Brothers,* 353.

10. HBS to William Lloyd Garrison, November, 1853, BPL.

11. HBS to Wendell Phillips, February 23, 1853, HO. Stowe also went to great lengths in her letter of December 16, 1852, to Eliza Cabot Follen, Dr. Williams's Library, London, to explain the declining enrollments of Lane Seminary in a more favorable light.

12. HBS to [Henry Wadsworth Longfellow], February 1, 1853, HO.

13. HBS to William Lloyd Garrison, December 12, 1853, as quoted in *William Lloyd Garrison, 1805–1879: The Story of His Life Told by His Children,* 4 vols. (New York: Century Co., 1889), 3:401.

14. Henry B. Stanton, as quoted in Perry, *Radical Abolitionism,* 14.

15. S. Pugh to Ann Warren Weston, June 6, 1853, BPL. Although I have found no direct documentation of meetings between Stowe and Garrison before she left for England, I am assuming on the basis of this warm personal endorsement of Garrison that they had met, perhaps in her comings and goings at the Boston Anti-Slavery Society.

Eliza Wigham, Stowe's Quaker hostess in Edinburgh, advised against "writing to prompt her, or to warn her" against schismatic antislavery groups, figuring that "if she has informed heself respecting W.L.G[arrison] in America, it shows her alive to the matter"; see Mrs. Eliza Wigham to [M. A. Estlin?], December 4, 1853, BPL.

16. Ann Warren Weston to Deborah Weston, February 7, 1853, BPL.

17. HBS to Lord Denman, January 20, 1853, HL.

18. Even Garrisonians who took a strong stand in favor of women's participation in abolitionist politics invoked the rhetoric of women's retirement from public debate. For a very interesting example that invokes Stowe's Mrs. Bird, see "The Cause of Woman," *Independent*, February 16, 1854, p. 52.

19. HBS to George Beecher, February 20, [1830?], Acquisitions, SD.

20. HBS to Edward Baines, February 28, 1853, Katharine S. Day Collection, SD.

21. *Journal of Charles Beecher*, 136–37. At the Exeter Hall meeting Harriet sat in a "side gallery," according to the *New York Daily Times*, May 30, 1853, p. 3.

22. *Journal of Charles Beecher*, 36.

23. She sometimes addressed the ladies privately, but we have no record of what she said because Charles Beecher, who accompanied her to England for the express purpose of being her recording secretary, was of course not present at these meetings of the ladies. At the Duchess of Sutherland's he reported that "the ladies drew together into a small apartment, the gentlemen were requested to withdraw, and Hatty addressed the ladies." He determined to ask her what she said, but apparently forgot, for his journal makes no further reference to the event. Charles was present at the Quaker Ladies Meeting for Free-Labor in London where Harriet spoke, but he mentioned only that her voice was "low and sweet" and left no record of her remarks. In the meantime Charles Beecher addressed a crowd of 4,000 at the Anti-Slavery Society meeting at City Hall in Glasgow. See *Journal of Charles Beecher*, 85, 39, 115.

24. HBS to Eliza Cabot Follen, December 16, 1852, Dr. Williams's Library, London. See also SM, 1:268; and Wilson, *Crusader in Crinoline*, 337.

25. "Many thanks for thy kind offer of a perusal of Mrs. Follen's letter," wrote Eliza Wigham, "but we have seen it through Hannah Webb's kindness & have been very much interested"; see Eliza Wigham to [M. A. Estlin?], December 4, 1853, BPL. See also Eliza Wigham to M. A. Estlin, March 22, 1853, BPL; and Mrs. A. Tribe to M. A. Estlin, September 9, 1853, BPL. Follen also showed the letter to George Eliot, who responded, "The whole letter is most fascinating and makes one love her"; see George Eliot to Mr. and Mrs. Charles Bray, March 12, 1853, in *The George Eliot Letters*, 9 vols., ed. Gordon S. Haight (New Haven, Conn.: Yale University Press, 1954–1978), 2:92.

26. Franklin organized public libraries and lit the streets of Philadelphia by putting himself "as much as I could out of sight"; his "frequent Successes" with this method led him to "heartily recommend it", see *The Autobiography of Benjamin Franklin*, ed. Leonard W. Labaree et al. (New Haven, Conn.: Yale University Press, 1964), 143.

27. *Journal of Charles Beecher*, 51–52.

28. SM, 1:xvi. *Journal of Charles Beecher*, 31.

29. As quoted in Fladeland, *Men and Brothers*, 357.

30. *Journal of Charles Beecher*, 57–58.

31. Eliza Wigham to [M. A. Estlin?], April 28, 1853, BPL.

32. S. Pugh to A. W. Weston, June 6, 1853, BPL. See also W. Smeal to M. A. Estlin, May 17, 1853, BPL. Only one observer felt that Stowe had not been even-handed. "In my opinion Mrs. Stowe had not acted either with fairness or magnanimity

to the Ladies A[nti-] S[lavery] S[ociety] in Glasgow," wrote R. D. Webb to E. F. Weston, April 27, [1853?], BPL.

33. Rice, "Controversies over Slavery in Scotland," 43–44.

34. Fladeland, *Abolitionists and Working-Class Problems*, 50–51; Fladeland, *Men and Brothers*, 347–48. "Consumption of the Products of Slave Labor in England," *National Era*, October 10, 1850, p. 161.

35. *Journal of Charles Beecher*, 61, 64, 67, 68. Fladeland, *Men and Brothers*, 370.

36. *Journal of Charles Beecher*, 119, 115.

37. Mrs. Isabella Massie to M. A. Estlin, May 20, 1853, BPL.

38. William Wells Brown to William Lloyd Garrison, May 17, 1853, in *Journal of Negro History* 10 (July 1925), 545. Henry Bibb, on the other hand, was in England for the express purpose of working for the free-produce cause; see Fladeland, *Men and Brothers*, 269.

39. *Journal of Charles Beecher*, 115; SM, 2:83.

40. William Wells Brown to William Lloyd Garrison, May 17, 1853, in *Journal of Negro History* 10 (July 1925), 545.

41. Eliza Wigham to [M. A. Estlin?], April 28, 1853, BPL.

42. Mrs. Isabella Massie to M. A. Estlin, May 20, 1853, BPL.

43. See the cartoon in the *New York Pick*, May 28, 1853, clipping, SD. S. Pugh to Ann Warren Weston, June 6, 1853, BPL. The Chapmans were their hosts in Paris.

44. *Journal of Charles Beecher*, 69–70. SM, 1:261. Dickens and Stowe did not develop a warm personal relationship. When Dickens invited her to dinner she was too tired to go (see SM, 2:31).

45. Klingberg, "Harriet Beecher Stowe and Social Reform in England," 551.

46. Josephine Donovan, *"Uncle Tom's Cabin": Evil, Affliction, and Redemptive Love* (Boston: Twayne Publishers, 1991), 3.

47. Fladeland, *Abolitionists and Working-Class Problems*, 60.

48. George Fitzhugh, *Cannibals All! Or, Slaves without Masters*, ed. C. Vann Woodward (Cambridge, Mass.: Belknap Press of Harvard University Press, 1960), xxiv–xxvi. I thank Travis Hedrick for drawing my attention to Fitzhugh.

49. Arthur Helps to [Charles Eliot Norton], July 9, 1852, HO.

50. Klingberg, "Harriet Beecher Stowe and Social Reform in England," 543, makes the erroneous assumption that Stowe agreed with these views.

51. HBS to Arthur Helps, August 22, 1852, Acquisitions, SD. Arthur Helps to HBS, October 9, 1852, HO.

52. Richard Whately, Archbishop of Dublin, to HBS, September 22, 1852, folder 241, Beecher-Stowe Collection, SchL.

53. Klingberg, "Harriet Beecher Stowe and Social Reform in England," 551. SM, 2:121.

54. Stowe's defense of the Sutherlands against charges that they had harshly evicted tenants on their highland estates is of a piece with these conciliatory positions; see SM, 1:308–13. CES to Rev. Dr. Nelson, August 21, 1857, BPL. For the pervasive anarchism of antebellum reform thought, see Perry, *Radical Abolitionism*, and Ann D. Braude, *Radical Spirits: Spiritualism and Women's Rights in Nineteenth-Century America* (Boston: Beacon Press, 1989).

55. A photocopy of the "Address" is included as a frontispiece in the *Journal of Charles Beecher*; it may also be found in Wilson, *Crusader in Crinoline*, 341–42.

56. Klingberg, "Harriet Beecher Stowe and Social Reform in England," 548. Fladeland, *Men and Brothers*, 355. Stowe had her revenge on the *New York Observer* when its editor, Irenaeus Prime, came to England during her tour and was denied a

seat at the British anniversary meeting of the Bible Society because of his proslavery views.

57. SM, 1:308–13. CES to Rev. Dr. Nelson, August 21, 1857, BPL.

58. HBS to Lord_____[probably Shaftesbury], January 7, 1853, Harriet Beecher Stowe Collection, UVa.

59. These volumes are on loan from the Connecticut Historical Society to the Stowe-Day Library.

60. HBS to Duchess of Sutherland, May 9, [1853], Harriet Beecher Stowe Collection, UVa. This bracelet is in the possession of the Stowe-Day Foundation.

61. HBS to Cassius M. Clay, February 8, 1853, Berg Collection of English and American Literature, NYPL.

62. HBS to "Dear Sir" [Henry W. Longfellow], February 19, 1853, HO. "Mrs. Stowe at Stafford House," *London Times*, May 9, 1853, p. 5.

63. HBS to Duchess of Sutherland, March 24, 1853, Harriet Beecher Stowe Collection, UVa.

64. This figure is an estimate based on (1) the $20,000 Penny Offering; (2) the $20,000 Stowe had received from Jewett for *Uncle Tom's Cabin*; (3) additional receipts of approximately $20,000 from continuing sales of *Uncle Tom* and from *The Key to Uncle Tom's Cabin*, which the *London Times* reported (May 9, 1853, p. 5) sold 60,000 copies in three days.

65. CES to HBS, August 8, 1853, Acquisitions, SD.

66. Isabella Beecher Hooker to John Hooker, July 4, 1852, Isabella Hooker Collection, SD.

67. Isabella Beecher Hooker to John Hooker, June 26 [and 27], 1852, Isabella Hooker Collection, SD. *Journal of Charles Beecher*, 363 n124. CES to HBS, July 11, 1853, Acquisitions, SD.

68. CES to HBS, July 31, 1853, Acquisitions, SD.

69. *Journal of Charles Beecher*, 257, 333, 140.

70. HBS to Eliza Cabot Follen, December 16, 1852, Dr. William's Library, London.

71. Eliza Cabot Follen to Maria Weston Chapman, March 12, [1853?], BPL; Mrs. Eliza Wigham to [M. A. Estlin?], April 28, 1853, BPL; HBS to Earl of Carlisle, Earl of Shaftesbury, G. W. Alexander, and Joseph Sturge, n.d. [before February 12, 1856], with replies from the Earl of Shaftesbury, February 12, 1856, and the Earl of Carlisle, February 27, 1856, BPL. Dorothy Sterling, ed., *We Are Your Sisters: Black Women in the Nineteenth Century* (New York: W. W. Norton, 1984), 189–93, prints some revealing letters from Emma Brown, a pupil at Miss Miner's school.

72. HBS to Earl of Carlisle, Earl of Shaftesbury, G. W. Alexander, and Joseph Sturge, n.d. [before February 12, 1856], with replies from the Earl of Shaftesbury, February 12, 1856, and the Earl of Carlisle, February 27, 1856, BPL. HBS to Wendell Phillips, n.d., HO. John W. Blassingame, ed., *The Frederick Douglass Papers: Series One: Speeches, Debates, and Interviews*, 4 vols. (New Haven, Conn.: Yale University Press, 1982), 2:448n14.

73. Wilson, *Crusader in Crinoline*, 371.

74. In a published letter to her Scottish hosts stowe reported that she had used money from the Scottish National Penny Offering to put one thousand copies of *Uncle Tom's Cabin* and the *Key* in the hands of home missionaries and also made from the same fund a contributuion of $1,000 to Miss Miner's school. See "Letter from Mrs. H. B. Stowe, to the Ladies' New Anti-Slavery Society of Glasgow," November 18, 1853," pamphlet, SD.

75. HBS to Earl of Carlisle, Earl of Shaftesbury, G. W. Alexander, and Joseph

Sturge, n.d. [before February 12, 1856], with replies from the Earl of Shaftesbury, February 12, 1856, and the Earl of Carlisle, February 27, 1856, BPL. Samuel May, Jr., to Maria Weston Chapman, November 13, 1857, BPL. Stowe also wrote a separate letter to the Duchess of Argyle to report on her use of money entrusted her to redeem slaves; see HBS to Duchess of Argyle, June 17,[1856], Harriet Beecher Stowe Collection, UVa. Ruth Bordin, *Woman and Temperance: The Quest for Power and Liberty, 1873–1900* (Philadelphia: Temple University Press, 1981), 74.

76. Harriet Jacobs [Linda Brent], *Incidents in the Life of a Slave Girl, Written by Herself,* edited by Jean Fagan Yellin, (Cambridge, Mass.: Harvard University Press, 1987); the quotation in on p. 77.

77. See the correspondence between Harriet Jacobs and Amy Post, in Jacobs, *Incidents in the Life of a Slave Girl,* 231–35. Jacobs also thought that her daughter, Linda, might accompany Stowe on her English tour as a "representative of the Southern states." Stowe condescendingly explained that such petting as her daughter would receive at the hands of the English would not be good for her.

78. HBS, *A Key to Uncle Tom's Cabin,* 155–68; the quotation is on p. 155. HBS, *The Edmondson Family and the Capture of the Schooner Pearl* (Cincinnati, Ohio: American Reform Tract and Book Society, 1856); I am grateful to Michelle Cliff for calling this volume to my attention. See also *Journal of Charles Beecher,* 117, and Isabella Beecher Hooker to John Hooker, June 10, 1852, Isabella Hooker Collection, SD.

79. For Mary Webb, see HBS to Lady Hatherton, May 24, 1856, Harriet Beecher Stowe Collection, UVa; HBS to Mr. and Mrs. Baines, May 24, 1856, Acquisitions, SD; HBS to Duchess of Argyle, June 17, [1856], Harriet Beecher Stowe Collection, UVa; and SM, 2:100. For Miss Greenfield, see SM 1:320, 2:100, 139; and *Journal of Charles Beecher,* 91.

80. HBS to the Duchess of Argyle, April 2, 1858, Harriet Beecher Stowe Collection, UVa.

81. *Journal of Charles Beecher,* 306.

82. HBS to Duke and Duchess of Argyle, September 4, [1853], UVa.

83. CES to HBS, July 22, 1853, Acquisitions, SD.

84. *Journal of Charles Beecher,* 116, 129. The silver inkstand is in the Stowe-Day Foundation.

85. HBS to Isabella Beecher Hooker, July 19, [1856–1860], Joseph K. Hooker Collection, SD; HBS to Henry Ward Beecher, June 4, [1852], Beecher Family Papers, SML; Thomas Beecher to Isabella Beecher Hooker, November 18, 1852, Joseph K. Hooker Collection, SD; Due Bill, Anti Slavery Fair, 1857–1858, BPL; HBS to Elizabeth Barrett Browning, n.d., Harriet Beecher Stowe Collection, UVa. Betty Fladeland mentions that Stowe's trip to the British Isles gave a boost to such traditional methods of women's political activism; see *Men and Brothers,* 358.

86. HBS to William Lloyd Garrison, November, 1853, BPL.

87. William Lloyd Garrison to [Harriet Beecher Stowe], November 30, 1853, in *The Letters of William Lloyd Garrison,* 4: 280–86.

88. HBS to William Lloyd Garrison, November 30, 1853, BPL.

89. Perry, *Radical Abolitionism,* 84.

90. William Lloyd Garrison to [Harriet Beecher Stowe], November 30, 1853, in *The Letters of William Lloyd Garrison,* 4: 280–86. HBS to William Lloyd Garrison, December, 1853, BPL.

91. HBS to William Lloyd Garrison, December 19, 1853, BPL.

92. HBS to William Lloyd Garrison, February 18, 1854, BPL.

93. HBS to Henry Ward Beecher, January 13, 1852, Beecher Family Papers, SML.

94. HBS to William Lloyd Garrison, December 22, 1853, BPL.

95. HBS to William Lloyd Garrison, n.d. [December 1853–Winter 1854], Acquisitions, SD; HBS to William Lloyd Garrison, February 18, 1854, BPL.

Chapter 21

1. Elizabeth Stuart Phelps, *Chapters from a Life* (Boston: Houghton Mifflin, 1897), 134–35.

2. Philena McKeen and Phebe F. McKeen, *Annals of Fifty Years: A History of Abbot Academy, Andover, Andover, Mass., 1829–1879* (Andover, Mass.: Warren F. Draper, 1880), 51–52, 48.

3. Henry Ellis Stowe to HBS and CES, 1856, folder 285, Beecher-Stowe Collection, SchL.

4. CES to HBS, January 5, 1857, Acquisitions, SD. HBS to Eunice Beecher, July 26, [1857], Beecher Family Papers, SML.

5. Isabella Beecher Hooker to John Hooker, July 17, 1857, Isabella Hooker Collection, SD.

6. CES to HBS, June 11 and 12, 1849, Acquisitions, SD.

7. HBS to Henry Ellis Stowe, n.d. [December, 1855], folder 183, Beecher-Stowe Collection, SchL.

8. HBS to Sarah Howe Allen, October 22, 1854, Harriet Beecher Stowe Collection, UVa.

9. Mary Beecher Perkins to Isabella Beecher Hooker, n.d. [1856], Joseph K. Hooker Collection, SD.

10. HBS to Henry Ellis Stowe, n.d. [December, 1855], folder 183, Beecher-Stowe Collection, SchL.

11. HBS to Mary Beecher Perkins, December 24, [1855], Helen D. Perkins Collection, SD.

12. Phelps, *Chapters from a Life*, 29, 33.

13. Henry Ward Beecher, "The Crisis," *Independent*, March 2, 1854, p. 65.

14. HBS, "An Appeal to the Women of the Free States of America, On the Present Crisis in Our Country," *Independent*, February 23, 1854, p. 57.

15. HBS to William Lloyd Garrison, February 18, 1854, BPL.

16. "Congress," *Independent*, March 16, 1854, p. 88, and March 23, 1854, p. 96. HBS to the Duchess of Sutherland, March 26,1854, Harriet Beecher Stowe Collection, UVa.

17. "Congress," *Independent*, June 1, 1854, p. 173.

18. See Michael Fellman, "Rehearsal for the Civil War: Antislavery and Proslavery at the Fighting Point in Kansas, 1854–1856," in Perry and Fellman, eds., *Antislavery Reconsidered*, 287–307.

19. CES and HBS to Mr. Phillips, June 11, 1854, BPL.

20. HBS to Duchess of Argyle, June 17, 856, Harriet Beecher Stowe Collection, UVa.

21. HBS, *Dred: A Tale of the Great Dismal Swamp, Together with Anti-Slavery Tales and Papers, and Life in Florida after the War*, 2 vols. (Boston: Houghton Mifflin, 1896), 1:263–264; hereafter referred to in text as D.

22. Perry, *Radical Abolitionism*, 234.

23. Foster, *Rungless Ladder*, 79.

24. Judith Fetterley, "Introduction," *Provisions: A Reader from 19th-Century American Women* (Bloomington: Indiana University Press, 1985), 15.

25. CES to Mr. Phillips, June 11, 1856, BPL.

26. Isabella Beecher Hooker to Mary Hooker Burton and Alice Hooker Day, June [19], 1856, Isabella Hooker Collection, SD.

27. HBS to Mr. Phillips, July 13, [1856], with a note from CES to Mr. Phillips, BPL.

28. HBS to Mr. Phillips, n.d. [between April 19 and July 29,1856], Katharine S. Day Collection, SD.

29. Nathan Hale, Jr., to Edward Everett Hale, April 23, 1857, box 18, Hale Papers, Smith College.

30. Mary Beecher Perkins to Thomas Perkins, August 13–15, 1856, Katharine S. Day Collection, SD. See also Mary Beecher Perkins to Thomas Perkins, August [17]–20, 1856, and August 23–25, 1856, Katharine S. Day Collection, SD.

31. "The Political Crisis in the United States," *Edinburgh Review* 104 (October 1856): 561–597, 565. *Dred* did better in the United States when compared to population, selling 150,000 in the first year; sales in Great Britain for the same period were 165,000; see Wilson, *Crusader in Crinoline*, 419.

32. HBS to Lady Byron, October 16, 1856, folder 245, Beecher-Stowe Collection, SchL.

33. Lady Byron to HBS, October 18, 1856, folder 245, Beecher-Stowe Collection, SchL.

34. HBS to Lady Byron, October 24, [1856], folder 245, Beecher-Stowe Collection, SchL. Mary Beecher Perkins to Thomas Perkins, November 2–7, [1856], Katharine S. Day Collection, SD.

35. HBS to the Duchess of Argyle, September 15, [1856], Harriet Beecher Stowe Collection, UVa.

36. Nathaniel Hawthorne, "Mrs. Hutchinson," in *The Complete Writings of Nathaniel Hawthorne*, 22 vols. (Boston: Houghton Mifflin, 1900), 17:1–12; quote from 1–2.

37. HBS to Lady Byron, October 24, [1856], folder 245, Beecher-Stowe Collection, SchL. CES to HBS, October 6, 1856, Acquisitions, SD.

38. CES to HBS, n.d. [1856], Acquisitions, SD. HBS to the Duke of Sutherland, November 21, [1856], Katharine S. Day Collection, SD.

39. CES to HBS, November 25, 1856, Acquisitions, SD.

40. CES to HBS, December 30, 1856, Acquisitions, SD. CES to Samuel Foote, March 9, 1857, Foote Collection, SD. Isabella Hooker to John Hooker, June 28, 1857, Isabella Hooker Collection, SD.

41. CES to HBS, n.d. [before March], [1857]; February 2, 1857, and February 23, 1857; all in Acquisitions, SD.

42. CES to HBS, February 2, 1857, Acquisitions, SD.

43. CES to HBS, n.d. [before March], [1857], Acquisitions, SD.

44. HBS to Lady Byron, October 16, 1856, folder 245, Beecher-Stowe Collection, SchL.

45. HBS to [Edward] Baines, October 25, [1856], Katharine S. Day Collection, SD. Fanny Kingsley to HBS, n.d. [1856], folder 242, Beecher-Stowe Collection, SchL.

46. Mary Beecher Perkins to Thomas Perkins, November 2–7, [1856], Katharine S. Day Collection, SD.

47. Mary Beecher Perkins to "Katy" [Catherine Perkins Gilman], October 23–[c. 26], [1856]; Mary Beecher Perkins to Thomas Perkins, August 23–25 and August 29, 1856—all in Katharine S. Day Collection, SD.

48. Mary Beecher Perkins to Thomas Perkins, August 29–30, September 10–11, [1856], Katharine S. Day Collection, SD.

49. Mary Beecher Perkins to [Perkins family], October 16 and October 11–13, [1856], Katharine S. Day Collection, SD.

50. Mary Beecher Perkins to Isabella Beecher Hooker, n.d. ("Sunday"), [1856], Joseph K. Hooker Collection, SD.

51. HBS to "Dear Sir," November 1, 1856, Harriet Beecher Stowe Collection, UVa.

52. *Journal of Charles Beecher*, 79.

53. *Journal of Charles Beecher*, 192, 216.

54. *Journal of Charles Beecher*, 151–52. This "fall" into high culture of a Protestant is described with rich irony in Harold Frederic's novel *The Damnation of Theron Ware* (1896).

55. For Mark Twain's travel letters to the *Alta California*, see Kaplan, *Mr. Clemens and Mark Twain* 35, 43, 48, 51, 52, 56, 71, 82, 114.

56. Lawrence W. Levine, *Highbrow/Lowbrow*.

57. *Journal of Charles Beecher*, 63.

58. *Journal of Charles Beecher*, 227–28.

59. Lawrence Buell juxtaposes passages from Emerson, Hawthorne, Ik Marvel, and Maria Cummins to suggest the continuities between serious and popular writing in antebellum America. The tendency that we in the twentieth century have "to see the New England Romantics in our image" he calls "perhaps the main obstacle to historically faithful interpretation"; see Lawrence Buell, *New England Literary Culture: From Revolution through Renaissance* (Cambridge: Cambridge University Press, 1986), 56–83; the quotation is on p. 83.

60. See Kaplan, *Mr. Clemens and Mark Twain*, 71.

61. D. B. Lawler to Samuel Foote, September 2, 1854, Foote Collection, SD.

62. Mary Beecher Perkins to Thomas Perkins, November 2–7, [1856]; November 12 [and 16], [1856]; November 28–December 3 [1856], and December 21–25, [1856]; January 22–28, [1857] and May 17, [1857]—all in Katharine S. Day Collection, SD.

63. CES to HBS, December 30, 1856, and October 6, 1856, both in Acquisitions, SD.

64. Mary Perkins to Thomas Perkins, n.d. [January after the 10th, 1857]; and January 18–20, 1857, Acquisitions, SD.

65. HBS, "Sojourner Truth, the Libyan Sibyl," *Atlantic Monthly*, (April 1863), pp. 473–81. "Letter from Sojourner Truth," in the Boston *Commonwealth*, July 3, 1863, p. 1. I am grateful to Lyde Cullen Sizer for this reference. Mary Perkins to Thomas Perkins, [March] 15–18, [1857], Acquisitions, SD.

66. CES to HBS, February 16, 1857, Acquisitions, SD.

67. Mary Beecher Perkins to Thomas Perkins, n.d. [January after the 10th, 1857]; January 18–20, 1857; [March] 14–18, [1857]; March 5, [1857]; April 7, 1857; [March] 14–18 [1857]; April 29–May 7, [1857]—all in Katharine S. Day Collection, SD.

Chapter 22

1. CES to HBS, March 2, 1857, Acquisitions, SD. Mary Hooker Burton to John Hooker, June 21, 1857, and Isabella Beecher Hooker to John Hooker, June 28, 1857—both in Isabella Hooker Collection, SD.

2. Thomas K. Beecher to CES, February 14, 1857, with a note from CES to HBS, Acquisitions, SD.

3. Isabella Beecher Hooker to John Hooker, June 28, 1857, Isabella Hooker Collection, SD.

4. Isabella Beecher Hooker to John Hooker, May 19, 1857, and John Hooker to Isabella Beecher Hooker, May 20, 1857—both in Isabella Hooker Collection, SD. CES to HBS, November 25, 1856, and May 4, 1857—both in Acquisitions, SD.

5. CES to HBS, February [16], 1857, Acquisitions, SD.

6. CES to HBS, January 5, 1857, Acquisitions, SD.

7. CES to HBS, March 2, 1857, Acquisitions, SD.

8. CES to HBS, February 23, 1857, Acquisitions, SD.

9. For a letter about Eunice Beecher, see HBS to Hatty Beecher, March 20, 1859, folder 103, Beecher-Stowe Collection, SchL. CES to HBS, March 2, 1857, Acquisitions, SD.

10. HBS to Isabella Beecher Hooker, July 19, [1856–1860], Joseph K. Hooker Collection, SD.

11. Isabella Beecher Hooker to John Hooker, June 28, 1857, Isabella Hooker Collection, SD.

12. Isabella Beecher Hooker to John Hooker, July 17, 1857, Isabella Hooker Collection, SD. HBS to Lyman Beecher n.d. [after July 9,1857], White Collection, SD.

13. Isabella Beecher Hooker to John Hooker, July 17, 1857, Isabella Hooker Collection, SD.

14. HBS to Eunice Beecher, July 26, [1857], Beecher Family Papers, SML.

15. CES to his children, July 29, 1849, Acquisitions, SD.

16. HBS to Catharine Beecher, August 17, [1858], folder 97, Beecher-Stowe Collection, SchL.

17. HBS to Henry Ward Beecher [and Eunice], August 30 [1859], Beecher Family Papers, SML.

18. HBS to Catharine Beecher, August 17, [1858], folder 97, Beecher-Stowe Collection, SchL.

19. HBS to Eunice Beecher, July 26, [1857], Beecher Family Papers, SML.

20. Quoted in C. E. Beecher, *Life*, 340–41.

21. Catharine Beecher to Leonard Bacon, September 28, 1857, Collection of American Literature, BL.

22. Sklar, *Catharine Beecher*, 238–39, 246.

23. Catharine Beecher to Leonard Bacon, August 27, 1857, and October 16, 1857—both in Collection of American Literature, BL.

24. Sklar, *Catharine Beecher*, 248, 256.

25. Elaine Showalter, *A Literature of Their Own: British Women Novelists from Brontë to Lessing* (Princeton, N.J.: Princeton University Press, 1977), 144.

26. Sara Parton, "Notes on Preachers and Preaching" (1869), as quoted in Kelley, *Private Woman, Public Stage*, 291. Kelley is richly suggestive on the subject of women's domestic ministries. An early article on women's challenge to the clerical establishment is Christine Stansell's "Elizabeth Stuart Phelps: A Study in Female Rebellion," *Massachusetts Review* 13 (1972): 239–56. See also Phelps, *Chapters from a Life*, 98–99 and Douglas, *The Feminization of American Culture*.

27. HBS, *The Minister's Wooing* (Boston: Houghton Mifflin, 1896) (hereafter referred to parenthetically in the text as MW); Elizabeth Stuart Phelps, *The Gates Ajar* (Boston: Fields, Osgood, & Co., 1869). I am indebted to Peggy McIntosh for pointing out the similarity between Stowe's and Phelps's criticisms of the male religious establishment. For Phelps, see Stansell's "Elizabeth Stuart Phelps" and Lori

Duin Kelly's *The Life and Works of Elizabeth Stuart Phelps, Victorian Feminist Writer* (Troy, N.Y.: Whitson, 1983).

28. Foster, *The Rungless Ladder*, 86–128, esp. 104, 111, 128. See also Lawrence Buell, "Calvinism Romanticized: Harriet Beecher Stowe, Samuel Hopkins, and *The Minister's Wooing*," in Ammons, ed., *Critical Essays*, 259–281.

29. See especially Elizabeth Ammons, "Heroines in *Uncle Tom's Cabin*" and Dorothy Berkson, "Millennial Politics and the Feminine Fiction of Harriet Beecher Stowe," in *Critical Essays*, ed. Elizabeth Ammons, 152–65 and 244–58, respectively; Laurie Crumpaker, "Four Novels of Harriet Beecher Stowe: A Study in Nineteenth-Century Androgyny," in *American Novelists Revisited: Essays in Feminist Criticism*, ed. Fritz Fleishman (Boston: G. K. Hall, 1982), 78–106; Jane Tompkins, "Sentimental Power: *Uncle Tom's Cabin* and the Politics of Literary History," in Tompkins, *Sensational Designs*. Their analyses of Stowe's transformation of patriarchal values have shaped my understanding of Stowe's fiction. See also Gillian Brown, "Getting in the Kitchen with Dinah: Domestic Politics in *Uncle Tom's Cabin*," *American Quarterly* 36, no. 4 (Fall 1984): 503–23 and Amy Shrager Lang, "Slavery and Sentimentalism: The Strange Career of Augustine St. Clare," *Women's Studies* 12 (1986):31–54.

30. I suspect that Stowe felt doubly called upon to answer Edwards because she, as an artist, could not help responding to his images.

31. I am indebted for this observation to Richard Shapiro, a student in my class on "Roots: Literatures of America," taught at Trinity College in the spring of 1983.

32. HBS to Henry Ward Beecher, August 30, [1859], Beecher Family Papers, SML.

33. HBS to Susan Howard, June 10, 1860, quoted in Annie Fields, ed., *Life*, 280–281.

34. HBS to Martha [Wetherill], December 13, 1860, Katharine S. Day Collection, SD.

35. Mary Beecher Perkins to Harriet Beecher Stowe, November 19, 1848, White Collection, SD.

36. Frederick Perkins's difficulties in settling down continued long after college. His inability to choose either the right profession or the right wife marked the childhood of his daughter, Charlotte Perkins Gilman. See Ann J. Lane, *To Herland and Beyond: The Life and Work of Charlotte Perkins Gilman* (New York: Pantheon Books, 1991), 25–34.

37. Isabella Beecher Hooker to John Hooker, June 20, 1852, Isabella Hooker Collection, SD. For a letter in which she seeks advice on handling her children, see Isabella Beecher Hooker to Harriet Beecher Stowe, July 31, 1849, folder 39, Beecher-Stowe Collection, SchL.

38. HBS to Catharine Beecher, August 17, [1858], folder 97, Beecher-Stowe Collection, SchL.

39. HBS to Henry Ward Beecher [and Eunice Beecher], August 30, [1859], Beecher Family Papers, SML.

40. HBS to Hatty Beecher, May 14, [1859?], folder 104, Beecher-Stowe Collection, SchL. HBS to Mrs. Edwards A. Park, n.d., BPL. To this invitation to tea Professor Park scrawled in response, "I will go, if I can get away at 8 o'clock." For Stowe's use of Park's *Memoir of the Life and Character of Samuel Hopkins, D. D.* (1852), see Foster, *Rungless Ladder*, 87–90. Buell, "Calvinism Romanticized," follows closely Stowe's use of this and other sources by and about Hopkins.

41. Dorothy Berkson, "Millennial Politics," 246–248, points out the "radical political implications" of Stowe's critique of Calvinism.

42. Foster, *Rungless Ladder*, 115.

43. HBS, "Walnut Hills," *Autobiography*, 2:131.

44. Judith Fetterley, "Introduction," *Provisions*, 8.

45. Buell, "Calvinism Romanticized," in Ammons, ed., *Critical Essays*, 269; Foster, *Rungless Ladder*, 69.

46. For an analysis of the Victorian home as a spiritual center, see Colleen McDannell, *The Christian Home in Victorian America, 1840–1900* (Bloomington: Indiana University Press, 1986).

Chapter 23

1. Ellery Sedgwick, "*Atlantic Monthly*," in *American Literary Magazines: The Eighteenth and Nineteenth Centuries*, ed. Edward E. Chielens (New York: Greenwood Press, 1986), 50.

2. Douglas, *The Feminization of American Culture*, 6.

3. Brodhead, *The School of Hawthorne*. See also Levine, *Highbrow/Lowbrow*.

4. CES to HBS, May 4, 1857, Acquisitions, SD.

5. Edward Everett Hale, *James Russell Lowell and His Friends* (Boston: Houghton Mifflin, 1899), 167.

6. For full and well-documented discussions of the "Whist Club," the "Town and Country Club," and the "Saturday Club," see Martin Duberman, *James Russell Lowell* (Boston: Houghton Mifflin, 1966), 162–64, 183–97.

7. Mark A. DeWolfe Howe, *The "Atlantic Monthly" and Its Makers* (Boston: Atlantic Monthly Press, 1919), 19.

8. In the literary memoirs of the period a number of the participants conflate the Saturday Club and the Atlantic Club (for example, Edward Everett Hale, *James Russell Lowell and His Friends*, 156–58). While the two had many joint members, the Saturday Club was the older and larger organization; as Thomas Wentworth Higginson pointed out in *Cheerful Yesterdays* (Boston: Houghton Mifflin, 1898; reprint, New York: Arno Press/New York Times, 1968), 176, it was "very clearly discriminated" from the "Atlantic Club" in Longfellow's journals. The distinction between the two clubs is carefully drawn in Edward Waldo Emerson, *The Early Years of the Saturday Club, 1855–1870* (Boston: Houghton Mifflin, 1918), 11–29.

9. Howe, *The "Atlantic Monthly" and Its Makers*, 20.

10. For descriptions of the "Stowe dinner," see Higginson, *Cheerful Yesterdays*, 176–80; and Thomas Wentworth Higginson to Louisa Storrow Higginson, July 10, 1859, in *Letters and Journals of Thomas Wentworth Higginson, 1846–1906*, ed. Mary Thacher Higginson (Boston: Houghton Mifflin, 1921), 106–10. A number of literary historians assume that women were regularly present at meetings of the Atlantic Club (see, for example Wilson, *Crusader in Crinoline*, 438–39), but Higginson says that this was "the only one to which ladies were invited" (*Cheerful Yesterdays*, 176), and I have found no evidence to the contrary. As Susan Coultrap-McQuin highlights, no women writers were invited to the twentieth anniversary celebration of the *Atlantic* in 1877. Not until the Holmes breakfast in 1880 and the birthday celebration for Stowe in 1882 were women included. See Susan Coultrap-McQuin, *Doing Literary Business: American Women Writers in the Nineteenth Century* (Chapel Hill: University of North Carolina Press, 1990), 2–5.

11. Duberman, *James Russell Lowell*, 185.

12. Barrett Wendell, a student of Lowell's at Harvard, taught the first course in

American literature at Harvard and published the fruit of his classroom lectures in *A Literary History of the United States* (1900), a book so provincial that one critic proposed to retitle it *A Literary History of Harvard University, with Incidental Glimpses of the Minor Writers of America.* He argued that the flowering of American letters was due to the genius of a homogeneous people, and its decline followed from the unhealthy addition of immigrants to the old American stock. See my "'Harvard Indifference,'" *New England Quarterly* 44 (September, 1976), 364, and Duberman, *James Russell Lowell,* 363. For a case study of the way in which a male writer's reputation was fostered by the male networks of publishers, college friends, and relatives, see Jane Tompkins, "Masterpiece Theatre: The Politics of Hawthorne's Literary Reputation," in her *Sensational Designs,* 3–39. In *Doing Literary Business,* 39, Coultrap-McQuin calls attention to the importance of these male networks, particularly the Saturday Club.

13. Katherine C. Grier, *Culture and Comfort: People, Parlors, and Upholstery, 1850–1930* (Rochester, N.Y.: Strong Museum, 1988) illustrates in lavish detail the transformation of the parlor. She also (p. 88) alludes to the contemporary equation of parlors with "shrines."

14. Foster, *Rungless Ladder,* 134–40, compares Hawthorne's and Stowe's Italian novels.

15. Fred Stowe to CES, October 26, 1859, folder 286, Beecher-Stowe Collection, SchL.

16. HBS to [John James] McCook, August 4, 1893, on loan from the Connecticut Antiquarian and Landmarks Society of Connecticut, Inc. to the SD. HBS to James T. Fields, [July, 1860], Fields Papers, HL. The commonplace book in which Stowe recorded her notes for *Agnes of Sorrento* is held by SD.

17. I am indebted for this observation to a conversation with Richard Brodhead. See, for example, "Roba di Roma," a long serial travelogue that began in the *Atlantic* in 1858. Many of *The Atlantic* writers had lived in Italy, where there was a large contingent of American artists. James Russell Lowell and his wife came at William Wetmore Story's urging to spend a few years; they lived first in Florence in the rooms that the Brownings had recently vacated, and then "settled in Julia Ward Howe's old rooms in Rome" (Duberman, *James Russell Lowell,* 117–18).

18. Tompkins, *Sensational Designs,* 34. Brodhead, *The School of Hawthorne,* 72, points out that *The Marble Faun,* "set in a museum world: a world furnished with and organized around works of art," embodies the changes that are taking place in publishing as high art was distinguished from popular art.

19. Review of *The Marble Faun, Atlantic Monthly,* April 1860, p. 510.

20. Samuel Clemens, *The Adventures of Huckleberry Finn* (San Francisco, Calif.: Chandler Publishing Company, 1962), 278.

21. See Buell, *New England Literary Culture,* chapters 1–3, for an analysis of the transformation of the ideal of "genteel amateurism" in American letters into literary professionalism. Brodhead, *The School of Hawthorne,* provides a splendid analysis of the way the emergence of high art led to the development of a new authorial persona for Hawthorne.

22. Richard Brodhead makes this point about the international novel in "Towards a Theory of Literary Access" (Paper presented at the Modern Languages Association annual meeting, New Orleans, 1989).

23. Clifford E. Clark, Jr., *Henry Ward Beecher: Spokesman for a Middle-Class America* (Urbana: University of Illinois Press, 1978), 71, 159.

24. Hawthorne and Fields were part of the same Cambridge networks. Haw-

thorne had just heard before sailing that he had been elected to the Saturday Club; Fields would be elected in 1864; see E. W. Emerson, *The Early Years of the Saturday Club*, 207, 356.

25. Coultrap-Mcquin, *Doing Literary Business*, 94–95. Judith A. Roman, *Annie Adams Fields: The Spirit of Charles Street* (Bloomington: University of Indiana Press, 1990), 18. HBS to Annie Fields, May 28, [1860], Fields Papers, HL.

26. Phelps, *Chapters from a Life*, 146–47.

27. For Julia Ward Howe's comment, see Duberman, *James Russell Lowell*, 192.

28. Roman, *Annie Adams Fields*, passim. Donovan, *New England Local Color Literature: A Women's Tradition* (New York: F. Ungar Publishing Co.,1983), 38–39.

29. Brodhead, *The School of Hawthorne*, 55.

30. T. W. Higginson to Louisa Storrow Higginson, July, 1861, in *Letters and Journals*, 111. Howe, *The "Atlantic Monthly" and Its Makers*, 52. In *Doing Literary Business*, Coultrap-McQuin introduces the concept of the "gentleman publisher" to describe James T. Fields and others who served during the beginning of the professionalization of literature.

31. HBS to James and Annie Fields, n.d. [c. February, 1861], Fields Papers, HL.

32. HBS, "A Card," *Independent,* November 21, 1861, p. 1.

33. Buell, *New England Literary Culture*, 57.

34. HBS to Theodore Tilton, December 18, [1860], Katharine S. Day Collection, SD.

35. CES to HBS, October 6, 1856, Acquisitions, SD. Stowe may have returned to her Maine novel in 1857, when, on her trip to Brunswick after Henry's death, she visited Casco Bay and Orr's Island. In his *Life*, 326–27, Charles Stowe says that *The Pearl of Orr's Island* was written simultaneously with *The Minister's Wooing*. I suspect that he confused the simultaneous writing of *Pearl* and *Agnes*. It is quite clear from Stowe's frantic attempts to keep *Pearl* and *Agnes* going at the same time, and her finally breaking off *Pearl* half-way through, that this novel was not completely written, or even very far along, when she began the serialization in the *Independent*.

36. HBS, *The Pearl of Orr's Island* (Boston: Houghton Mifflin, 1896), 8; hereafter cited parenthetically in the text as POI.

37. This statement has been made most prominently by Leslie Fielder in *Love and Death in the American Novel* (New York: Criterion Books, [1960]).

38. See my *Solitary Comrade: Jack London and His Work* (Chapel Hill: University of North Carolina Press, 1982), 94–111, for a discussion of *The Call of the Wild* as a transformation of London's initiation into working-class manhood.

39. HBS to Hatty Stowe, January 6, 1861, folder 106, Beecher-Stowe Collection, SchL.

40. For a suggestive treatment of the attraction of Stowe and other women writers to the character of Miranda in *The Tempest*, see Elaine Showalter, *Sister's Choice: Tradition and Change in American Women's Writing* (New York: Oxford University Press, 1991), 22–41.

41. HBS to Hatty Stowe, February 12, [1861], March 6, [1861], and January 9, [1861], folders 106–108, Beecher-Stowe Collection, SchL. For Hatty's unhappy love affair, see HBS to Hatty Stowe, March 4, [1859], March 14 [and March 20], [1859], and May 6, 1859, folder 104, Beecher-Stowe Collection, SchL.

42. HBS to James T. Fields, January 16, 1861, Fields Papers, HL.

43. HBS to Hatty Stowe, March 18, [1861], folder 108, Beecher-Stowe Collection, SchL.

44. HBS to Hatty Stowe, March 18 [1861], folder 108, and HBS to Hatty Stowe,

n.d. [February 10, 1861] and February 21, 1861, folder 107, Beecher-Stowe Collection, SchL. See also Annie Fields, *Life*, 288.

45. Fred Stowe to CES, December 18, 1859, folder 286, Beecher-Stowe Collection, SchL. HBS to Hatty Stowe, May 2, 1861, and May 10, 1861, folder 110, Beecher-Stowe Collection, SchL. HBS, "Getting Ready for a Gale," *Independent*, April 15, 1861, p. 1.

46. HBS, "Getting Ready for a Gale," *Independent*, April 25, 1861, p. 1. She expressed similar sentiments in "Letter from Andover," *Independent*, June 20, 1861, p. 1.

47. "The War and Slavery," *Independent*, May 9, 1861, p. 4.

48. Henry Ward Beecher, "On the War," sermon preached at Plymouth Church, Sunday eve, April 14, 1861, *Independent*, April 18, 1861, p. 1.

49. HBS, "Lazarus at the Gate," *Independent*, August 7, 1862, p. 1; "Simon the Cyrenian," *Independent* July 31, 1862, p. 1.

50. HBS, "Letter from Andover," *Independent*, June 13, 1861, p. 1.

51. HBS to Hatty Stowe, June 18, 1861, folder 111, Beecher-Stowe Collection, SchL.

52. HBS, "To Our Readers," *Independent*, December 5, 1861, p. 1.

53. Judith Fetterley provocatively suggests that *The Pearl of Orr's Island* is as close as Stowe came to writing an *Uncle Tom's Cabin* of women's oppression. Like the Christ on whom they were modeled, Tom and Mara are more powerful in death than in life. But the death that was so empowering in *Uncle Tom's Cabin* does not work the same way in *The Pearl of Orr's Island*—although clearly Stowe meant that it should. The problem, Fetterley suggests, is that Stowe could not imagine a world in which gender distinctions fell away like the shackles of the slave; see Fetterley, "Introduction," *Provisions*, 13, 12.

54. Kirkham, "Introduction," *The Pearl of Orr's Island* (Hartford, Conn.: Stowe-Day Foundation, 1979). Sarah Orne Jewett to Annie Fields, July 5, 1889, in Ammons, ed., *Critical Essays*, 212.

55. HBS to Hatty Stowe, [January, 1862], folder 113, Beecher-Stowe Collection, SchL.

56. Catharine Beecher to Henry Ward Beecher, February 17, 1860, quoted in Caskey, *Chariot of Fire*, 190.

57. HBS to Hatty Stowe, [January, 1862], folder 113, Beecher-Stowe Collection, SchL.

58. Catharine Beecher to Leonard Bacon, April 24, 1862, Collection of American Literature, BL.

59. HBS to Annie Fields, [1862], Fields Papers, HL. Henry Ward Beecher to Hatty, Eliza, and Georgiana Stowe, [1862], Katharine S. Day Collection, SD. There is no clear evidence that Stowe formally joined the Episcopal Church, but she increasingly participated in Episcopal services.

60. Calls for immediate emancipation appeared in columns by Daniel Curry, "What Will He Do with It?," *Independent*, June 19, 1862, p. 1, and Horace Greeley, "The Nation's Opportunity: A Theme for Independence Day," *Independent*, June 26, 1862, P1; HBS, "Simon the Cyrenean," *Independent*, July 31, 1862, p. 1; Stowe criticized those who urged emancipation on the grounds that it was essential "to the safety of the white race," but her invocation of "plagues" suggests her own implication in an economy of white self-preservation. HBS, "Prayer," *Independent*, August 28, 1862, p. 1.

61. Horace Greeley, "The Prayer of Twenty Millions," *New York Tribune*, August 20, 1861.

62. HBS, "Will You Take a Pilot?," *Independent,* September 11, 1861, p. 1.

63. CES, "Cotton Philanthropy," *Independent,* May 30, 1861, p. 1. HBS, "Letter from Andover," *Independent,* June 13, 1861, p. 1. The quotation is from HBS, "Letter from Andover," *Independent,* June 20, 1861, p. 1. See also HBS, "Letter to Lord Shaftesbury," *Independent,* August 1, 1861, p. 1.

64. HBS to James Fields, November 13, 1862, and November 19, 1862, Fields Papers, HL. HBS to Hatty Stowe, November 4, 1862, and November 10, [1862], folder 119, Beecher-Stowe Collection, SchL.

65. Mary Beecher Perkins and HBS to Henry Ward Beecher, typescript, November 2, [1862], Beecher Family Papers, SML.

66. Isabella Beecher Hooker to Alice Hooker Day, November 22,1862; Isabella Beecher Hooker to John Hooker, November 25, [1862]—both in Isabella Hooker Collection, SD.

67. Isabella Beecher Hooker to John Hooker, November 25, [1862], and November 26, 1862, Isabella Hooker Collection, SD; HBS to Henry Ward Beecher, September 11, 1863, Beecher Family Papers, SML.

68. Isabella Beecher Hooker to John Hooker, November26[–27], 1862, Isabella Hooker Collection, SD. HBS to James Fields, November 27, 1862, Fields Papers, HL.

69. Isabella Beecher Hooker to John Hooker, November 25,[1862], Isabella Hooker Collection, SD. Hatty Stowe to Eliza Stowe, December 3, 1862, folder 120, Beecher-Stowe Collection, SchL. HBS to CES, December 6, 1862, folder 81, Beecher-Stowe Collection, SchL.

70. Wilson, *Crusader in Crinoline,* 486–87.

71. Clifford, *Henry Ward Beecher,* 152. Frederick Stowe to CES and HBS, September 26, 1862, folder 287, Beecher-Stowe Collection, SchL.

72. HBS to Duchess of Argyle, June 1, 1863, Harriet Beecher Stowe Collection, UVa. HBS to Henry Ward Beecher, August 20, 1863, Beecher Family Papers, SML. HBS to Frederick Stowe, July 11, 1863, Katharine S. Day Collection, SD.

73. HBS to Henry Ward Beecher, August 20, 1863, Beecher Family Papers, SML. HBS to Annie Fields, July 26, [1864], Fields Papers, HL. HBS to CES, November 15, 1863, and November 22, [1863], folder 82, Beecher-Stowe Collection, SchL. HBS to Hatty Stowe, n.d. (postmarked November 27, 1863), folder 127, Beecher-Stowe Collection, SchL.

74. HBS to Hatty Stowe, "Thursday Eve" (postmarked December 3, 1863), folder 127, Beecher-Stowe Collection, SchL.

75. Frances Foote Godkin to Katherine Rockwell, n.d. [c. December,1863], Foote Collection, SD. CES to HBS, n.d. [November, 1856?], Acquisitions, SD.

76. HBS to Eliza, Hatty, and Georgiana Stowe, June 1, 1862, folder 115, Beecher-Stowe Collection, SchL; HBS to Hatty Stowe, "Thursday Eve" (postmarked December 3, 1863), folder 127, Beecher-Stowe Collection, SchL.

77. HBS to Hatty Stowe, January 26, [1861], folder 106, Beecher-Stowe Collection, SchL.

78. HBS to Hatty and Eliza Stowe, August 14, [1859], folder 105, Beecher-Stowe Collection, SchL.

79. HBS to Hatty Stowe, November 2, 1863, Folder 126, Beecher-Stowe Collection, SchL. For electrical treatments, see HBS to Hatty Stowe, November 2, 1863, folder 126, Beecher-Stowe Collection, SchL (the quote is from here); HBS to James Fields, November 3, 1863, Fields Papers, HL; and HBS to Hatty Stowe, n.d. (postmarked April 13), [1864], folder 131, Beecher-Stowe Collection, SchL. For sleeping pills, see HBS to Hatty Stowe, n.d. [December 17, 1863], folder 128, Beecher-

Stowe Collection, SchL. For Dr. Taylor's movement cure, see HBS to Sara Parton, October 21, 1868, Parton Papers, Smith College; HBS to Eliza and Hatty Stowe, December 15, [1869], folder 150, Beecher-Stowe Collection, SchL; and HBS to CES, September 2, [1871], folder 89, Beecher-Stowe Collection, SchL.

80. HBS to [Frederick William] Gunn, copy in another hand, October 12, [1862], Beecher Family Papers, SML; Charley Stowe to CES, November 3, 1863, folder 296, SchL; Charley Stowe to HBS, December 1862, folder 296, Beecher-Stowe Collection, SchL.

81. HBS to [Frederick William] Gunn, January 18, 1864, Beecher Family Papers, SML. Charley Stowe to CES, January 22, 1864, folder 296, Beecher-Stowe Collection, SchL. Adam Korpalski, *The Gunnery, 1850–1975: A Documentary History of Private Education in America* (Washington, Conn.: Adam Korpalski, 1977), 19.

82. HBS to [Frederick William] Gunn, January 18, 1864, June 6 [and 7], [1864], and July 21, 1864—all in Beecher Family Papers, SML. HBS to Annie Fields, November 29, 1864, Fields Papers, HL.

Chapter 24

1. HBS to Eliza, Hatty, and Georgiana Stowe, October 5, 1863, folder 125, Beecher-Stowe Collection, SchL.

2. HBS to Eliza, Hatty, and Georgiana Stowe, October 5, 1863, folder 125, Beecher-Stowe Collection, SchL. Harriet's figure of $500 per year seems ridiculously low as an estimate of her literary earnings. I suspect that she deliberately underrepresented this source of income as part of her austerity campaign.

3. Entry by Charles Stowe, December 27, 1913, Stowe Guest Book; HBS to CES, November 16, 1862, pasted in Stowe Guest Book, Katharine S. Day Collection, SD.

4. HBS to CES and children, October 8, [1862], folder 80, Beecher-Stowe Collection, SchL.

5. HBS to James Fields, November 3, 1863, Fields Papers, HL.

6. HBS to the Duchess of Argyle, June 1, 1863, Harriet Beecher Stowe Collection, UVa.

7. James M. McPherson, *Battle Cry of Freedom: The Civil War Era* (New York: Oxford University Press, 1988), 686.

8. HBS to James Fields, October 12, 1863, Harriet Beecher Stowe Collection, UVa; HBS to James Fields, October 27, [1863], Fields Papers, HL.

9. James Fields to HBS, October 29, 1863, folder 261, Beecher-Stowe Collection, SchL.

10. HBS, *Household Papers and Stories* (Boston: Houghton Mifflin, 1896), 15. here after cited parenthetically in the text as HP.

11. This was suggested to me by Wilson's comment that her *House and Home Papers* had "much of the flavour of the *Autocrat* in them"; see Wilson, *Crusader in Crinoline*, 496.

12. From the data he analyzed Lawrence Buell concluded that although "nineteenth-century New England women writers were actually more professionalized than their male counterparts," the domination of the marketplace by men led to "male consolidation of power, including power over canon formation, rather than the female literary culture that accounted for a greater percentage of the literary producers and consumers of the period than a roll call of eminent literary names would suggest" (*New England Literary Culture*, 54.)

13. I have borrowed here the apt words of Richard Brodhead describing the "museum world" in which Hawthorne set *The Marble Faun*; see *The School of Hawthorne*, 72.

14. HBS to James Fields, November 3, 1863, Fields Papers, HL.

15. For this portrait of Holmes I have drawn on Roman, *Annie Adams Fields*, 135–36, and Higginson, *Cheerful Yesterdays*, 88–89.

16. HBS to William Lloyd Garrison, in another hand, November,1867, BPL.

17. HBS to Annie Fields, "Monday morning somewhere in December 1867 for sartin," Fields Papers, HL. For Stowe's interest in the work of Elizabeth Comstock, a Quaker who visited the penitentiaries, army hospitals, and camps, see HBS to Annie Fields, November 29, 1864, Fields Papers, HL.

18. Caskey, *Chariot of Fire*, 193.

19. Kaplan, *Mr. Clemens and Mark Twain*, 182.

20. HBS to Hatty Stowe, April 9, [1864], folder 131, Beecher-Stowe Collection, SchL.

21. HBS to Hatty Stowe, April 9, [1864], and n.d. (postmarked April 13), [1864], folder 131, Beecher-Stowe Collection, SchL.

22. HBS to Annie Fields, May 1, [1864], Fields Papers, HL.

23. HBS to James Fields, June 3, 1864, Fields Papers, HL.

24. HBS to James Fields, March 2, [1864], Fields Papers, HL.

25. All of the information about her proposed continuation of the domestic papers is from HBS to James Fields, n.d. [before November 9], [1864], Fields Papers, HL. For Mme Demorest, see Frank Luther Mott, *A History of American Magazines*, 5 vols. (Cambridge, Mass.: Harvard University Press, 1938), 3:325.

26. HBS to Henry Ward Beecher, February 2, 1864, Beecher Family Papers, SML.

27. HBS to James Fields, n.d. [after November 29], [1864], Fields Papers, HL. On the personal cost of writing *Pearl* and *Agnes* simultaneously, see HBS to Hatty, Eliza, and Georgiana Stowe, October 5, 1863, folder 125, Beecher-Stowe Collection, SchL.

28. CES to HBS, April 1, 1868, Acquisitions, SD.

29. HBS to James Fields, September 6, [1865], Fields Papers, HL. For the many editions of *Little Foxes*, see Margaret Holbrook Hildreth, *Harriet Beecher Stowe: A Bibliography* (Hamden, Conn.: Archon Books, 1976), 88–89. The royalty figures are from the manuscript business records of Ticknor and Fields, MS Am 2030–2 (47), p. 166, HO.

30. William G. McLoughlin, *The Meaning of Henry Ward Beecher: An Essay on the Shifting Values of Mid-Victorian America, 1840–1870*, (New York: Alfred A. Knopf, 1970), 176–77.

31. In *The Marble Faun* Hawthorne demonstrated this point in the career of Hilda, the copyist, whose reverence for the Old Masters was so great that she renounced her own pretensions to art; see Brodhead, *The School of Hawthorne*, 80.

32. HBS to Annie Fields, August 16, 1867, Fields Papers, HL. HBS to James Fields, July 13, [1867?], Fields Papers, HL. James Russell Lowell reportedly refused to undertake the editorship of the *Atlantic* unless Nichols, who had edited his poems, agreed to read proof; Nichols's services went well beyond reading proof to correcting authors when they misquoted authorities or fell into grammatical inaccuracies. For George Nichols, see Arthur Gilman, "Atlantic Dinners and Diners," *Atlantic Monthly*, November 1907, p. 647.

33. HBS to Mrs. Reed, September, [1866], Harriet Beecher Stowe Collection, UVa.

34. HBS to Jame Fields, December, [1866?], Fields Papers, HL. See also HBS to James Fields, August 11, [1864], HO.

35. For the importance of Robert Bonner and the *New York Ledger* to women's writing, see Mary Kelley, *Private Woman, Public Stage*, 3–6, and passim. Bonner paid Henry Ward Beecher $25,000 for the serialization of *Norwood*.

36. HBS to James Fields, September 6, [1865], HL.

37. Wilson, *Crusader in Crinoline*, 510.

38. HBS to James Fields, n.d. ("Sunday Eve"), [1865], Fields Papers, HL.

39. HBS to James Fields, May 16, [1865], and HBS to James Fields, June 18, 1865, Fields Papers, HL.

40. HBS to James Fields, May 16, [1865], Fields Papers, HL.

41. HBS to James Fields, n.d. [1866], Fields Papers, HL.

42. HBS to James Fields, October 18, [1866], Fields Papers, HL.

43. HBS to James Fields, September 3, [1867], Fields Papers, HL.

44. HBS to CES, n.d. [1863–1864], folder 93, Beecher-Stowe Collection, SchL. See also HBS to CES, September 27, [1864?], folder 83, Beecher-Stowe Collection, SchL.

45. HBS to Annie Fields, November 29, 1864, Fields Papers, HL. See HBS, "The New Year," HP, 425–37.

46. Fred Stowe to HBS, January 6, 1864, copy in HBS's hand, folder 267a, Beecher-Stowe Collection, SchL. See also HBS to Catharine Beecher and Mary Beecher Perkins, n.d. [1867?], folder 97, Beecher-Stowe Collection, SchL.

47. Isabella Beecher Hooker to John Hooker, October 16, 1864, Isabella Hooker Collection, SD.

48. HBS to "Daughters all," November 13, 1864, folder 133, Beecher-Stowe Collection, SchL.

49. HBS to [Duchess of Argyle], February 19, 1866, Harriet Beecher Stowe Collection, UVa.

50. HBS to [Duchess of Argyle], February 19, 1866, Harriet Beecher Stowe Collection, UVa.

51. HBS to William Lloyd Garrison, January 2, 1866, BPL.

52. William Lloyd Garrison to Annie Fields, February 2, 1865, Fields Papers, HL.

53. HBS to [Duchess of Argyle], February 19, 1866, Harriet Beecher Stowe Collection, UVa.

54. HBS to Henry Ward Beecher, October 8, 1866, Beecher Family Papers, SML.

55. HBS to Eunice and Henry Beecher, September 23, [c. 1866], Beecher Family Papers, SML.

56. HBS to James Fields, June 18, 1865, Fields Papers, HL. See HBS, "The Noble Army of Martyrs," HP, 438–48.

57. CES to James Fields, December 6, 1866, Fields Papers, HL.

58. HBS to James Fields, October 18, [1866], Fields Papers, HL.

59. HBS to James Fields, n.d. (after October 18, [1866]), Fields Papers, HL.

60. HBS to James Fields, February 8, [1867], Fields Papers, HL.

61. HBS to James Fields, February 9, 1867, Fields Papers, HL.

62. HBS to James Fields, August 8, [1867], Fields Papers, HL.

63. HBS to James Parton, February 6, 1868, Parton Papers, Smith College.

64. CES to HBS, April 1, 1868, Acquisitions, SD.

65. HBS to James Fields, February 9, 1867, Fields Papers, HL.

Chapter 25

1. Robert Tomes, "The Americans on Their Travels," *Harper's New Monthly Magazine* (June, 1865), p. 57. I thank William Stowe for this reference.

2. Mabel Abigail Dodge (Gail Hamilton) to CES, July 11, 1870, folder 257, Beecher-Stowe Collection, SchL.

3. HBS to Charles Beecher, May 29, 1867, in C. E. Stowe, *Life*, 401–2. HBS to Henry [Allen], n.d. [February, 1867], Harriet Beecher Stowe Collection, UVa.

4. HBS to CES and children, March 10, 1867, folder 85, Beecher-Stowe Collection, SchL.

5. HBS to CES and children, March 10, 1867, folder 85, Beecher-Stowe Collection, SchL.

6. Arthur Foote to Eliza Foote, April 4, 1867, Foote Papers, SD.

7. HBS to Charles Beecher, incomplete, April 17, 1867, folder 98, Beecher-Stowe Collection, SchL.

8. CES to James Fields, March 23, 1867, Fields Papers, HL.

9. HBS to Hatty Stowe, April [7, 1867], folder 138, Beecher-Stowe Collection, SchL.

10. HBS to Lady Amberley, June 23, 1870, copy, SD; original in the Library of Congress.

11. HBS to CES, March 11, [1868?], folder 86, Beecher-Stowe Collection, SchL.

12. HBS to James Fields, [February, 1864], Fields Papers, HL.

13. HBS to James Fields, February 8, [1867], Fields Papers, HL.

14. HBS to James Fields, February 8, [1867], Fields Papers, HL.

15. HBS to James Fields, February 19, [1867], Fields Papers, HL.

16. For Calvin Stowe as audience for *Oldtown Folks*, see HBS to James Fields, February 9, 1867, Fields Papers, HL, and CES to HBS, April 1, 1868, Acquisitions, SD.

17. HBS to James Fields, n.d. [1868?], Fields Papers, HL.

18. HBS to James Fields, January 20, [1867], Fields Papers, HL. Oliver Wendell Holmes, "The Guardian Angel," serialized in the *Atlantic Monthly* January 1867 to December 1867.

19. HBS, "The Mourning Veil," *Atlantic Monthly*, November 1857, pp. 63–70. In Stowe's story a prosperous mother is sent by accident a mourning veil in an order of hats and other gay apparel. After her daughter dies unexpectedly, the mother dons the veil. In the sententious voice of Hawthorne's "The Minister's Black Veil," Stowe asks, "But how did the flowers of home, the familiar elms, the distant smiling prospect look through its gloomy folds,—emblem of the shadow which had fallen between her heart and life? . . . Now the outer world comes to thee through the *mourning veil*!"

20. Stowe v. Thomas, Circuit Court, E. D. Pennyslvania, October Term, 1853, Case No. 13,514, in Steven and Toledo, *Federal Cases, Circuit and District Courts* (1789–1880), vol. 23, p. 207.

21. HBS to James Fields, January 20, [1867], Fields Papers, HL.

22. See Tompkins, *Sensational Designs*, 10–11, and Brodhead, *The School of Hawthorne*, 15n24.

23. Brodhead, *The School of Hawthorne*, 80. I am drawing on Brodhead's discussion, 55–57, of Fields's simultaneous creation of "literature" as a market category and of Hawthorne as a classic writer.

24. I am drawing here on Brodhead, *The School of Hawthorne*, 17–47.

25. HBS to James Fields, n.d. [1868?], Fields Papers, HL.

26. HBS to James Fields, August 8, [1867], Fields Papers, HL.

27. HBS to Annie Fields, August 16, 1867, Fields Papers, HL.

28. HBS to James Fields, February 19, [1867], Fields Papers, HL.

29. HBS to James Fields, August 8, [1867], Fields Papers, HL.

30. HBS to Annie Fields, August 16, 1867, Fields Papers, HL.

31. Annie Fields, *Life,* 316.

32. HBS to Annie Fields, July 27, 1868, Fields Papers, HL.

33. HBS to Hatty and Eliza Stowe, August 10, 1865, folder 134, Beecher-Stowe Collection, SchL.

34. Isabella Beecher Hooker to Alice Day, July [13], 1867, Isabella Hooker Collection, SD.

35. HBS to Eliza and Hatty Stowe, n.d. [September?, 1867?], folder 139, Beecher-Stowe Collection, SchL. I suspect that this letter was written in September 1867, for by December of that year it would appear that Fred had been institutionalized for three months.

36. HBS to Eliza and Hatty Stowe, n.d. [December?, 1867?], folder 139, Beecher-Stowe Collection, SchL.

37. Fred Stowe to Eliza and Hatty Stowe, December 15, 1867, folder 288, Beecher-Stowe Collection, SchL.

38. HBS to Rebecca Harding Davis, January 31, [1869], Harriet Beecher Stowe Collection, UVa.

39. HBS to James Fields, n. d. [February? 1868?], Fields Papers, HL.

40. HBS to James Fields, n.d. [October, 1867], Fields Papers, HL. See also HBS to James Fields, October 19, [1867], Fields Papers, HL.

41. HBS to James Fields, n.d. [1867], Fields Papers, HL.

42. HBS to James Fields, n.d. [after November 21], [1867], Fields Papers, HL.

43. HBS to James Parton, February 6, 1868, Parton Papers, Smith College.

44. James Parton to HBS, February 14, 1868, folder 255, Beecher-Stowe Collection, SchL.

45. HBS to James Fields, n.d. [1868], Fields Papers, HL. HBS, "Little Captain Trott," *Atlantic Monthly,* March 1869, pp. 300–304. HBS, "Tribute of a Loving Friend to the Memory of a Noble Woman," *Atlantic Monthly,* February, 1869, pp. 242–250.

46. HBS to James Fields, per secretary, December 24, 1868, Fields Papers, HL.

47. HBS to James Fields, "Private," n.d. [c. July, 1868], Fields Papers, HL.

48. HBS to Eliza and Hatty Stowe, December 4, [1869], folder 150, Beecher-Stowe Collection, SchL.

49. HBS to Mrs. Underwood, December 31, [1869], Harriet Beecher Stowe Collection, UVa.

50. HBS to Eliza and Hatty Stowe, April [or March] 17, 1869, folder 145, Beecher-Stowe Collection, SchL.

51. HBS to Charles Stowe, May 29, 1867, in C. E. Stowe, *Life,* 402.

52. HBS to Annie Fields, March 13, 1868, Fields Papers, HL.

53. HBS to Hatty [and Eliza] Stowe, September 25, [1869], folder 149, Beecher-Stowe Collection, SchL.

54. Caskey, *Chariot of Fire,* 203.

55. HBS to Hatty Stowe, n.d. (postmarked April 8) [1869], folder 146, Beecher-Stowe Collection, SchL.

56. HBS to Hatty Stowe, April 12, [1868?], folder 140, Beecher-Stowe Collection, SchL.

57. HBS to Henry Ward Beecher, October 8, 1866, Beecher Family Papers, SML.

58. HBS to CES and children, March 10, 1867, folder 85, Beecher-Stowe Collection, SchL.

59. Alice Dike to HBS, February 17, 1868, Acquisitions, SD.

60. HBS to Annie Fields, first pages missing, [after April 8], [1869], Fields Papers, HL. For a discussion of Annie's involvement with charity work, see Roman, *Annie Adams Fields*, 75–88.

61. HBS to William Lloyd Garrison, in the hand of a secretary, November 9, 1868, Katharine S. Day Collection, SD.

62. HBS to Henry Ward Beecher, first part missing, n.d. [c. 1868], Beecher Family Papers, SML.

63. HBS to "Dear Sir," n.d. [c. 1868–70], Katharine S. Day Collection, SD.

64. Christopher Foote to George Foote, November 7, 1869, Foote Collection, SD. C. E. Stowe, *Life*, 402.

65. HBS, *Oldtown Folks*, 2 vols. (Boston: Houghton, Mifflin, 1896) 1:33; hereafter cited parenthetically in the text as OF.

66. HBS to James Fields, in the hand of a secretary, December 24, 1868, Fields Papers, HL.

67. HBS to James Fields, n.d. [1868 or 1869], Fields Papers, HL.

68. Henry May, "Introduction," *Oldtown Folks*, edited by Henry May (Cambridge, Mass.: Harvard University Press, 1966), 35.

69. Maria Weston Chapman to HBS, July 6, [1869], folder 254, Beecher-Stowe Collection, SchL.

70. Lydia Maria Child to Harriet Sewall, September 30, 1869, in *The Collected Correspondence of Lydia Maria Child, 1817–1880,* ed. Patricia Holland, Milton-Meltzer, and Francine Krasno (Millwood, N.Y.: Kraus Microform, 1980), microform 72, letter 1908. I am grateful to Caroline Karcher for this reference.

71. May, "Introduction," 36.

72. HBS to James Fields, n.d. [before May 15], [1869], Fields Papers, HL.

73. HBS to Hatty Stowe, May 18, 1869, folder 147, Beecher-Stowe Collection, SchL.

74. HBS to Rebecca Harding Davis, January 31, [1869], Harriet Beecher Stowe Collection, UVa.

75. "Mrs. Stowe's 'Oldtown Folks,'" *Nation*, June 3, 1869, p. 437.

76. HBS to Annie Fields, misdated by Stowe May 9, [June 9, 1869], Fields Papers, HL.

77. HBS to James Fields, May 10, 1870, Fields Papers, HL.

78. Bret Harte, "Review of *Oldtown Folks*," *Overland Monthly*, October 1869, p. 390, reprinted in Ammons, ed., *Critical Essays*, 206.

79. HBS to J. R. Osgood, July 6, [1869], HO.

80. HBS to J. R. Osgood, n.d. [1869], Fields Papers, HL.

81. Roman, *Annie Adams Fields*, 73–75, 89. HBS to Annie Fields, November 29, 1864, Fields Papers, HL.

82. HBS to J. R. Osgood, June 30, [1869], Fields Papers, HL.

83. HBS to James Fields, August 14, [1869], Fields Papers, HL.

84. HBS to James Fields, February 13, 1870, Fields Papers, HL.

85. Wilson, *Crusader in Crinoline*, 531.

86. HBS to E. L. Godkin, draft, [Summer, 1869], folder 256, Beecher-Stowe Collection, SchL.

87. HBS to Annie Fields, misdated by Stowe May 9, [June 9, 1869], Fields Papers, HL.

88. Mott, *History of American Magazines*, 3:332–33; the quote from Clapp is in Chielens, *American Literary Magazines*, 361. The bias against literary women evident in the *North American Review*, *Knickerbocker's*, *Graham's Magazine*, and the *Atlantic Monthly* was pronounced enough to draw comment from literary historian Fred Pattee, as Fetterley notes, "Introduction," *Provisions*, 19.

89. "Review of *Chimney Corner*," *Nation*, April 23, 1868, pp. 334–35, reprinted in Ammons, ed., *Critical Essays*, 203-5.

90. Mott, *History of American Magazines*, 3:339.

91. HBS to E. L. Godkin, draft, [Summer, 1869], folder 256, Beecher-Stowe Collection, SchL.

92. The information in this paragraph is drawn from a letter Isabella Beecher Hooker sent to the *Nation*; see I.B.H. [Isabella Beecher Hooker] to the Editor, *Nation*, November 12, 1868, pp. 391–93. See also HBS, "A Brave Noble Book," *National Anti-Slavery Standard*, December 31, 1868, p. 3 (from the *Hartford Courant*).

93. Eleanor Flexner, *Century of Struggle: The Woman's Rights Movement in the United States* (Cambridge, Mass.: Belknap Press of Harvard University Press, 1959), 179–80. The Sorosis Club appealed to professional women, who at this time were primarily literary women. A list of members published in conjunction with its second anniversary included "thirty-eight engaged in literature, six editors, twelve poets, six musical artists, twenty-five authors, two physicians, four professors, two artists in painting, nine workers in art, nine teachers, ten lecturers, one historian, one author of scientific works, and three known philanthropists." See "Sorosis," *Revolution*, March 31, 1870, p. 202.

94. "Dallas Galbraith," *Nation*, October 22, 1868, p. 330.

95. Mott, *History of American Magazines*, 3:334–35.

96. "Dallas Galbraith," *Nation*, October 22, 1868, pp. 330–31.

97. "Hedged In," *Nation*, April 14, 1870, pp. 244–45.

98. James had also written the scathing review of Davis's *Waiting for the Verdict* that Stowe had objected to; see Sharon M. Harris, *Rebecca Harding Davis and American Realism* (Philadelphia: Temple University Press, 1991), 136–37, 142.

99. "Dallas Galbraith," *Nation*, October 22, 1868, p.331. "Mrs. Stowe's 'Oldtown Folks,'" *Nation*, June 3, 1869, p.437.

100. "Injurious Works and Injurious Criticism," *Nation*, October 29, 1868, p. 346.

101. I.B.H. [Isabella Beecher Hooker] to the Editor, *Nation*, November 12, 1868, p. 392.

102. Theodore Tilton to Elizabeth Cady Stanton, November 1, 1868, *Revolution*, November 5, 1868, p. 273. This is precisely the context that Jane Tompkins recovers in "Sentimental Power: *Uncle Tom's Cabin* and the Politics of Literary History."

103. E.C.S. [Elizabeth Cady Stanton], "Anna E. Dickinson," *Revolution*, November 5, 1868), p. 261.

104. HBS to Sara Willis Parton, October 24, [1868], Parton Papers, Smith College.

Chapter 26

1. HBS to James Fields, November 6, [1868], Fields Papers, HL. Stowe's reply was published in the *National Anti-Slavery Standard*, December 31, 1868.

2. I.B.H. [Isabella Beecher Hooker] to the Editor, *Nation*, November 12, 1868,

pp. 391–92; Isabella Beecher Hooker to Robert Allen, November 28, 1868, Isabella Hooker Collection, SD.

3. As quoted in Angela Y. Davis, *Women, Race and Class* (New York: Random House, 1983), 82.

4. Elisabeth Griffith, *In Her Own Right: The Life of Elizabeth Cady Stanton* (New York: Oxford University Press, 1984), 123.

5. Griffith, *In Her Own Right*, 132–33.

6. "The McFarland Case," *Nation*, May 12, 1870, pp. 300–301. Ellen Carol DuBois, "Nineteenth Century Woman Suffrage Movement," in *Capitalist Patriarchy and the Case for Socialist Feminism*, ed. Zillah Eisenstein (New York: Monthly Review Press, [1978?], c. 1979), 145–46.

7. Ellen Carol DuBois, ed., *Elizabeth Cady Stanton/Susan B. Anthony: Correspondence, Writings, Speeches* (New York: Schocken Books, 1981), 95.

8. HBS to James Parton, copy in a contemporary hand, June 1, 1869, Parton Papers, Smith College.

9. Mary Beecher Perkins to HBS, March 10, [1850], White Collection, SD.

10. "The Byron Scandal," *Revolution*, October 28, 1869, pp. 262–63.

11. Gail Hamilton to her sister, October, 1867, in *Gail Hamilton's Life in Letters*, 2 vols., ed. H. Augusta Dodge (Boston: Lee and Shepard, 1901), 1:604.

12. James Parton to Mr. Osgood, June 12, 1869, Harriet Beecher Stowe Collection, UVa.

13. HBS to James Osgood, per secretary, June 23, 1869, Fields Papers, HL.

14. HBS, "The True Story of Lady Byron's Life," *Atlantic Monthly*, September 1869, pp. 295–313; quote is on p. 304.

15. Oliver Wendell Holmes to HBS, July 4, 1869, folder 258, Beecher-Stowe Collection, SchL.

16. Griffith, *In Her Own Right*, 127.

17. Susan B. Anthony to Paulina Wright Davis, n.d. [July or August, 1869], Isabella Hooker Collection, SD.

18. Griffith, *In Her Own Right*, 130.

19. Isabella Beecher Hooker to HBS, [April-May?], 1869, and Elizabeth Cady Stanton to Isabella Hooker, April 27, [1869], Isabella Hooker Collection, SD.

20. Elizabeth Cady Stanton to Paulina Wright Davis, n.d. [July or August 1869], Isabella Hooker Collection, SD.

21. Susan B. Anthony to Isabella Beecher Hooker, August 9 and [10], 1869, Isabella Hooker Collection, SD.

22. Elizabeth Cady Stanton to Paulina Wright Davis, n.d. [July or August 1869], Isabella Hooker Collection, SD.

23. HBS to Sara Willis Parton, February 15, [1868], Parton Papers, Smith College.

24. Gail Hamilton, *Woman's Wrongs: A Counter-Irritant* (Boston: Ticknor and Fields, 1868), 97.

25. HBS to Sara [Willis Parton], July 25, [1869], Parton Papers, Smith College.

26. HBS, "What Is and What Is Not the Point in the Woman Question," *Hearth and Home*, August 28, 1869, p. 568.

27. HBS, "The Woman Question," *Hearth and Home*, August 7, 1869, p. 520.

28. HBS, "What Is and What is Not the Point in the Woman Question," *Hearth and Home*, August 28, 1869, p. 520. In January 1871 Victoria Woodhull appeared before a congressional committee and made this same argument that women were already entitled to vote. Subsequently Stanton's National Woman's Suffrage Association embraced both Woodhull and her strategy and urged women to flock to the

polls; see DuBois, ed., *Elizabeth Cady Stanton/Susan B.Anthony*, 101–3; HBS to George Eliot, May 25, [1869], Berg Collection of English and American Literature, NYPL.

29. For Lucy Larcom, see HBS to Mr. Pettingill, February 10, 1869, Acquisitions, SD.

30. HBS to Ralph Waldo Emerson, 1869, HO. Emerson declined on the grounds of his already burdensome commitments; see Ralph Waldo Emerson to Isabella Beecher Hooker, October 9, 1869, Joseph K. Hooker Collection, SD.

31. Elizabeth Cady Stanton to Susan B. Anthony, December 28, 1869, as quoted in Griffith, *In Her Own Right*, 131. See also HBS and Isabella Beecher Hooker to Susan B. Anthony, [December, 1869], in Jeanne Boydston, Mary Kelley, and Anne Margolis, *The Limits of Sisterhood: The Beecher Sisters on Women's Rights and Woman's Sphere* (Chapel Hill: University of North Carolina Press, 1988), 278–79.

32. Susan B. Anthony to Isabella Beecher Hooker, n.d. [December,1869]; Susan B. Anthony to HBS and Isabella Beecher Hooker, December 29, 1869—both in Isabella Hooker Collection, SD. "The Born Thrall," *Revolution*, December 30, 1869, p. 408. I.B.H.[Isabella Beecher Hooker], "Happy New Year," *Revolution*, January 6, 1870, pp. 10–11.

33. HBS to William Dean Howells, n.d. [July, 1869], HO. HBS to Sara [Willis Parton], July 25, [1869], Parton Papers, Smith College.

34. HBS to Eliza and Hatty Stowe, n.d. (postmarked August 1), [1869], folder 148, Beecher-Stowe Collection, SchL.

35. HBS to Hatty Stowe, n.d. (postmarked August 16), [1869], folder 148, Beecher-Stowe Collection, SchL.

36. In her protest against the negative review of *Oldtown Folks* that appeared in the *Nation*, Stowe wrote, "The book is not sensational & can make no headway with those whose taste is formed by Lady Audley & Mrs. Henry Ward but the London Examiner & another English paper have notices as appreciative & more appreciative than I expected It is not a book to go with a rush"; see HBS to Annie Fields, May 9, [1869], Fields Papers, HL.

37. HBS to Sara and James Parton, n. d. [September? 1869], Parton Papers, Smith College.

38. Alice Crozier, "Harriet Beecher Stowe and Lady Byron," in Ammons, ed., *Critical Essays*, 191.

39. Harriet Beecher Stowe to Lady Byron, June 2, 1857, folder 245, Beecher-Stowe Collection, SchL.

40. HBS, "The True Story of Lady Byron's Life," 304.

41. "The Byron Controversy," newsclip, Byron Scrapbook, SD.

42. Justin McCarthy, "Mrs. Stowe's Last Romance," Letter to the Editor of the *Independent*, August 26, 1869, p. 1, reprinted in Ammons, ed., *Critical Essays*, 169–72.

43. HBS to William Patton, September 10, 1869, Authors Collection, Smith College.

44. "The Byron Controversy in Germany," Byron Scrapbook, SD.

45. Despatch from *Atlantic Telegraph*, London, September 3, [1869], Byron Scrapbook, SD.

46. HBS to James R. Osgood, n. d. [1869, after mid-August], Fields Papers, HL.

47. HBS to Sara and James Parton, n.d. [September? 1869], Parton Collection, Smith College.

48. "The Moral of the Byron Case," *Revolution*, September 9, 1869, p. 152. Also published in *Independent*, September 9, 1869, p. 1, and reprinted in Ammons, ed., *Critical Essays*, 174–76.

49. Elizabeth Cady Stanton to Isabella Beecher Hooker, September 1, 1869, Isabella Hooker Collection, SD.

50. "The Moral of the Byron Case," *Revolution*, September 9, 1869, p. 152. Lydia Maria Child also came strongly to Stowe's defense in "The Byron Controversy," *Independent*, October 14, 1869, p. 1. Child, who had heard the outline of the story about the Byrons from Mrs. Follen, took a line of argument similar to Stowe's and defended Lady Byron as "a Christian saint." I am grateful to Caroline Karcher for this reference.

51. Linda Gordon, *Woman's Body, Woman's Right*, 104; emphasis in original.

52. In only a few places does Stowe place her material in the wider context of women's inequality. Near the conclusion of her expanded 482-page investigation she asks, "Is it true, then, that a woman has not the same right to individual justice that a man has?"; see *Lady Byron Vindicated: A History of the Byron Controversy, from Its Beginning in 1816 to the Present Time* (Boston: Fields, Osgood, & Co., 1870), 405.

53. HBS to William Patton, September 10, 1869, Authors Collection, Smith College.

54. "The Byron Revelations," *Independent*, August 26, 1869, Byron Scrapbook, SD.

55. James Russell Lowell to Edmund Quincy, September 15, 1869, in *New Letters of James Russell Lowell*, ed. M. A. DeWolfe Howe (New York: Harper & Brothers, 1932), 146.

56. Henry Ward Beecher to HBS, August 24, 1869, Katharine S. Day Collection, SD.

57. HBS to James R. Osgood, n.d. [after mid-August], [1869], Fields Papers, HL.

58. HBS to Fields and Osgood, in another hand, September 23, 1869, Fields Papers, HL.

59. HBS to James R. Osgood, October 16, [1869], Fields Papers, HL.

60. Card signed by CES, n.d. [1869], Fields Papers, HL.

61. HBS to James R. Osgood, n.d. [1869], Fields Papers, HL.

62. HBS to Osgood, n.d. [1869], Fields Papers, HL.

63. HBS to Osgood, n.d. [1869], Fields Papers, HL.

64. Isabella Beecher Hooker to Fields and Osgood, November 29, [1869], Fields Papers, HL.

65. Caskey, *Chariot of Fire*, 315. The address of Dr. Taylor's is recorded in HBS to "children," December 25, 1872, folder 156, Beecher-Stowe Collection, SchL.

66. HBS to Hatty and Eliza Stowe, n.d. (postmarked November 22), [1869], n.d. (postmarked December 4), [1869], and n.d. [December 7, 1869]—all in folder 150, Beecher-Stowe Collection, SchL.

67. HBS to Hatty and Eliza Stowe, n.d. [November–December,1869], folder 150, Beecher-Stowe Collection, SchL.

68. HBS to William Patton, September 2, 1869, Acquisitions, SD.

69. HBS to Henry Ward Beecher, n.d. [after mid-August, 1869], Beecher Family Papers, SML.

70. In "Tried as by Fire," Woodhull claims she was married at fourteen and that her son's retardation stemmed from her having ignorantly "surrender[ed] my maternal functions to a drunken man." Her biographer, underscoring her tendency

to exaggerate the perfidy of her first husband, says she was not yet sixteen when she married Canning Woodhull (who was an alcoholic) and that her son's problems were not congenital but stemmed from a fall from a window at age two; see Emanie Sachs, *The Terrible Siren: Victoria Woodhull, 1838–1927* (New York: Harper and Brothers, 1928), 22, 26. It is conceivable that her son was under the care of her drunken husband at the time of the fall.

71. In response to statements at the Rutland Free Convention of 1858, Stephen S. Foster announced that "every family is a little embryo plantation, and every woman is a slave breeder,—in the eye of her husband is a slave, and the breeder of slaves,— and hence comes all the trouble"; quoted in Perry, *Radical Abolitionism*, 230. For a splendid discussion of the slavery/marriage analogy, see Braude, *Radical Spirits*, 130– 31.

72. HBS to Eliza and Hatty Stowe, n.d. (postmarked December 4), [1869], and "Tuesday" [probably December 7], [1869], both in folder 150, Beecher-Stowe Collection, SchL.

73. CES to James Fields, January 1, 1870, and HBS to James Fields, January 1, [1870]—both in Fields Papers, HL.

74. HBS to Hatty and Eliza Stowe, December 15, [1869], folder 150, Beecher Family Papers, SchL.

75. HBS to Annie Fields, n.d. [c.1870], Fields Papers, HL.

76. HBS to Horace Greeley, December 19, 1869, quoted in Wilson, *Crusader in Crinoline*, 546–47.

77. Notice of *Lady Byron Vindicated*, *Nation*, January 6, 1870, p. 2.

78. HBS to George Eliot, December 10, 1869, in Haight, ed., *The George Eliot Letters*, 5:71.

79. From *Fun Magazine*, 1869, reproduced in Wilson, *Crusader in Crinoline*, opposite p. 538.

80. Howe, *The "Atlantic Monthly" and its Makers*, 49–50.

81. "The Christian Union," *Revolution*, January 6, 1870, p. 7.

82. HBS to Henry Ward Beecher, first pages missing, n.d. [c. 1874–1875], Beecher Family Papers, SML.

83. HBS to Henry [and Eunice] Beecher, August 30, [1859], Beecher Family Papers, SML.

84. HBS to CES, n.d. [1870], folder 88, Beecher-Stowe Collection, SchL.

85. Wilson, *Crusader in Crinoline*, 556–57.

86. HBS to Henry Ward Beecher, October 13, [1870s], Beecher Family Papers, SML.

87. Eugene Benson, "George Sand and the Marriage Question," *Revolution*, July 7, 1870, pp. 1–2.

88. HBS to Henry Ward Beecher, n.d. [June?, 1870], Beecher Family Papers, SML.

89. HBS to [Mary Ashton (Rice)] Livermore, n.d. [August?, 1870], BPL.

90. HBS to Henry Ward Beecher, n.d. [June?, 1870], Beecher Family Papers, SML.

91. HBS to Henry Ward Beecher, n.d. [July?, 1870], Beecher Family Papers, SML.

92. HBS to Henry Ward Beecher, n.d. [July?, 1870], Beecher Family Papers, SML.

93. HBS to Henry Ward Beecher, n.d. [June?, 1870], Beecher Family Papers, SML.

94. "Another Delicate Subject," *Nation*, July 14, 1870, pp. 21–23.

95. HBS to Henry Ward Beecher, n.d. [August?, 1870], Beecher Family Papers, SML.

96. HBS to [Henry Ward Beecher], 1st two pages missing, reply to the *Nation*, n.d. [July?, 1870], Beecher Family Papers, SML.

97. HBS to Henry Ward Beecher, n.d. [July? 1870], Beecher Family Papers, SML.

98. HBS to [Mary Ashton (Rice)] Livermore, n.d. [August?, 1870], BPL.

99. *Nation,* June 9, 1870, p. 360.

100. HBS to [Mary Ashton (Rice)] Livermore, n.d. [August?, 1870], BPL.

101. Boydston, Kelley, and Margolis, *The Limits of Sisterhood,* 279–80ff.

102. Lydia Maria Child to Lucy Osgood, February 12, 1872, in Child, *Collected Correspondence,* microform 77, letter 2038. I am grateful to Caroline Karcher for this reference.

103. HBS to Henry Ward Beecher, June 21, 1870, Beecher Family Papers, SML.

104. HBS to [Edward Everett] Hale, April 14, 1869, Acquisitions, SD.

105. HBS, *Pink and White Tyranny* (Boston: Houghton Mifflin, 1896), 424.

106. Victoria C. Woodhull, "Tried as by Fire; or, The True and the False Socially" (New York: Woodhull & Claflin, 1874), 6–7.

107. Isabella Beecher Hooker to Susan B. Anthony, March 11 and 14, 1871, Isabella Hooker Collection, SD.

108. Catharine Beecher to Leonard Bacon, March 9, 1872, Collection of American Literature, BL.

109. See DuBois, ed., *Stanton/Anthony,* 105.

110. This series of events is recounted in HBS to Henry Ward Beecher, December 22, 1872, Beecher Family Papers, SML.

111. HBS to Hatty and Eliza Stowe, December 19, 1872, folder 156, Beecher-Stowe Collection, SchL.

112. HBS to George Eliot, March 18, 1876, Berg Collection of English and American Literature, NYPL.

113. HBS to [Mrs. Mary Claflin], August 22, 1874, copy, SD; original in the Hayes Library.

114. HBS to Mary Claflin, [December 24, 1872], copy, SD; original in the Hayes Library.

115. HBS to Henry Ward Beecher, "Sunday Eve^g" [c. 1872], Beecher Family Papers, SML.

116. HBS to [Duchess of Argyle] n.d. [late winter–early spring 1871], Harriet Beecher Stowe Collection, UVa. HBS to [Elizabeth Lyman], n.d., copy, SD; original in the Connecticut State Library.

117. HBS to Eliza Stowe, May 11, 1873, folder 157, Beecher-Stowe Collection, SchL.

118. HBS to "My dear Jack," n.d., Beecher Family Papers, SML.

119. HBS to Henry Ward Beecher, n.d., Beecher Family Papers, SML.

120. HBS to Eunice Beecher, January 13, 1876, Beecher Family Papers, SML.

121. HBS, *Pink and White Tyranny,* 455.

122. HBS, *My Wife and I; or Harry Henderson's History* (Boston: Houghton Mifflin, 1896), 92.

123. HBS to Mrs. Underwood, December 31, [n.y.], Harriet Beecher Stowe Collection, UVa. When J. B. Ford & Co. brought it out in book form, *My Wife and I* sold over 50,000 copies. If Stowe's reputation was declining in the wake of the Byron scandal, it still had a long way to go.

Chapter 27

1. HBS to Annie Fields, November 2, 1870, and November 4, 1870, Fields Papers, HL.

2. HBS to Mary Beecher Perkins [October 19 or 26, 1870], Helen D. Perkins Collection, SD.

3. HBS to Mary Beecher Perkins, [October 19 or 26, 1870], Helen D. Perkins Collection, SD; HBS to Hatty Stowe, October 11, 1870, folder 151, Beecher-Stowe Collection, SchL.

4. HBS to Mary Beecher Perkins, October 11, [1870], Helen D. Perkins Collection, SD.

5. See, for example, HBS to Mary Beecher Perkins, December 3, 1879, folder 99, Beecher-Stowe Collection, SchL.

6. HBS to Hatty and Eliza Stowe, October 30, 1870, folder 151, Beecher-Stowe Collection, SchL.

7. HBS to Mary Beecher Perkins, October 15, [1870], Helen D. Perkins Collection, SD.

8. HBS to Mary Beecher Perkins, [October 19 or 26, 1870], Helen D. Perkins Collection, SD.

9. Henry Ward Beecher to Lyman Beecher, March 18, 1843, folder 41, Beecher-Stowe Collection, SchL.

10. Harriet Foote to Eliza Foote, March 2[9] and 30, April 1, 6, and 7, 1837, Foote Collection, SD.

11. William H. Beecher to Beecher family, August 21, 1841, Acquisitions, Circular Letters, SD.

12. HBS, "A Look Beyond the Veil," *Christian Union*, November 5, 1870, p. 277, clipping at SD.

13. Fred Stowe to HBS, February 5, 1871, folder 288, Beecher-Stowe Collection, SchL.

14. HBS to [Annie Fields], December 27, 1874, Fields Papers, HL.

15. HBS to Hatty and Eliza Stowe, April [or March] 17, 1869, folder 145, Beecher-Stowe Collection, SchL. HBS to Hatty Stowe, April 12, [1868], folder 140, Beecher-Stowe Collection, SchL.

16. I am indebted for this perceptive observation to Esther Robbins, a tour guide at the Stowe House in Hartford.

17. HBS to James Fields, May 10, 1870, Fields Papers, HL.

18. HBS to Annie Fields, March 2, 1872, Fields Papers, HL.

19. HBS to George Eliot, April 15, 1869, Berg Collection of English and American Literature, NYPL.

20. HBS to George Eliot, February 8, 1872, Berg Collection of English and American Literature, NYPL.

21. HBS to Annie Fields, April 30, [1872], Fields Papers, HL. See also C. E. Stowe, *Life*, 491.

22. HBS to Annie Fields, August 21, 1872, Fields Papers, HL. HBS to Hannah Foote, August 5, 1872, Foote Collection, SD; HBS to Annie Fields, August 20, [1872], Fields Papers, HL.

23. HBS to Mary Claflin, October 10, 1872, copy, SD; original in Hayes Library.

24. HBS to CES, n.d., in C. E. Stowe, *Life*, 493.

25. HBS to Hatty and Eliza Stowe, November 9, [1872], folder 155, Beecher-Stowe Collection, SchL.

26. HBS to Annie Fields, November 22, 1872, Fields Papers, HL.

27. HBS to Hatty and Eliza Stowe, November 9, [1872], folder 155, Beecher-Stowe Collection, SchL.

28. HBS to Hatty and Eliza Stowe, December 25, 1872, folder 156, Beecher-Stowe Collection, SchL.

29. HBS to CES, March 11, [1868?], folder 86, Beecher-Stowe Collection, SchL.

30. HBS to Hatty and Eliza Stowe, December 19, 1872, folder 156, Beecher-Stowe Collection, SchL.

31. HBS to Hatty and Eliza Stowe, December 19, 1872, folder 156, Beecher-Stowe Collection, SchL.

32. HBS to "children," misdated by Stowe September 23, [December 23, 1872], folder 156, Beecher-Stowe Collection, SchL.

33. HBS to Charles Stowe, September 28, [1873], folder 186, Beecher-Stowe Collection, SchL.

34. HBS to Charles Stowe, September 28, [1873], folder 186, Beecher-Stowe Collection, SchL.

35. Hatty Stowe to Eliza Stowe, October 12, [1873], folder 269, Beecher-Stowe Collection, SchL.

36. Hatty Stowe to Eliza Stowe, October 19, [1873], and Hatty Stowe to Eliza Stowe, October 26, 1873, folder 269, Beecher-Stowe Collection, SchL.

37. Hatty Stowe to Eliza Stowe, October 26, 1873, folder 269, Beecher-Stowe Collection, SchL.

38. Hatty Stowe to Eliza Stowe, October 12, [1873], folder 269, Beecher-Stowe Collection, SchL.

39. Hatty Stowe to Eliza Stowe, October 26, 1873, folder 269, Beecher-Stowe Collection, SchL.

40. Hatty Stowe to Eliza Stowe, October 26, 1873, folder 269, Beecher-Stowe Collection, SchL.

41. Hatty Stowe to Eliza Stowe, October 26, 1873, and November 2, 1873, folder 269, Beecher-Stowe Collection, SchL.

42. HBS to_____, incomplete letter, transcript, SD; original at the Oliver Wendell Holmes Library, Phillips Academy, Andover, Mass.

43. McCullough, *Brave Companions,* 50.

44. HBS to Mary Claflin, November 6, 1873, copy, SD; original in the Hayes Library. HBS to Charles Stowe, October 28, 1873, in C. E. Stowe, *Life,* 499.

45. HBS to [Annie Fields], December 27, 1874, Fields Papers, HL. Stowe makes a similar recommendation to Henry Ward Beecher; see HBS to Eunice Beecher, January 10, 1884, Beecher Family Papers, SML.

46. HBS to George [Bissell, her banker], November 4, 1873, folder 262, Beecher-Stowe Collection, SchL.

47. HBS to [James Redpath], February 13, 1874, Harriet Beecher Stowe Collection, UVa.

48. HBS to Mr. Williams, June 8, 1874, Katharine S. Day Collection, SD.

49. HBS, *Woman in Sacred History: A Series of Sketches Drawn from Scriptural, Historical, and Legendary Sources* (New York: J. B. Ford and Company, 1874), p. 2 of unpaginated introduction. HBS to Charles Stowe, September 27, 1879, folder 209, Beecher-Stowe Collection, SchL.

50. HBS, "Introduction," *Woman in Sacred History,* not paginated, but p. 2.

51. Mary De Jong calls attention to the tension in scripture biography between

"desires to claim the authority of sacred literature and to use the appeals of secular fiction," and she also comments on the "erotic fantasies" invited by the portrayals of biblical heroines; see Mary De Jong, "Dark-Eyed Daughters: Nineteenth-Century Popular Portrayals of Biblical Women," *Women's Studies: An Interdisciplinary Journal* 19, nos. 3–4 (1991):283–308, esp. 286, 293.

52. HBS to Susie Munroe Stowe, July 23, 1878, folder 201, Beecher-Stowe Collection, SchL.

53. HBS to Charles Stowe, October 8, 1877, folder 192, Beecher-Stowe Collection, SchL.

54. Eunice Beecher to HBS, October 27, 1877, folder 58, Beecher-Stowe Collection, SchL.

55. HBS to Susie Munroe Stowe, December 2, 1879, folder 214, and HBS to Mary Beecher Perkins, December 3, 1879, folder 99, Beecher-Stowe Collection, SchL.

56. HBS to Christopher Spencer Foote, December 8 and 9, [1878?], Acquisitions, SD.

57. HBS to Charles Stowe, February 5, 1879, folder 195, Beecher-Stowe Collection, SchL.

58. HBS to Susie Munroe Stowe, February 9, 1879, folder 204, Beecher-Stowe Collection, SchL.

59. Sklar, *Catharine Beecher*, 266, 329n17.

60. HBS to [Catharine Beecher], n.d., folder 100, Beecher-Stowe Collection, SchL. Sklar, *Catharine Beecher*, 272.

61. HBS to Mrs. Munroe, January 3, 1879, folder 207, Beecher-Stowe Collection, SchL.

62. HBS to Susie Munroe Stowe, March 8, 1882, folder 227, Beecher-Stowe Collection, SchL.

63. HBS to Susie Munroe Stowe, November 20, 1879, folder 212, Beecher-Stowe Collection, SchL.

64. HBS to Susie Munroe Stowe, April 18, 1879, folder 204, Beecher-Stowe Collection, SchL.

65. HBS to "Friends All," December 23, 1880, folder 170, Beecher-Stowe Collection, SchL.

66. HBS to Susie Munroe Stowe, May 6, 1881, folder 224, Beecher-Stowe Collection, SchL.

67. HBS to Charles Stowe, March 7, 1879, folder 196, Beecher Stowe Collection, SchL.

68. HBS to Henry Ward Beecher, January 27, 1882, Beecher Family Papers, SML.

69. HBS to Isabella Beecher Hooker, February 1, 1883, Joseph K. Hooker Collection, SD.

70. HBS to Charles Stowe, n.d. [December 31, 1876], folder 189, Beecher-Stowe Collection, SchL.

71. HBS to Charles Stowe, February 28, [n.y.], folder 232, Beecher-Stowe Collection, SchL.

72. HBS to Charles Stowe, February 4, [1881], folder 221, Beecher-Stowe Collection, SchL.

73. HBS to Edward Everett Hale, March 3, 1872, Katharine S. Day Collection, SD.

74. HBS to Susie Munroe Stowe, March 8, 1882, folder 227, Beecher-Stowe Collection, SchL.

75. HBS to Mary Claflin, December 17, 1884, copy, SD; original in the Hayes Library.

76. HBS to Mary Claflin, August 12, [1880–1882], copy, SD; original in the Hayes Library).

77. HBS to Mary Claflin, May 12, 1881, copy, SD; original in the Hayes Library.

78. Juliet A. L. Tappan to HBS, May 8, 1880, Isabella Hooker Collection, SD.

79. HBS to "My Dear 'little Lucy,'" December 4, 1883, Katharine S. Day Collection, SD; HBS to Mary Claflin, fragment, n.d., and December 24, [1883], copies, SD; originals in Hayes Library.

80. HBS to Samuel Clemens, [1876?], copy, SD; original in Mark Twain Papers, Bancroft Library, University of California at Berkeley.

81. HBS to James and Annie Fields, January 29, 1874, Fields Papers, HL.

82. HBS to Mary Claflin, January 30, 1880, copy, SD; original in Hayes Library.

83. HBS to Hatty Stowe, July 27, 1882, folder 175, Beecher-Stowe Collection, SchL.

84. HBS to Hatty Stowe, August 27, 1882, folder 176, Beecher-Stowe Collection, SchL.

85. HBS to James Fields, February 13, 1870, Fields Papers, HL.

86. Gilman, "Atlantic Dinners and Diners," pp. 650–51, 652. Wilson, *Crusader in Crinoline*, 609–10, and Coultrap-McQuin, *Doing Literary Business*, 2–6.

87. HBS to Hatty and Eliza Stowe, June 20, 1882, folder 174, Beecher-Stowe Collection, SchL.

88. Wilson, *Crusader in Crinoline*, 612–14, 617.

89. Annie Fields, "Poem to HBS, June 14, 1882," HO.

90. Gilman, "Atlantic Dinners and Diners," 657.

91. HBS to "Dear Friend" [Annie Fields], September 24, 1884, Fields Papers, HL.

92. HBS to H. O. Houghton, December 3, 1880, HO.

93. HBS to H. O. Houghton, April 15, 1885, HO.

94. HBS to H. O. Houghton, September 3, 1885, HO.

95. HBS to H. O. Houghton, September 3, 1885, HO.

96. HBS to Estes & Lauriat, October 3 and October 8, 1885, Katharine S. Day Collection, SD. Calvin's failing health prevented her from accomplishing this; see HBS to Estes & Lauriat, December 30, 1885, Katharine S. Day Collection, SD.

97. Thomas Bailey Aldrich to HBS, November 6, 1886, HO.

98. HBS to Mary Beecher Perkins, December 3, 1879, folder 99, Beecher-Stowe Collection, SchL.

99. HBS to Mary Claflin, January 20, [1881], copy, SD; original in the Hayes Library.

100. HBS to Susie Munroe Stowe, March 19, 1884, folder 230, Beecher-Stowe Collection, SchL.

101. HBS to Mary Claflin, December 17, 1884, copy, SD; original in the Hayes Library.

102. HBS to Henry Ward Beecher, September 8, 1885, Beecher Family Papers, SML.

103. HBS to Isabella Beecher Hooker, January 22, 1885, Joseph K. Hooker Collection, SD.

104. HBS to Mrs. Jervis Langdon, February 5, 1885, Mark Twain Memorial, Hartford, Conn.

105. Descriptions of Georgie's symptoms can be found in the following letters:

HBS to Charles Stowe, July 26–27, 1876, folder 190; HBS to Hatty Stowe, August 11, August 15, and August 16, 1876, folder 160; HBS to Charles Stowe, October 8, 1877, folder 192; and HBS to Eliza Stowe, November 1, [1879], folder 166—all in Beecher-Stowe Collection, SchL; HBS to [Annie Fields], December 2, 1880, Fields Papers, HL; HBS to CES and "housefolk," June 21, [1881], folder 91, Beecher-Stowe Collection, SchL.

106. Ann Douglas Wood, "'The Fashionable Diseases": Women's Complaints and Their Treatment in Nineteenth-Century America," *Journal of Interdisciplinary History* 4 (Summer 1973):25–52, esp. 37–39. Taking a more temperate approach, Barbara Sicherman, "The Uses of a Diagnosis: Doctors, Patients, and Neurasthenia," *Journal of the History of Medicine and Allied Sciences* 32, no. 1 (1977): 33–54, points out that the diagnosis of "neurasthenia" allowed doctors to address a wide range of psychosomatic complaints that otherwise might not have fallen under their purview.

107. HBS to Charles Stowe, December 1, [1877], folder 183, Beecher-Stowe Collection, SchL; HBS to Sarah Beecher, December 22, 1877, folder 94, Beecher-Stowe Collection, SchL.

108. HBS, manuscript, "The Other World," August 5, 1887, Joseph K. Hooker Collection, SD.

109. Hatty Stowe to _____, January 29, 1890, HO.

110. Extract of Hatty Stowe's letter of January, 1890, copied in Susan T. Howard to Annie Fields, n.d. [c. January, 1890], Fields Papers, HL.

111. An autographed copy of this motto, dated March 24, 1896, and several undated copies, are in the Katharine S. Day Collection, SD.

112. HBS to Mary Beecher Noyes, May 28, 1893, Acquisitions, SD.

113. HBS to Oliver Wendell Holmes, February 5, 1893, Library of Congress.

114. Obituary clipping, Cincinati Historical Society.

115. Charles Dudley Warner to Annie Fields, September 5 and September 19, 1897, Fields Papers, HL. Hatty and Eliza went to live with Charles Stowe in Simsbury, Conn.

116. HBS, "Last Will of Harriet Beecher Stowe," November 3, 1885, copy, SD; original in Probate Court, City of Hartford, Conn., vol. 158, pp. 588–89.

117. Sarah Orne Jewett to Hatty and Eliza Stowe, October 8, n. y. [1896], folder 280, Beecher-Stowe Collection, SchL.

Select Bibliography

PRIMARY SOURCES

Manuscript Collections

Beinecke Rare Book and Manuscript Library, Yale University, New Haven, Connecticut
  Collection of American Literature
Boston Public Library
  Anti-Slavery Collection
Cincinnati Historical Society
  Green Papers
  Green-Roelker Papers
Clement Library, University of Michigan, Ann Arbor, Michigan
  Weld-Grimké Papers
Clifton Waller Barrett Library, University of Virginia, Charlottesville, Virginia
  Harriet Beecher Stowe Collection (#6318-C)
Henry E. Huntington Library, San Marino, California
  Fields Papers
The Historical Society of Pennsylvania, Philadelphia, Pennsylvania
Houghton Library, Harvard University, Cambridge, Massachusetts
  Houghton Papers
  Norton Papers
  Ticknor and Fields Business Records
Library of Congress, Washington, D.C.
  Holmes Papers
Mark Twain Memorial, Hartford, Connecticut
Middlesex County Historical Society, Middletown, Connecticut
New York Public Library
  Berg Collection of English and American Literature
Arthur E. and Eliza Schlesinger Library on the History of Women in America, Radcliffe College, Cambridge, Massachusetts
  Beecher-Stowe Collection
Sophia Smith Library, Smith College, Northampton, Massachusetts
  Authors Collection
  Parton Papers
Sterling Memorial Library, Yale University, New Haven, Connecticut
  Beecher Family Papers

Stowe-Day Library, Hartford, Connecticut
  Acquisitions
  Copies
  Foote Collection
  Katharine S. Day Collection
  Isabella Hooker Collection
  Joseph K. Hooker Collection
  Helen D. Perkins Collection
  Mary K. Talcott Collection
  White Collection
Dr. Williams's Library, London, England
  Mary Estlin Papers

Nineteenth-Century Newspapers and Periodicals

Atlantic Monthly
Godey's Lady's Book (also called *Godey's Magazine and Lady's Book* and *Godey's Lady's Book and Ladies' American Magazine*)
Hearth and Home
The Independent
The Nation
The National Era
New-York Evangelist
New York Observer
The Revolution

Works by Harriet Beecher Stowe

Books

Primary Geography for Children, on an Improved Plan with Eleven Maps and Numerous Engravings. Cincinnati, Ohio: Corey & Fairbank, 1833.

The May Flower and Miscellaneous Writings. Boston: Phillips, Sampson, 1855. (Originally published in 1843.)

Uncle Tom's Cabin; or, Life Among the Lowly. 2 vols. Boston: Houghton, Mifflin and Co., 1896. (Originally published in 1852.)

A Key to Uncle Tom's Cabin; Presenting the Original Facts and Documents upon Which the Story is Founded. Together with Corroborative Statements Verifying the Truth of the Work. Boston: John P. Jewett and Co., 1853.

Sunny Memories of Foreign Lands. 2 vols. Introduction by C. E. Stowe, Boston: Phillips, Sampson, and Company, 1854.

Dred: A Tale of the Great Dismal Swamp, Together with Anti-Slavery Tales and Papers, and Life in Florida after the War. 2 vols. Boston: Houghton, Mifflin and Co., 1896. (Originally published in 1856.)

The Minister's Wooing. Boston: Houghton, Mifflin and Co., 1896. (Originally published in 1859.)

Agnes of Sorrento. Boston: Houghton, Mifflin and Co., 1896. (Originally published in 1862.)

The Pearl of Orr's Island. Boston: Houghton, Mifflin and Co., 1896. (Originally published in 1862.)

Household Papers and Stories. Boston: Houghton, Mifflin and Co., 1896. (Originally published in 1865–1867.)

Little Foxes. Boston: Ticknor and Fields, 1866.

Oldtown Folks. Boston: Houghton, Mifflin and Co., 1896. (Originally published in 1869.)

Lady Byron Vindicated: A History of the Byron Controversy, from Its Beginnings in 1816 to the Present Time. Boston: Fields, Osgood, & Co., 1870.

Pink and White Tyranny. Boston: Houghton, Mifflin and Co., 1896. (Originally published in 1871.)

My Wife and I; or, Harry Henderson's History. Boston: Houghton Mifflin and Co., 1896. (Originally published in 1871.)

Woman in Sacred History: A Series of Sketches Drawn from Scriptural, Historical, and Legendary Sources. New York: J. B. Ford and Company, 1874.

Poganuc People. Boston: Houghton, Mifflin and Co., 1896. (Originally published in 1878.)

Articles and Pamphlets

"Uncle Enoch." *New-York Evangelist* 6 (May 30, 1835): 88.

"Trials of a Housekeeper." *Godey's Lady's Book,* 18 (January, 1839): 4–6.

"The Only Daughter." *Godey's Lady's Book* 18 (March 1839): 117.

"Olympiana." *Godey's Lady's Book* 18 (June 1839): 241–43.

"The Drunkard Reclaimed." *New-York Evangelist* 10 (November 30, 1839): 189–90, and 10 (December 7, 1839): 193–94.

"Eliza: From My Aunt Mary's Bureau." *Godey's Lady's Book* 20 (January 1840): 24–26.

"Sketches from the Note Book of an Old Gentleman. No. 1. The Old Meeting House." *Godey's Lady's Book* 21 (August 1840): 61–63.

"Mark Meriden." *Godey's Lady's Book* 22 (June 1841): 242–44.

"The Canal Boat." *Godey's Lady's Book* 23 (October 1841): 167–69.

"A Parable." *New-York Evangelist* 13 (February 24, 1842): 29.

"The Unfaithful Steward." *New-York Evangelist* 13 (April 7, 1842): 53.

"The Dancing School." *New-York Evangelist* 14 (April 6, 1843): 53, and 14 (April 13, 1843): 57.

"The Coral Ring." In *The Christian Souvenir* , edited by Isaac F. Shepard, 265–81. Boston: H. B. Williams, 1843. Reprinted in *Godey's Lady's Book* 36 (June 1848): 340–43.

"Literary Epidemics—No. 2." *New-York Evangelist* 14 (July 13, 1843): 109.

"Old Testament Pictures—No. 1." *New-York Evangelist* 15 (November 14, 1844): 18.

"Immediate Emancipation: A Sketch." *New-York Evangelist* 16 (January 2, 1845): 1.

"The Interior Life, or Primitive Christian Experience." *New-York Evangelist* 16 (June 19, 1845): 97.

"Lord, if though hadst been there!" *New-York Evangelist* 16 (September 11, 1845): 145.

"What Will the American People Do?" *New-York Evangelist* 17 (January 29, 1846): 17, and 17 (February 5, 1846): 26.

"Jesus." *New-York Evangelist* 17 (February 19, 1846): 29.

"Feeling." *Godey's Lady's Book* 36 (February 1848): 102–4.

"Atonement—A Historical Reverie." *New-York Evangelist* 19 (December 28, 1848): 205.

"Introduction." *The Incarnation; or, Pictures of the Virgin and Her Son,* by Charles Beecher. New York: Harper & Brothers, 1849.

"Earthly Care a Heavenly Discipline." Boston: American Tract Society, n.d. [c. 1850].

"The Freeman's Dream; A Parable." *National Era* 4 (August 1, 1850): 121.

"Heinrich Stilling." *New-York Evangelist* 22 (February 6, 1851): 21.

"Religious Scoffers." *Independent* 4 (May 20, 1852): 82.

"An Appeal to the Women of the Free States of America, On the Present Crisis in Our Country." *Independent* 6 (February 23, 1854): 57.

The Edmondson Family and the Capture of the Schooner Pearl. Cincinnati, Ohio: American Reform Tract and Book Society, 1856.

"The Mourning Veil." *Atlantic Monthly* 1 (November 1857): 63–70.

"Getting Ready for a Gale." *Independent* 13 (April 25, 1861): 1.

"Letter from Andover." *Independent* 13 (June 13, 1861): 1.

"Letter to Lord Shaftesbury." *Independent* 13 (August 1, 1861): 1.

"Will You Take a Pilot?" *Independent* 13 (September 11, 1861): 1.

"A Card." *Independent* 13 (November 21, 1861): 1.

"To Our Readers." *Independent* 13 (December 5, 1861): 1.

"Simon the Cyrenian." *Independent* 14 (July 31, 1862): 1.

"Lazarus at the Gate." *Independent* 14 (August 7, 1862): 1.

"Prayer." *Independent* 14 (August 28, 1862): 1.

"Sojourner Truth, the Libyan Sibyl." *Atlantic Monthly* 11 (April 1863): 473–81.

"Tribute of a Loving Friend to the Memory of a Noble Woman." *Atlantic Monthly* 23 (February 1869): 242–50.

"Little Captain Trott." *Atlantic Monthly* 23 (March 1869): 300–304.

"What Is and What Is Not the Point in the Woman Question." *Hearth and Home* 1 (August 28, 1869): 520–21.

"The True Story of Lady Byron's Life." *Atlantic Monthly* 24 (September 1869): 295–313.

"A Look Beyond the Veil." *Christian Union* 2 n.s. (November 5, 1870): 277.

OTHER SOURCES

Books

Allmendinger, David F., Jr. *Paupers and Scholars: The Transformation of Student Life in Nineteenth-Century New England.* New York: St. Martin's Press, 1975.

Ammons, Elizabeth, ed. *Critical Essays on Harriet Beecher Stowe.* Boston: G. K. Hall, 1980.

The Annual Catalogue of the Hartford Female Seminary. Hartford, Conn.: E. Gleason, Printer, 1839.

Baym, Nina. *Woman's Fiction: A Guide to Novels by and about Women in America, 1820–1870.* Ithaca, N.Y. Cornell University Press, 1978.

Beard, George M. *American Nervousness: Its Causes and Consequences.* New York, 1881.

Beecher, Catharine E. *The Biographical Remains of Rev. George Beecher, Late Pastor of a Church in Chillicothe, Ohio, and Former Pastor of a Church in Rochester, New York.* New York: Leavitt Trow, and Co., 1844.

———. *Educational Reminiscences and Suggestions.* New York: J. B. Ford and Co., 1874.

———. *Essay on Slavery and Abolitionism, with Reference to the Duty of American Females.* Philadelphia: Henry Perkins Boston: Perkins & Marvin, 1837.

———. *Suggestions Respecting Improvements in Education.* Hartford, Conn.: Packard & Butler, 1829.

———. *A Treatise on Domestic Economy*. New York: Schocken Books, 1977. (Originally published in 1841.)

Beecher, Charles. *The Incarnation; or, Pictures of the Virgin and Her Son*. New York: Harper and Brothers, 1849.

Bibb, Henry. *The Narrative of the Life and Adventures of Henry Bibb, Written by Himself*. In *Puttin' on Ole Massa* , edited by Gilbert Osofsky. New York: Harper & Row, 1969.

Bidstrup, P. Lesley. *Toxicity of Mercury and Its Compounds*. New York: Elsevier, 1964.

Blassingame, John W., ed. *The Frederick Douglass Papers*. Vol. 2, *Series One: Speeches, Debates, and Interviews*. New Haven: Yale University Press, 1982.

Bordin, Ruth. *Woman and Temperance: The Quest for Power and Liberty, 1873–1900*. Philadelphia: Temple University Press, 1981.

Boydston, Jeanne, and Mary Kelley and Anne Margolis. *The Limits of Sisterhood: The Beecher Sisters on Women's Rights and Woman's Sphere*. Chapel Hill: University of North Carolina Press, 1988.

Braude, Ann D. *Radical Spirits: Spiritualism and Women's Rights in Nineteenth-Century America*. Boston: Beacon Press, 1989.

Brickley, Lynn. "Sarah Pierce's Litchfield Female Academy, 1792–1833." Ed. D. Diss., Graduate School of Education, Harvard University, 1985.

Brodhead, Richard. *The School of Hawthorne*. New York: Oxford University Press, 1986.

Brumberg, Joan Jacobs. *Fasting Girls*. Cambridge, Mass.: Harvard University Press, 1988.

Buell, Lawrence. *New England Literary Culture: From Revolution Through Renaissance*. Cambridge: Cambridge University Press, 1986.

Butler, Marilyn. *Maria Edgeworth: A Literary Biography*. Oxford: Clarendon Press, 1972.

Cabot, Mary R., ed. *Annals of Brattleboro, 1681–1895*. 2 vols. Brattleboro, Vt.: E. L. Hildreth & Co., 1922.

Carby, Hazel V. *Reconstructing Womanhood: The Emergence of the Afro-American Woman Novelist*. New York: Oxford University Press, 1987.

Caskey, Marie. *Chariot of Fire: Religion and the Beecher Family*. New Haven, Conn.: Yale University Press, 1978.

Catalogue of Hartford Female Seminary Officers, Teachers, and Pupils, of the Hartford Female Seminary for the Summer Term of 1828. Hartford, Conn.: Published by the Seminary, 1828.

Catalogue of the Officers, Teachers, and Pupils of the Hartford Female Seminary for the Two Terms of 1829. In *Suggestions Respecting Improvements in Education*, by Catharine Beecher. Hartford, Conn.: Packard & Butler, 1829.

Catalogue of the Hartford Female Seminary, Together with an Account of the Internal Arrangments, Course of Study, and Mode of Conducting the Same. Hartford, Conn.: George F. Olmsted, 1831.

Cayleff, Susan E. " *Wash and Be Healed*": *The Water-Cure Movement and Women's Health*. Philadelphia: Temple University Press, 1987.

Chase, Richard. *The American Novel and Its Tradition*. Garden City, N.Y.: Doubleday, 1957.

Chielens, Edward E. *American Literary Magazines: The Eighteenth and Nineteenth Centuries*. New York: Greenwood Press, 1986.

Child, Lydia Maria. *The Collected Correspondence of Lydia Maria Child, 1817–1880*.

Edited by Patricia G. Holland, Milton Meltzer, and Francine Krasno. Millwood, N.Y.: Kraus Microform, 1980.

Cist, Charles. *Cincinnati in 1841: Its Early Annals*. Cincinnati, Ohio: Author, 1841.

Clark, Clifford E., Jr. *Henry Ward Beecher: Spokesman for a Middle-Class America*. Urbana: University of Illinois Press, 1978.

Clark, Victor S. *History of Manufactures in the U. S., 1607–1860*. Washington, D. C.: Carnegie Institution of Washington, 1916.

Clemens, Samuel. *The Adventures of Huckleberry Finn*. San Francisco: Chandler, 1962. (Originally published in 1885.)

Cott, Nancy F. *The Bonds of Womanhood: "Woman's Sphere" in New England, 1780–1835*. New Haven, Conn.: Yale University Press, 1977.

Coultrap-McQuin, Susan. *Doing Literary Business: American Women Writers in the Nineteenth Century*. Chapel Hill: University of North Carolina Press, 1990.

Craft, William, and Ellen Craft. *Running a Thousand Miles for Freedom*. New York: Arno Press New York Times, 1969.

Cross, Barbara M., ed. *The Autobiography of Lyman Beecher*. 2 vols. Cambridge, Mass.: Harvard University Press, 1961.

Dannenbaum, Jed. *Drink and Disorder: Temperance Reform in Cincinnati from the Washingtonian Revival to the WCTU*. Urbana: University of Illinois Press, 1984.

Davis, Angela Y. *Women, Race and Class*. New York: Random House, 1983.

Donegan, Jane B. *"Hydropathic Highway to Health": Women and Water-Cure in Antebellum America*. New York: Greenwood Press, 1986.

Donovan, Josephine. *New England Local Color Literature: A Women's Tradition*. New York: F. Ungar Publishing Co., 1983.

———. *"Uncle Tom's Cabin": Evil, Affliction, and Redemptive Love*. Boston: Twayne, 1991.

Douglas, Ann. *The Feminization of American Culture*. New York: Alfred A. Knopf, 1977.

Duberman, Martin. *James Russell Lowell*. Boston: Houghton, Mifflin, 1966.

DuBois, Ellen Carol, ed. *Elizabeth Cady Stanton/Susan B. Anthony: Correspondence, Writings, Speeches*. New York: Schocken Books, 1981.

Dudden, Faye. *Serving Women: Household Service in Nineteenth-Century America*. Middletown, Conn.: Wesleyan University Press, 1983.

Eckhardt, Cecilia. *Fanny Wright: Rebel in America*. Cambridge, Mass.: Harvard University Press, 1984.

Emerson, Edward Waldo. *The Early Years of the Saturday Club, 1855–1870*. Boston: Houghton, Mifflin and Co., 1918.

Fiedler, Leslie. *Love and Death in the American Novel*. New York: Criterion Books, [1960].

Fields, Annie Adams. *Life and Letters of Harriet Beecher Stowe*. Boston: Houghton, Mifflin and Co., 1897.

Finley, Ruth E. *The Lady of Godey's: Sarah Josepha Hale*. Philadelphia: J. B. Lippincott, 1931.

Fitzhugh, George. *Cannibals All! or, Slaves without Masters*. Edited by C. Vann Woodward. Cambridge, Mass.: Belknap Press of Harvard University Press, 1960.

Fladeland, Betty. *Abolitionists and Working-Class Problems in the Age of Industrialization*. Baton Rouge: Louisiana State University Press, 1984.

———. *Men and Brothers: Anglo-American Antislavery Cooperation*. Urbana: University of Illinois Press, 1972.

Flexner, Eleanor. *Century of Struggle: The Woman's Rights Movement in the United States.* Cambridge, Mass.: Belknap Press of Harvard University Press, 1959.

Foote, Abram W. *Foote Family: Genealogy of Nathaniel Foote of Wethersfield.* Vol. 1. Rutland, Vt: Marble City Press/Tuttle Company, 1907.

Foote, John P. *Memoirs of the Life of Samuel E. Foote.* Cincinnati, Ohio: Robert Clarke & Co., 1860.

Foster, Charles H. *The Rungless Ladder: Harriet Beecher Stowe and New England Puritanism.* Durham, N. C.: Duke University Press, 1954.

Frederic, Harold. *The Damnation of Theron Ware.* New York: Holt, Rinehart and Winston, 1960. (Originally published in 1896.)

Fredrickson, George M. *The Black Image in the White Mind: The Debate on Afro-American Character and Destiny, 1817–1914.* New York: Harper & Row, 1971.

Garrison, Wendell Phillips, and Francis Jackson Garrison. *William Lloyd Garrison, 1805–1879: The Story of His Life Told by His Children.* New York: Century Co., 1889.

Gilbert, Sandra M., and Susan Gubar. *The Madwoman in the Attic: The Woman Writer and the Nineteenth-Century Literary Imagination.* New Haven, Conn.: Yale University Press, 1979.

Gordon, Linda. *Woman's Body, Woman's Right : A Social History of Birth Control in America.* New York: Grossman, 1976.

Gossett, Thomas F. *"Uncle Tom's Cabin" and American Culture.* Dallas, Tex.: Southern Methodist University Press, 1985.

Grier, Katherine C. *Culture and Comfort: People, Parlors, and Upholstery, 1850–1930.* Rochester, N.Y.: Strong Museum, 1988.

Griffith, Elisabeth. *In Her Own Right: The Life of Elizabeth Cady Stanton.* New York: Oxford University Press, 1984.

Gusfield, Joseph R. *Symbolic Crusade: Status Politics and the American Temperance Movement.* Urbana: University of Illinois Press, 1983.

Haight, Gordon S., ed. *The George Eliot Letters.* 9 vols. New Haven, Conn.: Yale University Press, 1954–1978.

Hale, Edward Everett. *James Russell Lowell and His Friends.* Boston: Houghton, Mifflin and Co., 1899.

Hale, Sarah Josepha. *Woman's Record; or, Sketches of all Distinguished Women, from "The Beginning" till A. D. 1850. Arranged in Four Eras. With Selections from Female Writers in Every Age.* New York: Harper & Brothers, 1853.

Haller, John S., Jr. *American Medicine in Transition, 1840–1910.* Urbana: University of Illinois Press, 1981.

Hamilton, Gail [Mary Abigail Dodge]. *Gail Hamilton's Life in Letters.* 2 vols. Edited by H. Augusta Dodge. Boston: Lee and Shepard, 1901.

Harden, O. Elizabeth McWhorter. *Maria Edgeworth's Art of Prose Fiction.* The Hague, The Netherlands: Mouton, 1971.

Harris, Sharon M.. *Rebecca Harding Davis and American Realism.* Philadelphia: University of Pennsylvania Press, 1991.

Harrold, Stanley. *Gamaliel Bailey and Antislavery Union.* Kent, Ohio: Kent State University Press, 1986.

Hedrick, Joan D. *Solitary Comrade: Jack London and His Work.* Chapel Hill: University of North Carolina Press, 1982.

Higginson, Mary Thacher, ed. *The Letters and Journals of Thomas Wentworth Higginson, 1846–1906.* Boston: Houghton, Mifflin and Co., 1921.

Higginson, Thomas Wentworth. *Cheerful Yesterdays.* Boston: Houghton, Mifflin and Co., 1898. Reprint. New York: Arno Press/*New York Times,* 1968.

Hildreth, Margaret Holbrook. *Harriet Beecher Stowe: A Bibliography.* Hamden, Conn.: Shoestring Press, 1976.

Howe, Mark A. DeWolfe. *The "Atlantic Monthly" and Its Makers.* Boston: Atlantic Monthly Press, 1919.

Hurley, Daniel. *Cincinnati: The Queen City.* Cincinnati, Ohio: Cincinnati Historical Society, n.d. [c. 1983].

Jacobs, Harriet [Linda Brent, pseud.]. *Incidents in the Life of a Slave Girl, Written by Herself.* Edited by Jean Fagan Yellin. Cambridge, Mass.: Harvard University Press, 1987. (Originally published in 1861.)

Jones, Jacqueline. *Labor of Love, Labor of Sorrow: Black Women, Work and the Family from Slavery to the Present.* New York: Vintage Books, 1986.

Kaplan, Justin. *Mr. Clemens and Mark Twain: A Biography.* New York: Simon and Schuster, 1966.

———. *Walt Whitman: A Life.* New York: Simon and Schuster, 1980.

Kelley, Mary. *Private Woman, Public Stage: Literary Domesticity in Nineteenth-Century America.* New York: Oxford University Press, 1984.

Kerber, Linda. *Women of the Republic: Intellect and Ideology in Revolutionary America.* Chapel Hill: University of North Carolina Press, 1980.

King, Margaret [Rives]. *Memoirs of the Life of Mrs. Sarah Peter.* Cincinnati, Ohio: Robert Clarke and Co., 1889.

Kirkham, E. Bruce. *The Building of "Uncle Tom's Cabin."* Knoxville: University of Tennessee Press, 1977.

Kolodny, Annette. *The Land Before Her: Fantasy and Experience of the American Frontiers, 1630–1860.* Chapel Hill: University of North Carolina Press, 1984.

Korpalski, Adam. *The Gunnery, 1850–1975: A Documentary History of Private Education in America.* Washington, Conn.: Author, 1977.

Labaree, Leonard W., Ralph L. Ketcham, Helen C. Boatfield, and Helene H. Fineman, eds. *The Autobiography of Benjamin Franklin.* New Haven, Conn.: Yale University Press, 1964.

Lane, Ann J. *To Herland and Beyond: The Life and Work of Charlotte Perkins Gilman.* New York: Pantheon Books, 1991.

Lebsock, Suzanne. *The Free Women of Petersburg: Status and Culture in a Southern Town, 1784–1860.* New York: W. W. Norton, 1985.

Levine, Lawrence W. *Highbrow/Lowbrow: The Emergence of Cultural Hierarchy in America.* Cambridge, Mass.: Harvard University Press, 1988.

Lewis, R.W.B. *The American Adam: Innocence, Tragedy, and Tradition in the Nineteenth Century.* Chicago: University of Chicago Press, 1955.

Lowell, James Russell. *New Letters of James Russell Lowell.* Edited by Mark A. DeWolfe Howe. New York: Harper & Brothers, 1932.

McCray, Florine Thayer. *The Life-Work of the Author of "Uncle Tom's Cabin."* New York: Funk & Wagnalls, 1889.

McDannell, Colleen. *The Christian Home in Victorian America, 1840–1900.* Bloomington: Indiana University Press, 1986.

McKeen, Philena, and Phebe F. McKeen. *Annals of Fifty Years: A History of Abbot Academy, Andover, Mass., 1829–1879.* Andover, Mass.: Warren F. Draper, 1880.

McLachlan, James. *American Boarding Schools: A Historical Study.* New York: Charles Scribner's Sons, 1970.

McLoughlin, William G. *The Meaning of Henry Ward Beecher: An Essay on the Shifting Values of Mid-Victorian America, 1840–1870*. New York: Alfred A. Knopf, 1970.

McPherson, James M. *Battle Cry of Freedom: The Civil War Era*. New York: Oxford University Press, 1988.

Mansfield, Edward D. *Memoirs of the Life and Services of Daniel Drake, M. D., Physician, Professor, and Author; With Notices of the Early Settlement of Cincinnati and Some of Its Pioneer Citizens*. Cincinnati, Ohio: Applegate and Co., 1855.

———. *Personal Memories: Social, Political, and Literary, with Sketches of Many Noted People, 1803–1843*. Cincinnati, Ohio: Robert Clarke & Co., 1879.

Merideth, Robert. *The Politics of the Universe: Edward Beecher, Abolition, and Orthodoxy*. Nashville, Tenn.: Vanderbilt University Press, 1968.

Merrill, Walter M., and Louis Ruchames, eds. *The Letters of William Lloyd Garrison*. 6 vols. Cambridge, Mass.: The Belknap Press of Harvard University Press, 1875.

Mintz, Steven. *A Prison of Expectations: The Family in Victorian Culture*. New York: New York University Press, 1983.

Mott, Frank Luther. *A History of American Magazines*. 5 vols. Cambridge, Mass.: Harvard University Press, 1930–1968.

Norton, Mary Beth. *Liberty's Daughters: The Revolutionary Experience of American Women, 1750–1800*. Boston: Little Brown, 1980.

Perry, Lewis. *Radical Abolitionism: Anarchy and the Government of God in Antislavery Thought*. Ithaca, N.Y.: Cornell University Press, 1973.

Phelps, Elizabeth Stuart. *Chapters from a Life*. Boston: Houghton, Mifflin and Co., 1897.

———. *The Gates Ajar*. Boston: Fields, Osgood, & Co., 1869.

Plymouth Collection of Hymns and Tunes. New York: A. S. Barnes & Co., 1856.

The Pocket Register for the City of Hartford, to Which is Added a Brief Sketch of the Reception of General La Fayette. Hartford, Conn.: Benjamin H. Norton, 1825.

Poovey, Mary. *The Proper Lady and the Woman Writer: Ideology as Style in the Works of Mary Wollstonecraft, Mary Shelley, and Jane Austen*. Chicago: University of Chicago Press, 1984.

Raboteau, Albert J. *Slave Religion: The "Invisible Institution" in the Antebellum South*. New York: Oxford University Press, 1978.

Reed, Ishmael. *Flight to Canada*. New York: Random House, 1976.

Regulations of the Hartford Female Seminary, Together with a Catalogue of the Officers, Teachers, and Pupils of the Same for the Two Terms Ending October 26, 1830. Hartford, Conn.: Hudson & Skinner, 1830.

Richards, Leonard L. *"Gentlemen of Property and Standing": Anti-Abolition Mobs in Jacksonian America*. New York: Oxford University Press, 1970.

Roman, Judith A. *Annie Adams Fields: The Spirit of Charles Street*. Bloomington: University of Indiana Press, 1990.

Rorabaugh, William. *The Alcoholic Republic: An American Tradition*. New York: Oxford University Press, 1979.

Rosenberg, Charles E. *The Cholera Years: The United States in 1832, 1849, and 1866*. Chicago: University of Chicago Press, 1962.

Rosenblatt, Paul C. *Bitter, Bitter Tears: Nineteenth-Century Diarists and Twentieth-Century Grief Theories*. Minneapolis: University of Minnesota Press, 1983.

Rothman, Ellen K. *Hands and Hearts: A History of Courtship in America*. New York: Basic Books, 1984.

Rugoff, Milton. *The Beechers: An American Family in the Nineteenth Century.* New York: Harper & Row, 1981.

Sachs, Emanie. *The Terrible Siren: Victoria Woodhull, 1838–1927.* New York: Harper and Brothers, 1928.

Schuckers, Jacob William. *The Life and Public Services of Salmon Portland Chase.* New York: D. Appleton and Company, 1874.

Showalter, Elaine. *A Literature of Their Own: British Women Novelists from Brontë to Lessing.* Princeton, N.J.: Princeton University Press, 1977.

_____. *Sister's Choice: Tradition and Change in American Women's Writing.* New York: Oxford University Press, 1991.

Sklar, Kathryn Kish. *Catharine Beecher: A Study in American Domesticity.* New York: W. W. Norton, 1976.

Slotkin, Richard. *Regeneration through Violence.* Middletown, Conn.: Wesleyan University Press, 1973.

Smith, Henry Nash. *Virgin Land: The American West as Symbol and Myth.* Cambridge, Mass.: Harvard University Press, 1950.

Stampp, Kenneth. *The Peculiar Institution: Slavery in the Ante-Bellum South.* New York: Alfred A. Knopf, 1956.

Steiner, Bernard Christian. *History of the Plantation of Menunkatuck and of the Original Town of Guilford, Connecticut.* Baltimore: Author, 1897.

Sterling, Dorothy, ed. *We Are Your Sisters: Black Women in the Nineteenth Century.* New York: W. W. Norton, 1984.

Stowe, Charles Edward. *Life of Harriet Beecher Stowe, Compiled from Her Letters and Journals.* Boston: Houghton, Mifflin and Co., 1889.

Stowe, Charles Edward, and Lyman Beecher Stowe. *Harriet Beecher Stowe: The Story of Her Life.* Boston: Houghton, Mifflin and Co., 1911.

Sutherland, Daniel E. *Americans and Their Servants: Domestic Service in the United States from 1800 to 1920.* Baton Rouge: Louisiana State University Press, 1981.

Talcott, S. V. *Talcott Pedigree in England and America from 1598 to 1876.* Albany, N.Y.: Weed, Parsons and Company, 1876.

Trollope, Frances. *The Domestic Manners of the Americans.* Edited by Donald Smalley. New York: Alfred A. Knopf, 1949. (Originally published in 1832.)

Trumbull, J. Hammond, ed. *Memorial History of Hartford County, Connecticut, 1633–1844.* 2 vols. Boston: Edward L. Osgood, 1886.

Tyler, Alice Felt. *Freedom's Ferment: Phases of American Social History from the Colonial Period to the Outbreak of the Civil War.* 2d ed. New York: Harper & Row, 1962.

Tyrrell, Ian. *Sobering Up: From Temperance to Prohibition in Antebellum America.* Westport, Conn.: Greenwood Press, 1979.

Vanderpoel, Emily Noyes. *More Chronicles of a Pioneer School: From 1792 to 1833.* New York: Cadmus Book Shop, 1927.

Van Why, Joseph S., and Earl French, eds. *Harriet Beecher Stowe in Europe: The Journal of Charles Beecher.* Hartford, Conn.: Stowe-Day Foundation, 1986.

Warden, Robert Bruce. *An Account of the Private Life and Public Services of Salmon Portland Chase.* Cincinnati, Ohio: Wilstach, Baldwin & Co., 1874.

Warren, Joyce A. *Fanny Fern: An Independent Woman.* New Brunswick, N.J.: Rutgers University Press, 1992.

White, Alain C. *The History of the Town of Litchfield, Conn., 1790–1920.* Litchfield, Conn.: Litchfield Historical Society, 1920.

White, Deborah Gray. *Ar'n't I a Woman? Female Slaves in the Plantation South*. New York: W. W. Norton, 1985.

Wilson, Edmund. *Patriotic Gore: Studies in the Literature of the American Civil War*. New York: Oxford University Press, 1962.

Wilson, Forrest. *Crusader in Crinoline: The Life of Harriet Beecher Stowe*. Philadelphia: J. B. Lippincott, 1941.

Woolf, Virginia. *A Room of One's Own* New York: Harcourt, Brace and Co., 1929.

WPA. *Cincinnati: A Guide to the Queen City and Its Neighbors*. Cincinnati, Ohio: The Wiesen-Hart Press, 1943.

Wyatt-Brown, Bertram. *Lewis Tappan and the Evangelical War Against Slavery*. Cleveland, Ohio: Case Western Reserve Press, 1969.

Articles

Ammons, Elizabeth. "Heroines in *Uncle Tom's Cabin*." In *Critical Essays on Harriet Beecher Stowe*, edited by Elizabeth Ammons. Boston: G. K. Hall, 1980.

Bambara, Toni Cade. "The Emancipatory Impulse in American Literatures." Lecture delivered at the Center for the Humanities, Wesleyan University, September 17, 1990.

Beecher, Henry Ward. "The Fugitive Slave Bill at Its Work." *Independent* 2 (October 3, 1850): 162.

Berkson, Dorothy. "Millennial Politics and the Feminine Fiction of Harriet Beecher Stowe." In *Critical Essays on Harriet Beecher Stowe*, edited by Elizabeth Ammons. Boston: G. K. Hall, 1980.

Boydston, Jeanne. "The Pastoralization of Housework." In *Home and Work: Housework, Wages, and the Ideology of Labor in the Early Republic*. New York: Oxford University Press, 1990.

Brodhead, Richard. "Sparing the Rod: Discipline and Fiction in Antebellum America." *Representations* 21 (Winter 1988): 67–96.

———. "Towards a Theory of Literary Access." Paper presented at the annual meeting of the Modern Languages Association, New Orleans, December, 1989.

Brown, Gillian. "Getting in the Kitchen with Dinah: Domestic Politics in *Uncle Tom's Cabin*." *American Quarterly* 36, no. 4 (Fall 1984): 503–23.

Brown, William Wells. "Letter to William Lloyd Garrison, May 17, 1853." *Journal of Negro History* 10 (July 1925): 544–45.

Buell, Lawrence. "Calvinism Romanticized: Harriet Beecher Stowe, Samuel Hopkins, and *The Minister's Wooing*." *ESQ: A Journal of the American Renaissance* 23 (Fall 1978): 119–32. Reprinted in *Critical Essays on Harriet Beecher Stowe*, edited by Elizabeth Ammons. Boston: G. K. Hall, 1980.

Burstyn, Joan. "Catharine Beecher and the Education of American Women." *New England Quarterly* 47, no. 3 (September 1974): 386–403.

Carpenter, Lynette. "S/he Who Discover a New Pleasure: Cincinnati's Semi-Colon Club and the Woman Intellectual." Paper presented at the annual meeting of the National Women's Studies Association, Minneapolis, June 1987.

Child, Lydia Maria. "The Byron Controversy." *Independent* 21 (October 14, 1869): 1.

Cott, Nancy F. "Passionlessness: An Interpretation of Victorian Sexual Ideology, 1790–1850." *Signs: Journal of Women in Culture and Society* 4 (Winter, 1978): 219–36.

Crumpaker, Laurie. "Four Novels of Harriet Beecher Stowe: A Study in Nineteenth-

Century Androgyny." In *American Novelists Revisited: Essays in Feminist Criticism* , edited by Fritz Fleischmann. Boston: G. K. Hall, 1982.

De Jong, Mary. "Dark-Eyed Daughters: Nineteenth-Century Popular Portrayals of Biblical Women." *Women's Studies: An Interdisciplinary Journal* 19, nos. 2–4 (1991): 283–308.

DuBois, Ellen Carol. "Nineteenth Century Woman Suffrage Movement." In *Capitalist Patriarchy and the Case for Socialist Feminism,* edited by Zillah Eisenstein. New York: Monthly Review Press, [c. 1979].

Fellman, Michael. "Rehearsal for the Civil War: Antislavery and Proslavery at the Fighting Point in Kansas, 1854–1856." In *Antislavery Reconsidered : New Perspectives on the Abolitionists* , edited by Lewis Perry and Michael Fellman. Baton Rouge: Louisiana State University Press, 1979.

Fetterley, Judith. "Introduction" to *Provisions: A Reader from 19th-Century American Women.* Bloomington: Indiana University Press, 1985.

Gilman, Arthur. "Atlantic Dinners and Diners." *Atlantic Monthly* 100 (November 1907): 646–57.

Gordon, Ann D. "The Young Ladies' Academy of Philadelphia." In *Women of America*: *A History,* edited by Carol Ruth Berkin and Mary Beth Norton. Boston: Houghton Mifflin and Co., 1979.

Grimké, Angelina. "Letters to Catharine Beecher." In *The Feminist Papers,* edited by Alice Rossi. New York: Columbia University Press, 1973.

Grimké, Sarah. "Letter on the Equality of the Sexes and the Condition of Women, 1837." In *The Feminist Papers,* edited by Alice Rossi. New York: Columbia University Press, 1973.

Halttunen, Karen. "Gothic Imagination and Social Reform: The Haunted Houses of Lyman Beecher, Henry Ward Beecher, and Harriet Beecher Stowe." In *New Essays on "Uncle Tom's Cabin,"* edited by Eric J. Sundquist. Cambridge: Cambridge University Press, 1986.

Hawthorne, Nathaniel. "Mrs. Hutchinson." In *The Complete Writings of Nathaniel Hawthorne,* vol. 17. Boston: Houghton, Mifflin and Co., 1900.

Hedrick, Joan D. " 'Harvard Indifference.' " *New England Quarterly* 49 (September 1976): 356–72.

——. " 'Peaceable Fruits': The Ministry of Harriet Beecher Stowe." *American Quarterly* 40, no. 3 (September 1988): 307–32.

Kelley, Mary. "At War with Herself: Harriet Beecher Stowe as Woman in Conflict within the Home." *American Studies* 19 (Fall 1978): 23–40.

Kirkham, E. Bruce. "Introduction" to *The Pearl of Orr's Island,* by Harriet Beecher Stowe. Hartford, Conn.: Stowe-Day Foundation, 1979.

Klingberg, Frank J. "Harriet Beecher Stowe and Social Reform in England." *American Historical Review* 43 (1937–1938): 542–52.

Knight, Kate Brannon. "The Harriet Beecher Stowe Collection." In *History of the Work of Connecticut Women at the World's Columbian Exposition, Chicago, 1893.* Hartford, Conn., 1898.

Lang, Amy Shrager. "Slavery and Sentimentalism: The Strange Career of Augustine St. Clare." *Women's Studies* 12 (1986): 31–54.

McCullough, David. "The Unexpected Mrs. Stowe." In *Brave Companions: Portraits in History.* New York: Prentice Hall, 1992.

Margolis, Anne Throne. "A Tempest Tossed Spirit: Isabella Beecher Hooker and Woman Suffrage." In *The Isabella Beecher Hooker Project,* edited by Anne Throne Margolis. Hartford, Conn.: Stowe-Day Foundation, 1979.

May, Henry. "Introduction" to *Oldtown Folks,* by Harriet Beecher Stowe. Cambridge, Mass.: Harvard University Press, 1966.

Monaghan, E. Jennifer. "Literacy Instruction and Gender in Colonial New England." *American Quarterly* 40 (March 1988): 18–41

Mullen, Harryette. "Runaway Tongue: Resistant Orality in *Uncle Tom's Cabin, Our Nig, Incidents in the Life of a Slave Girl,* and *Beloved.*" Paper presented at the American Studies Association annual meeting, New Orleans, November 1990.

Parker, the Rev. E. P. "Harriet Beecher Stowe." In *Eminent Women of the Age: Being Narratives of the Lives and Deeds of the Most Prominent Women of the Present Generation,* edited by James Parton. Hartford, Conn., 1869.

Rice, C. Duncan. "Controversies over Slavery in Eighteenth and Nineteenth Century, Scotland." In *Antislavery Reconsidered: New Perspectives on the Abolitionists,* edited by Lewis Perry and Michael Fellman. Baton Rouge: Louisiana State University Press.

Riley, Joanne. "Tarquinia Molza (1542–1616): A Case Study of Women, Music, and Society in the Renaissance." In *The Musical Woman: An International Perspective* , vol. 2, edited by Judith Lang Zaimont. New York: Greenwood Press, 1987.

Rotundo, E. Anthony. "Romantic Friendship: Male Intimacy and Middle-Class Youth in the Northern United States, 1800–1900." *Journal of Social History* 23 (Fall 1989): 1–25.

Saum, Lewis O. "Death in the Popular Mind of Pre–Civil War America." In *Death in America,* edited by David E. Stannard. Philadelphia: University of Pennsylvania Press, 1975.

Scott, Anne Firor. "The Ever-Widening Circle: The Diffusion of Feminist Values from the Troy Female Seminary, 1822–72." In *Making the Invisible Woman Visible* by Anne Firor Scott. Urbana: University of Illinois Press, 1984.

Shepperson, George. "Harriet Beecher Stowe and Scotland, 1852–3." *Scottish Historical Review* 32, no. 113 (April 1953): 40–46.

Sicherman, Barbara. "The Uses of a Diagnosis: Doctors, Patients, and Neurasthenia." *Journal of the History of Medicine and Allied Sciences* 32, no. 1 (January 1977): 33–54.

Sklar, Kathryn Kish. "All Hail to Pure Cold Water." In *Women and Health in America,* edited by Judith Walzer Leavitt. Madison: University of Wisconsin Press, 1984.

———. "The Founding of Mount Holyoke College." In *Women of America: A History,* edited by Carol Ruth Berkin and Mary Beth Norton. Boston: Houghton Mifflin, 1979.

Smith-Rosenberg, Carroll. "The Female World of Love and Ritual: Relations between Women in Nineteenth-Century America." *Signs: Journal of Women in Culture and Society* 1 (Autumn 1975): 1–26.

Spillers, Hortense J. "Changing the Letter: The Yokes, the Jokes of Discourse, or, Mrs. Stowe, Mr. Reed." In *Slavery and the Literary Imagination,* edited by Deborah E. McDowell and Arnold Rampersad. Baltimore: Johns Hopkins University Press, 1989.

Stansell, Christine. "Elizabeth Stuart Phelps: A Study in Female Rebellion." *Massachusetts Review* 13 (1972): 239–56.

Stepto, Robert. "Sharing the Thunder: The Literary Exchanges of Harriet Beecher Stowe, Henry Bibb, and Frederick Douglass." In *New Essays on "Uncle Tom's*

Cabin," edited by Eric J. Sundquist. Cambridge: Cambridge University Press, 1986.

Stevenson, Louise L. "Sarah Porter Educates Useful Ladies, 1847–1900." *Winterthur Portfolio* 18, no. 1 (Spring 1983): 39–59.

Stowe v. Thomas. Circuit Court, E. D. Pennsylvania, October Term, 1853. In vol. 23, *Federal Cases, Circuit and District Courts 1789–1880,* (1853):207.

Sullivan, Sherry. "Strategies for Success: Gender and the Production of the American Giftbook." Paper presented at the Eighth Berkshire Conference on the History of Women, Douglass College, June 10, 1990.

Sundquist, Eric J. "Introduction" to *New Essays on "Uncle Tom's Cabin,"* edited by Eric J. Sundquist. Cambridge: Cambridge University Press, 1986.

Talcott, Mary K. "Historical Sketch of the Seminary." In *The Hartford Female Seminary Reunion.* Hartford: Case, Lockwood & Brainard Company, 1892.

Tompkins, Jane. "Masterpiece Theatre: The Politics of Hawthorne's Literary Reputation." In *Sensational Designs: The Cultural Work of American Fiction, 1790–1850.* New York: Oxford University Press, 1985.

———. "Sentimental Power: *Uncle Tom's Cabin* and the Politics of Literary History." In *Sensational Designs: The Cultural Work of American Fiction, 1790–1850.* New York: Oxford University Press, 1985.

Truth, Sojourner. "Letter from Sojourner Truth." (Boston) *Commonwealth* 1, no. 44 (July 3, 1863): 1.

Tucker, Louis L. "The Semi-Colon Club of Cincinnati." *Ohio History* 73, no. 1 (1964): 13–26.

Warhol, Robyn. "Letters and Novels 'One Woman Wrote to Another': George Eliot's Responses to Elizabeth Gaskell." *Victorian Newsletter* 86 (Fall 1986): 8–14.

———. "Toward a Theory of the Engaging Narrator: Earnest Intervention in Gaskell, Stowe and Eliot." *PMLA* 101, no. 5 (October 1986): 811–18.

Welter, Barbara. "The Cult of True Womanhood, 1820–1860." *American Quarterly* 18, no. 2 (Summer 1966): 151–74.

Wood, Ann Douglas. "'The Fashionable Diseases': Women's Complaints and Their Treatment in Nineteenth-Century America." *Journal of Interdisciplinary History* 4 (Summer 1973): 25–52.

Woodhull, Victoria C. "Tried as by Fire; or, The True and the False Socially." New York: Woodhull & Claflin, 1874.

Zboray, Ronald J. "Antebellum Reading and the Ironies of Technological Innovation." *American Quarterly* 40, no. 1 (March 1988): 65–82.

Index